*Understanding Sexuality*

# Understanding Sexuality

ADELAIDE HAAS, Ph.D.

Professor
The Department of Communication

KURT HAAS, Ph.D.

Professor
The Department of Psychology

*both of*

The State University of New York
The College at New Paltz
New Paltz, New York

**TIMES MIRROR/MOSBY**
**COLLEGE PUBLISHING**

ST. LOUIS · TORONTO · BOSTON    1990

*Editor*   Pat Coryell
*Senior Developmental Editor*   Michelle A. Turenne
*Project Editor*   Carol Sullivan Wiseman
*Production Editor*   Barbara Merritt
*Designer*   Rey Umali
*Production*   Jeanne Genz, Barbara Merritt
*Illustrator*   J.P. Tandy & Associates, Inc. and Donald O'Connor Graphic Studio
*Cover Art*   Chagall, Marc, *Birthday* (L'Anniversaire) (1915). Collection, The Museum of Modern Art, New York. Acquired through the Lillie P. Bliss Bequest.

Credits for all materials used by permission appear after the Index.

Printed in the United States of America

**Library of Congress Cataloging-in-Publication Data**

Haas, Adelaide.

   Understanding sexuality / Adelaide Haas, Kurt Haas. — 2nd ed.
      p.   cm.

   Rev. ed. of: Understanding sexuality / Kurt Haas. 1987.
   Includes bibliographic references.
   ISBN 0-8016-6131-5
   1. Sex.   2. Sex customs— United States.   I. Haas, Kurt.
II. Haas, Kurt. Understanding sexuality.   III. Title.
HQ21.H24   1990
306.7—dc20                                          89-20377
                                                         CIP

C/VH/VH   9   8   7   6   5   4   3   2

# About the Authors

**ADELAIDE HAAS** is Professor of Communication at the State University of New York, College at New Paltz. Her doctoral work at Columbia University on sex differences in the language of children was cited for its distinction. Dr. Haas's research in female/male communication, sex roles, and relationships has been published in a variety of professional journals, including *Psychological Bulletin* and *Sex Roles: A Journal of Research*. Her work on conversations and interactions of women and men has been reported in many popular newspapers and magazines. Dr. Haas has been awarded numerous research grants and has consulted extensively in her research and clinical capacities.

**KURT HAAS** received his Ph.D. in clinical psychology from Pennsylvania State University. He has taught at Bowling Green State University and is currently Professor at the State University of New York, College at New Paltz. Dr. Haas has been a U.S. Public Health Service Fellow, holds the Diplomate in Clinical Psychology, has also been awarded numerous research grants and is consultant to several mental health and treatment facilities. His previous books and publications reflect his interest and work in abnormal behavior and counseling and in psychological and sexual adjustment.

*To our children, Ruth and Joseph, and to all children. May they grow and live in a wiser, more loving, and peaceful world.*

# Foreword

**EDWARD M. BRECHER**

*(1912-1989)*

Sex education did not exist in the United States at either the school or the college level until 1937, when Dr. Alfred C. Kinsey taught his first course in human sexuality at Indiana University. He found no textbooks he could use; indeed, he could find very little information available to pass along to students. So he launched his own study of sexual behavior, using his students themselves as his first informants. The massive Kinsey reports—among the three or four most important contributions to the study of sex—were the outcome.

Students and instructors no longer have to begin virtually from scratch in their study of human sexuality. Dr. Adelaide Haas and Dr. Kurt Haas provide a clear, easily understood textbook that moves from a description of ancient sexual practices, beliefs, and restrictions in Chapter 1 to an informative analysis of early and current research. Along the way, they provide useful information to help readers better understand and enjoy their own sexuality.

This knowledge must not be taken for granted. As recently as 1941 the Supreme Court of Connecticut officially held that it was illegal for a physician to reveal to a married patient the facts about pregnancy prevention—even though the patient suffered from a life-threatening condition in which childbearing probably would prove fatal. If the patient didn't want to die in childbirth, the court ruled, she and her husband should abstain from sex altogether. In contrast, today, in Chapter 14 students will find practical, consumer-oriented information. They can read about the advantages and disadvantages of nearly a dozen reliable birth control techniques and then make a decision that is both informed and personally comfortable.

Students should recognize, too, that for many children and young people of college age as recently as a few decades ago, the wall of sexual secrecy was impenetrable. Many unmarried teenagers became pregnant, for example, because the relationship between sexual intercourse and pregnancy (see Chapters 8 and 15) had been kept a secret from them. Some brides went to bed on their wedding night in utter ignorance of what was about to happen to them. The kind of information the authors present in Chapter 5 concerning the means to satisfying sexual arousal, intercourse, and orgasm was either unavailable or suppressed.

Some young men of the pre-Kinsey generation were able to secure some of the sexual information they needed from their peers; but it was typically tainted with vast quantities of *mis*information, especially misinformation about women (see Chapter 3). They learned nothing, for example, about the role of the clitoris in female sexual response and very little about the fact that women, as well as men, experience orgasm. Thus young women suffered from a double dose of ignorance: the ignorance (mistakenly labeled "innocence") in which they themselves were being kept and the mixture of ignorance and misinformation with which their future lovers and husbands were reared.

Well aware of this heritage of potential ignorance and misinformation, the authors take great care in Chapters 3, 4, 5, 6, and 7 to teach and encourage women and men to learn their own and their partner's sexual needs, anatomy, and physiology. Couples are helped to communicate so that they can better understand their own motives and attitudes and appreciate those of their partner (see Chapters 10 and 11).

The tide began to turn when in 1930 an English gynecologist, Dr. Helena Wright, wrote *The Sex Factor in Marriage*. She told women readers two simple facts that had long been kept secret: how they could teach themselves to reach an orgasm and how they could thereafter teach their husbands to bring them to orgasm.

"The publisher and I expected the whole edition to be seized, banned, and destroyed," Dr. Wright later recalled, "so we grabbed the first copies off the press and buried them in secret places—two in England and one in France." Thanks in good part to the courage of pioneers like Dr. Wright, such precautions are no longer needed. *Understanding Sexuality* is filled with factual and practical information that need not be hidden but should be shared by all women and men.

Consider also the information concerning homosexuality contained in Chapter 13. Thirty years ago, state legislatures dared not use the *word* homosexuality when passing laws making homosexual acts a cause for imprisonment—in some cases lifelong imprisonment. To protect the innocence of those who might read the law, they frequently called homosexuality "the crime against nature." Writers who wanted to avoid mentioning the term used derogative phrases such as "the sin that dares not speak its name."

In this text the authors present an enlightened and sensitive discussion of homosexuality (Chapter 13), as well as of heterosexual alternatives (Chapters 9 and 12). They examine timely issues such as "coming out," the impact of AIDS, erotica, and nonmarital sexuality. They rationally describe and discuss the variety of choices that are part of human sexual need and expression.

The authors explore, too, the growth and evolution of sexual awareness. They show the development of sexuality in children and adolescents in Chapter 8. In Chapters 11 and 12 they portray the experiences and concerns associated with sexuality during the adult years through old age. Special attention is given also to sexuality among those who are single. This focus spans the entire spectrum from young unattached college students, to separated or divorced adults, to people who in their older years lose the person with whom they have shared most of their life (Chapters 9 and 12).

A generation or two ago the nouns *syphillis* and *gonorrhea* were rarely printed in newspapers or magazines; the vaguer term "venereal disease" was coined to help keep readers ignorant of this aspect of sexuality. In at least one state during the 1950s, moreover, it remained a criminal offense for anyone to tell how to protect against VD when having sexual intercourse. In Chapter 16, readers will find, spelled out in useful detail, all the information they are likely to want or need concerning AIDS, herpes, syphillis, gonorrhea, and other sexually transmitted diseases—including practical ways to minimize the risk of infection.

*Understanding Sexuality* presents a comprehensive overview of complex and technical scientific topics in a practical and highly readable style that students will find not only comprehensible but enjoyable. While the text can and should be studied, it can also be read much as a novel is read *by those eager to learn what is going to happen on the pages ahead*. Having just read the textbook myself, continuously, from cover to cover, I came away with a deep respect for the authors' achievement and with a sober, almost poetic, remark by the late comedian, W.C. Fields, fresh in my mind:

Sex isn't the best
thing in the world, or
the worst thing in
the world—but there's
nothing else
quite like it.

# Preface

Sex is a serious topic. The well-being of individuals, couples, families, and even an entire society can depend on matters that are fundamentally sexual. This does not mean that the tone of a human sexuality textbook needs to be pompous or somber. We are fully aware of the importance of sexual matters but also recognize their joyful potential. In the second edition, we continue our tradition of writing with a gentle touch, warmth, and even a bit of humor to spark interest, ease tension, and facilitate learning.

Both of us at different times have written about human sexuality. Adelaide Haas approached her task from the perspective of her specialties, female/male communication and interpersonal relationships. Kurt Haas has written as a psychologist. Although a few years went by before the obvious became apparent, we finally realized we could have a far better, more integrated approach if we worked together. As a team we bring the complementary skills of a woman and a man, a communications specialist and a clinician, parents of grown children, and over 25 years of college teaching. Our aim, through this blending of backgrounds, is to write a book that is informative, balanced, lively, and useful.

## AUDIENCE

Our textbook draws from the social, behavioral, biological, and health sciences. We know that students come to human sexuality courses from all of these areas and many others. A typical class may include people majoring in nursing, business, psychology, women's studies, physical education, science, engineering, and every one of the liberal arts. Further, while most will likely be traditional young college students, older returning men and women have become an increasing and important part of every classroom.

With such a varied audience, we have written the textbook so that it can stand on its own. Students can come from any college discipline and need not have any special prerequisite course. This means, also, that readers may be in 2- or 4-year college programs. In most instances the book will prove equally suitable for college women and men in their beginning years or those further advanced in their programs. The material included and the level of presentation are intended to be understandable and useful to the widest number of students regardless of their background preparation and goals.

## CONTENT HIGHLIGHTS

Every student is a potential (and sometimes current) spouse, parent, lover, and professional. Each is a consumer and user of knowledge. For this reason *Understanding Sexuality,* whenever appropriate, includes information that is instructive, practical, and useful. We want to help enrich our reader's sexuality, health, and life.

**Consumer oriented and practical** A major objective is to present a personally useful book. To achieve this goal we have made the text as relevant and accurate as possible. Whether we are discussing childbirth or contraception, we present sound suggestions and alternatives, advantages, and disadvantages. A small sample of such features includes maintaining sexual health; how to select appropriate contraception; understanding the other sex; handling obscene telephone calls; how to help yourself or seek professional treatment; overcoming shyness; and alternatives for unplanned pregnancy.

**Information, not anxiety**   Too much that is written about sexuality reinforces fear or is prejudicial. There are serious and sensitive issues that need to be discussed in a human sexuality textbook, but triggering anxiety or indicating disapproval is not likely to result in effective learning. For this reason our descriptions of sexually transmitted diseases and our reports on sexual victimization are realistic but reassuring. We point out that although herpes is a common, often annoying infection, it is rarely dangerous. Or whereas AIDS is extremely serious, it can be prevented by measures we explain in clear detail. The topic of sexual abuse is similarly treated. Victims may be traumatized by sexual assault, but prevention is possible and professional help is available to assist a full recovery. As we point out in our chapter on Family Planning and Birth Control, studies clearly show it is far more effective to teach the use of contraceptives than to try to intimidate and manipulate adolescents. Accurate information, much more than fear, brings about responsible behavior.

**Currency**   Several chapters and sections in *Understanding Sexuality* discuss new and current material that is covered in few other texts. These unique topics include the role of stress and fitness in sexual function and a thorough coverage of attraction and love, integrating physical, social, and psychological factors. Other contemporary concerns brought up-to-date include the sexuality of the physically, developmentally, visually, or hearing disabled; the latest developments in the epidemiology and management of AIDS; and the effects of the July 1989 Supreme Court decision on abortion.

**Sexual signals**   Communication is the means by which people come to know and relate to one another. It is at the core of every relationship and more often than not determines sexual and affec-

tional satisfaction. Unlike many texts, we devote an entire chapter to spoken and unspoken communication (Chapter 10). We want students to learn the words, body signs, and signals that play such an important role in sexual communication. The last section of the chapter gives specific advice so that readers can better understand others and improve their own communication process.

**Single adults**   Recognizing that one in every five Americans is now single persuaded us to devote an entire chapter to their needs and concerns (Chapter 9). The sexual and affectional behaviors, life-styles, and interests of single people, including the never married, the divorced, and the widowed, are discussed in detail. We pay particular attention to college students and their lives on campuses. In addition to presenting the issues and the advantages and disadvantages of being single, we also discuss the numerous singles' groups and services.

**Gender similarities and differences**   The social, psychological, and biological determinants of gender, as well as the resultant differences between women and men, are the focus of two chapters (Chapters 6 and 7). But unlike most texts, we pay careful attention to gender similarities. Whether we discuss physical strength, intellectual aptitudes, or emotional needs, we demonstrate that while there may be some differences between men and women, more often than not their attributes considerably overlap. Women and men are far more similar than they are different. It is this recognition that can bring about better communication between the sexes and add immeasurably to relationships.

**Personable writing style**   Written in a personal, conversational style, our goal is to make this text as reader-relevant and technically clear as possible. Information is drawn from the laboratory, numerous investigations, and other writers. All writers are not equally skilled in their scholarship and not all that is written is valid. For this reason we avoid excessive citation and, while remaining nonjudgmental, select and synthesize information so that students can understand and apply research and data.

# NEW TO THIS EDITION

So much has happened in human sexuality since we started the first edition of *Understanding Sexuality* in the beginning of the 1980s. AIDS has clearly surfaced as a factor without precedent. Not only is it a severely serious sexually transmitted disease, but it has stimulated wide-ranging scientific research and investigation. It has had, too, a profound effect on the sexual and affectional behavior of virtually every woman and man, old and young. It has prompted consideration and reconsideration of traditions, values, and beliefs. No one in the 1990s can ignore AIDS. For these reasons, in this second edition we have closely examined the impact of AIDS, and stress understanding the means of infection, as well as prevention.

Numerous other topics have been added or more thoroughly discussed in this second edition:

- A full chapter on Health: Ability and Disability (Chapter 18)
- Two new chapters on Sex as Business (Chapter 19) and Sex and the Law (Chapter 20)
- A reorganized presentation of sex education in the chapter on Childhood and Adolescence: Growing Up Sexual, for a more logical content sequence
- Consideration of the advantages of chorionic villus sampling over amniocentesis
- Presentation of a cross-cultural perspective allowing our own standards and behavior to be seen in context
- A more complete description of female circumcision
- An expanded discussion of all aspects of hysterectomy
- A review of the influences of the media and rock lyrics on teenage sexuality
- New research on gender-related behaviors such as aggression and nurturance
- Updated reports on teenage pregnancy and runaways
- Closer examination of the varieties of rape, date rape, psychological and physical sexual coercion and abuse, and the means of prevention
- Updated birth control methods, abortion technology, and legal considerations
- Reexamination of homophobia and its current consequences
- Discussion of the bisexual spouse
- Description of the new climate of sexual conservatism
- Consideration of pornography, erotica, and adult videotapes for home use
- The role of attractiveness in marriage, and marital and partnership alternatives
- 150 new research, scholarly, and investigational citations

While we have added a very substantial amount that is new, we have retained all first edition materials and features that were very favorably received and believed to be of particular value. Our aim remains to be informative, data based, practical, and consumer-oriented.

# NEW FULL COLOR SECTIONS

To enhance the visual appeal and excitement of the text, full color sections have been added to the discussions of sexual behavior, pregnancy, and sexual problems and solutions. In addition, the use of a second color has been retained elsewhere to accentuate the illustrations and design.

# ORGANIZATION

*Understanding Sexuality* is organized into seven sections; each includes topics that are related or congruent. Instructors may choose to follow the numerical succcession of sections and chapters. There is, however, enough flexibility built in to allow alternative arrangements or to omit particular chapters. We begin with "Perspectives," which is an examination of our origins and a brief report of basic sex research. Both history and scientific sex investigation have helped shape current thinking. The second part of the textbook, "Female and Male: Sex and Gender," explains the anatomical, physiological, and gender function of both sexes, as well as sexual intercourse.

"Our Sexual Selves," Part Three, presents human sexuality in a developmental context. We report on childhood and adolescence and focus, too, on single people from youth through old age. Part Four, "Sexual Connections: Relating to Others," provides substantive coverage of the many ways human beings form friendships and partnerships. In this section we also give practical pointers showing how relationships may be improved.

Part Five, "Reproduction," is a comprehensive, consumer-oriented presentation of pregnancy, family planning, fertility, abortion, and adoption. We want readers to be informed and aware of alternatives and options so that they can make reasoned decisions.

The same theme of helping students to be knowledgeable and judicious carries over to Part Six, "Sexual Health." We present a realistic but understanding discussion of sexually transmitted diseases and problems in sexual function. We also emphasize disease prevention and are reassuring about dysfunction and disability. We hope to allay some of the hysteria and misinformation conveyed by the media. Finally, Part Seven, "Sex and Society," includes several contemporary topics: exploitation, commercial sex, victimization, and abuse. These issues are of growing concern. An increasing wealth of research and writing is clarifying their social and personal impact.

## PEDAGOGICAL FEATURES

*Understanding Sexuality* contains a variety of learning aids to assist instructors and to enhance student learning.

**Chapter objectives**   Each chapter opens with the identification of four to six objectives. These help label and reinforce the goals of the chapter.

**Margin notes**   Margins are often used to provide additional information such as definitions, notes and tips, and cross-references to related discussions within the text. These aids are designed to assist student comprehension, to help apply the content learned, and to enhance overall visual appeal.

**Focus boxes**   In each chapter, focus boxes provide additional topics to stimulate student involvement. Some selected topics include women's and men's health care, the ethics of AIDS, surrogate parenthood, and systematic desensitization.

**In sum**   Unique to this text, interim summaries within each chapter recap previous content and immediately reinforce important and difficult concepts for students.

**Self-assessments**   Two types of self-assessments appear in the text and actively involve the reader. *Test Yourself* briefly quizzes student knowledge and awareness of pertinent topics such as sexual intercourse, sexual infections, and marriage and relationships. The correct answers are in the appendix at the end of the text.

*Ask Yourself* challenges students to identify their beliefs, attitudes, and abilities on more personal topics such as communication, partner compatibility, readiness for marriage, parenting, birth planning, stress, and fitness. Interpretations are provided to make the scores relevant to students, and suggestions are made for increasing awareness.

**Tips**   Helpful hints and practical advice are found in every chapter. Several tips on timely topics such as avoiding rape and coping with break-up have been highlighted for added emphasis and easy identification.

**Illustrative materials**   Instructionally oriented photographs, line art, tables, and case notes are included to highlight the key points and objectives of each chapter and to help students better understand important concepts and applications.

**Chapter summaries**   A final summary of the major points and their significance to students concludes each chapter.

**For thought and discussion**   Four to eight study questions are presented at the end of each chapter as additional learning aids. These can be used to stimulate classroom discussion.

**Documentation**   The most up-to-date and informative documentation has been used and is referenced at the end of the chapter.

**Suggested readings**   For those students who want to obtain more information about a particular topic, additional and timely resources have been included. These have been annotated in order to explain their relevance to the chapter material.

**Appendix**   Correct answers to the *Test Yourself* assessments have been conveniently arranged in one location at the end of the text. Scoring interpretations can be found within the appropriate assessment box.

**Comprehensive glossary**   At the end of the text, all terms defined in the margins, as well as other pertinent terms, are gathered into a comprehensive glossary. The glossary is cross-referenced providing the page locations where each term is described.

## ANCILLARIES

A carefully prepared and tested quality ancillary package is available to instructors who adopt *Understanding Sexuality*. These materials can greatly assist teaching and learning. We, as well as the publisher, have made a conscientious effort to produce supplements that are extraordinary in utility and quality. Each of the ancillaries has been reviewed by several instructors, and we have subsequently refined them to ensure clarity, and accuracy. More comprehensive information about the ancillaries, in addition to that presented in the following summary descriptions, is available from the publisher.

**Instructor's manual and test bank**   The instructor's manual begins with conversion notes, which are found in the opening paragraph of each manual chapter. These notes describe how the content and focus of chapters in *Understanding Sexuality* correlate with coverage of similar material in several other leading human sexuality textbooks. Instructors using textbooks other than those reviewed will also find the conversion notes useful in gaining an overall understanding of the content and focus of each chapter.

The instructional portion of the manual is a valuable tool. It features: chapter overviews, objectives, lecture outlines, notes and activities for teaching each chapter, assessments, media resources—including software—and full-page transparency masters of helpful illustrations and charts. The manual is perforated and three-hole punched for convenience. We have also prepared an extensive test bank, which contains over 2,000 multiple choice, true-false, matching, and essay questions. Test questions have been evaluated by reviewers for clarity, accuracy, and level of difficulty.

**Computerized test bank**   New with the second edition, qualified adopters of this text may request a Diploma Computerized test bank package compatible with the IBM PC, Apple IIc, Apple IIe, and Macintosh microcomputers. This software is a unique combination of user-friendly computerized aids for the instructor. The following summarizes these software aids:

- Testing. A test generator allows the user to select items from the test bank either manually or randomly; to add, edit, or delete test items through a preset format that includes multiple choice, true-false, matching, or essay options; and to print exams with or without saving them for future use.
- Grading. A computerized record keeper saves student names (up to 250), assignments (up to 50), and related grades in a format similar to that used in manual grade books. Statistics on individual or class performance, test weighting, and push-button grade curving are features of this software.
- Tutoring. A tutorial package uses items from the test bank for student review. Student scores can be merged into the grading records.
- Scheduling. A computerized databook makes class planning and schedule management quick and convenient.

**Sexuality student manual**   New with the second editon, *Healthy Sexuality: A Self-Assessment Manual* was prepared by M. Patricia Fetter, Ph.D., of Northeastern University. The comprehensive manual offers invaluable help to students by reinforcing concepts presented in the text and integrating these with innovative activities. Reviewed for clarity and accuracy, the guide provides the following:

- Learning objectives
- Terminology review
- A variety of questions to help students prepare for tests
- Abundant activities and exercises to encourage students to apply what they have learned from their text to their daily lives

**Overhead transparency acetates**   Fifty-four important illustrations, tables, charts, and diagrams are available as acetate transparencies in two-color and four-color. These transparencies can greatly assist classroom learning, facilitate discussion, and help in the explanation of challenging concepts.

**Human sexuality self-assessment software**

This interactive disk allows students to assess their personal values, attitudes, and knowledge. Approximately 100 short questions are asked about values, beliefs, and habits, after which the student receives suggestions for increasing and maintaining a sexually informed attitude. It is available to adopters of the text for both IBM and Apple personal computers.

## ACKNOWLEDGMENTS

The reviewers of our manuscript, selected by Times Mirror/Mosby, made a countless number of excellent and useful suggestions that we incorporated whenever possible. At each stage of our manuscript we looked forward to their special viewpoints and perceptions. We express our gratitude and appreciation for their insights and contributions.

Second Edition

**Elwin M. Barrett**
*Wichita State University*

**Lynn White Blanchard**
*University of North Carolina, Chapel Hill*

**Teresa Jean Byrne**
*Kent State University*

**Verna Buchanan**
*Wichita State University*

**Jan Campbell**
*California State University, Chico*

**Dennis M. Dailey**
*University of Kansas*

**Kelli R. McCormack**
*Western Illinois University*

**Dennis Morton**
*Pierce College*

**Susan Sprecher**
*Illinois State University*

First Edition

**Lorraine A. Baillie**
*Texas Tech University*

**Martha W. Bristor**
*Michigan State University*

**Rodney M. Cate**
*Oregon State University*

**Randall R. Cottrell**
*University of Oregon*

**James G. Dedic**
*Cypress College*

**John D. DeLamater**
*University of Wisconsin, Madison*

**Randy D. Fisher**
*University of Central Florida*

**Ann Springer**
*Hillsborough Community College*

**Richard D. Stacy**
*University of Nebraska, Omaha*

**W. Fred Stultz**
*California Poltechnic State University, San Luis Obispo*

**Barbara Szekely**
*Southwest Texas State University*

**Caryl N. Utigard**
*Highline Community College*

**Robert F. Valois**
*University of Texas, Austin*

**Paul R. Vaughan**
*Mankato State University*

**Charles Verschoor**
*Miami-Dade Community College*

**Linda D. Wolfe**
*University of Florida*

**Lin Smiklo Fox**
*Kean College of New Jersey*

**Michael Gonzales**
*University of California, Irvine*

**Robert Kaplan**
*Ohio State University*

**Mary Ann Klausner**
*Cypress College and Fullerton College*

**Lynette Lawrance**
*University of North Carolina, Greensboro*

**Leslie G. McBride**
*Portland State University*

**Judith A. Nevin**
*University of Arizona*

**Bruce Palmer**
*Washington State University*

**Robert H. Pollack**
*University of Georgia*

**Patty Reagan**
*University of Utah*

**Kathryn M. Rickard-Figueroa**
*Colorado State University*

**Barbara A. Rienzo**
*University of Florida*

**Lauralee Rockwell**
*University of Iowa*

**Laurna Rubinson**
*University of Illinois, Urbana/Champaign*

**Jerry S. Strouse**
*Central Michigan University*

**William R. Terrell**
*University of Minnesota*

**Priscilla White**
*University of Tennessee, Knoxville*

**R.N. Whitehurst**
*University of Windsor*

**William L. Yarber**
*Indiana University*

A special acknowledgment is owed numerous friends, students, volunteers, and colleagues who contributed information, photographs, suggestions, and personal histories to our text. We are indebted to the following colleagues at the State University of New York, College at New Paltz: Douglas Baker, Ph.D., Allen Bogarad, Ph.D., Anthony Dos Reis, Ph.D., Susan Puretz, Ph.D., and Professors Joseph Owens and Donald Wildy. We also acknowledge the helpful contributions of Robert Nacamu, Ph.D., Rutgers University, and particularly Robert Owens, Ph.D., State University of New York at Geneseo. Our thanks, too, to Herbert Weinman, M.D., for his review of materials concerning current medical practice.

Deep appreciation is owed to a very special colleague and friend, a pioneer in and a contributor to sexology, the late Edward Brecher. His intelligence, wit, generosity, and enthusiasm for his subject and for life continue to be an inspiration to us and are gratefully acknowledged.

Much credit must go to the excellent staff of our publisher, Times Mirror/Mosby College Publishers. We thank Jean Babrick, Supplements Developmental Editor, and numerous members of the production staff who helped make this text informative and appealing. Special gratitude is owed Michelle Turenne, Senior Developmental Editor. Her intelligent, patient, and detailed readings and reviews, as well as her numerous suggestions and instructions, were practical and helpful. Her contributions at every stage are highly valued.

**Adelaide Haas**
**Kurt Haas**
*New Paltz, New York*

# To the Student

Few topics have as much potential for stimulating differing attitudes and opinions as does human sexuality. Ample disagreement exists about nearly all sexual behaviors: masturbation, premarital intercourse, homosexuality, and dozens of other erotic and related practices. Among the thousands of students at any college there will be many men and women who have had intercourse with several different partners. But there will also be large numbers who defer such intimacy until they marry. A very substantial portion of the students, too, will feel joy and comfort in their sexuality, while quite a few others may experience disappointment, conflict, and guilt.

We recognize that we are a heterogeneous nation, composed of very many different cultural, religious, and ethnic groups. Through our heritage all of us bring different values, perceptions, and practices concerning sexuality. We believe that we understand these differences and respect them. In this text we do not propose any single standard to govern the sexual behavior of everyone. We *do not* urge either a "permissive" or a "conservative" lifestyle. We fully believe it is the right of all women and men to act on the basis of their own heritage and ethical values.

But we are advocates of knowledge. More often than not, what is most damaging to our human and sexual potential is misinformation and lack of information. Our hope in this text is to convey accurate and meaningful information. We want students to know. And because we also want readers to think, we do not shy away from debate. We include many controversial topics and examine them from different viewpoints in order to stimulate discussion and thought. The objective is to reach, through information and communication, a better understanding of our own sexuality and that of others.

# Contents in Brief

# Contents

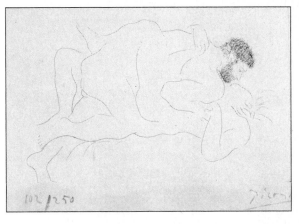

*Part One*

# PERSPECTIVES

*Chapter 1*

# Origins and Directions

*When you finish this chapter, you should be able to:*

Describe how in some societies, home and mothering roles for women and provider roles for men might have originated.

Trace how past civilizations and Judeo-Christian beliefs influence sexual practices and laws today.

Explain how Romanticism and Victorianism both succeeded and failed in their attempts to modify and channel sexual behaviors.

Describe how our sexual attitudes and practices have been influenced and changed in the last several decades by the social climate and our own cultural heritage.

We will begin our search for information by looking back, seeing from where we have come. We may think our feelings, motivations, and beliefs are totally our own creation. But when we stop and consciously think about it, most of us realize that nearly the exact opposite is true. The foods we eat, the clothing we wear, the political and religious convictions we hold are only in small part uniquely ours. Our sexual attitudes and the part we play in life as a woman or a man are derived from the generations that preceded us. For all of us, our behavior is the outcome not only of innate physical need but also of an accumulation of rules and customs that began ages and ages ago. In this chapter we cannot review all the complex economic, religious, and social factors that together form our human heritage. But we can take a peek at our origins and spot some of the paths into which we have been directed.

# THE DISTANT PAST
## *Homo sapiens sapiens*

*Homo sapiens sapiens*
Scientific term used to designate the modern form of human beings who first appeared roughly 40,000 years ago.

Some 40,000 years ago, anthropological evidence suggests, women and men appeared who could fit right in to society today. These *Homo sapiens sapiens* were probably as bright and resourceful as any human today. How these early people lived can be deduced in at least two ways. First many groups of *Homo sapiens sapiens* left behind an abundance of tools, gravesites, works of art, and debris. A careful examination of such artifacts often leads to intelligent guesses about the users' needs and customs. A second source of information is provided by examining the lives of isolated bands of humans like the Bushmen in Africa, the Eskimos, the Australian aborigines, and the Laplanders in far Northern Europe. Until recently, these groups hunted, foraged, farmed, herded, and organized their lives perhaps somewhat like those of early *Homo sapiens sapiens*.

Almost from the beginning it appears as if human life-styles differed. For example, there is evidence for at least two kinds of group living. Sometimes only a dozen people shared the same hut, cave, or other homesite. At other times, living arrangements were shared by 30, 40, or more *Homo sapiens sapiens*. The smaller units may have been family groupings with parents, children, grandparents, and perhaps an aunt or uncle. In these groups it is possible that **monogamy,** one wife married to one husband, or some equivalent form of coupling was common.

*monogamy*
A marital arrangement in which one person has only one partner or spouse.

*polygamy*
A marital arrangement in which one person has more than one partner or spouse.

*nuclear family*
A small unit consisting only of parents and children.

Other groups of early people seemed to have lived together in large clan-type arrangements that may have included several parents, distant cousins, and friends. Some of these larger units appear to be the result of something like **polygamy,** one person having several marital partners. It is also possible that a number of men and women lived together in a kind of group "marriage," where sexual or affectional partnerships were often temporary and changing (Fagan, 1983; Wedgwood, 1985).

The **nuclear family,** just parents and children living together, the pattern personally most familiar to us, was probably not common in the early history of the human race. Life was likely often too precarious to allow just a father, mother, and children alone to endure. It was not until the Middle Ages in Europe that the nuclear family seemed to emerge. It gradually became the dominant kinship grouping in Western nations but not in much of Africa, Asia, and South America.

Many scholars believe that the first modern humans made distinctions between the sexes in terms of their work, authority, and responsibilities. Women were the gatherers and farmers and took care of the children. Men, who were stronger, were assigned to hunt, protect the group, and compete with each other for leadership. But a few scientists have questioned this reconstruction of early human life. Tanner and Zihlman (1981) suggest that even 10,000 years ago, often both women and men were engaged in obtaining food and caring for children, and either may have ruled the group or clan. What seems most likely is that in the *division of labor,* just as with marital arrangements, different human groups reached different solutions.

In India, families typically include uncles, aunts, and grandparents. The latter often play an important role in raising children.

**Sex and birth**  Cartoonists enjoy depicting our distant ancestors, "cavemen," as hulking, unintelligent creatures carrying huge clubs. Actually, early human beings were apparently just as sensitive and creative as people today. Many of

## Sexual Knowledge

Most of us are convinced that we know a great deal about human sexuality. Actually very few of us are as expert as we believe. Test your own knowledge by circling true or false for the following statements. Answers are located in the Appendix p. 577. If you get 16 or more correct (80%) you are quite well informed and will enjoy learning more. But do not be discouraged if you get 10 or more wrong. Very few people who have not specifically studied human sexuality answer most of these questions correctly.

T  F  1. Most adolescent boys masturbate, but girls rarely do.

T  F  2. A married adult who masturbates is probably abnormal.

T  F  3. Most married couples sometimes engage in oral-genital contact.

T  F  4. Homosexual women and men are considered mentally ill by psychiatrists.

T  F  5. About one out of five young men has had at least one homosexual experience.

T  F  6. You can tell if a woman is a virgin since she will have a hymen blocking entry into the vagina.

T  F  7. During menstruation nearly all women are very irritable and depressed.

T  F  8. Sexual desire can be created by aphrodisiacs like Spanish fly.

T  F  9. Boys are almost always much better in mathematics and arithmetic than girls.

T  F  10. A good way to avoid pregnancy when having intercourse is for the man to withdraw his penis just before he ejaculates.

T  F  11. When a woman does not have an orgasm as a result of intercourse, it is almost always because the man is a poor lover.

T  F  12. When a woman has an orgasm, she ejaculates fluid much like a man.

T  F  13. People who live together for a few years before they marry almost always have a very happy and enduring marriage.

T  F  14. Almost all wives and husbands occasionally have extramarital intercourse.

T  F  15. Pregnant women should not have intercourse after the third month of pregnancy.

T  F  16. Herpes is a very serious infectious disease that causes uterine cancer and birth defects.

T  F  17. Condoms are an ineffective means of birth control.

T  F  18. Nearly all women who have an abortion become seriously depressed.

T  F  19. The inability to have an erection is almost always caused by hidden psychological problems.

T  F  20. Exhibitionists, men who expose their genitals, usually become rapists.

the homesites that have been excavated reveal cleverly made tools and beautifully decorated implements. In France alone, more than 70 sites of primitive cave art have been found. A good deal of this art depicts daily life and its concerns. Scenes depicting the hunt, farming, and fighting are common and rendered with skill.

Many early artistic efforts, 20,000 to 30,000 years ago, seem to have a sexual content. The famous so-called Venus of Willendorf is a 4-inch-high figurine

*erotic*
Sexual or related to
sexuality.


*coitus*
Sexual intercourse.

The so-called Venus of
Willendorf is one of
hundreds of similar
figurines. The exaggerated
sexual characteristics
suggest it may have had
some fertility or erotic
significance.

made of limestone. This small statue has an elaborately wavy hairdo, and emphasizes the breasts, buttocks, and belly. Many scientists suspect this Venus may have had a religious significance. It could have been used as a charm to assure fertility or might have been an icon to be worshipped. Still another possibility, however, is that the female figurine and male ones, emphasizing the penis, may be ancient **erotic** art intended to be sexually stimulating (Malinowski, 1985).

Despite their intelligence and erotic sensitivity, what little evidence we have shows that for tens of thousands of years, many groups of *Homo sapiens sapiens* probably did not understand the role of sexual intercourse in reproduction. Men and women had **coitus,** and sometimes there was pregnancy and sometimes not. It must also have been observed that pregnancy usually started after childhood and that women usually menstruated when they were not pregnant or nursing. But putting all this together and concluding that men fathered children may have required too vast a deductive leap (Tannahill, 1981).

It may, at first, seem difficult to believe that only several thousand years ago many people with our brains and capabilities did not clearly connect coitus with birth. Imagine, however, the conditions under which Stone Age women and men lived. Food was scarce and undernourishment common, and with almost no knowledge of sanitation or medicine, life was short and uncertain. Under such conditions fertility in both sexes may have been low and successful pregnancy not as frequent as it is today. Probably all women in a group had intercourse, but only a few now and then gave birth. Further, if some budding scientist among these primitive people suspected that coitus led to pregnancy, there was likely an example of a woman who had frequent intercourse yet never gave birth.

Until the last century, anthropologists reported isolated groups of people living in New Guinea and Australia who did not understand how conception took place. But one does not have to seek out remote aboriginal human beings. Still today a counselor occasionally needs to help a person who has no clear idea about pregnancy. A prosperous businesswoman recalled that when she was an adolescent, only 20 years before, she had discovered the pleasure of sexual intercourse with a neighborhood boy. Her sheltered upbringing suggested that what she was doing was "wrong," but she did not at all understand that it could lead to pregnancy. When she became pregnant at age 15, it was a traumatic experience that left a serious emotional wound.

Some scientists have speculated that as long as our distant ancestors saw coitus as simply a pleasurable act, not much different from massaging a friend, there was little reason to create many restrictions. It is possible, therefore, that for most of human life there may have been little anxiety about sex and relatively few rules about its appropriateness.

Just how and when humans learned about the male role in reproduction is not known. We surmise that in many cultures the facts of human reproduction became known anywhere from 5000 to 10,000 years ago. As *Homo sapiens sapiens* began to hunt less and to farm more, people began to have time to talk, observe, think, and investigate. Perhaps more important, as animals were herded and domesticated, the role of males eventually became obvious. Keeping heifers together did not result in calves. But when a bull entered the herd, cows soon became pregnant. The conclusion was inescapable. Males fathered children; males were indispensable in procreation (Fagan, 1983).

Once the man's role in reproduction became known, it was not only women who could talk about their children. Men, too, could speak of their daughters and their sons. Tannahill (1981) proposes the controversial notion that the discovery of the father's role in reproduction may have caused men to overreact. Before this knowledge, she guesses, men were surely thought irrelevant to procreation. Women, the source of life, may have had their power and authority magnified. After the revelation of their vital role in birth, however, men may have seized authority. Most of all, to assure the validity of their fatherhood, men may have curtailed the sexual freedom of women. "A man might have a harem if he chose, and if he could defend it, but the concept of 'my son' required the woman to be monogamous" (Tannahill, 1981, p. 47).

It is guessed that the knowledge of procreation benefited both sexes. It enabled them to control their own lives more than ever before. If they did not want to be parents, they may have been able to escape this role and responsibility by avoiding intercourse. Perhaps with knowledge of the role of coitus, both sexes became much more selective in choosing intimate partners. Knowing that intercourse carries enormous possible consequences could have given rise to the complex courtship and selection behaviors still practiced today.

### Ancient times

We make a monumental leap ahead in time when we jump from *Homo sapiens sapiens,* 10,000 years ago, attempting to understand reproduction, to the first civilizations in the fourth millenium B.C. By this time in the Middle East, the Sumerians had founded cities such as Ur and Kish. They had considerable technical knowledge about agriculture and worked a variety of metals into weapons, ornaments, and tools. In this creative civilization, **polyandry**, one woman having several "husbands," seemed quite commonplace for a substantial period. Then in about 2350 B.C. a Sumerian king, Urukagina, claimed credit for putting an end to polyandry and reversed marriage customs. One husband and several wives now became the norm, a practice called **polygyny**. How many women a man could marry depended in the main on his wealth. King Solomon, ruler in ancient Israel in 955 B.C., was reported to have had 700 wives (Wedgwood, 1985).

**Babylon**  By 1700 B.C. Babylon, another Middle Eastern nation, led the world in medicine, astronomy, and philosophy. The major achievement, however, may have been the code written for and by the king, Hammurabi. Among the many detailed regulations of the *Code of Hammurabi* is a clear definition of marriage and divorce proceedings. A woman could divorce a cruel husband and a man take a second wife if the first did not have children.

There are regulations, too, governing seduction and infidelity. Husbands were permitted to keep two "mistresses," but if they seduced an innocent young girl, they might be punished by beheading. If a wife was unfaithful, she could be bound and tossed into the river to drown. But if the infidelity was caused by the husband's neglect or ineptness, the unfaithful wife might just be thrown in the Tigris or Euphrates River without being tied up. Many of the 70 rules regulating Babylonian sex and marriage are still reflected in laws today.

**Israel**  The Code of Hammurabi may have significantly influenced the Hebrew people, who formed the original and influential nation of Israel, 3000

---

Imagine what life might be like if you lived among a group of women and men who were trying to survive and reproduce, but none of them knew about proper nutrition, how disease is caused by microorganisms, and how pregnancy occurs.

*polyandry*
One woman having several husbands.

*polygyny*
One man having several wives.

The Code of Hammurabi.

years ago. The Old Testament commanded the people of Israel to multiply and be fruitful. Nonreproductive behaviors such as masturbation, withdrawal before ejaculation to prevent conception, and homosexuality were serious offenses. Infidelity was also prohibited and in fact considered so evil that it was forbidden in the words of Jehovah. The seventh of the Ten Commandments clearly states, "You shall not commit **adultery.**"

In ancient Israel, as in all the Middle Eastern civilizations, women had few legal rights and little property, and they were largely limited to being wives and mothers. Some jobs were open to them, as entertainers, cooks, or scribes (secretaries) for example, but men dominated and led. Although there are a few notable exceptions, women were rarely rulers, priests, or prophets.

We may see these laws and customs of ancient Israel as derivatives of their own and their neighbors' Stone Age heritage. But as far as the Hebrew people were concerned, their practices were absolutely correct for the authority of God stood behind them. When Jesus and his followers built the New Testament on the foundations of the Hebraic writing, the religious, social, and sexual rules of the ancient Near Eastern cultures soon became the standard by which most people of the Jewish and Christian faiths would for 2000 years lead their lives (Pagels, 1988).

**Jesus of Nazareth**  According to most Christian teaching, Jesus is the son of God. He was conceived in purity and born of a virgin; his was not a sexual conception. Although there is disagreement, most clergy believe that throughout his own life he remained **celibate.** As a prophet and preacher 2000 years ago, Jesus spoke throughout the land of Israel. But although he had much to say about piety, love, and compassion, he said almost nothing about sexuality. In general, Jesus seemed to follow the traditional Jewish teaching. He celebrated marriage and encouraged family. He condemned lust and particularly adultery. In one of his earliest sermons he said, "Everyone who looketh on a woman to lust after hath committed adultery with her already in his heart" (Matthew 5:28).

Although Jesus said little about homosexuality, intercourse, prostitution, and many other sexual issues, his followers searched his words for guidance.

*adultery*
Married persons having sexual relations with someone other than their spouse.

*celibate*
Not having sexual relations.

To this day, Christians ranging from the most liberal to those who consider themselves fundamentalists derive different meanings from the reported thoughts of Jesus. One of the first who interpreted the teachings of Jesus concerning sexuality was Paul of Tarsus. Deeply influenced by the more ascetic elements in early Greek philosophy, he was unsympathetic to the "base" physical demands of the body. Homosexuality and masturbation were "evil," heterosexual intercourse quite suspect, marriage a concession to the weakness of the flesh, and only celibacy truly acceptable in a Christian. In the New Testament, St. Paul announces in Galatians 5:16-17, "This I say then, Walk in the Spirit, and ye shall not fulfill the lust of the flesh. For the flesh lusteth against the Spirit, and the Spirit against the flesh: and these are contrary the one to the other . . ."

**India**   In the Middle East 2000 years ago, the Jewish, Christian, and later the Islamic faiths seemed to question sexuality. The sexual drives of women and men needed careful regulation. Islam, the Muslim faith, also insisted women had to be robed and veiled. In contrast, Hinduism in India talked about a journey through this life that may be different for every person. If it is your *karma*, meaning your destiny in this incarnation, to be poor, or idealistic, or lascivious, so be it! Your work, wealth, and interactions with others, your sexual practices are what they are. Every person's karma is unique, and there are few absolutes. Thus it is that Hindu priests could advise that courting another person's spouse is not recommended, but if it is your karma to be driven by love to this extreme, there are proper ways of conducting the seduction.

The tolerance, the seemingly fatalistic shrug about human behavior and particularly about sexuality, that accompanies so much Hindu thought sounds strange to those raised in the Judeo-Christian world. But Western religious tradition often divides that which is sexual and physical from that which is spiritual and divine. In contrast, Hinduism attempts to integrate sexuality with all

The Hindu concept of karma, inevitable fate or destiny, is believed by some to be an obstacle to social and technological change in India. Do you agree?

Erotic acts depicted on the wall of an ancient Indian temple.

of life. The unity achieved between women and men in the sexual act can be conceived as part of a vast cosmological principal that ties together all peoples, things, and places. Consequently, erotic acts among people, and even between the gods themselves, are often carefully and gracefully depicted on the walls of Indian temples and holy places.

Perhaps the most famous writing that has survived from antiquity that is specifically sexual in content is the Hindu book the *Kamasutra*. The revered Indian sage Vatsyayana wrote the *Kamasutra* (meaning "love precepts") for he believed that even exciting and pleasurable as sexual intercourse is, it is an art that must be diligently studied to obtain the greatest joy. Men and women, the *Kamasutra* instructs, must give highest priority to the pleasures of the senses. For example, there are 10 possible kinds of kisses ranging from the very subtle kiss of a lover's reflection in the water to the highly erotic means of stimulating a partner's lips and mouth with the tongue. Each needs to be carefully learned (Burton, 1985).

We do *not* want to give the impression that India and the Hindu faith are entirely tolerant of all forms of sexuality. Over the past 1500 years many different shifts in Hindu thought and practices have occurred. Some Hindu sects have focused almost completely on the spiritual and renounced many physical needs and pleasures. Today, while elements of some of the erotic realism and acceptance of early Hinduism are still apparent, India, in comparison with the United States, must be considered a modest and conservative society.

### The western world

**Greece and Rome**   We can leave the Middle East and India and begin our study of the modern Western world with the great Greek thinker Aristotle. Writing 2000 years ago, Aristotle described sexual interactions as natural mammalian events. He recognized that both women and men had powerful sexual drives and described orgasm as a pleasurable climactic occurrence. He also, but erroneously, suggested that in women it played an important role in preparing the uterus for reproduction.

Aristotle wrote and worked in a time when Greece felt powerful and was making enlightened experiments in democratic government. Greek statues, architecture, philosophy, and science celebrated strong, free, and beautiful women and men. People from many lands lived in ancient Greece, and vastly different customs and outlooks were tolerated. Greek life itself was dominated by numerous gods and goddesses who ruled every aspect of existence. *Zeus* was the chief god; *Nike* was the goddess of victory; *Aphrodite* was the goddess of sexual intercourse; and her son *Eros* was the god of the emotion love. Nearly every problem could be solved and almost any life-style could be justified by referring to the proper deity.

As the Greek world declined and the Roman Empire rose, Romans copied much of the life, art, philosophy, and theology of the Greeks. But one should not get the impression that Greek, and later Roman, life was entirely dedicated to beauty, science, knowledge, and tolerance. Both empires seemed to be almost continuously involved in wars and economic crises. Disease and poor sanitation often cut life short. Political plots, intrigues, and Caesars often brought suspicion, fear, and violence into every citizen's life.

In this turbulent atmosphere while much sexual freedom and experimenta-

As reflected in Bernini's *Apollo and Daphne*, Greek life was dominated by gods and goddesses.

tion were common, there were also restrictive countertrends. From one year to the next, there was ample contradiction. At times, for example, male homosexuality and **lesbianism** were tolerated or idealized. At other times these sexual preferences were severely punished. **Prostitution,** both male and female, and sexual activities involving groups of women and men were as often celebrated as they were denounced as unhealthy and condemned. The status of women, too, was contradictory. Many were confined to their homes and virtually regarded as the property of their husbands. Other women demanded and obtained the right to vote. Sometimes, too, in Greece and in Rome, women rose to positions of power and political dominance. Greece and Rome not only left us with a heritage of science, medicine, learning, and the beginnings of democratic government, but also many of the often conflicting views of the meaning of sexuality and the roles of women and men (Davis, 1984).

**Catholicism** By the year 300, Christianity, which had taken firm hold in the Middle East, spread to Rome and became the official faith of the vast and heterogeneous Empire. The Roman converts to the new Christian faith were re-

*lesbianism*
Female homosexuality. The word comes from the Greek island of Lesbos, said to be inhabited in ancient times by women who preferred the company of women.

*prostitution*
Engaging in sexual activities for money.

## The Mob and Witchcraft

In old Europe authorities suspected sexuality; the mob, too, expressed its attitudes. In Hungary, in the thirteenth century, a group of people appeared who were certain that the plagues then sweeping Europe were the product of lust and sin. These mobs marched from town to town, growing in size and fury. They sang hymns, bore wooden crosses, and publicly confessed and often reenacted their bodily desires. To display their penitence, mob members carried whips with which they *flagellated*, meaning whipped, themselves, with passion and abandon.

The seeming antisexual fury of the mob may well have had disguised erotic motives. The orgy of suffering for the sin of lust sometimes turned into group sexual activities or rape. The crowds got carried away with the very acts they were supposedly repenting. By the seventeeth century many flagellant groups had become so obviously sexual that the practice was strictly prohibited by Emperor Charles IV and Pope Clement (Tannahill, 1981).

Perhaps the most notorious example of antisexual fury that swept through most of early Europe and eventually the newly discovered American continent started in the fifteenth century. The medieval mind sought blame for every catastrophe. When there was drought, often a locally un-

popular person was believed responsible. When there was disease, minorities such as Huguenots, Jews, or dissident Catholics became the scapegoats. Who was to blame for the unsavory carnal impulses of men? Women, it was women who stimulated the lowest and basest need of even the most decent male! "Woman is a temple built over a sewer," the medieval banner read. Women

Witch-burning.

During the fourth century the Roman Catholic Church, but *not* its near twin the Eastern Orthodox Faith, insisted on priestly celibacy, total abstinence from all sexual activity.

pelled by what was depicted as the military, material, and sensual excesses of the Roman world. Many Catholic priests insisted on enduring monogamy, intercourse limited to reproduction, and purity as a goal for all men and women. St. Augustine (354-430), who lived in Carthage and Rome, may have set the Christian moral tone for centuries. As a young man he had numerous affairs and fathered a child outside of marriage. But in his early 30s he sought forgiveness and converted to Catholicism. In his preaching and writing, St. Augustine increasingly condemned sexuality. He eventually maintained that all sexual intercourse is sinful and that every child is therefore conceived in an impure act and must be cleansed of this sin.

By the fourth century, the campaign against the sins of the flesh included prohibitions on many forms of sexual expression and focused particularly on the question of priestly celibacy. Should the Roman Catholic clergy be allowed to continue to have sexual intercourse and marry or should they personally tes-

stirred men's passions. Since lust was the work of the devil, it supposedly followed logically that women were in league with the devil; they were witches.

The passionate distrust of women resulted in periodic outbreaks of mob torture and murder. Supposedly to bring order and sense to this persecution, two German monks—Johann Sprenger and Heinrich Kraemer—carefully and precisely described how to detect witches and how to deal with them. Their book, *Malleus Maleficarum* (The Witches' Hammer, 1487), served for centuries as the official policy manual for many in the church and government. The *Malleus* contains precise descriptions of the *incubi*, the male demons who seduce women, and the *succubi*, the devilish females who provoke and stimulate males. Since women were held responsible for most carnal lust, the monks recite in graphic detail how to strip a woman and investigate every orifice, so that if a devil is hiding anywhere, it can be found.

Many women who were mentally ill were likely to be brought before the inquisitorial courts and their hallucinations accepted as validated proof of their conspiracy with demons. Still other women, whose only "crime" was that they were different, were tortured until they "confessed" the most bizarre sexual acts. Ultimately, over the centuries, the *Malleus Maleficarum* fanned a witchcraft hysteria that was responsible for hundreds of thousands of women, and a good many men and children, too, being accused, tortured, and burned at the stake.

It should be emphasized that it did not take much to become a victim of the witchcraft paranoia. In most instances an accusation of lust and sorcery, no matter how unsubstantiated, resulted in the death of the innocent person. The charge of witchcraft was irrefutable. The *accusation alone was enough* for torture and death to follow. One outcome of these terroristic injustices was the demand, as humanity emerged from the Middle Ages, for laws protecting the rights of the accused. Cross-examination of the accuser, the need for concrete and confirming evidence of guilt, and the abolition of torture became part of the legal code of most advanced nations.

We have another, less enlightened, heritage from the witchcraft centuries. Faded remnants equating women with sex and witchcraft are still with us in our language. Every time we describe a woman as "bewitching," or "charming," or "spellbinding," we unknowingly acknowledge the medieval idea that women are in league with the devil (Pagels, 1988; Wedgwood, 1985).

tify to their commitment to the divine by total chastity? The problem was vigorously, sometimes violently, debated in churches, forums, and councils for several centuries. Finally Pope Leo IX (1048-1054) formally ended clerical marriage and commanded celibacy for all priests.

**Protestantism**   After more than 1000 years of uninterrupted Catholic supremacy in Europe, dissent and protest gave rise to an alternate form of Christianity. The Protestant religious reformation, roughly 400 years ago, questioned, revised, and reformulated Catholic doctrine. In its attitudes toward sexuality, Protestantism seemed then, as many faiths are today, somewhat ambivalent. Martin Luther, the moving force behind the Reformation, exemplifies the conflict, for he appears both restrictive and also quite frank about sexuality. He warned of the consequences of lustful thoughts and of masturbation. Yet, at the same time, Luther was intrepid enough, after decades of living as a

This sixteenth century painting by Albrech Durer shows a wife locked into a chastity belt, a device making it impossible for her to have sexual intercourse until she is released. These belts were often the butt of humor. The wife is shown slyly stealing money from her husband's purse to give to her lover so he can have a spare key made.

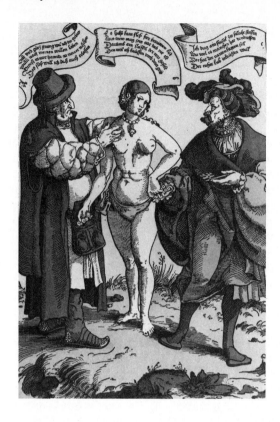

celibate priest, to renounce his vow of chastity and marry a young woman (Lowenich, 1983). A famous bit of advice, a humorous verse, attributed to Luther suggests he also, in a way, understood the healthy need for sexual satisfaction in both men and women:

> A week two
> Is the woman's due
> Harms neither me nor you,
> Makes in a year, twice fifty-two.

In contrast to Luther, who had some sympathy toward sexuality, John Calvin seems quite a strict theologian. Calvin, a sixteenth century Protestant leader, was an extremely able thinker, zealously devout, but also austere. On pain of imprisonment, women and men were not allowed to dance together. Adultery, as well as writing or painting anything that could be interpreted as erotic, might be punishable by death at the stake.

In England 300 years ago the followers of John Calvin, called Puritans, waged a long and bitter struggle against what they saw as a corrupt and unfaithful government and church. Eventually the Puritans fled and settled in what are now the New England states. The Puritans brought with them their convictions that men and women were by nature sinful. Only long and hard work could rehabilitate human beings and help them resist temptation. They forbade dancing, gambling, performing in theater, drunkenness, and any sexual activity except that for the purpose of reproduction within marriage. To violate any Puritan rule was an offense that could result in imprisonment, exile, or worse.

While the Puritans were stern and forbidding, another branch of Protestantism arose in the sixteenth century that contested the Christian doctrine of the Trinity and many of the views of Calvin and Luther. Early Unitarians, (because they believed in the oneness—unity—of God), evolved into what is today considered a liberal denomination. Recently, for example, this church helped write and distribute a sex instructional book that clearly and in detail informs young children about topics such as masturbation and intercourse (Chapter 8). Protestant beliefs, and to an extent most other religious faiths as well, have within them advocates of viewpoints on sexuality that range from what may be described as very liberal to highly conservative.

---

Our attitudes and beliefs are the outcome of our individual needs and our collective human history. The earliest human beings probably lived in groups, perhaps with few rules governing sexual conduct. About 5000 years ago, when the relationship between sexual intercourse and reproduction became clear, many different sexual customs and marital arrangements evolved.

Partnership styles in ancient Middle Eastern cultures tended to be strictly regulated, but ranged from polyandry to polygyny. This setting contributed to the marriage, sexual, and family practices of Judeo-Christian faiths. At the same time, there were other points of view. Much of the vast Indian nation and the Greco-Roman Empire appeared to have a relatively open attitude toward sexuality. Eventually, however, Judeo-Christian practices prevailed in Europe and became the basis of most Western values and laws.

*In Sum*

---

## MODERN BEGINNINGS
### Science and romance

Despite the condemnation of the pleasures of the flesh in old Europe, sexuality did not fade away. A drive as powerful as the sexual-reproductive need apparently cannot be ruled out of existence. While some sects prohibited dancing, dancing nevertheless continued. While authorities periodically campaigned against adultery and prostitution and drove suspected culprits from their towns, these behaviors continued and were often comically depicted in plays and songs.

Most significant for the study of sexuality, many scholars and scientists remained aware of the importance and complexity of human sexual needs. Even during the sternest days of European history, the works of great Greek thinkers like Aristotle were preserved and studied. Sixteenth century physicians dared to directly examine human anatomy and function. Careful dissections revealed the exact placement and much of the work of the vital organs. In this atmosphere an Italian doctor, Gabriello Falloppio (1523-1562) carefully probed the sex structure. He was particularly interested in pregnancy and presented a rough but relatively factual account of women's reproductive organs.

The *fallopian* tubes were, of course, named after him. Falloppio himself coined the terms *placenta* and *vagina* (Chapters 3 and 15).

Sexual behavior too was opening up for study. Many clergy and philosophers still condemned almost all forms of sexual behavior, but scientists wanted to know more. Disease, particularly if it seemed to be sexual in origin, was seen as fit punishment for sin. It was certainly not a condition to be treated or alleviated. But John Hunter (1728-1793), a Scottish scientist, took a different view. For him sexual infections were like other illnesses, puzzles to be understood and cured. In May 1767 he made two tiny incisions in a healthy penis and introduced a bit of gonorrheal discharge from an afflicted patient. Within a few days the healthy patient too had gonorrhea. Hunter concluded that if a means could be found to keep the gonorrheal discharge away from a healthy organ, the disease might be prevented. Equally important, gonorrhea was not a punishment but simply another infectious disease (Chapter 16) (Rapport and Wright, 1952).

**Romanticism**    Although a few scholars, physicians, and clergy kept the scientific study of sexuality alive, much of European thought was eventually dominated by **Romanticism,** a view that idealized love and emphasized emotion, imagination, and adventure. For centuries Europeans had been suspicious of and uneasy about sex. Then, starting about 400 years ago, a gentle means was found to divert and repress sexuality. Romantic love was not a new idea; it even appears in the Old Testament, in a culture considerably different from that of the West. But the fable of innocent boy and virginal girl falling hopelessly in love, the eternal "Romeo and Juliet," grew and prospered and continued until our present era.

The romantic notions of sensual innocence coupled with adventure to win one's true love gave birth to thousands of legends. After the initial attraction, it was the man who fought, labored, journeyed, and sacrificed so that he could win his lady. Sometimes the two lovers themselves are caught in intrigue and drama, but eventually they emerge triumphant and stand proudly at the marriage altar. They will live, the myth asserts, happily ever after.

Many of us today think of romanticism as a trivial device making for a worn-out, low-grade melodrama. But the idea of romantic love was a moving and profound discovery, a "truth" that guided many great European thinkers and artists. The famous eighteenth century French philosopher and revolutionary, Jean Jacques Rousseau (1712-1778), proclaimed the romantic ideal just as fervently as he hailed political freedom.

The social climate was undergoing rapid changes in France. Rousseau looked at the "modern" state and announced that all its customs, traditions, laws, and institutions did nothing but seduce and corrupt. Every government must be dismantled, and men and women must be returned to nature. In this natural world, the true and positive essence of every human being would emerge. In this natural world, the sexes would find they were destined for each other. There would be *one* woman right for just one man, and one man perfectly suited for just the proper woman. This was, Rousseau taught, the will of God, the law of nature, and the outcome of reason.

A century after Rousseau, Elizabeth Barrett Browning, the renowned English poet, put into words the ideal, totally romantic image of love. Her own

*Romanticism*
An emphasis on the nonphysical, spiritual, and ideal aspects of love and sexuality.

Many people still believe the romantic notion that there is only person (Miss, Ms. or Mr. Right) eminently suitable for them. Actually both research and experience show that there are likely many people with whom they could have an equally satisfying relationship and truly happy marriage (Chapters 11 and 12).

courtship contained all the elements of romanticism at its best. The attraction between Elizabeth Barrett and Robert Browning was, according to them, overwhelmingly intellectual and emotional, not physical. Their courtship was conducted by letter in a prose filled with only the purest sentiments of affection. When she was 44 years old in 1850, Elizabeth Barrett Browning wrote her husband what may well be the greatest romantic poem of the English language.

How do I love thee? Let me count the ways.
I love thee to the depth and breadth and height
My soul can reach, when feeling out of sight
For the ends of Being and ideal Grace.
I love thee to the level of everyday's
Most quiet need, by sun and candlelight.
I love thee freely, as men strive for Right;
I love thee purely, as they turn from Praise.
I love thee with the passion put to use
In my old griefs, and with my childhood's faith.
I love thee with a love I seemed to lose
With my lost saints—I love thee with the breath,
Smiles, tears, of all my life!—and, if God choose,
I shall but love thee better after death.
*(Sonnets from the Portuguese* [XLIII])

Romanticism idealized love and emphasized adventure.

## Victorianism

As the Middle Ages were ending, the knight became the symbol of romantic love. But knightly kindness and purity were little more than fiction. Romantic legend and royal reality were two different things. By the eighteenth century, revolutions tore through Europe. Ordinary people who were supposed to adhere to the strictest code of romantic sexual morality, found out that the doings between knights, ladies, and lords were a bit different from what they had been led to believe. In the royal houses, through books, plays, and operas, the sexual games and erotic intrigues became widely known and talked about. The appetite for young men of Catherine I of Russia became legendary. Louis XV in Paris reigned over a troubled Empire, but his mistresses multiplied as did his group sexual festivities (Tannahill, 1981).

The sexuality modeled by the aristocracy often encouraged ordinary people to experiment. Perhaps neither men nor women needed to be ashamed of their biology, and marriage was not sacred as church leaders insisted. In Europe and in North America communal groups sprang up of women and men who practiced nudism or lived together without being married. By the end of the eighteenth century, the American statesman, Benjamin Franklin, talked and wrote about his own vigorous sexuality and advised young people how to enjoy their sensual desires. Sex remained highly suspect, however, and Romanticism was still alive. The small rebellious forays into a more candid sexuality were met by a counterforce of moral purity when 18-year-old Princess Victoria mounted the throne of England.

Victoria became queen of the most powerful empire in the world. In the nineteenth century, England was a nation that imagined itself not only the military but also the moral leader of all humanity. Given such enormous power and prestige, Victoria and many of the British aristocracy set out to end the "depravity" among royalty and among the common folk. They were driven, they declared, to protect women and the family. Even more important, nineteenth century scientists had "discovered" that sexual activity leads to physical and emotional debilities. Sex drained vital bodily fluids and energies and could threaten the progress and dynamism of an increasingly powerful England. A decent husband, guarding his own and his wife's health (and the prosperity of Great Britain), had sexual intercourse no more than once a month. (Gay, 1983; Money, 1985).

*Victorianism*

**Victorianism** was a crusade not only for purity of thought and act but also for ignorance. No boy or girl, nor most women, were to know anything about sexuality. The campaign for purity and ignorance may be said to have begun when the Queen directed parliament in 1857 to ban obscene books. At first books that were obviously erotic in content were seized and destroyed. Soon, however, even great classics fell victim. The works of Shakespeare, Milton, and Dante, and even the Bible were carefully reviewed, and any passage that was suspect in even the remotest way was diligently edited out.

Following Victoria's lead, women's legs disappeared throughout England. Women wore layer on layer of stiffly starched, bulky skirts, so that no suggestion of legs, let alone buttocks, was perceptible. Modesty would not even permit a woman to disrobe in a doctor's office. Physicians kept dummies and the women patients would point to the place on the model where they felt pain.

The extreme modesty initiated by Queen Victoria may strike us as amusing.

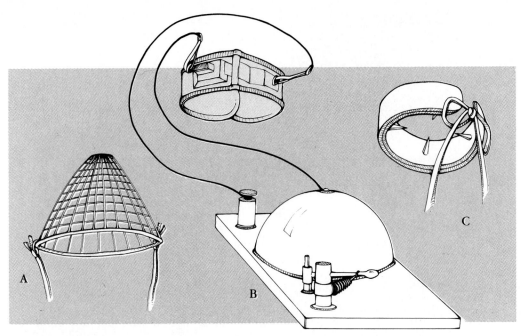

*Figure 1-1*
These Victorian devices were considered humane ways to prevent male erection and masturbation during sleep. A century ago they were thought far better than harsh beatings to punish "self abuse." Masturbation was held to result in loss of health and sanity. **A,** The mesh metallic cage was slipped over the penis and the straps locked together in back. **B,** Bell wired to a metal ring that slipped over the penis. If the boy's penis erected it expanded the ring, making a connection transmitted to the bell, which then rang, waking the child and his parents. **C,** This device was slipped snugly around the boy's penis and tied to his body. If the penis expanded, it was pricked by the sharp metal points.

Eventually, for example, furniture and piano legs were also covered up lest viewing them suggest "shocking" thoughts. When asking for chicken, white or dark meat was requested, not a leg or breast. Many Victorian practices, however, were punitive. To prevent boys from **masturbating**, special cages were manufactured that were locked over their penises at night. Some of the cages, to be more effective in preventing erections, had spikes sticking out of them (Figure 1-1).

Girls, too, were carefully watched, and any sign that they touched their genitals was sternly punished. Physicians warned that women who masturbated were particularly likely to suffer paralysis and insanity. Following the mood of the times, many doctors also announced that their investigations proved women were interested in being mothers and never derived any pleasure from sexual intercourse. It was a woman's duty to lie still, to sacrifice herself, and, in a ladylike way, to permit her husband to use her body to satisfy his animal needs. To suggest that women could enjoy intercourse, or actively participate in it, was more than shocking; it was disgusting (Brecher, 1980).

Victorianism succeeded in convincing generations of women and men that sex was a dirty business. It was best not to think or know about it and to get it

*masturbating*
Self-stimulating the sexual organs until climax is reached. The practice is now known to be common and normal (Chapter 8).

Nineteenth century Victorianism insisted on a strict morality. At the same time prostitution and other secret forms of sexual expression flourished.

Victorian prohibitions were particularly strict for women. Men were permitted more leeway. This double standard is more fully discussed in Chapter 2.

The most enduring legacy of the Victorian era may be the strongly held belief that, in matters sexual, ignorance is best. Many people still hold the view that the child or adolescent who knows nothing will not "get into trouble." Frequently, of course, the opposite is true.

over with swiftly and efficiently. But sex continued. Men and women had intercourse during marriage and even before. Some of the most sensual poetry ever written emerged from this guilt-ridden age. What's more, there was a rich underground market for erotic writing and pictures, some of which still seem unusually explicit today. Prostitution flourished in almost every city of any size. Despite the Victorian insistence on absolute sexual innocence and ignorance for women, or perhaps because of it, in 1850 more than 8000 prostitutes were known to the police to be operating in the streets of London. Another example was found in the busy and thriving industrial city of Leeds, where a historian counted 41 churches and chapels as opposed to 451 taverns and 98 brothels (Gay, 1983).

The Victorians may sound like a strange and distant people. The men dressed in black and wore top hats. The women wore crinolines. They lived in gaslit houses with ornate draperies and heavily upholstered furniture. By law, Sunday was set aside as a time of worship and most forms of entertainment were forbidden. But these nineteenth century ladies and gentlemen lived in a world not very different from our own. During this century England became the leading industrial power on earth. Its fast railways, mines and factories, ships, telegraph, and compulsory education marked it as a wealthy, modern nation.

The expansion and the riches of England convinced some that they were, in Thomas Macaulay's words (1855), "the greatest and most highly civilized people that ever the world saw." But not everyone was comfortable with the self-confident morality of Great Britain. Many wrote about a sense of loss, a fear that events were moving too fast and that human relationships could not stand the ever-changing technology and progress. In addition, the views of Charles Darwin (1809-1882) on the evolution of human beings seemed to question the very foundation of English and of all Judeo-Christian thought. The Victorian decades generated a great deal of conflict and stress. Many of our sexual doubts, anxieties, and inhibitions today are traceable to our Victorian heritage.

---

*In Sum*

Sexual restrictions have always existed on one level, and violation of these restraints on another. People have not always acted as society, religion, or the law has prescribed. In more recent centuries, the influence of Romanticism has been to idealize sexual attraction and to see it as spiritual and affectionate, almost without any physical component. Victorianism emphasized purity and ignorance and imposed a stern morality that reached into every aspect of human life.

---

## The twentieth century

**The first decades**   Victorian attitudes and mores lasted until well into this century. At the same time scientific investigation and thought were growing at an accelerated pace. In Europe intrepid thinkers and physicians such as Sigmund Freud and Henry Havelock Ellis (Chapter 2) were using the methods of science to study sexuality. Their findings that masturbation is common and harmless and that women have sexual desires helped dispel the punishing misconceptions of Victorianism. In the United States Margaret Sanger's tireless campaign to provide women with safe and reliable contraception (Chapter 14) promised to give women more personal freedom and greater reproductive choice than they had ever known.

By the time World War I ended in 1918, fashions, dance, and literature throughout North America had undergone rapid and liberating changes. The so-called Roaring Twenties saw young men and women flirting, dating, and dancing together intimately and confidently. Writers such as Ernest Hemingway (*The Sun Also Rises*, 1926) were describing lives that were adventurous, courageous, and free. The automobile, now within the economic reach of most middle class citizens, not only enabled young couples to get away but gave them a totally private place to talk about and explore their sexuality.

The 1930s saw the "Great Depression," and economic hardship came to almost every life. But the rejection of Victorian restrictions and of deliberate ignorance continued to grow. People wanted to know, and pioneering books such as Theodore van de Velde's *Ideal Marriage* (1926) told them in detail how to enjoy healthy sexual relations.

**1940s to 1950s**   In the 1940s the United States engaged in the largest war in its history. Sixteen million men and one hundred fifty thousand women served in the armed forces. They were taken from their homes during the years normally reserved for courtship and marriage to fight a fearsome and formidable enemy.

Dr. van de Velde managed to combine socially "proper" beliefs—"Marriage is sacred to the believing Christian"—with what was then thought outrageously shocking advice. He suggested, for example, that oral-genital sexual contact is a proper and enjoyable preliminary to intercourse.

At first women recruited into the services served as secretaries and nurses, but events soon changed this. By the end of the war, women were flying fighter and bomber aircraft across oceans. They were huddled with men facing combat areas, handling the most complex communication and electronic equipment. On the homefront, too, the jobs normally filled by the sixteen million young men at war were vacant. For the first time, massive numbers of women worked in factories, on the assembly line, in shipyards, and in mines. The popular image, celebrated by cartoons, songs, and motion pictures, was of "Rosie the Riveter," a strong determined young woman holding a heavy rivet gun, an essential in the war effort.

After the war, it should be pointed out, most women, "Rosie" included, returned to conventional domestic roles in their homes. It was not until a decade had passed that strong feminist movements emerged and progress was made toward equal opportunity, and financial, social, and psychological dignity.

Just as women were achieving a measure of recognition outside the home, sexual mores were shifting ever so slightly. For a young man and woman to live together or have intercourse before marriage was reprehensible in 1933 but hinted at in 1943. The men were going to war, their "sweethearts" might never see them again, and a few stolen moments together before the soldier left became the subtle theme in many Hollywood motion pictures and popular novels.

Whether for good or ill, too, the "pin-up" picture emerged into the open. Servicemen took with them photos of actresses like Betty Grable and Rita Hayworth. They were partly undressed, but still, in keeping with the morality of the forties, breasts and genitalia were clearly covered.

With the end of the war, the baby boom started. After 4 years of war and separation of young women and men, there was a deluge of marriages and childbirths in the late 1940s. This was also a time for celebration and innovation. All that was new and much that was daring seemed promising. In this atmosphere in 1948, the Kinsey studies of male sexuality (Chapter 2) were published, a work the authors considered a dull, narrowly scientific volume that might sell 1000 copies to physicians and scholars. But the reverse was true: so hungry was the population for information that the first printing of the book sold out in weeks. Subsequent printings by the many tens of thousands were not able to keep up with the demand.

*pornography*
Sexually explicit books and films intended to be arousing.

Information based on Kinsey, *Playboy,* and other sources of sex research is detailed in Chapter 2.

It may have been the totally unexpected popularity of the original Kinsey study that triggered the beginning of what can best be called a sex industry. To be sure, there has always been underground **pornography,** sexually explicit films and books secretly available if you knew the proper dealer or store. But in 1953, the first edition of *Playboy* magazine appeared on the public newsstands. Right there, for all to see, no longer hidden, was a magazine devoted to pictures of seminude women, and titillating stories and articles. The magazine was an immediate success. Its ability to associate a sense of affluence with a seemingly innocent, although exploitive, sexuality seemed to meet the needs of the postwar generation. *Playboy* brought "soft-core" pornography into the open, became one of the best-selling magazines of all time, and stimulated hundreds of imitators.

**1960s**   By the late 1950s and early 1960s, sexuality in the media and as entertainment had become acceptable or close to it. Elvis Presley, the Beatles, and numerous other rock musicians sang about love and gyrated their bodies with intent and provocation. Perhaps the most important event during this era was the development and availability of oral contraception, "the pill." Now for the first time there was a totally reliable contraceptive that did not interfere at all with coitus. A woman who took the pill every night was totally protected and could be spontaneous with her lover.

Whether it was "the pill," rock and roll music, the opposition to the Vietnamese war, the mushrooming Civil Rights movement, or the growing availability of marijuana and other drugs, a new attitude seemed to develop. Many adolescents and young adults strove to be "hip," meaning up-to-date, unconventional, and rejecting of old rules and standards. The themes of this "hippie" revolution were "hang loose," "question authority," "drop out," and "make love, not war." This was a time for experimentation and no field or institution was exempt. Some students and teachers founded nontraditional colleges. Personal and sexual relationships of every type and variety were encouraged, both for those who were single and many of those married (Chapter 12). The new counterculture prescribed a distinct manner of dress, essentially the same for young women and men. The hair was long; jeans, beads, leather boots, and fringes were the order of the day. Genuinely rebellious hippies were never more than a small minority, but their **hedonism,** sexual liberality, and questioning of authority affected all Americans and brought about a decade of experimentation (D'Emilio, 1988).

*hedonism*
Pleasure seeking; it was coined by the ancient Greeks to describe a philosophy of life dominated by seeking physical and psychological comfort, beauty, and joy.

**1970s and 1980s**  During these decades the often cited "sexual revolution" triggered by the rebellion and counterculture of the preceding decade seemed to take hold. The United States Supreme Court legalized abortion throughout the land. Its rulings on pornography and prostitution appeared to embolden both enterprises. Movie houses and newsstands merchandising the most sexually explicit material became common in every town of any size. Group sex clubs, massage parlors, and the like opened in dozens of cities around the nation (Chapter 19).

In the colleges, what were once strictly gender-segregated dormitories now included both women and men. When once only a small proportion of adolescents had premarital intercourse, it now became common (Chapter 8). In fact, the frequency of intercourse among all people, married and unmarried, with their spouse and with others, increased (Chapters 9, 12, 13).

Perhaps one of the most significant and enduring effects of the almost revolutionary changes in sexual attitude was the very substantial increase in the proportion of unmarried couples living together. Before the 1950s such couples, then often described as "living in sin," were uncommon, particularly among those who were middle class. By the 1980s the picture had changed. Living together, without marriage, has become much more acceptable and several million couples now have such relationships (Chapters 8, 9, 12).

During this last generation, too, the feminist movement seems to have made considerable gains. Women are now employed in virtually all jobs and professions and their income is becoming more equitable. A new sensitivity has also emerged concerning issues such as harassment, so that many women and men feel more comfortable with one another in both work and social situations (Chapters 10, 20).

Many students can remember some of the seventies and the marked changes in attitudes and behavior that occurred then and still affect us today. Can you identify some current attitudes that have been influenced by the seventies?

Interest in sex education in the schools and colleges also grew. Where sex had once been a topic not to be discussed at all, or if addressed confined to whispered exchanges, a need was now seen to provide accurate information to young people. Although some argued "the more you know the more you do," a growing consensus held that it was through knowledge that individuals could make intelligent sexual decisions. Chapter 8 examines attitudes and approaches toward sex education.

Thanks to Masters and Johnson, sex therapy also became established. In fact, even the most conventional magazines, particularly those aimed at women, were filled with articles advising pleasurable, orgasmic, and sexually enhancing techniques. Sexual satisfaction was a promise held out to all.

## LOOKING AHEAD

Trends often continue. Perhaps equality for women and men will flourish and grow. It is possible, too, that personal and sexual freedom will increase. But at the same time, countertrends are evident. Sexually explicit materials and entertainment have been curtailed in many areas (Chapters 19, 20). In the last few years, the age of first intercourse has increased and the number of different sexual partners has declined. There seems to be a shift, too, among young men and women from focusing on sexuality to more emphasis on the emotional and affectional aspects of becoming a couple. Perhaps the tragedy of AIDS has accelerated a trend already present, or it may have created one out of necessity. It does seem evident that more and more people are moving into monogamous relationships (Chapters 9, 12, 13).

What we are today and what we will become tomorrow reflect our history and heritage.

Sexuality during adolescence, and among those younger, has come under renewed scrutiny and its appropriateness more closely examined. Abortion and sex education, which seemed assured several years ago, have once again become the centers of controversy. In the 1970s there was a "sexual revolution"; free and open attitudes often seemed to be encouraged. In the late 1980s and '90s we may be witnessing a countertrend—a new sexual conservatism. It is, of course, impossible to predict what will happen 2 years or even 6 months from now. But it is clear that sexual attitudes and behavior are fluid and changing, so that what seems appropriate in one age may be thought improper in another.

### Ethnocentrism and cross-cultural perspectives

A glance at our history has shown that sex is one of the most regulated of all human activities. Although our sexual needs are deeply biologically rooted, we modify them by what we learn, and the prescriptions of our parents, culture, and faith. We, in turn, as friends, mothers, fathers, or educators, teach what we consider proper sexual behavior to others. After all, our way, many of us are convinced, is the best way. In our sexual outlook, as in many other areas of our lives, we are **ethnocentric**; we judge right and wrong from our own perspective. We have learned to regard our own ways as correct and tend to look down on the behavior of others as erroneous or morally wrong.

*ethnocentric*
Believing one's own sexual and social standards are correct and other's wrong.

Yet, throughout the world, standards of sexual propriety differ. Anthropologists have shown how often societies have totally different standards of sexual conduct. Tribal societies often offer vivid contrasts. In the South Pacific, for example, while the Manus of New Guinea view most sexual expression as shameful, the people on the Island of Mangaia seem freely to celebrate the pleasures of sexuality. In Africa the Nyakyusa of Tanzania strictly limit the sexual interest of youngsters. When boys reach the age of 10, they are required to leave their parents' village and establish their own settlement a distance away. Youngsters move out because they should not see or be tempted by the sexual activities of adults. The Nyakyusa have an intense dislike of childhood sexuality and particularly of relations between the younger and older generations. In sharp contrast, another tribal group in East Africa, and not too far away, the tall stately Masai, accept that men in their 30s may seek the companionship of young girls (Malinowski, 1985; Rosman and Rubel, 1981).

We do not have to travel to obscure islands or to visit tribal societies to show the marked differences that exist in sexual standards and practices. The major nations of the world often differ substantially in their mores. In North America masturbation is considered by most people to be a common and normal practice. In many African nations such as Nigeria, masturbation is viewed as childish and shameful. In the United States, extramarital sexual affairs are strongly disapproved by most couples (Chapter 12). In France, when a husband or wife has an affair, the news is likely to be met with an understanding shrug of the shoulders. The feeling is "such things happen all the time and it is nothing to get very excited about" (D'Emilio and Freedman, 1988; Oshodin, 1984).

We limit marriage to one partner, and divorce is quite common. In several major Islamic (Moslem) nations (Morocco, Libya, Saudi Arabia, Iraq, and others) a man may have several wives, although divorce is infrequent. There is also a sharp difference in dress. Throughout most of North and South America and Europe women are encouraged to dress attractively, sometimes even provocatively. In the Moslem states, women must be modestly completely covered and their faces veiled. Also, they are traditionally kept apart from men in their social and recreational activities.

Within the United States and Canada there are widely discrepant community standards. In many states homosexual behavior or an unmarried man and woman living together is legally forbidden. In a few areas a couple that engages in oral-genital sexual contact is committing a felonious act and may be prosecuted (Chapter 20).

Religious groups have also often taken strong opposing positions. The Roman Catholic Church and some Orthodox Jewish and fundamental Protestant faiths vigorously oppose abortion. At the same time many people in these faiths, or with other religious traditions, firmly uphold freedom of choice. There are similar differences in attitudes toward premarital intercourse, contraception, and masturbation. What one group opposes another may tolerate and a third even encourage. At the same time, every group believes it is correct, that the viewpoint it teaches—its sex education—is morally and ethically right.

Ethnocentrism has some value. It helps a group solidify and ensures a considerable degree of social cohesiveness and loyalty. But ethnocentrism carried too far produces a rigid society and intolerant individuals.

There is an antidote to ethnocentrism and that is to learn and understand other people's cultures, beliefs, and practices. Granted, it is easy to look at others and whisper "immoral," "sick," or "kinky." But if we are to leave ourselves open to growth, we need to know that our convictions may not be the only valid ones. An intellectually honest student and a careful teacher maintain a *cross-cultural perspective*. They recognize and understand that to the questions posed by sexual and affectional needs, other people have reached other answers that make sense to them.

A cross-cultural perspective allows us to see also how much a drive as potent as sex may be modified by custom and practice. Equally important, a cross-cultural approach helps us compare our traditions with those of other nations, faiths, and people. It aids us in evaluating the effectiveness, the strengths and weaknesses, and the validity of our own rules.

In short, our heritage and our directions are ambivalent ones. Our society and our individual psyches are loaded down with ambiguous directions and conflicting messages. In this setting, every person needs to chart her or his own course based on solid information, understanding, responsibility, and good will. (Money, 1985; D'Emilio, 1988).

---

*Summary*

Human sexual behavior is a product of our biology and of numerous cultural, religious, and individual experiences and influences. The present species of humans appeared some 40,000 years ago and may have lived in fairly large groups or bands. About 5000 years ago, when humans began to settle and farm, various family forms evolved along with numerous regulations governing sexual relations. In the Middle East laws and attitudes coming from several cultural sources eventually became the basis for Judeo-Christian belief and teaching concerning family life and morality. At roughly the same time, the Hindus in India often saw sexuality as an integral part of both physical and spiritual needs.

Two thousand years ago the Greek and Roman empires and their relatively candid views of sexuality were gradually replaced by the rapidly growing Roman Catholic faith that insisted on priestly celibacy and advocated significant sexual restraint. Fifteen hundred years later, as the Protestant Reformation swept through much of Europe, some sexually repressive sects emerged; the Puritans, for example, banned most social and nearly all physical sexual contact. This inhibited atmosphere sometimes spawned hidden sexual frenzies such as flagellation and the witchcraft mania. At the same time, there were still enlightened voices both in the clergy and, particularly often, in medicine.

During the last several hundred years the Romantic and the Victorian eras both emphasized sexual attraction as a spiritual, nonphysical event. Marriage was often idealized, though in reality, the inhibiting morality of Victorianism often severely oppressed women and men. Though the Victorian age had its share of secret eroticism, it was punitive overall, and it left many anxieties still evident today.

During the last decades, trends toward greater personal and sexual freedom and equality between men and women have been evident. At the same time, a new emphasis on monogamy and more conservative values has appeared. Given the many different pressures, viewpoints, and practices in our own nation and societies around the world, most people need to learn and to work toward an informed and ethical standard. A cross-cultural perspective, an insightful look at our ethnocentrism, can help us responsibly fulfill our sexual and human needs.

---

1  What can the study of people as they lived tens of thousands of years ago tell us about human sexuality today? How did the understanding that coitus led to reproduction influence the needs and behaviors of men and women? Do you agree with the hypotheses presented in the textbook?
2  How has your own religious background influenced your views on sexuality and your behavior? Consider how some of your sexual practices may conflict with a strict interpretation of your religious faith.
3  Evaluate your attitudes toward premarital intercourse, abortion, homosexuality, fidelity, and divorce, and try to trace the roots of your feelings.
4  As the book explains it, how did the Judeo-Christian and Hindu attitudes toward sex differ?
5  Explain the hidden sexual motives of the flagellants and witch burners. Give examples of other instances with which you are familiar where there seem to be hidden sexual motives.
6  Test your own ethnocentrism. Name some of the ways you believe your own sexual attitudes and practices are better than those of others. How is ethnocentrism a barrier to understanding and growth?
7  It has been said that we are still recovering from a debilitating sexual disorder called Victorianism. Evaluate the extent to which you believe people are still sexually repressed or burdened by feelings of shame or guilt.

*For Thought and Discussion*

*References*

Altherr, T.L. *Procreation or pleasure? Sexual attitudes in American history.* New York: Krieger, 1983.

Brecher, E.M. *The sex researchers.* Boston: Little, Brown, 1980.

Burton, A. *The Kama Sutra of Vatsyayana.* Berkeley, Calif.: Berkeley Publishers, 1985.

Davis, N. *The rampant god: Eros throughout the world.* New York: Morrow, 1984.

D'Emilio, J., and Freedman, E.B. *Intimate matters: a history of sexuality in America.* New York: Harper & Row, 1988.

Fagan, B.M. *People of the earth: an introduction to world prehistory.* Boston: Little, Brown, 1983.

Gay, P. *The bourgeois experience: Victoria to Freud. Vol. I. Education of the senses.* New York: Oxford, 1983.

Lowenich, W. *Martin Luther: the man and his work.* Minneapolis, Minn.: Augsburg Publishing House, 1983.

Malinowski, B. *Sex and repression in savage society.* Chicago: University of Chicago Press, 1985.

Money, J. *The destroying angel.* Buffalo, NY: Prometheus Books, 1985.

Oshodin, O.G. The sexual life-styles of polygynous African men. *Journal of Sex Education and Therapy,* 1984, *10*(2), 37-40.

Pagels, E. *Adam, Eve, and the serpent.* New York: Random House, 1988.

Rapport, S., and Wright, H. (editors): *Great adventures in medicine.* New York: Dial Press, 1952.

Rosman, A., and Rubel, P.G. *The tapestry of culture.* Glenview, Ill.: Scott, Foresman, 1981.

Tannahill, R. *Sex in history.* New York: Stein & Day, Publishers, 1981.

Tanner, N.M., and Zihlman, A.L. *Woman the gatherer.* New Haven, Conn.: Yale University Press, 1981.

Wedgwood, C.V. *The spoils of time: A world history from the dawn of civilization through the early Renaissance.* New York: Doubleday, 1985.

*Suggested Readings*

Davis, N. *The rampant god: Eros throughout the world.* New York: Morrow & Co., Inc., 1984.
> Sex customs and beliefs are the concern of this book. The writing and style are uneven but in all quite captivating.

Gibson, I. *The English vice: beating, sex, and shame in Victorian England.* New York: Grove Press, 1984.
> A highly readable and knowledgeable description of the conflicting moral/sexual views, practices, and vices during Victorian times.

Gordon, B. *Jennifer fever: older men, younger women.* New York: Harper & Row, 1988.
> The relationships that develop between younger women and middle aged men, a practice more common in other societies, are examined in a breezy, sometimes humorous, often dramatic way.

Pagels, E. *Adam, Eve, and the serpent.* New York: Random House, 1988.
> The biblical story of the creation is reconsidered from an historical perspective. Pagels' readable book illuminates early Christian thinking regarding human freedom, religion, and sexuality.

Tannahill, R. *Sex in history.* New York: Stein & Day, 1981.
> This highly witty, literate, and penetrating history of sexual behavior, customs, literature, and ideology should be a must on everyone's reading list.

*Chapter 2*

# Studying Human Sexuality

**When you finish this chapter, you should be able to:**

Identify some of the contributions to the study of sexuality and some of the misconceptions of Freud, Ellis, and Krafft-Ebing.

Describe some of the work of major researchers such as Kinsey, Masters and Johnson, and Blumstein and Schwartz.

Explain how a scientific survey, case study, experiment, and observation are conducted.

Describe statistical terms such as mean, correlation, and significance.

Modern science is little more than a hundred years old. Toward the end of the nineteenth century, technology, experimentation, and scientific inquiry advanced rapidly in the United States and Western nations. Chemists, engineers, and other physical scientists announced fundamental discoveries and inventions such as x-rays, radio, and the airplane. Medicine conquered yellow fever, was attacking other infectious diseases with vigor, and was beginning to perform complex surgery. In this atmosphere, social scientists, too, were prompted to be courageous. It was time to look objectively at a topic that was often politely ignored or even diligently suppressed. In this chapter some of the major explorers of human sexuality will be presented along with a sample of their findings. We will also learn how modern sex research is conducted and evaluate the meaning and validity of its conclusions.

## PIONEERS: EARLY EXPLORERS

The scientific exploration of human sexuality is only about a century old. This does not mean that sex was ignored throughout human history. Galen, a physician in both Greece and Rome 2000 years ago, described the coital positions he believed best for fertility and reproduction. He drew his conclusions from listening to his patients and from animal observations. Galen is also credited with identifying and naming gonorrhea and attempting treatments that had some effectiveness. So thorough were Galen's reports and his work on anatomy and physiology that his conclusions, both accurate and erroneous, dominated medical thinking until the fourteenth century. Unfortunately, however, in medieval Europe sex research was usually suppressed and it was not until the nineteenth century that it again reappeared (Chapter 1).

### Krafft-Ebing (1840-1902)

One of the first modern investigators of human sexuality was Richard von Krafft-Ebing, a psychiatrist who practiced in Germany and Austria. He worked and wrote at a time when Victorianism and Romanticism sternly, though inconsistently, repressed sexual needs.

Krafft-Ebing's intention to explore and document human sexuality was honest and diligent, but his attitude was distorted by two factors. First he was a product of his time. He looked at sex with some suspicions and misgivings. Second, he was a medical doctor in the employ of the police and as such had maximum opportunity to see people seriously sexually maladjusted. The result was that Krafft-Ebing's writings and case citations seem somewhat lurid. The readers of his books, particularly his 1902 volume, *Psychopathia Sexualis,* are led to the conclusion that since everyone the doctor describes is sexually disturbed, sex might well be a fearsome activity. We wrote the following case study in the style of Krafft-Ebing to suggest the cases seen by him and the emotional writing style he used.

Richard von Krafft-Ebing

> CASE 30. During the month of June, 1896, quite a number of young girls had been struck in the genitals on the street in broad daylight. On the 2nd of July the perpetrator was caught in the act. V., twenty years of age, was hereditarily heavily tainted; when fifteen years old he had been sexually excited to a high degree at the sight of a woman's buttocks. From that time on it was this part of the female body which attracted him in a sensuous manner and became the object of his erotic fancies and dreams, accompanied by pollutions (ejaculation). Soon this was coupled with the lascivious desire to slap, hold, pinch, or strike the genitals of women. At the moment when he in his dreams performed this act, pollution took place.

Krafft-Ebing appeared particularly uncomfortable with female sexuality. He supported the **double standard,** the view that men may tolerably engage in premarital and other sexual activities, but women may not.

*double standard*
The conventional attitude that permits men more sexual freedom than women.

> The unfaithfulness of the wife, as compared with that of the husband, is morally of much wider bearing and should always meet with severer punishment at the hands of the law. The unfaithful wife not only dishonors herself, but also her husband and her family, not to speak of the possible uncertainty of paternity (Krafft-Ebing, 1902).

The attitudes and recommendations of Krafft-Ebing powerfully influenced several generations of doctors and disturbed millions of readers. However misdirected we may consider his orientation today, his examinations and case recordings were performed with meticulous care. Despite his biases and errors, Krafft-Ebing told doctors, scientists, and scholars that the study of sex, *sexology*, was legitimately their business. Krafft-Ebing directly helped pave the way for Havelock Ellis and Sigmund Freud and for the researchers working today.

To guard against people reading his books and becoming sexually excited, Krafft-Ebing wrote many of his descriptions in Latin.

### Henry Havelock Ellis (1859-1939)

In 1896 Henry Havelock Ellis, an English gentleman, but also a courageous and open-minded scientist, published the first of seven volumes of his *Studies in the Psychology of Sex*. The books revealed how people around the world, and in other times, dealt with sexuality. Much to the surprise of his reading audience, the restrictive views shared by the Victorian countries were *not* the ideal upheld by all other societies. Ellis, for example, examined the Victorian belief that modesty requires that most parts of the body be hidden by clothing. He found that human beings were completely inconsistent. Europeans, English, and Americans were scrupulously careful to hide their penis, breasts, vagina, buttocks, and adjacent areas. In contrast, the Japanese often bathed together totally in the nude. Furthermore, many African groups once considered covering sexual areas improper and provocative. At the other extreme, the Islamic nations, Turkey and Arabia, were adamant about requiring the female face to be hidden, while American, British, and European ladies painted their faces to emphasize their lips, cheeks, and eyes.

Henry Havelock Ellis

Central to Ellis's thesis was the notion that to understand sex, scientists needed to reach far outside the Victorian West. Even more important, Ellis was convinced that what his compatriots thought of as "civilization," meaning their own cultural preferences, had actually handicapped normal sexuality.

Havelock Ellis collected hundreds of what he called histories of sexual development. Since he was a doctor, many came from patients who sought his help. Many others turned up on his travels and still others were mailed to him by people who read his books. If nothing else, the positive tone of Ellis's writings was a welcome reassurance to his readers. He made it clear that no one single sexual standard applies to all people everywhere in the world. Responsible adults from diverse national, religious, and ethnic backgrounds have evolved different, and for them suitable, standards of modesty, marriage, and sexual behavior. Further, many of the beliefs held by Victorians concerning sexual behavior were misinformed and often unjustly punitive.

Ellis pointed out that around the world, different nations and societies had evolved many contrasting rules and practices concerning modesty, morality, and sexuality. (See ethnocentrism and cross cultural perspectives in Chapter 1.)

### Sigmund Freud (1856-1939)

Few people have had as profound or as broad an effect on the understanding of human motivation and behavior as has Sigmund Freud. His analysis of the psyches of men and women has influenced physicians, novelists, historians, and social scientists from many different specialties. Few of Freud's ideas or observations have gone unchallenged, but it is likely that his name and much of his writing will continue to be recognized for its uniqueness and creativity.

Freud was born and worked in Vienna, Austria, until the homicidal religious persecution initiated by the Germans caused him to flee to London in 1938. He was trained as a medical doctor and specialized in neurological illnesses. Soon, however, he became more and more interested in psychological complaints and explored where the fears, phobias, and pains of his patients ac-

Sigmund Freud

tually originated. Influenced by Krafft-Ebing, Freud at first attributed psychological disorders to masturbation. But Freud was not content with this explanation. His almost compulsive analysis of everything his patients said forced him to conclude it was not sexual indulgence, but rather sexual deprivation, that ultimately transformed itself into neurotic symptoms.

Based on his analysis of hundreds of patients, Freud was convinced that sexual impulses and needs are in the main quite good. But when these drives are continually devalued, pushed aside, ignored, and finally **repressed,** symptoms of stress and conflict are bound to result. The clearest instance of this, according to Freud, occurs when sexual repression results in a condition called *conversion hysteria*. This is a neurosis characterized by the paralysis of limbs, visual or hearing impairments, or other physical symptoms. We wrote the following case study to suggest the cases seen by Freud.

*repression*
The rejection from conscious awareness of thoughts or impulses that are painful, disagreeable, or unhealthy.

Emily, a 19 year old, shy, young woman, went with her fiancé to a garden party given by his parents. A game was started in which the young people chased and tagged one another. Emily had to chase her fiancé up a small hill and when she reached the top was so out of breath that she gasped, panted, became dizzy and finally fainted. When she revived she reported she had lost her hearing. A few days later, Emily insisted that her wedding be postponed. The family sought expert medical advice, but seven months after the incident Emily could still not hear and still refused to marry. Finally she was brought to see a psychoanalyst.

The freudian trained doctor asked Emily to relax and talk freely. Over the course of months Emily's story was pieced together. When Emily was ten years old, her young and shiftless Uncle moved in with the family and was given the bedroom next to hers. Emily immediately liked him, admired his stories and soon had a crush on him. Often she could hear him go into his room, undress and go to bed. Fairly soon after the Uncle moved in, Emily began to hear the maid's voice in her Uncle's room. Listening carefully she could even hear some of their words, then their heavy breathing and gasps. She realized they were having intercourse and became both sexually aroused and frightened. To prevent becoming excited Emily soon began putting her hands over her ears, and burying her head in her pillow so that she heard nothing.

When all the circumstances were clear, the analyst helped his patient understand that her recent deafness was brought on by her breathless panting while chasing her fiancé in the garden game. These sounds unconsciously reminded Emily of the noises made by her uncle and the maid doing something she both desired and also feared. Her defense when she was eleven was deafness, blocking up her ears. Now that she was faced with marriage and sexual intercourse, which she also feared, she again resorted to deafness.

For Freud, conversion hysteria clearly pointed out the unconscious struggle between sexuality and morality. Actually, there were supposedly three components in this drama within the mind. The so-called *id* (primitive sexual and aggressive drive) was pitted against the *ego* and the *superego*. The ego was the *reality principle*. It was our own civilization, our culture telling us what we can or cannot get away with. The superego was conscience, it was the *ethical and moral principles* "learned at the mother's knee," telling us what is right or wrong, praiseworthy or wicked.

Freud, much to the consternation of his contemporaries, saw sexuality as part of the id, beginning in infancy. He believed sexual and psychological needs evolved together. Every child was seen passing through several psychosexual stages. At first psychological-sexual gratification was obtained through the mouth. This **oral stage** lasted from birth until the first year of life. The **anal stage** followed, gratification now being achieved by defecation and other toilet functions. Between the ages of 3 and 5 the child was said to be in the **phallic stage,** pleasure centered on the genitals.

Freud believed each stage left its mark. A child who was overindulged or frustrated at any particular stage might *fixate,* permanently carrying personal traits traceable to one of these early periods of life. Typical oral traits that might become permanent were said to include such behaviors as smoking and excessive talking. Anal traits that might become permanent might include stinginess or excessive cleanliness.

Freud also believed the phallic stage was critically, but differently, important to the maturation of boys and girls. During this stage, girls are likely to learn that boys have a penis. Finding this out, and seeing the importance supposedly granted to a male child, the girl develops *penis envy.*

Boys suffer a similar concern related to their own penis. Toward the end of the phallic stage they "fall in love" with their mother: the *Oedipus* complex. At the same time they are anxious that this incestuous wish will result in their penis being cut off by their father, *castration* fear. If this troubled period was mishandled, Freud believed the child's heterosexual identity would be impaired (Chapter 13). But if these oedipal needs were appropriately repressed, the youngster would learn to "act like a man," identifying with his father, so that he too might one day have a woman for his wife.

By the time boys and girls reach their fifth year, this considerable sexual turmoil is, according to Freud, eased by the **latency period.** Freud supposed that children's sexual drives are substantially reduced, almost quiescent, from the age of 6 until puberty, the beginning of adolescence. During this quiet time, sexual concerns are laid aside, while physical, intellectual, and emotional

**oral stage**
The period in life, according to Freud, in which psychological and sexual pleasure is obtained through the mouth.

**anal stage**
According to Freud, during the second and third years of life most pleasure concerns defecation.

**phallic stage**
Freud's third psychosexual stage: when pleasure is focused on the genitals.

**latency**
The time during which sexual drives are supposedly relatively dormant; from about age 6 to puberty, according to Freud.

*genital stage*
From puberty onward, Freud believed that psychosexual pleasure is mature and focused on coitus.

*psychoanalysis*
The technique proposed by Freud for treating personal and psychological disorders. It requires patients to speak openly and honestly to their therapist about their entire lives. Today there are many different forms of therapy and relatively few therapists still practice freudian psychoanalysis.

growth become dominant. If all goes well, by the early teenage years the child enters the **genital stage,** the period when she or he is ready to assume full adult psychosexual function.

Sigmund Freud wrote volumes, constantly polishing and revising what he produced until he died at the age of 83, a world-renowned authority. We cannot cover the entirety of the theory of **psychoanalysis,** and a great deal of what Freud wrote is no longer accepted. Few therapists still fully uphold hypotheses such as penis envy, latency, and psychosexual stages. Contemporary psychoanalysts also think Freud had an unfortunate tendency to exaggerate his views by choosing overly dramatic metaphors or terms, such as oedipal or superego. He also tended especially to misperceive and neglect the psychological needs and development of girls and women. Overall, however, a few freudian psychoanalytic concepts have found general support and we will summarize those that bear most directly on human sexuality (Freud, 1959; Gay, 1988).

1. Sexual drives are healthy biological needs and begin in infancy.
2. Every child is born with the potential for learning or developing a variety of different sexual interests and orientations.
3. Sexual drives may be unconscious and may underlie some attitudes and behaviors, even seemingly far removed from sexual needs.
4. The repression of sexual energies can lead to anxiety, depression, and other personality disturbances.

Krafft-Ebing, Freud, and Ellis were all physicians. Much of what they reported was based on their study of people who came to them for help. Krafft-Ebing's patients were often individuals who had violated the law. Freud tended to see upper-class Viennese who were relatively sophisticated, and Ellis saw women and men who had sexual problems. They had difficulty becoming aroused or having intercourse. Conclusions based on studies of patients are undeniably useful, but one needs to be careful not to generalize on this basis about the sexuality of healthy people. To explore sexual behavior in general we need to study individuals from all walks of life, young and old, women and men, healthy and sick, and coming from every social, religious, and ethnic group.

## SEX RESEARCH TODAY

Contraceptives, particularly the condoms used by men, are an effective way of preventing the transmission of many sexually infectious diseases (see Chapters 15 and 16).

The contemporary exploration of sexuality began slowly. At the beginning of this century, the silence compelled by Victorianism was clearly weakening. Then the First World War brought a new frankness into some sexual attitudes. For example, at first the government tried to prohibit servicemen from having intercourse with the numerous prostitutes who surrounded military bases. But eventually it was obvious that fraternization could not be stopped and that sexually infectious diseases were rapidly multiplying. As a result, the military adopted the nearly unprecedented realistic policy of recognizing sexual needs and supplying servicemen with *condoms* intended to prevent disease.

During the "roaring" twenties, the free feeling that followed the end of the war helped women reject long Victorian skirts and crinolines. Short skirts, cheek-to-cheek dancing, and the new inexpensive Model T Fords led to a heady feeling of liberation in both sexes. In this atmosphere, Dorothy Bromley and F.H. Britten conducted one of the first scientific surveys of sexual behavior. Unlike Freud, Ellis, and Krafft-Ebing, who were physicians working largely with people with problems, Bromley and Britten studied normal young women and men. They administered a fairly brief questionnaire to 1364 students at 46 colleges. Their publication, *Youth and Sex* (1938), showed that male and female students, the social and educational elite of society, were, for that day, fairly active sexually. Most had masturbated, many had extensive petting experience, and quite a few had intercourse. This enterprising beginning blazed a trail soon to be followed by increasingly thorough sex research.

## Alfred Kinsey (1894-1956)

Little more than a generation ago, the most detailed and comprehensive surveys ever conducted about human sexuality came into being through the efforts of Alfred C. Kinsey. Kinsey was not a sexologist, but he was a scrupulously careful scientist. He was a professor of entomology, content with classifying and recording the varieties of wasps and other insects. But in 1937 Indiana University asked him to teach a course in sex education and marriage. In his efforts to prepare for the new assignment, Kinsey read widely and found that although much was believed about sex, there was relatively little research from which to draw valid conclusions. Human sexuality needed to be thoroughly investigated.

Alfred C. Kinsey

Kinsey assembled a team of social science research experts, and together they developed a precise, probing questionnaire and interview. They checked and rechecked their results and produced a now classic study on the sexual behaviors of men and women. In all, they interviewed over 11,000 people and asked hundreds and hundreds of questions. The result was that the team collected literally millions of bits of information and provided data that scientists still find useful.

The two Kinsey books, *Sexual Behavior in the Human Male* (1948) and *Sexual Behavior in the Human Female* (1953), detail precisely who does what, how often, and with whom. For example, Kinsey and his associates recorded the weekly frequency of married intercourse according to age, education, and religious affiliation. What emerged from this enterprise were two 800-page books filled with page after page of charts that the authors believed would be of interest to only a few medical and mental health professionals. But what turned out to be the case was that the public was so hungry for accurate information that the books became sensational best sellers.

Anthony Comstock, a tireless crusader for what he considered decency, succeeded in having the federal government pass the *Comstock Laws* in 1873, forbidding the mailing of sexual and related literature. Since much of Kinsey's work occurred before those laws were repealed in the 1960s, some officials then argued that Kinsey's questionnaires and books should be declared obscene and the researchers should be indicted.

The Kinsey surveys were conducted over a generation ago, and much of the information is now outdated. For example, Kinsey devotes an entire chapter to human sexual contact with animals, an experience that is rare today. In addition, the proportion of people who have premarital intercourse or oral-genital contact has increased substantially as we will see in Chapters 5, 9, and 12.

A more serious criticism of the Kinsey studies is that they did not fairly sample all segments of the American population. Most respondents were middle to upper class Protestants, living in cities. Older people, those in rural areas, and other religious and ethnic groups were underrepresented. Black Americans were in large part omitted. The Kinsey findings have also been criticized for relying too heavily on volunteers. This is a deficiency common to most sex research since one must volunteer to participate, thus eliminating the experiences and histories of nonvolunteers. The behavior of nonvolunteers may differ

The Kinsey surveys are imperfect and have shortcomings, but they still stand as models for other researchers, often providing information with which present-day scientists can compare their results.

somewhat from the behavior of people who volunteer to participate and discuss their sexuality. Nevertheless, the Kinsey findings are still recognized as monumental contributions to our understanding of human sexuality.

The information collected by Kinsey and his associates is now a half century old. But the thoroughness with which thousands of people were interviewed left behind a wealth of data that is too rich to be just filed away. As a result, what is now called the Kinsey Institute, under the direction of Dr. June Reinisch, is reinterviewing a substantial portion of the 11,000 subjects originally examined. The Institute hopes to find the consistencies, as well as the changes, in the sexual lives of the original participants. The effects of illness and aging on sexual behavior are also being studied (Hall, 1986).

### Morton Hunt

Twenty years after Kinsey, sex research was no longer a lonely or uncharted enterprise. Numerous investigators, physicians, and counselors wrote about their findings and observations. One of the most conscientious attempts to bring the Kinsey findings up to date was reported by Morton Hunt (1974). In order to get a representative **sample,** Hunt researchers selected the names of 2000 women and men from telephone books in 24 cities scattered around the United States. The subjects picked were telephoned and invited to participate in a small group discussion of sexual behavior. Despite reassurances about the credibility, anonymity, and scientific importance of this conference, only about a fifth of the people telephoned appeared for the discussion. Following the talk, subjects were given a 1000-item questionnaire to fill out, exploring a full range of their sexual behavior.

*sampling*
A method for studying a large population by selecting a small representative segment. Since we cannot survey all people in the United States, we select a sample.

Hunt tried to replicate the Kinsey findings. He was hampered by the fact that his research techniques were far from perfect. For example, 80% of those contacted for the survey did not respond. Might the sexual behaviors of these nonvolunteers be different from those who volunteered? Other critics have suggested that answering a 1000-item questionnaire has to inevitably result in fatigue and quick thoughtless responses just to get the task completed. But despite these shortcomings, the Hunt survey portrayed much of the detail of sexual activities in the 1970s. Other researchers have been particularly pleased by being enabled to compare the Kinsey data of the 1940s with the Hunt information gathered in the 1970s. This has helped make clear how much sexual behavior can change over the course of a generation.

### Shere Hite

Shere Hite's surveys of sexuality were conducted from a feminist perspective. She felt that many of the sexual needs and feelings of women, and in some ways those of men, were underreported. Hite tried to focus her questionnaire on how people experience sex in their lives. Her report on female sexuality in 1976 gave the results of a questionnaire completed by 3000 women. In 1981 *The Hite Report on Male Sexuality* revealed how 7000 men came to terms with their sexuality.

Hite's work demonstrated the importance of clitoral stimulation for orgasm in women and the need for touch in men. For both she showed the significance of the emotional component in sexuality.

Hite's work has often been criticized as biased, scientifically weak, and drawing broad conclusions based on a relatively special population. For instance, the researcher stated that she mailed out over 100,000 questionnaires to women and received only 3000 back. Further, the people who answered appeared to be well educated, liberal, and unusually sexually aware. Many of the questions in the survey have also been pointed out to be suggestive. For example, an inquiry about how "frustrated" you feel if you do not have an orgasm may be quite leading. The Hite studies have serious limitations. But both books with their many self-descriptions and anecdotes sometimes provide enlightening reading. Hite's responders frequently let us know a good deal about the emotional, as well as the physical, details of their sexuality.

We wrote the following to suggest the type of self-description quoted in Hite's work:

> I like being with Terry. It's important to me that we make love together. And it's very good. Both our orgasms are very good. But when I'm alone, when I excite myself and I go on to masturbate, it's sometimes a lot better. I feel almost embarassed to write this down since it may not sound very loving. But Terry and I do love each other very much. It's just that when I masturbate and have an orgasm alone, it's very powerful. I feel it creep up on me. It comes from down in my legs, deep in my belly, and it's just sometimes really powerful. Maybe, I've thought, this orgasm is more powerful or deeper because I'm alone. I don't have to be concerned about Terry. I don't have to think about how I appear to another person. I can be totally uninhibited by myself.

The latest Hite book, *Women and Love: A Cultural Revolution* (1987), may be the most controversial of all Hite's work. Her percentages are considered much too high by many sexologists. Hite reports that 70% of the women in her study who are married 5 years or more are having extramarital relations; 87% said that they had their deepest emotional (not physical) relationship with a woman friend. Nine out of ten felt harassed by the men they loved, and 98% wished for more communication and closeness with their male partners.

Like Hite's earlier works, this report has been criticized for its ideological tone and scientific weaknesses. Hite said she sent out 100,000 questionnaires and got back only about 4.5%. This low response rate in itself assures a highly biased volunteer group who are very likely to respond because they have a grievance. One off-the-record critic has said, "It is not only the obvious man-bashing that bothers me, but the reporting as scientific fact what is no more than a collection of gripes." Hite's work is questionable, but it must also be acknowledged that she does document that there are very many women who find their relationships with men unsatisfying and lacking particularly in emotional closeness.

## Magazine surveys

Magazines that are directed primarily toward women or toward men have conducted a number of surveys that are noteworthy because of the large numbers of readers involved. In 1980 *Redbook* magazine surveyed 20,000 of their female readers and 6000 of their male partners about the quality of their relationships. Among many other new findings, the magazine reported that oral-genital contact was experienced by nine out of ten of the couples responding to the magazine's questionnaire (Sarrel and Sarrel, 1980). In 1987 *Redbook* again

Readers of special magazines often respond in very large numbers to surveys and questionnaires. Even if the respondents are not a fair scientifically selected sample of the entire population they help researchers understand the sexuality of the groups that identify with that magazine.

questioned 26,000 women readers and found most heartily enjoyed their sexuality and the intimacy it often evoked. Comparable magazines, *Cosmopolitan* and *Playboy,* increased the number of respondents by surveying hundreds of thousands of their readers (Cook et al., 1983; Wolfe, 1981). They reported their audiences quite sexually active. Most respondents began having sexual intercourse in their adolescent years and many had several different sexual partners before they were 30 years old.

Magazine survey findings such as these are often valuable. They report the results of questionnaires given to hundreds of thousands of readers. The information revealed, however, is often scientifically limited. It may well be that the findings reported by such research apply only to a proportion of the younger and more educated women and men who typically read *Redbook, Playboy,* and *Cosmopolitan.*

### Blumstein and Schwartz

*cohabiting*
Living together without being married. The term is usually used to describe a heterosexual relationship.

One of the largest couple investigations conducted in recent times was by Phillip Blumstein and Pepper Schwartz (1983). This team studied both heterosexual and homosexual partners who were either married or **cohabiting.** They evaluated 12,000 mail questionnaires, directly interviewed 300 of the couples responding, and 18 months after the initial contact sent half the couples follow-up questionnaires. The researchers contributed many interesting findings; just a few will be mentioned here. Among heterosexual partners, males more often initiate sexual contact. Among heterosexual and homosexual couples, the frequency of sexual intercourse declined gradually in an analogous manner the longer the pair remained together. The Blumstein and Schwartz research is not without flaws: its sampling and follow-up questioning are often uneven. Overall, however, it is so insightful that we will refer to it often in subsequent chapters.

### Masters and Johnson

William H. Masters, a gynecologist, and Virginia E. Johnson, trained in psychology (and husband and wife), took the study of human sexuality in a new direction. Recognizing the shortcomings of questioning people about their sexuality, they determined to study male and female behavior directly. Their subjects were observed in a medical laboratory. Ingenious cameras and other recording apparatuses were constructed so that masturbation, coitus, orgasm, and other sexual behaviors could be recorded. In this way, over the last 30 years, both researchers have been able to describe the physiological and psychological events that lead women and men from first sexual excitation to climax and the period of relaxation that follows.

To be historically fair, Masters and Johnson were not the first to study sexuality directly. A few early Greek physicians, 2000 years ago, tried to understand how seminal fluid resulted in pregnancy by witnessing coital activities. In more recent times, early in this century, the famous psychologist John Watson, the founder of behaviorism, measured the physiological changes that occur during sexual intercourse. While a professor at Johns Hopkins University, he connected several measuring instruments to his body and that of his female partner. Word of his research leaked out and caused considerable furor. The university and Watson's wife, as well as legal authorities, denounced his work.

Virginia Johnson and
William Masters

The information obtained from the study was never made public and Watson
was dismissed from Johns Hopkins in 1920 (Schultz and Schultz, 1987).

Soon after their innovative laboratory observations began, Masters and
Johnson used the information they gathered from measuring tens of thousands
of heterosexual and homosexual responses to devise means to treat sexual
problems. The procedures they advocated departed sharply from previous psychotherapeutic attempts that offered mainly discussion and counseling. Masters and Johnson insisted that their patients learn about their own physical
function and actually practice various massage, masturbatory, and coital techniques with their own partner in complete privacy. This treatment was direct,
relatively quick (about 2 weeks), and claimed to be highly effective (Chapter
17).

The pioneering work of Masters and Johnson has not escaped criticism. It
is argued that what people do in a medical laboratory setting while being photographed and observed could in some ways misrepresent actual sexual behavior. Doubt has also been cast on their treatment results. Zilbergeld and Evans
(1980) point out that some of the work of these sex researchers has not been
confirmed by other scientists. Further, little is known about how Masters and
Johnson selected subjects and how representative their research participants
were of the population as a whole. Most of all, Zilbergeld and Evans suggest
that the Masters and Johnson claims of very high success rates treating both
heterosexual and homosexual people must be looked at with skepticism. Masters and Johnson seemed to report therapy a success even when a person was
just *beginning* to show a little improvement. To be fair, however, like most
studies in an area as difficult as human sexuality, the Masters and Johnson efforts are imperfect but have contributed substantially to our knowledge of the
sexual function of women and men (Masters, Johnson, Kolodny, 1986).

### Richard Green

Sex research need not always involve thousands or even hundreds of subjects
to enable us to gain some insights. Richard Green (1987) a psychiatrist, began

The Masters and Johnson
and other therapies to treat
sexual difficulties are
described in Chapter 17.

## The Hazards and Ethics of Research

In this text we report the results of many different investigations of human sexuality. Readers should be aware that even the most careful and scientific study is offensive, even infuriating, to some people. The Kinsey investigations in the 1940s, and the work of Masters and Johnson 10 years later, brought sacks full of hate mail. Efforts were made to charge the investigators with committing criminal acts and a few political, clerical, and journalistic spokespersons denounced their work as immoral or subversive. Sex researchers today are often less likely to be officially harassed, but considerable opposition to sexology, the scientific study of sex, still remains.

Sex researchers who are trained professionals are very concerned about protecting their subjects. The American Psychological Association (APA), the American Association of Sex Educators, Counselors, and Therapists (AASECT), the Society for the Scientific Study of Sex (SSSS), the American Medical Association (AMA), and other professional groups have drawn up the most stringent guidelines to protect participants in sex research and in treatment. These standards guard both the investigator, from accusations of malpractice, and the subjects, from any sort of physical or psychological injury. These ethical requirements prohibit sexual intimacy or other exploitation and assure the subjects that their identity and records will be kept completely confidential. No legitimate investigator will ever request any behavior or act that is abusive or violates ethical standards. Central to all the safeguards is the rule of *informed consent*. This means that all participants in research or treatment shall know as fully as possible the methods and aims of the project so they can, with full knowledge, agree (or not agree) to take part.

examining effeminate behavior in boys a generation ago. He followed 44 boys who had been referred to him for treatment primarily because their behavior was judged "extremely effeminate." Many of these boys played almost exclusively with girls, often dressed in female clothing, shunned vigorous or typical male games, and/or played with dolls. Over the course of nearly 2 decades, Green found that despite the attempts of counselors or parents to influence the boys' sexual orientation, three fourths of the original 44 children were homosexual or bisexual by the time they reached their twenties. To help validate these findings, Green compared a group of boys of similar ages who engaged in more typical masculine games and behaviors and found only one who was bisexual.

Green's work suggests homosexual and heterosexual orientation is evident early in life. Can one say that playing feminine games causes boys to have a homosexual orientation? Or, could it be that an inherent biologically given sexual need led these boys to more feminine activities? The study says a good deal, too, about how we differentiate childhood games and activities into masculine and feminine. If we did not label activities as girl or boy games, how might this affect gender and sexual orientation? Like many good studies, large or small, Richard Green's work raises a number of substantial questions that need to be examined further (Chapter 13).

By the end of the nineteenth century, despite inhibiting Victorian attitudes, scientific progress and inquiry were accelerating. In this atmosphere, Krafft-Ebing was one of the first pioneers to look at and write about sexuality in a scientific manner. At about the same time, Havelock Ellis showed that sexual mores varied greatly from one society to another. A third pioneer, Sigmund Freud, announced that he had discovered that sexual repression, and not license, could cause psychological disorders. All three explorers were physicians and their observations may not adequately describe the sexual behavior of all people.

The first large-scale investigation of sexual behavior was conducted by Alfred Kinsey. Although the sample of people studied was not entirely representative, the work is so thorough that many of the findings are still applicable today. Subsequent researchers such as Morton Hunt and Blumstein and Schwartz have updated and added to previous information. Their surveys are vulnerable to volunteer error and the likelihood that respondents are not always truthful. Masters and Johnson have largely avoided these problems by moving sex research into the laboratory where they studied and recorded sexual responses directly. Sex research is difficult and requires trained scientific skill but increasingly more valid information is accumulating.

## TECHNIQUES OF SEX RESEARCH

Sexologists, like other scientists, rely on a number of research methods in their attempt to understand human sexuality. Unlike most other scientists, however, sex researchers are working in an area that people consider private. Many men and women are reluctant to participate in sex research. As a result, sex researchers need to devise procedures and employ techniques that are scientifically productive yet still respect individual needs and sensitivities. One way in which personal hesitation to participate in sex studies has been overcome is for investigators to rely on anonymous surveys and confidential interviews.

### Interviews and surveys

Surveys are the most popular way to obtain information about sexual behavior. If we want to know how often newly married people have intercourse, we might simply mail a questionnaire to 1000 couples whose marriages have recently been listed in city records. We could even send our surveyed group a calendar and request that for the next 6 months they mark the time and day when they have intercourse and then mail the completed diaries to us. In this way we rely much less on memory and may get a more accurate record of the frequency of marital intercourse.

Surveys are also often conducted through personal interview. If we want to know how and when people first learned about sex we could just knock on 100 doors, or make 100 telephone calls, and question those who respond to our inquiry. But a truly reliable survey is not as easy to conduct as it may sound. We need to be aware of several important requirements for survey research whether it involves an anonymous mailed questionnaire or a private interview.

## Sex Research

| Research | Year(s) | Comment |
|---|---|---|
| Alfred Kinsey and associates: *Sexual behavior in the human male; Sexual behavior in the human female* | 1948, 1953 | In a pioneering undertaking, thousands of men and women were carefully interviewed about their sexual behavior. Despite some sampling shortcomings and the age of the research, these studies remain highly informative and worthwhile. |
| Masters & Johnson: *Human sexual response; Human sexual inadequacy* | 1966 to present | Virtually for the first time, photographed and physiologically recorded thousands of instances of sexual arousal, orgasm, masturbation and coitus. Devised short effective treatment for sexual problems. Conclusions have been said to be distorted by laboratory procedures and research weaknesses. Overall, the findings continue to make an invaluable contribution to understanding sexuality. |
| Morton Hunt: *Sexual behavior in the 1970s* | 1974 | Hunt showed both consistencies and changes in sexual behavior a generation after the Kinsey findings. Research weaknesses limit the validity of some of the observations. |
| Blumstein & Schwartz: *American couples* | 1983 | A careful but limited study of the sexual and affectional behavior of couples. |
| Shere Hite: *The Hite report on female sexuality; The Hite report on male sexuality; Women and love.* | 1976, 1981, 1987 | Although Hite's findings are guided by a controversial point of view and not representative of the population as a whole, her case reports are often insightful. |
| Magazine surveys: *Redbook, Cosmopolitan, Playboy* | 1980, 1983, 1987 to present | Magazine research has the advantage of surveying well over 100,000 readers. Findings can be revealing but often apply more to the magazine's readers than they do to all adults. |

*representative sample*
A small group that is very much like the entire population from which it comes.

**Sampling** We cannot ask every married couple in North America how often they have intercourse. We will instead have to rely on a **representative sample.** That is, we will survey a small and manageable group of people that is very much like the entire population in whom we are interested. In the Kinsey studies on male sexuality, the investigators tried to make sure that the men they sampled were as close as possible to the population as a whole in terms of age, religious affiliation, education, and other such variables. For example, if by chance the researchers question only men who are college graduates about foreplay, they might falsely conclude that all men enjoy extensive foreplay. This would be a false conclusion because it has been found that male interest in foreplay is somewhat related to education. Often, the greater the amount of formal schooling, the higher the likelihood of foreplay. A first requirement, therefore, for every survey that intends to make statements for a *whole population* is that it be representative, including an equitable proportion of old and young, urban and rural, and so on.

Representative samples can be obtained in several ways. We will describe two. First, we can try to match the number of college graduates, different occupational groups, and so forth in our sample with the proportion of each group in the entire population. Another possibility is to select people by **random sample.** The assumption is that if we pick subjects simply by chance, then there is an excellent probability that the representation of various groups will be fair. Since, for example, nearly every adult in the United States has a social security number, we might just pick every ten thousandth number and send a survey questionnaire to this person to be filled out. Obtaining a good representative sample by random or *proportional selection* may sound difficult, but social scientists now have computerized techniques that make such selection processes routine.

Another requirement of surveys is that they need to be of sufficient size. Can one question 29 women about their premarital sexual experiences and then draw conclusions for all 40 million single women in the United States? Probably not. In order to yield accurate information, samples need to be large enough (as well as representative) lest their conclusions be meaningless. Sample size has been thoroughly explored so that expert researchers have formulas available to tell them the number of people they will need. Although there are exceptions, we can say as a rough rule of thumb that a sexuality survey should question at least several hundred people, if the results are to have meaning.

**Questions** Surveys depend on questions. Whether a survey employs a questionnaire or depends on face to face interviews, questions must be asked cor-

*random sample*
A small group selected by chance procedures from a larger population.

A good interviewer spends considerable time talking informally to a subject in a relaxed setting, establishing good rapport, before taking careful notes.

rectly. In both situations inquiries need to be asked or written in an unbiased accurate manner. Interviewers need to be painstakingly trained not to reveal shock, approval, or any personal attitudes when they question. On paper, questions need to be similarly unprejudiced in their appearance. For example, asking, "Have you ever had extramarital intercourse?" is likely to lead to a "No," and close off a sensitive area. It would be much more productive to say, "Please describe your extramarital sexual experiences."

It is especially important to ask questions that are neutral and not leading when an emotionally charged issue is examined. As a class exercise, half of the students polled their dormitory suites and asked, "Should there be a constitutional amendment prohibiting abortions for all women no matter what the reason?" In response to this question 32% of those polled said "Yes." The other half of the students asked "Should there be a law protecting the life of unborn children?" To this question 68% of the students said "Yes." Based on the answers to the first question, one could argue that most people are for the freedom to choose an abortion. The second question suggests that most people are against it. Often you can get the result you want by constructing a question that biases the answer. We want to emphasize that a scientific survey is not simply a casual question and answer session. Whether a surveyor uses a printed questionnaire or a carefully planned interview, the interrogation is designed with painstaking skill and care.

**Volunteer error**   Most surveys of human sexuality rely heavily on volunteers. The purpose of the research is clearly stated, reassurance concerning the confidentiality of the data is given, and people are invited to participate. For example, in the Hunt (1974) survey, a sample of over 2000 people was chosen who appeared to represent the national population in terms of gender, marital status, race, and other important variables. But, as we noted a few pages earlier, only one in five eventually agreed to participate. In the Hite surveys, less than 5% volunteered. We know from previous research that volunteers in sex surveys often tend to have a more active and more colorful history. It may be that people who have the confidence to talk about themselves also have enough self-assurance to be more sexually adventuresome. Knowing this, we wonder how much the sexual habits of the few who volunteer accurately reflect the feelings and conduct of the many who do not. This means that the results of any investigation that depends only on a relatively small number of volunteers must be interpreted with great caution (Barker and Perlman, 1975).

### Observation

Observation, watching and recording a subject's behavior, is a well-established scientific technique. Careful observations of infants, for example, have shown how skills such as perception, language, and reasoning develop. Observation of animals, such as gorillas and wolves, in their natural state has shed light on questions concerning aggression and communication. In many of these studies, the observer needed only a notebook. In others, motion picture and other photographic equipment was used to record every aspect of the subjects' behavior for careful analysis.

In most observational studies, it is important that the observer blend in, that he or she not intrude and thereby change the behaviors that have been targeted for study. Monica Moore (1985), for instance, was interested in how

A major advantage of observational research is that scientists do not have to rely on the subjects' imperfect memories and sometimes not too truthful self-reports.

## Which Sex Research Is Legitimate?

If you become a participant in sex research you may have to reveal some very sensitive concerns and experiences. You will need to be unusually honest and forthcoming. Unfortunately, an individual occasionally will pose as a sex researcher in order to uncover intimate details of your life, or to become aroused (Chapters 19, 20). Which of the following appears to be legitimate sex research, the only kind in which you should take part?

1. A telephone caller tells you that your name has been chosen at random. She would like your cooperation in important research on the biology of sexual experiences. If you consent she will first send you a questionnaire to fill out. Next you may be asked to report to the well-known university hospital in your town. The caller has identified herself as Dr. Pavarotti, but has answered very few of your questions. She tells you that when you receive the questionnaire, you will also get a consent form and a booklet describing all procedures.

2. Several days ago you returned home with your new baby. A telephone caller, who stated he was Dr. Caruso, said he read your name in the births column of the newspaper. Since he is doing research on child care for the famous university hospital in your town, he would appreciate it if you would answer some questions over the telephone. He asks whether you are breast-feeding, how much larger your breasts have become, whether you enjoy breast-feeding, if you feel sexually aroused while nursing, how you like to have your breasts caressed, etc.

3. You have received a questionnaire in the mail. It is to be returned to Dr. Kiri at a Post Office box number, although the questionnaire states that the research is being carried out for the famous university in your town. The questionnaire requires that you describe your masturbatory, heterosexual, and homosexual history and experiences in detail. You are asked to sign the form and give your address as a way of pledging that you have answered every question honestly.

---

women and men get to know each other in a cocktail lounge. The researcher observed patiently for hours, appearing like a customer in order to understand the movements the women particularly, used to start a relationship (Chapter 10).

In some situations more is required than just being unobtrusive. Anthropologists have long been aware that they get their most meaningful data and are best able to understand a society when they participate in it. In the same way, some studies of sexuality have involved **participant observation.** This requires that the scientist both be a participant and simultaneously retain enough objectivity to observe and record. Several studies of homosexual interactions and of *swinging* (couple sexual exchanges) have involved participant observers (Chapters 12 and 13). By both participating and observing, a disciplined social scientist is often able to learn far more than is possible by even the best interview or questionnaire.

While observations in the natural setting may usually be preferable, sometimes they are not possible or ethically desirable. For these reasons, Masters and Johnson (1986) investigated sexual response by bringing nearly 700 women and men into their laboratory. There, physiological instruments could

*participant observation*
A method of studying behavior by actually becoming part of the group to be studied and engaging in some of its activities.

be used to evaluate such things as blood flow, vaginal chemistry, penile erection, and other sexual biological processes.

A clear advantage of observation is that it permits trained scientists to directly collect and interpret data. In contrast, when sex researchers need to rely entirely on questions, "What happens when you have an orgasm?" investigators are completely dependent on the subject's intelligence, memory, and frankness. But observer studies have disadvantages, too. Perhaps the most vexing problem is that observation may result in subjects subtly altering their behavior. They may act a little differently when being observed in contrast with how they ordinarily behave in complete privacy.

### Case studies

Case studies permit researchers to concentrate on studying a few people with great care. Such research can result in new discoveries or answer specific questions.

So far we have mentioned survey and observational research that has involved many hundreds, even hundreds of thousands, of subjects. But such massive numbers may not always be necessary. Sometimes the careful study of only a handful of people can assist our understanding of sexuality. When only a few people are investigated, it becomes more important than ever to guard against bias, faulty observations, and unwarranted conclusions. With these cautions in mind, we present an example of an informative case study.

During the first part of the 1980s it became apparent that a new and fatal disease, AIDS (acquired immune deficiency syndrome), had appeared. It seemed primarily to infect homosexual men and secondarily intravenous drug users and blood product recipients. As more was understood about the disease, it appeared possible that heterosexual transmission might also occur. To answer the question of the possibility of heterosexual transmission, Robert Redfield (1985) and his associates examined the wives and children of seven male heterosexual AIDS patients. They found that in five cases the wives had evidence of infection, but only one of the eleven children was positive (possibly because of close contact with infected blood). This made it clear that heterosexual intercourse could transmit the virus. The fact that 10 of the 11 children were not positive suggests ordinary close household contact may not usually be sufficient for transmitting the ailment. We will discuss this new and threatening sexually transmitted disease further in Chapter 16. For now we want to make it clear that we can also learn a great deal by case studies.

### Experiments

There are many ways in which information can be gathered. Our list is not complete, but we do want to mention experiments. Experimental analyses are a favorite for scientists because they enable investigators to exercise unusual control of the conditions they are studying. They can ask a precise question and often get a detailed answer. For example, a great many questions have centered on the degree to which male and female hormones determine behavior. Are human beings who are more active sexually simply responding to the demands of their own body chemistry? To answer these questions, experiments have been conducted with both human beings and animals. Usually the experimenter randomly assigns each subject to a *control* or an *experimental group.* The two groups should be as much alike as possible. But the control is administered a harmless substance, a **placebo.** These subjects serve as a base for comparison. In contrast, the experimental group is given sex hormones. The results

*placebo*
A harmless substance that sometimes "works" only because it is believed to work.

Although human and animal behavior differ substantially, research with monkeys and other species sometimes gives revealing hints about the possible meaning of human drives and needs.

of such experiments over the years (Chapters 3 and 4) have shown that while animals such as rats and chimpanzees are often clearly affected by the administration of sex hormones, human behavior is altered only subtly or indirectly by hormonal biochemistry.

Experimentation is still not a common way to study sexuality. Scientists cannot ethically inject humans with hazardous chemicals or expose them to new or different sexual partners and measure the effects. Nevertheless, experimental methods appropriately used with animals and sometimes with people can contribute to our knowledge of sexuality.

An investigator usually makes sure the research is "double blind." Neither the subjects nor the experimenter know who is getting a placebo and who the real thing.

---

There are many ways of scientifically exploring human sexuality. In sex research, surveys are the most commonly used technique. They can provide much information, but care must be taken that the population questioned is representative. Equally important, the distortions that occur as a result of volunteer error and biased questions need to be avoided. Observational methods allow direct recording, measurement, and photography of subjects. Case studies and experiments can also be useful, but as in all scientific investigations care must be taken to assure that conclusions drawn are accurate and meaningful.

*In Sum*

---

## STATISTICAL DESCRIPTION

### Averages

Statistical descriptions are an indispensable tool in all the sciences and equally necessary when talking about sexuality. One of the most frequent terms we

Mean and median are technically "measures of central tendency," telling us the middle score in a range of scores.

will use is *mean*, which is a synonym for average. This is calculated by adding all scores and dividing by the total number of scores. The *median* is the score or number in the middle of a range of scores. If we asked everyone in a classroom to line up by size, the person in the middle would be the median height. Half the class would be taller and half shorter. The *mode* is the most common or frequent score. In our example, the modal height would be that which appeared most often.

We also need to know how much scores vary. How much behavior differs from one person to the next is reported by the *range*. Knowing the range is important because it can demonstrate that a mean or median is not necessarily the "normal" score. For example, a healthy 60-year-old couple may be having intercourse three times a week and then read the average for their age is once a week. If, like many people, they confuse average with good or normal, they may erroneously worry that they are too active. But if they know that the range among similar older couples is between two and fifteen times monthly, they will be not only better informed but also reassured.

### Correlation

When any two factors (marital happiness, income, age, years of education), correlate, it means they move in parallel fashion. If the correlation is quite high, say .8, it means that as one factor goes up (or down), the other follows closely. For example if age and marital happiness correlated .8 we could be fairly certain that the older a couple the happier would be their marriage.

Two students are discussing whether or not "it pays to get good grades." The advocate states that, "the higher your grade point average, the more money you'll be offered on your first job." The problem is readily resolved by calculating a statistic called the *coefficient of correlation*. It measures the degree to which any two variables are related. A correlation can range from 0, demonstrating absolutely no relationship, to 1.0, showing a perfect correspondence. Suppose, for example, we did a careful study of all graduating seniors and compared their grade point averages to their starting salaries. If the investigation found a correlation of 1.0 it would mean that there was a perfect relationship between grades and money. The higher the grade point average the higher the salary offer. But what if, as is more likely, the correlation was found to be 0? This would mean that grades and money are not at all related. Someone with low grades just as often winds up with a high salary as someone with high grades.

Computers have greatly facilitated statistical research.

## How Can Sex Be Scientifically Investigated?

The following questions were asked in a sex education class. Each question reflects a personal value—a judgment concerning sexual activity. As such, none of the questions can be scientifically answered, but each can be reworded so that a trained researcher can obtain important information about human sexual attitudes and behaviors.

Be a scientist. Rewrite each question in the space provided so that it can be objectively investigated. (See Appendix p. 578 for answers.)

1. Is sexual intercourse outside of marriage wrong?

   _____

   _____

   _____

2. When a person habitually masturbates does it mean she or he is immature?

   _____

   _____

   _____

3. Should a person be allowed to have more than one spouse?

   _____

   _____

   _____

4. Is it true that a bad sex life causes divorce?

   _____

   _____

   _____

   _____

5. Should nudity be permitted in public parks and beaches?

   _____

   _____

   _____

6. Is having sexual intercourse every day too much?

   _____

   _____

   _____

   _____

Correlation may be as low as 0 or as high as 1.0. In reality the actual number that is found by calculation is usually somewhere in between these two extremes. For example, studies of marital happiness and sexual satisfaction have found a correlation of about .5. This suggests that happiness and satisfaction are related, but given the relatively low correlation coefficient, only weakly. A researcher might say that there is a tendency, although not a strong one, for marital happiness and sexual satisfaction to go together.

So far we have been talking about positive correlations. Correlations may also be *negative*. A study of the relationship between church attendance and divorce showed a correlation of −.3. This coefficient demonstrates a very slight tendency for fewer divorces among the more frequent churchgoers. Notice that whether a correlation is positive or negative is only an expression of the direction of the relationship. A positive correlation means both factors go up or down together. A negative correlation means that when one measure goes up, the other goes down. A correlation of −.8 is just as strong as one that is .8 (+ is usually omitted). The only difference between the two numbers is that they indicate varying directions.

## Research Methods: Advantages and Limitations

Sex researchers need information. They cannot generalize from their own experience or like a novelist try to imagine how other people feel and act. The methods sex researchers use differ and none are perfect. The information we have now gives us a good approximate idea concerning human sexuality. Continuing research and future exploration will refine our techniques and knowledge.

| Technique | Advantages | Cautions |
|---|---|---|
| Surveys | Permit research on very large numbers of people. | It is difficult to get a sample of people who accurately reflect the entire population being studied. |
| | Interviews permit questioner to be flexible, following up a productive lead with additional inquiries. | Spoken and written questions need to be phrased very carefully to avoid biasing the answer. |
| | Mail questionnaires are a relatively inexpensive and rapid way of obtaining information from large numbers of people. Their anonymity helps subjects be truthful. | Most people do not answer mail questionnaires, leading to volunteer error. Further, even though their answers are anonymous, what people say about themselves is not always accurate. |
| Observation | Behavior and activities of research interest can be measured or recorded directly. | Presence of observers and recording devices may alter behavior. |
| | Researchers need not depend on the subjects' memory or truthfulness. | Not all behaviors or feelings can be seen, measured, or observed. |
| Case studies | Permit in-depth study of a few people, sometimes for long periods of time. | May not be able to generalize results based on just a few case studies. |
| | Can give researcher valuable insights and understanding of cause and effect. | The causes of specific behaviors often differ considerably from one person to the next. |
| Experiment | Provides scientific control over what is being studied so we can be reasonably certain of cause and effect. | Many human feelings, experiences, and behaviors cannot, for ethical or scientific reasons, be studied experimentally. |

NOTE: Sometimes more than one research method may be applicable. It may happen, too, that a question may not be answerable because of scientific or ethical considerations.

What research methods could be used to answer the following questions?

1. What are the effects of drinking wine on the length of sexual intercourse and the feelings experienced during orgasm?
2. What proportion of college students routinely use contraception (and what type) during intercourse?
3. Are singles' bars effective places to meet new friends?
4. Can a married person who is experiencing sexual problems with her or his spouse be helped by having an "affair"?
5. What are the causes of the sexual disturbance known as exhibitionism (exposing oneself)?

The most common mistake people make about correlation is to believe that it means causation. Correlation is *not* necessarily cause. It is simply an expression of a relationship. The fact that marital happiness and sexual satisfaction have a fair correlation does not mean one has caused the other. There may well be a third factor, say a personality variable such as flexibility or freedom from anxiety, that contributes to both.

## Significance

At the end of nearly all research the question is raised whether the numbers revealed are *real* or just the result of *chance*. If 100 elementary school children were given a test of mathematical ability and the mean score for boys was 83 while the average for girls was 76, is this difference "real", or in the language of statistics, is it *significant?*

Using any one of several formulas to compute *significance* enables us to make a probability statement about any score. Thus a significance of .10 would show that there was a 1 in 10 probability that the difference in the boys' and girls' mathematics scores was not real but was caused by chance. In the mathematics research, actual calculation showed a significance of .50. This means that a math difference of 7 points between males and females in this study would have been obtained by chance in one of every two test administrations. It is reasonable then to conclude that this 7-point score difference was meaningless or insignificant.

Whenever we are presented information based on seemingly impressive statistics, it is often necessary to inquire whether the numbers have been subjected to a test of significance. We need to have a trained view toward sex research so that the scientific exploration of human sexuality can move ahead.

A difference is significant (for example in the average IQ scores obtained by a group of girls in contrast with those of boys) when it is so large that the probability is strong that it could not have occurred by chance or measuring errors.

---

Most sex research findings require a statistical description. Research results are often reported in terms of averages, whether a particular trait or behavior correlates with another, and their significance, or the likelihood that a finding is caused by chance.

*In Sum*

---

*Summary*

As the present century began, a number of pioneers worked to understand sexuality. Krafft-Ebing made some positive contributions, although overall he seemed to regard sexual behavior with suspicion. Henry Havelock Ellis, a little later, showed sexual expectations to vary from nation to nation and argued that European and American standards were overly repressive. Sigmund Freud, too, contended that sexuality was healthy, and that its suppression, rather than its exercise, might lead to psychological disorder.

The Kinsey studies were unique in their thoroughness. They were based on a decade of work and interviews with over 11,000 people. The Kinsey team found that many sexual behaviors questioned in the 1940s, such as masturbation, were frequent and found in healthy women and men. Subsequent research by Morton Hunt and many others has updated and modified our understanding of sexual behavior.

In the 1960s Masters and Johnson did the first large-scale direct study of the actual physical sexual sequence from arousal to orgasm. In a medical laboratory they photographed and measured the responses of men and women in sexual activities. This work also led to a better understanding of sexual problems and resulted in effective and rapid treatment methods.

Sex researchers, like other scientists, depend on a number of scientific tools. A great deal of sex research is conducted through surveys, which may involve subjects being interviewed directly or asked to fill out questionnaires. Such surveys need to minimize volunteer error and also carefully phrase questions in order to assure the most truthful and accurate results. Scientific research may also involve observational studies with the investigator just watching subjects or sometimes participating to an extent. When such research is not possible, investigators may try to simulate a real-life situation in a laboratory. Often experiments can be carried out in such a setting. Still other information about sexual behavior is obtained from careful and thorough case studies.

The results of scientific sex research are usually reported statistically. The frequency of behavior is described in terms of a mean, median, or mode. Correlation is an indication of the degree to which two or more measures are related. The significance of a result denotes the statistical probability that a research finding is valid.

---

*For Thought and Discussion*

1 Krafft-Ebing, Freud, and Ellis each contributed to new attitudes and understanding of sexuality. Contrast their different approaches and contributions.
2 The Kinsey and Masters and Johnson studies moved sexology fully into the twentieth century. What were their approaches and contributions? If both teams of researchers announced their work and results today, would they be subjects of harassment or criticism?
3 What problems face researchers who use survey techniques to gather information?
4 Set up research projects that might be best carried out by the following methods: observation, experimentation, case studies.
5 Think of actual or possible studies in which the following are useful: mean, mode, median, range, correlation, significance.
6 Do you think the ethical restraints of sex research described in this textbook are sufficient? How would you modify ethical guidelines either to offer greater protection to subjects or to give sexologists more freedom to investigate or participate?

---

*References*

Barker, W.J., Perlman, D. Volunteer bias and personality traits in sexual standards research. *Archives of Sexual Behavior*, 1975, 4, 161-171.
Blumstein, P., Schwartz, P. *American couples*. New York: Wm. Morrow, 1983.
Cook, K., Kretchmer, A., Nellis, B., Lever, J., and Hertz, R. The *Playboy* readers' sex survey (Part 3). *Playboy*, May, 1983.
Ellis, H.H. *Studies in the psychology of sex*. London: F.A. Davis Co., 1906.
Freud, S. *Collected papers*. New York: Basic Books, 1959.
Gay, P. *Freud*. New York: Norton, 1988.
Green, R. *The "sissy boy syndrome" and the development of homosexuality*. New Haven, Conn.: Yale University Press, 1987.
Hall, E. Profile, June Reinisch, New directions for the Kinsey Institute. *Psychology Today*, June 1986, 33-39.

Hite, S. *The Hite report: a nationwide study of female sexuality.* New York: Macmillan, 1976.

Hite, S. *The Hite report on male sexuality.* New York: Knopf, 1981.

Hite, S. *Women and love: a cultural revolution in progress.* New York: Knopf, 1987.

Hunt, M. *Sexual behavior in the 1970s.* Chicago: Playboy Press, 1974.

Kinsey, A.C., Pomeroy, W.B., and Martin, C.E. *Sexual behavior in the human male.* Philadelphia: W.B. Saunders, 1948.

Kinsey, A.C., Pomeroy, W.B., and Martin, C.E. *Sexual behavior in the human female.* Philadelphia: W.B. Saunders, 1953.

Krafft-Ebing, R. *Psychopathia sexualis.* Stuttgart, Germany, 1902.

Masters, W., Johnson, V.E., and Kolodny, R.C. *Masters and Johnson on sex and human loving.* Boston: Little, Brown, & Co., 1986.

Moore M.M. Nonverbal courtship patterns in women: context and consequences. *Ethology and Sociobiology,* 1986, 6(4), 237-247.

Petersen, J.R., Krechmer, A., Nellis, B., Lever, J., and Hertz, R. The *Playboy* readers' sex survey (Part 1). *Playboy,* January, 1983, p. 108; March 1983, p. 90.

Redfield, R.R. et al. Frequent transmission of HTLV-III among spouses of patients with AIDS-related complex and AIDS. *Journal of the American Medical Association,* 1985, *235,* No. 11, 1571-1574.

Rubenstein, C., and Tavris, C. Special survey results: 26,000 women reveal the secrets of intimacy. *Redbook,* September 1987, *169,* p. 147.

Sarrel, P., and Sarrel, L. The *Redbook* report on sexual relationships. *Redbook,* October 1980, pp. 73-80, and February 1981, pp. 140-145.

Schultz, D.P., and Schultz, S.E. *A history of modern psychology.* New York: Harcourt Brace Jovanovich, 1987.

Wolfe, L. *The Cosmo report.* New York: Arbor House, 1981.

Zilbergeld, B., and Evans, M. The inadequacy of Masters and Johnson. *Psychology Today.* August 1980, pp. 29-43.

*Suggested Readings*

Brecher, E.M. *The sex researchers.* Boston: Little, Brown, 1980.
A highly readable description of sex research beginning over a century ago with Havelock Ellis and Krafft-Ebing up to the work of Masters and Johnson. The author also discusses topics like falling in love and swinging.

Gay, P. *Freud.* New York: Norton, 1988.
A careful, well documented, and often captivating history and exploration of Freud and his theories.

Kinsey, A.C. et al. *Sexual behavior in the human male.* Philadelphia: W.B. Saunders, 1948; *Sexual behavior in the human female.* Philadelphia: W.B. Saunders, 1953.
Although sexual behaviors have changed somewhat, these studies remain the most substantive ever conducted. The books are filled with very informative tables, figures and other statistical details.

Hite, S. *Women and love, a cultural revolution in progress.* New York: Knopf, 1987.
Almost the opposite of the Kinsey work. Whereas Kinsey is dull reading, Hite's approach is quite personal. Nevertheless, Hite tells us what many thousands of women are thinking and experiencing.

Petersen, J.R. et al. The *Playboy* readers' sex survey. *Playboy,* January, March, 1983.
Entertaining and enlightening reading, but it must be remembered that the survey used a somewhat unreliable questionnaire and tapped a select audience.

# Part Two

# FEMALE AND MALE
## Sex and Gender

*Chapter 3*

# The Biological Woman

**When you finish this chapter, you should be able to:**

Describe the location and function of the vagina, clitoris, hymen, cervix, and uterus.

Explain the role of the ovaries and fallopian tubes in pregnancy.

Describe how to examine and care for your genital and reproductive organs.

Explain how hormones regulate sexual and reproductive function and evaluate their medical use.

Give an explanation of the menstrual cycle and describe its physical and psychological effects on some women.

Identify erogenous areas and explain their role in arousal.

We are women or men because of our biology. Human males and females have anatomical features so distinct we cannot possibly confuse the two sexes. Less obvious—but equally important—are the hormones, chemicals released directly into the bloodstream, that substantially shape male and female physiology. All of this, being woman or man, begins at conception, 9 months before parents proudly proclaim, "It's a girl (or boy)." In subsequent chapters, we will study conception, the moment when sex is determined, and also examine how society conditions boys and girls, that is, teaches them roles and behaviors believed appropriate to their gender (Chapters 6 and 7). In this chapter and in Chapter 4 we focus on the sexual anatomy and physiology of women and men so that we can understand their individual biological makeup.

## GENITAL AND REPRODUCTIVE ORGANS

As different as they seem in an adult man and woman, the sexual-reproductive systems of both sexes have similar embryological beginnings. Within the earliest weeks of fetal life, the future egg-producing structures in females and the analogous sperm-producing organs in males start as nearly identical glands. Almost simultaneously, tubes are formed that will eventually transport sperm in men and eggs in women. During the later stages of fetal growth, the penis and female genital folds develop from similar rudimentary folds of tissue. But however identical their origins, within 3 months after conception the developing infant has visible sexual and reproductive organs marking it girl or boy (Figure 3-1).

### Vulva

At 3 months of age in utero the fetal *vulva* can be seen in girls and the penis in boys. The vulva is not a specific female organ, but refers to the more external

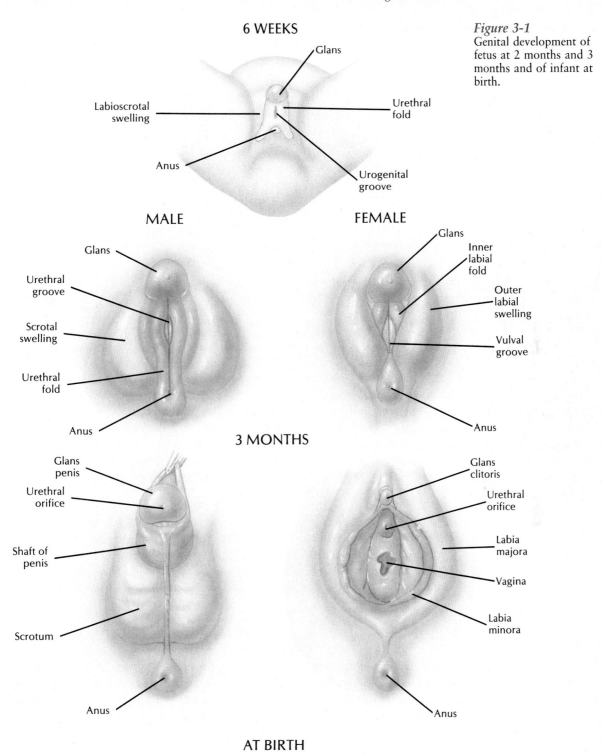

**6 WEEKS**

Glans

Urethral
fold

Labioscrotal
swelling

Anus

Urogenital
groove

*Figure 3-1*
Genital development of
fetus at 2 months and 3
months and of infant at
birth.

**MALE**

**FEMALE**

Glans

Urethral
groove

Scrotal
swelling

Urethral
fold

Anus

Glans

Inner
labial
fold

Outer
labial
swelling

Vulval
groove

Anus

**3 MONTHS**

Glans
penis

Urethral
orifice

Shaft of
penis

Scrotum

Anus

Glans
clitoris

Urethral
orifice

Labia
majora

Vagina

Labia
minora

Anus

**AT BIRTH**

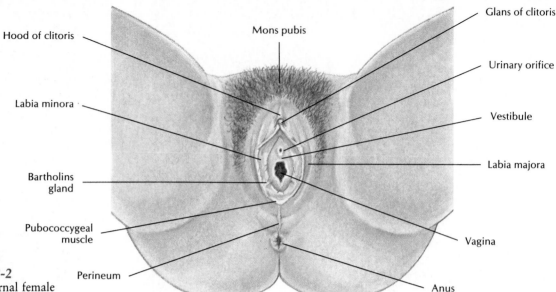

Hood of clitoris

Labia minora

Bartholins gland

Pubococcygeal muscle

Perineum

Mons pubis

Glans of clitoris

Urinary orifice

Vestibule

Labia majora

Vagina

Anus

*Figure 3-2*
The external female sexual-reproductive organs.

Many women (and men) are unfamiliar with their own genital and reproductive organs. Readers may find it worthwhile both to examine their own structures (sometimes using a mirror) and also to talk about their questions and discoveries with close friends who are informed or also reading this textbook.

parts of the genitalia, the *clitoris* and *vaginal* and *urethral* openings. At the top of the vulva there is a cushion of soft tissue, the mons pubis. This area, also called the *mons veneris* (from Latin, meaning Mound of Venus), will be covered with hair by the beginning of the adolescent years. Starting at the bottom of this pubic hill, when the vulva is fully developed, there will be two long folds of skin called the *labia majora*, or major or outer lips. These outer labia are externally covered with some hair, but the inner surface is smooth. Immediately inside the majora are the inner or minor lips, the *labia minora*. In an adult woman the lips may appear to close off the vagina but they can easily be parted with the fingers (Figure 3-2).

The inner lips are smaller and thinner than the majora, pinkish to dark in color, and their appearance varies somewhat from woman to woman (see Figure 3-3). The labia minora are hairless, run along the vaginal opening, and come together toward the top of the vulva to form the *hood* covering the clitoris. The inner lips are quite amply endowed with blood vessels and nerve endings and as a result are sensitive to sexual stimulation.

### Vestibule

The inner lips enclose an area sometimes called the *vestibule*, since this is, in effect, an entryway to the vagina. Within and toward the top of the vestibule lies the urethral opening, the passageway for urine. A little beneath the urethra is the vagina. In virginal women, both openings are small and sometimes not easily seen at first. Unlike the male, in whom the urethra has both excretory and sexual functions, the female urethra passes only urine and is not involved in erotic activity.

The vestibule also contains ducts from *Bartholin's glands*, small bodies inconspicuously located on either side of the vagina. These glands were once thought to produce ample vaginal fluid particularly during periods of sexual arousal. Masters and Johnson (1986), however, found that they secrete only a

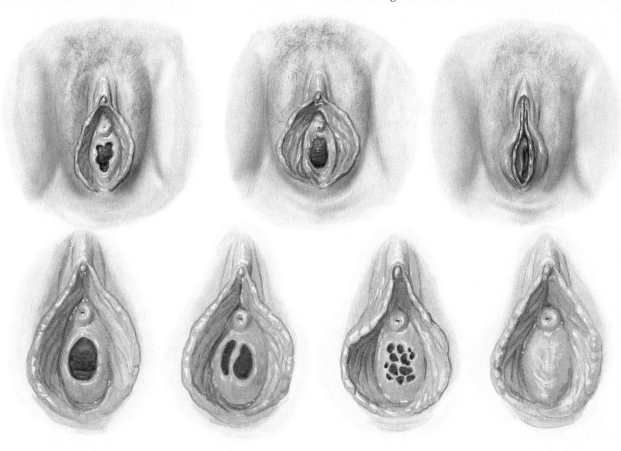

*Figure 3-3*
There are differences in the appearance of female genitalia. The lips and folds about
the vagina may be fairly large, small, or petal-like. A woman who has not had
intercourse may have little or no hymen, or one with several openings.

few tiny drops of lubricant and are not a vital source of vaginal moisture. At
present the role of Bartholin's glands is not certain.

## Vagina

The *vagina* is a tubular organ, technically the terminal point of the *uterus*, and
is about 10 cm (4 inches) long. In the resting state its walls touch each other,
but during sexual excitation there is sufficient expansion to admit an erect penis. During childbirth, powerful uterine muscles push the infant through the
vagina, and this organ opens to a diameter of 15 cm (6 inches) or more. This
allows passage of an infant's head and shoulders. On occasion, however, during birth the opening may have to be surgically widened to prevent tearing
(Chapter 15).

**Hymen**  The *hymen* is a mucous-lined membrane that is located at and partially closes off the entrance to the vagina. Some hymens are minimal and
never noticed even in an adolescent who is not sexually experienced. A few can
be large and a very few so thick as to make inserting a penis difficult. In most

situations, however, the hymen is present, but the opening, even in a young girl, is usually large enough to admit a tampon. As girls grow to adulthood, the hymen often changes. It may be widened by masturbation or, for no known reason, show several small openings, enlarge, or thin out. Despite legends to the contrary, for many women, the hymenal opening is large enough to permit first intercourse with relatively little discomfort. Occasionally, however, a more obtrusive hymen will require gradual gentle stretching by finger (or medically) a week or two before coitus to permit sexual relations to be comfortable (Figure 3-3).

The hymen has no known biological function, but folklore, custom, and tradition are rich with tales and myths. Folklore has it that virginity can be verified by an intact hymen; but given the normal variations in thickness and appearance, this is a *totally false notion*. Nevertheless in some cultures there are elaborate ceremonies in which the bed sheets are examined for the blood supposedly spilled when the husband first tears the virgin bride's hymen.

### Clitoris

The clitoris, a small, sensitive organ, is located at the top end of, and is enclosed by, the labia minora. Ordinarily, the clitoris itself is covered by its hood: the *prepuce*. Gently sliding the hood back reveals the rounded clitoral tip or *glans*, which is a small pea-sized body. The average glans is about 5 mm (⅕ inch) in diameter, and the visible clitoris is less than 1 cm (⅓ inch) or so in length. These averages are approximations for there is considerable variation in the size and prominence of the clitoris (see Figures 3-2 and 3-3).

*corpora cavernosa*
Spongelike cells and tissues that can fill up with blood, enlarging or erecting the clitoris and the penis (Chapter 4).

The clitoris is made up of bodies of spongy erectile tissue, the **corpora cavernosa.** During sexual excitation the clitoris may fill with blood (like the penis, Chapter 4) and become swollen and slightly enlarged. But in most women, even a clitoris that has been sexually stimulated is *not* prominently hard or obvious. The clitoris is not a penis, nor is the penis a clitoris. At the same time it must be recalled that the two organs share a developmental history. Both arise from the same embryological folds and have similar spongy erectile tissue and blood supply. Masters and Johnson (1986) suggest that the penis is exterior, while most of the clitoris is interior. If one considers the organs in their entirety, then they may be more similar than is visibly evident.

*ovulation*
This occurs when the internal female reproductive organs, the ovaries, release an egg ready for fertilization.

The function of the clitoris, outside of being a center for pleasure, is not clear. Most female mammals have a clitoris fairly similar to that seen in human beings. In some species, clitoral manipulation seems to be important in regulating hormonal secretions and bringing about **ovulation.** In a few animals, it may be necessary to stimulate the clitoris in order for vaginal intercourse to take place, although it is not known whether pleasure or orgasm is experienced. In humans the clitoris could be said to have a secondary reproductive function. The pleasure communicated by this organ during intercourse, in many women, might encourage future coitus, an act that can lead to pregnancy (Daley and Wilson, 1983).

The role of the clitoris in providing sexual pleasure has been misunderstood by many societies. In the Western nations, particularly during the Victorian era, some physicians removed or cauterized (burnt out) part or all of the clitoris for a number of different conditions ranging from "nymphomania" to epilepsy. Krafft-Ebing (Chapter 2) was among the doctors who eventually counseled a more "humane" female operation, removal of a section of the clitoral hood to "stop masturbation and avoid its evil consequences."

If the clitoris was feared a hundred years ago, then the reverse was true in the 1930s. Medical writers and marriage advice books rediscovered the importance of the clitoris and typically advised its careful stimulation so that women fully enjoyed their sexuality. This led to some excess since the clitoral glans is often highly sensitive and it is difficult for many women to receive direct touch or pressure. For most women the preferred stimulation, much of the time, leaves the hood in place, and touch is subtle and indirect (Chapter 5, Rubenstein, Tavris, 1987).

Even during coitus, regardless of the position the couple uses, the penis does not ordinarily contact the clitoris. Most often the coital thrusting results in the labia being pushed and pulled, sliding the hood over the clitoral glans and providing pleasurable sensations.

The clitoris is a sensitive sexual organ. Touch that is indirect, subtle, and light is often considered stimulating.

**Circumcision**   In ancient Egypt, and in a few tribal societies and less developed countries today, female "circumcision" was, or is, practiced. (The term *circumcision* means "cutting around" and is more correctly applied only to the penis [see Chapter 4].) The female circumcision ritual may be performed at birth, during childhood, or at puberty. Part or all of the clitoral hood, the clitoris itself, or surrounding labial tissue may be removed. In a few instances the inner vaginal lips may also be sewn partly closed (Tannahill, 1981).

Female circumcision often has deep cultural roots. It persists despite educational efforts made by the World Health Organization and other agencies to eliminate the practice. But there is increasing awareness too of the considerable risk of hemorrhaging, scarring, and infection, and that the operation may be sexually disabling. Fran Hosken (1979) acknowledges the social, symbolic, and religious significance of this rite but suggests, too, that for some people it may be a way of controlling women and denying their sexuality.

### Sexual arousal

The clitoris, the vagina, and several related structures all respond to sexual stimulation. When a woman experiences **sexual arousal,** through touch, caress, or thought, blood flows rapidly into the genital area. As a result the labia majora part slightly, the inner lips double in size, and their color becomes deeper. The clitoris may also increase slightly in length and diameter, and the hood expands and thickens.

*sexual arousal*
Heightened state of sexual excitement and interest.

A half minute or so after the woman is sexually aroused, the vagina becomes lubricated. This slippery moistness was once believed the result of secretion of Bartholin's glands (see Figure 3-2), but Masters, Johnson and Kolodny (1986) contend the vagina is lubricated by a process analogous to sweating. They had their laboratory subjects insert a small camera enclosed in a plastic penislike device into their vagina so that its activity during arousal could be measured. This work suggested the swelling of erectile tissue in the vulva, during arousal, forced out fluid stored between cells (Chapter 5).

There are many misconceptions about vaginal lubrication. To begin with, the amount of lubrication is *not* a reliable indicator of a woman's readiness for coitus. Moisture may be scant or plentiful and a woman may want or not want sexual relations. There is also considerable variation from one woman to another and from situation to situation. The result is that the amount of vaginal lubrication is usually not an indication of a woman's sexual interest, capacity, or arousal.

The consistency, taste, and odor of vaginal secretion also vary a good bit. Many sexual partners report the lubricant to be appealing and sexually stimulating. Sometimes vaginal moisture that is extremely bitter or acidic may suggest a possible infection, so that self-examination and perhaps medical help is advisable (Chapter 16).

When lubrication is continuously scant it may be the result of some anxiety on the part of the woman, inadequate preparation, or inadequate foreplay. If relationship difficulties do not seem to be responsible, the occasional use of a lubricant may help. Ordinary saliva is often sufficient, but sometimes a small amount of a water-soluble solution or gel, such as K-Y lubricating jelly, is worthwhile.

During female sexual arousal a host of other changes occur throughout the body. The uterus becomes elevated; the breasts may increase in size; the nipples may erect. The whole body may seem to become tensed. We will detail these and related changes further in Chapter 5.

*orgasm*
Sexual climax—the intensely pleasurable feelings usually ending stimulation of genital organs (clitoris, vagina, or penis).

**Clitoris and Grafenberg**   For most of this century, the clitoris was believed the *only* center for female arousal and pleasure. But not every observer agreed. Sigmund Freud (1959) was of the opinion that clitoral stimulation, particularly **orgasm,** is immature. Almost no one today agrees with this idea, but for years most psychoanalysts maintained that a climax achieved by clitoral touch was too identical with masturbation to be considered "adult." Only an orgasm attained through vaginal friction was supposedly acceptably grown-up and normal.

The belief in the superiority of vaginal stimulation and orgasm faced a good many difficulties. For one, microscopic tissue examination revealed that the vagina is skimpily supplied with nerve endings, while the clitoris is richly endowed. Most important, Masters and Johnson (1986) pointed out that in direct observations and recordings of coitus or masturbation (Chapter 2), the clitoris is nearly always the center of attention. During masturbation women typically stimulate the clitoral area with their finger or perhaps an electrical vibrator. During intercourse, the penis moving in and out of the vagina pushes and pulls the inner vaginal lips, causing the clitoral hood to slide over the small, delicate organ. Further, even when in rare instances, a woman reaches climax solely by having her body massaged or her breasts stimulated, visual records using a photographic vaginal insert (Chapter 2) show it is the clitoris in which the orgasm is physiologically centered.

The clitoris seemed to have won the day and the argument seemed finished. Then the claim for vaginal sensitivity was given new life a few years ago through the efforts of John Perry and Beverly Whipple (1981). They followed up the work of a little known physician of a generation ago, Ernest Grafenberg, and concluded that there is a highly sensitive erotic center in the anterior wall of the vagina. This erotic zone (called the *Grafenberg* or *G spot*) lies along the course of the urethra. It was said to be surrounded by delicate erectile tissue similar to that found in the penis and clitoris.

Perry and Whipple studied women's responses during intercourse and mas-

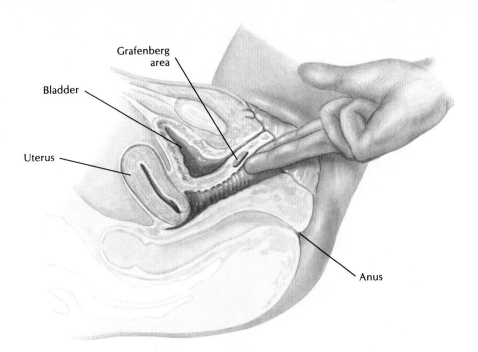

Grafenberg
area

Bladder

Uterus

Anus

*Figure 3-4*
A few women say they
have found the Grafenberg
area by inserting most of
the middle finger into the
vagina and pressing
toward the front. Some
intercourse positions may
be conducive to
stimulating the G spot
(e.g., woman over a supine
man or man entering the
vagina from the rear while
both partners lie on their
sides [see Chapter 5]).

turbation, and reported that many women experienced two different kinds of orgasms, clitoral and vaginal. Supposedly, too, vaginal orgasm often resulted in an "ejaculated" fluid said to be chemically similar to that produced by the male during climax (Chapter 4).

Perry and Whipple point out that their research is much more than simply of academic interest, because it offers sex therapists a new insight with which to help women become orgasmic. They do *not* argue that either a clitoral or vaginal orgasm is superior, more adult, or more desirable. But they do suggest that the rediscovery of the Grafenberg area demonstrates that women have more than one source of sexual pleasure.

At this point the Perry and Whipple work remains controversial. Undoubtedly, sensitive areas in the vagina contribute to sexual pleasure for many women. On the other hand, doubt has been cast on the hypothesis that a specific vaginal area is as highly responsive and pleasure-giving as Grafenberg advocates suggest. Most researchers report that less than 10% of women have an area of sensitivity on the front wall of the vagina that could be called a G spot (Alzate and Londono, 1984).

## Uterus

The **uterus** and vagina are in a sense two ends of a tubular-shaped organ. The vagina, at the lower end, opens to the outside and receives the penis during coitus. The uterus at the upper end is a highly fibrous, elastic structure that houses the developing infant for 9 months. In a young woman who has never been pregnant, the uterus is a compact 7 cm (3 inches) long and its walls are about 2 cm (1 inch) thick. With pregnancy it expands enormously, so it is capable of holding 10 to 15 pounds of baby and fluid. After childbirth the uterus returns to its nonpregnant size and shape fairly well. After **menopause** the uterus usually shrinks even further.

*uterus*
A pear-shaped organ in which the fertilized egg implants and develops into a fetus.

*menopause*
The time when menstruation, the monthly period, completely ends.

*Part Two*

Part Two

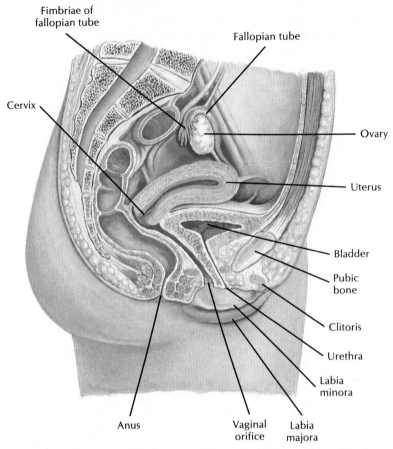

*Figure 3-5*
The female
sexual-reproductive system.

Fimbriae of
fallopian tube

Fallopian tube

Cervix

Ovary

Uterus

Bladder

Pubic
bone

Clitoris

Urethra

Labia
minora

Anus

Vaginal
orifice

Labia
majora

The uterus is flexibly held in place by a number of ligaments. This gives the organ considerable freedom to grow, a situation necessary in pregnancy. It also means, however, that the uterus may not be centrally positioned. Normally, in a standing woman, it lies horizontally with its top toward the front of the body (see Figure 3-5). In a few women, the uterus may be tipped toward the back. Such variations in position were at one time blamed for any number of ills including infertility, backache, and abnormal menstrual bleeding. Current medical opinion stresses the need for careful diagnostic study of all gynecological symptoms instead of just attributing them to a supposedly malpositioned uterus (Krupp and Chatton, 1989).

The uterus has basically three layers: the thin resilient outer cover, called the *perimetrium*; the thick middle muscular layer, called the *myometrium*; and the critically important inner layer, the *endometrium* (see Figure 3-6), which consists of mucous like tissue. Each month the endometrium thickens and its blood supply increases in readiness to begin pregnancy. If **implantation,** a fertile egg attaching to the endometrium, does not take place then the rich uterine tissue breaks down and along with blood is washed off and shed, appearing as menstrual fluid (the menstrual cycle is described later in this chapter).

*Implantation*
The fertilized egg attaching to the uterine wall.

Most of the uterus is firm, but flexible, myometrial tissue. These interlaced muscle fibers expand enormously during pregnancy and also gain considerable strength. When the fetus is fully developed these muscles, responding to hormonal signals, contract in powerful rhythmic spasms. The contractions increase in intensity and frequency as the moment of birth nears; this is why parents and doctors time the length of contractions and the period in between contractions (Chapter 15).

**Cervix**  The lower and narrow end of the uterus is called the neck or, in Latin, *cervix*. It is a small but highly elastic body that in adult women is half the size of the uterus. A portion of the cervix, about 1 cm (½ inch), extends into the vagina. There the small *os* (Latin for opening), not much bigger than a capital *O*, is usually plugged by mucus. The several cervical glands secrete a sticky substance that is resistant to the passage of sperm except during ovulation. Then the chemical character changes and sperm can pass through the os easily. This same *mucoid plug* may also be present throughout pregnancy, shielding the uterus from bacteria and other foreign matter.

### Ovaries, fallopian tubes

The *ovaries* are the *gonads*, meaning the reproductive glands, of women. (The testicles are the male gonads—Chapter 4—and both arise from the same embryological tissue.) The two ovaries are light, small (1½ inches long) organs that look a little like large almonds. They lie on each side of the uterus, almost resting in the curve of the fallopian tubes. Each ovary is held in place by ligaments, which are strong solid cords of tissue. The ovaries have two functions: (1) they produce *sex hormones*, secreting *estrogen* and *progesterone* directly into the bloodstream; and (2) they develop and release the *ova*, or eggs, that are the female reproductive cells.

**Ova**  At puberty, by about age 12 or 13 (Chapter 8), the ovaries contain about 40,000 undeveloped, microscopic eggs. Each egg, or *ovum*, is surrounded by nutrients and cells secreting supportive hormones. These very tiny capsules of tissue are called *ovarian follicles*. Each lunar month, that is, about every 28 days, one ovum that has grown to maturity is discharged from its follicle—a cycle that will continue from puberty to menopause.

The sequence leading to the discharge of a mature egg from the ovary is not completely understood. It has been observed that each month several follicles begin development. Then, within several days, one follicle accelerates its growth, while the rest regress and eventually disintegrate. Soon the one maturing egg in its capsule, now called a **graafian follicle,** moves next to the ovarian wall. Then the expanding follicle opens and the egg is discharged through the thin, delicate membrane of the ovary. *Ovulation* has occurred. An egg, now roughly a fifth the size of a period on this page, has left the ovary and is ready to enter the fallopian tube where fertilization by a sperm could take place.

The discharged ovum leaves behind its follicle, still inside the ovary. The remains of the follicle is transformed into the **corpus luteum** (Latin for yellow body). Its function will be to produce progesterone and some estrogen—chemicals that ready the uterus to receive the egg—and if implantation occurs, to maintain pregnancy. If pregnancy does not take place, the corpus quickly ceases its function and soon after degenerates.

When the ovum breaks through or ruptures the ovarian follicle, it sometimes causes a tiny amount of bleeding or "spotting" and mild cramping.

*graafian follicle*
A capsule on the ovary from which a mature egg is discharged.

*corpus luteum*
Structure that forms on the ovary, producing progesterone.

When two different eggs have been released and fertilized by two different sperm at the same time, fraternal twins develop. They are no more alike than ordinary brothers and sisters.

If shortly after fertilization an egg divides or breaks in two, identical twins, infants with the same hereditary makeup, may result.

Women who have this *Mittelschmerz* (German for midtime pain) can often pinpoint their time of ovulation with considerable precision. This is the time of greatest fertility. Intercourse within a day or so of ovulation is quite likely to result in pregnancy (Chapters 14 and 15).

Ordinarily the ovaries alternate. The left ovary releases an egg one month, and the right ovary releases an egg the next month. Ultimately in the course of a reproductive lifetime, a woman will ovulate about 450 times. If a woman has only one ovary she may release an egg only every second month and reduce her chances of becoming pregnant. Occasionally, both ovaries discharge an ovum simultaneously, or one ovary releases two eggs. If both eggs become impregnated, *fraternal twins* may be born.

**Fallopian tubes**  The distance between the ovaries and uterus is "bridged" by the 10 cm (4 inch) *fallopian tubes*. At the uterine end these curving tubes are attached. On the ovarian side the tubes broaden out into fingerlike projections, called *fimbriae* (Latin for fringes), that loosely surround but do not physically connect to the ovary. The ovum, expelled from its capsule, must make a short but remarkable voyage. After leaving its ovarian follicle, the egg must find its way into a fallopian tube. The transportation is apparently the result of a sweeping chemical action. This draws the ovum close to the fringed end and ultimately into the funnel-shaped opening of the fallopian tube (see Figure 3-6).

In the tube the ovum makes a tortuous journey helped along by muscular action and microscopic hairlike structures called *cilia*. If *fertilization* is to take place, that is, a sperm is to enter the egg, it has to occur during the *first 24 hours* that the egg is in the *beginning third of the fallopian tube*. The sperm may have been deposited in the vagina as little as an hour before, or as much as a couple of days earlier. If fertilized, the ovum begins to divide and grow

*Figure 3-6*
The internal female sexual-reproductive organs: the uterus, fallopian tubes, and vagina are shown in section to illustrate the internal anatomy.

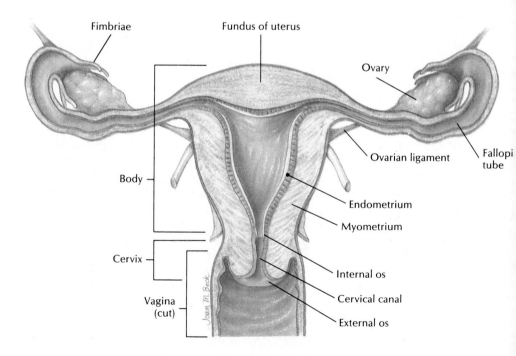

## HORMONES

**Hormones** are chemicals produced by structures called ductless glands. They are called ductless because the hormones are *released directly* into the *bloodstream*. Although the quantities of hormones involved are extremely small, their impact on the body is considerable. In effect, hormones act as messengers instructing various body organs and tissues to grow or subside. To simplify the matter, we will concentrate, in this chapter, on the hormones most directly involved in a woman's sexual and reproductive function.

It should also be noted that while we describe feminizing hormones in this chapter, and masculinizing in the next, both sexes share a similar biochemistry. Men and women *both* have female and male hormones. In women the feminizing hormones predominate, and in men the reverse is true.

### Pituitary and hypothalamus glands

Deep within the skull, at the base of the brain, are two small structures that work in concert, the *hypothalamus* and beneath it the *pituitary*, a ductless gland. The function of the hypothalamic area is to trigger the pituitary into producing *follicle stimulating hormone* (FSH) and *luteinizing hormone* (LH).

Follicle stimulating hormone is a *gonadotropin*, a sex gland regulator. In women FSH prompts the growth of the ovarian follicles leading to the production of an egg. Luteinizing hormone is also a gonadotropin. In females it brings

*hormones*
Internally produced chemicals that stimulate and regulate many different bodily functions and behaviors.

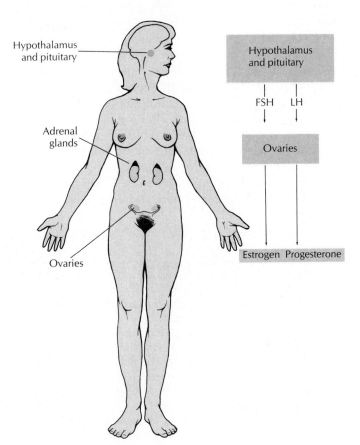

*Figure 3-8*
Hormones in women.

on ovulation, the release of the mature egg from the follicle.

The pituitary gland also secretes *prolactin*. The full function of this hormone is not known. It is, however, directly involved in *lactation*, the production of breast milk. Prolactin builds up during the later months of pregnancy and stimulates the milk glands in the breast, readying them for nursing. (If nursing does not occur, lactation gradually ceases in several weeks.)

### Estrogen and progesterone

Estrogen may be prescribed for transsexual men who want to be women. It is often effective in giving men a more feminine appearance (Chapter 6).

Estrogen, often called the feminizing hormone, is produced primarily in the ovaries. Estrogens help determine the embryo's sexual development, and at puberty they accelerate the growth of breasts, the vagina, the clitoris, and internal uterine organs. Estrogen is also responsible for the softer, more rounded adult female body and its typical hair distribution. (Sometimes balding men take estrogen in an attempt to restore their hair—a very unsound medical practice.) Psychologically, estrogens have been identified with nesting, mothering, and submissive behavior. But given society's role in teaching gender roles, there is considerable question whether these are hormonally or socially determined traits in women (Chapter 6).

Progesterone is produced mainly by the corpus luteum in the ovary. It helps regulate menstruation and prepares the uterus to receive and nourish the fertilized egg. It may also have some moderating influence on sexual motivation. When relatively high levels of progesterone are present in women (or men), there is often a reduced level of sexual activity. During later pregnancy progesterone may be 25 times higher than usual and thus biologically reduce sexual motivation. In men there may be cyclical periods of high progesterone too, perhaps resulting in a period of lower sperm count and potency. The inhibitory effects of progesterone on sperm production have led to some experimental attempts to use it as a male contraceptive (Chapter 14).

Women also produce masculinizing hormones called *androgens* (Chapter 4). Minute quantities of several different androgens are produced by the ovaries and the adrenal glands. In females androgens seem to contribute to the growth and development of infants and children. One particular androgenic hormone, testosterone, may play a role in determining the level of sex drive in both sexes. This function is much clearer in lower level mammals. It is difficult

*Table 3-1*

**Female Hormones**

| Hormone | Source | Function |
|---|---|---|
| Luteinizing hormone (LH) | Pituitary gland | Prompts ovulation and stimulates follicle to produce progesterone (in men, helps in production of androgens) |
| Follicle stimulating hormone (FSH) | Pituitary gland | Encourages follicle growth and production of estrogen (in men, aids in sperm development) |
| Prolactin | Pituitary gland | Stimulates milk production in pregnant women |
| Estrogens | Ovaries, small amounts in adrenals (in men, small amounts in testes) | Encourage female physical growth particularly during fetal development and puberty |
| Progesterone | Ovaries, small amount in adrenals (in men, small amounts in testes) | Prepares uterus for pregnancy and contributes to the menstrual cycle; moderates sex drive |

to determine the effect of a single factor in women and men because of the many psychological and environmental variables involved in determining the level of sexual interest.

Both men and women share most of the same hormones. Nevertheless the proportion of male and female hormones is usually quite different in each sex. The level of estrogen, for example, may be 15 times as high in women as in men. It should be noted that the actual amount of hormone present may not be as important as the proportion of androgen to estrogens in determining the degree of masculine or feminine physical characteristics

### Hormones as treatment—caution!

Hormones are potent biochemicals. As knowledge of their production and function has increased, so too has the frequency of their use as medication. Often the proper administration of hormones in a person who is deficient is vital to restore health. But hormone treatment may also carry a risk.

Estrogenic substances known commercially as Menrium and Premarin are frequently prescribed to women to help regulate the menstrual cycle to relieve menopausal symptoms. They are generally effective, but common side effects include skin rashes, nausea, and breast tenderness. A more serious though rare complication is the formation of blood clots that may eventuate in stroke or heart attack.

The most infamous hormone may be *diethylstilbestrol (DES)*, a synthetic estrogen. A half century ago DES was used for problem pregnancies. 1950s estimates suggest that perhaps a million mothers had been given the drug to prevent possible miscarriage, bleeding, and spontaneous abortion. The drug seemed effective, but long-term observation showed it created serious problems.

Males whose mothers took DES while they were in the embryonic may show uneven testicular development and as adults could have a low sperm count. Females exposed as embryos may have fertility and pregnancy difficulties as adults. Most startling was the finding that during adolescence a small number of "DES daughters" developed breast and, particularly, vaginal cancers. Women who have surgically lost considerable vaginal tissue or reproductive capability have successfully sued the drug manufacturers. Today, because of the possible hazards in the use of hormones, much more caution is used in the prescription of all of these powerful biochemicals (Krupp and Chatton, 1989).

## PHEROMONES

Hormones are chemicals produced by us that help regulate our own body processes. **Pheromones** may be produced by us and influence the bodily processes of others. Pheromones achieve their effect primarily by being excreted through the skin and body openings so that other organisms can smell their presence. Female moths, for example, secrete *bombykol* during their period of sexual receptivity. Smelling this induces male moths to pursue the female. Female dogs in heat produce odors that lure males from as much as a mile away.

The question as to whether or not humans produce pheromones, chemicals that attract partners, has been investigated for decades. Current research suggests that women may vaginally secrete a pheromone called *copulin,* particu-

Both sexes share most of their hormones. Men produce small amounts of progesterone and estrogen in their gonads and adrenal glands.

larly in periods of sexual excitation and also around the time of ovulation. Some men have observed that they are sexually excited by vaginal smells, a phenomenon that would be particularly useful for reproductive purposes. The woman secreting copulins around the time of ovulation is giving a cue, a scent signal, as Hopson (1979) puts it, that encourages intercourse at her most fertile time.

But are copulin and similar substances really pheromones? In animals pheromones have an almost reflexive effect on the behavior of others. The male moth or dog that smells the female pheromone is almost compelled to copulate. Human beings may be too far along the intellectual ladder to be compelled by an odor to engage in a complex set of mating behaviors. Our sense of smell has taken a back seat to sight and, most importantly, to thought and communication (Chapter 10). Human pheromone-like substances, if they exist at all, might be perceived only at an unconscious level. One researcher has observed that if we do detect their presence, they may just register with us like a subtle encouraging smile (Liebowitz, 1983).

### Menstrual synchrony

Another way in which the presence of pheromones has been evaluated is by the observation that women living together sometimes tend to harmonize their menstrual cycles. This **menstrual synchrony** has been noticed in college dormitories. Graham and McGrew (1980) observed female college students for close to a half year. At the beginning of the study, friends newly sharing living quarters averaged 11 days apart in their time of menstruation. After only 3 months, cycles averaged only 6 days apart. Further, those women who were closer friends, spending more time together, more rapidly developed menstrual synchronization.

What role do pheromones play in this synchronization? There is little conclusive evidence. But it seems as if very subtle odors in one person, smells not readily detectable on a conscious level, may trigger menstrual responses in another. In one experiment a female subject daily placed an extract of concentrated perspiration from an unknown donor on her lip. The concentrate presumably contained pheromones but had no readily detectable smell. Nevertheless over a 4-month period the woman who had the perspiration applied to her came closer and closer to the menstrual cycle of the distant donor (Russell et al., 1977). It seems as if human biological function, and perhaps behavior, could in some ways be influenced by pheromones or similar chemical factors.

## MENSTRUATION

Menstruation, the monthly period, is an essential part of every woman's reproductive capability. The menstrual cycle typically begins between ages 10 and 15. For many girls the start of their period is a time of pride and satisfaction; they now believe themselves to be fully women. For others, who are uninformed or misinformed, menstruation can be accompanied by fear and guilt. Even relatively enlightened parents and friends may erroneously caution adolescent girls that they can no longer engage in vigorous sports and have to sit, talk, and act "like ladies" (Chapters 6 and 7). The end of menstruation may also be troubling for some women. Menopause, which usually occurs in the late 40s, may cause both physical and psychological distress. A few

A clean body is sexually attractive, but the excessive use of deodorants may mask pleasing natural scents.

*menstrual synchrony*
The possibility of women who live together to follow a similar menstrual cycle.

## Three Women Learn About Menstruation

When I was around 10 years old, my mother took me aside and said she had something to tell me about being a woman. She was very apologetic and kept saying she really did not know that much about what she was going to say but that I had to learn it sooner or later. Anyway, she began to tell me I would have bad cramps and bleed once a month for a few days. She said it had something to do with pregnancy, but she did not explain it very clearly. I remember most of all her using the word "bleed" over and over, and I hated it. Anyway, I let her finish. I felt sorry for her since I knew what a nasty family she had come from and how my father had not been at all nice to her before they split up. Anyway, I let her finish and thanked her. I never told her that I already knew a lot about it from my girlfriend Karen and her high school biology book. I was just depressed that she did such a poor job telling me.

I guess I was lucky. I never had a special time set aside when anyone told me. I feel like I always knew. I think my parents made an effort to tell me about sex from the time I was born. They got me books like the *Grow Series* that explains all kinds of things in pictures and language I could understand as a child. By the time I was 12 I found myself explaining it to other girls. I felt very happy and grown up. If I wanted to, I could become a mother some day.

My older sister told me about menstruation. She called it "falling off the roof." Mom had told her to tell me. She was not too clear about the reasons, but she did say it was perfectly normal. She told me that she had discovered it herself when she found blood in her panties one evening. At first she thought she had had a bowel movement she was unaware of. Surprisingly she told Mom, and Mom explained it somehow. Anyway, I was sent back to Mom and told to tell her I knew all about it now. The next thing my mother and father told me was that when it happened I would be a young lady and I was not to rough-house or fool around with boys. I mean it was just about what they make fun of when you hear them say, "Now you are a woman." Goodbye to climbing, running and chase games, especially with boys. Well anyway, that lasted for a while. But later I found out on my own that I could still play any game I wanted and I wouldn't get hurt or pregnant. In fact, it was then that I joined the school track team, but my parents didn't like it.

*(Authors' Files)*

women feel they have lost a part of their femininity, and some may become quite depressed. Others, however, feel free of the worry of unwanted pregnancy.

## Menstrual phases

The term **menstruation** comes from Latin and means "monthly." Usually the cycle is about 28 days, one lunar month, but individual cycles as short as 3 weeks or as long as 5 weeks are not unusual. Menstruation *seems* to occur for only a few days every month. Actually, the cycle is a continuous process controlled by complex neurological signals and several different hormones. For descriptive purposes, the cycle can be divided into four overlapping phases.

The first phase occurs when menstrual bleeding has ended; the pituitary begins to produce large amounts of follicle stimulating hormone and small quantities of luteinizing hormone. The result is that, as we saw a few pages back, ovarian follicles begin to mature, leading to the name *follicular phase*. The de-

*menstruation*
The monthly vaginal discharge of blood and the lining of the uterus.

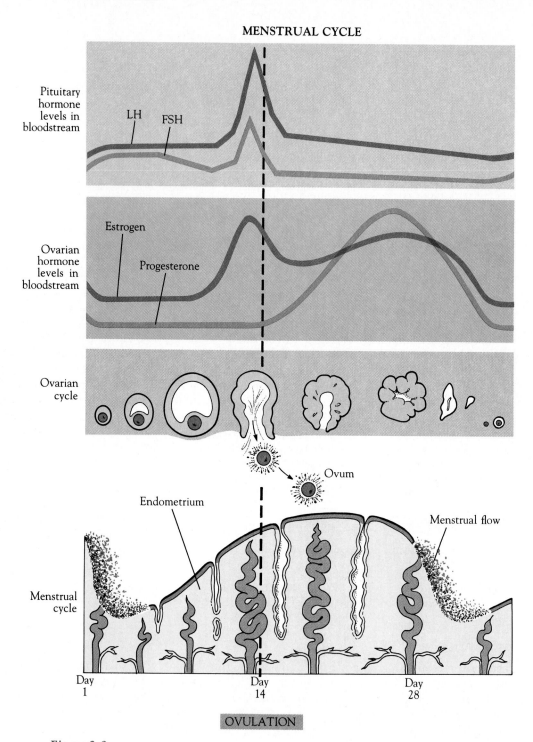

**MENSTRUAL CYCLE**

Pituitary
hormone
levels in
bloodstream

LH    FSH

Ovarian
hormone
levels in
bloodstream

Estrogen

Progesterone

Ovarian
cycle

Ovum

Endometrium

Menstrual flow

Menstrual
cycle

Day
1

Day
14

Day
28

OVULATION

*Figure 3-9*
The menstrual phases. For most women, the complete menstrual cycle is between 24 and 34 days. Longer or shorter periods are common.

veloping follicles produce estrogens that cause the uterine endometrium to thicken and bring about other changes favorable to potential pregnancy. The follicular phase lasts about 12 days.

Toward the end of the follicular phase, the amount of luteinizing hormone increases, triggering ovulation, the discharge of the graafian follicle. In a 28-day cycle this second or *ovulation phase*, generally occurs about 14 days before the next menstrual period. Some women experience Mittelschmerz (as noted before) but for most, the follicular and ovulation phases are a time of well-being. Sexual interest, vigor, and affection are often at a peak. Many report that they are also more resistant to stress and disease. Part of this good feeling may be attributed to hormonal influences, but it is likely that psychological factors also play a role (Boston Women's Health Book Collective, 1985).

Ovulation is ordinarily the time of greatest fertility. But since ovulation varies a good deal in many women, it is difficult to pinpoint fertility or infertility (Chapter 14).

The third phase is the *luteal phase*. This lasts about 10 days and is dominated by high progesterone levels. The endometrium is now a rich mixture of blood and nourishing substances ready for the implantation of a fertilized egg. If implantation does occur, the uterine lining, now host to an **embryo,** remains intact, and within a few days the woman notices she has missed her usual menstrual period. A missed period is a fairly good, although not absolute, sign that pregnancy has begun (Chapter 15).

*embryo*
The unborn infant during the first 2 months of pregnancy.

If a fertilized egg is not implanted, the corpus luteum regresses and estrogen and progesterone levels decline. The final effect is a degenerative change in the endometrial lining of the uterus. The menstrual cycle has moved to the fourth phase.

In the last phase, menstruation, blood and tissue from the endometrium and mucus and dead cells from the cervix and vagina are released. In the course of about 4 days, some 4 tablespoons of this bloodlike flow are shed. Toward the end of menstruation, the low levels of estrogen trigger an increase in follicle stimulating hormone, thus beginning the follicular phase again.

We began our description with the follicular phase, which starts when menstrual bleeding has *ended*. When women want to calculate the day during which they ovulate, for family planning or other purposes, they usually start their count with the *beginning* of menstrual flow. That is counted as day one of the entire cycle (Chapters 14 and 15).

## Dysmenorrhea

Many women feel some mild discomfort during menstruation. A few complain of severe cramps and pain, a condition called *dysmenorrhea.* Dysmenorrhea should always be carefully diagnosed since hormonal imbalance, uterine growths, or infection may occasionally be responsible. When there is no physical cause, anxiety, stress, or other emotional disturbances may sometimes be at the root.

Current views hold that in the majority of cases dysmenorrhea *is* physically caused and probably the result of an excess in the body's production of *prostaglandin*, a biochemical that assists muscle contraction. Penny Budoff, a physician, in her book *No More Menstrual Cramps and Other Good News* (1980), reports that women who take medication that reduces prostaglandins have obtained significant relief from dysmenorrhea. Aspirin is a weak antiprostaglandin. More potent medications are available by prescription and include Motrin and Ponstel.

Menstrual cramps may be a result of stress, or they may be physically caused. They are not imaginary and it is often wise to seek medical help.

## Toxic shock syndrome

A few years ago, media attention focused on a condition called *toxic shock syndrome* (TSS). TSS prompted numbers of women to look at tampons with distrust and study every vaginal discharge with suspicion. Subsequent work

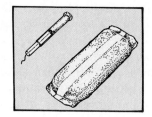
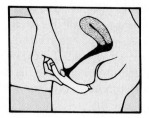

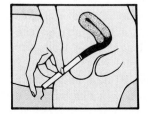
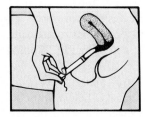
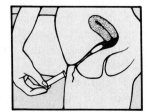

*Figure 3-10*
Women today wear sanitary napkins *(top right)* or insert tampons *(bottom)* to absorb the menstrual flow. During the heaviest period of flow women average about four or five napkins or tampons a day. Other methods to absorb or catch the menstrual blood, such as a cup or sponge, have been attempted, but no satisfactory alternative to tampons or napkins is currently available.

has shown that the infection may occur only if a tampon, a diaphragm, a contraceptive sponge, or any other vaginal insert is retained beyond the period recommended.

TSS results when the vaginal insert encourages overgrowth of bacteria. These microorganisms produce toxins that are absorbed by the body. The result usually is high fever, rash, and vomiting—symptoms often associated with poisoning. This is a very serious but rare condition. It can be avoided if vaginal inserts are sanitary and not retained longer than medically recommended (Benson, 1989).

### Menstruation myth and intercourse

Menstruation, more than many other biological functions, is surrounded by misunderstanding, superstition, and a host of moral and religious proscriptions. Perhaps menstruation has been so mythologized because there was really no way for early human beings to understand its normal reproductive function. Menstrual blood, contrary to other losses of blood, was not associated with a wound or injury.

For some early people the fact that women bled and did not die suggested that they were superhuman beings, perhaps goddesses or witches. For others, the menstrual flow seemed an indication of uncleanliness. In ancient Sumeria, women wore a towel, a "blood bandage," for the 6 days of their period. During this time, they were alleged to contaminate anything they touched. After the period ended, a ritually cleansing bath, a practice still found among some religious groups today, was prescribed so that the woman was again "clean" and could be readmitted to the company of men (Tannahill, 1981).

Echoes of the ancient theme that the menstruating woman is unclean or especially vulnerable still appear in beliefs that forbid women to swim, climb, or follow any of their usual pursuits during menstruation. Most of all, it is widely supposed that menstrual women must not sexually approach their husbands.

Menstruation is not a magical occurrence, but an ordinary and healthy biological event. The fact is, also, that menstruation affects different women dif-

It has long been recognized that a woman is less likely to become pregnant if she has intercourse during her menstrual period. Menstrual intercourse is an old but undependable method of birth control. It is not at all reliable since some women ovulate while menstruating.

ferently, so that one can not make blanket statements. Many women find that most of their periods bring no special discomfort, but once in a while they feel abdominal cramps or fatigue. Other women may feel bloated, complain of breast tenderness, backache, or emotional sensitivity for a few hours or for a few days. Some find physical exercise helpful in relieving symptoms, whereas others note difficulties while engaging in athletic activities (Puretz, In press, 1988). Some women or their partners feel sexually uninterested and unreceptive during much of the menstrual period, but others find the opposite true, saying that intercourse or masturbation often feels particularly good. The point is that it is perfectly safe for a healthy woman to continue all of her usual activities, including sexual ones, during her menses if she feels comfortable doing so (Asso, 1983).

### Premenstrual distress

Without looking at a calendar, most women know when they are about to begin menstruating. Studies show that about 70% of menstrual women experience a mild to moderate degree of breast tenderness, abdominal discomfort, fatigue, or some emotional changes. For most women these premenstrual signs are minimal and not disruptive. But a few suffer substantial distress, including severe cramping and depression. It has even been claimed that some women are more violence or accident prone during the premenstrual days (Hopson and Rosenfeld, 1984).

Until a few decades ago, physicians did not distinguish the possible discomforts of menstruation itself from the distress that sometimes occurs just before

This 1822 painting by Charles Auory pokes fun at the family trying to cope with mother's headache. A century ago, quite often, neither women nor menstrual distress were treated seriously.

the period. Then a British physician, Katherina Dalton, proposed that premenstrual discomforts should be considered a distinct clinical entity. She coined the term *premenstrual syndrome* (PMS) and held that a progesterone deficiency caused the symptoms.

Over the years several hundred symptoms and behaviors have been attributed to the premenstrual period. It has been reported that premenstrual women are more likely to commit suicide, get lower test scores, perform poorly on mechanical tasks, and be more aggressive. Physical symptoms reported have ranged from headaches to pain in the feet. One interesting contribution was by an investigator who carefully combed through crime statistics. He concluded that women commit nearly half of all their crimes in the several days preceding the menses or in the week following the start of the actual flow. Readers can figure out why these findings are correct but also meaningless.

In a comprehensive review of the scientific literature, Mary Parlee (1976) carefully examined the reports of premenstrual women being clumsy, pained, and unstable. She showed that few research investigations had adequate control groups. For the sake of comparison the studies of PMS should have measured the emotional states of menstrual women and other women and men, but they did not. Parlee also found that a great many of the tests used to measure personal characteristics were biased or depended heavily on self-report. This suggests that if the subject thought she was supposed to be mean before her menses, she was likely to rate herself crabby, even if in actuality she was not. Parlee concluded that many of the old notions and most of the supposed scientific findings of a deeply disturbed premenstrual state for all women have little foundation in fact. In her view, women with PMS generally did as well on IQ tests, in school examinations, in athletic events, and on the job as they did in their non-PMS state. Later work by Janet Hopson and Anne Rosenfeld (1984) was in agreement. They combed very carefully through the last decade's research and suggested that up to 10% of premenstrual women may actually have two or more severe symptoms. But 90% have no, few, or only mildly distressing complaints.

### Current views

There is consensus that some women experience some premenstrual pain, emotional fluctuations, and fatigue, but there is disagreement about most of the other behaviors and emotions supposedly characterizing the days before menstruation.

If PMS is a syndrome, its cause is not certain. It does seem likely that significant hormonal fluctuations and/or an excess of prostaglandins before the actual menses play a role. It is also argued that negative social attitudes toward women and menstruation, as well as job and family stress, may contribute to premenstrual symptoms.

The treatment of PMS is not yet standard. Progesterone, anti-prostaglandin medications like Ponstel, Motrin, and aspirin (mentioned under dysmenorrhea) may relieve many PMS complaints. Elimination or reduction of caffeine, proper diet, and exercise have also been found helpful. In addition research has shown that sometimes a *placebo* is effective. One result of this is that a great many substances have been suggested to alleviate PMS, including zinc, tranquilizers, and vitamins.

Most woman are equally fit psychologically and physically in all phases of the menstrual cycle.

In general, it is now recommended that women with distressing premenstrual symptoms receive a complete physical and sometimes psychological evaluation. Gynecological problems, life stressors, and hormonal changes may all play a part in PMS. After possible causes are investigated, a woman experiencing PMS can work out an individual treatment program tailored to her own needs (Asso, 1983).

## MENOPAUSE

The cessation of menstruation (menopause) is a perfectly normal, healthy developmental event. It begins sometime during the 40s for nearly all women. At this time they notice that their periods are becoming less regular. There are alterations, too, in the amount of flow. Instead of a monthly menses and a considerable discharge, the flow may occur more frequently and be scant. Or several months may occur between periods. Eventually, by the late 40s, a third of all women have stopped menstruating. By age 50, 8 out of 10 no longer have monthly periods (Benson, 1989).

The direct cause of menopause is a steady and continuing decline in the production of estrogen by aging ovaries. This decrease along with other hormonal changes also has some side effects. One major consequence is vasomotor instability. This means there are momentary bursts of capillary expansion that result in a warm flushed feeling called **hot flashes.** These sensations around the neck or head last a half minute or more and may occur just once or twice or a dozen times a day. Vaginal changes are also fairly common and include some organ shrinkage and drying. A few women also report some vagi-

*hot flashes*
Occasional warm sensations about the head and neck common in menopausal women.

Menopause and aging need not be a barrier to happy marriage or remarriage.

nal bleeding, itching, and pain. Some women also note a weakening of their bone structure, *osteoporosis,* and an aging of their skin.

A great many other physical and psychological changes have been attributed to menopause. These include fat on the thighs, loss of muscle tone, and high blood pressure. Mental health problems, too, including depression, fatigue, and loss of libido, have been said to be caused by menopause. To evaluate the validity of these claims, Sonja McKinlay studied 8000 women aged 45 to 55. Her findings showed that the stereotype of the complaining, deteriorating menopausal woman is "patently false" (Eastman, 1985): menopause may bring some health concerns but generally "the menopause does not make women sicker and does not cause any significant increase in the use of medical care."

While menopause does not necessarily result in despair, ill health, or a loss of sexual interest, it can be a challenge. Society does emphasize youth and instills a fear of becoming older. A few women are anxious about aging and others are saddened by knowing they are past the childbearing years. At the same time, many look forward to the cessation of menstruation. If they have often suffered menstrual distress, menopause may relieve their discomfort. Even if menstruation has usually been free of difficulty, menopausal women need no longer take precautions against pregnancy. Women can look forward to menopause, seeing it as a period that can present new perspectives and opportunities. (Raymond, 1988).

If menopause adjustment problems seem significant, counseling is one option. Often this can be provided by a therapist who is sensitive to the questions that accompany life passages from youth to middle age and the older years. There are also women's support groups in which women help one another informally by sharing insights, warmth, and understanding. Restructuring one's habits and moving toward a healthier life-style may also be useful.

If menopausal medical problems persist, hormonal therapy under a health provider's supervision may be attempted. Small amounts of estrogen and progesterone are unlikely to have undesirable side effects and can relieve the vasomotor instability resulting in hot flashes. Hormonal creams may also be smoothed around the vaginal area to help relieve some genital discomfort. On the other hand, if vaginal dryness during sexual relations is a complaint, this can often be helped by a little surgical jelly or saliva.

---

*In Sum*

Hormones are chemical messengers produced by glands that regulate sexual and other body activities. The pituitary is involved in the production of follicle stimulating hormone and luteinizing hormone. These biochemicals help monitor the menstrual cycle and the function of the ovaries. The ovaries produce estrogen and progesterone, both closely tied to female development and function. Hormones may be used in treatment but must be employed with caution. Pheromones may help arouse sexual interest in others although this observation is still not confirmed in humans.

The menstrual cycle begins with follicular development and ends with a shedding of blood and endometrial and other tissue when a fertilized ovum is not present in the uterus. There are some negative attitudes and considerable misinformation concerning menstruation. Most women, however, can continue their usual activities throughout the cycle. Some women may experience physical and psychological distress just before or during menstruation but treatment is available. Tampons may be used with safety, but to avoid toxic reactions they should be kept in place no longer than is recommended. Menstruation ceases, and menopause occurs during the late 40s, and is sometimes accompanied by some discomforts that can be treated.

---

## BREASTS

The female breasts are *not* genital or reproductive organs. Technically, both male and female breasts are *mammary glands*. They are organs found in all mammals and are used to suckle the young. Ordinarily, only female breasts, responding to hormonal triggers activated by pregnancy and birth, produce milk. This nourishing fluid is usually perfectly suited, and medically preferred, for feeding infants. Male breasts are fundamentally the same as female ones although not as well developed. Yet if males are given the proper hormones, their breasts increase slightly in size and they can even lactate.

### Anatomy and physiology

The adult female breast, and in vestigial form the male breast also, consists of glandular tissue with ducts opening to the nipple. The glandular clusters are loosely cushioned with fibrous and fatty tissue. If there is a considerable amount of fatty and related tissue, the breast appears large and feels soft. But the dimensions of the breast are related neither to their sensitivity nor to their ability to lactate.

The breast is tipped by a *nipple* that may be small, inverted, or as large as a half inch. Around the nipple there is a light pinkish to deep brown area, the *areola*, which may be almost absent or have a diamenter of as much as 3 inches. The nipple itself is basically muscle tissue with numerous tiny openings prepared to deliver milk to a sucking infant. The nipple may become erect during sexual arousal, as a result of caressing, oral, or other stimulation, or even from something as impersonal as cold weather.

The areola and nipple are more amply endowed with nerve endings than the rest of the breast, and many women find that having their nipple, or sometimes areola, touched is especially sexually pleasing. Some men also report that having their breasts touched can be pleasurable. Some women, and a few men, have achieved orgasm simply through breast manipulation. This may be the result of *conditioning*, the person having *learned* to associate breast touch with other sexual activity that eventually leads to climax (Chapters 5 and 13).

In most of the world today, the breasts have a sexual connotation and are touched and caressed during intimate relations. But the interest in breasts is not universal. Before the massive influence of Western culture through books, movies, and television, the breasts were not considered particularly erotic in parts of Africa and the East. Further, while nearly all of our human sexual behaviors, ranging from vaginal coitus to mouth-genital contact, is found among mammals, and especially primates, there is no evidence of breast interest among other mammals (Broude and Green, 1976; Ford and Beach, 1980).

*Figure 3-11*
The female breast. Breasts are mammary glands; their function is to produce milk to nurse infants.

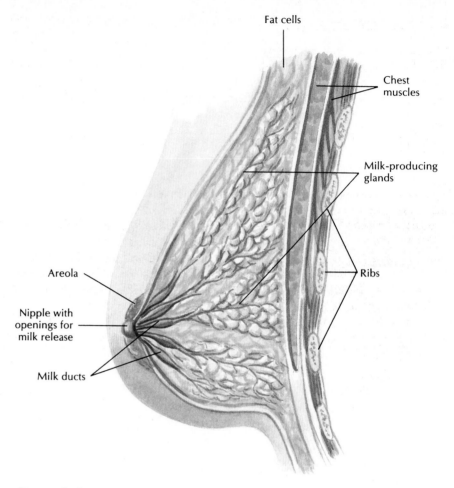

Fat cells

Chest muscles

Milk-producing glands

Ribs

Areola

Nipple with openings for milk release

Milk ducts

The function of the breasts to produce milk for nursing is unrelated to breast size or shape.

## Size and shape

The focus on female breasts as a sign of attractiveness has motivated a multitude of industries from clothing manufacturers to surgeons to try to reshape this gland. Surgery can alter the breast. A woman who has very large and hanging breasts that are a source of discomfort may find breast reduction surgery worthwhile. Breast size has also been enlarged by medical implants or tissue grafts, but such procedures are not always satisfactory and side effects such as infection may result.

Creams and massagers and the like to augment or redefine breast appearance are heavily promoted in some magazines geared to younger readers. These treatments are worthless, but usually harmless. Breast exercises conscientiously designed and dutifully carried out have little effect on mammary size, but they may develop the underlying chest musculature and result in a healthier appearing and more upright bosom.

Finally, despite the emphasis placed on the female breasts, their dimensions may not be as important to men as the media would have us believe. In a *Playboy* magazine poll of over 100,000 readers, the vast majority of the young men respondents, 72%, said breast size is unimportant. Personality and social factors were more valued (Petersen et al., 1983).

### Breast Lumps and Cancer

In an effort to reassure women, the Harvard University Medical School health newsletter (*Medical Forum*, 1984) makes the clear, although not too sensitive statement, "Half of all women have lumpy breasts." Then more to the point, "Lumpy breasts in themselves have no serious consequences." The message is that irregularities in breast tissue; nodules, cysts, and variously shaped lumps are common and do not usually require medical treatments. Breast cancer also is infrequent among young women but increases with age. After age 50, 3% of women have malignant breast growths. Despite the low incidence of breast cancer among younger women, self-examination is a must. Most breast disorders are detected by women themselves doing their own examination. The accompanying illustration shows a recommended self-examination routine. This inspection should take place monthly, after the menstrual period. All new lumps, particularly those that appear hard or persistent or do not diminish during the menstrual cycle, should be called to a doctor's attention. By about age 30, according to the recommendation of the American Cancer Society, an additional breast examination, *mammography*, should be per-formed every 2 to 3 years. This is a special breast x-ray procedure that can spot even small breast growths. A mammogram is recommended every 1 to 2 years between ages 40 to 49, and every year at age 50 and thereafter. Women who have a family history of breast cancer or are otherwise at greater risk may require yearly mammographic evaluations.

### Tip
### Breast Self-Examination

In front of a mirror: Examine your breasts visually with (1) your arms at your sides, (2) raised above your head, and (3) resting on your hips. Look for any swelling, puckering, dimpling, or changes in the skin or nipple.

Lying down: Lying on your back place a small pillow under your right shoulder. Now examine your right breast with your left hand. Think of your breast as a spiral and work your way completely around and slowly inward. Feel gently and firmly for any irregularity, lump, or thickening. Gently pinch your nipple, checking for any discharge. Now do the same for your left breast (Boston Womens Health Book Collective 1985).

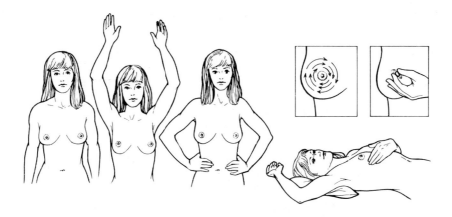

A support brassiere worn during nursing or vigorous exercise may help breasts retain their shape.

## EROGENOUS AREAS

So far, discussing the biological woman, we have focused our attention primarily on the genital and reproductive organs. Actually many parts of the body are importantly involved in sexual behavior, although they have no direct coital function. Nongenital body areas that are sexually sensitive to pressure, stroking, and touch are called *erogenous*. In general, these areas are similarly responsive in women and men.

To some extent what is and is not erogenous is determined by the nerve supply to that area. The lips are amply endowed with pressure-sensitive nerve endings so that it is not surprising that they play an important role in sexual stimulation. On the other hand, custom, individual experience, and cultural traditions also determine what is believed to be erogenous. The female breasts, for instance, are not particularly well supplied with nerve endings, yet they have an important sexual role in many societies.

Given individual experience and learning, *every* part of the body is potentially erogenous. The entire *skin* is in fact a single organ and a fairly responsive one at that. Thus every inch of skin could become erogenous. To avoid mentioning every anatomical location that one person or another may consider erotic, we will mention only a few regions more commonly considered erogenous in Western nations.

Below the waist, one of the most sensitive and also most commonly overlooked spots is the *perineum*, the small area between the anus and the vulva. This space is well endowed neurologically and shares many of the same nerves as the genital organs themselves. Some people find that bicycle or horseback riding leaves them sexually stimulated, although many are not aware that it was direct pressure on the perineal area that led to their arousal.

The *anus* and the *rectum* may provide erotic pleasure. The circle of muscles controlling anal opening and closing has numerous nerve endings, some of which are shared with the genitalia. The sensitivity of this area may account for the fact that about one third of all *heterosexual* partners have tried anal intercourse (Chapter 5).

The inner thigh and the buttocks are protected areas in that they are rarely touched by another except for sexual purposes. Consequently, many women find that touch or stroking may be arousing.

When one thinks of erogenous areas above the waist, the breasts are likely to come to mind first. But the breasts themselves are only moderately sensitive. As we noted before, it is the areola and the nipple that are often most easily stimulated. Further, Masters and Johnson (1986) report that a third of women are not pleased by breast or nipple touch. Most women in fact experience times during menstruation, for example, when such stimulation may feel uncomfortable (Rubenstein, Tavris, 1987).

A less immediately obvious part of the upper body that may be erogenous is the hair. Many people recognize the pleasure in running their fingers through their partner's hair or holding and caressing their head. Olivia Vlahos (1980) describes numerous ways different cultures have treated hair in an erogeneous way. Perhaps the Tchikrin Indians of the Amazon have evolved the most original custom. Among these people, biting off the lashes of one's lover is considered a special erotic treat. A generation ago, teenagers in the United States gave "butterfly kisses." While necking, they pressed their eyes against the other's cheek or mouth and blinked, lightly brushing their partner with their eyelashes.

Outside of the genitalia, the lips, mouth, and tongue may be the most sensitive erogenous areas. Mouth sexual involvement seems a distinct part of our biological heritage. Many mammals, particularly primates, use their mouth and tongue to touch and explore. Some monkeys even seem to engage in

The lips and mouth are highly erogeneous areas.

mouth-to-mouth contact very similar to kissing among humans. Extensive and intimate kissing is a source of sexual pleasure and stimulation for most couples and found in nearly all societies. In fact, the mouth may well be the most universal nongenital, erogenous area (Liebowitz, 1983).

## *Summary*

The sexual organs of women and men have identical embryological beginnings. In women the vulva describes the external genital area including the major and minor vaginal lips and the clitoris. During sexual excitation, the vagina lengthens and moistens and the clitoris enlarges. The clitoris is composed of erectile tissue and is usually thought responsible for pleasurable orgasmic feelings. Its role has often been poorly understood, and misinformation is still common. It also seems likely that some areas within the vagina itself are pleasure sensitive. The vagina, in sexually inexperienced women, may sometimes be partly obstructed by a thin membranous tissue called the hymen.

The uterus is a highly fibrous and elastic structure housing the developing infant for 9 months and ultimately contracting powerfully during the birth process. The ovaries lie over the uterus and produce the sex hormones estrogen and progesterone, as well as ova. The fallopian tubes take up the ova and pass the eggs along to the uterus, but fertilization of an ovum by a sperm needs to occur in the fallopian tube. If fertilized, the egg begins to divide and grow and within a few days is implanted within the nourishing uterine wall. Each month the endometrial layer of the uterine wall enrichs and thickens, preparing for a fertilized egg. If an egg is not fertilized, hormonal changes trigger a shedding of the endometrium, other uterine tissue, and blood. This monthly flow is called menstruation.

Hormones are chemicals that direct many of the body's sexual and reproductive functions. The pituitary gland releases prolactin, follicle stimulating hormone, and luteinizing hormone. The latter two signal the ovaries to produce estrogen and progesterone. These hormones are involved in the growth of the ovarian follicle, ovulation, menstruation, and the maintenance of feminine physical characteristics. Pheromones are chemicals that may elicit sexual arousal in other persons.

Menstruation is a normal monthly occurrence, although misinformation abounds. Most women have little or no menstrual discomfort, but some experience cramping or emotional unevenness. When distressing symptoms occur just before the onset of the period, the condition may be called PMS. A small percentage of women suffer serious PMS distress, which may be the result of hormonal changes or stress. Intercourse and accustomed activity, even if rigorous, is safe for most women during menstruation and is a matter of individual choice. Menopause may be accompanied by some discomfort and conflicting emotions, but most women adjust well to the cessation of menstruation.

The breasts are mammary glands used to nurse the young. They are the focus of much aesthetic and sexual attention in Western societies. Most breast lumps are harmless. Cancer often can be effectively detected by self-examination.

Erogenous areas are body locations that are sexually sensitive to touch and caress. These include the lips, mouth, breasts, hair, thighs, and buttocks.

1 Many people have little information, or considerable misinformation, about the genital organs, particularly the vagina. How can this be explained?
2 What are the role of the clitoris, the Grafenberg area, and the vagina in orgasm?
3 How might anxiety and negative social attitudes help cause menstrual pain and distress?
4 Why do the breasts seem important in sexuality when they play only a secondary role in reproduction?
5 Is a good understanding of a woman's body and how it functions important for men as well as women?

Alzate, H., and Londono, M.L. Vaginal erotic sensitivity. *Journal of Sex & Marital Therapy,* 1984, *10,* 49-56.
Asso, D. *The real menstrual cycle.* New York: Wiley, 1983.
Benson, R.C. (editor): *Current obstetrics and gynecology: diagnosis and treatment,* 5th ed., Los Altos, Calif.: Lange Medical Publishers, 1989.
Boston Women's Health Book Collective. *The new our bodies, ourselves.* New York: Simon & Schuster, 1985.
Broude, G.J., and Green, S.J. Cross cultural codes on twenty sexual attitudes and practices. *Ethology,* 1976, *15,* 409-429.
Budoff, P.W. *No more menstrual cramps and other good news.* New York: G.P. Putnam, 1980.
Daley, M., and Wilson, M. *Sex evolution and behavior.* New York: Willard Grant Press, 1983.
Eastman, P. Menopause and mental health. *Psychology Today,* February, 1985, 12ff.
Ford, C.S., and Beach, F.A. *Patterns of sexual behavior.* Westport, Conn.: Greenwood Press, 1980.
Freud, S. *Collected papers.* New York: Basic Books, 1959.
Graham, C.A., and McGrew, W.C. Menstrual synchrony in female undergraduates living on a coeducational campus. *Psychoneuroendocrinology,* 1980, *5*(3), 245-252.
Hopson, J.S. *Scent signals: the silent language of sex.* New York: Morrow, 1979.
Hopson, J., and Rosenfeld, A. PMS: puzzling monthly symptoms. *Psychology Today,* August 1984, 30-35.
Hosken, F.P. *The Hosken report: genital and sexual mutilation of females.* Lexington, Mass.: Women's International Network News, 1979.
Krupp, M.A., and Chatton, M.J. *Current medical diagnosis and treatment.* Los Altos, Calif.: Lange Medical Publishers, 1989.
Liebowitz, M. *The chemistry of love.* Boston: Little, Brown & Co., 1983.
Masters, W., Johnson, V.E., and Kolodny, R.C. *Masters and Johnson on sex and human loving,* Boston: Little, Brown & Co., 1986.
Medical Forum. Lumpy breasts. *The Harvard Medical School Health Letter,* November, 1984, *IX* (13), 3 ff.
Parlee, M.B. The premenstrual syndrome. In Kaplan, A.G., and Bean, J.P. (editors). *Beyond sex role stereotypes: readings toward a psychology of androgyny.* Boston: Little, Brown & Co., Inc., 1976.
Perry, J.D., and Whipple, B. Pelvic muscle strength of female ejaculators: evidence in support of a new theory of orgasm. *Journal of Sex Research,* 1981, *17*(1), 22-39.
Petersen, J.R., Kretchmer, A., Nellis, B., Lever, J., and Hertz, R. The *Playboy* readers' sex survey (part 3). *Playboy,* May, 1983, 126 ff.
Puretz, S.L. Menses and exercise: attitudes and action. *Journal of Sports Medicine and Physical Fitness,* In press. 1988.
Raymond, C.A. Studies question how much role menopause plays in some women's emotional distress. *Journal of the American Medical Association,* June 24, 1988, *259,* (24), 3522-3523.

Rubenstein, C., and Tavris, C. Special survey results: 26,000 women reveal the secrets of intimacy. *Redbook*, September 1987, *169*, 147.

Russell, M.J., Switz, G.M., and Thompson, K. Olfactory influences on the human menstrual cycle. Paper presented at the meeting of the American Society for the Advancement of Science, San Francisco, June 1977.

Tannahill, R. *Sex in history*. New York: Stein & Day, 1981.

*Suggested Readings*

Asso, D. *The real menstrual cycle*. New York: John Wiley & Sons, 1983.
> An authoritative and comprehensive book and very interesting. It is fairly short and well worth reading.

Boston Women's Health Book Collective. *The new our bodies, ourselves*. New York: Simon & Schuster, 1985.
> A sympathetic and sensitive discussion of a woman's body and her sexuality. Offers much useful advice.

Grant, T. *Being a woman*. New York: Random House, 1988.
> An up-to-date and provocative review of what being a woman means today.

Kitzinger, S., McKenna, N.D. *Women's experience of sex*. New York: Putnam, 1983.
> Reading this book is an engrossing experience. Although one may not always agree with the views, they are presented with clarity and conviction.

Ladas, A.K., Whipple, B., and Perry, J.D. *The G spot and other recent discoveries about human sexuality*. New York: Holt, Rinehart & Winston, 1982.
> An entertaining and persuasive book written with a self-help orientation. The G spot may not be all the authors contend, but it seems worthwhile to know about it.

## Chapter 4

# The Biological Man

** When you finish this chapter, you should be able to:**

Describe the structure and function of the penis and testicles.

Explain the role of Cowper's glands, the prostate, and sperm in reproduction.

Explain sexual arousal, erection, and ejaculation in men.

Describe the role of masculinizing hormones in contributing to male behavior and sexual interests.

Describe the erogenous areas in men.

Biologically, man may seem a relatively simple sexual-reproductive organism. Like most other male mammals, his reproductive role in continuing the species seems only a momentary one. The male body manufactures and stores sperm and possesses a penis, a physical means to introduce the germinal material into the female. The sperm itself is a richly complex seed. It determines the sex of the child and half of its hereditary makeup. In this section we look at the biological man, in most ways physically similar to woman, but distinct in his genital and reproductive contributions.

## Test Yourself

### What Do You Know About Men?

Test your knowledge of the biological man by filling in the blank spaces. Choose the appropriate word or phrase from those listed below. Be cautioned; there are more terms than necessary. Answers are located in the Appendix on p. 579.

1. Erection of the penis occurs when the _____ rapidly fills with _____.
2. The sperm count in an average ejaculation is usually between _____.
3. Normal men have small amounts of the feminizing hormone _____ just as normal women have very small amounts of the equivalent masculinizing hormone _____.

4. The _____ is a small gland in the lower abdomen that helps produce semen in which sperm thrive.
5. Men do not have _____ cycles although a few appear to undergo some regular shifts in mood that may be the result of biochemical changes.
6. Testosterone is a _____ secreted by the testes.
7. Circumcision of all male infants is _____ considered medically necessary.
8. Penis size is _____ related to sexual satisfaction.

**Choices**

| | |
|---|---|
| 10 and 20 | almost always |
| closely | male sex hormone |
| not | prolactin |
| no longer | menstrual |
| absolutely | prostate |
| clitoris | estrogen |
| androgen | spongy tissue |
| erectile muscle | blood |
| spinal fluid | 200 and 400 million |
| female sex hormone | pheromone |

**Interpretation**

If you filled in all 10 blank spaces correctly, you know a good deal about the biology and function of men. A score of seven or better is also fairly good. Do not be discouraged if you got most wrong. Many of us know relatively little about our own sexuality or that of the other sex. Public schools do not ordinarily provide a good opportunity for learning.

This 500-year-old Peruvian pottery was designed to celebrate the penis.

## GENITAL AND REPRODUCTIVE ORGANS
### Penis

The *penis*, the male reproductive organ, has been the object of considerable artistry and mythology. Many earlier societies built massive replicas of it. Some carried amulets carefully shaped like penises and often rendered in gold or other precious materials. Two thousand years ago the Romans worshipped Priapus. He was a fertility god who although quite small had an enormous penis. Statues of Priapus were asked to bring good fortune in business, strong children, and a robust old age. The function of the penis was poorly understood but it was believed to bring power and prosperity. Today we know the penis is a sexual and reproductive organ, but its physiology and anatomy are still not clear to many.

The penis is a tube-shaped external organ consisting essentially of three internal cylinders. These cylinders are composed of cells that have pinhead-sized spaces between them. The cavelike appearance of this spongy tissue is the source of the anatomical names. The two *corpora cavernosa* form the top of the penis and the *corpus spongiosum* forms the bottom. (See Figure 4-1.) The *urethra,* the passageway for urine, is located within the corpus spongiosum toward the bottom center. From the *meatus,* the opening at the tip of the penis, the urethral canal (bladder to meatus) measures about 20 cm (8 inches) in length.

Besides being a passageway for urine, the urethra also transports *semen,* a thick whitish solution carrying *sperm,* the male reproductive cell. At the base of the penis, inside the lower abdomen, muscular tissue surrounds the urethra. One prominent muscle is the *bulbocavernosus.* It helps start and stop urinary flow and also propels semen to the outside.

All three spongy cylinders of the penis have a common sheathlike covering. As a result, the penis appears to be a single round structure. But when the penis is **erect,** the corpus spongiosum stands out as a visible ridge on the underside of the organ. Its outline can be seen and felt by light fingertip touch.

Female fertility figures were also venerated. The Venus of Willendorf, described in Chapter 1, is an ancient example.

**erect**
When the penis lengthens, thickens, and stands upright at an angle to the body. Erection is usually the result of sexual stimulation.

*Figure 4-1*
The penis: the male reproductive organ.

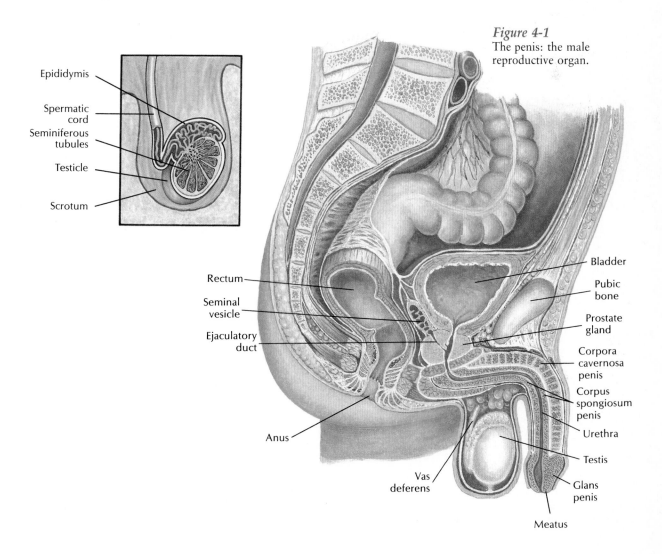

Epididymis
Spermatic cord
Seminiferous tubules
Testicle
Scrotum

Rectum
Seminal vesicle
Ejaculatory duct
Anus
Vas deferens

Bladder
Pubic bone
Prostate gland
Corpora cavernosa penis
Corpus spongiosum penis
Urethra
Testis
Glans penis
Meatus

The penis is similar in size among most men. Folktales and gossip to the contrary, penis size is not an indication of sexual ability or competence.

**Size**   Size variation in human penises is not very great. Most men have a penis about 4 inches in length when flaccid (not erect) and 6 inches, more or less, when erect. The erect diameter is about 1 inch (3 cm). There is no reliable correlation between body proportions and penis size. A tall muscular man and a short thin one frequently have penises of about the same size. There is also some tendency for penises to "even out" when erect. Relatively small flaccid penises sometimes enlarge more than larger ones, so that they both roughly equal about 6 inches when fully erect. Penis size is also not related to masturbation or amount or type of sexual activity. In addition, "back of the magazine" advertisements to the contrary, men cannot reliably increase the size of their penises by exercise or any apparatus.

Despite relatively little variation in penis size, a few men have somewhat larger or smaller penises. Adolescent boys and men, including those with average-size penises, often have some concern about their dimensions (Hite, 1981). Some of this anxiety may be traceable to the notion that bigness equals masculinity or is in some way better. It may also be due to the fact that men may misperceive their own penis size. They do not realize that looking down at their own penis visually (and falsely) shortens it. When they look straight on at another man in the locker room, his penis is bound to look bigger.

*Figure 4-2*
Interior structure of the penis.

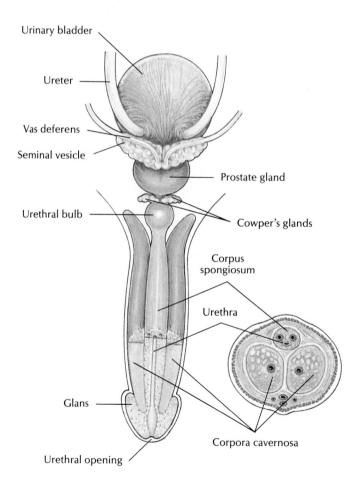

An interesting look at women's point of view concerning size resulted from a *Forum* magazine investigation (Nobile, 1982). One hundred sexually active women were asked about their choices. The majority agreed that if they had to specify a preference, it would be for an average-sized organ, not markedly large nor too small. At the same time, three out of four stated that penis size did not actually affect their relationships. They were much more interested in a man's feelings and attitudes than his dimensions.

Fisher, Branscombe, and Lemery (1983) studied the significance of penis size from another perspective. Is big more attractive and arousing to women and men? The researchers asked both sexes to read sexually stimulating material that differed only in its description of the size of the penis. The men and women whose readings included references to large penises did not differ in their sexual arousal from the subjects reading about average-sized organs. The researchers concluded that "penis size may be as unimportant on a psychological level as it appears to be on a physical level."

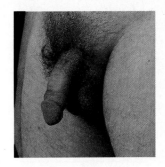

Circumcised penis.

**Glans**   The head of the penis is called the *glans,* Latin for acorn, which is what it resembles. The rim of the glans is called the *corona.* The glans, and even more the corona, are richly supplied with nerve endings and contribute substantially to the pleasurable feeling experienced during sexual activity. The small triangular area on the underside of the glans, where the *frenulum,* a delicate strip of skin, is attached to the head, is also very reactive. It seems particularly responsive to touch that is light and soft.

The entire penis responds to stimulation with at least two other areas being sources of distinct pleasure. The underside of the shaft of the penis, meaning the entire body below the corona, seems sensitive to gentle friction. Another area is at the base of the penis. Some men report that they can be brought to orgasm by them or their partner circling the base with their fingers and stroking.

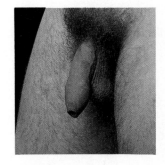

Uncircumcised penis.

It is not necessary for most uncircumcised men, but if there is smegmatic irritation, they can easily draw back their foreskin and gently clean the glans and penis with soap and water.

The skin covering the shaft of the flaccid penis is loose and folded and ordinarily forms a hood over the glans, which is called the *foreskin* or *prepuce.* The prepuce can easily be drawn back, exposing the glans when the penis erects. The foreskin and glans are lubricated by *smegma,* a glandular secretion, which may sometimes accumulate under the prepuce and become irritating.

**Circumcision**   One of the most ancient sexual and religious rituals is circumcision, the surgical removal of the foreskin of the penis. In this operation the prepuce is drawn forward past the corona and a small part of this foreskin is cut off. This permanently eliminates the hooded appearance of the unerect penis and exposes the glans. The surgery takes only minutes and is usually performed a few days after the child's birth. Among the Australian aborigines and the African Kikuyu, circumcision takes place at puberty, frequently as an initiation to manhood.

Anthropological evidence suggests that the practice was prevalent in Egypt as long as 5000 years ago. Ultimately, however, it was adopted by the Hebrew people. In Genesis 17, God makes a covenant with the patriarch Abraham to be the God of his people and lead them to their land. "And you shall circumcise the flesh of your foreskin; and it shall be a token of the covenant betwixt me and you."

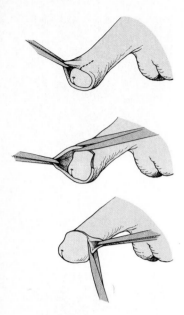

*Figure 4-3*
In circumcision, a portion of the foreskin is removed. In the procedure, the foreskin is pulled forward and the flap cut around the penis.

There is more variation in testicular and scrotal size than there is among penises. One man may seem to have a scrotum almost twice as large as another.

Circumcision of male babies is done in many parts of the world today, by people of the Jewish and Islamic faiths and in some African cultures. The early Christians also circumcised their young babies, but the procedure was debated, and the New Testament (Acts 15) takes a stand against it. Some Jewish authorities too, like the twelfth century scholar and physician Maimonides, were doubtful of the value of circumcision and questioned the continuation of the practice. Nevertheless the procedure endured, and by the late 1800s had become widespread in the United States. It was held to be a worthwhile health practice.

In the United States, for most of this century, physicians believed that the foreskin covering the head of the penis provided fertile ground for bacteria and infection. Other investigators reportedly found links between an uncircumcised penis and phallic or prostate cancer in men, and cervical cancer in their wives. Finally, many doctors warned that if the foreskin is not removed during infancy when it is a minor task, some medical reason may compel the operation in adulthood when it can be painful and serious. As a result, in the United States today it is estimated that 8 out of 10 male babies, regardless of religious background, are circumcised (Romberg, 1985).

Careful epidemiological studies have failed to show any health advantage of circumcision. Comparisons of the populations of the United States and Israel, where nearly all males are circumcised, and nations such as Sweden, where almost none are, show no practical differences in the rates of cancer in men or in women or in any other medical or sexual problem. In fact, the uncircumcised penis may have a slight advantage because the covering skin may protect the glans from irritation. The surgery also carries a risk, although it is slight. Excessive bleeding, infection, and scarring are possible consequences of circumcision (Romberg, 1985).

The evidence now suggests that male (and female) circumcision is not medically necessary. In 1975 the American Academy of Pediatrics established a special task force to study the operation, and after weighing all the evidence, concluded that circumcision should no longer be performed as a routine procedure. However, circumcision may continue to be performed because of its important symbolic or religious value.

### Scrotum and testes

**Scrotum** The *scrotum* is a puckered-looking pouch hanging behind the penis. It contains two *testes* (also called *testicles*), the gonads that produce sperm. Men usually become aware during childhood that their scrotum elongates during warm weather and contracts when they are cold. During sexual arousal and activity the scrotum also tightens, sometimes making this sac seem like a firm round ball. The loosening and tightening of the scrotum seem intended to help the gonads maintain a fairly stable temperature, just a little below ordinary body temperature. When the man is cold, the puckered scrotum brings the testes close to the body, utilizing every bit of warmth available. When the body is warm, scrotal elongation helps cool the gonads.

The likelihood that sperm will be impaired by heat was observed hundreds of years ago and became a primitive contraceptive technique. By taking frequent very hot baths, particularly before coitus, a man had a small chance of lowering his sperm count sufficiently to reduce the likelihood of pregnancy. It must be noted that this practice is practically worthless as a birth control procedure.

**Testes** The testes are rounded glands that are prolific manufacturers of sperm. They are about the same size, but the left one usually hangs lower in the scrotum, a fact recognized by the cut of pants made for men. A cross-section of a testicle reveals several hundred lobes containing tiny threadlike *seminiferous tubules*. The tubules are lined with germinal tissue and continuously produce sperm, millions of them in the course of a single day. As the sperm mature, they are moved out of the testes into an area called the *epididymis*, a very thin 20-foot-long coiled tube lying over the testes. Technically, it is the testis and the epididymis together that are properly called testicle. The sperm continue their maturation in the epididymis and afterward leave the testicle through the *vas deferens*, where they are stored awaiting their reproductive function (see Figure 4-1).

**Sperm** *Spermatozoa*, or sperm, are the male contribution to reproduction. These microscopic cells, in **semen**, leave the testicles via the *spermatic cord*, the name for the vas deferens with its accompanying nerves, blood vessels, and protective tissue. The cord travels up from the scrotum into the abdomen. Within the abdomen the vas deferens leads around the urinary bladder and eventually merges with the *seminal vesicles*. These saclike bodies secrete considerable fluid that sustains sperm. Next the vas turns downward, past the *ejaculatory ducts* and through the *prostate gland*, feeding finally into the urethra. The prostate also contributes fluid maintaining the sperm. The ducts carry sperm from the seminal vesicles into the urethra.

Before finishing this journey and ultimately leaving the body, sperm are also assisted by *Cowper's glands*. These two pea-sized structures are located just below the prostate. During sexual arousal they produce several drops of acid-neutralizing fluid, which are fed into the urethra and soon leak out of the penis.

We will describe the internal organs assisting the development and transportation of sperm later. First, a closer look at sperm.

The average adult man has a total of about 275 yards of seminiferous tubules producing sperm. As a result, in a typical **ejaculation** there are 200 to 400 hundred million or more microscopic spermatozoa. This means more sperm than there are people in the United States and Canada combined. While this is an impressive figure, it should also be realized that a large number are needed to maximize the likelihood of conception. A man with a total sperm count under 40 million is considered to have seriously impaired fertility (Chapter 14).

A mature sperm consists essentially of a head, a midpiece, and a very long tail (Figure 4-4). The powerful tail whips the sperm along so that it can make its way up through the female reproductive canal to the egg (Chapter 3). The head of the sperm contains *lysin*, a chemical antibody that helps dissolve the membrane of the female egg and allows the sperm to enter. Most important, the head contains the *DNA*, the basic genetic material, that will combine with equivalent DNA in the egg to begin the development of a human being.

Human cells contain 46 **chromosomes**, rodlike structures that genetically

The various birth control techniques, and their effectiveness, are discussed in Chapter 14.

*semen*
A whitish, creamy fluid containing sperm. About a teaspoonful is usually expelled as a result of climax.

*ejaculation*
The expulsion of semen and sperm, usually accompanying orgasm.

*chromosome*
The threadlike body in the nucleus of cells that carries the units of heredity.

*Figure 4-4*
*Left,* mature sperm cell;
*right,* head of mature
sperm cell.

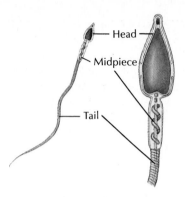

Head

Midpiece

Tail

program every individual. The sperm head contributes a total of 23 chromosomes and the egg the same number to produce the full genetic complement. An important distinctive contribution of the sperm is that it determines the sex of the future child. Each egg contains one sex-determining X chromosome, but each sperm may have either an X or Y sex determiner. When an X and X combine the result is ordinarily a girl; an X and Y produce a boy. Consequently, a woman fertilized by an X sperm will have a girl, but she will have a boy if fertilized by a Y-carrying spermatozoan.

There are some differences in the appearance, movement, and chemical structure of the X- and Y-bearing sperm. Several investigations have suggested that Y sperm (boy) move faster but are shorter lived. In contrast, X-carrying sperm (girl) are less agile and heavier and have greater endurance. Many have been found alive and vigorous, capable of fertilization, as much as 3 days after being deposited in the vagina. Can we take advantage of the ostensible differences between the X and Y sperm and thus choose the sex of our baby?

*Sex selection*  During the Middle Ages if a couple wanted a boy the man was advised to drink a cup of lion's blood before intercourse. A hundred years ago, if the husband and wife had intercourse during the morning, a girl was held to be the likely result. Today prescriptions are more scientific but the results are still controversial. Some physicians have suggested that the sex of the child may be determined by when coitus takes place. If a couple wants a boy, they should have intercourse very near the time of ovulation. Supposedly this maximizes the opportunity for the allegedly faster-traveling male carrying sperm to meet the egg. If a couple wants a girl, intercourse should take place several days before ovulation. This may enhance the chances of the slower-moving but more durable female determining sperm to meet the egg. Supposedly more X sperm will still be around 2 days after intercourse, when the egg is then released from the follicle and ready for fertilization.

Methods to find out when ovulation takes place are discussed under birth control techniques in Chapter 14. "Sex selection" kits based on ovulation are available in many pharmacies. Their effectiveness is doubtful.

A number of fertility clinics have introduced novel methods. One technique places semen in a nourishing fluid at the top of a laboratory glass tube. After several hours, many if not most of the faster-moving Ys have supposedly sped to the bottom of the tube. Meanwhile the sperm still toward the top of the glass column are supposedly extra rich in Xs. A woman can now be artificially inseminated with the X or Y concentrate, giving her a girl or boy as desired (Chapter 14).

Do sex selection techniques work? The normal male/female birth ratio is

106 males to every 100 females. Couples who try deliberately in one way or another to have a girl or a boy have changed this ratio only slightly. Self-monitored attempts such as timing coitus to coincide with, or come a few days before, ovulation seem the least successful. Careful laboratory methods to concentrate or separate Y and X sperm and then inseminate women appear to be a little more successful. Overall, however, the sex of a future child cannot yet be determined either very reliably or very easily (Shettles and Rorvik, 1984).

### Prostate and Cowper's glands

The prostate and the two Cowper's glands both contribute to the sustenance and transportation of sperm. The prostate gland is walnut size and lies just below the bladder. It is made of both muscular and glandular tissue and produces a clear, alkaline secretion that makes up 60% of the semen in which the sperm thrive (Table 4-1). This fluid also contains small amounts of the hormones called prostaglandins. This chemical may help the movement of sperm in the woman's reproductive tract by promoting subtle uterine contractions.

*Table 4-1*

**Ejaculate Composition**

| Source | Major components | Function | Ejaculate percentage |
|---|---|---|---|
| Testes and epididymis | 200-400 million sperm in fluid | Fertilize ova | 4% |
| Cowper's glands | Alkaline fluid | Support sperm, help neutralize normal acidity of urethra | 4% |
| Seminal vesicles | Fluid containing nourishing sugars | Activate and sustain sperm | 30% |
| Prostate gland | Alkaline fluid, prostaglandins | Activate sperm and encourage transport, neutralize normal vaginal acidity | 60% |

Data from Jones (1984).

The doughnutlike shape of the prostate allows it to surround and feed directly into the urethra. In boys the gland is quite small but it begins to grow during puberty. By the early 20s it reaches full size and then remains stable until the 50s. After the fifth decade it often enlarges and as a result may press on and narrow the urethra. This may reduce the force and volume of the urinary stream in older men and sometimes even prevent urination entirely—a medical emergency. In a few older men, malignant growths may start in the prostate, necessitating removal of this gland. (See Focus: Health Care for Men.) Detected early, these prostate cancers may be cured without damaging the ability to have sexual intercourse, although live sperm may no longer be ejaculated (Chapter 18).

Just below the prostate, on either side of the urethra, there are two Cowper's glands. These pea-sized bodies empty a few drops of liquid into the urethra during sexual arousal and before ejaculation. Like prostatic fluid, Cowper's secretions are alkaline and thus help neutralize the normal acidity of the urethra. This makes the passageway more hospitable to sperm. The acidic tendency of the urethra might otherwise damage or kill sperm.

Withdrawal is an ancient but not very effective birth control technique. Sperm may be introduced in the beginning of intercourse or semen ejaculated before it is expected and without marked feelings of orgasm.

The Cowper's secretion also has a slight lubricant function. A man, or his partner, sometimes notices a drop or two leaking from his meatus during sexual arousal. This is sometimes enough fluid to help act as a lubricant. More importantly, however, in some men, these few preejaculatory drops may contain significant numbers of sperm. It is uncommon, but women have become pregnant after only a brief penile insertion and withdrawal long before the man ejaculated. For this reason, because this early fluid may contain some stray sperm, birth control techniques like the diaphragm, foam, or condom must be applied before coitus begins (Chapter 14).

## AROUSAL, ERECTION, AND EJACULATION
### Erection

*tumescence*
The period of building up of sexual energy during arousal; penile erection.

The penis brings sperm to the vagina so that ultimately an egg can be fertilized. For the penis to enter the vagina, that is, for sexual intercourse to take place, it must usually be **tumescent,** that is, firm and fairly upright. Many other mammals, including dogs, have bony or cartilaginous tissue that helps stiffen their penises so they can enter the vagina. Human beings do not have any penile bones or cartilage and no musculature that directly hardens the male organ. Human erection is entirely dependent on the spongy cavernous cells within the phallus becoming engorged with blood.

When fully erect, incidentally, the penis does not stand straight out from the body. Most erections in younger men are above the horizontal. They range from slightly to moderately vertical. Very few are upright to the point where they nearly parallel the abdomen. Many erections also "tilt" a little bit. Kinsey (1948) found about a fourth lean to the left, but very few tilt right. Some penises curve. About a fourth curve up and 11% curve to the left. The lesson in all of this is that unlike the simple illustrations in books, normal penises may tilt, curve, and erect in individual ways.

The male erection is controlled by clusters of nerves called the *erection centers* in the spinal cord. These nerve clusters can be activated by excitatory neural impulses coming either from the penis itself or from the brain. When erection comes about through penile stimulation alone, the sequence is almost like an automatic reflex. It is similar to the knee jerk the doctor elicits when tapping a patient's knee with a hammer. When the penis or nearby skin is stroked or touched, sensitive nerve receptors convey the message to the erection center. This is located toward the lower end of the spinal cord, the *sacral area*. The sacral erection center then sends neural messages back, initiating rapid blood flow into the spongy cavernous cells of the penis, and producing erection.

Notice that this reflexlike erection comes about through penis stimulation alone. Just touching or rubbing the penis, even without sexual thoughts, can result in an erection. This is why, for example, the penis rubbing against shorts while a man jogs can send neurological signals to the erection center and produce erection. This means that male babies or children may erect simply in response to touching their penis, long before they apparently have any sexual information or interest.

We will describe sexual arousal in more detail in Chapter 5.

Erection may also be initiated through the brain, by conscious thought and perception. A man who has erotic fantasies, or whose brain interprets a situation as leading to sexual relations, such as kissing or disrobing, causes nerve

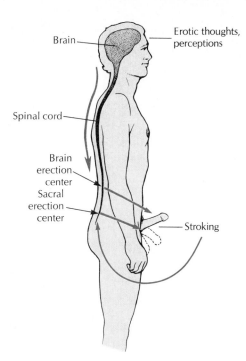

*Figure 4-5*
The erection center triggers the processes leading to erection. The center may be activated when the man perceives an erotic situation or his penis is stroked. Frequently, both situations occur simultaneously.

impulses to flow toward a second erection center. This is also located in the spinal cord, a bit above the sacral area. In this way a man may have an erection although his penis has not been touched, even through fantasizing, without any other person being present.

In reality, erection usually involves both processes, direct penile stimulation and the perception or thought that sex is beginning. We should point out also that just one source of stimulation, direct touch or sexual thinking, may often not result in an erection. As they get older, many men need both sources of arousal. They require foreplay preceding sexual relations. They kiss, embrace, and intimately touch their partner, but they must also have their penis stroked or massaged to obtain a satisfactory erection (Figure 4-5).

The erection of the penis comes about when nerve impulses from the erection centers direct the blood vessels of the penis to relax and dilate. Blood then rushes through several phallic arteries and smaller vessels, filling up the spongy, cavernous structure of the three tubelike penile bodies. As the blood collects within the cells, tissue becomes distended and subtly compresses the veins, thus restricting the blood flow out of the penis. Ultimately, since all the erectile tissue is enclosed by a tough fibrous membrane, the increasingly swollen size of the individual cells causes the penis to become hard, erect, and large.

Erection is not an all or none proposition. There is an almost infinite continuum ranging from a penis that is completely flaccid, to partially erect, to fully erect. Even a person who believes he has erection difficulties may actually be partly erect. He may be sufficiently firm, for example, to have coitus providing the couple is informed and knows what to do (Chapter 17). A full erection is not needed for orgasm and ejaculation.

It is common for the firmness of an erection to increase and decrease during

Erections are not all or none. A man with a partial erection may have a satisfying sexual experience.

## Health Care for Men

The genital and reproductive organs in men are generally healthy and durable. Nevertheless, self-examination and other good health practices should be routine. When a problem arises it is always a good idea to get medical help.

### Tip
### Penis and testes self-examination

The penis and testes should be examined about once a month. It is often convenient to do following the shower. The penis should be looked at for any lesion or discharge. It is *not* a good idea to "milk" the penis, squeezing the head to look for a discharge.

The testicles can be examined one at a time, by gently rolling them between the thumb and first few fingers. Penile cancer is rare and testicular malignancies are uncommon, but in your self-exam be alert for any swelling or lumps.

### Prostate

The prostate gland is sometimes the site of minor infections. Symptoms of infection (prostatitis) include burning on urination, urinary frequency, and a clear to milky discharge from the penis. (A pussy, painful discharge could be gonorrhea— see Chapter 16.)

In some men prostatitis follows extraordinary sexual activity, such as four orgasms in as many hours. But the condition is also found in celibate clergymen. As a result some physicians blame prostatitis on overactivity, and some on underactivity. Some occupational life-styles have also been cited, particularly those that require long

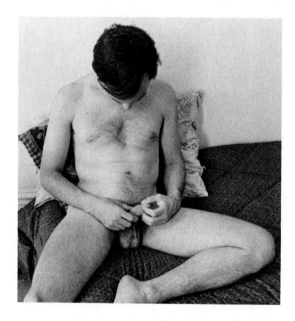

sexual activity. Informed men are aware of this and not disturbed by it. But those who are anxious can be further frightened when they feel erection decreasing. Their fear may then start a vicious cycle that results in losing their erection (Chapter 17).

Finally, given the several steps involved in erection, it should not be surprising that all men occasionally experience some erection difficulties. Blood vessels or circulation may be impaired by illness or medication, allowing relatively little blood to fill the spongy tissue of the penis. Neural impulses to or from the erection center may be diverted by conflicting messages, such as fear or anger. In fact, fear particularly can block the usual erectile impulses from both spinal cord erection centers, resulting in a flaccid penis. In Chapter 17 we will pay particular attention to the faulty learning and negative emotions that can impair sexual arousal in men and women and describe effective treatment.

In Chapter 18 we will describe how nerve injury and illness may impair erectile ability.

sitting. The causes of prostatitis remain debatable but treatment with antibiotics is usually successful.

The prostate gland sometimes becomes cancerous as men get older so that a yearly prostate examination is suggested for all men past 40. Since the gland is close to the rectum, a physician can easily insert a lubricated, gloved finger into the anus and feel the prostate. If the gland appears hard or enlarged, it could indicate disease and warrant further diagnosis. For a prostate examination a man is usually asked to bend over and spread his buttocks with his hand. The exam is not painful (Krupp and Chatton, 1989).

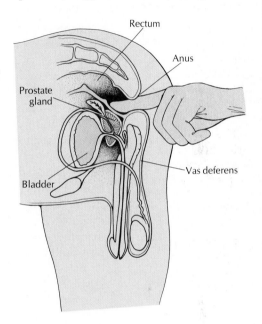

## Ejaculation

The penis is well formed for its reproductive function. Once erect it can be placed in the vagina. Assuming the woman is aroused and lubricated (Chapter 3), the smooth, relatively soft glans can be moved back and forth without damaging vulnerable vaginal structures. Finally, as orgasm and ejaculation, the expulsion of semen from the urethra, approach, the erect penis grows even slightly larger. This seems to assure that sperm will be deposited well back in the vagina, maximizing the chances of conception.

Coitus, or any other form of sexual stimulation, initiates a neurological reflex in the spinal cord. As a result, the ejaculatory center sends out nerve impulses causing the scrotal muscles to raise the testicles and starting contractions in the epididymis and vas. Simultaneously, the seminal vesicles, prostate, and Cowper's glands begin their pulsations, adding momentum to the sperm and fluid. All these secretions combined provide sugars and other nourishments and the highly alkaline environment necessary for sperm survival. If the semen should enter the vagina, its alkalinity will help neutralize the normally acidic vagina so that the sperm can survive for a few days.

Ejaculation in men is actually a two-stage event. In the first phase, as a result of sufficient sexual stimulation, the reflex begins. The vas deferens, the prostate, and seminal vesicles contract rhythmically, forcing semen into the urethra. This is called **emission**. At this point the man experiences the sensations of *ejaculatory inevitability*. He feels he has reached an orgasmic brink. Ejaculation and climax will come very quickly. He cannot stop it.

The second ejaculatory stage, **expulsion**, rapidly follows the first with little or no additional sexual stimulation. In this second phase the combined contractions of the prostate, urethra, bulbocavernosus and associated muscles, and the penis create the force necessary to expel the semen. The neck of the urinary bladder also shuts tightly, preventing semen from entering or urine mixing with the ejaculate. The ejaculatory contractions discharging semen begin at about 1-second intervals. After three or four such spurts, the time between pulsations lengthens. After another three or so pulsations they fade away entirely.

The buildup of excited sexual feelings leading to ejaculation is communicated to and from the so-called pleasure center of the brain. What happens has been likened to water surging into a lake created by a dam. Just as the water increasingly piles up against the restraining dam, the pleasurable neural impulses experienced during sexual excitation load up the nervous system and brain. Finally a point is reached where the dam can no longer contain the massive flood. The nervous system, too, can no longer accommodate the increasing excitatory load. The dam bursts and the nervous system discharges. For the man the sudden neural discharge means both ejaculation and accompanying pleasurable feelings called orgasm.

Ejaculation and orgasm in men usually happen simultaneously. But it is possible for one to happen without the other. Orgasm without ejaculation is common in young boys before puberty. It may also happen in men who are older, have prostatic disease, or are using some medications. Ejaculation without orgasm seldom occurs in healthy men but is not unusual in those with spinal cord or other neurological impairment (Chapter 18).

The ejaculatory expulsion of semen varies from one occasion to the next and from one man to another. Sometimes in young men, semen spurts forth with enough force to travel a foot or more. At other times it may simply ooze from the urethra. The force of the ejaculation can depend on the man's age, health, time since previous ejaculation, and degree of sexual excitation.

Finally, it should be noted that we have been discussing ejaculation and orgasm to understand the man's contribution to reproduction. But as we will see in Chapters 5 and 12, orgasm is not always necessary for a man or a woman to find a sexual interaction satisfying.

### Sleep, erection, and orgasm

Nearly all men are aware that they frequently have erections while asleep and often wake up with an erect penis. Many men have also experienced an ejaculation while sleeping. This last phenomenon is commonly called a *wet dream* or more clinically a **nocturnal emission**.

*emission*
The first stage of the ejaculatory process.

*expulsion*
The second stage of the ejaculatory process. The seminal fluid in the urethra is expelled from the body.

*nocturnal emission*
Ejaculation of semen during sleep.

Sexual arousal during sleep is not limited to men. Measurements of the clitoris and the vagina demonstrate that a degree of nighttime sexual arousal happens in women, too. Both the penis and the vagina show the increased blood flow that indicates arousal in both sexes (Chapter 3).

One explanation for erections and sexual arousal is that the person is having an erotic dream. People sometimes do recall vivid sexual dreams, but this may not always be the case. Infants and children, presumably not yet sexually motivated, may also show arousal while sleeping. Further, careful physiological observation has shown that the muscular tension that accompanies full waking sexual excitement is missing during sleep (Fisher et al., 1983).

**Orgasm** Sexual arousal during sleep is very common but nocturnal emissions, or orgasms, are a less frequent experience. About eight out of ten men and close to half of all women recall having at least one orgasm while asleep. The range for both sexes is very considerable. Most adults seem to have only a few nocturnal orgasms in their lifetime. On the other hand, a few women and men say they have such orgasms several times a month (Petersen et al., 1983).

During medieval times, nocturnal ejaculations and orgasms were believed to be the work of the Devil and his demons (Chapter 1). The male demon (incubus) had coitus with women during their sleep and the female demon (succubus) seduced men. Current explanations are more biological.

A long-held popular view argued that nocturnal orgasms in men were the result of pressure created by the buildup of semen in the vas and other reproductive structures. Women, it was believed, had an orgasm while asleep to relieve accumulated sexual tensions. Both hypotheses are unlikely. Semen does not build up in the testicles or prostate, and orgasms while sleeping are only modestly related to the amount of sexual activity. People who are less sexually active, or entirely inactive, are sometimes a little more likely to have an orgasm while sleeping. But even people who have sexual relations daily may have nocturnal climaxes. Neither seminal pressure nor sexual tension is now considered a satisfactory explanation.

Too tight pajamas, too warm a bed, a full urinary bladder, and certain sleep positions have also been said to account for nocturnal orgasms. But here, too, evidence is lacking. What seems most likely is that ejaculation and orgasms while sleeping are reflexive events ordinarily occurring during **REM** sleep. These orgasms, like arousal, seem the result of the automatic initiation of the orgasm center in the spinal cord.

Once the orgasmic process is under way, it likely stimulates an erotic dream fragment. The whole sequence happens rapidly, usually in under a minute. Nevertheless most people awakened by the orgasm and fleeting erotic dream typically insist the entire process took longer.

Sexual arousal, nocturnal emissions, and orgasms are involuntary. Some adolescents, however, need to be reassured that what has happened is outside their control and entirely harmless. Adults may also be anxious, being particularly disturbed by the dream that accompanied their nocturnal climax. This is sometimes the case when a brief dream seems to involve sexual behavior the person does not consciously approve. A husband dreaming of having sexual relations with a co-worker may feel conscience-stricken about his nocturnal emission. He may need help understanding that both the orgasm and the

A healthy attitude toward oneself and others and a fit life-style are reflected in an appealing personality and appearance.

*REM*
A sleep stage marked by rapid eye movement, dreaming, and a relatively active nervous system.

*guilt*
The anxious feeling that one has done something ethically or morally wrong.

dream are normal events he cannot control and for which he need not feel **guilt.**

---

*In Sum*

Women and men are physiologically distinguished by their sexual-reproductive organs and biochemistry. The male organ, the penis, contains cavernous and spongy tissue, which when filled with blood becomes erect enabling coitus to take place. Physical as well as psychological sexual excitation can cause penile erection. Circumcision of the foreskin is no longer recommended as medically routine. The testicles are important in the production and storage of sperm. The prostate gland contributes much of the semen, a fluid in which the sperm thrive. At the height of sexual stimulation ejaculation occurs, resulting in hundreds of millions of sperm being released. The head of the sperm contains the male's genetic contribution and sex determinant. If the sperm fertilizes a female egg, conception has taken place and pregnancy begins. Erection and orgasm may occur during sleep, both being involuntary, relatively automatic events.

---

## HORMONES

Hormones are chemical messengers that instruct the growth and function of various body organs and tissues. As we saw in Chapter 3, the pituitary and hypothalamus glands work together to produce FSH and LH. FSH cannot stimulate an ovarian follicle in men because none exists. It does, however, affect the testes, encouraging the production of sperm. LH, the luteinizing hormone, also targets the testes stimulating the production of testosterone (Figure 4-6).

### Androgens

*masculinizing*
Producing the physical and behavioral characteristics of men.

The *androgens* are **masculinizing** hormones largely produced in the testes. Smaller amounts are secreted by the adrenals. Like their female estrogenic equivalents, androgens play a vital part during fetal development and at puberty. The increasing amounts present during puberty accelerate genital maturation and produce the angular, muscular adult male body.

The androgens constitute several hormones, the most important of which is *testosterone*. This biochemical appears to be the main determinant of the sex drive. Sometimes a man, or a woman, who is having difficulty becoming aroused or orgasmic has a testosterone deficiency. But as we will see in Chapter 17, it is far more likely for sexual problems to be the result of other reasons.

Testosterone may also play a role in aggressive and competitive behavior. Experiments with animals have shown that the administration of this hormone to white rats, for example, increased their aggressiveness. But it must be remembered that among human beings it is difficult to separate the biological contribution from roles and behaviors encouraged or prescribed by society. We will examine this more closely in Chapters 6 and 7, (Gallagher, 1988).

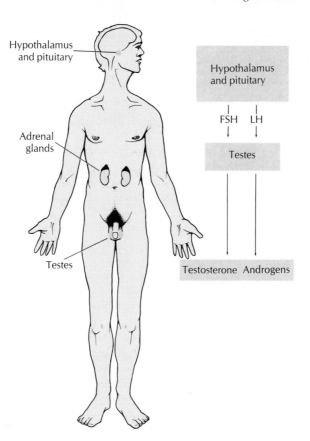

*Figure 4-6*
Hormones in men.

## Estrogens

Both men and women have estrogenic and androgenic hormones, although the amounts differ considerably. In both sexes the adrenal glands produce small amounts of these sex hormones and the ovaries or testes the rest. In women the ovaries produce proportionately large amounts of estrogen and progesterone and very small quantities of androgen. In men the ratio is reversed, with the testes producing minute amounts of estrogen and progesterone and a much greater quantity of androgens. For example, the daily production of testosterone in men is about 7 mg and that of women 0.5 mg.

The role of estrogens, **feminizing** hormones, in men is not clear. These chemicals may help preserve the quality of the body's bone, hair, and skin structure. Progesterone in men may affect sperm production. Because large amounts of this hormone in men may reduce sperm development, it could eventually be useful as a male contraceptive (Chapter 14).

Men and women share most of the same hormones. Those designated *male* are found in much greater proportion in men, often being 10 to 30 times as great as they are in women.

## Pheromones

Pheromones are chemicals secreted through the skin and other body openings that sexually arouse or attract others. The evidence that women produce pher-

Men and women share the same hormones, but the estrogen/androgen ratio between the sexes differs considerably. Chapter 3 discusses female hormones.

*feminizing*
Producing the physical and behavioral characteristics of women.

*Table 4-2*

**Male Hormones**

| Hormone | Source | Function |
|---------|--------|----------|
| Luteinizing hormone (LH) | Pituitary gland | Stimulates production of testosterone |
| Follicle-stimulating hormone (FSH) | Pituitary gland | Stimulates production of sperm cells |
| Androgens | Mainly in testes, small amounts in adrenals (for women small amounts in ovaries) | Encourage physical male growth, especially during fetal development and puberty |
| Testosterone | Mainly in testes and small amounts in adrenals (for women small amounts in ovaries) | Stimulates and maintains sex drive; may encourage aggressive behavior |

Data from Jones (1984).

omones is questionable (Chapter 3). Whether men do is even more debatable. We know that few if any male mammals secrete pheromones. It seems always to be the female dog, cat, fox, or hippopotamus that secretes chemicals that attract males and announce that she is sexually receptive (Wallace, 1980).

Among humans, men have been hypothesized to produce *exaltolide*, a chemical with a musky smell somewhat similar to the scents used in some body lotions (White, 1981). Exaltolide is thought to be released in perspiration and be detectable in male urine. The scientific evidence is limited, but on the other hand, many people find their partners' smell, particularly during sexual relations, very arousing. Liebowitz (1983), in fact, suggests there is a "chemistry" of love. Partners may be attracted to one another by biological cues, smells, needs, and perceptions of which they are not aware.

The research on the possibility of human pheromones hints that perhaps men and women should not be overly scrubbed and chemically deodorized. The person who is clean but still permits some of his or her biological scent to come through, may be more successful in attracting others.

## EROGENOUS AREAS

*Erogenous areas* are nongenital parts of the body that are particularly sensitive to sexual stimulation. Men, like women (Chapter 3), typically report that areas richly supplied with pressure-sensitive nerve endings can be a source of sensual pleasure. As a result, the lips and mouth, the scalp, and in fact most of the face often play an important part in sexual interaction. On the lower half of the body, men like women, find the perineal area (in men, between the scrotum and anus) and the inner thighs sources of pleasure.

Any part of the body may be eroticized. Individual experience and preference are important determiners of what is an erogenous area.

Every part of the body, whether with many or with few nerve endings, is potentially erogenous. A person may learn, for example, that touch of his neck or upper back is sexually stimulating if it is usually associated with simultaneous or subsequent sexual activities. In other words, all parts of the skin can be considered erogenous. Although any area of the male body may be or become erogenous, the anus and the breasts are often not thought about. Both have abundant nerve endings and are quite sensitive to touch.

## Male Menstrual Cycles—Menopause?

Men and women share the same hormones. Both sexes have androgens and estrogens. The follicle-stimulating and luteinizing hormones so prominent in bringing about menstruation in women are present in men too. Although the amounts of FSH and LH in men are small, might they not produce some changes possibly resembling menstruation?

There is evidence that men, like women, have some hormonal cycles. Urine tests for androgens in men have shown a tendency for hormonal fluctuations. Over periods of 3 to 8 weeks the amount of androgen seems to slowly rise and decline rhythmically. In some men, too, there may be synchronous changes in sexual interests and feelings (Liebowitz, 1983).

In her book *Outrageous Acts and Everyday Rebellions,* Gloria Steinem, a feminist leader,

Supposedly a few men in their forties or fifties find younger women particularly attractive.

asks how our views of men and women might change if men did menstruate (see the section on premenstrual syndrome in Chapter 3). She suggests that if men had periods, many of the myths and misconceptions concerning menstruation might long since have been corrected.

**Menopause?** Men do not menstruate and do not experience menopause. Supposedly a few men in their forties or fifties enter a "silly season," when they buy a flashy sports car or become enamored of much younger women. If this happens at all it may be more the result of a bit of social rebellion rather than any hormonal alteration. Sperm count and reproductive capability in men slowly decrease but most continue to be able to impregnate a woman until their seventies or even eighties.

A small proportion of men, however do experience fairly marked declines in testosterone as they pass middle age. This often results in a combination of symptoms that physicians have called the male climacteric. In their 60s they may report feeling chronically fatigued, have a poor appetite, and have lost much of their interest in sex. Note, however, that the term *male climateric* is in dispute and that only about 1 in 20 men manifest the signs suggestive of an accelerated physical or sexual decline (Gallagher, 1988).

What is erroneously called "male menopause" is best explained by later life events. Children leave home; physical limitations create stress, job and career pursuits become more problematic and retirement and death may appear to loom ahead. These events rather than any innate physical change may lead men (and women) to feel unattractive and withdraw intellectually as well as psychologically and sexually. For some men, however, these same stressors act as a stimulus. Instead of resulting in falsely labeled "menopausal" symptoms, they can prompt men (and women) to explore new directions and live productively in their later years (Chapter 12) (Krupp and Chatton, 1989).

**sensuous**
Pleasing to the senses. Often used to mean sexually pleasing.

Among homosexual men, breast and anal activity is common. Some breast stimulation by hand or mouth is frequent, and nearly all of these men have had anal intercourse (Chapter 13). Among heterosexual men, up to a fifth report the anal area is involved in some sexual activity. Very few, only about one in twenty, say they derive **sensuous** pleasure from breast or nipple touch (Cook et al., 1983; Masters and Johnson, 1979; Petersen et al., 1983).

Masters and Johnson observed that compared with women many heterosexual men found relatively fewer areas of their body erogenous. This may be the result of socialization. Many men, it is contended, have not learned to experience most parts of their body as erogenous despite an area's potential (Chapter 17).

### In Sum

Hormones are biochemicals that regulate the body's sexual growth and function. Men have larger quantities of androgens, and these hormones play an important role in stimulating male development and maintaining the sex drive. Pheromones, chemicals that sexually attract, have been hypothesized to be secreted by men, but the evidence is uncertain. Erogenous areas are nongenital parts of the body that may be particularly sensitive to touch or that because of learning or cultural preference play a role in sexual arousal. In men, the perineum, thighs, lips, and mouth are usually erogenous and involved in sexual interaction.

### Summary

The male sexual-reproductive organ, the penis, consists of cylinders with spongelike tissue that fill up with blood to produce an erection. Penis size and structure are fairly similar in most men, but numerous misconceptions exist about this organ. The penile glans and corona appear most responsive to sexual stimulation, but the entire organ is also sensitive. Circumcision is an important religious or cultural rite, but it has no definite health advantages.

The testicles in men produce sex hormones and sperm. Sperm are microscopic cells consisting of a head and long tail to enable them to swim toward the egg after being deposited in the female reproductive tract. The head of the sperm contains the genetic material, including a gender-determining X or Y chromosome, which if united with a female egg will result in the beginning of life.

Sexual arousal and erection in men may be initiated by physical or psychological stimuli. After sufficient sexual stimulation, ejaculation occurs. Hundreds of millions of sperm cells and sustaining fluid from the seminal vesicles, prostate, and Cowper's glands are expelled in several orgasmic pulsations.

Hormones are internally secreted chemicals that regulate the body's growth and function. The pituitary gland and the testes manufacture a number of hormones essential to sexual function, reproduction, and the biological determination of sex. Both men and women have masculinizing androgens and testosterone and feminizing estrogens and progesterone.

Erogenous areas are nongenital parts of the body that are particularly sensitive to sexual stimulation. These areas may be well supplied with nerve endings, such as the mouth, or they may be associated with sexuality because of past experience or cultural preference. In men the thighs, anus, hair, lips, and mouth are often highly erogenous.

*For Thought and Discussion*

1  Biologically the man's role in reproduction is momentary, whereas a woman may be committed for a year or more. In your view how does this physical difference affect the sexuality of both sexes and their relationships with one another?

2  What are some common misconceptions about the penis and erection? How does such misinformation affect the attitudes and beliefs of children and adults?

3  How are the sexual organs of men and women similar, and how are they different?

4  How can erection, and sometimes ejaculation, during sleep be explained? Should parents prepare young adolescents for such experiences?

5  Can you detect regular mood swings, or varying emotional rhythms, in yourself or in others?

6  How may individual experience and learning result in body areas that are erogenous?

*References*

Blumstein, P., and Schwartz, P. *American couples.* New York: Wm. Morrow, 1983.

Cook, K., Kretchmer, A., Nellis, B., Lever, J., and Hertz, R. The *Playboy* readers' sex survey (Part 3), *Playboy,* May 1983, 126.

Fisher, C., et al. Patterns of female sexual arousal during sleep and waking: vaginal thermo-conductance studies. *Archives of Sexual Behavior,* 1983, *12,* 97-122.

Fisher, W.A., Branscome, N.R., and Lemery, C.R. The bigger the better? Arousal and attributional responses to erotic stimuli that depict different size penises. *Journal of Sex Research,* 1983, *19,* 337-396.

Gallagher, W. II. Sex and hormones. *The Atlantic Monthly,* March 1988, pp. 77-82.

Hite, S. *The Hite report on male sexuality.* New York: Alfred A. Knopf, 1981.

Jones, R.E. *Human reproduction and sexual behavior.* Englewood Cliffs, N.J.: Prentice-Hall, Inc., 1984.

Krupp, M.A., and Chatton, M.J. *Current medical diagnosis and treatment.* Los Altos, Calif.: Lange Medical Publishers, 1989.

Liebowitz, M. *The chemistry of love.* Boston: Little, Brown & Co., 1983.

Masters, W., and Johnson, V. *Homosexuality in perspective.* Boston: Little, Brown & Co., 1979.

Nobile, P. Women's penis preferences. *Forum,* September 1982, pp. 23-28.

Petersen, J.R., Kretchmer, A., Nellis, B., Lever, J., and Hertz, R. The *Playboy* readers' sex survey, (Parts 1 and 2). *Playboy,* January 1983, p. 108; March 1983, p. 90.

Romberg, R. *Circumcision: the painful dilemma.* South Hadley, Mass.: Bergin and Garvey, 1985.

Shettles, L.B., and Rorvik, D. *How to choose the sex of your baby: a complete update on the method best supported by the scientific evidence.* New York: Doubleday, 1984.

Steinem, G. *Outrageous acts and everyday rebellions.* New York: Holt, Rinehart & Winston, 1983.

Tannahill, R. *Sex in history* New York: Stein & Day, 1981.

Vlahos, O. *Body, the ultimate symbol.* New York: Lippincott, 1980.

Wallace, R.A. *How they do it.* New York: Morrow, 1980.

White, D. Pursuit of the ultimate aphrodisiac. *Psychology Today,* September 1981, pp. 9-11.

*Suggested Readings*

Altherr, T.L. (editor): *Procreation or pleasure? Sexual attitudes in American history.* New York: Krieger, 1983.

> Written with a sense of humor, this book covers the continuing debate about the "purpose" of sex. Also includes some delightful anecdotes about our forebears.

Daley, M., and Wilson, M. *Sex, evolution, and behavior.* New York: William Grant Press, 1983.

> Takes the view that our sexual behavior is largely the result of our biological heritage. Suggests that society is likely to continue to find conflict in its efforts to channel deeply rooted and inherent drives.

Liebowitz, M. *The chemistry of love.* Boston: Little, Brown & Co., 1983.

> Many people talk loosely about a "chemistry" attracting people to one another. Do humans have pheromones, chemicals that attract? The author explains how biochemistry may play a role in attraction, affection, and sexual arousal.

Robinson, B.E., and Barrett, R.L. *The developing father.* Beverly Hills, Calif.: Sage, 1986.

> Shows how men, supposedly neither hormonally nor neurologically prepared for a sustained parental role, can be caring and intelligent fathers.

*Chapter 5*

# Arousal, Intercourse, and Orgasm

**When you finish this chapter, you should be able to:**

Explain the importance of foreplay in sexual relations and list some different techniques.

Describe positions commonly used for coitus and note possible advantages for each.

Identify sexual relations that are variations on coitus.

Evaluate the role of orgasm in satisfactory sexual relations.

Provide suggestions to improve the quality of sexual relations.

Describe the sexual response cycle as conceptualized by Masters and Johnson.

Sexual intercourse (coitus), the placing of the penis into the vagina, is a common, straightforward biological act found in all mammals. Among humans, however, this elementary physical activity has attained remarkable significance. Hundreds of words are used to describe it, although nearly all have been deemed unfit to say out loud. Even more numerous than synonyms for coitus are the countless rules and customs dictated by society, religion, and law. One can understand much of this concern and anxiety, because intercourse is an act upon which the continuation of the family, in fact the very survival of the species, depends.

Coitus is part of a larger sexual response cycle that, we will see, has been described somewhat differently by several authorities. For the sake of clarity we first present intercourse as a sequence involving three phases: arousal, coitus itself, and finally orgasm. To be sure, this is a simplified outline but one that will help present the fundamental information.

## Test Yourself

### What Do You Know About Sexual Intercourse?

Fill in the blank spaces or circle the right answer.
Answers are located in the Appendix p. 579.

1. Foreplay (caressing and petting before beginning coitus) should last _____ minutes.
2. It is very important for a man and a woman having intercourse to climax at the same time. Circle *True* or *False.*
3. When a woman does not have an orgasm it is almost always her partner's fault. Circle *True* or *False.*
4. How common are oral sexual relations—stimulating the penis or vagina by mouth? Circle a, b, or c.
   a. Almost everyone does it.
   b. Only about 1 in 50 couples engage in oral relations.
   c. Most young adult American couples frequently use this technique.
5. A man must always have a firm and erect penis to enjoy intercourse. Circle *True* or *False.*
6. When it is said that a person is multiorgasmic, it means she or he may have several _____ .
7. A woman who does not have a sexual climax is sexually inhibited. Circle *True* or *False.*
8. How frequent is the coital position where the woman is supine and the man on top of her? Circle a, b, or c.
   a. Only inhibited people use this position.
   b. About 1 in 10 couples frequently use this position.
   c. Almost everyone uses this position at least once in a while.
9. During sexual relations a person who masturbates or stimulates his/her partner's genitals by hand is reverting to unhealthy childish behavior. Circle *True* or *False.*
10. How many times can most men and women climax in a day? (Pick a number for men and for women.) _____ _____

### Interpretation

If you got nine or ten questions correct, you are fairly knowledgeable about human sexuality. Even a score of seven or eight is good. You know more than most people. Scores of five and six are average. A score of four or less suggests you have had little opportunity to become informed about sex or were given a good deal of misinformation. Now is the time to become well informed.

## AROUSAL—FOREPLAY

*copulation*
Usually reserved to describe intercourse in animals; coitus is human sexual intercourse.

Among mammals coitus is not usually possible until the female or the male, or both, have been sufficiently *aroused,* that is, physically prepared for **copulation.** The sexual organs need to be readied so that the penis can be placed in the vagina and sperm eventually released. Animal arousal is usually quick, lasting only a few seconds or a minute or two. Dogs, lions, and elephants, for example, briefly smell and may lick one another's genitals. Arousal in whales is more gradual. Male grey whales swim alongside the female and use their enormous bodies to gently but increasingly brush and nudge the cow. After several hours of touch, the female may turn on her back, signaling she is ready to copulate.

Arousal among women and men, although far more highly evolved, resembles that found in other mammals. When people touch, caress, and kiss—physically and psychologically preparing for coitus—it is called **foreplay.** This preliminary pleasurable sexual stimulation leads to the dilation and lubrication of the vagina (Chapter 3) and the erection of the penis (Chapter 4) so that coitus can take place.

Foreplay behaviors are similar but not identical in all nations and peoples of the world. Kissing and embracing are universal means for heterosexual and homosexual women and men to become aroused and prepared for sexual relations, but there are some cultural differences. What is widely accepted and common in one place may be infrequent in another. Americans usually touch the female breast, but many African societies pay relatively less attention to this part of the body. Similarly, while we may think of stimulating the genitals by mouth as exciting precoital activity, very few heterosexual couples in Nigeria or Japan include this form of arousal (Oshodin, 1984). Members of some South Sea Island societies pull, prod, and tickle genital organs, a practice that is not common in western nations. Even within our own society there may be some cultural differences. Couples with strong religious feelings, for example, often use fewer oral stimulation techniques. There are, too, substantial individual variations. We will mention several common arousal techniques but recognize that many couples may prefer only a few of those mentioned or have devised some of their own which are original (Hite, 1987; Rubenstein, Tavris, 1987).

## Appearance

Most discussions of arousal techniques (foreplay) omit an important ingredient—appearance, which creates a mood. Some couples consider a scrubbed, after-the-shower look highly inviting. Others like erotic clothes or nightwear. Petersen et al. (1983) found one third of the men in their survey, and about half of the women, often wore "sexy" underwear or nightclothes. Another appearance element often neglected is posture. The sexual partner lying in bed, smiling invitingly while watching the intended partner move about the room, looks very different than one who is reading a book or watching television. The way a person appears can be a nonverbal (Chapter 10) arousal technique.

## Touch and kiss

Touch, one of the warmest and most affectionate of human behaviors (Chapter 10), is probably the most universal arousal technique. Virtually all partners caress and touch each other's erogenous areas (Chapters 3, 4) before coitus. Even the ancient Indian *Kamasutra,* 1500 years ago, carefully spelled out the various touches and their significance. Lovers were advised that the throat was to be scratched gently with the fingernail, the navel to be patted softly, the foot pressed with the toe, and the head and hair caressed with the fingertips. Only after much gentle devotion to these areas were the thighs, abdomen, and breasts to be touched.

*Kissing,* meaning the lips and mouth in mutual contact, is a very common arousal behavior. **Deep kissing** is also widely accepted and not new. In the seventh century, a Chinese physician, Tung-hsuan, wrote in his manual on sexuality that kissing should be delicate, a soft caress and gentle touching of lips to

*foreplay*
The sexual arousal process in humans. The touching, caressing, and kissing that partners engage in often leading to intercourse.

*deep kissing*
Open mouth kissing that may also involve the tongue.

Touch and kissing are
common foreplay
behaviors.

lips with a first time partner. Later on, as intimacy grows, the passionate exploration of one's partner's mouth was prescribed. It was through kissing and
the fondling it encouraged, Tung-hsuan wrote, that the "Jade Stalk [penis]
stiffened and the Cinnabar Cleft [vagina] moistened as if by some hidden
spring" (Tannahill, 1981).

Intimate sexual kissing is not, however, practiced by all societies. In the
United States, Canada, and Britain during Victorian times (Chapter 1) deep
kissing was considered indecent and "animalistic." Oshodin (1984) points out
that extensive and intimate kissing is not accepted in many African nations. In
these cultures, older generations do not deep kiss either before or during coitus. The younger generation and those influenced by the West have only recently included this sexual practice.

A few couples include a degree of pain in their touch and kiss. They may
playfully bite the other's lips, breast, or ear, teasingly pinch or spank, or enjoy
activities such as paddling the other or pulling their nipples. Wolfe (1981) and
Petersen et al. (1983) suggest that about 10% of their respondents sometimes
enjoyed some degree of pain during foreplay. Most of this apparently was
mainly play-acting involving little actual pain.

People who enjoy receiving
or giving *serious* sexual
pain are discussed in
Chapter 20.

### Undressing and talk

Some people find that scents, a little wine and other substances increase their
sexual interest and feelings (see aphrodisiacs, Chapter 19). Wolfe (1981) found
that 90% of her women respondents feel that a man undressing them is highly
arousing. They were excited by a man gently and seductively disrobing them.
A woman undressing a man is not as common, but based on interviews is
clearly stimulating also. In fact, among all couples, heterosexual as well as homosexual, undressing is considered a potentially exciting form of foreplay
(Blumstein and Schwartz, 1983).

For many partners, talk is an essential arousal technique. The couple may
talk about their feelings, their emotions, or their love. Or they may speak more

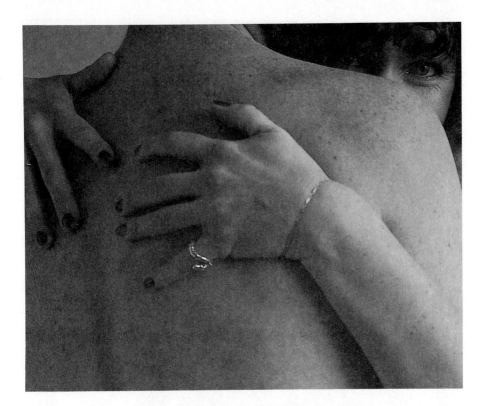

Most women and men find undressing and nudity highly arousing.

about the sexual interaction taking place. Sometimes they taunt or tease one another by verbalizing the erotic things they are doing or will do (Chapter 10). Love talk may range from the most romantic and passionate declarations of affection to the bluntest-seeming obscenities. Typically, too, as arousal progresses speech becomes sporadic, the voice deepens, and phrases may be hoarsely enunciated. Petersen et al. (1983) found about half of the people they surveyed sometimes enjoyed "talking sexy" as part of sexual relations. Hite (1987) on the other hand, contends that most women are dissatisfied because too little talk takes place during or before arousal. She reports that eight out of ten of her sample wanted more talk about feelings, needs, and affection.

### Genital touch, hand and mouth

During arousal nearly all men and women touch, stroke, and caress their partner's genitals. This can be arousing for both. At the same time, both sexes sometimes report that their partner is lacking in skill. According to Blumstein and Schwartz (1983) and Wolfe (1981) men can be both too firm and too direct. The woman may want genital play to begin gradually. First, perhaps some light touch and stroking of her thighs, moving gradually to the vaginal area. Then, after sufficient time, gentle indirect touch of the clitoris can begin.

Foreplay, like nearly every other aspect of sexual relations, is highly individual. The touch or kiss one person enjoys may mean little to another.

Some men note that women do not stimulate their penises properly. They report their partner is unaware of how their penis should be held or the rhythm with which it should be stroked. They may find their partners impatient, seeming to want them to respond too quickly, expecting them to erect too rapidly (Cook et al., 1983).

This graceful early nineteenth century Indian painting depicts simultaneous fellatio and cunnilingus—a technique found in most societies.

*cunnilingus*
Stimulating the female genitalia by mouth.

*fellatio*
Stimulating the penis by mouth.

Approximately half of all heterosexual couples often include oral-genital activities in their sexual relations. Simultaneous cunnilingus and fellatio are colloquially called 69.

Genital touch may be oral. The mouth may be used to stimulate the woman's genitals (cunnilingus). The man's penis may be taken in the mouth (fellatio). **Cunnilingus** can involve sucking and licking the vaginal lips and clitoris and insertion of the tongue into the vagina. **Fellatio** can be limited to sucking the glans of the penis or the whole organ may be taken in the mouth and stroked up and down with lip and tongue pressure. Such oral activity may be quite extensive and include touch and stroking with the fingers as well. Oral-genital contact need not be just an arousal technique. Many couples continue fellatio or cunnilingus to orgasm.

Cook et al. (1983) and Petersen et al. (1983) found that almost all the women and men in their survey had both performed and received oral-genital stimulation. The number who performed it frequently, however, was somewhat lower. Sixty-four percent of single men and 47% of married men performed cunnilingus often. The figures for women were not too different. Fifty-five percent of single women and 49% of married women frequently performed fellatio. Among homosexual couples, oral-genital contact is a more frequent and often much preferred means of sexual stimulation (Chapter 13).

### Fantasy

*Sexual fantasies* are mental images of erotic experiences. They are one of the main means to arousal when a person masturbates. There is no one to touch or kiss, so that thought must be depended on to produce sexual stimulation (Chapter 8). However, fantasy may also be used when there is a partner present. It can enhance other means of sexual arousal or be used by itself.

During foreplay fantasy may start with the first touch, sight, or even thought of the person with whom one will soon have sexual relations. Picturing what will happen and what each partner will experience, do, and say can be a potent means of arousal. The fantasy may also involve picturing oneself with people other than the present partner. Imagining sexual relations with another person, or two or more at the same time, is common and frequent (Zimmer et al., 1983).

Many people are aware that their partner may fantasize sexual relations with another while intimate with them. Often this is not a cause for concern. However, Apfelbaum (1980) notes that thinking about others could cause conflict. He describes what might happen if one partner finds the other fantasizing while they are having sexual relations. If the partner feels the other's arousal is caused by imagination, the almost reflexive response might be: "What's wrong with me?" To Apfelbaum this situation suggests people whose sexual and affectional relationship may be deficient. Sexual fantasies, Apfelbaum writes, are "cut off parts of us signaling wildly to get back in." We need to be in touch with ourselves, understanding our motives and conflicts and those of our partners so we can ably function in the real world, not relying on fantasy.

A more positive view of fantasy sees imagination as a help to sexual arousal. Fantasy permits us to experience in a controlled and harmless manner something we find intriguing but would never want to experience in reality (Klinger, 1987).

> I like to imagine I'm being spanked, and very hard. In my fantasy it hurts only as much as I want it to.

> My fantasy is to be forced to have sex by a whole group. It's very, very exciting. But it's my fantasy so I can control everything about it. I would never want that to happen in reality. That's the difference. Fantasy I can control. Reality I don't.
>
> *(Author's Files)*

Fantasies apparently can invigorate a sexual relationship that has become dull or routine. It may not be necessary for a man to play drunken sailor while the woman acts the part of prostitute. But some couples have found a degree of fantasy and imaginary play-acting a pleasurable stimulus. Zimmer et al. (1983) looked at the fantasies of sexually distressed and nondistressed men and women and found few significant differences. Most couples at least occasionally fantasize during sexual relations. According to Zimmer, this does not ordinarily indicate sexual or marital difficulty. Fantasy is viewed simply as a harmless way to enhance sexual arousal.

Fantasy, it should be noted, is not reserved just for intimate partnership situations. Fantasies or daydreams may arise at any time during the day or night. They may be initiated by the sight of an appealing person or by a recollection of a past experience, or they may seem to appear almost randomly. One interviewee said, "If I were to ring a bell every time I fantasized about sex, I'd be ringing it most of the day" (Klinger, 1987).

Schwartz and Masters (1984) interviewed 120 women and men and found most had about eight fantasies a day, ranging from very brief, just momentary,

Erotica, sexually stimulating reading or film may be used, along with fantasy to assist arousal (Chapter 19).

to quite long and detailed. A few people had as many as 40 or more fantasies daily. Among heterosexual men and women, the most common fantasy was making love with a different partner, followed next by visualizing a sexual encounter that was to an extent forced. The fifth most common fantasy for men was group sex, and for women an encounter with another woman. Homosexual men first fantasized images of the male anatomy and second, relations with a lover. The third most frequent fantasy was sexual contact with women. Lesbians had forced sexual encounters with women as their first fantasy and encounters with men ranked third. In the authors' view, fantasies hint at sexual and intimacy needs that may be either conscious or unconscious. Schwartz and Masters contend that the fantasies they uncovered suggest that at some level nearly all men and women seem to want more sexual excitement and variety. Because reality does not provide it, imagination frequently does.

### Time and progression

Arousal cannot be rushed. While some people feel 5 minutes of foreplay is sufficient, many others want a half hour or more. Some couples say prolonging foreplay leads to more satisfying coitus and orgasm.

Individual arousal techniques differ, but there is a common thread running through most. Arousal is usually a progression of increasingly intimate behaviors. The partners often begin slowly with touch, embracing, and kissing. There is also an element of advance and retreat. Stimulation is begun, continued, and then withdrawn. The couple may pause, rest, and talk. Then, once again, it begins, perhaps this time unfolding a little more, progressing a little farther. Eventually foreplay becomes more and more intense. After caresses and kisses, it may move to mutual genital play by hand or mouth. Complete undressing and then coitus may follow.

Many marriage counselors and writers of sex advice books suggest the progression from kissing to coitus may be too rapid for most people. Wolfe (1981) who tabulated the results of a questionnaire given to more than 100,000 women noted that half wanted foreplay to last up to a half hour. Another 15% wanted a full hour of arousal preceding intercourse. At the same time, the actual reported length of foreplay for most people is between 5 and 15 minutes. It appears that for many women, and often for men, too, sexual stimulation (foreplay) progresses too rapidly. It leads too quickly to coitus. One result may be that coitus is uncomfortable or that orgasm does not occur. Many partners are advised to discuss their individual needs and perhaps extend foreplay (Scarf, 1987; Hawton, 1985).

## COITUS

Coitus is a relatively simple behavior. Yet its consequences can be enormous. A single coital act may in some instances result in a forced marriage, an unwanted birth, a serious sexual disease, and/or extraordinary shame and guilt. Sometimes a partnership is torn apart because a spouse has sexual intercourse outside the marriage. Even more serious, people have been severely punished or imprisoned because they violated a social rule concerning the propriety of coitus (Chapter 20). Andrea Dworkin (1987) a controversial feminist, argues women should start refusing to have coitus. "Intercourse is the pure, sterile, formal expression of men's contempt for women." Dworkin sees the very act of sexual intercourse, the woman opening herself up for the man's penetration, as political subjugation. Coitus, in Dworkin's view, is innately a means to assure and perpetuate the powerlessness and exploitation of women.

Most prolonged intercourse probably does not have any health consequences. The couple who is used to an hour or so of lovemaking is unlikely to experience any discomfort. Longer periods of intercourse, those lasting 2 to 3 hours, may result in some complaints. Both sexes may feel a burning sensation upon urination. Sometimes there is also some lower abdominal or genital pain. But these and similar complaints ordinarily clear up with a few days of rest (Krupp and Chatton, 1989).

**Fellatio and cunnilingus**   Oral sexual activity may be used as foreplay or a couple may continue fellatio and cunnilingus to orgasm. Until recently cunnilingus and fellatio were considered perverse. As late as the 1920s a psychiatric text described oral-genital activity as a "deviation often associated with dementia [insanity]." Even today, in many areas a spouse can sue for divorce because the marital partner insists on cunnilingus or fellatio. In fact, in many states and in many other nations as well, oral sexual contact, even with one's own spouse, is a felony. Fellatio and cunnilingus are defined as **sodomy,** a legal term, describing a sexual act considered unnatural or deviant.

Some men or women accept oral sex but do not want to give it. A central issue for many is the taste of semen. Some find it sexually stimulating to have their partner climax orally. Others say the salty flavor and milky feel of semen is unpleasant. Partners involved in cunnilingus may object that the vagina has an undesirable taste. Actually, a healthy, clean vagina has a subtle sexual scent which many partners find erotically arousing. If there is a distinct bitter taste or unpleasant smell it may suggest a vaginal infection and should motivate the woman to get a medical evaluation (Chapter 16).

The mixed or negative attitudes of many couples concerning fellatio or cunnilingus should be discussed openly and truthfully. Acceptable solutions can be worked out only when a couple talks about their feelings and shares their needs and preferences.

**Anal intercourse**   About 30% of all heterosexual couples have had anal intercourse. Among male homosexual couples the incidence is over 90%. In both groups, however, the proportion who regularly include anal intercourse is much lower. It averages about 10% for heterosexuals and 50% for homosexual males (Blumstein and Schwartz, 1983; Cook et al., 1983; Hunt, 1974).

In heterosexual anal intercourse the male usually inserts his penis into the anal canal of his female partner. Occasionally, however, the reverse occurs with the female inserting a finger, vibrator, or similar object into the rectum of her male partner. During anal intercourse the woman does not usually reach orgasm, but the man who is using her rectum in the same way he would her vagina ordinarily climaxes. Males may also ejaculate when a penis, fingers, or vibrator is inserted into their anus. This happens partly because the object put in the rectum reaches the length of the canal to touch and stimulate the prostate (Chapter 4).

Anal intercourse is held to be satisfying by a few couples, but it also carries some risks. The healthy penis and vagina are relatively free of harmful microorganisms. The anus, however, contains bacteria that can be troublesome if introduced to the male urethra or female vagina. Consequently, couples who have anal-vaginal intercourse are advised to take extra care with personal hy-

About half of the states have adopted "consenting adult" laws. These statutes say the private sexual behavior of consenting adults that injures no one shall not be interfered with by courts or police (see Chapters 13 and 20).

*sodomy*
A broad legal term for a variety of sexual acts, including oral-genital contact, that are considered unlawful.

The positions assumed for heterosexual anal intercourse are the same as for vaginal intromission from the rear. The two should not be confused. *Anal* means the penis is placed in the rectum, while in *vaginal rear coitus* only the vagina is entered.

giene. They should have vaginal coitus first, followed and ended by anal intromission. The rectal bacteria should not be carried into the vagina. The anal-rectal canal is also easily bruised, permitting the entry of microorganisms. Anal intercourse is now considered a "high risk" behavior, since it is a likely means to transmit infection with the AIDS virus (Chapter 16). Both homosexual men and heterosexual men having anal intercourse should use a condom.

**Skin to skin**   Coitus usually means receiving the penis in the vagina. But the penis or the vagina may be rubbed against any part of the body and pleasurable sexual feelings follow. The penis may be put, for example, between the thighs (*intercrural coitus*) or between the buttocks (*intergluteal coitus*). In intercrural coitus, the woman can hold her legs fairly tightly closed and entry can take place from front or behind. With sufficient lubrication and with a partner whose thighs (or buttocks) are fairly ample, the fit is tight and the sensations for the man are satisfying.

Women can simulate intercourse by placing their genitals against their partner and pressing or rubbing against them. One way this is frequently done is by the man placing his thigh between the woman's legs, snugly against her vaginal area. This technique is sometimes used by heterosexual couples either in combination with a penis-stimulating skin-to-skin activity or in conjunction with coitus. The technique is found quite often among lesbian partners (Chapter 13).

When the man puts his penis between the woman's breasts, it is called *intermammary coitus*. Frequently a lubricant is used and the woman may help by holding her breasts together to make a snugger fit.

These skin-to-skin coital variations are sometimes recommended as techniques to avoid pregnancy or the possible transmission of sexual infections. Because the penis remains outside the body, touching only skin, disease is unlikely and pregnancy is impossible. Some obstetricians also recommend these techniques as a safe way for pregnant women to have intercourse in the weeks before birth if vaginal intromission would be unwise.

The bidet, on the left, found in most of Europe, permits men and women to wash their genitals before and after sexual relations.

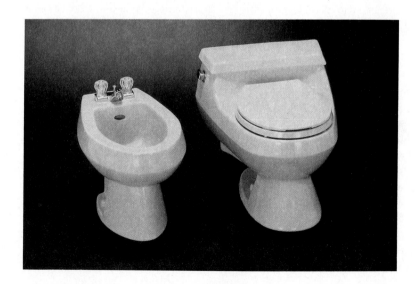

## Frequency and partners

During the 1800s and particularly in the Victorian era (Chapter 1), many clergy and quite a few physicians held that sexual intercourse was either so demeaning or fatiguing that it should be indulged in no more than once a month. In a day when contraception was still neither reliable nor widely practiced, these prescriptions did have a dampening effect on family size. But probably the couples who limited coitus to once every 3 or 4 weeks felt quite frustrated. If we look at studies over the past four decades on the frequency of intercourse, it is apparent that most people want sex fairly often. Currently, during the early years of marriage or cohabitation, most younger adults have coitus 3 or 4 times weekly, and many nearly every day. As the relationship continues and the partners age, the frequency slowly declines. Yet by the time women and men are well into middle age, they still have intercourse about once or twice a week, considerably more than the Victorian ideal (Chapters 1, 12).

Although age and partner availability have an obvious impact on coital frequency, other factors have also been reported to affect sexual practices. The Kinsey studies (1948, 1953) found that adults who had a high school education spent less time on foreplay and were less likely to use varied sexual techniques than those with more education. People who describe themselves as very religious were also less sexually active. Many religious husbands and wives had intercourse less than half as often as comparable couples who did not profess strong adherence to a faith.

More current studies, such as those by Blumstein and Schwartz (1983), suggest the impact of education on sexual activity has diminished. The frequency of intercourse for couples is now quite similar regardless of schooling or social background. More revealing evidence comes from careful in-depth interviews conducted by Lillian Rubin (1976). She talked with 50 high-school-educated working-class couples and 25 from middle-class backgrounds in the San Francisco area. Despite an initial reluctance to talk frankly, Rubin eventually helped the women and men to trust her and be remarkably honest. One result was that she was able to report that 70% of her working-class couples had tried oral-genital sexual contact. This figure is far above that reported much earlier by Kinsey. It also shows the increasing similarity of sexual behavior in working- and middle-class people. It may well be that in the United States individual factors—personal likes and preferences—rather than social status are determining the type and frequency of sexual intercourse.

*Physical health may play a larger role in determining the frequency of sexual intercourse than age alone. Older women and men who are healthy and have an interested partner may have coitus 2 to 4 times weekly or more (Chapter 12).*

**Partners and Coolidge**    A few homosexual men and couples who exchange partners (Chapters 12 and 13) may literally have hundreds of sexual partners in a lifetime. But this is not typical. A large proportion of women and men have few partners. To begin with, about 10% to 20% of all American men and women have only one sexual partner. They meet, marry, or otherwise become partners and have intercourse with no one else.

About one third of women and men have five or fewer different sexual partners in a lifetime. A much smaller proportion, roughly a fifth, say they have had 25 or more partners (Cook et al., 1983; Petersen et al., 1983; Wolfe, 1981). Another study by Blumstein and Schwartz (1983) seemed to tap more sexually conservative people. This report suggests that only 7% of men and 3% of women have had as many as 20 sexual partners.

Is there an innate need for a variety of partners? Often this question is answered by citing the *Coolidge effect*. The term comes from an apocryphal story.

> President Calvin Coolidge and his wife Grace were touring a large farm. Grace Coolidge was first shown some chicken pens and noticed a powerful looking rooster. She asked how often the rooster mated. "Dozens of times a day," was the reply. Mrs. Coolidge responded, "Please tell that to the President." Shortly afterward the President passed the same chicken coops and also asked about the rooster. When he was given the same information about the very active rooster, Calvin then asked, "Same hen?" The answer was negative. "No, each time the rooster mounts a different bird." The President seemed thoughtful for a moment and then requested, "Please tell that to Mrs. Coolidge."

Animal research can give an insight into human behavior, but cattle, rats, and apes are only distant evolutionary relatives of humans. We cannot be certain that what is true for them holds for people too.

Experiments with animals have demonstrated that most males will copulate almost every time a new, receptive female is presented. A bull placed with a cow may mount her once or twice and then appear disinterested. But if different cows are presented to the bull he may copulate with a dozen animals in a 24-hour period.

The Coolidge effect, the renewal of potency and sexual interest when a new receptive partner is presented, has also been observed among female animals. The female chimpanzee is in heat for about 6 days every 5 or 6 weeks. During this period she will spend a sizable portion of each day mating with every adult male in her troop (Dewsbury, 1981).

The Coolidge effect may be reflected in human behavior. New couples do have a considerably higher rate of sexual intercourse than those who have been living together for several years (Chapter 12). As we noted before, both swingers and some homosexual men report the invigorating effects of meeting a new partner (Chapters 12 and 13). Dewsbury (1981) suggests, however, that the Coolidge effect may not be a result of novelty and newness. It may simply be a response to a partner who indicates availability. Among animals, it is only when the potential sexual partner signals sexual receptivity that copulation takes place. When a new animal indicates disinterest copulation does not take place.

Similarly, in humans who are swingers interest in new partners may be environmental. They are in an atmosphere, a party, where sexual relations are the theme. That is the expected activity for the night. A new partner is often particularly stimulating, but there may be as many social and environmental reasons for the Coolidge effect as there are innate biological ones.

---

*In Sum*

Sexual intercourse can be described as a sequence of activities beginning with arousal and then progressing through coitus to orgasm. Arousal takes place through foreplay. The partners usually kiss, touch, caress, and stimulate one another in various genital and oral interactions. Sexual fantasy is common and may contribute to arousal.

Coitus begins after arousal and usually lasts 3 to 10 minutes. Many different positions are possible but lying face to face, side by side, and rear entry are fairly common. Each has some advantages and partners have individual preferences. Intercourse may be varied by prolonging coitus, including cunnilingus, fellatio, and other erotic practices.

The frequency with which a couple has intercourse may depend more on individual than social or educational factors. Generally young and new partners are likely to have intercourse more often. A few men and women have a substantial number of partners but most have fewer than five during their lifetime. Whether there is an innate drive for a variety of sexual partners has not been clearly answered.

---

## ORGASM

Orgasm is the pleasurable sexual feeling that often climaxes coitus, masturbation, or other erotic activity. It has been described in language that is cool and scientific, as well as in words that ring with poetry and passion. Technically, orgasm, as we saw in Chapters 3 and 4, is a physiological reflex, a neuromuscular discharge of sexual excitation. Individuals asked to describe their own orgasm sometimes provide much more color.

> It starts deep, deep down in my belly. Sometimes it seems to have roots, strong, deep roots from up in my breasts, to down in my legs. It seizes me. It grabs all of me. My vagina and my clit, they seem swollen up. I feel I'm one gigantic sex organ. Then it comes. A gigantic tidal wave; it just throws me. It rushes over me. I have giant crashing wave after wave of pure pleasure. I scream and I scream. It's so unbelievably good. It's fabulous.
>
> *(Author's Files)*

All healthy human beings generally find orgasm satisfying. It feels good, but just how good varies a great deal. Some people, like the woman quoted above, suggest that their orgasms are intensely pleasurable. They may scream or groan with delight. For others orgasm may be soothing. They are pleased and relaxed. Their climax has capped an enjoyable sexual experience.

Orgasms may differ with the partner, the mood, the setting, and the sexual experience. Some men and women also report that a particular kind of sexual activity in their opinion provides better orgasms. In one survey, Cook and his associates (1983) found that most heterosexual women and men chose coitus as the activity giving the best orgasm. A third voted for fellatio-cunnilingus and a fifth selected masturbation. Homosexual men selected anal intercourse, and lesbians chose cunnilingus as their best source of orgasm (Chapter 13). Other reports, such as those of Masters et al. (1986), have suggested that many men and women—perhaps close to half—frequently say that masturbation is the source of most intense orgasms.

### Refractory periods and multiple orgasms

After orgasm and ejaculation men are aware that their erection will subside and their sexual arousal diminish. They need to rest before they can begin sexual activity again. Masters and Johnson (1986) called this involuntary rest the **refractory period.** Much as they might like to have sexual intercourse again, males have to wait several minutes, hours, or days before they are able to become sexually aroused and their penis can erect. In their laboratory, Masters and Johnson found a few young men whose refractory periods were very brief. Within a minute or two they were ready to masturbate or have sexual inter-

*refractory period*
The period following orgasm during which further sexual arousal and orgasm cannot occur.

Just as in younger men, there is considerable variation in the sexual needs and behaviors of older people. Although most men in their 50s and 60s have a refractory period lasting an hour or more, a few can be aroused after resting only 10 to 20 minutes (Chapter 12).

*multiorgasmic*
Capable of having several orgasms during coitus or similar sexual activity.

Men past their 50s often find orgasm more variable. They may enjoy coitus but no longer invariably climax (Chapter 12).

course again. In this way, in the course of an hour, they might have five or six orgasms. It is more usual, however, for the refractory period in younger men to last 10 minutes to a half hour. In those who are considerably older, in their 50s and 60s, the time needed before the penis can be restimulated may vary from an hour to a day or more.

Many women do not usually have a distinct refractory period. After a sexual climax they do not need to rest in the same way as men. Some women seem to maintain their arousal and follow one orgasm with another. In this way they may have two, three, four, or more orgasms in an hour or so of coitus, masturbation, or other sexual activity. Other women report, however, that continued stimulation following orgasm is unpleasant and that they require a period of time to regain sexual interest.

Fisher (1982) and Masters and Johnson (1986) suggest that nearly all women may be potentially **multiorgasmic.** They may never have experienced more than one orgasm during coitus with their partner, but if coitus, masturbation, or any other source of satisfying sexual stimulation continues for an hour or so, they are likely to climax more than once. In practice perhaps about 10% of all women are frequently multiorgasmic (Wolfe, 1981). Some of these women report, however, that only masturbation either by hand or with a vibrator usually provides more than one orgasm.

### Orgasm in females and males

The male climax usually follows a consistent pattern. There is a progression of excitation resulting in a sudden ejaculatory release (Chapter 4). Some women have essentially a similar orgasmic experience. But while men ordinarily describe only this one kind of orgasm, women report others (Chapters 3, 7). For some women, there is no sudden trigger-like release, but a more gentle pleasant peak followed by an enjoyable downward slide. For a few others the orgasm seems to approach slowly, increase subtly, and then be sustained for a minute or more. These and many other orgasmic patterns may remain constant for a woman for most of her life. But they may also change. Many women report that how they experience orgasm depends a good deal on arousal, the situation, their partner or subtle relationship feelings not easily explained (Rubenstein, Tavris, 1987; Scarf, 1987).

Women are also aware that their orgasm seems more variable than that experienced by men. Males usually, though not invariably, have an orgasm. For many women, even if their partner and the circumstances of their sexual activity are exciting and satisfying, orgasm may not be the outcome. Describing the proportion of women who have orgasm has occupied writers since earliest times. The figures also conflict. We suspect that it is a matter of whom you interview and how you measure. If 20-year-old single women masturbate in a laboratory, one set of conclusions is likely to emerge. If 50-year-old married women are asked to recall the percent of the time they have orgasm, another set of figures will be produced.

We have carefully considered several different studies beginning with the Kinsey work 40 years ago and conclude:

- Two thirds of women usually experience orgasm as a result of coitus.
- Over three fourths of women usually experience orgasm as a result of coitus and/or their partner stimulating their genitalia manually or orally.

- Nearly all women can reach orgasm using a vibrator, their hand, or another masturbatory technique.

(Data from Blumstein and Schwartz, 1983; Hunt, 1974; Kinsey et al., 1953; Rubenstein, Tavris, 1987; Waterman, Chiauzzi, 1982.)

The same research from which we draw these statistics has also shown that one woman in 10 has not had an orgasm. Study of this 10% of nonorgasmic women has demonstrated that most might better be thought of as **preorgasmic.** They are potentially orgasmic but have not masturbated or been in sexual situations that would lead to climax. They are women who can learn the type of sexual activity, partner, or circumstances, as de Bruijn (1982) has demonstrated, that will lead to orgasm.

Orgasm may involve a number of psychological and learning elements, as well as physiological ones. Women do seem to learn to climax as they and their partners become more aware of needs and preferences. Wolfe (1981) showed that only 10% of women reported that their first sexual relationships resulted in orgasm. Yet a dozen years later orgasm is the result of coitus for the large majority of all women (de Bruijn, 1982).

**Clitoris**   The clitoris is the small, pea-shaped pleasure-sensitive organ located just beneath the top of the inner vaginal lips central to orgasm in women (Chapter 3). During coitus the penis usually does not contact the clitoris directly. Masters and Johnson (1986), among others, suggest that this clitoral placement could help account for the variability of female orgasm during coitus. It may also be the reason, at least in part, why orgasm is almost certain if the woman or her partner stimulates the clitoris by hand, mouth, or other means.

In addition, the likelihood of clitoral stimulation and the probability of orgasm may be increased by an extended period of foreplay and/or coitus. After intromission, many men have an orgasm within about 5 minutes. Wolfe (1981) reported that one third of the women she surveyed required 10 to 20 minutes. Five percent needed an hour of coitus or its equivalent to climax. The point is these women could and did have satisfying orgasms, although they required more time than was usual for many men.

Hock (1983) believes orgasm may be more likely if the clitoris and the vagina are both involved during coitus. The entire front wall of the vagina is held to be sexually and neurologically sensitive. Hock writes that during coitus, "the female orgasm results from successful stimulation of . . . the female orgasmic reflex consisting of clitoral *and* anterior [front vaginal] wall simultaneous stimulation . . ." (p. 166). It may be that clitoris and vagina are part of a unified sensory complex, and function together to provide sexual feelings and climax.

Some coital positions have also been thought more likely to result in orgasm. In face-to-face coitus when the woman is on top, the man supine, she can more easily control the degree to which her clitoris is stimulated by the man's penis. Some doubt, however, has been cast on the orgasmic potential of this position by the research of Myers and his colleagues (1983). They report that the woman on top has no clear climactic advantage. Yet, individually, many women still affirm their enjoyment of this position.

A final point must be cleared up. Some women and men believe there is

*preorgasmic*
Not yet having experienced orgasm.

The clitoris has been called a miniature penis. One could also call the penis an enlarged clitoris. The point is that both are pleasure-sensitive organs richly endowed with nerve endings. They arise from the same germinal and embryonic tissue during the early weeks of life (Chapters 3 and 4).

## The Pleasure of Sex

"Sex is one of the nine reasons for reincarnation," wrote the late, controversial novelist Henry Miller. "The other eight are unimportant." "Keeping Sex in Your Relationship," in Chapter 12, shows ways in which satisfying erotic relations may be maintained. The following additional suggestions can help keep the pleasure in sex.

### Sex is more than orgasm

In the view of many sex therapists, too much has been written about orgasm, particularly in women. Magazine articles, advice books, even television talk shows, often focus attention on orgasm. However, the climax is just one part of a much larger sexual interaction that involves touch, kiss, caress, and warm affectionate feelings. Coitus has many purposes. Its aims may be to express love, experience physical pleasure, reproduce, or bond a relationship. In this sexual gestalt, the orgasm is important, but it is not the only goal. Waterman and Chiauzzi (1982), for example, did a careful statistical analysis of the sexual techniques and satisfactions of 42 young couples. Both women and men were able to rate sexual pleasure as high whether it occurred with or without orgasm (see "Goal-Free Sex" in Chapter 17).

### Communication, yes: interrogation, no!

Couples need to talk honestly with each other. Instead of routinely asking, "Did you come?" it is far better, after sexual relations, to discuss feelings, needs, and preferences. A sex counselor has suggested that good sexual-affectional relations may depend much more on communication than on any technique or achievement in bed. Chapter 10 outlines specific ways in which communication can be facilitated.

### Accentuate the positive

Life is uncertain. A baking masterpiece last week may turn out to be soggy cake when made today. We may have prepared brilliantly for a placement interview but some little error puts us on the wrong track and we fail to get the job. An intelligent, caring couple doing all the right things may nevertheless spend an unsatisfied hour in sexual relations. Sexual satisfaction can be elusive. It is influenced by all sorts of environmental pressures, fears, and stresses. For many different reasons, both known and unknown, sex can sometimes be dull, frustrating, or difficult. The opposite is true, too. Sexual relations that appear to be routine can turn into an exciting, emotionally and physically gratifying experience. It is part of the complexity of sex that it is somewhat unpredictable. In fact it may well be this unpredictability that helps keep sex interesting. A positive outlook will assure us that just as there are unexpected disappointments, there will be many unanticipated pleasures.

The clitoris itself may be very sensitive, and pulling back the hood and touching the organ may feel uncomfortable. Clitoral stimulation that is varied and subtle and leaves the hood in place is preferred by many women.

something wrong if a woman or a man does not have an orgasm through coitus alone. This is partly a reflection of several decades of sex and marriage advice books that attached major significance to orgasm and especially to coital climax. Current views hold it is equally desirable and normal if orgasm is the result of coitus alone or coitus and/or touch by hand, mouth, or other means. It is very much a personal or a partnership decision which mode of stimulation is preferred (Hawton, 1985).

**The orgasmofib** Nearly everyone has faked an orgasm, a white lie we call an **orgasmofib.** Petersen and his associates (1983) report that two thirds of the women and one third of the men they surveyed reported having faked an orgasm. We suspect in-depth interviews with people older than those in the Petersen sample might reveal orgasm faking in both sexes approaching 100%. The major reason people fake orgasm is to please their partner and/or to end what may seem like a prolonged and fruitless endeavor.

> I've lied about having an orgasm. I want her to think she's very sexy and always gets me off. I groan and throb and really do an act.
>
> I've faked coming. It makes him feel good to think he's made me come.
>
> *(Author's Files)*

There is also an element of face-saving in faking orgasm. The man may want to continue to project an unblemished image of confidence and sexuality. Fatigue may be another reason. A woman may be tired of her partner's persistence. She can stop him only by pretending she has climaxed. On occasion a woman or man may fake an orgasm to avoid talking about it or sex in general. They may resent being questioned. The frequent inquiry, "Did you come?" is not one that ordinarily stimulates good communication. It is more likely to lead to an untruthful "yes" than to honest communication.

Finally, the myth of the simultaneous orgasm must take blame for some orgasmofibs. The same sex and marital advice books that may misdirect women and men concerning coital orgasms also often advance the notion of simultaneous climaxes. In the 1950s and '60s a great many couples were instructed to fine tune their sexuality so that they might climax mutually. The men and women who still have this simultaneous goal in mind may be motivated to fake orgasm. They want their partner to know they have reached the goal together.

Today it is recognized that orgasm is not a tape at the end of a race that both partners have to break together. Sometimes orgasms do occur simultaneously, and a few couples may even be expert in achieving this end. But for most people, whether or not orgasms are mutual is not critically related to the satisfaction obtained in their sexual relations.

## SEXUAL RESPONSE CYCLES

The topics we have discussed—arousal, coitus, and orgasm—are part of a cycle of sexual response. An early Greek physician saw the cycle consisting of 12 steps, beginning with "apprehension": seeing and sensing another with whom to make love. Around the turn of this century, Havelock Ellis (Chapter 2) viewed sexual interaction simply as tumescence and detumescence. *Tumescence* literally means swelling and often refers to penile erection and vaginal lubrication. The second phase, *detumescence,* was the physical and psychological release of energy through orgasm. In this section we will look at two recent descriptions of the phases of sexual response and present what they have revealed about human sexuality.

*orgasmofib*
This term for faking orgasm will not be found in any dictionary. Its originator is Donna Davis, a State University of New York communications instructor. She points out that many common human experiences and behaviors lack an adequately descriptive word.

Enjoying a mutually satisfying relationship.

### Kaplan's three stages

Helen Kaplan (1987), a noted sex therapist, conceives of sexual relations as involving three stages: *desire, excitement,* and *orgasm.* This concept came from Kaplan's work as a therapist. She saw sexual problems usually falling into one of these three categories. A person might not desire sexual relations; might desire them but be unable to be excited (aroused); or might fail in the attempt to have orgasm. Based on this understanding of sexuality, Kaplan was able to focus specifically on the sexual problems of her clients and provide appropriate treatment (Chapter 17).

A second contribution made by the three-stage sexual response model is its clear description of desire. Kaplan sees sexual desire as a physically and intellectually distinctive event. It precedes biological arousal and involves thought, motive, and plan. The person whose sexual interest is heightened seeks sexual

*Figure 5-4*
Three-stage model of the sexual response cycle suggested by Helen Kaplan (1979).

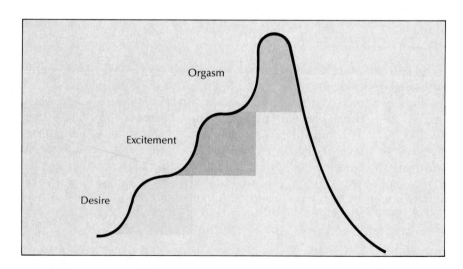

excitation. But powerful as the desire motive can be, it is not indispensable to sexual relations. Kaplan points out that women and men may be physically aroused, have intercourse, masturbate, and engage in other sexual activity to the point of orgasm, on a strictly reflexive basis (Chapters 3 and 4). Desire need not always accompany sexual activity.

Kaplan's model is appealing. Its delineation of the role of desire contributes to a fuller understanding of sexuality. It may, for example, be differences in sexual desire from one person to the next that account for the considerable variability of people's sexual behavior. The three-stage model is also easy to comprehend and immediately seems to fit our personal experience. But this model has not been widely accepted. For many, it lacks specificity, not sufficiently detailing what happens on a physiological level through the several steps of sexual response.

### Masters and Johnson: four-stage model

The most well-known and accepted description of the stages of sexual response is that proposed by Masters and Johnson. Beginning two decades ago, this team examined 10,000 instances of sexual activity for 694 men and women in their laboratory (Chapter 2). They reported that the entire coital sequence involves four steps: *excitement, plateau, orgasm,* and *resolution.* The investigators pointed out that while variability exists in the duration, quality, and progression of the steps from one person to the next, all people and both sexes share very similar patterns (Masters, Johnson, and Kolodny, 1986).

Two biological processes are essential to the Masters and Johnson model. The first is *vasocongestion,* which describes the increased blood flow to and enlargement of the genitals, breasts, and other body tissues (Chapters 3 and 4). The second process, *myotonia,* refers to the buildup of tension and energy in nerves and muscles. The entire body becomes prepared: physically flexed for sexual activity.

**Excitement**   The first sexual response stage, excitement, may be prompted by erotic thoughts, sights, or the physical contact of foreplay. In men the most marked aspect of the excitement phase is vasocongestion of the penis, resulting in erection (Chapter 4). In women the excitatory vasocongestion results in enlargement of the clitoris, expansion of the vaginal lips, and in varying degrees, moistening of the vaginal walls in a process called *transudation* (Chapter 3). Women and sometimes men may also experience some breast and nipple enlargement, and both sexes show increased perspiration, heart rate, and respira-

Kaplan points out that desire is not always necessary to have coitus. A person who does not especially want intercourse at the moment can often be physically aroused by a partner stimulating her or his genitals.

*Figure 5-5*
*Left,* The four-stage sexual response cycle is similar in most males. A refractory period (*dotted line*) usually follows orgasm. *Right,* The four-stage sexual response cycle often varies among women. The three examples show that Ann is multiorgasmic while Beth reaches plateau but no orgasm. Carol's response cycle is similar to that of a male. Numerous other variations are possible. (Modified from Masters, Johnson, and Kolodny, 1986.)

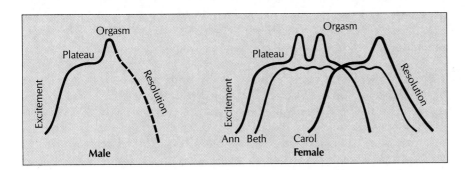

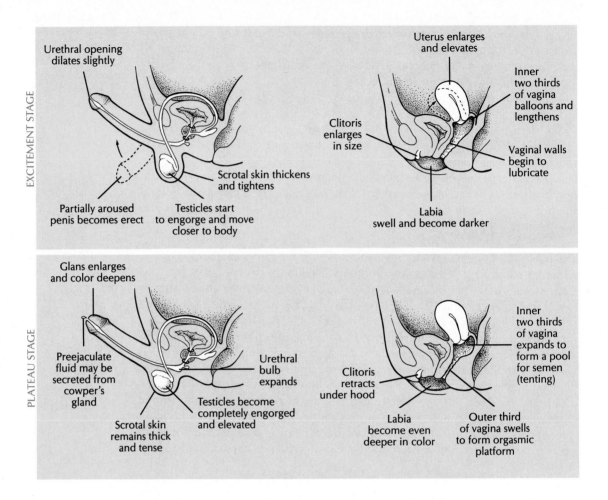

EXCITEMENT STAGE

Urethral opening
dilates slightly

Partially aroused
penis becomes erect

Testicles start
to engorge and move
closer to body

Scrotal skin thickens
and tightens

Uterus enlarges
and elevates

Clitoris
enlarges
in size

Inner
two thirds
of vagina
balloons and
lengthens

Vaginal walls
begin to
lubricate

Labia
swell and become darker

PLATEAU STAGE

Glans enlarges
and color deepens

Preejaculate
fluid may be
secreted from
cowper's
gland

Scrotal skin
remains thick
and tense

Testicles become
completely engorged
and elevated

Urethral
bulb
expands

Clitoris
retracts
under hood

Inner
two thirds
of vagina
expands to
form a pool
for semen
(tenting)

Labia
become even
deeper in color

Outer third
of vagina swells
to form orgasmic
platform

tion. Internally in women, the increased myotonia pulls the uterus up, bringing the cervix with it. It is hypothesized that these vaginal and uterine changes provide the best possible environment for sperm to be deposited and for conception to take place.

The excitement phase with its penile erection and vaginal lubrication may proceed smoothly or be uneven. Vasocongestion can wax and wane. It is normal and fairly common for vaginal lubrication and erection to increase, decrease, and increase during a sexual encounter. The man who senses a decrease in erection and becomes fearful is inflicting on himself a *self-fulfilling prophecy*. The man or woman who thinks or worries "I'm losing it" may be setting himself or herself up to actually become unaroused (Chapter 17).

**Plateau**    The plateau stage for both sexes is much like moving into high gear. The increase in muscle tension, which began during excitement, becomes more marked and now often extends to the neck, face, hands, and feet. The person may have a look of extreme concentration. The lips may appear swollen, the face may seem enlarged, breathing becomes faster, blood pressure rises, and the heart rate often increases to as much as 180 beats per minute. Skin color

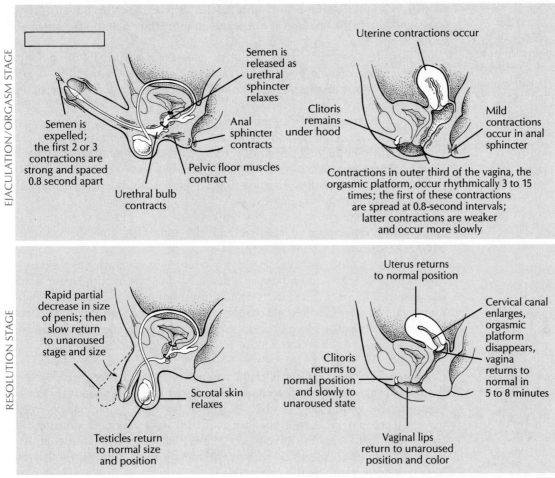

EJACULATION/ORGASM STAGE

Semen is released as urethral sphincter relaxes

Uterine contractions occur

Semen is expelled; the first 2 or 3 contractions are strong and spaced 0.8 second apart

Anal sphincter contracts

Pelvic floor muscles contract

Urethral bulb contracts

Clitoris remains under hood

Mild contractions occur in anal sphincter

Contractions in outer third of the vagina, the orgasmic platform, occur rhythmically 3 to 15 times; the first of these contractions are spread at 0.8-second intervals; latter contractions are weaker and occur more slowly

RESOLUTION STAGE

Rapid partial decrease in size of penis; then slow return to unaroused stage and size

Scrotal skin relaxes

Testicles return to normal size and position

Uterus returns to normal position

Cervical canal enlarges, orgasmic platform disappears, vagina returns to normal in 5 to 8 minutes

Clitoris returns to normal position and slowly to unaroused state

Vaginal lips return to unaroused position and color

*Figure 5-6*
The sexual response cycle. Note that this depicts only the genital changes during the four phases of the response cycle. Actually the entire body is involved (see text).

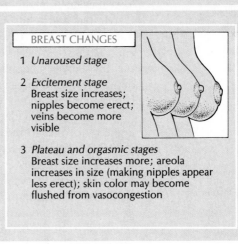

BREAST CHANGES

1 *Unaroused stage*

2 *Excitement stage*
Breast size increases; nipples become erect; veins become more visible

3 *Plateau and orgasmic stages*
Breast size increases more; areola increases in size (making nipples appear less erect); skin color may become flushed from vasocongestion

may deepen and reddish or brownish patches appear over the abdomen, chest, back, and face. This **sex flush** is noticeable in more than half of all women and a fourth of men.

In men the erection that began during excitement reaches its full potential with further increases in penis diameter. At the same time, seminal fluid gathers in the prostatic urethra in preparation for the transportation of sperm during orgasm.

In women, the swelling that started during excitement becomes more marked. The female breast and areola can become even more prominent. The vasocongestion in the outer third of the vagina causes these tissues to enlarge. This reaction, termed *orgasmic platform,* narrows the vaginal opening by a third or more. The result is a vagina that accommodates the penis snugly. The inner two thirds of the vagina expands a bit more during the plateau phase, while the uterus elevates, a reaction called "tenting." This may lengthen the coital canal, facilitating intercourse, and also ultimately contributing to the passage of sperm for reproductive purposes.

The clitoris, which might have roughly doubled in size during excitement, is now highly sensitive and withdraws reflexively under its hood where it is very responsive to indirect stimulation. Simultaneously the inner lips enlarge significantly and become brighter and deeper in color. Masters and Johnson contend that once this vaginal lip color change occurs, if appropriate stimulation continues, orgasm will invariably follow.

**Orgasm**   Orgasm or climax is at the summit of the sexual response cycle although it lasts only 3 to 15 seconds. During the quarter minute or so of orgasm, muscle spasms may be felt throughout the body. Some people will be quiet; others may seem to grunt just as if they were lifting or working. The entire being may seem to convulse and the genitals to pulsate. Although boys and aged men may experience orgasm without ejaculation, this is the key biological event of male orgasm (Chapter 4).

Masters and Johnson found orgasm in women to involve muscular contractions in the uterus, as well as in the outer third of the vagina. The first several contractions can be intense and occur at about 1-second intervals. Gradually the time between contractions lengthens and the pleasurableness of each wave diminishes. Mild orgasms, the researchers point out, may involve three or four contractions, although a very profound climax may number a dozen or more.

Do women "ejaculate" during orgasm? Ladas, Perry, and Whipple (1982) argue that some women expel a fluid much like semen without sperm. Heath (1984) contends that female ejaculate may even be quite substantial, enough to wet the bed. Masters et al. (1986) point out that in careful investigations with over a thousand women in their sex therapy program, only a handful reported fluid emission accompanying orgasm. They contend that chemical analysis has in most cases shown the liquid is actually urine. This is said to have been squeezed from the urethra by the muscular straining that occurs during sexual arousal and stimulation. But they also agree that in a very few instances women may ejaculate a type of fluid that is not urine. The controversy continues. What is clear is that most women do not routinely ejaculate. When fluid does appear, it may be urine or be chemically analogous to seminal emission.

### Afterplay

*Afterplay* is an uncommon word, certainly much less likely to be recognized than *foreplay*. But most sexologists now see what happens immediately after coitus and orgasm (afterplay) as an important part of intercourse. Halpern and Sherman, in their book *Afterplay* (1979), argue that much as dessert may color our feelings about the whole meal, afterplay critically influences how we feel about sexual intercourse.

Halpern and Sherman (1979) interviewed 234 men and women to uncover what most couples liked and did not like after intercourse. Nearly all women and men agreed that their favored afterplay involved touch. They wanted to be held, stroked, and embraced. Many also liked loving words, relaxing, some food and drink, and showering together.

Afterplay activities that were disliked included, surprisingly, going to sleep. This involved one partner going to sleep and essentially shutting out the other person. Watching television, smoking, leaving, questioning sexual performance, and talking about other partners were also disliked.

A common thread runs through the afterplay activities that were desired and those that were rejected. After intercourse some people feel awkward and perhaps vulnerable. They have opened themselves up and been unusually self-revealing. In all these situations, what is wanted is some continuity of intimacy and good feeling. The man and woman want to go on, for a while at least, feeling valued, trusted, liked, and cared about. Activities after coitus that ignore the partner, or that shift too suddenly from sharing to individual needs, are likely to end intercourse on a negative note. As one interviewee said, "I like to reenter the real world gradually."

**Resolution**   If orgasm has occurred or sexual stimulation ends after the excitement or plateau phase, resolution begins. During this fourth and last sexual response stage, within 5 to 15 minutes the body returns to its prearousal state. Muscle tension is relaxed; heart rate, breathing, and blood pressure return to normal. The sex flush disappears but may leave a film of perspiration. The penis, vagina, lips, clitoris, and nipples lose their expansion in size.

A variety of emotions are experienced following orgasm. Some people laugh, others cry; some feel wide awake and energetic; others are exhausted and want to sleep. Although biology may contribute, it is likely that the emotional context of the sexual situation weighs heavily in determining postorgasmic feelings. For example, orgasm experienced at night with a loved spouse may cause the partners to feel tenderness, affection, and fatigue. When the orgasm occurs through masturbation or with a new partner, the individual may feel released, energetic, and ready to get on with other activities (Halpern and Sherman, 1979).

This four-step description of human sexual response is not accepted by all authorities, and many disagree with specific details. But Masters and Johnson have provided a physiological model; a framework within which to understand human sexual activity and conduct further research.

*In Sum*

Orgasm is the pleasurable experience climaxing sexual relations. The orgasm of men coincides with ejaculation and is relatively consistent. That of women is more varied. Many women and men may have several orgasms, although men nearly always require a brief rest first. The clitoris is the sensory center for female orgasm, although a number of different means may be used to bring about a sexual climax. Both sexes may occasionally fake an orgasm.

The sexual response cycle has been differently described by several writers, with the Masters and Johnson outline among the most prominent. According to them, excitation occurs first, a period when men and women become physically and psychologically ready for coitus. Next there is a plateau phase when vasocongestion and myotonia intensify. Orgasm is the next phase and this is marked by ejaculation in men. The last stage of sexual response is the resolution period when the body returns to a normal, nonsexually excited condition. Part of the resolution stage in males, and to a more subtle degree in some women, is a *refractory* period lasting several minutes to a few hours when it is difficult for them to become sexually excited again.

*Summary*

Sexual intercourse may be described in terms of arousal, coitus, and orgasm. Arousal usually involves the partners kissing, embracing, and touching erogenous areas. Fantasy may assist arousal and subsequent coitus. Following sufficient foreplay, the couple is physically and psychologically ready for coitus.

Coital techniques can be many but most involve the couple facing one another lying, standing, or sitting, or rear entry positions. Personal preference plays a large part in determining which positions are particularly pleasurable, although some coital techniques may have specific advantages. Most couples try to vary their positions and their coital behaviors by cunnilingus or fellatio and other innovations. Couples may also interact sexually without having orgasm as their goal.

The frequency with which couples have sexual intercourse varies widely. Generally, younger and healthier couples average about three times weekly, while older partners estimate once a week. Most people have five or fewer different partners in their lifetime, although a small portion of women and men have many more. Whether there is an innate biological drive for humans to have a variety of sexual partners is not yet clear.

Orgasm climaxes coitus and is a pleasurable sensation lasting several seconds. Nearly all men experience orgasm and ejaculation, but the climax for many women is often more varied. Among the women who report they do not usually reach coital orgasm, nearly all climax with masturbation or similar techniques. It has been suggested that female orgasm may involve sensitive areas within the vagina, as well as the clitoris. Both women and men may have several orgasms, although most men and many women usually need to rest after climax before excitation can take place again.

The sexual response cycle has been described in many different ways with the most well-known being that of Masters and Johnson. They scientifically studied masturbation and intercourse and report that whether the sexual behavior occurs alone or with a partner, four stages are involved: excitation, plateau, orgasm, and resolution. During each stage there are marked internal and external physiological changes involving the whole body and not just the sexual-reproductive organs. During the excitement stage, the penis erects, and the vagina moistens and the clitoris enlarges. During the plateau phase, neuromuscular and vasocongestive body changes continue and the entire organism has an intense concentrated appearance. With orgasm, males ejaculate and both sexes experience spasms of pleasurable sensation. During the final stage, resolution, the genitals and the body's physical and psychological state return to a nonaroused, resting condition.

---

*For Thought and Discussion*

1 What is the purpose of arousal in human beings and in other mammals? How is arousal in humans and mammals different, and how is it similar?
2 Describe the basic positions for intercourse and discuss some of their common variations. What are the supposed advantages for different coital positions?
3 What is the average frequency of coitus for younger and for older couples? What factors other than desire may determine frequency? What recommendations might you make to help a couple prevent boredom? What is the Coolidge effect?
4 Describe the sexual response cycle, and its specific effects on men and women, as suggested by Masters and Johnson.
5 How may orgasm differ for women and men? Why do some women not have orgasm with coitus but then climax through masturbation?
6 What are the differences among vaginal, G-spot, and clitoral orgasms? Do you believe these distinctions are valid?
7 What is afterplay, and what is its function in sexual intercourse?

---

*References*

Apfelbaum, B. Why we should not accept sexual fantasies. In Apfelbaum, B. (editor): *Expanding the boundaries of sex therapy,* rev. ed., Berkeley, California: Berkeley Sex Therapy Group, 1980.
Blumstein, P., and Schwartz, P. *American couples: money, work, and sex.* New York: Morrow, 1983.
Cook, K., Kretchmer, A., Nellis, B., Lever, J., and Hertz, R. The *Playboy* readers' sex survey, Part 3. *Playboy,* May 1983, 126.
de Bruijn, G. From masturbation to orgasm with a partner: how some women bridge the gap—and why others don't. *Journal of Sex and Marital Therapy,* 1982, 8, 151-167.
Dewsbury, D.A. Effects of novelty on copulatory behavior: the Coolidge effect and related phenomena. *Psychological Bulletin,* 1981, 89, 464-482.
Dworkin, A. *Intercourse.* New York: The Free Press, 1987.
Ellis, H.H. *Studies in the psychology of sex.* London: F.A. Davis Co., 1906.
Fisher, H.E. *The sex contract.* New York: William Morrow, 1982.
Ford, C.S., and Beach, F.A. *Patterns of sexual behavior.* Westport, Connecticut: Greenwood Press, 1980.
Halpern, J., and Sherman, M. *Afterplay.* New York: Stein & Day, 1979.
Hawton, R. *Sex therapy: a practical guide.* New York: Oxford University Press, 1985.
Heath, D. An investigation into the origins of a copious vaginal discharge during intercourse: "enough to wet the bed"—that "is not urine." *The Journal of Sex Research,* 1984, 20 (2), 194-215.
Hite, S. *Women and love: a cultural revolution in progress.* New York: Knopf, 1987.
Hock, Z. The G spot. *Journal of Sex and Marital Therapy,* 1983, 9, 166-167.

Hunt, M. *Sexual behavior in the 1970s.* Chicago: Playboy Press, 1974.

Kaplan, H. *Sexual aversion, sexual phobias, and panic disorders.* New York: Brunner-Mazel, Inc., 1987.

Kinsey, A.C., Pomeroy, W.B., and Martin, C.E. *Sexual behavior in the human male.* Philadelphia: Saunders, 1948.

Kinsey, A.C., Pomeroy, W.B., and Martin, C.E. *Sexual behavior in the human female.* Philadelphia: Saunders, 1953.

Klinger, E. The power of dreams. *Psychology Today,* October 1987, 37-44.

Krupp, M.A., and Chatton, M.J. *Current medical diagnosis and treatment.* Los Altos, California: Lange Medical Publishers, 1989.

Ladas, A.K., Whipple, B., and Perry, J.D. *The G spot and other recent discoveries about human sexuality.* New York: Holt, Rinehart, and Winston, 1982.

Masters, W.H., Johnson, V.E., and Kolodny, R.C. *Masters and Johnson on sex and human loving.* Boston: Little, Brown & Co., 1986.

Oshodin, O.G. The sexual life-styles of polygynous African men. *Journal of Sex Education and Therapy,* 1984, *10* (2), 37-40.

Petersen, J.R., Kretchmer, A., Nellis, B., Lever, J., and Hertz, R. The *Playboy* readers' sex survey (Parts 1 and 2). *Playboy,* January 1983, 108; March 1983, 90.

Rubenstein, C., and Tavris, C. Special survey results: 26,000 women reveal the secrets of intimacy. *Redbook,* September 1987, *169,* 147.

Rubin, L.B. *Worlds of pain: life in the working class family.* New York: Basic Books, 1976.

Scarf, M. *Intimate partners: patterns in love and marriage.* New York: Random House, 1987.

Schwartz, M.F., and Masters, W.H. The Masters and Johnson treatment program for dissatisfied homosexual men. *American Journal of Psychiatry,* 1984, *141,* 173-181.

Tannahill, R. *Sex in history.* New York: Stein & Day, 1981.

Waterman, C.K., and Chiauzzi, E.J. The role of orgasm in male and female sexual enjoyment. *The Journal of Sex Research,* May 1982, *18*(2), 146-159.

Wolfe, L. *The Cosmo report.* New York: Arbor House, 1981.

Zimmer, D., Borchardt, E., and Fischle, C. Sexual fantasies of sexually distressed and nondistressed men and women: an empirical comparison. *Journal of Sex and Marital Therapy,* 1983, *9,* 38-50.

---

## Suggested Readings

Comfort, A. *The joy of sex: a gourmet guide to lovemaking.* New York: Simon & Schuster, 1985.

> A delightful book to read, although each sexual technique may not be acceptable to everyone. Many consider this book a warm and erotically illustrated sex guide for adults.

Coward, R. *Female desires: how they are sought, bought, and packaged.* New York: Grove Press, 1985.

> Women's desires and sexuality are considered from a psychoanalytic point of view.

Olds, S.W. *The eternal garden: seasons of our sexuality.* New York: Times Books, 1985.

> A sensitive book containing case studies that shed light on sexuality at different ages and stages of life.

*Chapter 6*

# Becoming a Woman or a Man
*Gender determinants*

***When you finish this chapter, you should be able to:***

Explain how sex and gender are determined.

Distinguish among genotype, phenotype, autosomes, and sex-linked characteristics.

Describe some of the ways society teaches children gender identity and gender roles.

Explain the more traditional view of gender and show how this is changing.

Identify and discuss some of the advantages and disadvantages of sex reassignment surgery.

How does a person become a woman or a man? In Chapters 3 and 4 we saw that normally in the third month after fertilization the sex of the fetus becomes clear. The embryo that is genetically XY (boy) will have produced androgens, while one that is chromosomally XX (girl) will have produced estrogens, resulting in the physical development of a man or woman. In this chapter we will talk less about biological sex and more about gender. *Gender* describes the psychosocial attitudes and perceptions that define a person as female or male. *Sex* is the result of biology—chromosomes and hormones. Gender is largely the result of cultural and personal values, traditions, and expectations. In this chapter we look at how our society identifies and encourages what it considers proper feminine or masculine characteristics and behaviors.

## PRIMARY, SECONDARY, TERTIARY

Several years ago, a young jockey fell off a horse and was taken unconscious to an emergency room. There, the first discovery the attendants made as they loosened the clothing was that the "man" had small but developed female breasts. After taking care of the medical emergency, the doctor palpated the jockey's lower abdomen and felt the outlines of a uterus and also saw the vaginal opening. If it had been necessary, a tissue sample from the jockey would have shown XX chromosomes, proving conclusively that the young "man" was indeed a woman. The explanation was simple. The woman had dressed herself and posed as a man so that she could enter a professional sport that until recently accepted only males.

### Primary sex characteristics

Whether we are men or women is decided at three levels—primary, secondary, and tertiary. *Primary sex characteristics* are fundamentally biological. This is why once the jockey was physically examined it was clear that "he" was female. A man has a penis, prostate, and a high level of androgens. Women have vaginas, uteruses, and higher levels of estrogens. Primary characteristics define men and women in terms of their sexual reproductive roles. Women, like all mammalian females, are biochemically and structurally designed to be impregnated, carry the growing fetus, and finally give birth to it. Males are built so that they can impregnate.

Primary sexual characteristics are usually readily identifiable. We can tell when we look at a horse, monkey, or newborn infant whether it is male or female. On the primary level, sex is a dichotomy; we are either boy or girl, and there are usually no in-betweens. On rare occasion, a baby is born whose structural and physiological sex is confused. **Hermaphrodism,** having the physical characteristics of both sexes, is uncommon, but when it does occur, it only underlines that a person has to be either one sex or the other. As we will see shortly, hermaphrodites are usually medically assisted to live as members of the gender to which they most seem to belong.

### Secondary sex characteristics

The injured jockey looked externally like a man, but as soon as her body was seen, it was obvious she was a woman. The jockey's disguise depended on her ability to imitate male *secondary sexual characteristics*. Secondary sexual traits are features, largely hormonal, that distinguish femaleness and maleness, but are not essential to reproduction. Men generally have facial hair, lower-pitched voices, wider shoulders, and a larger structural frame than women. Women usually have softer and more rounded body contours, wider hips, and fuller breasts. Awareness of these secondary man/woman differences enabled the jockey to lower her voice through careful practice and cut her hair in the masculine fashion. She was small and slim like many women, but then nearly all men jockeys are also. With a bit of clothing rearrangement she was able to hide her breasts. Based on secondary sexual characteristics, only someone who saw that she awoke each morning without a stubbly growth of beard on her face might have cause to suspect she was a woman.

Notice that secondary sexual characteristics are not either/or, but are on a **continuum.** Both men and women have hair, but men usually have more all

A person's sex is the result of biology. Gender is a result of attitudes and behaviors that are learned.

*hermaphrodism*
A rare condition in which a person partly has the genital organs of both sexes.

*continuum*
An uninterrupted series or scale used to signify the degree to which a trait is present.

When women and men dress alike and have similar hair styles, their sex may not be obvious.

over their body. Yet some men have relatively little hair and a few women have enough facial hair to grow a nice moustache. Both sexes have breasts, but women usually have more tissue, making their breasts more prominent. Yet anyone who has seen an obese man in a bathing suit knows men can have large and female-appearing bosoms.

Voice characteristics are also on a continuum. Most men are somewhat heavier and taller than women; they also have larger larynxes and therefore deeper voices. But size alone does not determine all voice qualities, so that a few men speak in the soprano or alto range. Occasionally, too, a woman naturally speaks or has learned to speak in a voice like that of a tenor or baritone. In general, the secondary sexual qualities that differentiate women and men overlap.

### Tertiary sex characteristics

Primary and secondary sexual qualities are *maturational*. They are due to physical growth, developing gradually from the moment of conception. Sex differences that are described as *tertiary* are in large part *acquired*, that is, they are learned. In much of the world, men are taught and expected to be aggressive, and to be the household member who works outside the home to support the family.

Women, from the traditional perspectives, are often encouraged to be **nurturant** and to be the adult who takes care of the home and children. Men curse, women cry; boys play cops and robbers and girls play house; men wear pants and women dresses. In every instance, there is no clear physical reason why the activity could not be reversed. The young jockey was very effective playing the role of a male on a tertiary level. She wore pants, swore in the

*nurturant*
Tending to take care of, bring up, or support and encourage.

clubhouse, and showed she could take even the roughest race with appropriate toughness.

### Consistency

Primary, secondary, and tertiary sex characteristics need not be consistent. A few men who are clearly reproductively male and have all the usual secondary male sexual characteristics may play the role of woman on a tertiary level. A heterosexual man who remains at home cooking, cleaning, and caring for children may be seen both as a man on primary and secondary levels and as "feminine" based on tertiary qualities. A heterosexual woman who has the distinctive sexual qualities of a female may defy conventional social stereotypes and be a rugged construction worker. As our society becomes more open, the traits that define male and female at the tertiary and sometimes even secondary levels seem to be becoming more flexible. Fewer and fewer emotional, behavioral, and intellectual qualities, careers, and aptitudes are now seen as invariably female or male.

## THE CHROMOSOMAL CONTRIBUTION

The physical differences between men and women, basically the primary and secondary sexual characteristics, stem from our chromosomal makeup. As we saw in Chapter 4, an X chromosome from each parent normally results in a girl and a maternal X coupled with a paternal Y produces a boy.

The determination of biological sex only begins with the pairing of an X or Y chromosome and their genetic complement. For at least the first 2 months of intrauterine life the infant can not readily, by looking, be called a boy or girl. (Chapter 3, Figure 3-1). By 3 months, if the egg was originally fertilized by an X chromosome the undeveloped gonads, the sex glands, ordinarily evolve into rudimentary ovaries. In the presence of a Y chromosome and hormones secreted by the embryo, the gonads become testes.

Once testicular and ovarian development has begun, both organs begin to play critical roles in sexual differentiation. The ovaries produce estrogenic hormones and the testes produce androgenic hormones that stimulate the growth of appropriate female or male structures. The process is not simple however. For example, it appears that high levels of feminizing hormones are not entirely necessary in order for a fetus to develop as a female. This is not comparable for males. If particular androgens are not sufficiently produced, a genetically XY fetus could develop some female sex organs. This observation has led to the idea that regardless of an X or Y pairing, the embryo begins as female and will develop as such unless critical masculinizing hormones are added.

The increasing understanding of the many complex steps involved in the determination of sex has led several investigators to point out there is considerable latitude and room for contradiction in what constitutes biological maleness and femaleness. Pillard and Weinrich (1987) suggest that behaviors or traits in women and men that seem more appropriate to the other sex may in large part be due to variations in fetal hormones and genetics.

The X and Y chromosomes, along with the 44 others, contain many thousands of **genes**. The chemical **deoxyribonucleic acid** (DNA), found in each gene, controls the growth and development of every cell tissue, organ, and structure.

*gene*
The basic unit of heredity transmitted on the chromosome.

*deoxyribonucleic acid*
Abbreviated DNA, the chemical found within the genes that carries the genetic instructions to each cell.

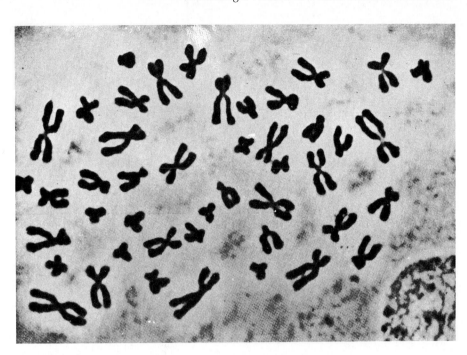

*Fig. 6-1*
Chromosomes of normal human cell (×2,000).

The genes passed on to the child come equally from each parent. Typically this causes children to have, for example, their "father's big hands," or their "mother's eyes." But children are not just a stewlike combination of their parents. A child may fail to resemble either the mother or father. The causes of this are many, but a good deal has to do with the fact that some genes are dominant and some recessive. A *dominant gene* is one whose instructions almost always prevail. A *recessive gene* manifests itself, that is, controls the development and appearance of some structure, only when both a maternal and paternal recessive are paired. For example, for simplicity's sake, say that the gene for brown eye color is dominant while that for blue is recessive. If one parent contributes brown eye color genes to the offspring, and the other provides blue eye color genes, the child will have brown eyes. If both the mother and father contribute blue eye genes even though they both have brown eyes, the baby will have blue eyes.

### Genotype and phenotype

A second reason why parents and children are not precise copies of one another is the difference between genotype and phenotype. A person's *genotype* is the genetic makeup, the DNA potential. *Phenotype* is the outward expression, the behavioral manifestation of the gene. A woman who comes from a religious background that forbids dancing may have inherited her mother's slim and supple body, her father's long limbs, and excellent perceptual and motor skills. She may have all the physical attributes necessary to make her a first-rate ballet dancer, but her potential, her genotypical traits, may never become phenotypical because her culture forbids dancing.

The distinction between genotype and phenotype is often made dramatically clear when comparing the educational achievements of children born in

It is difficult to know all the potential talents we possess, our genotype, unless we have a chance to learn or try out most skills.

## Boy, Girl, or Both

In ancient Greek mythology, the handsome, muscular messenger of the gods, Hermes, courted the beautiful goddess of love, Aphrodite, and they produced a true male-female person with the full sexual characteristics of both a woman and a man, called a *hermaphrodite*. Very few people actually have all the hormonal and physical structures of both sexes. "True" hermaphrodism is rare; only a handful of such people have been identified in recent times. But every year, 1000 or more children are born who have some mix of primary or secondary sexual characteristics. (These people are more accurately called pseudohermaphrodites.)

In infants who are chromosomally male (XY), there may be insufficient androgen production during the critical months before birth. As a result a baby may be born with a small and poorly developed penis and testes. Or a boy may produce sufficient male hormone but his tissues and cells could be incapable of utilizing it. This means that the small amounts of estrogen produced by the male testes and adrenal glands dominate, resulting in a male baby who has a small shallow vagina. Because estrogen production, however tiny, continues and androgen is still not effective, as the child grows past puberty he may develop breasts and some of the rounder and softer contours of women. This is the most common form of male hermaphrodism and is called *testicular feminization syndrome*.

In genetic women (XX), the most frequent form of hermaphrodism is the result of the erroneous production of masculine hormone by the adrenal glands (hence called *androgenital syndrome*). Such infants are likely to have normal female internal reproductive organs but only a small or partial vagina. The clitoris may be quite enlarged, and sometimes a penis is present.

Hermaphrodism in female infants may also be induced by hormones administered to the mother for medical reasons. One common condition is called *progesterone-induced hermaphrodism*. In these fetuses both male and female genitals may be present but either or both may be reduced in size or appear very rudimentary.

The study of hermaphrodism provides a dramatic illustration of the effects of biology and environment on sex identification. Several studies have focused on hermaphroditic children born with about the same mix of physical sexual characteristics. Often the decision as to whether to call one of these children a boy or girl is momentary, a decision made by the doctor at the time of birth. In several studies of such relatively quick gender assignments, it has been found that most children and their parents stick with the assigned gender. Children labeled male are brought up as and feel themselves to be boys. The same is true for girls. This provides evidence for those who argue that important as biology may be, upbringing, learning, and environment play significant

the United States with those of their immigrant parents. The child is a physician, a professor, or successful business person. The child's parents, however, were laborers or janitors. A substantial part of the successful offspring's ability must have come from the parents, but the parents lacked money and educational opportunity so that their genotypical aptitudes could not be outwardly or phenotypically expressed.

In short, the genetic instructions received by every child at birth are vast and complex. Few human characteristics are simply genetically determined. In most instances, the best we can do in predicting a child's hereditary makeup is to make a probability statement. For example, when a child comes from two

roles in bringing about gender identity

The photograph on the right shows a young woman who at birth had been called a female although she had only a small and partial vagina. Examination also showed undescended testes in her lower abdomen. Nevertheless, having been called a girl by the doctor the youngster was treated as such by everyone and considered herself a girl. A medical examination after puberty to diagnose why she was not menstruating showed she had no ovaries or uterus. Her vagina was very short and her breasts were small. Most critical of all, her chromosomal typing showed she was clearly male, XY.

In this instance, as in most cases of hermaphrodism discovered late in childhood, the person had already taken on a gender identity. Even though her gender affiliation conflicted with her chromosomal sex typing, it was considered psychologically most appropriate to medically assist the sex with which she had identified. The person pictured believed she was a woman and was helped to remain so. Surgery removed the internal testes. The vagina was lengthened so it was sufficient for intercourse, and hormonal supplements were prescribed. Like almost all hermaphrodites, this woman would never be able to reproduce, but she continued to live a well-adjusted life as a female.

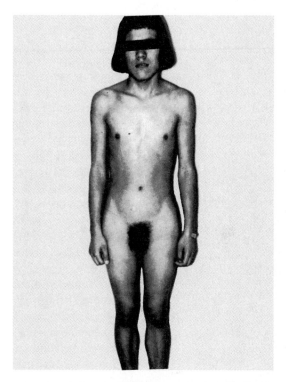

This female hermaphrodite has an enlarged clitoris and a fused labia, which resembles a male scrotum. Her physical and muscular build resemble that of a male.

tall parents we can say that the odds are eight in ten that he or she will also be tall. But there are so many different genes and interactions involved in height that occasionally tall parents also have short children. Most children will receive many of their parents' hereditary characteristics, but given the numerous possibilities involved in which sperm will fertilize which egg, children may also seem to share very few of their parents' physical attributes.

## Sex-linked characteristics

Are there sex-linked hereditary attributes, qualities that are an inevitable consequence of being a woman or a man? For example, are men invariably better

*Table 6-1*

**Qualities of Sex and Gender**

| Sexual Characteristics | Definition | Male | Female |
|---|---|---|---|
| Primary | Anatomical and physiological features permitting the person to play a male or female reproductive role | XY chromosomes, penis, testes, androgens, seminal vesicles | XX chromosomes, vagina, ovaries, estrogens, fallopian tubes |
| Secondary | Physical qualities usually distinguishing female from male but not critical to reproduction | Large body size, small hips, ample body and facial hair, angular body, low voice | Small body size, large hips, little body and facial hair, soft contours, high voice, fuller breasts |
| Tertiary | Gender differences that appear to be acquired as a result of social learning and related processes and thus can vary from one culture to the next | *Wearing pants, breadwinner, engineer, aggressive, football, tough | *Wearing dresses, homemaker, nurse, submissive, modern dance, tender |

*These are traditional qualities assigned women and men. They are changing as equality between the sexes increases.

*sex chromosomes*
Chromosomes that influence the determination of biological sex.

*autosome*
A chromosome that does not determine sex but carries other genetic instructions.

Until recent times, childbirth was a considerable hazard, one that a woman might not survive. Today childbirth is safer and more women than men live to old age.

in mathematics, taller, or more aggressive? To understand the biological contribution to gender we must first also understand the difference between **sex chromosomes** and **autosomes.**

Human beings have, as we have pointed out, 22 pairs of autosomes, chromosomes that carry all sorts of genetic instructions *except* sex. Both women and men also have a twenty-third pair, sex chromosomes that ordinarily help program the child to be female or male. The DNA of the sex chromosome transmits the instructions that eventuate in the development of genitalia, a reproductive apparatus, and a body type that is consistent with that of a man or woman. This same single sex chromosome does not appear to possess genes concerning attributes like intellectual potential, hair curliness, or finger dexterity; hence these traits are not sex-linked. These features appear to be autosomal. They are independent of whether a person is a woman or a man (Bleier, 1984).

There are also some clearly sex-linked traits. Disorders such as *hemophilia* (excessive bleeding) and some varieties of color blindness are found almost exclusively in men.

Longevity has also been postulated to be sex-linked. Today the life expectancy for men is 70 years and for women 77. According to the National Center for Health Statistics in Washington, D.C., during the first 4 years of life about 10 males per 1000 die compared with 8 females per 1000. At age 20 there are about 1.5 male deaths per 1000 and only .5, a third as many, for females. At 50, male deaths are 8 per 1000 and female only half as much. Today, at every age level, women seem more likely to survive than males (Dranov, 1981).

Let's return to the question we started with: Are there sex-linked hereditary attributes? The answer is *yes*, but perhaps not as many as were once assumed. We would have to say that one type of hemophilia is sex-linked, as are all primary and secondary sexual characteristics. An argument can also be made for

### What Is My Gender Biography?

By filling in the blank spaces below, you can construct a biography of your gender awareness and identity. An analysis is provided in the Appendix on p. 580.

I first became conscious that I was a (boy/girl) _____ at about the age of _____ . It is hard to remember, but I think (describe a person or event that helped your awareness) ___ _____ _____ made me conscious I was a boy/girl. I was (never, often, sometimes) _____ teased that I was actually a member of the other sex. Teasing like this always made me feel _____ .

I think there was a person of my own sex after whom I modeled myself. I believe this person was _____ . I guess I may have copied some of this person's (walk, talk, dress, etc.) _____ .

When I was growing up it was (important, unimportant) _____ that I dress and act like members of my own sex. I do remember dressing and acting like a person of the other sex. This made me feel _____ .

I have thought about being the other sex. I think about this (rarely, often) _____ , and consider the thoughts (pleasant, disturbing, neutral) _____ . Overall I am (satisfied, neutral, dissatisfied) _____ with my own sex.

Children look like their parents because they have inherited their genes.

## In Our Genes?

Dee Shepherd-Look (1982) points out that our society shares widely held and "pervasive concepts that prescribe how each sex ought to perform." These *sex role stereotypes* insist that men are invariably sexually assertive, aggressive, and inclined to want a variety of partners. Women, it is held, are much more sexually passive and desirous of enduring relationships. These traits do exist in many men and women, but what is their source?

*Sociobiologists* argue that most human behavior is rooted in our biology, specifically in our genes. They contend that all species evolve strategies to assure reproduction—their continuity. Those that are not reproductively successful, of course, disappear. Human sexual behavior, it is maintained, has also evolved to meet this important reproductive goal.

Sociobiologists like Symons (1981) say that early emerging men and women had to have different reproductive strategies. A man maximized his reproductive chances if he had coitus with as many women as possible. This means that the evolutionary selective process weeded out men who were sexually hesitant, not very responsive, or unappealing. In contrast, men who were most sexually aggressive and promiscuous had the most offspring. They passed on their aggressive sexuality genes to numerous male children.

Women, sociobiologists hypothesize, had to adopt a different reproductive strategy. They have an important 9-month or much longer possible investment in every sexual act. Thus it is in the woman's interest to select her mate very carefully. It is also in her and the potential baby's interest that the mother try to commit the father, involving him in helping care for the newborn.

The ultimate outcome of these differing needs and reproductive strategies, it is supposed, is that the men who survived through hundreds of thousands of years of evolution are easily sexually aroused, aggressive, and inclined to wander. Women, on the other hand, are born to be sexually very selective. They are "nesters," providing a stable environment for their infants, and are intent on bringing the man into an enduring relationship.

A view opposing the sociobiological position sees *learning* as central to the determination of sexual behaviors. Shepherd-Look (1982) believes that society continuously teaches boys and girls how they are supposed to conduct themselves. Each sex learns not only what toys to play with but how to act and feel sexually. In their book, *Not in Our Genes,* Lewontin, Rose, and Kamin (1984) contend that human behavior is actually quite flexible. Social learning and cognition can emphasize, cultivate, or minimize any number of supposed female or male traits.

Men may appear more sexually aggressive

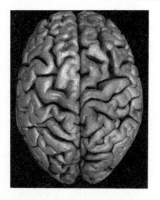

The brain.

longevity probably being in part sex-linked. But a great many other attributes, such as intellectual abilities and most personality, psychological, and behavioral traits, are likely autosomal. We will look at sex-linked and autosomal characteristics more fully in Chapter 7 when we examine the similarities and differences between men and women.

## THE BRAIN

The brain is the supreme organ of our body. Viewed from the outside, it seems to be only a firm gelatinous mass, but it is packed with tens of billions of nerve cells that directly or indirectly control every bodily function. The brains of the two sexes differ slightly. Those of women are a bit smaller and usually weigh

than women and less inclined to marry. The proof that these may be learned characteristics becomes evident when one finds other nations in which these behaviors seem to be turned around. There are South American Indian cultures where men play a primary parenting role. There are also societies in which men are relatively sexually passive. Among the very tall, lean, and graceful Wodaabe nomads of Niger, it is the men—and not the women—who lavishly use cosmetics, feathers, cloth, and beads to decorate themselves. Our culture, and not our genes, teaches and shapes most of the behaviors that we traditionally think of as being distinctively masculine or feminine.

Beryl Benderley (1987) stakes out her position by research, as well as on political grounds. In her book, *The Myth of Two Minds,* she reports that she intended to do nothing more than examine the evidence for three apparently scientific truths. First, that men and women think and act differently; second, that these differences have a definite physiological base, and third, that the traditional roles women and men assume in society are also biologically based. Benderley carefully evaluated numerous studies and arguments and was forced, she states, to conclude that the supposed scientific findings were little more than personal opinion or bias. There are physical differences, but their effects on intellectual and personality attributes are minimal. The alleged biological differences between men and women "have no bearing at all on the great issues that face our society: how to apportion power, work, and responsibility."

## Interaction

In broad terms the discussion of gender determinants divides itself roughly into those who take an environmental position and those suggesting that biology or nature is the root cause of male and female behavior. This is an ancient debate, a resolution of which may lie in the fact that both sides seem to be edging toward an acceptance of interaction. Often it appears as if biology and learning are working together to produce behaviors that we label feminine or masculine. Just such an interaction can be seen in the recreation often chosen by men and women. Even during the preschool years, boys have tighter grips and throw harder. Girls show more body flexibility and fine muscle control. Parents may enlarge these small differences by teaching boys to throw and catch and girls to dance ballet. But enough overlap in abilities is actually present to reverse the teaching. Boys can dance and girls can catch. Whether small inherent differences in abilities will be assigned just to one sex, or cultivated in both, is a social and not a biological decision (Doyle, 1985).

---

just a little under 3 pounds. The male brain is ordinarily slightly larger and weighs a bit over 3 pounds. If we look at a man's or woman's brain we see that it appears the same for both sexes. On the outside the brain is richly convoluted. Right down the middle of the brain, from the front to the back, is a groove seemingly separating the organ into two halves, the right and left hemispheres.

For centuries there was speculation as to whether the two connected hemispheres had different functions. It was realized over 300 years ago that the left hemisphere controls most right side body activities and the right hemisphere controls the left side of the body. Around the end of the nineteenth century, a neurologist in England had a patient whose right hemisphere was severely

A little bit of difference in brain size between women and men doesn't seem to mean much. In Chapter 7 we will see that intelligence in both sexes is similar.

damaged. This patient's major loss was in visual skills. At about the same time, in Europe, other physicians treating people with left hemisphere damage announced that this injury impaired language abilities. The deduction was made that the brain consists of two separate parts, each controlling specialized human abilities.

*hypothesis*
A scientific guess based on limited information.

A few decades ago, the observation that the two hemispheres appeared to differ somewhat in their function led to research that suggested the "right brain" vs. "left brain" **hypothesis.** The function of the left brain was said to include realism as well as language. The right had creativity and visual aptitudes. While both hemispheres were utilized by all people, if you were a very verbal person, then supposedly the left brain dominated. If you were more right hemisphere influenced, then your talents lay in inventiveness and perception. It was not a far step from this contention to suggest next that women were allegedly innately more talkative and concerned mainly with day-to-day affairs because they were "left brain dominant." Men were held to be less practical but more creative because they were ostensibly born right brain individuals.

Numerous researchers proposed further inherent differences between male and female brains. (1) The brains of girls experience rapid periods of growth at different ages compared to boys. This was held to help explain some of the maturational unevenness between the sexes during childhood and puberty (Chapter 8). (2) The female brain hemispheres were said to be more integrated and more flexible. When either hemisphere is damaged in a woman, the other hemisphere is likely to compensate. (3) Men seem more inclined, it was contended, to rely more totally on the right hemisphere. As a result they are also less flexible in shifting use when either half of the brain is damaged (Tan-Willman, 1981).

Some books and programs allege that they can teach people specific left or right brain skills, but their effectiveness is controversial.

Jerre Levy (1985) is an investigator who has spent over a decade studying how the two hemispheres function and influence behavior. In her review of the evidence she finds reason to debate the hypothesis that the two brain hemispheres always function separately among different people and between the two sexes. She points out that often when the two hemispherical portions are surgically disconnected each functions quite well with relatively little loss in most abilities. Further, when one hemisphere is extensively damaged the remaining undamaged half, in both sexes, frequently assumes many of the functions once thought limited to the other hemisphere. Her review of the evidence leads Levy to conclude that people are not irrevocably "left brained" or "right brained." Instead it could be that development of either hemisphere can be neglected or stimulated and improved. Levy's work suggests that many of the supposed differences in abilities and behaviors between women and men may result from brain "learning" rather than from hemispherical structures that are inborn and unchangeable.

---

**In Sum**

Primary sexual characteristics refer to the reproductive organs that distinguish women from men. Secondary characteristics are also physiological but not related to reproduction. These attributes, such as hair distribution and body contours, are often on a continuum, the sexes overlapping. Tertiary traits are usually the result of learning and social expectation. Some human characteristics such as hemophilia and perhaps longevity are genetically sex-linked. Most qualities present in men and women, however, such as intellectual ability and personality, seem to be autosomal, genetically independent of sex. Learning may account for some sex differences in brain function.

## SOCIAL LEARNING

From the moment a child is born it is taught what it means to be boy or girl. To begin with, many parents have two alternative names, Joseph or Josephine, David or Ruth, that they will assign depending on whether the baby is a girl or boy. Next, many traditional parents will buy pink for girls and blue for boys. Before too long the child will be given dolls or trucks, and as he or she gets older will be told to "act like a man," or "be a little lady." Family and friends create an environment that teaches the child whether to become a woman or a man and how to act appropriately. In fact, all of society plays a role in showing children how to be girls or boys. These educational pressures literally begin at birth, continue during childhood, and often intensify during adolescence. It seems nearly everyone, teachers, television, neighbors, books, and even strangers—passersby—play a role in instruction. All of these teaching and learning processes together are called *social learning* and we will describe three particularly influential methods of bringing about **gender identification** and **gender roles:** (sometimes called sex roles), channeling, modeling, and reinforcement. (Simmons, Blyth, 1987).

### Channeling

People tend to like and accept as "natural" whatever is familiar. If we dress a girl in pink, tie ribbons in her hair, and give her dolls, she will become accustomed to these things and want them. Similarly, boys given tools and balls and dressed in blue overalls will come to feel most comfortable with these objects. The process of assigning a child an environment that is consistent with his or her perceived gender is termed *channeling*.

Channeling appears to begin right at birth. Shepherd-Look (1982) reports an investigation in which parents of infants only a day old were asked to rate different babies on several personality traits. When the adults were told the babies were girls, they rated them high on features such as "delicate" and "pretty." When the infant was identified as a boy, characteristics such as "coordinated" and "hardy" were dominant. It was the labeling of the sex of the child that accounted for the difference in perception. Parents seem to start the channeling long before the child can understand their expectations.

Guidance and channeling of a child's interests are continuous. Adults do this not only by the clothing and toys they buy but even by the conversations they have with children. Boys are far more likely to be told why the car is accelerating, and girls why the cake came out dry. Schools often continue the channeling. Until recently, boys were assigned to shop classes, and girls to sewing and cooking.

### Modeling

A *model* is a real or fictional person whom a child may observe and imitate. During the early years, girls usually have a wider selection of live models than boys. Mothers traditionally were the persons who were home most of the time

*gender identity*
A person's inner belief or sense of being a woman or a man.

*gender role (sex role)*
The different behaviors and attitudes our society expects of women and men.

During the middle years of childhood children increasingly imitate the behaviors of the same-sex adult models.

and who were the primary caretakers. Babysitters and elementary school teachers are typically female. The only male model available to young boys was usually an older brother or the father. One result of this is that young males may participate in "female" activities like cooking or playing with dolls during their early years. Only a few years later, by about age 5, when channeling and male models have had their effect, they are likely to reject these interests.

Television and motion picture characters are also models for sex role behavior. In many, if not most, programs and films, male characters are leaders, solve problems, are aggressive or violent. Females are passive, polite, and sometimes emotional or intuitive. Even when women are heroes, leaders, or successful, sometimes they are inspired by or take orders from a man.

Most children watch 4 to 6 hours of television a day. As a result, much of what they consider appropriate male or female behavior is modeled after what they have seen on television.

Many television commercials seem to have particularly fixed images of male and female behavior. Women discuss which laundry product to use and worry about keeping their floors clean and shiny and their bodies deodorized. Men choose beer, jeans, or tools that enhance their competence, masculinity, and authority. Given the models continuously depicted on television as appropriate to men and women, it is not surprising that children often have firm views of what they strongly believe to be the only "proper" male and female behavior. To be a "man" they think you need to be tough, combative, and domineering. Women are viewed as domestic, motherly, and dependent. Television and films have made progress in portraying men and women in more realistic and up-to-date ways, but older portrayals of "proper" gender behavior still occur daily. A common result is that quite early many adolescent girls still reach the erroneous conclusion that they have to choose between being *either* tough and career-oriented "like a man," *or* caring and "stay at home" as in the traditional role of wife and mother (Archer, 1985; Lengermann and Wallace, 1985; Williams, LaRose, and Frost, 1981).

## Reinforcement

An event following a behavior that strengthens that behavior is called a *reinforcer*. In human situations a reward, which can be as subtle as gentle praise or as explicit as money, usually acts as a reinforcer. People often are not *aware* they are being reinforced and learning a particular behavior (Maier, 1988). In the development of gender, or sex roles, children are often reinforced for behaviors that are consistent with adult gender expectations. For example, a young girl imitating her mother may put on her dress and high-heeled shoes. The mother seeing this may reinforce the activity by smiling and saying, "Hi, little lady. I see you're dressed for a day in the city." Boys doing the same thing, wearing the mother's clothing, may be ignored, that is, not reinforced. They may even be "punished," by the mother saying, "Hey, silly, boys don't wear high heels."

A large variety of behaviors could be listed for which one sex but not the other is reinforced. The boy who comes home dirty or bruised after a rough football game or a fight may well receive admiration or congratulations from his father or an older brother. A girl similarly disheveled is likely to be scolded. In contrast, a girl very neatly, fashionably dressed will probably be reinforced by admiring comments. A boy could well be punished by being sarcastically called "cute," or when older, a dandy.

One of the central behaviors for which boys and girls are differently reinforced is talking and listening. Beginning in early childhood, middle-class parents are more likely to look at their little girls face to face and talk to them. Conversations with boys are more often quick directives and "yes" or "no" answers. As children get older, talk is increasingly differentially reinforced by listening and attending more to the comments and feelings of girls and less to those of boys. Eventually, girls learn both to talk more fully about their own emotions, and listen—with "hmms" and nods of the head—to encourage other girls to be open with them.

One result of this different reinforcement of communication techniques in childhood is that sometimes adult men and women are dissatisfied with their conversations. A woman wants to talk about her job and her difficult boss with her male friend. The man responds that if the boss makes the work so unpleasant she should file a grievance. As far as the man is concerned that ends the conversation. The woman, on the other hand, is not looking for advice. She understands her options. She has learned to communicate as a means of exploring and relieving feeling. The man sees communication as a means of addressing problems and resolving them (Chapter 10) (Pearson, 1985).

## Cognition

Human responses are based on more than behaviors learned through channeling, reinforcement, and imitation. A good deal of what we do results from our attempt to understand our own needs and environmental demands. Much of the time we think about who we are, what is expected and demanded of us, and what we should do. We try to make sense out of what is happening around us and act in ways that are appropriate. Our ability to perceive, to understand, in short to think, is called **cognition**.

The human ability to think, to use cognitive abilities, develops slowly from birth on. At first thinking is relatively primitive, rigid, and awkward. In terms

*cognition*
Thinking, understanding, reasoning, planning, deciding, and all the processes involved in thought.

of sex, most children who are 2 to 3 years old answer correctly and consistently the question of whether they are a boy or girl. At this age, they often perceive the world in very strict gender terms. Mommies are girls; daddies are boys. Girls have long hair and boys short. Looking through a picture book, some preschoolers insistently exercise their newly acquired cognitive ability to categorize all living things as male or female. Whether they see people, bears, or fish, they look for cues such as length of hair, dress, or body size that will tell them the person or animal is a "boy" or "girl."

When children sex type others, they are *labeling*. Society uses labels as a convenient shorthand. A child wearing pants and playing rough and tumble games is labeled a boy. Another child who cries easily and plays "house" is labeled a girl. Learning labels not only enables children to assign them, but it tells the child a good deal about himself or herself. If I am called a boy, then I must play rough games and not cry. A label becomes critical in establishing identity, who I am. For this reason a child constantly called cruel, sissy, or dumb is likely to assume the identity suggested by the label.

The cognitive limitations of young children during their first few years frequently result in their reaching conclusions about gender based only on their own narrow family experiences. Mommies like fried eggs and daddies like them scrambled. Mommies all brush their hair and drink wine. However inaccurate the beliefs that youngsters have about women and men, they often strongly adhere to them and are disturbed when someone acts in a way that they feel is not appropriate for their sex. One young girl, seeing a photograph of a Scotch bagpiper in kilts, was convinced that he had to be a "lady" because "she's wearing a skirt." When told that this was a man who lived in another country, the child said, "That's dumb," and tried to tear the picture.

As children get older, their cognitive skills mature. They begin to understand that sex typing need not be based on superficialities. The Scotch bagpiper is a man because he has male genitalia and he remains a man even when he wears a skirt. The development of thinking abilities permits children to be secure in the knowledge that they are male or female and will stay that way even if they do something supposedly appropriate to the other sex.

A child brought up in a traditional family usually has firm ideas of appro-

*Table 6-2*

**Cognitive Development of Sex and Gender**

| Example | Cognitive Concept | Approximate Age (Years) |
|---|---|---|
| "I'm a girl." | Personal gender identity | 2 |
| "Johnny is a boy." | Gender classification of children | 3 |
| "Mommy is a girl." | Gender classification of adults | 3 |
| "Pink is prettier than blue." | Preference for objects associated with own sex | 4 |
| "Boys have short hair." | Rigid gender expectations | 4 |
| "I'll cook 'cause I'm a girl." | Rigid gender-role behaviors | 5 |
| "I want to be like Mommy." | Identification with same-sex parent | 5 |
| "Girls can be pilots, too." | Relaxation of gender stereotypes | 13 |

Data from Doyle, 1985; Maccoby, 1980.

priate male and female behaviors. During adolescence, however, along with the maturation of cognitive skills, many become more flexible in their expectations concerning sex-role characteristics (Table 6-2).

## SCHOOL YEARS

The school years, from nursery school to the beginning of high school, deserve special mention. This decade seems to solidify the sense of gender. During these years, boys and girls heighten their awareness of being a male or female, their gender identity. Along with their identity they continue to learn gender roles, the attitudes and behaviors that our society expects of boys and girls.

One- and two-year-old children of both sexes play together and alongside one another seemingly unaware of any gender distinction. But 4- and 5-year-olds divide themselves into boy and girl groups. True, a girl may play with boys; being a "tomboy" is often accepted. But a boy who is involved in girl's play is very likely to be labeled a "sissy," and parents may worry whether he is developing normally (Maier, 1988).

The games and activities of girls and boys in the early school years typically differ. Girls are likely to play with dolls and dress up. They construct familiar scenarios ("I'm taking care of the baby, and you be the grandma"), jump rope, and play games with rules. Traditional games for similar aged boys involve ball throwing, running, hiding, climbing, and real or play fighting. There is considerable imaginary play, too, often based on adventure. ("We're astronauts and we have to bail out.") Girls and boys sometimes play together, but traditionally this behavior is not approved and such cooperation is short lived (Sadker and Sadker, 1985).

During their early school years girls and boys solidify their sense of gender.

### Classroom

Beginning at age 4 or 5, the schoolroom becomes central to the child's life. During the 10-month school year, children will spend more time in contact with teachers and fellow students than with their own parents and families. Much more than geography, spelling, and arithmetic is taught in the classroom. Through modeling, channeling, and all the other social learning techniques, many instructors and schools still teach traditional gender roles (Lengermann and Wallace, 1985; Pogrebin, 1980).

- In many textbooks and stories, historical leaders and achievers are usually male. Women typically play a subservient role. Contrast General George Washington with Betsy Ross, whose contribution to the American Revolution was that she sewed the flag.
- Boys are more often steered into mathematics, science, and business courses and girls into teaching, English, sociology, and psychology.
- Girls and boys are frequently given different school chores. Boys are asked to carry, build, fix, or paint. Girls are called to help rearrange, decorate, straighten, and clean up.
- Some classroom texts still feature males in more active and dominant roles. Men are scientists, laborers, farmers, or firefighters. Women are portrayed as nurses and secretaries. Often, too, boys in schoolbooks tend to be depicted in vigorous play while girls watch them from a window.

Myra and David Sadker (1985) believe boys are given an advantage in society by what happens in the classroom. They conducted a 3-year study of elementary school classrooms. In one experiment they showed teachers films of class discussions and asked the viewers to record who talked more, girls or boys. The teachers almost all agreed that the girls were talking much more than the boys. In reality, however, the boys outtalked the girls three to one. The researchers concluded, "stereotypes of garrulous and gossipy women are so strong that teachers fail to see this communications gender gap even when it is right before their eyes."

Equally as critical as teachers not seeing how much more boys talk than girls, they reportedly encourage boys to talk, and often discourage girls. This can be seen by how teachers respond to both sexes when they speak out. The Sadkers write that boys are more assertive in the classroom. They were 8 times more likely than girls to call out an answer. According to the investigators, when boys called out an answer the teacher was likely to accept it: "Yes, that's right." When a girl intruded an answer, even if correct, the teacher often reprimanded, "In this class we don't shout out answers, we raise our hands."

Teachers were also reported to be twice as likely to give boys instructions in how to do things for themselves. With girls, teachers more often do the task for them. A possible result, the Sadkers suggest, is that boys are encouraged toward independence and self-reliance and girls toward dependence.

### Tradition and change

Through work and play, in school and at home, many boys are taught to be competitive, assertive, and independent. Girls learn to collect dolls, take piano lessons, clean, and cook. The way many children are socialized often results in women whose goal it is to be wives, and men who intend to be heads of households. A large number of people are comfortable with and happily seek these roles. They want to be a traditional husband or wife.

Girls and boys are often treated differently in the classroom because many elementary school teachers assume they need to be. But even teachers who try to provide equal opportunity may unconsciously respond differently to the two sexes.

Is it possible to be a basically traditional wife or husband and also a parent who encourages one's children to make the most of their abilities regardless of whether they are boys or girls?

Many other people have taken part in the changes occurring in gender roles and expectations during this decade. Schools and textbooks are increasingly trying to balance their presentation of female and male models. Teachers attempt to give equal attention and encouragement to both sexes. A very large and increasing number of women and mothers work outside the home. Many parents avoid overemphasizing customary gender roles. They buy tools for their girls and encourage their sons to play "house."

In her book *Growing Up Free* (1980), Letty Pogrebin suggests one way to encourage children to be more open about sex (gender) is to give young boys and girls ample time to play together. In these situations the children themselves, sometimes guided by adult models, can reinforce skills and good deeds rather than activities supposedly appropriate to only one gender.

Some schools have introduced courses such as "Family Living," where both sexes are taught household and mechanical skills. The Future Homemakers of America, an extracurricular school organization once restricted entirely to girls, now has over 10% of its 400,000 members who are boys. Athletic programs, which a decade ago were exclusively female or male, are much more integrated. The federal government, under Title IX, a statute that mandates equal educational opportunity regardless of sex, requires that sports be open to all. If current trends continue then it is possible that there will eventually be far less fixed definition of the sports, personal traits, interests, and vocations appropriate for men or women.

Encouraging boys and girls to play together may result in their being more open about sex roles.

For some, change is occurring too rapidly. They are reluctant to see women and men working at jobs once reserved just for one sex. They question whether a healthy family will survive when traditional sex roles are relaxed. Others believe change is occurring too slowly. They contend that many parents say they are raising their children in more flexible ways but are still modeling traditional roles. Similarly, having a handful of boys in a cooking class or one or two girls in woodworking shop seems only a token gesture. Ending discrimination based on sex is seen as still more of an ideal than a reality. Lengermann and Wallace (1985) believe that equal treatment must start very early. Women will not achieve equality in the home or in the workplace until they too, in their youngest years, are encouraged toward the skills and the independence now often reserved for boys.

---

*In Sum*

From the moment of birth children are taught how to be male or female. Parents and friends continuously guide each child's interests, often channeling girls to games like house and boys to football. Society also provides models, men and women who by example encourage boys and girls to act, dress, and work like them. Children themselves begin to think of the world as divided into two sexes and often try hard to be like the adult members of their own gender. Many behaviors and traits labeled masculine or feminine are the result of cultural practice, but in some instances there may also be a biological contribution. Currently many parents and schools try to be flexible about gender roles and give both girls and boys a full range of opportunities.

---

## QUESTIONS OF GENDER AND IDENTITY

The roles of men and women are changing. Men can be first-rate nurses, and women can be excellent firefighters. Men can be caretakers raising children, and women can be corporate executive officers. Both sexes, too, may find members of the other sex, their own, or both sexes attractive to them. At the

Gender identity, feeling and acting like a man or a woman, is the result of biology, environment, and social learning.

same time, most people, however nontraditional, have a firm sense of their own biological and psychological identity. They know that they are women or men, and by and large dress and act like members of their own sex. But this is not always the case. There are people who like to imitate some of the appearance of the other sex. There are those, too, who would like to change their physical sex. They are uncomfortable not only with their tertiary but also with their primary and secondary sexual characteristics and want to change them. A study of both these situations can help us better understand questions of sex and gender.

### Transvestism: men dressing as women

*Transvestites* are certain of their physical sexual identity but seem drawn to some of the superficial tertiary characteristics of the other gender. Transvestites (Latin: *trans* = cross, *vestia* = dress) are men who enjoy or are aroused by wearing women's clothing. Most are heterosexual and the majority are married. A few may also be homosexual or consider themselves bisexual, having relations with both sexes.

Transvestites are men who enjoy or are aroused by wearing women's clothing.

When transvestites cross-dress they may wear an entire woman's wardrobe—undergarments, dress, coat, pocketbook, and hat—or just a few articles. The man who only partially dresses is likely to select panties, brassiere, stockings, and other intimate apparel. Sometimes the clothing is contemporary, but frequently it is drawn from the fashions popular in the 1940s and 1950s.

The "TV" who dresses completely may also appear in public passing as a woman. Because there are 100,000 or more transvestites, there are also clubs in many areas where transvestites meet, fully dressed, socialize, and talk over common interests (Wise, 1982).

Some cross-dressers who concentrate on only a few items of clothing de-

Transvestism in women is rare. Few consistently dress as men for sexual pleasure.

pend on the attire to become aroused. They may then masturbate or have sexual relations with their wives or friends. It has been estimated that about a third of wives who know of their husbands' transvestism incorporate it into their relationship. But some wives are very distressed and leave the marriage or insist that the husband get treatment.

Attempts to explain cross-dressing have not been conclusive. To begin with, there are degrees of transvestism. Some cross dress relatively little, and others do so very often and wear full outfits with cosmetics and wigs. Research suggests few if any distinct differences in the family or childhood of cross-dressers. There is also no consistent evidence supporting a hormonal explanation. Another hypothesis is that cross-dressing began as sexual play. Most transvestites report cross-dressing as early as 7 years of age. Some can recall putting on their mother's or sister's clothes for no known reason, but then perhaps accidentally associating sexual excitement with the act (Bullough et al., 1983).

> I put on my sister's panties and I liked the silky feeling. I don't think I had any sexual intention when I started, but the silky feel felt good and I started touching my penis and playing with it. It felt good so I did it a lot the next few years. That's how I sort of stumbled into it, I guess, when I was nine years old.
>
> *(Author's Files)*

Another explanation, proposed by some transvestites, holds that transvestism is a conscious escape from the gender demands, pressures, and rigidities of being a man. When they dress as women, men can wear more colorful and provocative clothing and assume a whole new identity. Their dress provides them relief from the **stereotyped** image of a tough, assertive, always masculine man.

For psychiatrists, confirmed, in contrast to very occasional, transvestism is abnormal, confused fetishistic sexual behavior. Transvestism is labeled a compulsive need to wear female clothing—a fixation. The transvestite is described as a disordered person who instead of focusing on a relationship is attached to inanimate objects: feminine clothing. Cross-dressers themselves contend they are not abnormal. They protest that society and psychiatry should understand that their behavior is innocent and harmless. They want to be seen as enjoying an alternate but legitimate source of sexual arousal (Goldman, 1988).

### Transsexualism

For most people sex is determined at fertilization. The father's chromosomal contribution determines whether they will be female or male (Chapter 4). On rare occasion, there is conflict—fetal hormones and chromosomes do not agree; hermaphrodism may be the result. There is, however, another possibility of sex confusion. A person may be clearly male or female, with chromosomes and hormones seemingly in agreement, and yet want to change his or her biological sex. Such persons are unhappy both with their sex and the gender roles assigned. They want to join the other sex psychologically and physically.

*Transsexuals* are biological women and men who feel like and identify with members of the other sex. This gender/sex discrepancy is much publicized but fairly uncommon. There are only about 20,000 transsexual people in the United States, and the majority are men who want to be or already have become women.

*stereotyped*
Preconceived, fixed, or biased.

We will discuss sexual *fetishism* in Chapter 20.

A study of transsexuality emphasizes the power of gender. It appears so potent that it motivates a few adults to reorient their physical sex. Transsexual men and women endure the discomforts and risks of major surgery to bring their sex into line with what they believe is their gender (Bullough, Bullough, and Smith, 1983).

Transsexual individuals typically report that since childhood they have felt "trapped in the wrong body." One transsexual man asked why he would willingly undergo radical surgery, removing his penis, replied:

> I have no choice. Right now I am a disabled person. I feel crippled. I have parts attached to my body that do not belong there. I want to become a physical woman so that I can really be myself.
>
> *(Author's Files)*

Several causes for transsexualism have been proposed. Some psychologists suggest that transsexualism is the outcome of parents consciously or unconsciously guiding their children to identify with the other gender. Occasionally a transsexual man recalls his parents telling him they would have preferred he was a girl and sometimes labeling or treating him as a girl. In other instances, children appear to voluntarily model themselves after a favored other-sex adult. A transsexual woman recalled that even as a young child she wanted to be like her 10-year-old brother. She imitated his vigor, voice, walk, and habits. By the time she was 10 and he 20 she was lifting weights just as he did.

Most often the background of transsexual men and women is not very revealing. Vern and Bonnie Bullough and Richard Smith (1983) studied 33 male-to-female transsexuals and found few distinctive historical features. As children most showed minimal interest in sports and also reported some long periods of unhappiness. Otherwise the 33 subjects studied were much like other children. These slight differences appear to be insufficient explanations for transsexualism.

Because transsexual women and men frequently come from ordinary backgrounds, attention has turned to their biochemistry. Perhaps transsexual women have too high an androgen balance and men too much estrogen (Chapters 3 and 4). Some transsexual men occasionally appear to have a more feminine, and transsexual women a more masculine, body structure (before surgery) than most other men and women. Nevertheless, glandular evaluations in adults have not found consistent hormonal discrepancies that might account for transsexuality. It has been suggested that perhaps hormonal triggers are involved during the fetal period before birth. Thus far neither this nor any other single explanation appears to account for all instances of transsexualism (Bullough, Bullough, and Smith, 1983; Goldman, 1988).

The causes of transsexualism are not certain, but what is known is that transsexual women and men are ordinarily not homosexual. If they do have sexual relations with a person of their own sex they imagine it to be a heterosexual act. A transsexual man explained:

> When I had sex with John before my operation I imagined his penis in my anus was actually in my vagina. I also would not let him touch or see my penis. I convinced myself that despite this organ which I hated, I was a woman . . .
>
> *(Author's Files)*

Most homosexual people, like heterosexuals, are comfortable and content with their biological sex. Transsexual women and men are not happy with their sex; they want to change it.

**Sex reassignment**  Transsexual awareness of the need to change may start as early as age 3 or may not become clear until adolescence. Typically many transsexual people attempt to suppress their need, marry, and become parents. Many also seek psychotherapeutic help. But psychiatry is apparently not necessarily successful, and the urge to change genders and sex remains (Pauly, Edgarton, 1986).

Before the days of modern surgery, people who were transsexual had to be content to dress in the clothes of the other sex and assume their speech, behaviors, and attitudes. There are numerous stories and folktales of people who disguised themselves and passed for years as members of the sex with which they identified. As early as 400 B.C., the great Athenian poet Agathon reportedly received his friends looking like a Greek matron, dressed in a flowing yellow tunic, a fitted vest, high tight-laced boots, and an elaborate hair net. Today many but not all transsexual people seek what is called *sex reassignment surgery*. There are about a dozen reputable clinics, usually attached to major hospitals, that perform this surgery.

A responsible clinic does not perform surgery simply on demand. Most also have a sex or gender **dysphoria** program that helps evaluate and guide potential patients. A first step is usually educational and evaluational. The potential patient is educated about the procedure she or he will undergo and the likely results. They learn that once the penis is removed, or the vagina altered, they have taken an irreversible step. They also need to know that they will not become a fully sexually capable woman or man, but only approximate the physical appearance and function of the sex they wish to be. Neither men nor women can be provided with functioning reproductive organs and they will remain chromosomally XX or XY (woman or man), just as they were born.

*dysphoria*
Unhappiness; a gender or sex dysphoria clinic is for people who are unhappy with their gender and sex.

The genitalia after sex reassignment surgery. *A,* Male to female; *B,* female to male.

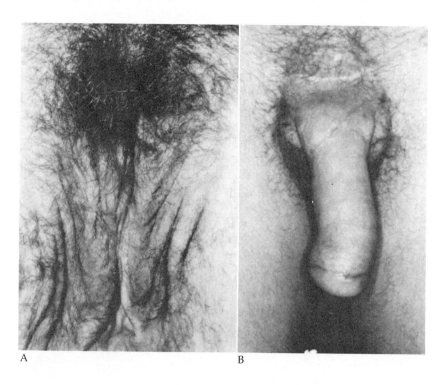

A                                    B

What follows next is often a 1- to 2-year period when the patient is given hormones and encouraged to dress and act like the desired gender. Estrogenic hormones give men a little breast growth, a more ample head of hair, softer skin texture, and some body rounding. The hair of the beard usually remains and has to be removed by electrolysis. Women treated with androgens often find some facial and body hair, diminution or end of menstruation, and increase in muscular bulk.

During this trial period, patients are encouraged to speak frankly with their families and friends and explore the effect the reassignment surgery will have on their jobs and lives. They must also attend to numerous legal details, such as modifying their driver's license, life insurance, and so on. If all goes well, then eventually many patients may be selected for surgery.

For men, sex reassignment surgery means removal of the testes and penis and creation of an approximately 3-inch-deep pubic pouch that resembles a vagina. If there has been careful dissection of nerve pathways in the penis some of this tissue may be rescued and anchored within the vaginal pouch. In such instances the man (now woman) may have some limited pleasurable vaginal feeling during intercourse. The breasts may also be enlarged by implants and plastic surgery employed to imitate curved hips and buttocks.

For women, sex change surgery often requires breast reduction or removal and perhaps abdominal, hip, and other reconstructive procedures. The vaginal lips may be partially amputated and the uterus and ovaries removed. Masculine genitals may be imitated by fusing labial tissue to resemble a scrotum (filled with soft plastic testicles). A penis may be devised by taking 5 inches of cartilage from the upper leg, shaping it, and covering it with labial tissue. Such an appendage may resemble a semierect penis. A penis might also be fashioned from abdominal tissue and then sewn near or over the clitoris, which has been enlarged by androgens. Erection may be accomplished by the person pumping air into an inflatable tube implanted in the penis. This device is similar to the prosthesis described in Chapter 17 and used for men who have serious erectile problems. If surgery is successful and the clitoris enlarged and preserved, there may be some pleasurable feeling during intercourse.

Gerry is a 43-year-old former woman who is considered a top foreign auto engine mechanic. Excerpts from an interview follow.

*Question:* Why do you want to be a man?

*Answer:* I don't want to be. I am a man. It just so happens I was not born with the right body. But I am a man. I like working on engines. I like getting grease under my fingernails. I'm very strong; I can lift anything in the garage. I talk like a man and cut my hair like a man . . . . My hobbies are a man's. I watch the ball game; I smoke cigars. I drink beer . . . . I bowl.

*Question:* How did this start? Tell me about your life.

*Answer:* I was a tomboy, I guess. I always played with the boys. I thought girls silly. I didn't like their things. I liked being rough and tough. The boys always accepted me . . . . I changed a little in high school. I started hanging out with the girls. I giggled and things like that. I thought I had to do it. I got married after high school. My daughter is 22 years old now. She lives with my ex-husband. I've been divorced and on my own 17 years now.

A sex reassignment operation is major surgery, often taking 4 to 6 hours. As in all surgery, complications may occur. Costs average over $10,000 and are seldom paid by medical insurance.

Dr. Reneé Richards, a
much publicized
transsexual, played
professional tennis first as
a man and then as a
woman.

*Question:* When did you first recognize you are transsexual?

*Answer:* I left my husband. I had read about it. I went to New York and ended
up at the clinic. I took different jobs. I started hormone treatments. It gave me a
little beard, a little deeper voice. I already had muscles. It made them bigger.

*Question:* What about your relationships?

*Answer:* In New York it was strange. I met Ralph. He was becoming a woman.
He was what they called a "he-she" then. He had a penis but his hormones gave
him a curvy figure. He had beautiful breasts and also beautiful eyes. We lived
together for a while. Then I came here.

*Question:* Are you a lesbian?

*Answer:* No. A lesbian is a woman who desires women. I am a man. Some
women are attractive to me. I don't find men sexually attractive to me. I have
friends who are women and who are men. But I don't have, haven't had, a relationship with anyone for a long time. I don't need sex that much.

*Question:* Are you happy with your sex change operation?

*Answer:* Yes and no. I go to New York every 6 months and they check me out
and adjust the hormone dose I get. I look on the outside like a man and that
makes me happy. But my sex, my penis doesn't work really. That's not so good.

*Question:* Do you feel you're abnormal?

*Answer:* No. Sometimes I think the world is abnormal. Why do we have to
make such a deal about whether you are a man or woman? If I like cars and
cigars why can't I just be a person who likes those things? Why do those things
have to be called manly and some other things womanly?

*Question:* You would like it if we stopped labeling gender. If we stopped saying that some characteristics and actions are masculine and other feminine.

*Answer:* Right. Then anyone could do whatever they wanted with their lives.

*(Author's Files)*

**Results**   The two most prominent gender dysphoria programs at Stanford in California and at Johns Hopkins in Baltimore no longer routinely perform reassignment surgery. The decision is based on studies that suggest that many people are not helped by such a radical procedure. They are conflicted as much after surgery as before. Disappointment is also common. Many patients fantasize that they will turn into lovely men or women. They find instead that they are simply somewhat altered copies of their former selves with their actual sexual capability considerably reduced. Many reassigned transsexuals also face social and job discrimination. Some friends and employers withdraw and no longer want to maintain contact (Lothstein, 1982).

However, sex reassignment surgery continues and may be increasing in popularity. Many transsexuals say they have been helped and are happier with themselves than they have ever been before. The best clinics carefully screen their clients; others will accept anyone who has money. Gender and sex counseling programs are also continuing and expanding because many specialists feel that gender identity questions are better answered by counseling and therapy rather than by surgery. At the least, counseling, even if it does not help, does leave the person physically intact. Surgery irreversibly alters an individual. Looking at all the evidence, it seems the most prudent alternative for a transsexual person is to carefully and for a considerable time try every other option before considering surgery (Pauly, Edgarton, 1986).

---

*Summary*

The sexual characteristics and behaviors that distinguish women from men are described as primary, secondary, and tertiary. The first two are basically biological, while the last is mainly acquired. A child's sex is determined by the genetic contribution of the father, but many other traits are the result of the gene combinations from both parents. Just what traits emerge is dependent not only on the presence of particular genes but environmental opportunity as well. Some phenomena such as hemophilia and longevity are sex-linked. Brain function and most intellectual and personality traits seem only minimally dependent on biological sex.

From the moment a child is born, social learning processes, such as channeling, modeling, and reinforcement, encourage traits and behaviors traditionally deemed appropriate for one sex or the other. In this environment, children begin to conceptualize the world as consisting of males and females, and they try to act like their own sex. Some traits such as aggression may be biological in origin, but societies tend to enlarge such differences. It is likely, too, that many other characteristics of men and women are the result of an interaction of biological predisposition and social learning. A study of transsexual women and men and transvestism reveals the importance and power of gender in determining personal happiness and sex identity. Today many educators, parents, and others advocate child-rearing practices that emphasize equal opportunity for every girl and boy, not locking either into inflexible gender roles.

*For Thought and Discussion*

1 What are primary, secondary, and tertiary sex characteristics? In contrast with some other cultures, what is our society's attitude toward and definition of secondary and tertiary characteristics?

2 What is meant by sex chromosome, autosome, genotype and phenotype, and DNA? What role do these play in determining female and male behavior?

3 Social learning suggests boys and girls are taught to be members of their gender. Give examples of how the following processes may serve that purpose: channeling, modeling, reinforcement, cognition.

4 What does transsexualism and transvestism teach us about biological sex and the qualities thought of as gender?

5 How have gender expectations and roles changed in the last 10 years?

*References*

Archer, S. Careers and/or family: the identity process for adolescent girls. *Youth and Society,* 1985, *16*(3), 289-314.

Benderley, B.L. *The myth of two minds: what gender means and doesn't mean.* New York: Doubleday, 1987.

Bleier, R. *Science and gender: a critique of biology and its theories on women.* Elmsford, New York: Pergamon, 1984.

Bullough, V., Bullough, B., and Smith, R. A comparative study of male transvestites, male to female transsexuals, and male homosexuals. *The Journal of Sex Research,* August 1983, *19*, 238-257.

Doyle, J.A. *Sex and gender: the human experience.* Dubuque, Iowa: Wm. C. Brown , 1985.

Dranov, P. New genetic findings: why women live longer. *Science Digest,* 1981, *89*, 32-33.

Freud, S. *Collected papers.* New York: Basic Books, 1959.

Goldman, H.H. *Review of General Psychiatry.* Norwalk, Connecticut: Appleton & Lange, 1988.

Lengermann, P.M. and Wallace, R.A. *Gender in America: social control and social change.* Englewood Cliffs, New Jersey: Prentice-Hall, 1985.

Levy, J. Right brain, left brain: fact and fiction. *Psychology Today,* May 1985, 38-44.

Lewontin, R.C., Rose, S., and Kamin, L.J. *Not in our genes: biology, ideology, and human nature.* New York: Pantheon, 1984.

Lothstein, L. Sex reassignment surgery: historical, bioethical, and theoretical issues. *American Journal of Psychiatry,* 1982, *139*, 417-426.

Maccoby, E.E. *Social development, psychological growth and the parent-child relationship.* New York: Harcourt Brace Jovanovich, 1980.

Maier, H.W. *Three theories of child development.* Lanham, Maryland: University Press of America. 1988.

Pauly, I., and Edgarton, M. The gender identity movement: a growing surgical-psychiatric liason. *Archives of Sexual Behavior,* 1986, *15*(4), 315-327.

Pearson, J.C. *Gender and communication.* Dubuque, Iowa: Wm. C. Brown, 1985.

Pillard, R.C., and Weinrich, J.D. The periodic table model of the gender transpositions: Part I. A theory based on masculinization and defeminization of the brain. *The Journal of Sex Research,* November 1987, *23*(4), 425-454.

Pogrebin, L. *Growing up free: raising your child in the '80s.* New York: McGraw-Hill, 1980.

Sadker, M. and Sadker, D. Sexism in the schoolroom of the '80s. *Psychology Today,* March 1985, 54-57.

Shepherd-Look, D.L. Sex differentiation in the development of sex roles. In Wolman, B.B. (editor). *Handbook of developmental psychology,* Englewood Cliffs, New Jersey: Prentice-Hall, 1982.

Simmons, R.A., and Blyth, D.A. *Moving into adolescence.* New York: Aldine De-Gruyter, 1987.

Symons, D. *The evolution of human sexuality*. Fair Lawn, New Jersey: Oxford University Press, 1981.

Tan-William, C. Cerebral hemispheric specialization of academically gifted and nongifted male and female adolescents. *The Journal of Creative Behavior,* Winter 1981, *15,* 276-277.

Williams, F., LaRose, R., and Frost, F. *Children, television, and sex role stereotyping.* New York: Praeger Publishers, 1981.

Wise, T. Heterosexual men who cross dress. *Medical aspects of human sexuality,* 1982, *16,* 11.

*Suggested Reading*

Blume, J. *Letters to Judy: what your kids wish they could tell you.* New York: Putnam: 1986.

Letters to Judy Blume reveal how children and adolescents really feel, and what they experience, about growing up and becoming men and women.

Dowling, C. *The Cinderella complex: women's hidden fear of independence.* New York: Summit Books, 1981.

The author makes a good case for the controversial contention that many women sabotage their own achievement and autonomy because they are fearful of independence. Leads readers to self-examination and gives some useful suggestions.

Doyle, J.A. *Sex and gender: the human experience.* Dubuque, Iowa: Wm. C. Brown Group, 1985.

A well-balanced presentation of what it means to be a woman or a man in today's world. Presents interesting research and differing viewpoints.

Goldberg, H. *The new male-female relationship.* New York: Morrow, 1983.

Emphasizes how both sexes may better understand one another when stereotypes are discarded.

## Chapter 7

# Being Woman or Man
## *Similarities and Differences*

**When you finish this chapter, you should be able to:**

Compare the physical abilities of women and men and explain how they might be the same or different.

Explain how female and male attributes overlap and how this demonstrates the sexes are more similar than different.

Explain differences and similarities in male and female sexuality.

Describe the personality traits and aptitudes often thought more characteristic of men and of women.

Identify how job stereotypes have substantially changed during this decade.

When we look at a woman and a man, the most obvious fact is often missed. It is easy to see that the sexes are ordinarily different in dress and physical appearance. What we frequently fail to see is the fact that both have hearts, brains, bones, joys, and worries that are not easily distinguished. Or, as Shakespeare suggested in *The Merchant of Venice,* although he was talking about religious rather than gender differences: all people have senses, passions, and affections. They are fed with the same food, hurt with the same weapons, subject to the same diseases, warmed and cooled by the same winter and summer.

Fundamentally similar as women and men are, most cultures seem to believe some features are more characteristic of one sex than the other. In our society many assume that women are endowed with greater verbal skills and men with higher mathematical aptitudes. Women are ostensibly more sexually inhibited and emotionally sensitive. We will examine these and other reputed gender differences and trace their origins.

# PHYSICAL ABILITIES

At birth and through most of life, gender differences in size, strength, and physical ability are often evident. Newborn boys are generally longer, have larger heads, and are heavier. Infant boys also lift their heads higher, pull harder on a ring, and typically have more muscle strength. These sex distinctions occur before there is much opportunity for learning or environmental influence, and may be attributable to the chromosomal differences between the sexes (Ambron, 1985).

All of the physical characteristics mentioned are averages. There is a range in physical size and strength in both boys and girls, and very considerable *overlap* as well. Some newborn girls are larger than boys and among older children, many boys are not as strong as the average girl.

There do not seem to be any differences in ages at which young children master basic motor skills such as sitting up, standing, and walking. Despite this equality, preschool boys tend to be better than girls at ball throwing, jumping, and climbing. Girls excel at hopping, balancing, and careful eye-hand coordination as is required in drawing with crayons and cutting with scissors. There may be a biological component in all these physical accomplishments, but there is likely a learned element also. Even before school begins, most boys are encouraged to play ball and most girls are encouraged to color and cut out (Pitcher, 1985).

Between the ages of 6 and 12, boys and girls usually draw abreast of one another and are about equal in their running and related athletic activities. As puberty nears, between 10 and 14 years of age, girls seem to accelerate. As a result, most pubertal girls at ages 13 or 14 are temporarily taller, sometimes stronger, and nearly always sexually more developed than boys of the same age (Chapter 8). After this gap is bridged, by ages 14 and 15, boys draw ahead of girls in height and strength. Men appear to develop a greater heart and lung capacity, and stronger, firmer musculature. Most women who stop sports at this age reach a plateau. The athletic abilities they had at 12 or 13 level off or even decline.

Part of the accelerated growth in male physical prowess is related to the increase in testosterone found in the postpubertal male. But another part of the gender difference results from the way in which adolescent boys and girls are socialized at home and in school. Traditionally, only men were given the opportunity and encouraged to make use of their physical abilities. Particularly after the onset of menses (Chapter 3), girls were instructed to stop running and climbing.

In recent years, women's athletics have received more attention and more financial support. Most schools today must accept girls, as well as boys, who want to participate in any sport. The results of this equal treatment are already appearing. Women have been found to have far more endurance than expected. They are competing successfully, for example, in Olympic events. A study of sports performance in the *Guinness Book of World Records* shows that women have improved dramatically since they began taking part, less than a decade ago (McWhirter, 1990).

Whether we measure running speed, assertiveness, sexual drive, or nearly any other characteristic, we will invariably find it to be shared by women and

Many preschool girls do as well as or better than boys in such traditional masculine activities as running and climbing.

Encouraging women to participate in all sports has resulted in increasingly better performance.

men. Most measurable human attributes of women and men overlap. The two sexes are much more alike than they are different.

## SEXUALITY

*libido*
Sexual interest and desire.

A commonly held belief is that men may often be inordinately driven by their sexuality. Their **libido** is held to be much greater than that of women. Men are easily stimulated and supposedly consider nearly every woman a potential partner. Women, on the other hand, according to the same popular view, want sex mainly in terms of a relationship. They are said to be selective in their choice of partners and less easily aroused. Are these alleged differences between the sexes real? We will consider three aspects of sexuality—desire, erotica, and orgasm—and see what these may tell us about the similarities and differences in the sexuality of women and men.

### Desire

Do men want more sex than women? One indication of sexual desire is the frequency of masturbation. According to the Kinsey studies in 1948 and 1953, 90% of adolescent boys, but only half as many girls, masturbated. Two decades later, Hunt (1974) found two out of three teenaged girls masturbated, a considerable increase over the earlier Kinsey results. More recent studies again

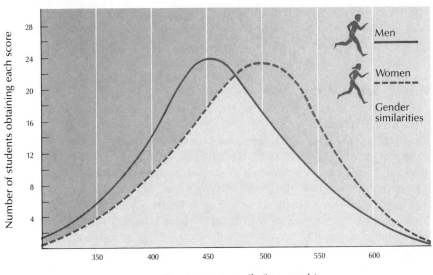

*Figure 7-1*
In a track training
program, 100 college
women and 100 college
men were asked to run a
mile. The average score for
women was 500 seconds
and for men 450. Their
achievement *overlapped*—
represented by the palest
portion of the two curves.
Most human traits and
abilities appear equally in
both sexes. When there are
differences between the
sexes, there is usually also
considerable overlap.

show an increase. By the 1980s, close to all adolescent males admitted masturbating and the percentage for females approached 80% (Atwood, Gagnon, 1987; Petersen et al., 1983).

There are also differences in the frequency of masturbation between adult men and women. During the adolescent years, most males masturbate between one and three times weekly and females masturbate once every week or two. But this difference narrows or perhaps even reverses itself later. During adulthood, women may masturbate as much as, or sometimes more frequently than, men. This observation has prompted the question, "Are women really masturbating more now, or are women perhaps less reluctant to talk about sexual behaviors when they are surveyed and interviewed?" (Hunt, 1974; Petersen et al., 1983; Rubenstein, Tavris, 1987; Wolfe, 1981).

Another way to measure desire is to compare how much coitus women and men want in a marriage. The Hunt (1974) and Kinsey (1948, 1953) studies showed that more than half of all couples questioned believe that their present frequency of intercourse is more or less right. An examination of a sample of younger couples, however, revealed some discrepancies. About 20% of the women and approximately 40% of the men in this sample wanted intercourse almost daily. A congruent finding was obtained by asking husbands and wives if they desired less coitus. The figures suggest that 2% to 5% of married men and 10% to 15% of the women believed intercourse occurred too often (Wolfe, 1981).

These data make it appear as if 5% to 20% of women want intercourse less often than their husbands. But there are findings that point in the opposite direction. Blumstein and Schwartz, for example, (1983) found that about 10% of wives sometimes want intercourse more often than their husbands. The picture seems mixed. The evidence conflicts, making it difficult to conclude that one sex consistently wants more intercourse than the other.

Sexual activity outside of marriage has also been used to gauge sexual desire. A generation ago, the number of men who had extramarital relationships

Chapter 2 describes survey
and other research
techniques and points out
some weakness in these
methods.

Marital sexual behavior is
explored in Chapter 12.

approximated 50%, while only 30% of married women had extramarital relationships (Kinsey et al., 1948, 1953). Through the decades, there has been a steady increase with some studies suggesting that for people marrying now, two thirds of the men and half of the women will have intercourse with someone other than their spouse. This increase for both sexes suggests that social learning and tradition, along with biological need, play a role in determining the likelihood of extramarital intercourse (Blumstein and Schwartz, 1983; Petersen, 1983; Wolfe, 1981).

Another means of evaluating sexual desire is to examine homosexual relationships. Studies of male and female homosexual activities seem to reveal important differences. A *small* proportion of homosexual men sometimes go to **gay** bath houses. Here along with steam rooms and massage there is dancing and sexual intimacy. Many people attending the baths have sexual relations with two, three, or more men in several hours. There is no equivalent facility for homosexual women. At most some women go to **lesbian** bars where the main objective will be to socialize. Interviews with older homosexual men and women further highlight sexual differences. Close to half of all homosexual men report that they have had several hundred different partners. Among lesbians, most have had fewer than 20 partners in a lifetime (Chapter 13).

Finally, the most telling measure of sexual desire may be who makes the sexual invitation. Is it not, after all, much more often men, rather than women, who in one way or another ask for sexual intimacy? It is widely believed that men are the initiators, and women are more likely to be reluctant, hesitant, or rejecting. Perper and Weis (1987) investigated the sexual strategies of 77 college women in order to evaluate to what extent they suggested sexual contact. The subjects wrote essays describing how they seduce or reject a man. Among the techniques used to initiate sexuality were dressing invitingly, creating a romantic ambience, sexy talk, and touch (Chapter 10). To the researchers' surprise, nearly all (87%) of the women described sexual seduction strategies. The authors concluded, "Although popular and scholarly opinion may say that women behave hesitantly and reluctantly with men, the data obtained here flatly contradict the belief that women invariably defer to, or rely on, men to initiate sexual encounters" (p. 474).

The Perper and Weis study did not measure actual sexual activity, nor were the women observed directly. Their written descriptions were believed valid indicators of their behavior. Such research results cannot be conclusive, but they cast doubt on the notion that it is mainly men who first seek sexual gratification. The desire to start a sexual relationship may be just as prominent in many, if not most, women as in men.

### Erotica

Most **erotica**, meaning sexually arousing pictures, films, stories, and even articles of clothing, are directed at men. A generation ago, Kinsey (1948, 1953) wrote that while men enjoyed and could get excited looking at pictures of nude women or sexual scenes, erotica had little attraction for women. Researchers have since contested the Kinsey view and several studies have suggested that some women are just as interested in erotica as men.

It has been pointed out that stories, films, and the like, in which the personalities of the participants become alive, in which love plays a critical role in

*gay*
A slang term, now socially acceptable, used primarily in reference to homosexual men, but sometimes also for homosexual women.

*lesbian*
A female homosexual.

Four percent of men and about as many women are homosexual. Many more people have had some homosexual experiences. This sexual orientation will be described in Chapter 13.

*erotica*
Materials, books, pictures, films, that portray sex or sexual activity with the intent of arousing the viewer.

```
┌─────────────────────────────────────────────────────┐
│         ★ OUTSTANDING EROTIC MOVIES ★                │
│        for Ladies, Gentlemen and Couples              │
│                    ★ ★ ★                              │
│  GIRLS TALKING DIRTY..Many different stories featuring sex │
│                       action that will turn you on.   │
│  BARE BOYS...........Ladies: Watch ten male strippers take │
│                       it all off.                     │
│  SWINGING COUPLES.....Bisexual foursome get it on every │
│                       possible way.                   │
│  MARRIED AND GAY......The story of a married man and his │
│                       boyfriend.                      │
│  GARDEN OF ORGASM.....Male and female nude dancers, models, │
│                       teasers, oral action, and more! │
│  WONDERFUL WOMEN......Three sexy ladies and a midget.  │
│  COUPLES IN LOVE......The film made by women, for women and │
│                       couples.                        │
│  JIGGLE AND DANCE.....All nude men in an erotic bouncing │
│                       contest.                        │
└─────────────────────────────────────────────────────┘
```

*Figure 7-2*
Some advertisements for erotica acknowledge the interest in sexually explicit entertainment among women as well as men.

sexuality, may be more stimulating to women. Women, it is said, often reject erotica not because it is unappealing, but because the quality is unacceptable. In contrast, if a woman feels that the couple portrayed is emotionally involved and that the woman is not being exploited, made into a "sex object," she may find scenes showing intercourse and oral relations quite stimulating (Athanasiou, 1980).

Julia Heiman (1975) proposed that some women may not be aware of, or revealing about, their own physical response to explicit erotica. While a man might feel his penis becoming erect, a woman might not know that vaginal changes are taking place indicating arousal. To demonstrate this, Heiman measured physiological reactions to sexually stimulating material. In her study each man wore a measuring gauge around the base of his penis. Each woman had a cylinder in her vagina that registered blood flow and pulse, indicators of sexual arousal. Subjects then listened to taped stories that were frankly erotic or romantic or both, in content. The result: both sexes were equally aroused by the uninhibited erotic stories. In this study, women did not seem to be more excited just by the romantic.

Several studies like Heiman's have measured the physical correlates of arousal and found them similar in both sexes. Other researchers have concentrated on how people behave and how they say they feel. Such research has revealed that in both women and men erotica may lead to sexual excitation and to intensification of the feelings accompanying sexual activity. In one study, adults who read and viewed erotic materials more often had intercourse in the following 24 hours than couples in a control group (Athanasiou, 1980).

Fisher and associates (1983) reasoned that previous attitudes might affect the responses of men and women toward erotica. In their research, explicit erotic passages detailing sexual activities were read by 67 male and 154 female college students. Experimental participants, both men and women, who had a favorable attitude toward erotica in general tended to be most aroused by the stories read. As might be expected, too, those women and men with unfavor-

## How Feminine or Masculine Are You?

The next section discusses masculine and feminine personality traits. Before beginning this part, test your own femininity or masculinity in terms of traditional definition. Try not to guess which traits are which and answer as honestly as you can. Circle the number that best describes you.

| Trait | Rarely or never | Sometimes | Usually or always |
|-------|-------|-------|-------|
| 1. Assertive | 0 | 1 | 2 |
| 2. Shy | 0 | 1 | 2 |
| 3. Independent | 0 | 1 | 2 |
| 4. Affectionate | 0 | 1 | 2 |
| 5. Athletic | 0 | 1 | 2 |
| 6. Yielding | 0 | 1 | 2 |
| 7. Defend own beliefs | 0 | 1 | 2 |
| 8. Loyal | 0 | 1 | 2 |
| 9. Self-reliant | 0 | 1 | 2 |
| 10. Easily flattered | 0 | 1 | 2 |

### Scoring

To find your femininity score, add the points you gave yourself on even numbered (2, 4, etc.) items. Your masculinity score is obtained by adding the points on odd numbered items.

### Interpretation

A score above eight in either masculinity or femininity is considered highly masculine or feminine. Scores between five and eight are common and suggest somewhat less pronounced male or female traits. When scores in both masculinity and femininity are in the six, seven, or more range it indicates an *androgynous* personality. People who are androgynous are considered to have a healthy combination of traditionally female and male personality traits.

Please note these personality trait scores are based on traditional views of what is masculine or feminine. This informal test is intended to make you more aware of sex typing, *not* to irrevocably label someone as high or low in feminity or masculinity. With increasing equality for the sexes, few if any traits appear to be definitely masculine or feminine (Bem, 1981).

---

able attitudes toward erotica, those who disliked sexual stories, were ordinarily least stimulated by the sexual material.

Research now suggests that women like men may be aroused by some erotic materials. Yet the sex industry still seems to cater largely to men. There are occasional attempts to produce a magazine or film appealing to women, but these efforts usually get only small audiences. Dozens of magazines like *Playboy* and *Penthouse*, and many that are far more sexually explicit, have tens of millions of male readers. The realities of business and commerce apparently indicate that a lot more sexually stimulating material will be sold if it caters to men (Cook et al., 1983).

Perhaps this demonstrates some continuing biological differences in women's and men's responses to sexual material, or maybe it shows only that much of what is thought erotic is actually so inadequate or offensive that many women find it unacceptable. A third possibility may be that many women are still reluctant, because of social standards, to permit their interest to show. We

*Erotica will be discussed more fully in Chapter 19.*

will need more research before we can be certain just how different or similar men and women are in their responses to sexually explicit material.

## Orgasm

Orgasm, the intensely pleasurable feelings that may climax sexual activity, has been described differently in women and in men. Among men, orgasm ordinarily involves a progressive buildup of excitation, resulting in pleasurably climactic release. Women may have a similar orgasmic pattern or they may feel pleasurable wavelike sensations or a number of small climaxes. Men usually have an orgasm as a consequence of intercourse. Many women also have an orgasm as a consequence of intercourse, but many others do not. Whether or not they experience orgasm with intercourse may depend on the occasion, the coital position, personal feelings, or other variables not readily defined. Yet despite these seeming differences, there is also at least one marked similarity. Both sexes almost always have an orgasm as a result of masturbation (Chapter 5).

There are also differences in the number of orgasms that may be experienced. Some women are multiorgasmic, having two, three, or more orgasms during a half hour to an hour or so of sexual activity. Few men are multiorgasmic in this sense, and most usually require a period of rest following ejaculation before they can begin coitus again.

## Conclusion

Is there a difference in sexual desire between women and men? Had this question been asked 100 years ago we might have confidently answered "yes," there is an enormous difference," (Chapter 1). At that time it appeared that women rarely masturbated and that they seemed to want little intercourse. Today it is no longer entirely clear which sex masturbates more often or desires intercourse more frequently. The response to erotica is similarly ambivalent. The marketplace suggests that men buy most erotica, but research shows that women can respond to sexually arousing materials also.

Sociobiologists (Chapter 6) insist that there is a difference in male and female sexuality and say it is, or was, a necessary one. They call attention particularly to the higher level of sexual activity among some homosexual men. This is seen as male behavior untempered by the moderating influence of a female. Sociobiologists contend that historically the continuation of the human species depended on the natural selection of men who were easily aroused and wanted many different sexual partners. This hypothesis is supported, it is argued, by the biochemical evidence. The hormone mainly responsible for the sex drive, testosterone (Chapter 4), is 20 times more plentiful in men than in women. Further, in controlled studies with older women, those who received testosterone, rather than a placebo, had a much higher frequency and intensity of sexual arousal (Gallagher, 1988; Symons, 1981).

From the social learning perspective, the evidence for a difference between female and male sexuality is considered slight. Whatever distinctions do appear are attributed to culturally induced attitudes and behaviors. The higher level of sexual activity, for example, of some homosexual men is explained in terms of socially imposed expectations. Men, whether gay or not, it is contended, have been conditioned by society to act "macho" and sexy. The homosexual man

Female and male orgasms may be alike in many ways since the nerve endings responsible for orgasm are located in the clitoris and the head of the penis. These organs have similar embryological beginnings.

# Who Are They?

Do women and men respond differently to erotica? Four people, two women and two men, were given an erotic videotape *(Undress Me, Slowly)* and instructed to watch it alone, privately in their homes. Their descriptions and reactions to the film follow. Try to match the person with the description. (Answers are provided below.)

Person 1: Woman, age 43, divorced 3 years and living alone

Person 2: Woman, age 23, never married and sharing an apartment with her older sister

Person 3: Man, age 24, newly married

Person 4: Man, age 37, married for the second time

## Description A

I found the film fair. It had its good points and bad. I didn't like the gigantic close-ups of a woman's head doing oral sex with the man. That gigantic head bobbing up and down over a penis. That's not a turn on. That's boring. The same with those love scenes where he's on top. All you see really is his rear end going up and down. That's just not exciting. . . . What I did like was the scene where they met. They became very excited about each other. I think it was real. You could see his fingers tremble as he was unbuttoning her skirt along the side. They really seemed into one another. . . . I found the foreplay scenes very good. The actual intercourse was just not well done. It was boring, monotonous. Not a turn on. Some people would be offended.

## Description B

The film was terrific. A real turn on. It started slowly. They talked a lot but you could see they were eyeing each other. They liked each other. The first time she touched him was really well done. You could feel there was passion. The only thing, maybe it was a little too open. Showing the vagina, the penis like that, in close up, it puts you off a little bit.

## Description C

When I put the film on the VCR I wasn't sure how I'd feel. Believe it or not I'd never seen a porn film before . . . but when it came to it, I liked it. It was a turn on. I'd seen nude bodies before. . . . We often go to a swimming spot in the mountains where people sun themselves and swim without any clothing on. It's always been exciting for me to lie around in the sun. Sometimes people look at me. Sometimes I look at them. But a porn flick . . . that was something else. I thought at first, this is not real. You can't really get interested. But I did get turned on. It was interesting, too, to see what the woman did when she was aroused. She stretched and tightened her body. She touched herself. I liked seeing the man's erection. You could tell they loved it. Well, in spite of some doubts about it, I liked it.

## Description D

I was raised to consider sex a very private thing. You did it in private, and you didn't talk about it except in a very general way. I didn't think I'd like seeing this erotic film. I'd seen one 4 years ago, and frankly it didn't do much for me. It had a nasty quality about it. But times have changed, and I guess I've changed too. Well, maybe things haven't changed all that much. This film was technically a lot better than the old one. There was a story line that was sort of hokey but I could get into it. As far as being a turn on, well parts were and parts weren't. I liked when the actors were getting excited, undressing each other. You knew they would soon be into it. But I think much too much time was spent showing genital action . . . in-out-in-out-in-out. Sure this is what sex is like, but I think the genital shots were overdone. But all in all, the film was ok. No one gets hurt, some people might find it a turn on.

## Answers: Who are they?

Description A: Person 4
Description B: Person 3
Description C: Person 2
Description D: Person 1

*(Author's Files)*

could supposedly be especially driven to prove his masculinity by having many partners (Chapter 13).

The significance of the higher level of testosterone in men is also debated. One view holds that testosterone may lead only to greater physical activity generally and society channels this into sexual or aggressive behavior. Other investigators point out that the amount of testosterone may itself not be that important. It is hypothesized that females are more sensitized and responsive to this hormone. Only a minute amount in a woman may have the same sexual effects as a much larger amount in a man.

Is the sexuality of women different from that of men? There are likely some ways in which men and women inherently differ. Society also seems to have magnified or perhaps distorted some of these differences. Overall, however, it seems as if in the sexual and affectional areas the attributes of the two sexes overlap. Women and men are much more similar than they are different.

---

Women and men are structurally quite similar. There are however some inborn and some culturally induced distinct characteristics and skills. The increasing participation of women in athletics has revealed abilities once socially discouraged. There may be some differences between men and women in sexuality. On the other hand, compared to a generation ago, distinctions in masturbation, desire, and arousal are much less marked than they once appeared. The remaining differences in sexuality may be partly inherent and the result of social learning. Given the large overlap in both physical traits and sexuality, women and men appear to be much more similar than different.

*In Sum*

---

## PERSONALITY TRAITS

An ancient Chinese folksaying contends that men have marble and women have waxen minds. Centuries have passed, but it is still commonly believed that men are decisive, while women act with uncertainty. Many of us have *gender stereotypes,* fixed and biased notions about the personalities of women and men. The stereotypes about the personality traits of women and men usually cluster along the following lines. Men are seen as competent, independent, aggressive, logical, and adventurous. The stereotypical traits for women suggest that they are gentle, talkative, and affectionate.

These perceptions are not limited to our own society. Williams and Best (1982) studied male and female characteristics in nations around the world. Respondents in 30 different countries were presented with a list of 300 adjectives and asked to associate them with women or men. The findings were surprisingly consistent. Men were almost unanimously described as being more assertive, independent, and dominant. Women were seen as primarily dependent, timid, and nurturant.

Remember that these are gender stereotypes. They are beliefs held by many men and women about the alleged characteristics of their own and the other sex. These are opinions and the fact that these assumptions are held by many people or by prestigious people does *not* automatically make them any more valid. We will look at several of these traits and see what research actually shows.

### Aggression, nurturance

Aggression and nurturance may be more typical of one sex than the other. Boys tend to play "cops and robbers," while girls play "house." The behavior of preschool middle class American boys and similar groups of girls has been observed in different play environments. In most such settings the children act differently depending on their sex. The girls spend a good deal of time being nurturant, taking care of everyone. They tend to set up rules for play so all will have fun and take part. The boys more typically start their play with friendly roughhousing, which may lead to some fights. In general, the boys' aggressiveness is often aimed at the establishment and maintenance of dominance (Pitcher, 1985).

These distinctive male/female patterns of interaction also appear in adulthood. Even at leisurely social events, many men seem to compete aggressively. They try to impress one another, to be "top dog," by telling jokes, boasting of success, or just talking so much that they dominate the conversation. Women do not usually display as much aggressive behavior, but seem to agree to act tactfully and sympathetically toward each other. While one woman talks, the other's face and posture signals she hears what is being said. Rather than two women trying to top each other, the listener often indicates her support and encouragement by nods and "mmhmms" (Pearson, 1985).

As an explanation, animal research often shows aggressive traits tied to testosterone and nurturance to estrogens (Chapters 3 and 4). Either aggression or nurturance often can be stimulated in a male *or* a female rat just by adjusting the hormonal balance. Allied with this is the sociobiological thesis that nurturant behavior has to be innate in women, that it is virtually an "instinctive," imperative because it is necessary for women to provide and care for their infants (Chapter 6).

Biology may be part of the story, but testosterone provides only an incomplete explanation for human male aggression. Testosterone levels fluctuate daily and vary from one man to another. The amount of testosterone present is usually not correlated with the degree of aggressiveness. Very aggressive men may or may not have more testosterone than men who are relatively nonaggressive. Similarly, attempts to show a direct relationship between estrogens and caring attitudes in women have not been very conclusive. After a comprehensive review of the literature, Pleck (1981) wrote that there may be considerable evidence for hormonal factors in animals playing a role in their aggression. Hormonal studies in humans, however, are not sufficient to predict aggressiveness in women and men.

Melson and Fogel (1988) reexamined nurturance and suggest boys may be as nurturant as girls but primarily when they are younger. In one investigation, 71 boys and girls between 2 and 6 years old were brought into a room, one by one, where they saw a baby sitting in an infant seat with a mother nearby. A significant number of the children responded to the baby. They smiled, offered a toy, talked to or touched the infant. "Surprisingly there were no differences between boys and girls in how much they . . . interacted with the infant" (p. 42). But this equality of nurturant interest in babies does not continue. By the time children near puberty, boys pay less and less attention to infants, while girls seem to feel interested in and comfortable with caring for them. Melson and Fogel suggest that boys' nurturant needs do not disappear spontaneously

If females did not have a strong inborn nurturant need, it is argued that they would abandon their babies. Male apes and monkeys, for example, have nothing to do with infants and may even kill them.

Male aggression

but are discouraged by society. In contrast, as they get older, girls are increasingly delegated to take care of babies and given the knowledge that will enable them to do so.

Observations by social scientists often point more to culture than to biochemistry. The amount and kind of aggression and of nurturance can be highly dependent on the characteristics encouraged by each society. In an exhaustive cross-cultural examination, Ronald Rohner (1976) studied data from 101 groups of people. As might be expected, in almost all, boys were described as more aggressive than girls. But what was also interesting was that the more the society encouraged aggression in boys, the more aggression was also evident in girls. In other words, societies that stimulate a high level of aggressiveness turn out aggressive males, but they also encourage the same quality in females. When aggressiveness is not encouraged, such as among the peaceful Chenchu of southern India, aggression is almost equally uncommon among boys and girls. Apparently there may be innate differences in aggressiveness and nurturance between women and men. Society, however, may play a significant role in bringing out or moderating these traits.

### Achievement, success

*Achievement,* the motive to do one's best, to succeed and increase one's status or wealth, is closely related to aggressive drives. Measurements of this need have been made by pencil and paper tests asking questions such as "Would you rather get the best grades in class or be the most well-liked student?"

Other researchers have shown subjects pictures of people in various activities, like a boy playing a violin, and asked them to make up a story to accompany the picture. Frequently the pictures from a psychological test called the *Thematic Apperception Test (TAT)* have been used. The assumption is that stories such as, "The boy is practicing hard so that he can be a concert artist," express a great deal of achievement motivation. A story like, "He hates practicing and would rather play ball," shows little achievement motive.

The evidence for a difference in achievement needs between men and women has pointed in both directions. For a while, it seemed clear that men nearly always rank higher in achievement needs. Then it was observed that in homes in which parents rewarded early independence—children chose their own clothes, did household chores, and so on—boys and girls showed nearly equally high achievement needs. There were also homes that encouraged achievement for boys but not for girls. The achievement need seemed quite dependent on parental direction (Maccoby, 1980).

The achievement issue attained a new focus when Colette Dowling, in her book *The Cinderella Complex* (1981), suggested that some women are afraid of being too successful and independent. They avoid success because they are anxious that it may appear to decrease their femininity or cause difficulties in relationships with their spouse or family. Put in another way, many women choose not to achieve outside the home since in their social milieu this "non-achievement" may lead to greater reward and recognition ("she's a fine wife and mother") than being a business or professional success. Some women may, as a result, appear to have lower achievement needs because they are deliberately holding back (Forbes and King, 1983).

Achievement

## Androgyny

Sandra Bem (1981) has developed a psychological test that measures the "masculinity/femininity" of an individual's personality. Subjects rate themselves on 60 personality traits and then add up their gender score. Characteristics such as ambition, forcefulness, self-reliance, independence, and analyticity are considered masculine. The reputed feminine traits include adaptability, helpfulness, reliability, tactfulness, and theatricality.

A number of investigators using the Bem scale have shown that women and men who adhere strictly to the personality attributes supposedly typical of their sex tend to be quite inflexible in many areas of their life. In contrast, Bem reported that about a third of Stanford University students, in California, had a pretty fair mixture of "masculine" and of "feminine" traits in their self-descriptions. These students were reported to date more, to be generally happier, and to get better grades.

People who exhibit both male and female personality characteristics have been called androgynous. They are a combination of *andro* and *gyne,* Greek for male and female. These are *not* sexually confused persons (Chapter 6) but people who possess character traits customarily labeled male or female. An androgynous man may be nurturant and warm, along with being traditionally aggressive and independent. An androgynous woman may be assertive and adventurous, so-called masculine traits, along with being affectionate and supportive, the last two customarily thought of as feminine characteristics.

Those who advocate androgyny want boys and girls to be raised together, sharing learning, growth, toys, and play. Playing together and being treated equally, it is contended, would eliminate the early childhood period of sex role stereotyping during which boys learn to become aggressive and girls learn to become caring. Freed from sex role stereotypes, it is argued, each person might learn to be assertive and tender, leading and following. Healthier attitudes, greater male/female understanding, and a more satisfying sexuality are thought to be the result (Cook, 1985).

Androgyny has been questioned. Kimlicka and associates (1983), for example, asked 204 women to complete the Bem sex-role inventory and other tests. Kimlicka and associates found that women who scored high in androgyny, as expected, tended to be better adjusted. A closer look showed that those scoring high in masculinity alone were also happier and had greater self-confidence. Perhaps some traits that are thought of as masculine, such as independence and assertiveness, and not androgyny, bring about a satisfying life in our society. Kimlicka's research prompted a reexamination of the fuller meaning of both androgyny and masculinity.

Other questions have been directed at the wisdom of calling personality traits masculine or feminine. Might it not be better to characterize personality attributes along some other dimension, say, social desirability? Being supportive, for example, is generally more desirable than being negative. Another suggestion has been to abandon the concept of androgyny altogether since it might unintentionally be continuing sex stereotypes. Women and men, it is argued, should be encouraged to maximize their best qualities without labeling them with any gender designation. In the long run, it may be that people who are resourceful, who act appropriately as each new situation arises, are best adjusted and most successful. It is their ability to understand, to analyze situa-

The androgynous person may get along better with both sexes since she or he shares some of the personality traits of both men and women.

Many nursery and other preschool facilities now encourage boys and girls to play and work together and learn from each other.

### Playing Dumb

How often do you know an answer but remain quiet, letting someone else appear more competent? Traditionally, women have seemed to "play dumb" more often than men. Hughes and Gove (1981) wondered just how frequently younger adults still hide their competence. They surveyed 2248 women and men over 18 years of age, representing a broad variety of groups and locations within the United States. The respondents were asked, "Have you ever pretended to be less intelligent or knowledgeable than you really are?" The subjects were also asked in which of seven situations they played dumb: (1) with a date, (2) with spouse, (3) with boss, (4) with coworkers,

(5) with friends, (6) with strangers, and (7) with children.

The results of the survey showed that if there was a tendency for women to play down their skills and abilities, it has noticeably diminished. In this research, it was found that men, not women, more often play dumb. Men were roughly twice as likely to play dumb both with their bosses and coworkers, than were women. Hughes and Gove concluded, "in fact, more men than women play dumb in nearly every situation—with friends and strangers, with bosses and coworkers, with dates and children."

tions and act productively, rather than traits called female or male that makes them more effective human beings (Cook, 1985; Lyons and Green, 1988).

### Conclusion

Almost two decades ago, Eleanor Maccoby and Carol Jacklin (1974) spent most of 3 years searching through over 2000 books and articles describing sex differences. They found many distinctions between the two sexes clearly explained, but few were backed by consistent experimental evidence. One distinction that did stand out was aggression: males were often found somewhat more aggressive than females. Even boys as young as 2 years were occasionally more verbally and physically forceful than girls. At the same time it was evident that aggression often appeared in both sexes and could be stimulated or moderated by parents, school, and society.

Achievement needs seem to be almost equal in both sexes, but they are often stimulated differently. Females are likely to achieve more in situations where competition is minimized. Males often respond to competition with greater effort to achieve.

Maccoby and Jacklin did not find evidence to conclusively say that personality differences are inborn or acquired. They did learn, however, the very considerable extent to which most personality attributes are closely shared by the sexes. Again, in personality, as in the other dimensions we have discussed, the two sexes are much more alike than they are different.

## APTITUDES

Are men or women smarter? Like all such questions, the answer is not a simple yes or no. Tests of general intelligence, such as the Wechsler Adult Intelligence

Scale, sometimes show an **intelligence quotient (IQ)** difference between the sexes. Before puberty, girls tend to receive slightly higher test scores than boys. By the later teen years, however, the IQ scores of adolescents are roughly equal. During adulthood when women and men are carefully matched for education and other background circumstances, it is difficult to find overall IQ differences between them. Perhaps the two sexes are not intellectually unequal but just develop at different rates (Ambron, 1985).

*intelligence quotient (IQ)*
Score obtained on an intelligence test.

### Mathematics

When general intelligence is separated into its components such as verbal, mathematical, and perceptual aptitudes, some gender differences have appeared. Camilla Benbow and Julian Stanley provoked a flurry of criticism and research activity when they announced that boys are better than girls in mathematics. They tested 9927 gifted children in the seventh and eighth grades and found, on average, the boys did better and more scored in the highest categories of mathematical aptitude. Benbow and Stanley reasoned that the children had taken the same math courses, were part of the same school system, and were equally intellectually gifted. Since the children had the same learning background and potential, Benbow and Stanley believed that the difference in mathematical aptitude between the boys and girls had to have, at least in part, a biological basis.

Gender differences in aptitude may be biological and/or cultural in origin.

A few years later, in response to criticism of their original work, the investigators reevaluated their methods and findings. Once again Benbow and Stanley (1983) concluded that the higher achievement of some boys in mathematical tasks is a fact, not a research error.

Other research has shown boys and men to be ahead in tasks often correlated with mathematics, such as quantitative and mechanical aptitudes. Boys tend to be better in visualizing an object like a cube or a gear and mentally figuring out its dimensions or uses. On tests requiring identification of tools and machine parts, boys and adolescent males also customarily do better than females. Most investigators have found boys are somewhat ahead of girls in mathematical and related tasks, but whether this is a cultural or a biological event is still being debated (Chipman et al., 1985).

### Language

Most evaluations of language in children have frequently shown girls to be ahead in verbal abilities. During the first few months of life babies cry and **vocalize.** Within 4 or 5 months they babble, combining vowels and consonants. A few months later they begin imitating some simple sounds made by others. By about 1 year of age most children say their first meaningful word. While there is a great deal of variation from child to child, in general girls appear to be somewhat ahead of boys in these early communication skills.

*vocalize*
Make sounds with the voice.

During later childhood, the difference in language abilities between many members of the two sexes may become marked. Boys between the ages of 3 and 10 more often have speech problems; more boys than girls are enrolled in speech or language therapy. Similarly, during the early school years, fewer girls are identified as having difficulties in learning to read.

Throughout adolescence girls typically do better in tests measuring verbal skills, reading, and language aptitude. They often have larger vocabularies, are

Women read much more than men. They buy many more books and borrow far more from libraries. Is this the result of social standards or inborn ability differences?

more accurate grammatically, and spell more correctly. Among individuals with less formal education, this sex difference may be even more pronounced. The young adult man with a minimal high school education is likely to read very little and his spoken grammar and articulation may depart considerably from standard English. Many women from the same socioeconomic groups with similar education often read more and use speech that is closer to the middle class norm (Pearson, 1985).

### Conclusion

Neither women nor men can claim to be intellectually superior as a group; though perhaps there are some specific aptitudinal distinctions. Girls and women as a group often get higher scores on tests measuring language skills. Mathematical and related tasks often seem to be better handled by boys and men. But when one actually compares individual test results, rather than averages, similarities rather than differences become apparent. Most boys and girls, women and men, get much the same scores, whatever aptitude is being measured. There is, in short, considerable overlap in all aptitudes for both sexes. The few distinctions that do occur often appear during infancy and childhood. These dissimilarities could have some biological roots, but school, social and learned expectations also clearly play an important role. We will not know just how much of the differences that have been observed are physically sex-linked or are caused by social learning until all people are provided equal opportunity and encouragement (Chipman et al., 1985).

## OCCUPATIONS

In a very distant past, 5000 and more years ago, hunting, gathering, and caring for the young were the essentials of human survival. In this primeval world, it

Men are increasingly assuming child-care roles once traditionally reserved for women, and women pursuing occupations once traditionally limited to men.

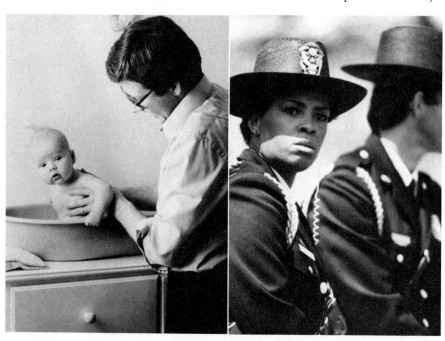

seemed only woman could sustain the life of the newborn. She was needed to nurse and care for the infants that followed each other every several years. No sooner did she stop nursing her 2- or 3-year-old, than, because her fertility was restored, she conceived again.

Man was usually stronger and faster than woman and, perhaps even more important, was basically free of child-rearing responsibility. As a result, he could spend days or weeks on the hunt and bring back whatever food he had killed or gathered. Thus some biological differences—pregnancy, lactation, and physical size—gave rise to a *division of labor*. This set in motion many of the occupational gender distinctions we still hold on to today (Chapter 1).

Woman as the homemaker and man as the breadwinner are vocational roles that may, historically, have had some biological basis. Most societies over the course of centuries have multiplied and elaborated these differences to produce *vocational stereotypes*. Just a generation ago, it was almost universally agreed that men worked outside the home and women were housewives. If women worked outside the home, they took on jobs that extended their caring or housekeeping role, such as teacher, nurse, or secretary. They also earned less money. Men were supposedly free to be whatever they chose, but they seldom assumed jobs that cultural forces, not biology, had set aside as "woman's work," such as telephone operator or airline stewardess. The man and the woman may not have liked the arrangement, but in the face of considerable social pressure there was little either could do (Benin, Agostinelli, 1988; Williams, Best, 1982).

Times, however, have changed and vocational stereotyping has decreased. Over the last decades, job titles have been revised to lessen vocational sex stereotyping (Table 7-1). Now many telephone operators are men; many police officers and business executives are women. There has been a steady growth toward equal representation by each sex in many occupations (Table 7-2). As might be expected, schoolchildren are often more flexible than adults in their career goals and aspirations. One study of 5600 high school seniors from 17 schools showed a marked redefinition of sex role expectation. Compared to

*Table 7-1*

**Unbiased Job Titles**

| Former title | Revised title |
| --- | --- |
| Airline stewardess | Flight attendant |
| Busboy | Waiter's assistant |
| Clergyman | Clergy |
| Credit man | Credit manager |
| Fireman | Fire fighter |
| Fisherman | Fisher |
| Foreman | Work supervisor |
| Laundress | Launderer |
| Maid | Household cleaner |
| Newsboy | Paper carrier |
| Office boy | Office helper |
| Saleslady | Sales clerk |
| Watchman | Guard |

*Table 7-2*

**Changes in Women's Employment**

| Occupation | Percentage of women | | | |
|---|---|---|---|---|
| | 1960 | 1972 | 1980 | 1990 (est.) |
| Accountants | 17 | 22 | 33 | 40 |
| Bank officers | n.l.* | 19 | 32 | 38 |
| Barbers | n.l. | 4 | 13 | 20 |
| Bus and other drivers | 1 | 4 | 8 | 12 |
| Engineers | n.l. | 0.8 | 3 | 5 |
| Lawyers and judges | n.l. | 4 | 12 | 16 |
| Physicians | n.l. | 9 | 12 | 16 |
| Sales clerks | 64 | 69 | 70 | 72 |
| School administrators | 25 | 26 | 36 | 40 |
| Social scientists | 19 | 21 | 35 | 40 |
| Teachers, college | 24 | 28 | 32 | 35 |
| Writers, artists, entertainers | 28 | 32 | 38 | 40 |

*In 1960, sex differences in employment were so pronounced that women were not even listed (n.l.) in many occupations. Source: U.S. Bureau of the Census, 1988 (1990 estimated percentages).

studies done 10 years previously, the vocational aspirations of girls and boys had considerably opened up. Nearly equal numbers of male and female students aimed for a variety of jobs and occupations ranging from accountant to zoologist (Sauter et al., 1980).

*In Sum*

There are few consistent personality differences between men and women. One that does appear frequently is aggression. Even if this trait is biologically rooted, it is heavily influenced by social learning and tradition. Many believe an androgynous combination of personality traits is a worthy goal in child rearing since it is held to lead to a more empathic, confident, and well-adjusted person. Most traits overlap so that comparisons between women and men show them to be much more alike than different.

Most aptitudes and abilities appear to be the same in women and men. There may be some differences in mathematical and language skills, possibly resulting from both biological and social circumstances. History, as well as biology, has contributed to limiting women and men to stereotyped occupational roles. Today the vocational prejudices that have defined jobs as appropriate only for one or the other sex are fading. The process is gradual, but it is now accepted that both sexes can capably be doctors, teachers, and firefighters.

## FINAL NOTE

It is not likely that women and men are exactly identical in every intellectual, social, and physical dimension. There may well be some sex-linked and innate differences in personality, aptitudes, and sexuality although distinctions do not make one sex better or worse than the other. What is most apparent is that in all areas, whether verbal skills, sexual motivation, or emotion, the sexes are much more alike than they are different.

Whatever the evidence for similarity, beliefs about inflexible differences between men and women persist. Some girls are brought up to think that they cannot do well in business. Others are taught that it is not ladylike to have healthy sexual needs. Men suffer also from prejudices that restrict their roles to narrowly defined masculine behaviors. A father may be convinced that it is unmanly to help raise his children or do housework. Beliefs such as these become **self-fulfilling prophecies.** They direct attitudes and expectations into traditional stereotypes. A society that maintains that ability and interest are unchangeably determined by X and Y chromosomes fails to look at the individual and denies each person her or his potential.

*self-fulfilling prophecy*
Making something happen (like failing a test) by convincing yourself it will happen.

*Summary*

Women and men are structurally fairly identical and respond to the same needs and emotions. When we speak in terms of averages some sex differences can be noted. From birth onward, males have usually tended to be larger, stronger, and more athletic than females. Currently, however, women's achievements in sports are increasing. In all physical skills and other human characteristics as well, there is considerable overlap between the sexes. In virtually all traits women and men seem more similar than different.

Traditionally, men have been described as having greater sexual interest than women. This observation has been supported by the seemingly greater frequency of male masturbation, interest in erotica, and sexual intercourse. Additional evidence has been suggested by the larger number of sexual relations among male as compared to female homosexuals. But as society becomes less restrictive and the role of women changes, these differences in sexual interest and activity seem to have become less marked.

Commonly held beliefs about the personalities of men and women maintain that men are more independent, aggressive, and logical. Women are supposedly more gentle and affectionate. Most of these stereotypes do not hold up to careful scientific scrutiny. Even when some personality distinctions do exist between the sexes, they are variations in degree rather than in kind. In all personality traits, substantial overlap exists between the sexes. Men and women are far more similar than different. People who have personality characteristics traditionally associated with males and also with females may be considered androgynous. They may develop their potential as people without regard to gender stereotypes.

Although no overall sex difference in general intelligence can be substantiated, males often show greater mathematical and mechanical aptitude, and females typically have greater language ability. But, again, there is great overlap in abilities between the sexes. Women may be successful mathematicians and engineers, and men may demonstrate their verbal skills as writers and speakers. Since our culture has tended to encourage different skills for each sex, it is difficult to determine to what extent mathematics and language distinctions are innate or learned.

Until recently, jobs were defined as clearly suitable just for women or men. The assumption was that most women would be homemakers or be employed as nurses, teachers, or secretaries. Men's jobs were far more varied. Today, job titles have been changed to free them from sex stereotyping. In the past two decades, there has been significant movement of women into areas of employment that were traditionally open only to men. Men too have increasingly assumed positions once largely reserved for women.

In personality, aptitude, and sexual interest, men and women are much more alike than they are different. Providing equal opportunity will allow every person to achieve full potential.

*For Thought and Discussion*

1  Which differences in physical ability between women and men seem more inherent and which more learned?
2  What evidence is there that the sexual interest or motivations of men and women differ? How and why do studies of homosexual behavior suggest distinctions in the sexual needs of women and men? How has society enlarged some seeming differences in the sexual interests and style of men and women?
3  How do both biology and learning influence personality traits like aggression, nurturance, and achievement in both sexes?
4  What proof is there, if any, that women or men are smarter? What specific aptitudes seem different in both sexes and why? How do innate and learned skills and attitudes contribute to job selection and career planning?
5  How do you feel about androgyny and about women and men fully sharing responsibilities and opportunities? What changes have you seen in the movement toward equal treatment of men and women?

*References*

Ambron, S.R. *Child Development.* New York: Holt, Rinehart, & Winston, 1985.
Athanasiou, R. Pornography: a review of research. In Wolman, B.B., and Money, J. (editors): *Handbook of human sexuality,* Englewood Cliffs, N.J.: Prentice-Hall, 1980.
Atwood, J.D., and Gagnon, J. Masturbatory behavior in college youth. *Journal of Sex Education and Therapy,* 1987, *13*(2), 35-42.
Bem, S.L. Beyond androgyny. Some presumptuous prescriptions for a liberated sexual identity. In Sherman, J., and Denmark, F. (editors): *Psychology of women: future directions of research.* New York: Psychological Dimensions, 1981.
Benin, M.H., and Agostinelli, J. Husbands' and wives' satisfaction with the division of labor. *Journal of Marriage and the Family,* May 1988, *50,* 349-361.
Benbow, C.P., and Stanley, J.C. Sex differences in mathematical reasoning ability: more facts. *Science,* 1983, *222,* 1029-1031.
Blumstein, P.W., and Schwartz, P. *American couples.* New York: Wm. Morrow, 1983.
Chipman, S.F., Brush, L.R., and Wilson, D.M. *Women and mathematics: balancing the equation.* Hillsdale, N.J.: L. Erlbaum Publishers, 1985.
Cook, E.P. *Psychological androgyny.* New York: Pergamon Press, 1985.
Cook, K., Kretchmer, A., Nellis, B., Lever, J., and Hertz, R. The *Playboy* readers' sex survey, (Part 3). *Playboy,* May 1983, 126.
Dowling, C. *The Cinderella complex: Women's hidden fear of independence.* New York: Summit, 1981.
Fisher, W.A., Branscombe, N.R., and Lemery, C.R. The bigger the better? Arousal and attributional responses to erotic stimuli that depict different size penises. *Journal of Sex Research,* 1983, *19,* 337-396.
Forbes, G.B., and King, S. Fear of success and sex-role: there are reliable relationships. *Psychological Reports,* 1983, *53,* 735-738.
Gallagher, W. Sex and hormones. *The Atlantic Monthly,* March 1988, 79-82.
Heiman, J.R. The physiology of erotica: women's sexual arousal. *Psychology Today,* April 1975, *8* (11), 90-94.

Hughes, M., and Gove, W.R. Playing dumb. *Psychology Today*, 1981, *15*, 74-80.

Hunt, M. *Sexual behavior in the 1970s*. Chicago: Playboy Press, 1974.

Kimlicka, T., Cross, H., and Tarnai, J. A comparison of androgynous, feminine, masculine, and undifferentiated women on self-esteem, body satisfaction, and sexual satisfaction. *Psychology of Women Quarterly*, 1983 (Spring), 7(3), 291-294.

Kinsey, A.C., Pomeroy, W.B., and Martin, C.E. *Sexual behavior in the human male*. Philadelphia: W.B. Saunders, 1948.

Kinsey, A.C., Pomeroy, W.B., and Martin, C.E. *Sexual behavior in the human female*. Philadelphia: W.B. Saunders, 1953.

Lyons, D.S., and Green, S.B. Sex role development as a function of college experiences. *Sex Roles*, 1988, *18*(1/2), 31-40.

Maccoby, E.E., and Jacklin, C. *The psychology of sex differences*. Stanford, Calif.: Stanford University Press, 1974.

McWhirter, N. (editor). *Guinness book of world records*. New York: Sterling, 1990.

Melson, G.F., and Fogel, A. Learning to care. *Psychology Today*, January 1988, 39-46.

Pearson, J.C. *Gender and communication*. Dubuque, Iowa: Wm. C. Brown, 1985.

Perper, T., and Weis, D.L. Proceptive and rejective strategies of U.S. and Canadian college women. *The Journal of Sex Research*. November 1987, 23(4), 455-480.

Petersen, J.R., Kretchmer, A., Nellis, B., Lever, J., and Hertz, R. The *Playboy* readers' sex survey (Parts 1 and 2). *Playboy*, January 1983, 108; March 1983, 90.

Pitcher, E.G. *Boys and girls at play: the development of sex roles*. Hadley, Mass.: Bergin & Garvey, 1985.

Pleck, J.H. Prisoners of manliness. *Psychology Today*, 1981, *15*, 69-83.

Rohner, R. Sex differences in aggression: phylogenetic and enculturation perspectives. *Ethos*, 1976, *4*, 57-72.

Rubenstein, C., and Tavris, C. Special survey results: 26,000 women reveal the secrets of intimacy. *Redbook*, September 1987, *169*, 147.

Sauter, D., Seidl, A., and Karbon, J. The effects of high school counseling experience and attitudes toward women's roles on traditional or nontraditional career choices. *Vocational Guidance Quarterly*, 1980, *28*, 241-249.

Symons, D. *The evolution of human sexuality*. Fair Lawn, N.J.: Oxford University Press, 1981.

U.S. Bureau of the Census. *Statistical abstract of the United States: 1988*. Washington, D.C.: U.S. Government Printing Office, 1988.

Williams, J.E., and Best, D.L. *Measuring sex stereotypes: A thirty-nation study*. Beverly Hills, Calif.: Sage, 1982.

Wolfe, L. *The Cosmo report*. New York: Arbor House, 1981.

---

*Suggested Reading*

Brothers, J. *The successful woman: how you can have a career, a husband, and a family—and not feel guilty about it*. New York: Simon & Schuster, 1988.
    A woman's guide to having and doing it all.

Doyle, J. *The male experience*. Dubuque, Iowa: Wm. C. Brown, 1983.
    A good attempt to describe the place of men and their varying and changing roles and responsibilities in today's society.

Fausto-Sterling, A. *Myths of gender: biological theories about women and men*. New York: Basic Books, Inc., Publishers, 1985.
    Anne Fausto-Sterling, a geneticist, presents evidence that disputes the hypothesis that the behavior of men and women is biologically and inherently different. A controversial and sometimes provocative book.

Tavris, C., and Wade, C. *The longest war*. New York: Harcourt Brace Jovanovich, Inc., 1984.
    A careful, sometimes subjective look at sex differences and an effort to improve male-female relationships.

## Part Three

# OUR SEXUAL SELVES

## Chapter 8

# Childhood and Adolescence
## Growing Up Sexual

**When you finish this chapter, you should be able to:**

Describe the growth of sexual awareness and behavior in infants and young children.

Define puberty and explain its effects on girls and boys.

Give a description of adolescent sexuality including masturbation, dating, petting, and intercourse.

Evaluate the relationship between adolescents and their parents.

Explain some of the causes and consequences of adolescent pregnancy.

Describe the character of, and necessity for, sex education.

A century ago it was widely believed, or perhaps more accurately it was hoped, that sexuality began in the early adult years. Some adolescent sexual stirrings were admitted, but actual physical experience was expected to take place later, only after marriage. Childhood was held to be unique. It was idealized as a time of innocence, free from the suspicious taint of sexuality (Chapter 1). Today, owing to the work of scholars such as Ellis, Freud, and Kinsey, we know that human sexual function begins with birth (Chapter 2). Just as infants take pleasure in eating and sleeping, they also seem to take delight in their sexual beings. In this chapter, we will trace the sexual development and activities of human beings from birth through adolescence.

## INFANCY

Children are sexual beings from the moment they are born. Sigmund Freud reported this observation, 75 years ago and shocked and outraged Europe (Gay, 1988). Often adults first become aware of their child's sexuality when they see their young son or daughter exploring his or her own genitals. Because this requires a fair amount of motor control, it is not likely to occur until many months after birth. But as early as during the first week of life, boys can be seen to have erections. Analogous to this, an early equivalent of vaginal lubrication may occur in girls after they are born. Both are reflexive reactions, although they do show that the child's sexual development has begun (Chapters 3 and 4).

The sexual interest and activities of infants are not limited to their genitals. Babies are highly responsive to skin contact. Body to body closeness and cuddling, as well as holding and stroking, produce smiles and pleasurable sounds. Such contact may not be sexual in an adult sense, but it does seem to stimulate sensual pleasure.

During the early months of infancy the mouth appears to be a special organ for pleasure. Children who nurse at their mother's breast and those who bottle feed can be seen toying with the nipple with their lips and tongue. Occasionally some boys have been observed to have an erection while sucking. This is likely not a direct sexual response, but suggests that the infant may be experiencing pleasure (Maier, 1988).

Interest in one's own, and other's, genitals may be evident during infancy.

Mothers, too, may have some sensual as well as emotionally satisfying feelings in response to nursing. Masters and Johnson (1966) observed that during nursing, much as in foreplay and intercourse, women's nipples may erect and the uterus rhythmically contract. A few mothers may be disturbed about their own good feelings or those of their child and have to be reassured that these responses are normal.

### One to two

Developmental patterns vary from child to child but the ability of infants to control their hands usually starts after the first half year of life. Wolman and

Money (1980) report that by 8 months of age the majority of children have begun to touch their own **genitals**. During the following months, pelvic rocking and thrusting develop. These motor skills are often sufficient to permit the child to masturbate, to stimulate the genitals until it appears that climax is reached. According to Kinsey et al. (1948, 1953), although only a few children reach orgasm during the first year of life, by the age of 2 a substantial number may have achieved a form of climax. The masturbatory techniques are often highly inventive, with dolls, blocks, pillows, toys, and blankets being used. One mother interviewed reported seeing her 19-month-old daughter masturbate to what appeared to be a climax.

> Kathy lay on her back and took her big stuffed Panda and wrapped her legs around it. Then she squeezed on it with her thighs and pulled it towards her. She pressed her vagina against it. She did this a few times and then rolled over with the Panda under her. She pressed her body against it and rocked her pelvis towards it too. Back and forth. After about two minutes of really working at this she seemed to have her climax. I mean she was really intense when she was doing it. Then, suddenly, she seemed flushed and sweaty and she just lay back and relaxed. Almost like an adult.

A few parents become disturbed when they notice any sort of sexual activity in their child. Some become almost phobic about touching their infants while washing, diapering, or dressing them. They do not want to brush against the penis or vulva because they have seen the pleasurable response this touch can evoke. Some adults are also careful in how they dress their children. They try to clothe them in garments that will not press or rub their genitals. These precautions will likely prove useless. Most youngsters will still in one way or another touch their sexual areas. Many children also appear to feel that clothing is a form of adult repression. The child removing his or her clothing and running around naked is engaging in a rebellious act frequently encountered between the ages of 1 and 2. Parents can expect their children to explore their genitals and go through periods when they reject clothing.

### Two to four

By the age of 2 or 3, it is common for children to show some affectional or sexual interest in each other. Sometimes sexual needs motivate what looks like wrestling or rough and tumble play. At other times, children may gently hug and kiss one another, or even pay attention to each other's genitals. Much of this play is in some measure the result of simple curiosity. It is the kind of inquisitiveness that results in boys comparing their penises or both sexes together studying how differently they are constructed.

At this age, too, attempts may be made at some form of sexual relations. Boys and girls, or members of the same sex, may lie together, holding, rubbing, and thrusting against each other. Estimates suggest that about half of all adults can remember such childhood erotic play, based on a combination of curiosity and pleasure (Kinsey et al., 1948, 1953; Roberts, 1981).

In Western nations, childhood sexuality is a source of considerable concern for many adults. From infancy onward, anxious parents may warn their children to keep their so-called private parts covered. Touching oneself in these areas, or even worse touching another, is strictly forbidden. Any violation of

*genitals*
The external sexual-reproductive organs; the penis and vagina.

Touching, hugging, kissing, pulling, and wrestling are common among young children. These behaviors may be a source of physical pleasure.

these rules can produce a scolding, a spanking, or an accusation of wickedness. As a result, many youngsters have learned by the time they are 3 or 4 that sex is supposedly fearful, shameful, and dirty. (See Focus: Do You Have Sex Guilt? later in this chapter.)

In several cultures, the sexual potential of infants and children seems to be more openly acknowledged. Until relatively recently, among the Yolunga people in Australia, sex play was taken for granted and it was not unusual to see very young children masturbate without being stopped. Among the Marquesa in the South Pacific, sex play often had a useful function. Crying infants were pacified by adults gently rubbing their genitalia. These people also believed that large labia were a sign of beauty. To encourage their growth, mothers occasionally pulled and rubbed the infant's labia hoping to make them more prominent and enhance their child's desirability as well as pleasure potential. Childhood attempts at coitus were accepted. Adults argued that since they were children, nothing serious, meaning no pregnancy, could occur (Ford and Beach, 1980). (See Focus: Restrictive to Permissive.)

## CHILDHOOD

At the beginning of childhood, at about 5 years of age, the child's biological maturity has considerably advanced. Boys and girls are physically capable of excellent motor control and because of increasing anatomical and hormonal development, much more sexually capable. It is not surprising, therefore, that by age 5, almost half of all children have experienced orgasm, or an equivalent, almost always the result of masturbation (Kinsey et al., 1948, 1953; Roberts, 1981).

By this period, kissing, cuddling, and embracing are also quite well developed. Some of this hugging takes place with adults as a form of parental affection, but some is a form of erotic play with other children. During the kindergarten year, distinct affectional partnerships can already be observed.

The kindergarten relationships sometimes seem to be authentic romances. The boy or girl waits for the special friend; they smile warmly and look at each other lovingly; they hold hands and embrace one another. They may even secretly try some sexual experimentation. When there are signs that two children especially like one another, other kindergarteners may gossip about them and taunt and tease. In fact, among children in this age group, gossip and speculation about who likes whom, and which two will supposedly eventually marry, is common.

By ages 7 or 8 kissing games may start. Curiosity is also likely to expand. Why do older girls have big breasts? Can other boys make their penis hard? Adult and parental sexual behavior sometimes becomes the object of unwanted attention. Inquisitive children may want to see their parents naked or having intercourse. Sometimes youngsters even become aggressively curious, picking up the babysitter's skirt or trying to persuade her or him to talk about sex.

Toilet activities are often especially fascinating for children. Possibly because of the proximity of excretory and sexual organs there is sometimes confusion between the two. The fact that parents label elimination as well as masturbation "dirty" may convince the child that defecating or urinating is a kind of sexual activity. It could take several more years before the child becomes a

Some children playing together make body motions while clothed that suggest coitus. Such behavior is usually upsetting to parents but can provide an opportunity for responsible and understanding sex education.

Kindergarten children can develop strong friendships that in some ways resemble adult romances.

young adolescent and begins to clearly differentiate toilet and sexual functions (Gay, 1988).

By later childhood, a year or two before **puberty**, a very small proportion of girls and boys experience coitus. Some of this occurs because older siblings or friends initiate the activity, but much is also the result of curosity. Estimates vary, but it is likely that almost 5% of children have their first intercourse before age 12. At this age, too, some erotic play with the same sex sometimes appears. Most will be limited to mutual masturbation, but the mouth and anus may also be involved (Kinsey et al., 1948, 1953; Roberts, 1981).

*puberty*
The period in early adolescence when a child becomes sexually mature.

### Personality

It should be remembered that sexual development occurs in a larger **context** of personality and gender maturation. The infant and childhood years are critical to the development of trust, self-identity, and basic feelings of security. Parents who are punitive of a child's sexuality are also likely to be harsh and unaccepting in general. These attitudes could result in a fearful, insecure person as well as one who is sexually handicapped. The point to keep in mind is that sexual feelings and behaviors are part of a total personality that is shaped by biological needs as well as parental and social influences.

*context*
The physical, psychological, and social environment.

---

Sexual interest and activity often begin during infancy and develop gradually until the beginning of adolescence. Although our society disapproves of childhood sexual experimentation, such play is common. By the end of childhood many girls and boys have developed some affectional relationships with other children. A few have also masturbated and a very small number have had sexual relations.

*In Sum*

---

## Restrictive to Permissive

Ford and Beach (1980) have described cultures on a continuum ranging from sexually *restrictive* to *permissive*. Restrictive cultures try to prevent children from learning about sex or give them fictional explanations of reproduction. Words to describe sexual activities are considered improper, and any form of nudity is forbidden. Premarital sex as well as masturbation are generally prohibited. Childhood sex play is almost always punished. For example, among the Ashanti in Ghana (Africa) parents expressly warn their children that touching or stimulating their genitals will result in ill health or misfortune.

Permissive societies, Ford and Beach (1980) write, do not permit "everything," nor are they without rules. *Incest,* sexual relations with close relatives, is typically prohibited as is abuse and exploitation. Such societies, however, appear to accept behavior that most other cultures reject. Childish sex play is usually fairly open. Masturbation is fully accepted and a variety of sexual behaviors are sometimes encouraged. Among the Chewa in Africa it was believed that children should be sexually active from the earliest ages to assure their fertility. In the Trobriand Islands, boys and girls from 6 or 7 years on may be taught intercourse and engage in coitus with other children and adults. Sex instruction begins early, and it is realistic and detailed. (Many of these native cultures have been influenced by the West and have become less permissive.)

Where on the anthropological restrictive-permissive scale does our society stand? The evidence is mixed. Most American families are not what Ford and Beach consider permissive. But neither are most homes as restrictive as they were a few generations ago, during the Victorian era (Chapter 1). Some parents and schools provide children with a fairly sound sex education and recognize childish sex play as usually harmless. At the same time there is sometimes opposition to all sex education and much that does occur emphasizes biology and restraint. Some states have laws prohibiting sexual relations before marriage, homosexuality, and many other common forms of sexual expression. Simultaneously, half of all states have abolished laws regulating private sexual acts between consenting adults (Chapter 20). As a whole, we cannot be easily described as either a restrictive or a permissive society. Perhaps we are somewhere near the center and occasionally drift toward one extreme or the other. Where do *you* stand on the restrictive to permissive continuum?

## ADOLESCENCE

### Puberty

During their childhood years, boys and girls are only partially sexually developed. In both sexes, the genitalia are small; secondary sex characteristics such as developed breast and beard are virtually absent; and reproduction is not possible. Then at about the time the teen years begin, fairly sudden and dramatic changes occur in hormonal chemistry. In a matter of a few years a child will be transformed into a young adult. *Puberty* is the term used to describe the period during which a child becomes sexually mature and reproductively capable.

In girls, pubertal changes may begin as early as age 10 or 11, or wait until the child is 13 or even older. When puberty does start, early signs ordinarily include breast enlargement, pubic and underarm hair, a slight lowering of vocal pitch, and a spurt in weight and height. The first menstruation, often an inconsistent and irregular discharge, frequently follows the earlier signs of puberty, although it may precede them (Chapter 3).

Puberty in boys begins later than in girls, so that males may be 14, 15, or even 16 before sexual maturation is evident. A typical first male sign is enlargement of the penis and testes followed by the appearance of pubic hair. Soon the voice deepens, height and weight increase rapidly, and toward the end of adolescence facial hair develops. Some boys also experience a nocturnal emission, often accompanied by a sexual dream. The child who is totally unprepared for this experience may find it frightening (Chapter 4).

The two sexes become reproductively capable during early **adolescence.** Live sperm, in sufficient quantity for fertilization, are produced by most boys within a year or two after puberty starts. The uterus and associated organs are sufficiently developed, and a monthly ovum is readied in most girls by age 14. Thus a large majority of 15-year-old boys and 14-year-old girls are biologically capable of being parents.

**Adjustment**   Puberty can be an uncomfortable period for youngsters. To begin with, the 10- and 11-year-old girls and boys who shared the same classes and many of the same games and interests now seem to develop in different directions. During the early pubertal years, girls tend to be developmentally about 2 years ahead of boys. It is common to see 13-year-old girls, tall and feminine and looking very much like young women, while boys the same age still appear as boys. In a few years the maturational level in both sexes will be equal, but at the beginning of adolescence, the uneven growth rate of boys and

*adolescence*
The period in human life between puberty and adulthood; usually the teen years from age 13 to 19.

The beginning adolescent years are marked by an accelerating interest in the other sex.

*Figure 8-1*
All these children are 14 years old. At this age girls are usually developmentally ahead of boys. In both sexes development varies widely in children of the same age.

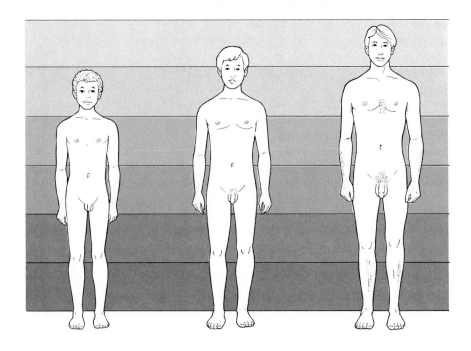

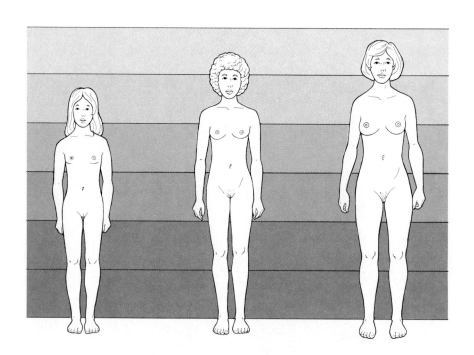

girls may result in some awkward moments for both. The seventh grade dance may see some uncomfortable partnerships between tall, sexually developed girls, and smaller child-appearing boys.

Another difficult adjustment for both girls and boys is compelled by the considerable maturational variation within each sex. Although one youngster may be quite well developed by age 13, another may not reach the same sexual-maturational level until age 17. The result is that in any group of young adolescents, some will appear almost fully grown and distinctly feminine or masculine, while other same-aged teenagers still appear to be children. The teenaged boys and girls who develop earlier often take great pride in their young adult body and dimensions. Those who develop later, although their slower maturation is normal, may worry that something is wrong or that they are somehow inadequate.

Parents and society often add to the self-consciousness boys and girls feel during puberty. In primitive cultures there is frequently a rite of passage. Children and adults celebrate the pubertal passage from child to adult with dance, feasting, prayer, and other initiation ceremonies. Remnants appear in our own society, such as confirmation in many Christian faiths and the Jewish bar mitzvah at age 13.

Parents often do their part to heighten their children's awareness of a transformation by suddenly restricting them. As puberty, and particularly the menses, begins, girls are likely to be told that now they are "women," and may no longer climb trees or play rough games. Boys who are still playing with girls may now be ridiculed by their pubertal friends and urged by their parents to pursue supposedly more masculine games like football. In a few instances, too, parents may appear to become somewhat distant. As fathers and mothers recognize the pubertal signs of sexual development in their children, some become reluctant to continue the physical affection, the hugs and kisses, they bestowed earlier. The result may be that the young adolescent sometimes feels rejected and isolated, ill at ease with his or her emerging adulthood.

Puberty and the early adolescent years means new bodies and new expectations, new emotional, school and parental demands. A person still in many ways a child is seemingly faced with a perplexing array of dilemmas. Anne Petersen (1987) carefully interviewed and tested over 300 teenagers to determine how well these challenges were handled. Peterson found girls and boys who matured most rapidly seemed to be more pleased with themselves and were more frequently viewed positively by their friends and by adults. But even adolescents who entered puberty later, generally did well. In fact as a whole, the sample Petersen studied managed the challenges of adolescence quite competently; 85% of her teenagers were satisfied and capable youngsters. Puberty and the early adolescent years present profound adjustment challenges, but the research suggests the large majority of teenagers cope nicely.

### Masturbation

*Masturbation* is the self-stimulation of the genitalia to orgasm. Most often it starts and is at a peak during adolescence. In some people, particularly younger children, masturbation may not result in **climax**. But the rhythmic massaging, stroking, or the like is kept up because it feels good. In a few instances, too, it is not the penis, vagina, or clitoris that is the object of mastur-

Menstruation is described in Chapter 3.

*climax*
Sexual climax is synonymous with orgasm.

batory attention. Although it is rare, there are people who can reach climax by stimulating their own breasts, anus, or other sensitized bodily part.

Nearly every boy and girl who masturbates is aware that it is disapproved by many adults. There are also ample historical precedents for fear. The Old Testament viewed masturbation as an unmitigated evil. Medieval physicians and Victorian experts were convinced masturbation caused insanity, tuberculosis, and blindness (Chapter 1). There were, surprisingly, a few enlightened voices. The seventeeth century physician, Sinibaldi, approved of masturbation, pointing out that not only did it allegedly prevent disease, but it supposedly improved the complexion. Until well into this century, however, the weight of religious, medical, and authoritative opinion was that masturbation was undesirable. Even relatively modern mental health experts joined the chorus, with

*Figure 8-2*
Masturbation.

Freud and other psychoanalysts pronouncing masturbation a childish fixation and evidence of immaturity (Gay, 1988).

Guilt about masturbation and fear of its alleged consequences can be emotionally destructive. The child, adolescent, or adult who is convinced masturbation is wrong, for whatever reason, may well develop any number of psychological symptoms. They may, for example, become anxious, isolate themselves, or seem very irritable and suspicious. We must stress, however, that not only is there no valid evidence that masturbation is evil or immature, but that everything we know today shows it is normal and harmless. Currently masturbation is recommended by some physicians and counselors as a healthy way to relieve sexual needs and tensions. Some sex therapists also suggest that masturbation should be learned to be a pleasurable experience so that it can contribute to gratifying sexual intercourse with a partner (Chapter 17).

Some sex therapists believe masturbation can help people learn about their own sexuality and could lead to satisfying coital relations with a partner (Chapter 17).

**Frequency**  For most girls and boys masturbation is the first frank sexual experience. In the 1940s, Kinsey and his associates reported that by the mid teens, close to 90% of males and about 50% of females masturbated. Studies in the 1980s show these percentages had increased. A fair estimate suggests that today nearly three fourths of all girls will be masturbating by adolescence and another 10% or so will wait until their 20s to start. By adulthood, 9 out of 10 men and 8 of 10 women masturbate (Atwood, Gagnon, 1987; Kinsey et al., 1948, 1953).

The frequency of masturbation varies considerably. Some adolescents and adults do so only occasionally, no more than a few times a year. Most teen-aged boys, however, masturbate two, three, or more times a week. Girls at the same age average about once a week. There is, however, very considerable variation. There are adolescents who masturbate every day, or more often, and those who do not masturbate at all.

It is important to note that masturbation does not automatically end with marriage or another form of lasting partnership. Masturbation is an enjoyable sexual activity that may continue in its own right, regardless of whatever other sexual opportunities are available. What does happen is that the monthly frequency of masturbation goes down or up depending in part on the availability of a partner.

Masturbation is a normal sexual activity that is found at all ages in most people whether single, married, or in a relationship.

**Techniques and fantasy**  Masturbation is usually a solitary experience. As a result, arousal and excitement often depend on imagining sexual happenings. Boys and men, perhaps more often than women, depend on erotic books, pictures, and films to stimulate thinking. Both sexes, however, also use their own fantasies to become aroused and accompany masturbation. Three fourths of women and men imagine intercourse with a friend. Relations with a stranger and group sex scenes are also popular. Less common, but encountered occasionally among many people, are fantasies of forced sex and/or homosexual relations (Table 8-1).

Most males masturbate by holding the erect penis in their hand and then stroking up and down. Some move the skin down and up and over the corona and glans. Others use a lubricant such as a surgical gel or baby oil and then glide their hand up and down the entire penis. Females, contrary to the common belief of many men, do not usually insert objects into their vagina. Most

People who fantasize forced sex do not usually long for such experiences in reality. In fantasy the force another person uses is totally controllable— completely safe. In the real world, force is uncontrollable and traumatic.

*Table 8-1*

**Fantasies While Masturbating**

| Fantasy | Percentage who said they often had fantasy* | |
|---|---|---|
| | Male | Female |
| Intercourse with friend | 75 | 80 |
| Intercourse with stranger | 47 | 21 |
| Group sex: intercourse with more than one person | 33 | 18 |
| Being seduced | 14 | 28 |
| Sex scenes involving force | 10 | 14 |
| Homosexual scenes | 7 | 11 |

Data from Friday, 1984; and Hunt, 1974.
*Many respondents reported they often had more than one fantasy, therfore totals add up to more than 100%.

female masturbation consists of rubbing or stimulating the clitoris and/or labia with one or several fingers. The breasts and nipples may be simultaneously stroked. A few members of both sexes sometimes touch or manipulate their anus while masturbating.

A small number of both adolescents and adults masturbate by rubbing or pushing against a pillow, mattress, or the like. Another increasingly popular technique is for a woman to use an electrical vibrator, which she applies to the genital area. There are also vibrators for men, as well as life-size, air-inflated female rubber dolls with advertised "realistic" vaginal and oral openings. These devices are employed by very few (Chapter 19).

### Beginning sexual relationships

There is a moment at some time during the early pubertal years when the familiar girl or boy, once played with or ignored, becomes warmly appealing. Childhood play now seems secondary as sexual needs assert themselves. The adolescent feels moved toward establishing a relationship much deeper and more intimate than anything experienced in childhood.

**Dating**   All societies devise ways in which adolescent boys and girls can pair off and eventually marry. Historically, and still in some nations today, the pairing was arranged by parents or marriage brokers. When the young women and men met, their encounter and all subsequent activities were frequently supervised by a chaperone. In our own society, adult-sponsored meetings are uncommon and chaperones rarer still. Adolescents meet one another in school, at a party, or in a common interest group such as a church club or hiking organization. In formal terms, American mate selection is through **free choice**. We may feel that free choice is quite normal, but it was a process that appalled our forebears for they believed that parental wisdom was far superior to adolescent decision.

A generation ago, adolescent pairing followed a largely standardized dating routine. The ritual could start as early as the beginning high school years, although some students might not participate until college. The method required

*free choice*
Selection of dates and future spouse by individuals and not their parents.

the boy to ask the girl for a date for a weekend evening. Good form necessitated the request be made no later than Wednesday; to ask after that was to risk rejection, whether or not the girl actually had another date.

At the appointed time the boy called for the girl in her home or college dormitory, and they went to a movie, party, or performance. This was followed by a visit to a candy or ice cream shop. Later on, in the boy's car, a corner of the lounge in her dormitory, or some other secluded spot, a good bit of necking was expected to take place.

Dating became quite an elaborate social game. Sociology texts written in the 1940s and 1950s recount the many complex and varied motives behind dates. Sometimes a girl would date a high-status male, perhaps because he was an athletic hero or had an impressive car, simply to elevate her own prestige. Boys might date because a girl had a reputation for being "easy," meaning sexually available. Both sexes could be motivated to date because the friendship might provide an entry into a prestigious circle of friends. The list of needs fulfilled by dating and the sexual and exploitative maneuvers were vast and frequently had little to do with friendship or entertainment. But for many adolescents, dating did provide a relatively easy and structured way of getting to know the other sex and initiate some degree of communication and sexual relationship.

For many couples dating is limited to one or two occasions. Then either the boy or girl decides they have little interest in the other, or someone more promising comes along, and the relationship ends. If dating continues then the couple may fall into the category of **going steady**. Ordinarily this means that the two see only one another and do not permit any dating or equivalent socialization with others. A few couples, however, let it be known that although they are going steady and that their relationship is most important, they are still free to date others (Peterson et al., 1983).

*going steady*
A relationship in which a couple who is dating agree to date only each other.

Dating helps define the qualities desired in a potential mate.

Older single people in their thirties, forties, and beyond often still follow the dating practices they learned as adolescents (Chapter 9).

*necking*
Kissing and hugging without other erotic touch.

*petting*
Kissing and erotically stimulating another person without having sexual intercourse.

First intercourse may occasionally be difficult because of a resistant hymen or an involuntary tightening of the vagina (Chapters 3, 17). Sometimes, too, a bit of vaginal bleeding occurs. The male may also lose his erection or climax almost immediately, and further attempts at coitus may only compound the problem. First attempts that are frustrating and fearful could cause persistent problems (Chapter 17).

**Dating today**   The dating ritual is still intact although in many parts of the United States its formality has lessened considerably. Some high school teenagers are unfamiliar with the date as such. They think of their circle of male and female peers as friends and they may talk on Thursday or Friday about what might be fun to do during the weekend. Further, while in the traditional date the male usually paid all expenses, in the more current form of friends doing things together, cost is likely to be shared.

In those groups that do not practice formal dating girl/boy protocol has also changed. In the traditional date it was only the man who could telephone the woman and make a date or start the going steady process. The girl may have hoped the boy would call, but she did not dare take the initiative. Today the girl as well as the boy can telephone, show a special interest, and try to encourage a relationship to continue.

**Petting, necking**   The generation before us made very careful distinctions among necking, light, and heavy petting. **Necking** was defined as kissing, with perhaps an occasional hug, but all important activity was really above the neck. Fifty years ago even relatively conservative parents might consent to their adolescent children doing a little necking in the living room after a date.

Light **petting** was a little more daring, involving primarily a good deal of embracing and the boy touching and caressing the girl's breasts. Heavy petting was defined as the manual or oral stimulation of the genitalia. When Kinsey and his colleagues (1948, 1953) interviewed 1940s adolescents, nearly all of them had necked or engaged in light petting. Even manual genital play had been experienced by 90% of the males and 50% of the females. But the "heaviest" petting, namely oral-genital contact, was true for only about a fifth of teenaged boys and girls. A half century later, the proportion of adolescents who have included such petting in their sexual interactions has increased to well over three fourths of the population (Hunt, 1974).

McCabe and Collins (1984) have found that some degree of light to heavy petting is now found on most first dates and in almost all relationships that go beyond several dates. These researchers administered dating questionnaires to college students and found that intimacy increased as dating continued. First dates often included light kissing and necking and perhaps breast touch. After several dates genital stimulation was frequent. Couples who considered themselves to be going steady often progressed to oral-genital contact and sexual intercourse. At the same time, a few young women and men surveyed continued to confine their dating sexual activity to necking and relatively light petting (Lawrance et al., 1984).

**Intercourse**   The proportion of adolescents having intercourse has steadily increased during this century. A generation ago fewer than half of all adolescents had sexual intercourse before marriage. When coitus did take place it was most likely only with the one person the teenager would eventually marry. Today by age 15 one sixth of all adolescents have had intercourse, and by age 20 the number approximates 7 out of 10. Furthermore, intercourse may take place after relatively short acquaintance.

But this is only a partial picture. For most young dating adolescents, the initiation of intercourse is still related to the degree the partners become involved with one another. McCabe (1987) studied 1637 young dating couples and found that while men often wanted intercourse earlier and more often, both sexes desired intercourse almost equally as their relationship deepened and became more committed. For many if not most teens, coitus occurs in the context of an ongoing "serious" relationship (See Sexual Standards, Chapter 9) (Coles and Stokes, 1985).

The beginning attempts at intercourse may or may not be satisfying. When first intercourse occurs in the context of an ongoing relationship it is more likely to proceed smoothly and be pleasurable for both. But for some youngsters the first experience can be a difficult and frightening one. One partner, or both, may feel coerced, intimidated, or tense. The very act of inserting the penis in the vagina can provoke anxiety for both the girl and boy. When questioned about their first experiences, over half of all women and nearly as many young men recall feeling afraid, disappointed, or worried. Typically there are concerns about being discovered, pregnancy, disease, and guilt. On the other hand, the first experience can also have affirmative elements. For some adolescents, beginning coitus brings intimacy, joy, pleasure, and fulfillment. Perhaps most important, for nearly all adolescents starting coitus leaves them with a mixture of positive as well as negative feelings (Coles and Stokes, 1985; Weis, 1985).

Given the impermanent nature of many adolescent relationships, there are few teenagers who have intercourse regularly. For most persons the years between ages 12 and 20 are marked by only brief periods in which coitus is a common sexual outlet.

The increasing danger of AIDS, acquired immunodeficiency syndrome (Chapter 16), has also entered the consciousness of adolescents. For many this has further decreased the availability of partners and the frequency of coitus (Carroll, 1988). As a result, masturbation remains the most common and dependable sexual activity for adolescents and, in fact, for many single people (Chapter 9) regardless of age.

**Homosexual relations**    During the adolescent years some teenagers explore sexual and/or affectional relations with members of their own sex. Such homosexual interactions may involve deep emotional feelings as well as mutual genital stimulation by hand or mouth, kissing and caressing and other sexual excitation. Cook et al. (1983) and the Kinsey surveys, (1948, 1953) suggest that about 10% of girls and 20% of boys have one, two, four, or more homosexual experiences during adolescence. For some these early homosexual contacts cause a good deal of anxiety and guilt. For others they are the beginning of an adult homosexual orientation. For most however these teenage homosexual experiences do not lead to adult homosexuality and are seen as attempts to examine and define sexual and affectional needs.

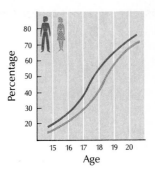

*Figure 8-3*
Percentage of unmarried people who have had intercourse by the ages indicated; the cumulative proportion of men and women having intercourse for the first time at each age differs slightly.
(Data: Coles, Stokes, 1985; Peterson, et al. 1983; and others.)

A few pages further on we will note one third of all adolescents do not regularly use birth control methods. There are nearly 1,000,000 teenage pregnancies every year.

Homosexuality, gay, and lesbian life-styles are described in Chapter 13.

*In Sum*

As the adolescent years begin, boys and girls experience a spurt in physical and psychological development. Pubertal changes often start earlier in girls than in boys and are frequently irregular, sometimes leading to some maturational unevenness and discomfort. By the middle teen years, both sexes are usually biologically fully developed. Masturbation is the most common adolescent sexual activity and despite beliefs to the contrary is harmless. Heterosexual relations also begin during this period, often with dating. Dating may lead to steady relationships and sexual intimacy. During early adolescence sex may be limited to kissing and petting, but for a small portion of teenagers coitus begins. Toward the end of adolescence over three fourths of boys and girls will have had intercourse. Homosexual experiences in adolescence are not infrequent, but most of the time do not seem to lead to this orientation.

## ADOLESCENTS, PARENTS, AND SOCIETY

Today sexual intercourse among adolescents is still disapproved by most parents, but many accept some petting and masturbation.

Human beings are biologically adult, meaning capable of reproduction, at the beginning of the second decade of life. In fact, in many less technologically advanced cultures and in our own past, postpubertal 15- and 16-year-olds had all the privileges and responsibilities of adulthood. Today our society's standard of living demands a long period of education and dependency. The result is that a *biological adult,* a person between ages 12 and 20, is still considered a child or minor according to most laws.

The conflict between the adolescent's physical adulthood and the way society and parents treat him or her as a child is sharply defined in the area of sexuality. Several decades ago, when Kinsey and his associates (1948) for the first time systematically explored sexuality, they were startled to find the potency of adolescent sexual energies. No group, they wrote, is more sexually capable or more active than teenagers between the ages of 16 and 20. Yet, despite the healthy sexual vigor of both teenage males and females, society makes virtually no provision whatsoever for its legitimate expression. In fact, the expected and ordinary sources of sexual outlet, Kinsey observed, are deemed illegal or socially disapproved. That is, coitus is forbidden, and masturbation is often frowned on.

Kinsey wrote several decades ago, but the picture does not seem to have changed much. To elicit the current feeling of adults about adolescent sexuality, Borhnstedt, Freeman, and Smith (1982) asked a representative sample of 1,002 residents of Los Angeles their attitude concerning a number of family situations.

66% of adults agree a father should tell a local pharmacist not to sell his son more condoms after the druggist reported the 14-year-old had bought some.

71% of the adults interviewed backed the idea that a 12-year-old should not read books that had a few sexual references or see a movie that contained some nude scenes.

84% of the adults would insist their 15-year-old son leave the door open when in his room with his girlfriend.

90% of those surveyed would not let their 15-year-old daughter spend the weekend with her college boyfriend.

Many adolescents and parents frequently disagree. They are in conflict about when they should be home at night, with whom they may be friends, and even what they may read or watch on television. These differences are often rooted in the adult expectation that adolescents should refrain from sexual activity.

## Church and state

Both the church and the state come to the aid of parents trying to curb the sexuality of their adolescent children. Masturbation, the most frequent adolescent sexual outlet by far, particularly comes in for powerful censure in the Judeo-Christian view. According to Genesis 38:8-10 when Onan "spilled his seed" on the ground, the Lord was displeased and He slew him. Some interpretations see Onan's act as an early form of birth control. Many other scholars see it as a condemnation of masturbation.

Civil law, too, can be harsh. In many states a woman must reach the age of 18 before she can legally give her consent to intercourse. Consequently, intercourse with a woman who is younger than 18, even if she is unquestionably willing or even clearly initiates the coitus, is illegal, an act of **statutory** rape. Thus in some states a 16-year-old boy, making love to his 17-year-old girlfriend, can, if apprehended, be convicted of rape and jailed for periods of up to 20 years. Fortunately for most adolescents this law is rarely applied (Chapter 20).

## The media

The world in which adolescents seek their appropriate place is not a simple one; it abounds with mixed messages. Their parents and their faith have probably counseled sexual restraint while a conflicting message is beamed at teenage boys and girls by the media (Chapter 19). Motion pictures, television, advertisements, and songs depict the allure of sexuality, the seeming joy of rebellion, the gratification that comes from being young and sexy. Lisa Ray and her colleagues (1988) did a content analysis of the lyrics of rock music from the 1950s to the 1980s. The researchers found that while most supposedly sang about "love," sexual references and persuasions were found in one third of all the lyrics. Some songs were relatively subtle like "I chose you for the one, now we're having so much fun." Other lyrics were more explicit: "I'm cryin' for it, dying' for it, ooh ooh, Baby, you know what I need." Still other songs were even more direct, including phrases like "I want to do it now," "It feels so good," "Baby make love to me, hard, hard, hard."

Eleven percent of the songs linked sex and violence such as in "Along came Jones," which describes a woman being assaulted, tied up, and a buzz saw being turned on. Given the conflicting advice thrust upon adolescents, the prohibitions of parents, and the encouragements by friends and much of the media, it is little wonder that for some youngsters, adolescence is often a period marked by confused and anxious sexual behaviors.

## Running away

The conflict between parents and their adolescent children is most sharply dramatized by the tendency of some teenagers to run away. Each year, a million adolescents in the United States flee from their homes. Some leave an abusive father or mother. Just as often, however, teenagers run away because they think they cannot really talk to their parents or hope to have their needs understood. Quite a few, too, are troubled by pregnancy, impending arrest or school failure. They believe they are escaping social and sexual restrictions and attitudes they consider unbearable.

Until the beginning of this century it was common for adolescents, children

Most of the major faiths still forbid masturbation. In 1988 Pope John Paul II reaffirmed the Church's strong opposition to masturbation as well as premarital intercourse.

*statutory*
According to the law or "statute." In this case, it means the act in and of itself is unlawful regardless of whether or not it was consenting.

## Ask Yourself: Do You Have Sex Guilt?

Circle the following statements (−1), (0), (+1) for False, Unsure, or True. Give your honest feeling and not the answer you believe is correct.

|  | False | Unsure | True |
|---|---|---|---|
| 1. High school sex education classes stimulate students to try sexual relations. | −1 | 0 | +1 |
| 2. Sexual relations before marriage are always wrong | −1 | 0 | +1 |
| 3. Masturbation is immature, childish behavior. | −1 | 0 | +1 |
| 4. Sex play in children should be strictly punished. | −1 | 0 | +1 |
| 5. The thought of having sexual intercourse often disgusts me. | −1 | 0 | +1 |
| 6. It's wrong to feel sexual desires for a person you don't even know. | −1 | 0 | +1 |

|  | False | Unsure | True |
|---|---|---|---|
| 7. Some sex practices, even if the partners fully agree, are unnatural. | −1 | 0 | +1 |
| 8. I always find sexy pictures and stories repulsive. | −1 | 0 | +1 |
| 9. Men are just interested in sex and will tell a woman anything to get it. | −1 | 0 | +1 |
| 10. Decent women don't really like sex but use it to trap a man. | −1 | 0 | +1 |
| Totals | | | _____ |

### Scoring

Add the total number of −1 and +1. Subtract the smaller number from the larger one. Be sure to assign the correct plus (+) or minus (−) sign.

aged 14 or 15, to leave home, become apprenticed to a tradesperson, marry, or just "seek their fortune." Today, some adolescents who run away still follow this tradition and manage to find a job and begin a career. Most teenagers who flee their homes, however, return and often with some professional help establish a better relationship with their parents. A few adolescents become persistent runaways, returning home, but then fleeing again.

Ultimately close to one in five of all runaways becomes involved in stealing, drug use, or prostitution. In fact, runaway teenagers are often a major source for the sex industry (Chapter 19). Toward the end of their teen years they may

### Interpretation

If you have a score of seven, eight, or more, you may have a good bit of sex guilt and sometimes find sex a distressing area in your life. Scores of four to seven suggest a fair amount of sex guilt, which might occasionally interfere a little with establishing good social and sexual relationships. Low scores, three or less, suggest just a little sex guilt, a situation that is fairly common. If your total adds up to a minus score, $-5$ or $-6$, you have very little if any sex guilt and should enjoy healthy sexual-affectional relations. High minus scores ($-9$ or $-10$) show that you are both well informed and free of most guilt feelings.

### Sex guilt

This informal survey is based on the work of D.L. Mosher (1980), who has extensively explored sex guilt and its impact. Sex guilt is an anxious, punishing emotion that is triggered by violating or thinking about violating very restrictive personal standards of sexual behavior. People very high in sex guilt often avoid sex topics or education and have difficulty becoming aroused and enjoying sexual relations even with their own spouses. In fact, sex guilt is one of the chief causes of the sexual problems discussed in Chapter 17.

Sex guilt frequently originates in childhood. Often people who have a great deal of guilt were punished as children for asking questions about sex, using sexual words, or touching their genitals. As adults, many youngsters raised in such circumstances believe sex is dirty, wrong, and immoral, and have very high restrictive standards.

### Reducing sex guilt

Severe sex guilt can be a handicapping emotion. It may also be difficult to overcome in a society such as ours that continually gives conflicting messages. Many parents and religious and other authorities stress restraint. They prohibit premarital intercourse and try to forbid petting and masturbation. At the same time the eroticism often found in movies, popular music, and television seems to be urging continual sexual adventure. Whichever way an adolescent or adult turns, they can feel they are displeasing someone or failing to live up to an expectation. The following suggestions can help alleviate some sex guilt and lead to more fulfilling relationships.

*Education* Learn about sexuality, contraception, different moral and ethical standards. Replace misinformation with knowledge.

*Recognition* Become aware that sex is an inherent and healthy part of life. It is neither dirty nor disgusting but a pleasurable and vital function.

*Ethics* Learn or develop an ethical code of sexual conduct that avoids coercion or exploitation. Let your attitude and behavior emphasize responsibility, affection, and sharing.

become sex entertainers such as topless dancers, appear in "adult" films, or engage in prostitution. While girls are much more involved in prostitution, boys too may sell sexual services (Chapter 19). As psychologist Nick Lestardo, director of Larkin Street Services in San Francisco, explains, "Male prostitution is a good way to make $75 to $200 a night. Many of these boys have already been sexually abused. They realize nobody will hire a 15-year-old for a conventional job. They hear, 'It's not so horrible.' Twenty-five bucks for 10 minutes sounds like a lot of money to kids" (Hersch, 1988).

Alone and adrift, many adolescent runaways may be exploited by unscrupulous adults.

We live in a relatively permissive society that in many ways encourages sexuality. At the same time we do not seem to equally encourage responsible and educated attitudes towards relationships and contraception.

## TEENAGE PREGNANCY

Every year close to a million unmarried women age 19 or younger unintentionally become pregnant. Over three hundred thousand fetuses will be aborted, while nearly a half million babies will be born. Put another way, each year 1 out of every 20 adolescent women has a baby. This teenage pregnancy rate is among the highest in the world. Comparing ourselves with other nations that are as, or more, sexually permissive than the United States is revealing. The United States teenage pregnancy rate is roughly double that of Canada and Sweden and 5 times higher than that of Holland or Switzerland (Maciak, et al., 1987).

Teenage pregnancies, particularly those in younger teenagers (age 15 or 16), are a considerable health risk. The babies are often underweight and have birth defects. They are also less likely to survive. Infant mortality in adolescents is almost twice that for women in their 20s. The mothers themselves more often have births complicated by medical problems. Just as important, there are several social hazards.

Most teenage mothers drop out of school. This means that they will have few or no job skills. There is also often considerable tension concerning whether the adolescent mother should marry or just what the responsibilities of the father are. Two additional difficult questions are, "Should the fetus be aborted?" and, if not, "Should the coming baby be given up for adoption?" (See Chapter 14.)

Ultimately two thirds of mothers choose not to abort, eight out of ten do not marry, and almost all keep their babies, not giving them up for adoption.

Sometimes these decisions work out well. The mother (occasionally with the father's help) establishes a healthy and stable environment. More often an adolescent pregnancy means a woman alone with limited ability to support herself who becomes dependent on government programs and agencies (Zelnick et al., 1981).

Probably one of the better courses to take, based on Bolton's (1980) findings, is for the adolescent mother to seek her parents' help. Often they are able to assist in caring for the child and letting the mother return to school. If she can complete her education, the chances become much more favorable for a meaningful career and a healthier atmosphere for the growing child.

Adoption and abortion are discussed further in Chapter 14.

## Causes

Whether we believe it immoral or natural, as we have seen in the previous pages, sexual activity between adolescent girls and boys is very common. Teenaged human beings are at a biological peak of energy, enthusiasm, and adventuresomeness. Stern adult warnings intended to control these qualities, and the sexuality that accompanies them, do not ordinarily succeed. Educational programs and psychological, physical, or even religious threats, seem to have limited effectiveness in promoting abstinence. For example, the Catholic Church takes a very firm stand against sexual relations before marriage. Despite this clear official position, the National Opinion Research Center (1981) found few young Americans who were persuaded. Based on their survey of 3,000 Roman Catholic people aged 14 to 30, they reported that only 17% considered premarital sex morally wrong.

According to Bullough (1981), the chief cause of teenage pregnancy is teenage sexuality. He argues that teenage intercourse and pregnancy are not signs of decadence, but rather that, "teenagers are biologically ready for sex, as they always have been. *Society,* by refusing to recognize this, *has made it a problem.* On the subject of [adolescent] sex, modern sophisticated Americans have buried their heads further into the sand than Victorian America ever did."

In addition to the primary biological reason for adolescent pregnancy, there are also psychological factors. Most pregnancy is not the result of a single and casual sexual contact. Usually the teenaged parents believed they were in love and had mentioned marriage. In 80% of cases the relationship was an affectional and a sexual partnership. When pregnancy occurred, both the boy and girl were unprepared, but typically neither blamed the other or reacted with hostility. Rosen (1981), in fact, found that pregnancies typically resulted from an ongoing relationship that on average had lasted 15 months. These were true partnerships and not casual sexual liaisons.

Adolescent pregnancy may also be the outcome of hidden emotional needs. What appears to be an accident may actually be an act motivated by unconscious drives. Although she may not be aware of it, a girl may think of pregnancy as a way of striking back at her parents or finding a person to love. A boy may be similarly driven to show off his maturity. For still other adolescents, pregnancy seemingly provides a means to keep a reluctant partner, or persuade him, or her, to get married. Powerful as such motives are, they are a poor basis for marriage, because marriages forced by pregnancy are estimated to have a failure rate at least twice as high as those when the woman is not pregnant (Rosen, 1981; Zelnick and Kantner, 1981).

## What Would You Do?

You are the chief administrator for a detention center for over 100 youthful offenders. Most of the boys and girls have been involved in minor offenses such as persistent school truancy, shoplifting, or running away, and their confinement will last only a few months. It has been discovered that most of the boys and girls in the center, ranging in age from 12 to 17, have been engaging in sexual activities including intercourse. Although housed in separate quarters, they frequently met each other on the grounds during outdoor sports periods and would sneak away into the shrubbery or an empty shed for sexual relations. Some of the adult counselors knew about this but did nothing to stop it. A commission was empowered to investigate the entire matter and make recommendations. Commission members, people of both sexes, and with medi-

cal, psychological, legal, and related backgrounds could not agree. Ultimately three separate recommendations were made. As chief administrator, which suggestion would you follow? Explain your rationale.

1. The girls and boys having intercourse and the counselors who knew what was happening were engaged in criminal behavior. Prosecute all under felony statutes to set an example for others in the future.
2. Give the boys and girls psychiatric treatment so that they can be rehabilitated and teach them to limit sexual activities to their future spouse.
3. Teach the counselors, so they in turn can educate the children in their charge, about contraception, relationships, and responsible sexual behavior.

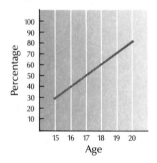

*Figure 8-4*
Percentage of adolescents who customarily use contraception: although adolescent use of contraception increases with age, many continue to employ techniques such as withdrawal whose reliability is low (see Chapter 14). (Data from Zelnick et al., 1981.)

## Contraception

The most direct cause of adolescent pregnancy may be ignorance of, or resistance to, contraception. Well over one third of adolescents who are sexually active do not consistently use contraceptives. Even more enlightening are studies that show that among many adolescents, first intercourse precedes contraceptive use by as much as a year. What this means is that the majority of teenagers have not been sufficiently prepared, either psychologically or educationally, to accompany coitus with contraception (Zelnick and Kantner, 1981).

Birth planning requires frank and explicit instruction. Classrooms need to be equipped with visual aids, contraceptive devices have to be demonstrated, and discussion has to be open and straightforward. Often "role playing," acting out different possible potential sexual situations, is particularly helpful. Equally important, educational efforts should start at the end of the elementary school years, for by that time sexual activity is already beginning for some students. All this is much easier said than done. As we will see, many groups remain fervently opposed to sex education in the classroom. As a result, less than a third of high schools and very few elementary schools realistically educate youngsters.

*In Sum*
Parents usually disapprove of many of their adolescents' sexual activities and their attempts to restrain their children often lead to considerable conflict.

Such disagreement between the two generations sometimes provokes adolescent rebellion and even running away. As a whole, older adolescents are sexually quite active. Because of the frequency of intercourse among adolescents and the uninformed or casual attitude toward contraception among many, the teenage pregnancy rate is quite high. Realistic sex and contraception education is clearly needed.

## Sex education

Children and adolescents spend nearly 40 hours every week in school. They learn a great deal about Shakespeare, the geography of the Plains states, physics, chemistry, and composition. Relatively little time, if any, is spent teaching them about the biology, psychology, and meaning of sex. The situation at home may be even more limited. Parents may teach their children all sorts of social skills and say nothing helpful about sex.

Sex education requires a recognition that often proves difficult for many adults. The sexuality of young people, of adolescents, has to be acknowledged. Young people are, after all, a very sexually active portion of the population. Whether parents like it or not, their sons and daughters will learn about sex. What children are taught will differ widely depending in good measure on the source.

In the Trobriands, a small volcanic chain of tropical islands made famous by anthropologists, sex education was quite direct. Until a few generations ago, these untroubled South Pacific lands seemingly had a very open attitude toward sexuality. Skill and subtlety in sexual relations were prized and children were taught by caring adults. It seemed logical and reasonable that sex be learned through observing and participating (Malinowski, 1985).

In North America, many younger children begin their inquiry about sex with their parents. They are curious about birth and their sexual organs, just as they are inquisitive about nearly everything else. "How do mommies have babies?" is as likely a question for a child to ask as "Why does it rain?" If the child is fortunate, the questions are answered with sensitivity and intelligence. The parents *provide as much information as the child can understand* and perhaps supplement this with *appropriate books*.

Parents or other adults are not, however, the most frequent source of sex information. Many fathers and mothers may be quite anxious about their own sexuality and fearful of their child's growing maturity. They are likely to respond to their child's questions by reprimands. Children are told not to think about such things or that they are too young to know. The result is that less than half adequately inform their children about AIDS, only a fourth tell them about sexual intercourse, and a fifth about birth control (Leo, 1986). Consequently, only a small proportion of children and adolescents cite their parents as a major source of useful and consistent sex information (Table 8-2).

Because parents are often not helpful, the most common source of information about sex during childhood and adolescence is other children. Six out of 10 children seem to depend on their peers to learn about sex. Most of the time the friends are about the same age, but often a slightly older girl or boy serves as a fount of wisdom. Many adults can recall listening intently as a child while a self-appointed teacher carefully revealed all there was to know about a topic

The utopian South Pacific Islands so often portrayed by novelists have virtually disappeared. Western religious values and social and economic practices have replaced ancient tradition.

Most children become curious about their own bodies and those of others by age 2 or 3. When their questions are ignored or punished, they may learn negative sex attitudes.

*Table 8-2*

**Sources of Sex Information**

| Source | Percentage reporting this a major source | Accuracy of information |
|---|---|---|
| Other children | 60 | Low to fair |
| Books | 20 | Generally good |
| Parents | 15 | Low to good |
| School | 10 | Generally good |

Estimates based on data from Davis and Harris, 1982; Gordon, 1986. (Percentages equal more than 100 because of dual sources.)

parents had refused to discuss. Often the information is a mixture of fact, fantasy, and misinformation (Davis and Harris, 1982).

> When I was 13, this older boy told me if you play with yourself, you'll get pimples. This stopped me from masturbating until I was in the eleventh grade and read that it wasn't true in my biology book.

> I was told by a girl I couldn't get pregnant if my boyfriend took it out right away. Like after we did it for a little while. Anyway, I was pregnant when I was 15.

> My friend told me blood would come (from my vagina) every couple of weeks when I turned 12. She told me it was to remind me of Christ's bleeding on the cross to save us from sin. I kept wishing I would never be 12.

*(Author's Files)*

Books and pamphlets appear to be a growing and usually worthwhile source of sexual information with about a fifth of all children depending upon them. Sometimes books are provided by parents who believe that this is a comfortable way to inform children. At other times public libraries, relatives, friends, or religious or social groups make books available. Magazines specifically directed at teenagers have also ventured some basic sex information articles.

Sex education courses in schools account for only a small portion of information. Only about 10% (Table 8-2) of all children say schools are a major source of instruction. This is because although the material presented in school is generally accurate, it tends to come much too late. Birth and contraception (if mentioned at all) are not likely to be covered until the last year or two in high school. By that time many adolescents are already sexually active, with coitus a distinct possibility. Thus, if sex education in the schools is to reach more children and have greater impact, it will have to come much earlier than it does at present.

Given the many sources for sex information—parents, friends, school, books—it would seem that nearly all adolescents know at least the fundamentals. Zelnick, Kantner, and Ford (1981) found, however, that over half of all adolescents were not knowledgeable about the menstrual cycle and the likelihood of pregnancy. They did not know how the two were related or when the period of maximum fertility occurred. Knowledge of contraception, ethical responsibilities, birth, disease, and abortion was similarly sketchy. As a result, many teenagers are likely to be involved in relationships and confronted by consequences they do not want.

For most adolescents, sexual relations including coitus precede adequate contraceptive information or practice.

Most children learn about sex from other children.

## Parents and schools

Parents are in a potentially excellent position to teach their children about sex. Not only are they generally trusted and admired, but they are seemingly easily available to discuss questions and concerns. They could also provide mature, responsible models (Fisher, 1986).

The following overview outlines just a few of the facts and attitudes that might be communicated by parents to their children at different ages:

Nearly all educators agree that sex education should be continuous and gradual. A child should not be able to identify any specific date when she or he learned about coitus or menstruation but rather believe that she or he has always known.

| Ages | |
|---|---|
| Birth to 4 | Recognize child's interest in male/female differences and explain role of each in reproduction; in response to child's questions or behavior, reassure that touching (or masturbating) own genitals is normal and pleasurable but private function; begin to use correct terms for penis, breasts, vagina, etc. |
| 4 to 8 | Discuss feelings, affections, sexual attractions, and interests; explain meaning of "obscene" terms and social usage; establish awareness of possible hazards from strangers who approach child or people who might be abusive |
| 9 to 13 | Talk about menstruation and pubertal changes, male and female reproductive roles, contraception, and abortion; discuss sexually transmitted diseases and prevention |
| 14 to 19 | Talk about going steady, petting, intercourse, and marriage; include topics such as love, exploitation, ethical, religious, and moral viewpoints; reinforce knowledge of contraception and sexually transmitted diseases |

In May 1988 the Surgeon General of the United States, C. Everett Koop, sent a booklet with detailed AIDS information to every home. This stimulated millions of parents and numerous school systems into frank and informative discussion.

Teachers, too, need to be taught about human sexuality.

Parents generally approve of schools including sex education in their curricula. According to a *Time* magazine nationwide poll (Leo, 1986), the vast majority of fathers and mothers support sex education in elementary and high schools. Ninety-five percent want youngsters 12 years and older taught about AIDS, 93% want sexually transmitted disease covered, and 89% want birth control taught. But according to the National Education Association only about a fifth of public elementary and high schools have substantial programs. An additional half of all schools mention reproduction and sexuality as segments of courses in biology. At the other end of the spectrum it is estimated that over a dozen states discourage or prohibit sex education courses or specific topics such as contraception (Gordon, 1986). The Anaheim experience, following, provides a graphic example.

**Anaheim**  Anaheim, California, is the home of Disneyland. In 1963 courses called Family Life and Sex Education were brought into the junior and senior high schools. The instruction included lectures and readings and also encouraged a great deal of student discussion. Nearly all areas of biological sexuality were covered as well as peer relationships, parent-child conflict, and moral and religious standards. As in *most* sex education courses, the general thrust of the Anaheim program was to *dissuade students* from early and premarital sexual experimentation.

The Anaheim program had the solid support of the school system and community. Ten years after its inception, its development and excellence drew national attention. It became a model for other junior and senior high schools. But this prominence apparently attracted opposition. A local Anaheim newspaper began to run articles attacking the program. Opponents of school sex education began to speak and campaign. Teachers, school board members, and supporters started to hear *false* charges that they were teaching children **per-versities.** They were alleged to be demonstrating sex in the classroom and were supposedly opposed to marriage. There were even those who saw sex education as a subversive plot to capture the innocent minds of children and overthrow the government.

These charges, no matter that they were false, plus harassment by anonymous telephone calls and letters, began to intimidate community and school supporters. Ultimately the tiny but highly vocal antisex education group dominated the school board and ended the program. A decade afterward, a reporter, James Collier (1981), wrote; "Eleven years later, despite a continued desire for the program by parents, school authorities, and the California State Department of Education, nobody has been able to revive it."

### Effects

Does sex education work? Does it really provide useful information and lead to responsible attitudes? Does it produce social benefits, such as lowering pregnancy and disease rates? Whether sex education meets any or all of these goals is not nearly as important to many as whether it promotes sexual activity. A major criticism of sex education is that telling adolescents about intercourse, contraception, and other intimacies will lead to an increase in sexual relations. Information is seen as removing an inhibitory barrier, encouraging sexual experimentation (Collier, 1981).

Despite rumors and misstatements to the contrary, sex education does *not* lead to an increase in sexual activity. A number of careful studies have shown that sexual relations or experimentation does not increase with education. Eisen and Zellman (1987) for example, interviewed 126 female and 77 male adolescents—white, black, and Hispanic—and found that participants in a sex education course "were no more likely to be coitally active than those who did not have any sex education."

*perversities*
Deviant or illegal sexual behaviors.

Sex education is often misrepresented and protested by small but effective groups of opponents.

Good sex education encourages people to use precautions.

Sex education in the schools also meets the goal of accurate information. Studies show that students typically end an educational program with new knowledge and understanding. Klein (1984) surveyed 285 midwestern high school students using the *Sex Education Program Outcome Questionnaire*. He found that teenagers greatly improved their knowledge in areas such as human reproduction, effectiveness of various contraceptives, and sexually transmitted disease. There were attitudinal changes as well. The high school adolescents felt more able to communicate their feelings and talk about their desire either to be or not to be involved with their partner.

It has been calculated that each unwanted birth ultimately costs society over $100,000. If sex education were required, the reduced birth rate could save the nation between 10 and 20 billion dollars.

A major justification cited for school sex education programs is the argument that they will reduce unwanted pregnancies. Sex education seems to have had some success. Maciak, et al. (1987) found that while teen pregnancy is still very high, over the last decade there is evidence of decline. Zelnick and Kim (1982), examined a nationwide selection of female and male teenagers who had sex instruction in school and contrasted them with students who had not had such education. Those who were educated more frequently used contraception, including the condom, and accounted for fewer infections and pregnancies. The pregnancy rate for all sexually active teenaged girls who were not given such an education was nearly 40%. Women who had a sex education course in school had a one third lower pregnancy rate. This suggests that between 100,000 and 200,000 pregnancies could be prevented each year if all adolescent girls and boys had a thorough sex education course.

*Summary*

Sexual activity begins in infancy and may involve genital play and masturbation. During early childhood, by 4 or 5 years of age, children frequently show an interest in the genitals of other boys and girls. Though such interest is normal, parents are often distressed and punitive when they become aware of their young child's sexual explorations. Affectional relationships may also begin for some as early as the kindergarten years.

During puberty rapidly accelerating physical and emotional changes culminate in a sexually mature male and female. During the pubertal years, girls often develop faster than boys and both sexes experience some irregularity in their growth. After puberty sexual activity greatly increases for girls and boys. For most, masturbation remains the main sexual outlet. Most also start dating and petting, and a few begin coitus. As adolescence progresses, intercourse becomes more common.

Adolescent sexuality is disapproved by most parents and can be a source of conflict between the two generations. Sometimes adolescents rebel against their parents, or fearing punishment, run away. Toward the end of adolescence most have had intercourse, but a sizable number have uninformed attitudes concerning contraception. As a result, teenage pregnancy and births are quite high. Realistic sex and birth control education is needed.

The majority of children obtain information about sex from other children that is often misleading. Parents and books are a second source. Parents who are motivated can be excellent teachers and there is a great deal of material available to help them. Education should begin in early childhood and be continuous. Despite community support for schools teaching sex education most emphasize biology and steer away from controversy. Sex education programs do not seem to increase or decrease the frequency of adolescent sexual relations. They do have a positive effect in lowering adolescent pregnancy and sexually transmitted disease.

---

1 Describe the infant behaviors that suggest sexual interests. How can parents help infants develop healthy sexual attitudes?

2 What games and activities during childhood may be the outcome of sexual interests? Why and how do young children confuse toilet needs with sexuality?

3 Describe the possible psychological and sexual effects on children of masturbation and sex play with other children.

4 Describe the major adjustment challenges imposed by puberty. What should adolescents be taught about masturbation, petting, and coitus?

5 Recall the sources and content of your own sex education. Were you misinformed? How did this information affect your sexual adjustment?

6 What are the causes of teenage pregnancy and why is this a social problem? What educational measures and what social changes might help alleviate teenage pregnancy?

*For Thought and Discussion*

---

*References*

Atwood, J.D., and Gagnon, J. Masturbatory behavior in college youth. *Journal of Sex Education and Therapy,* 1987, *13*(2), 35-42.

Bolton, F.G., Jr. *The pregnant adolescent: problem of premature parenthood.* Beverly Hills, Calif.: Sage, 1980.

Borhnstedt, G., Freeman, H.E., and Smith, T. Adult perspectives on children's autonomy. *Public Opinion Quarterly,* Winter 1981, *45* (4), 443-461.

Bullough, V.L. Myths about teenage pregnancy. *Free Inquiry,* 1981, *1,* 12-15.

Carroll, L. Concern with AIDS and the sexual behavior of college students. *Journal of Marriage and the Family,* May 1988, *50,* 405-411.

Coles, R., and Stokes, G. *Sex and the American teenager.* New York: Harper & Row, 1985.

Collier, J.L. Whatever happened to sex education? *Reader's Digest,* May 1981, 128-131.

Cook, K., Kretchmer, A., Nellis, B., Lever, J., and Hertz, R. The *Playboy* readers' sex survey (Part 3). *Playboy,* May 1983, 126.

Davis, S.M., and Harris, M.B. Sexual knowledge, sexual interest, and sources of sexual information of rural and urban adolescents from three cultures. *Adolescence,* 1982, *17,* 471-492.

Eisen, M., and Zellman, G.L. Changes in incidence of sexual intercourse of unmarried teenagers following a community-based sex education program. *The Journal of Sex Research,* November 1987, *23*(4), 527-544.

Fisher, T.D. Parent-child communication about sex and young adolescents' sexual knowledge and attitudes. *Adolescence,* 1986, *21,* 517-527.

Ford, C.S., and Beach, F.A. *Patterns of sexual behavior.* Westport, Conn.: Greenwood Press, 1980.

Friday, N. *My secret garden.* New York: Simon & Schuster, 1984.

Gay, P. *Freud.* New York: Norton, 1988.

Gordon, S. What kids need to know. *Psychology Today,* October 1986, 22-26.

Hersch, P. Coming of age on city streets. *Psychology Today,* January 1988, 28-37.

Hunt, M. *Sexual behavior in the 1970s.* Chicago: Playboy Press, 1974.

Kinsey, A.C., Pomeroy, W.B., and Martin, C.E. *Sexual behavior in the human male.* Philadelphia: W.B. Saunders, 1948.

Kinsey, A.C., Pomeroy, W.B., and Martin, C.E. *Sexual behavior in the human female.* Philadelphia: W.B. Saunders, 1953.

Klein, D. Knowledge, attitude, and behavioral changes as a result of sex education. *Journal of Sex Education and Therapy,* 1984 (Spring/Summer), *10*(1), 26-30.

Lawrance, L., Rubinson, L., and O'Rourke, T. Sexual attitudes and behaviors: trends for a ten year period, 1972-1982. *Journal of Sex Education and Therapy,* 1984 (Fall/Winter), *10*(2), 22-30.

Leo, J. Sex and schools. *Time,* November 24, 1986, 54-60, 63.

Maciak, B.J., Spitz, A.M., Strauss, L.T., Morris, L., Warren, C.W., and Marks, J.S. Pregnancy and birth rates among sexually experienced US teenagers—1974, 1980, and 1983. *Journal of the American Medical Association,* October 16, 1987, *258*(15), 2069-2071.

Maier, H.W. *Three theories of child development.* Lanham, Maryland: University Press of America, 1988.

Malinowski, B. *Sex and repression in savage society.* Chicago: University of Chicago Press, 1985.

Masters, W., and Johnson, V.E. *Human sexual response.* Boston: Little, Brown & Co., Inc., 1966.

McCabe, M.P. Desired and experienced levels of premarital affection and sexual intercourse during dating. *The Journal of Sex Research,* February 1987, *23*(1), 23-33.

McCabe, P.M., and Collins, J.K. Measurement of depth of desired and experienced sexual involvement at different stages of dating. *Journal of Sex Research,* 1984, *20,* 377-390.

Mosher, D.L. Three dimensions of depth of involvement in human sexual response. *Journal of Sex Research,* 1980, *16,* 1-42.

National Opinion Research Center. Dissent in the church. *Playboy,* 1981, 85.

Petersen, A.C. Those gangly years. *Psychology Today,* September 1987, 28-34.

Petersen, J.R., Kretchmer, A., Nellis, B., Lever, J., and Hertz, R. The *Playboy* readers' sex survey (Parts 1 and 2). *Playboy,* January 1983, p. 108; March, p. 90.

Ray, L., Soares, E.J., and Tolchinsky, B. Explicit lyrics: a content analysis of top 100 songs from the 50's to the 80's. *The Speech Communication Annual,* January 1988, *2,* 43-56.

Roberts, E.J. *Childhood sexual learning.* Paper presented at the meeting of the Society for the Scientific Study of Sex, New York, November 1981.

Rosen, R.H. *Couple relationships and family formation patterns of pregnant teenagers.* Association paper, Wayne State University, Detroit, Mich., 1981.

Weis, D. The experience of pain during women's first sexual intercourse: cultural mythology about female sexual initiation. *Archives of Sexual Behavior,* 1985, *14,* 421-428.

Wolman, B.B., and Money, J. (editors). *Handbook of human sexuality.* Englewood Cliffs, N.J.: Prentice-Hall, 1980.

Zelnick, M., Kantner, J.F., and Ford, K. *Sex and pregnancy in adolescence.* Beverly Hills, Calif.: Sage, 1981.

Zelnick, M., and Kim, Y.J. Sex education and its association with teenage sexual activity, pregnancy, and contraceptive use. *Family Planning Perspectives,* 1982, *14,* 117-126.

---

*Suggested Reading*

Anthony, J., Green, R., and Kolodny, R. *Childhood sexuality.* Boston: Little, Brown & Co., Inc., 1982.

A good general discussion of the sexuality of children and adolescents.

Leight, L. *The parents' guide to raising sexually healthy children.* New York: Macmillan, 1988.

Written in a clear, helpful style, this guide offers useful suggestions for promoting positive sexual attitudes in children.

Robinson, B. *Teenage fathers*. Lexington, Mass.: Lexington Books, 1988.
This handbook, geared to healthcare professionals, offers helpful suggestions for addressing the needs of young fathers.

Schultz, L.G. (editor). *The sexual victimology of youth*. Springfield, Ill.: Charles C Thomas, Publisher, 1980.
A collection of articles on the many ways children may be sexually abused and exploited, including pornography, incest, and prostitution. The material is uneven but generally informative.

# Chapter 9

# The Single Adult

**When you finish this chapter, you should be able to:**

Describe the different groups who are single.

Explain the various standards college students and other singles use in deciding the extent to which they will become sexually intimate.

Describe how the interests and activities of single college students and never married adults both differ from and resemble those who are divorced and widowed.

Evaluate some of the advantages and disadvantages of being single.

List some of the services offered to single people and explain their usefulness.

Remaining single was once seen as the unfortunate outcome of being too "choosey," shy, or unattractive. Becoming single through divorce or death was considered a tragedy. The assumption was that everyone would rather be married than live alone. Today there are 50 million people who are single. Most have never married and many others are divorced or widowed. This large group of women and men now represents one fifth of the nation, and they no longer conform to the old stereotypes. Many are choosing not to marry or remarry. Some prefer to live together, to cohabit, rather than to marry. Most also look at being single in a positive light. They see singleness filled with educational, economic, social, and many other advantages.

# WHO THEY ARE

The fact that 50 million Americans over age 18 are not married has brought about significant changes in society. There are housing areas designed just for single people. Many foods are packaged for those living alone. A variety of consumer goods and services address the needs and buying habits of unmarried women and men. It seems to be increasingly accepted that there are options besides marriage. A person may choose to become a spouse and parent, but it is just as legitimate to elect education or a career or to combine any of these or other personal goals.

Social change to accommodate single women and men has occurred. At the same time, however, the traditional family is still often seen as the center around which people's lives should revolve. The result is that many single people often feel isolated. They are not invited by married couples to have dinner or pursue recreations with them. The unmarried may also suffer disadvantages on the job or in housing. Apartment owners often distrust single women and men and are reluctant to rent to them. Employers are by law not supposed to discriminate, but some still hire married persons because they think they are more dependable. In several ways, society seems to misunderstand or be prejudiced against those who are not married.

**Stereotypes**   Despite increasing recognition of single people as a factor in society, stereotypes or biased convictions are plentiful. Divorced men and women are often seen as incompetents, unable to hold a partnership together. The never married man is likely to be pictured as a swinging bachelor, sexy and self-indulgent. The single woman in her 30s may be seen as so selfishly dedicated to her career that she has time for little else. Cargan and Melko's survey (1982) found seven persistent myths held by many married adults about single people. Singles were alleged to be: (1) immature, (2) deviant, (3) unwilling to accept responsibility, (4) very happy, (5) very lonely, (6) financially well-to-do, and (7) **workaholics.**

Cargan and Melko worked with over 400 single men and women. They noted first of all that several of the myths were contradictory. Single people were called both lonely and happy. Or they were said to work too hard and too long, but supposedly also lacked responsibility. In the researchers' view it was true that a few single people were sometimes immature or could be said to be workaholics. Overall, however, Cargan and Melko found beliefs about singles were little more than stereotypes, invalid and unsubstantiated judgments. Single men and women may share some life circumstances, but each is still a unique individual.

**Numbers**   The 50 million single people in the United States share the fact that they are not married. Otherwise they come from a diversity of backgrounds and have a variety of interests and goals. The majority of single people are women. Throughout the 20s single men actually outnumber single women, but then the longevity of women asserts itself. More men die at each age period than women. By age 30 there are only 75 single men to every 100 women. This unevenness in the ratio of women to men means that some women who want to marry have their chances diminished. It may also prompt

*workaholic*
A work "addict," someone too dedicated to her or his occupation.

At each adult age period more women survive than men, resulting eventually in many more single females than males. Women's longevity is discussed in Chapters 6, 7.

*Figure 9-1*
The curve shows the number of single men for every 100 single women at each age period. (Data from U.S. Bureau of the Census, 1984.)

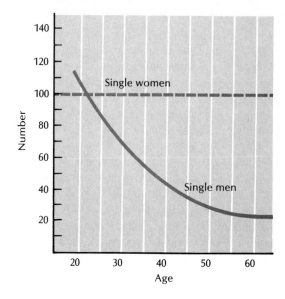

*Figure 9-2*
There are over 50 million single people in the United States: 13 million divorced, 11 million widowed, and 26 million never married. (Data from U.S. Bureau of the Census, 1988.)

women to look more favorably on singleness as a life option and maximize its advantages (Figure 9-1).

The largest group of single women and men are in their 20s and 30s and have not yet married. This group also includes about 14 million college students age 18 or over. Most people in this very large group of singles will eventually marry. Often, however, they are single for many years and live in a world quite different from those who are part of a couple (Figure 9-2) (U.S. Bureau of the Census, 1988).

People who are divorced or separated number about 13 million. This segment of the population has increased fairly rapidly overall since the beginning of the century (Chapter 12). Widows and widowers are the oldest singles. Most are past 60 years of age and have become single through the death of a spouse. There are now about 11 million widowed people, and this number can be expected to grow gradually as the entire population of the United States ages (U.S. Bureau of the Census, 1988).

### College students

We begin our description of single persons with college students. Open enrollment programs, admitting nearly all high school graduates or those with equivalent work, have resulted in over 14 million students. College is no longer just for the well-to-do. Most students have part time jobs and/or receive some form of financial aid. Colleges increasingly represent every cultural, economic, and ethnic group (U.S. Bureau of the Census, 1988).

It is important to recognize that college students today are not what they were when the Kinsey et al. studies (1948, 1953) were conducted over 40 years ago. College students then consisted mainly of the children of white, affluent parents. Partly as a result, the Kinsey studies found substantial differences in the sexual behavior of college women and men and those with less education. The former, for example, did much more petting but had intercourse for the first time a little later than young people with more limited schooling. College

The largest group of single women and men at present are in their 20s and 30s.

students today represent a broader cross section of the United States so that their behavior is likely more closely representative of all young Americans.

College offers single men and women a maximum opportunity to meet, socialize, and form alliances. Most colleges are coeducational, meaning that at these institutions people of both sexes are brought together in a situation that allows for freedom and interaction not previously experienced by them. The result is that during the college years, nearly all students have several different relationships, many involving a good deal of both emotional and physical intimacy.

**Residence halls**   At residential colleges, senior and graduate students may live off-campus in apartments or rooms, but the majority of undergraduates still live in dormitories. This makes these residences a center for much of their social and sexual activity. On many church-sponsored or conservative campuses, dormitories are strictly gender segregated. There are lounges where women and men may meet, but visiting in each other's rooms is prohibited. In other colleges, the trend has been to have sex-segregated as well as coeducational dormitories. In joint facilities, men and women may live in the same building in rooms next to one another, or some distance may be kept between the sexes by putting them on different floors or in different wings.

When coeducational dormitories were introduced about two decades ago, critics predicted rampant and unrestrained sexuality and a precipitous decline in academic achievement. In fact, open sexuality did not become the norm; and academic performance is not perceptibly different for students in coeducational or gender-segregated dormitories. But the coeducational dormitory did facilitate, as we will see later in this chapter, heterosexual friendship and intimacy. The access men and women had to each other's rooms has doubtlessly contributed to the general increase in sexual activity among college students over the past generation (Sherwin and Corbett, 1985).

The majority of college students live in dormitories, making their rooms centers for social and sexual activities.

**cohabitation**
Living together; usually refers to a woman and man who live together in an intimate relationship but are not married.

On many campuses throughout the United States, the dormitory provides the first **cohabitation** experience. The couple become friends, move on to sexual intimacy in his or her room, and gradually spend more and more time together. Eventually a roommate complains about the couple's activities in monopolizing the room and complex compromises may be worked out. Sometimes the couple agrees to have intercourse only when the roommate is away. At other times the roommate may be paid or helped to move elsewhere so that the couple can continue their cohabitation undisturbed. Most often the cohabitants move off campus to their own private room or apartment.

Not all students cohabit, but several surveys suggest that in many colleges about a third had a cohabitation experience before they graduate. This cohabitation may be quite brief, only a week or so, or last through most of the college years. It is important to point out also that there are institutions, frequently with a religious affiliation, where almost no students cohabit (Macklin, 1983; Risman et al., 1981).

Many college students seem to view living together in much the same way an earlier generation thought of going steady. The partners like one another; they have become closer as they have spent more and more time with each other. It seems a natural step for the two to eventually share their lives more fully. They feel comfortable and fulfilled cohabiting.

Cohabitation also has several disadvantages. It may involve students in a more extensive commitment than they desire. They may have to face, at the age of 18, 19, or 20, emotional and relationship problems encountered by married couples 5 to 10 years older and that much more mature and experienced. Another disadvantage felt by many couples living together is social and parental disapproval. This may take the form of the college evicting or expelling the couple or the parents withholding support. As it does for older adults, cohabitation has its pluses and minuses for college students.

**Sexual standards** The sexual behavior of college students is influenced by traditional and often personal standards. They may follow their parents' guidelines or those that they and their friends have thought about and discussed. The oldest historical guide is the *double standard*. This is the belief that some sexual behaviors are permissible for men but not for women. Since the Victorian era a variety of sexual behaviors have been tolerated among men but disapproved of for women (Chapter 1). Men might have intercourse before marriage, but not women. Men might be sexually aggressive, even coercive, but women were expected to be modest and demure.

According to DeLamater and MacCorquodale (1979), college students no longer support the double standard. Survey data from over 800 subjects showed that roughly two thirds of the college men and women had intercourse—with the proportion of males only slightly greater than the proportion of females. Consistent with this similarity, none of the men questioned said they supported the double standard and only 2% of the women said that they did (Table 9-1).

For students, the double standard appears to have been replaced by new beliefs. Research has suggested three standards governing sexual conduct, traditional, moderate, and permissive. These three moralities describe when sexual intimacy in a dating couple is likely to take place (Peplau, Cochran, 1980; Christopher, Cate, 1984).

The *traditional* couples believed that intercourse should occur only when the couple have clearly committed themselves to marry. The partners may engage in heavy petting, but intercourse is reserved for the time when future marriage is clear. The couples called *sexually moderate* said intercourse was acceptable as long as the couple was in love. They did not have to make a commitment to marry or even include it in their plans. When the couple reached the point in their relationship that they felt they loved one another, intercourse could follow.

The third group, the *sexually liberal or permissive,* viewed sexual intercourse as an outcome of friendship. If two people liked one another, if they thought sharing sexual intimacy would be mutually satisfying, they might have intercourse. Being in love, vowing to marry, was in their view almost irrelevant to enjoying oneself through sexual pleasure.

Sherwin and Corbett (1985) found similar standards in a large midwestern

The double standard is alive and well. Most college students, however, reject it. Some other adults still believe that premarital or extramarital intercourse may be tolerated in men but not in women.

*Table 9-1*

**College Sexual Standards**

| | Females (%) | Males* (%) |
|---|---|---|
| Believe in abstinence before marriage or engagement | 10 | 5 |
| Believe in double standard | 2 | 0 |
| Believe in liberal standard (intercourse is OK if both want it) | 15 | 40 |
| Believe in moderate standard (intercourse is OK if both are in love) | 60 | 40 |

Data from DeLamater and MacCorquodale, 1979; Peplau and Cochran, 1980; Christopher, Cate, 1984.
*Percentages do not equal 100 since all student opinion could not be classified.

state university. Their data went back 20 years, to 1963. Since that time there has been a very significant increase in the number of students having intercourse. To some observers it seemed as if no standards of any kind other than increasing "liberality" dominated the sexual behavior of the students, but a closer look at the data revealed this is untrue.

Between 1963 and 1984 the proportion of students having sexual intercourse increased 10 to 20 times. Most, however, was in the context of a relationship, namely among engaged or otherwise committed couples. Nine percent of couples dating casually had intercourse as opposed to 74% of those who were engaged. The authors of the research comment, "Although the norms have changed, they do not appear to have been abandoned in favor of 'free love' standards. Sexual intercourse is not routinely endorsed as an expected activity for all types of relationships."

**First intercourse**  In view of these differing sexual attitudes, ranging from traditional to liberal, it is revealing to know the circumstances of first intercourse among young single women and men. For most of this century, sexual intercourse between single people occurred when the two partners had made a commitment to marry. Until a generation ago, many women and men held the view that a man would not respect a woman who "gave herself freely." A woman was taught to hold back and only reward the man with intercourse when he had married her, or at the least proposed.

Zelnick and Shah (1983) asked 936 women and 670 men to describe their first sexual partner. For two thirds of the women their first partner was a man to whom they were engaged or with whom they were going steady. In contrast, among men, only a third of their first partners was a woman with whom they were going steady or to whom they were engaged. Based on this behavior, it appears as if many more young women adhere relatively closely to the traditional standard than do men.

The more liberal standard also seems to be upheld somewhat differently by the two sexes. Four out of ten men reported their first intercourse was with a friend or someone they had met quite recently. Among women the proportion who seemed to follow the liberal sexual standard was low. Only one out of ten reported first intercourse with a friend or recent acquaintance. First intercourse may not be the best way to evaluate the standards governing sexual intimacy. It does appear, however, that women tend a little more toward moderate and traditional standards and men toward liberal, men often wanting or pressing for intercourse earlier than women (Table 9-1; McCabe, 1987).

**Sexual activity**  Sexual behaviors are usually described in terms of averages and frequencies. We, too, will have to report college data in this way, but it should be realized that there is considerable variation. Students in a small women's or men's college have fewer opportunities for sexual contact than those living in a coeducational dormitory. Similarly, a college noted for its liberal policies will attract students whose sexual attitudes and standards are far different from those who go to a strict, religiously oriented institution. For example, we could say that based on estimates derived from several studies, over 70% of all males and close to two thirds of all females have coitus while in college. But it must be realized that in some colleges the frequency will be

*free love*
Usually used to mean sexual relations without commitment.

First intercourse is sometimes awkward or anxious (Chapter 8). It may leave the man or woman fearful of subsequent coitus. Sexual problems and their treatment are discussed in Chapter 17.

higher, approaching 80% or 90%. In other institutions, the number may be as low as 10% (Risman et al., 1981).

During the college years, the sexual behaviors that started during adolescence (Chapter 8) continue and increase. Petting experiences become more frequent and intimate. Touching and stimulating the genitals of a partner of the other sex is found in over 60% of college students. Stimulation of the partner's genitals by mouth (orally) occurs in over 40%. Necking and light petting, such as touching the female breast, are almost universal, found in over 90% (DeLamater and MacCorquodale, 1979; Petersen et al., 1983).

Sherwin and Corbett surveyed over 3000 students on an Ohio college campus from 1963 to 1984. They found a dramatic decrease in the number of virginal students. The decrease was most marked for women. Forty percent of the men were virgins in 1963 and 30% in 1984. Among women in 1963, 80% were virgins, but almost two decades later there were fewer than 40%. Sherwin and Corbett contend that these figures show that there may well have been a sexual revolution. Students and society in general may have become more sexually permissive. But looking at these statistics indicates that if there has been a sexual revolution, it seems to have affected mainly the behavior of women.

It is important to note, too, that college students are increasingly aware of AIDS (Chapter 16), and many are moderating their sexual behavior as a result. Leo Carroll (1988) gave a 23-page questionnaire to 447 students. He found that 15% said they had refrained, on occasion, from having intercourse because of a fear of AIDS. A small number, 3%, who once had several sexual partners said they had stopped their search for variety. Overall, the majority of women and men who were sexually active said that AIDS had made them more selective in their choice of partner.

The sexual activities of college students are varied and range from necking to intercourse, but for all of these young adults masturbation continues to be prominent. Nearly all young men masturbate as do the majority of women. During periods when students are engaged in an intimate relationship with a partner, there may be little or no masturbation. At other times, masturbation may occur a few times a week, daily, or more often. For the majority of college students, masturbation is still the most frequent source of sexual gratification (Atwood and Cagnon, 1987; Petersen et al., 1983).

**Ethnic differences**  As college campuses have become more representative of the American population as a whole, there has been a large increase in the number of blacks, Hispanics, Asians, and other minorities. Differences in sexual standards and behaviors exist among all these groups. Frequently the beliefs and practices of those from more traditional Hispanic and Asian backgrounds are more conservative than those of white Americans. Black sexuality, on the other hand, has often been described as more "liberal," black adolescents engaging in premarital relations a little more often and at earlier ages than whites.

These ethnic differences are reflected in the college population. Asian students, for example, may be surprised at the seeming sexual permissiveness of their white and black American peers. Several ethnic studies have primarily compared American white and Afro-American students. Zelnick and Shah (1983) surveyed 874 white and 732 black students of both sexes. They found

*Masturbation, discussed more fully in Chapter 8, is a common and normal sexual activity. It is found at all ages but is more frequent during adolescence and early adulthood.*

The sexual and social behavior of black and white college students, and those from most other ethnic backgrounds, is fairly similar.

Many students, from all ethnic backgrounds do not always use contraception consistently so pregnancy among college students is not rare.

that white women and men tended a little more often to insist on the traditional standard. They were more inclined to have intercourse only in the context of a committed relationship. A few more black men than white seemed to uphold the liberal sexual standard. Six out of ten black men, compared to four out of ten white, had intercourse with someone considered an acquaintance or friend.

Philip Belcastro (1985) also looked at the variety of sexual experiences of white and black students and found more similarities than differences. Black males had slightly more interracial sexual intercourse and masturbated a little less frequently than white males. White women students were more likely to have stimulated the man's penis by hand or mouth. But in nearly every other respect, frequency of intercourse, attitudes towards contraception—in fact in the majority of sexual behaviors—the two races appeared fairly identical. What seems to be happening is that when students from different ethnic backgrounds attend college, a leveling process takes place. Different sexual behaviors and standards probably tend to converge (Blumstein and Schwartz, 1983; Weinberg and Williams, 1988).

### *In Sum*

There are 50 million single people. They are never married, divorced, and widowed men and women. College students remain single longer than they did a generation ago. They are also starting sexual relations earlier, and most have had intercourse before graduation. Usually, college students have sexual relations only with the person with whom they are in love or to whom they are engaged. A small portion of students have liberal sexual attitudes that permit sexual relations with acquaintances and friends. The sexual behaviors of students from different ethnic backgrounds often converge during the college years.

### The never married

A generation ago it was often customary to marry soon after college or even high school graduation. Today many, if not most, college and high school graduates say they are postponing marriage until they are older. These people want to go to graduate school, learn a profession or trade, establish themselves in business, or for many personal reasons prefer to wait before they marry and start a family. Some plan not to marry at all.

People who put off getting married voluntarily elect to be single at least for a while. Other single adults would prefer marriage but are unable to find a partner. A few of these involuntary singles have emotional or physical problems. They may be psychologically disturbed or seriously overweight, or they may have other handicapping impairments. Most, however, are normal women and men who have not found a person with whom to have a committed relationship.

There are also women and men among the never married adults whose advanced training or career goals have kept them busy until they are beyond the time when most people marry (Chapter 12). Women particularly face a diminishing pool of eligible men their own age as they reach their late 20s. Despite greater social flexibility concerning gender roles (Chapters 6 and 7) many women and men still expect the husband to earn more or have the more important job. Phillis and Stein (1983) see a fair-sized segment of the never married adult population consisting of self-supporting, highly accomplished women. They may want to marry, but their achievement has priced them out of the marriage market. We need to reiterate, however, that many women and men do not have marriage as their overriding goal and have chosen to be single.

**Sexual activity**  The never married single, the post-college 25- to 35-year-old person, seems to have captured the imagination of the media and the public. Often these people are portrayed as swinging singles. They are alleged to meet in sophisticated bars and dance clubs, exchange a few words, and go on to what has become known as a "one night stand." The stereotype has them tumbling into bed in the late hours of the night and separating again the next morning, perhaps not even knowing each other's name.

Like most myths, there may be a grain of truth in this script. A few men and women who are single may for a time be sexually quite active. But most single people are far less sexually nontraditional than imagined. Petersen et al. (1983) showed that only about a third of younger single adults had intercourse as much as twice a week. Most also had only a small number of different partners, three or fewer in any one year.

Even the figures of Petersen and his associates may be high. They are based on the response of *Playboy* readers, a magazine that appears to attract people with more extensive sexual histories and more liberal attitudes. Working in Ohio, Cargan found comparatively low frequencies of sexual experience. Among his single subjects, one fourth said that they did not presently have any sexual partner at all. This was apparently not because these people were disinterested. They were willing to become sexually intimate, but a sizeable number of these singles had no one available. Cargan found, too, that many of those who were sexually active tended to behave much like married people. They averaged intercourse two or three times weekly and had only one partner. Many

Some single people have many different partners, but have intercourse less frequently than those who are married.

single people of both sexes are likely to be far less sexually active than is commonly portrayed (Cargan, 1980; Cargan and Melko, 1982).

In recent years, the sexual activity of single people has been further reduced by the fear of AIDS (Chapter 16). Sexual relations with a partner one has recently met and/or whose background is unknown is risky behavior. As a result many single people, although not all, avoid sexual relations with casual acquaintances and are quite careful in their choice of partners (Langone, 1988).

How satisfying is the sex life of a never married person? For a few, the freedom to explore relationships with many different people is an advantage that is enjoyed and treasured. For a few others, their heterosexual inactivity causes frustration and despair. Less than half say their sexual relations are satisfactory. Complaints frequently include feeling manipulated, relationships that are shallow, and difficulties being sexually aroused or reaching climax. These findings may be more understandable when contrasted with the sexual satisfaction of married people. Over one fourth of married couples say they are sexually dissatisfied. Being single can result in sexual frustration, but marriage also has a good share of discontented wives and husbands (Blumstein and Schwartz, 1983; Rubenstein and Tavris, 1987).

As pointed out earlier, single women increasingly outnumber single men. Laurel Richardson (1986) reports that this discrepancy has led to an increase in single women having affairs with married men. She talked with 700 women involved in such liaisons and did a detailed study of 55, asking how their relationship started, progressed, and ended. Although such affairs may prove to be frustrating and anxious, they can also apparently be rewarding. Richardson makes it clear that many women feel exploited and diminished, but a few others may derive affection, pleasure, and meaning from these arrangements.

For a few single people, masturbation becomes an important source of sexual gratification. Most single men and women masturbate at least occasionally, but some make this the focus of their sexual behavior. It is often difficult to find a willing and appealing partner, and the possibility of sexually transmitted infections (Chapter 16) has added additional incentive to masturbation. Betty Dodson, in her book *Sex for One: The Joy of Selfloving* (1988), suggests attitudes and techniques to enhance the masturbatory experience. In her view, adults need to be guided to overcome the deeply rooted **taboo** against masturbation and helped to see it as a wholesome way to experience sexuality.

*taboo*
Totally forbidden.

*homosexual*
A person whose sexual/affectional activity is predominantly or entirely with a person of the same sex.

**Homosexuality** The never-married singles include **homosexual** men and women. These are people who most often have sexual relations with those of their own sex. An estimate of this number is difficult to obtain. As we shall see in Chapter 13 the exact proportion of the population that is homosexual is not known. For one thing, a few people may be homosexual for a period of years and then be primarily heterosexual. Another statistical problem is that some homosexual women and men are married and thus clearly not members of the singles population.

Current estimates suggest that roughly one in ten unmarried persons from their 20s to their 50s is exclusively homosexual (Chapter 13). This means that it is likely for heterosexual people to meet or have as a friend a person who is gay or lesbian. It often comes as a surprise to both people that, while their sexual orientations differ, the fact that they are single gives them many congruent interests. Both are worried about sexual health, are likely to have grappled with relationship problems, have financial concerns, and have given considerable thought to the advantages and disadvantages of the single life. Both are also likely to have come to a city area for a job or for an enriched social life. Both have probably wrestled with loneliness and also been thankful for the freedom and flexibility their singleness has given them. Many homosexual men and women may be considered part of the single, never married community. They will probably find that being single, as much as any other personal characteristic, defines much of their life-style.

### Divorced singles

College and high school graduates can be thought of as entering the singles world as single. They may have had an important relationship during their school years, but most never truly considered themselves "coupled." Young adults just out of school *are* single, in contrast to older formerly married adults who must *become* single. Becoming single through a partnership breakup or divorce, finding oneself alone after years of what may have seemed to be an enduring relationship, is typically a painful experience.

There are over 13 million divorced women and men in the United States. Most are in their 30s and were married between 3 and 10 years. A small number, but still a sizable portion, were married for over 20 years. For all these people, whether they had a partner for 4 years or for 30, the prospect of living alone produces an intense reaction (Alvarez, 1982; U.S. Bureau of the Census, 1988).

To be sure, for a few women and men, when the marriage dissolves they are relieved or happy. Perhaps a third already have another satisfying relationship. Others may have been trapped in an abusive, unaffectionate, or dreary situation that drained their energy and enthusiasm. But most people feel a mixture of dread, depression, and loneliness. By psychiatric standards, marital dissolution is one of the most potent causes of stress and can lead to any number of physical and psychological illnesses (Chapters 12 and 17).

In addition to the psychological distress of marital dissolution there are important financial and other practical considerations that confront the single person. The end of a partnership can be a severe economic blow, particularly to the woman. Smaller, cheaper housing has to be found. A new job may be vital. The wife who left financial matters to her husband, who is now gone, may be completely at sea trying to cope. The husband who never helped run the home may find everyday chores, such as getting the children ready for school or doing laundry, overwhelming tasks after his wife has left. Even the most competent women and men often find how many details of living they left to their partner, which now need to be mastered. The process of becoming single again involves numerous physical, emotional, and practical challenges (Chapter 12).

**Reentry fear** The divorced person, perhaps more than any other single man or woman, is very likely to suffer from "**reentry fear**." Such persons will argue that they have become older and heavier, and they no longer know how to make themselves look attractive. Or they may contend that they were married so long, 7 or 12 years, that they have forgotten how to talk with unfamiliar

Divorce and death of a spouse cause similar emotions, including anger, fear, and depression. Men and women often need a year or more to readjust and regain their stability.

*reentry fear*
Anxiety concerning entering a situation in which a person once functioned.

members of the other sex. They no longer know the rules and rituals of dating. They feel unable to reenter the world of singles.

Much of the reentry doubt, the fear of seeming unattractive or awkward, may in reality be anxiety about rejection. The divorce itself may have been the ultimate rejection, and this is not a situation that is easily relieved. Alvarez (1982) suggests that many divorced men and women, trying to reenter, may rush into dating too soon. It is then that they are most vulnerable to rejection and most likely to feel self-conscious. Divorce should be followed by a period of "mourning." Perhaps for as much as a year, people should try to live a relatively quiet life, taking comfort from friends and family. This gives them a chance to rebuild their shattered self-image. Then they are ready to reenter the singles world with a degree of confidence and some stable direction.

When parents divorce, many children, particularly those who are younger, may feel uprooted and traumatized. Psychological counseling may be needed.

**Children**   The divorced parent faces many challenges and has unique opportunities while raising children alone. We will describe these in Chapter 12. A special problem the divorced parent faces is bringing home the new lover or date. The divorce itself will have been a difficult experience for the children. Many children often believe, erroneously, that they are at fault. At the same time they hope that something they can do or say will bring the missing parent back. When the divorced mother or father brings home a date some children react with fury. They may be fiercely jealous and possessive of the remaining parent.

Parents also worry about being poor role models. If their current friend stays overnight, how will the children react? The children know their parent has violated a deeply rooted social tradition that unmarried people do not go to bed together. Even more to the point, what will be the impact on children if they see a new friend, a different lover, in a few months? Mothers and fathers may be afraid they are setting an example for their children that might be considered immoral or promiscuous. Until the parent works out a satisfactory solution, helping the children to understand the adult's life and needs, sexual activities may be quite constrained (Alvarez, 1982).

Sometimes couples are able to have a "friendly" divorce, agreeing to separate and yet remain friends. These couples may continue sexual relations for some time.

**Sex**   The period following a break-up is stressful even for the person who has deliberately sought to end the relationship. It is not unusual, therefore, that during the difficult months following the end of the partnership, sexual activity is often quite limited (see Chapter 12).

Possibly because a new sexual partner is not available, almost 20% of couples continue to have intercourse with each other for several months after divorce. They are used to regular sexual activity, have no one else available, and find it comfortable to continue old habits. But this contact soon stops as many couples increasingly find that their sexual relationship creates new problems, stirring old and difficult emotions and causing one or both considerable distress (Cherlin, 1981).

About a fifth of all divorced men and women seem to plunge into sexual relations. For a time they appear interested in having intercourse with many different persons. This high level of sexuality following divorce may be an effort to find relief from loneliness or make up for lost time and opportunity. It could also be an attempt to rebuild one's self-image as desirable and worthy of attention and love (Brehm, 1985; Cherlin, 1981).

Divorce almost always requires a period to readjust and restabilize one's life.

Within about a year after divorce, fairly stable sexual patterns emerge. The woman or man who has been dating several people is likely to have reduced her or his activity considerably. The person at the other extreme, who has been reluctant to start dating or seeing any one at all, begins to emerge. Within a year after divorce most women and men are sexually active. The majority also report their sexual relationships to be satisfying, and some say they are better than during their marriage (see Chapter 12; Cherlin, 1981).

### Widowed

The painful emotions experienced after the death of one's marital partner are in some ways similar to the feelings after divorce. In both situations there can be anger, depression, and fear. In divorce angry emotions may dominate for some time before other emotions displace them. In widowhood, anger soon subsides, and depression becomes the overriding emotion. The person feels frightened and morose; life may look uncertain and hopeless. There are financial problems, new responsibilities, and pressing feelings of loneliness (Chapter 12).

It often takes about a year for women and men who have lost their spouse through death to readjust. During this first year of mourning the widowed person moves from poignant recollections of life as it was to making some plans for the future. At first every holiday, every family event, serves as a tearful reminder. Gradually the surviving spouse gains more and more independence. These women and men recognize that they can make it on their own (Balkwell, 1981).

Not every widow or widower is grieved and depressed. Sometimes the death of a spouse who was particularly difficult to live with or painfully ill is felt as a relief.

There are 11 million widowed people in the United States and the median age is in the mid-50s. Those on the younger side of this age gradually start attending social functions for singles and dating. Their self-doubts, self-consciousness, and reentry problems are similar to those faced by people of the same age who are divorced. It has been a long time since they, like the middle-aged divorced, have been in the singles world and the adjustment is not easy.

Widowers and widows who are in their 60s and beyond may not even try to reenter the singles and dating scene. Many of these men, and more often the women, continue to wear their wedding bands. It may be years after the spouse's death until they finally, if ever, remove it. They still feel married and avoid suggestions that they find someone else.

Glick (1980) reports that between ages 45 and 55, two thirds of the widowed men and little more than a third of the women remarry. The men tend to marry women close to their own age; the women, faced with fewer men their own age, often marry men 5 to 10 years older than themselves. After age 55 only 14% of the widows wed again. The proportion for men remains fairly high with 30% of the men over 55 marrying again. This discrepancy grows even larger in the 60s and 70s, with men remarrying 3 or 4 times as often as women. This difference in the frequency of remarriage between men and women is a reflection of a fact pointed out at the beginning of this chapter. There are many, many more single women available after 50 years of age than there are men.

**Sex**   When the widowed start dating, sexual activity may or may not be an objective. Those who are older often say they are looking mainly for companionship. These people may be over 70 and convinced that sex is no longer possible. Or there may be social obstacles; relatives and friends may disapprove of sexual activity. Some men and women withdraw from sexuality because of failing health or diminishing interest. A main problem, however, revealed by Brecher's extensive survey and analysis (*Love, Sex, and Aging,* 1984), is the older man or woman's inability to find a willing partner.

Some widowed men and women, particularly those in the 50- to 60-year-old bracket, socialize, date, and look for companions within the first year after the death of their spouse. Those who find a steady partner again or remarry almost always resume sexual activity. In fact, their frequency of intercourse is often higher than for couples of the same age who have been married for many years. The stimulus of a new sexual partner often appears to increase sexual interest, capability, and satisfaction (Brecher, 1984).

### Cohabiting

Being single does not necessarily mean living alone. A good proportion of singles cohabit, that is, live together in a sexually intimate relationship. Younger adults who cohabit often see their relationship as an alternative, a middle ground between marriage and remaining single. At the older end of the age scale, cohabiters may be widowed adults who share room, board, companionship, and sexual intimacy. They choose not to marry for personal reasons or because they would then lose Social Security or other financial benefits, or have to pay more in taxes. Tanfer (1987) suggests that, for many singles, cohabitation is a way of continuing to feel single, perhaps for years, while exploring the possibilities of a more permanent relationship.

Figures accumulating over the past two decades show living together is an increasingly common phenomenon. In the 1950s nonmarital partnerships were rare and constituted much less than 1% of all households. By the 1970s the number of households in which a woman and a man lived together without marriage had increased to over a million. The number climbed steadily and by

Many people past 50 remain almost as sexually active as younger women and men. A main factor in older people continuing sexual relations is whether they have a suitable partner. We will describe the sexuality of older persons in Chapter 12.

Alternatives to traditional marriage may include cohabitation as well as partnerships that permit extramarital relations. Such marital options are explained in Chapter 12.

Living together, without marriage, is an increasingly common phenomenon.

1990 it is estimated that there will be over 2 million cohabiting couples. This number might even be higher if some couples did not hide the fact they were cohabiting by pretending to be married. If trends continue, by the end of the century, 1 of every 20 partnerships may be cohabitant (DeMaris and Leslie, 1984; Tanfer, 1987; U.S. Bureau of the Census, 1988).

The number of people who cohabit has increased because society seems to be making it a little easier. College dormitories, as we pointed out at the beginning of this chapter, are mostly coeducational. This often makes it relatively simple for a woman and man to unofficially share a room. Apartment owners now seldom ask whether a couple to whom they are renting is married. Banks often lend mortgage money to partners who are cohabiting. Employers, too, who might once have discharged a worker who was in the old derogatory term "living out of wedlock" are now likely to overlook an employee's living arrangement.

A few states in the United States still prohibit cohabitation. Alabama, Idaho, Iowa, Ohio, Pennsylvania, Rhode Island, and Texas among others may charge people who cohabit with a misdemeanor and jail them for 6 months or a year. These laws are seldom enforced, so that most cohabiters do not concern themselves with legal statutes.

It might, however, benefit people who cohabit to be aware that some states recognize cohabitation as a form of marriage. In these states "common-law" marriage statutes consider a couple legally wed if they have lived together con-

To avoid judgmental terms, the Internal Revenue Service and the U.S. Bureau of the Census have originated the term *POSSLQ* (pronounced possl · cue), meaning Person of Opposite Sex Sharing Living Quarters.

## How Compatible Are We?

People who choose to live together sometimes believe that they are entering a partnership much like marriage. But unlike marriage, there are few traditions to guide such couples. Cohabitants may also not know one another as well or be as familiar with each other's day-to-day habits as people who have been engaged and then marry. A couple considering cohabitation might find the following informal questionnaire useful. Each partner should take the test separately and alone. When both partners have taken the test they should compare answers.

| Check Each Question: | Agree | Neutral | Disagree |
|---|---|---|---|
| 1. It's all right for my partner to invite friends to our home without my consent. | ____ | ____ | ____ |
| 2. If things work out between us, we will get married. | ____ | ____ | ____ |
| 3. Smoking is permitted in our home. | ____ | ____ | ____ |
| 4. Drinking is permitted in our home. | ____ | ____ | ____ |
| 5. All expenses, even if one of us eats more or uses the telephone more often should be shared equally. | ____ | ____ | ____ |
| 6. Our home should always be neat, picked up, and tidy. | ____ | ____ | ____ |

| Check Each Question: | Agree | Neutral | Disagree |
|---|---|---|---|
| 7. I like listening to the music my friend plays on the radio or stereo and what he (she) watches on television. | ____ | ____ | ____ |
| 8. Sex is very important in our relationship and each of us should do our best to please the other in any way desired. | ____ | ____ | ____ |
| 9. Cohabiting is not marriage so that it is acceptable if I sometimes have sexual relations with another person. | ____ | ____ | ____ |
| 10. We should always use birth control if we do not want pregnancy to occur. | ____ | ____ | ____ |

**Check Each Question:**

| | Agree | Neutral | Disagree |
|---|---|---|---|
| 11. If one of us wants to go out but the other doesn't feel good and wants to stay at home, both of us should stay at home. | ____ | ____ | ____ |
| 12. We should make a real effort to get to know and like each other's parents and relatives. | ____ | ____ | ____ |
| 13. We should set aside a time each week when both of us can talk freely about our relationship. | ____ | ____ | ____ |
| 14. We should spend most of our free time together and be each other's best friend. | ____ | ____ | ____ |
| Totals | ____ | ____ | ____ |

**Interpretation**

Whenever one partner marks *neutral,* and the other checks *agree* or *disagree,* it does not usually count as a significant conflict. It ordinarily means that the neutral partner is willing to go in either direction. Nevertheless, the meaning of each neutral should be discussed. It may reveal feelings and needs that were hidden rather than clearly articulated.

Truly incompatible answers, one *agrees* and the other *disagrees,* on just two or three items are usually not very meaningful. But there is an exception. A real disagreement about just one item, number 9, can be critically important. Even if this is the only area of conflict, it needs to be very carefully and honestly discussed.

When disagreements number five or six, it suggests that partners should wait just a bit before cohabiting. They may need to understand each other's habits and expectations a little better before moving in. Disagreements on over half the items, scores as high as ten or twelve, show the partners may not know each other well or have not had a chance to communicate honestly. They should consider ways to reconcile their needs, behaviors, and goals before contemplating cohabitation (Brehm, 1985; Macklin, 1983; Risman et al., 1981).

tinuously for several years. The number of years necessary for a couple to be considered legally married varies from state to state and may be as low as 3. There are probably numerous long-term cohabiting couples who are unaware that they are now legally married.

Some cohabiting couples have been living together happily for years. They say they are reluctant to get married because they fear it could end the novelty and excitement in their relationship.

**Sex and durability**    Are cohabiters enjoying a better sex life than people who are married? The answer is a qualified yes. People who cohabit often report having intercourse more frequently than comparable couples who are married. They also vary their sexual activity more than married people. Cohabiters, for example, use more different positions for coitus and spend more time caressing before coitus. Risman's (1981) study of cohabitation suggests that couples who live together are more like courting men and women than married ones. Though living together just as intimately, they may keep some of the romance and passion of their relationship intact a year or two longer than married people (Blumstein and Schwartz, 1983). We will look at this difference in sexual activity more closely in Chapter 12.

Although activity and satisfaction are higher among cohabiting couples compared to similar married men and women, this does not seem to make cohabiting relationships more durable. Divorce statistics are easy to obtain because each breakup needs to be legally recorded. The solidity of cohabiting relationships can only be approximated. There are couples whose cohabitation endures, lasting decades. But such partnerships are not typical. Most cohabiting relationships last several months, or at most about 3 or 4 years (Brehm, 1985; White, 1987).

No matter how close a couple is, or how deep their commitment, cohabitation is not marriage. Couples who cohabit can leave the partnership relatively easily. There are few or no legal or financial obligations, and dependent children are the exception. In contrast, married couples, even those who want to separate, are often kept together by the weight of social and religious authority and the many obligations to one another that they have accumulated. The relative ease of dissolving cohabitation, and the difficulty of ending marriage, can be seen as advantageous or disadvantageous depending on one's perspective (Macklin, 1983).

*egalitarian*
Equal; fair and equitable.

**Happy marriage?**    Does living together lead to happier marriage? The research and interviews of Blumstein and Schwartz (1983) suggest that cohabitants more often work out agreements about sharing household responsibilities. They are also more likely to tolerate outside relationships in general and are more **egalitarian.** Such attitudes might seem to have a positive impact on future marriage. Research findings have, however, not been conclusive. Some studies have pointed to *yes* as well as to *no* answers. Research has shown that younger couples who first live together are likely to have less satisfying marriages. Other investigators have reported that older couples, especially those who have been divorced, benefit by cohabitation. Divorced people who cohabit seem to have happier second marriages.

One of the most careful evaluations of the effects of cohabitation was carried out by DeMaris and Leslie (1984). They examined 309 married couples who had originally cohabited. The findings revealed that most of the couples believed their marriage was less satisfying than their cohabitation. Many seemed to be looking back and saying that while they were living together they spoke more openly and shared more of each other's lives. At the same time, they were unclear about their cohabitation's effect on their marriage. Whether cohabitation hurt or helped most of them was uncertain.

Psychologist James White (1987), in contrast, came to a favorable conclusion about 800 Canadian cohabitants he studied. Over the first few years of marriage, couples who had cohabited were almost twice as likely to stay married as those who had not. But whether these findings would apply to couples in the United States or elsewhere, or hold in the long run for the Canadians surveyed, is unclear.

Sharon Brehm (1985) looked at the research that examined the effects of cohabitation on marriage. Evaluations of marital satisfaction largely yielded similar results for those who did or did not live together before their wedding. There was also no difference in the divorce rate. Brehm writes:

> It does not appear, then, that cohabitation offers any kind of "cure" for the present divorce rate. Instead, it seems that cohabitation and marriage are essentially different relationship alternatives that people enter into for different reasons. We are more likely to cohabit with *or* marry someone than to cohabit with *and then* marry someone. Even if a couple does live together as a prelude to marriage, this experience appears to have little effect on their marital relationship.

## Celibacy

Celibacy is abstinence from sexual relations (Chapter 1). Celibacy may be voluntary, the result of personal choice, or it may be involuntary, imposed on a person. The period of time involved needs to be fairly substantial. Withdrawal from activity for a few weeks is not ordinarily considered celibacy. People who are celibate refrain from all forms of sexual activity with a partner for many months, often for years, and sometimes for a lifetime.

The Catholic faith, Buddhism, and several other religions require celibacy of some of their clergy. Otherwise celibacy is not common. The number of people who are voluntarily celibate is probably about 1%. Those who have celibacy imposed on them by illness, age, or social circumstances may number up to 10% (Brown, 1980).

The involuntarily celibate include people who are physically or psychologically handicapped, or socially rejected. Women and men who are imprisoned may also be prohibited sexual relations for many years. Such involuntary restrictions on sexual contact are frequently experienced as distressing and painful deprivations.

Involuntary periods of celibacy occur among many single people. There can be long months or years when the never married, divorced, or widowed are not involved in a relationship that provides sexual intimacy. In these instances some women and men can feel frustrated and depressed. Sometimes psychotherapy or counseling is needed to help people cope with involuntary celibacy (Brown, 1980).

There are single people, too, and a few who are married, who look on periods of celibacy as a time to restructure their lives and goals. Celibacy gives them an opportunity to reevaluate and grow. Such men and women choose to abstain from sexual relations to devote themselves fully to their work, their family, or other personal goals.

Celibacy is abstinence from sex with a partner. Many professionals contend that a person may masturbate and still be considered celibate.

A 32-year-old woman: I have been celibate for 5 months. I believe relationships with men are inherently exploitative and I do not want to involve myself in that. Not at this time. I want to reconsider all my needs and my directions.

A 19-year-old man: I bicycled through China for 7 months and was determined to remain celibate. That way I could put all my energies into my journey. I also did not want to seem the over-sexed American, chasing local women.

A 46-year-old woman: Being divorced makes the men think I'm an easy mark. I'm not. I want to think things over before I get involved again. I've been celibate for almost a year.

A 52-year-old man: My wife and I have taken a break from sex. I see this as a period to develop. For both of us to grow in new directions. I need to sleep alone a while longer to know where I want our relationship to go.

*(Author's Files)*

Voluntary celibacy has been suggested to help people readjust. Sex therapists may counsel clients to abstain while old negative attitudes are explored and new behaviors considered. Whelehan and Moynihan (1982), believe celibacy might provide an answer to sexual "burnout." Sometimes relationships can become too intense and demanding. In the view of these investigators voluntary celibacy can provide the refreshing break that helps reestablish a sense of equilibrium.

Celibacy has also been claimed to be invigorating and to contribute to health and a fit old age. Athletes may assert that several weeks of celibacy improves their performance. Artists may contend that celibacy helps their productivity. When they abstain from sexual intercourse they believe themselves to be more creative. At the same time, there are warnings that the sex drive must assert itself. Voluntary celibacy is held to be emotionally and biologically damaging. Brown (1980) has examined the scientific evidence and concludes that the data do not support the supposed health and creativity benefits of celibacy, nor its alleged ill effects. Voluntarily abstaining from sexual relations does not appear to affect vitality, artistic abilities, or physical prowess in one way or another. Celibacy is neither hazardous nor uniquely productive, although a few people who elect this option may believe it to be worthwhile.

## SINGLEHOOD: ADVANTAGES AND DISADVANTAGES

A generation ago choosing to remain single was considered an odd or unfortunate choice. Today society has much more positive attitudes toward being single, recognizing it as a legitimate option and life-style.

For many single people, being unmarried is a temporary state. These men and women believe they are single only until they find a partner. For those who are younger and more flexible, singlehood may be relatively brief. People who are older may not find a partner for a very long time, if at all. There is also a third group: women and men who choose to remain single. They like their unmarried life-style and have no intention of abandoning it. For all people who are single, whether briefly, for several years, or for a lifetime, there are advantages and disadvantages.

### Freedom, loneliness, health

The single person is free to come home early or late, eat out or in, travel, and change jobs with few constraints. Such persons can do almost anything at all with their lives without answering to anyone.

### Meet Three Single People

I'm not single entirely by choice. I have had chances to live with some men, probably marry and all, but the timing wasn't right and I wasn't sure about how I felt. I sort of broke those relationships off. I'm 32, and I do worry that the market out there is getting smaller. Most of my friends are married, some already for the second time. I go to social events, the ski club mixer, the dances held by the health club, and such. I do meet people, but either I'm not that interested or they are not. I'd like to be married, but maybe I just am not desperate enough. I'm content with my life. It's good.

I've been married, divorced, married and widowed. Now what? I'm only in my 40s, and most of the men I meet look for someone who's younger. I can't entirely blame them since I'm a pretty strong sort of woman and I guess I intimidate them. They probably feel they can get away with more with a younger woman. Anyway, I'm not that motivated to couple up again. I have found women friends who meet my needs, sometimes more than any of the men I have ever known. I also have a good job and money in the bank. I feel really independent. Maybe when I'm in my 60s I'll look for some old widower, just for the sake of having some company. But then, I have my women friends, so who needs it?

I was single until I married at age 33. I had a really good time as a young single, now that I think of it. But there was always pressure to marry from my parents, friends would fix me up, etc. I wasn't exactly your swinging single, but I did spend money on cars, women, restaurants, and so on. Anyway, my marriage lasted 10 years, and here I am single and poor. That's the important part. I have nothing in the bank, and child support costs me all the extra money I used to live on in style. You'd be surprised how many modern women, those who say they are liberated, care about how much money you make. I got serious with one woman, and then she found out I'm living on what little that's left after my divorce settlement, and she suddenly lost interest in me. I'd like to live with someone, have a serious relationship, but I guess it's the money, or something else—it could be something else—that's keeping me from it.

Nearly all single people, even if they have several friends, can feel very lonely. They may not have had a chance to talk with anyone for a week or more except for brief business conversations. If they go to a movie or restaurant and see everyone else coupled, they may feel out of place and embarrassed. On the other hand, in a survey of 356 single women, a good portion of those interviewed seldom felt lonely, and, for many that did, this feeling declined as time went by. The women adjusted well to being alone, particularly when they built quality relationships with friends (Essex and Nam, 1987).

Because single people usually live alone, some tend to slip into individualistic habits. Instead of going to bed at 11 PM and eating two or three meals at customary times, they can develop completely irregular routines. They may fail to take proper care of themselves and be sick more often. In a research program at Massachusetts General Hospital examinations of single and married men who were otherwise alike showed those living alone to have a higher incidence of heart disease, more depression, and more days of illness (Wolfe, 1982).

Being single sometimes means periods of loneliness.

### Variety and commitment

Single people have more varied friends and relationships. Their lives are enriched by knowing different people. Their sexuality may also be more innovative. According to Petersen et al. (1983), some single people were more likely to find sex more exciting by engaging in it in unconventional places, such as an automobile. Some single people also had more sexual partners than those who were married.

The old and familiar term for STD, sexually transmitted disease, is VD or venereal disease. Most STDs are treatable, but a few are very serious.

Many unmarried women and men seem to have more acquaintances and friends. But those who have sexual relations with many different people are at greater risk of coming in contact with a person who has a *sexually transmitted disease,* of which AIDS is the most serious (Chapter 16). Sometimes, too, having several friends is not as satisfying as having one person with whom one is involved in a solid relationship. Friendships can be superficial, while a committed relationship may be deeply rewarding.

### Work

Being single may permit one to spend more hours and days on one's career or job. Single people who like their work can give it their full attention and make the kind of progress that will earn them money and success. But without the pull of a family, those single people who are ambitious can become workaholics. Their jobs or professions may so consume their time and energy that they have room for little else. They could lose their friends and become narrow persons who can talk only about their work.

## Happiness

Weighing all the advantages and disadvantages, do single people have a greater or lesser potential for happiness? The answer, of course, is an individual one. Those who enjoy the flexibility and freedom available to single people may be happier remaining single. Others who want the structure and constancy of a partner may find marriage, or its equivalent, deeply satisfying. Glenn and Weaver (1988) tried to measure happiness by analyzing more than a decade of survey results for over 5000 young adults. The proportion of single men who said "very happy" when asked to describe how happy they were doubled in the last 15 years. When women were asked, more said they were happy today than did 10 years ago, although the increase was not as large as that for men. Of all the single groups, the never married were happiest and those who were divorced or separated were least content.

---

Never-married adults are the largest singles group. Most will eventually marry but many others elect to remain single. These singles often have more friends and a more varied sex life than do married couples. Few, however, live up to the stereotype of the adventurous young man or woman. As a group they rate themselves less sexually satisfied than married couples. Divorced and widowed people often find their new aloneness difficult and may face financial and psychological problems. Most who are divorced eventually remarry. Older men, and more so women, who want remarriage usually find it difficult to find sexual-affectional or matrimonial partners. The number of people who cohabit is now substantial and this form of partnership is increasingly socially accepted. Some people elect celibacy and believe it helps them reevaluate their relationships and goals. Remaining unmarried may be a chosen option or involuntary, and has advantages as well as disadvantages.

*In Sum*

---

## SINGLES GROUPS AND SERVICES

Despite the image, few single people regularly go to singles bars or find them a satisfying way of meeting people. To provide for the growing number of single people who want to meet others, a multifaceted industry has evolved consisting of newsletters, magazines, social groups, and services. One of the most well-known groups is Parents Without Partners (PWP), a nationwide organization with chapters in virtually every community. PWP meets regularly for business, educational, and social purposes. Single Professionals is another popular group that brings people together to share ideas and experiences and learn from one another. Most of all, such singles clubs provide a way for people to meet and begin friendships.

Networks, support groups, workshops, and similar opportunities are increasingly available for people who are divorced or widowed or who have never married. Churches and synagogues have also recognized the swelling numbers of single people. Weekend dances and social mixers are common. Just before the weekend, dozens of advertisements can be found in most larger newspapers from religious, community, ethnic, and similar organizations an-

## Personal Ads

**Hazel-eyed Brunette,** slim and vivacious, divorced, with grown children. Self-employed professional, 42 and ready to start enjoying life. Looking for congenial nonsmoker who likes suburban living, serious movies, flea markets, and antiques. Desire flexible, noncommitted relationship. Box 063.

**Tired of Singles Bars** and clubs, and intense women! Ready to settle down with an old-fashioned lovely lady who knows how to pamper a man. I'm muscular, 5' 8", 32, attorney, who likes to jog, bike and hike. Box 244.

*(Author's Files)*

Personal advertisements like these appear on the back pages of many magazines and increasingly in the classified section of local newspapers. Most are written by single, divorced, or widowed men and women looking for a possible spouse. A few magazines also accept advertisements placed by homosexual people. Despite the growing popularity of these advertisements many people are still suspicious of them. The stereotype is that only a desperate person will advertise and only an undesirable person will answer.

Michael Lynn and Barbara Shurgot (1984) from Ohio State University monitored the responses to personal advertisements in an Ohio magazine called *Living Single*. The number of ads placed by women was 190 and those put in by men 205. Male advertisers received an average of nine responses and women an average of eleven. Women placed slightly fewer ads and received slightly more responses.

The researchers also found that including certain physical descriptions in the advertisements helped draw more responses. Women who included the information that they were attractive or in some other way physically appealing got an average of fourteen responses. Those who said nothing about physical appeal only received seven. On the male side, those who said they were tall received more responses than those who indicated they were shorter.

Lynn and Shurgot (1984) are aware that self-descriptions tend to exaggerate desirable features. As a result, when the men and women who have contacted one another through a personal advertisement finally meet, one or both may be a little disappointed. Nevertheless people who answer advertisements generally agree that advertisers are usually friendly and decent women and men.

I've placed ads and answered ads. I've been told that the women may down play their weight a little, or take a few years off their age. But otherwise they're honest and nice people. Most of the men I've met have been professionals or business executives . . . but you get working people too. They're not creeps. They're the kind of people you might meet in church or at a neighbor's . . . nice, normal people.

■ ■ ■

There is a certain protocol in meeting. Let's say I put in an ad. They write to a box number and the magazine forwards the letters to me. They don't know my address or phone number. You do this because you have to be careful. If I'm not interested in their letter I send it back with a polite note that I can't follow up, that I'm busy now. If I am interested I write to their address or call them up. I then give them my work phone number and we talk. Then we set up a date for lunch in a restaurant. That way if he turns out to be a big bore I know I only have to put up with it for 45 minutes. But if we hit it off then we'll exchange home phone numbers and make plans to start dating.

*(Author's Files)*

A video dating service.

nouncing "Young Singles Dance: Adults 18 to 35" or "Maturity Mixer: Single Men and Women over 50."

### Dating services

If going to meetings with other single parents or attending church functions does not sound appealing, then a dating service might be appropriate. To provide for the millions of singles who are not meeting people they believe desirable, commercial dating services have sprung up. Some are simply newsletters that carry a few articles of interest to singles but consist mainly of page after page of partner-seeking advertisements.

Dating services may also introduce people directly. Applicants may be interviewed about their likes and dislikes and then an attempt is made at matching them. More elaborate versions of dating agencies may use psychological tests and computers. Clients fill out checklists containing hundreds of personal description items. They are then introduced to others who seem compatible.

Video dating services often combine personal checklist descriptions with videotapes of prospective dates. The client is shown videotapes of five or ten supposedly compatible single people. When two people like what they see on the screen, a meeting is arranged.

### Coping with shyness

Divorced and widowed people often have reentry problems; they no longer know how to date. Never married single people sometimes complain of shyness. They feel awkward and tense in the presence of the other sex. They lack confidence and fear rejection. They are afraid that if they make a friendly overture or invite another person, they will be turned down.

The number of people affected by shyness and dating concerns is considerable. A survey of nearly 4000 students at the University of Arizona found a third of the women and men were quite anxious about dating. These fears of-

*Some dating services restrict membership to those who have tested free of AIDS. Since members could have relations with those not in the club, such services may offer only a false sense of security.*

*People who are shy find it difficult to state their needs, to approach others, and to start a conversation.*

*assertiveness training*
A popular way to help
people overcome shyness.
This technique teaches
people to speak up, look
others in the eye, and state
their wants tactfully but
clearly.

*thought sharing*
Telling another person
one's idea, feeling, or
observation.

ten led to an avoidance of the other sex, or when friendship was started it
failed to progress to more intimate levels (Timnick, 1982).

Many singles groups and dating services, as well as colleges, often offer
workshops in overcoming shyness. Such brief courses usually involve about a
dozen single people and a leader. The group is urged to talk freely and openly
reveal their doubts and anxieties. They are also taught specific social skills.
They may learn **assertiveness,** that is, to speak up for themselves tactfully. Or
they may learn how to start a conversation with a stranger. One method, for
example, that breaks the ice and gives the single man or woman something to
talk about is called **thought-sharing.** Using this approach, getting to know
someone could begin with: "Hi, I was wondering if you had noticed how unusually beautiful the sky was earlier tonight" (or "how quiet it is in here," or
"what a cozy room this is").

Those who lack confidence and fear rejection (also discussed in Chapter 11)
learn how to work their way up from making minor requests with confidence
to major ones. One simple assignment might be to ask people one wants to
meet if they have seen any movies or theatrical productions recently that they
would recommend. Shyness and rejection fears can be formidable barriers, but
these hesitations can also be overcome. (Gilmartin, 1987).

## Summary

There are over 50 million single people, unmarried adults, in the United States.
This very large group includes never-married, divorced, and widowed women
and men. There are more unmarried women than men, and this is particularly
true among older people.

The majority of college students can be considered "single." In most colleges life revolves around the residence hall, which is frequently coeducational.
These dormitories housing both women and men seem to make social and sexual relations easier. Many students cohabit during their college years even if
only for a brief period. The proportion of students who have sexual intercourse has increased over the last several decades. This is especially true for
women. But most intercourse takes place in the context of a significant relationship. Despite the fact that intercourse and intimate petting are common,
masturbation is still the most frequent sexual outlet for college students. The
sexual and social behaviors of students of all ethnic backgrounds on campuses
seem similar and appear to reflect those of younger people as a whole.

Never-married adults constitute the largest group of singles. Most plan to
and will eventually marry. Others elect to remain single. Never-married adults
are often stereotyped as sexually adventurous. Some do have more varied relationships. Most, however, have intercourse less frequently than married couples and often say their sexual relations are not as satisfactory. A small number
of homosexual men and women are included in the never-married, single adult
group. Their experiences are defined as much by the fact that they are single as
by their orientation.

Divorced and widowed people become single after having been married.
Many feel angry and distressed and have difficulty reentering the singles world.
Both groups of adults may have few social and sexual relations for up to a year
after the marriage ends. After the first year, most divorced people have found
an affectional-sexual partner and often report their relations are more satisfac-

tory than in their marriage. Older widowed people may not resume affectional-sexual relations, but those in the 50s and 60s usually do.

Over 2 million single people cohabit, a partnership style that continues to increase in frequency. Cohabitation is still technically illegal in many states, but social disapproval has lessened considerably. The cohabitants may have a relationship that includes many of the elements found in marriage or their partnership may be quite flexible. Most cohabitations are relatively short-lived, but many others end in marriage. Cohabiting does not seem to improve or detract from a future marriage.

Periods of celibacy are common among single people. Celibacy that is involuntary may prove frustrating and stressful. Voluntary celibacy may be elected to enable a person to reevaluate relationships and purpose. Celibacy in and of itself confers no special health or creative benefits; nor is it harmful.

Being single has many advantages and disadvantages. On the positive side these include freedom, variety, and the opportunity to devote major energy to one's career. Negatives include loneliness and overcommitment to one's profession or job. Whether the pluses or minuses are more important is a decision each person must make individually.

Single adults meet in various ways. Singles organizations, dating services, church dances, taking courses, and newspaper advertisements can all be helpful in meeting others. Shyness and dating fears that may inhibit socializing can be overcome.

---

*For Thought and Discussion*

1 Define the different people and groups described by the word *single*. What effect has the growing number of single people had on society?
2 How do college students cope with being single both in school and after graduation? What effect have coeducational dormitories had on male/female relationships and future partnership styles?
3 Suggest ways in which women and men can prepare themselves for and lessen the pain of becoming single; the dissolution of a partnership.
4 In your experience, what are good ways for single people to meet? Evaluate the worth of singles bars, dating services, advertisements, and courses and workshops. How can dating fears be overcome?
5 Consider the different people, older and younger, who are single and describe the advantages and disadvantages for each. What social and related changes would you make that might improve the life of men and women and older and younger single people? How has AIDS affected single life-styles?

---

*References*

Alvarez, A. *Life after marriage: an anatomy of divorce.* New York: Simon & Schuster, Inc., 1982.

Atwood, J.D., and Gagnon, J. Masturbatory behavior in college youth. *Journal of Sex Education and Therapy,* 1987, *13*(2), 35-42.

Balkwell, C. Transition to widowhood: a review of the literature. *Family Relations,* January 1981, *30,* 117-127.

Belcastro, P.A. Sexual behavior differences between black and white students. *The Journal of Sex Research,* February 1985, *21*(1), 56-67.

Blumstein, P., and Schwartz, P. *American couples: money, work, and sex.* New York: William Morrow & Co., Inc., 1983.

Brecher, E. *Love, sex, and aging.* Boston: Little, Brown, & Co., Inc., 1984.

Brehm, S.S. *Intimate relationships*. New York: Random House, Inc., 1985.

Brown, G. *The new celibacy*. New York: McGraw-Hill, Inc., 1980.

Cargan, L. Singles: an examination of two stereotypes. *Family Relations*, 1980, *30*, 377-385.

Cargan, L., and Melko, M. *Singles: myths and realities*. Beverly Hills, Calif.: Sage Publications, Inc., 1982.

Carroll, L. Concern with AIDS and the sexual behavior of college students. *Journal of Marriage and the Family*, May 1988, *50*, 405-411.

Cherlin, A.J. *Marriage, divorce, remarriage*. Cambridge, Mass: Harvard University Press, 1981.

Christopher, F., and Cate, R. Factors involved in premarital decision-making. *Journal of Sex Research*, 1984, *20*, 363-376.

DeLamater, J.D., and MacCorquodale, P. *Premarital sexuality: attitudes, relationships, behavior*. Madison: University of Wisconsin Press, 1979.

DeMaris, A., and Leslie, G.R. Cohabitation with the future spouse: its influence upon marital satisfaction and communication. *Journal of Marriage and the Family*, February 1984, *46*, 77-82.

Dodson, B. *Sex for one: the joy of selfloving*, Avenel, N.J.: Crown Publishers, Inc., 1988.

Essex, M.J., and Nam, S. Marital status and loneliness among older women: the differential importance of close family and friends. *Journal of Marriage and the Family*, February 1987, *49*, 93-106.

Gilmartin, B.G. *Shyness and love: causes, consequences, and treatment*. Lanham, Maryland: University Press of America, Inc., 1987.

Glenn, N.D., and Weaver, C.N. The changing relationship of marital status to reported happiness. *Journal of Marriage and the Family*, May 1988, *50*, 317-324.

Glick, P.C. Remarriage: some recent changes and variations. *Journal of Family Issues*, December 1980, *4*, 445-478.

Kinsey, A.C., Pomeroy, W.B., and Martin, C.E. *Sexual behavior in the human female*. Philadelphia: W.B. Saunders Co., 1953.

Kinsey, A.C., Pomeroy, W.B., and Martin, C.E. *Sexual behavior in the human male*. Philadelphia: W.B. Saunders Co., 1948.

Langone, J. *AIDS: the facts*. Boston: Little, Brown, & Co., 1988.

Lynn, M., and Shurgot, B.A. Responses to lonely hearts' advertisements: effects of reported physical attractiveness, physique, and coloration. *Personality and Social Psychology Bulletin*, September 1984, *10*(3), 345-357.

Macklin, E. Nonmarital heterosexual cohabitation: an overview. In Macklin, E., and Rubin, R. (editors): *Contemporary Families and Alternative Lifestyles*, Beverly Hills, Calif.: Sage Publications, Inc., 1983.

McCabe, M.P. Desired and experienced levels of premarital affection and sexual intercourse during dating. *The Journal of Sex Research*, February 1987, *23*(1), 23-33.

Peplau, L.A., and Cochran, S.D. *Sex differences in values concerning love relationships*. Paper presented at the annual meeting of the American Psychological Association, Montreal, September 1980.

Petersen, J.R., Kretchmer, A., Nellis, B., Lever, J., and Hertz, R. The *Playboy* readers' sex survey (Parts 1 and 2). *Playboy*, January 1983, 108; March, 1983, 90.

Phillis, D.E., and Stein, P. Sink or swing? The life styles of single adults. In Allgeier, E.R., and McCormick, N.B. (editors): *Changing boundaries: gender roles and sexual behavior*. Palo Alto, Calif.: Mayfield Publishing Co., 1983.

Richardson, L. Another world. *Psychology Today*, February 1986, 22-27.

Risman, B.J., et al. Living together in college: implications for courtship. *Journal of Marriage and the Family*, 1981, *43*(1), 77-83.

Rubenstein, C., and Tavris, C. Special survey results: 26,000 women reveal the secrets of intimacy. *Redbook*, September 1987, *169*, 147.

Sherwin, R., and Corbett, S. Campus sexual norms and dating relationships: a trend analysis. *Journal of Sex Research*, August, 1985, *21*(3) 258-274.

Tanfer, K. Patterns of premarital cohabitation among never-married women in the United States. *Journal of Marriage and the Family,* August 1987, *49,* 483-497.

Timnick, L. How can you learn to be likable, confident, socially successful for only the cost of your present education? *Psychology Today,* August 1982, *16,* 42.

U.S. Bureau of the Census. *Current population reports.* Washington, D.C.: U.S. Government Printing Office, 1988.

Weinberg, M.S., and Williams, C.J. Black sexuality: a test of two theories. *The Journal of Sex Research,* May 1988, *25*(2), 197-218.

Whelehan, P.E., and Moynihan, F.J. Secular celibacy as a reaction to sexual burnout. *Journal of Sex Education and Therapy,* 1982, *8*(2), 13-15.

White, J.M. Premarital cohabitation and marital stability in Canada. *Journal of Marriage and the Family,* 1987, *49,* 641-647.

Wolfe, L. The good news. *New York,* January 4, 1982, 33-36.

Zelnik, M., and Shah, F.K. First intercourse among young Americans. *Family Planning Perspectives,* 1983, *15,* 64-70.

*Suggested Reading*

Broder, M., and Claflin, E.B. *Singlehood—after the sexual revolution: the complete guide to enjoying life on your own.* New York: Macmillan Publishing Co., 1988.

An upbeat, frank look at what it means to be single in a time of growing conservatism and preoccupation with sexually transmitted disease.

Cargan, L. and Melko, M. *Singles: myths and realities.* Beverly Hills, Calif.: Sage Publications, Inc., 1982.

The authors compare the stereotypes of single people, such as the lonely and the sexually active, with the reality. The report is based on a limited sample of singles, but gives some interesting insights into the life-styles of unmarried men and women.

Douglas, J.D., and Atwell, F.C. *Love, intimacy, and sex.* Newbury Park, Calif.: Sage Publications, Inc. 1988.

This careful review of the varieties of relationships is especially informative for single people, both younger and older.

Shahan, L. *Living alone and liking it.* New York: Stratford Press, Inc., 1981.

A well-written guide to the problems and solutions of living alone. Perhaps a little overly enthusiastic but helpful nevertheless.

*Part Four*

# SEXUAL CONNECTIONS
## *Relating to Others*

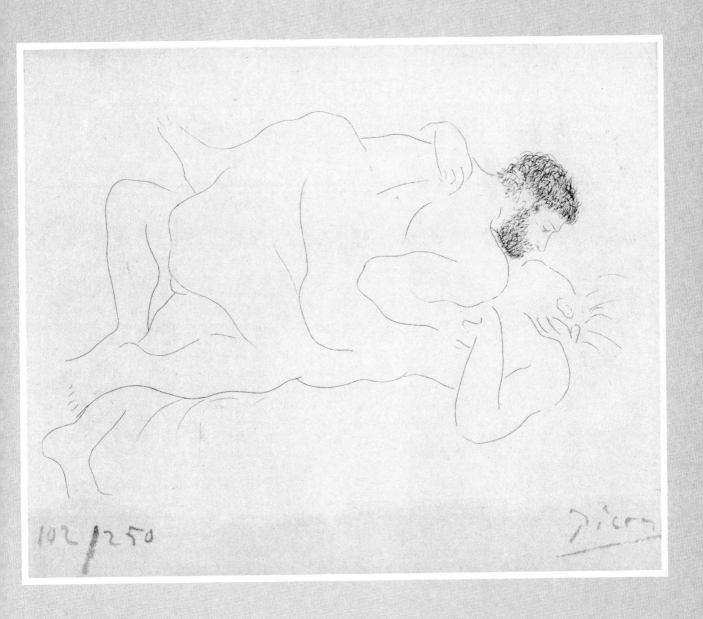

102/250                                    Picasso

# Chapter 10

# Sexual Signals
## Spoken and Unspoken Communication

**When you finish this chapter, you should be able to:**

Explain how and why words and phrases can have different meanings.

Identify body signals (unspoken communications) that are common in our society.

Describe how smiling, eye contact, touch, and posture can convey meaning.

Evaluate ways in which spoken and unspoken communication can have hidden or false meanings.

Apply techniques to improve your ability to understand and communicate.

There is a poignantly funny scene in Woody Allen's film, *Play It Again, Sam.* Allen and his date are sitting on a couch in a dimly lit living room and the woman has complained that other people are much too inhibited. The couple are turned towards one another and their postures, closeness, and the setting clearly suggest intimacy. The woman then leans toward Allen and states, "I believe in having sex as often, as freely, and as intensely as possible." Allen responds by embracing his date and trying to kiss her. But the woman acts shocked and says, angrily, "What do you take me for?" Allen backs away and shakes his head. He asks himself, "How did I misread those signs?" In this part of our text we will try to understand and answer Woody Allen's question. We will describe the ways in which men and women communicate about sexual and related feelings. We will discuss spoken communication as well as unspoken signaling. The intent is to help women and men communicate more clearly, enriching their lives and relationships.

# SPOKEN COMMUNICATION

Communication is the chief process through which people learn about cooking, religion, computers, in fact the entire world about us. Perhaps most important for our discussion, communication is the means by which people come to know and relate to one another. Communication requires that messages be sent and received. We are most aware of spoken words, but we also relate to others through written words, pictures, signs, hand gestures, facial expressions, clothing, and so on. In fact, it is impossible to be in the same place with someone else and not communicate, although the message may simply be, "Leave me alone."

## Words

Human beings are the only animals able to use a multiplicity of sound combinations to make words and convey meaning. Chimpanzees can learn to make a few vocal sounds and as many as a hundred or so manually signed words to form some very simple sentences. Birds, dogs, elephants, and most other animals make a number of sounds that communicate (Wallace, 1980). Human language, however, has literally hundreds of thousands of recognizable sound patterns. When these words are arranged in sentences, the grammatical combinations become infinite. Notice, in the following, how just a few similar sounds can convey several different meanings.

1. I love you.
2. I do love you.
3. I, love you?
4. I know I love you.
5. I have loved you.
6. I love you; I love you.

Although words, sentences, and all spoken language reveal a great deal about our feelings and thoughts, speech is not a perfect means of communication. We can say "I love you" very distinctly and still be misunderstood. A great many husbands, wives, friends, and lovers have heard these words and responded, "What do you mean?"

Imperfect as words are, they are still the clearest, most efficient, and direct way we have to convey a message. So long as what we say is said honestly, the chances are good that we will be understood. When we use words and sentences, spoken language, we have the best chance of communicating accurately.

Words, spoken language, are the simplest and most efficient way to convey a message. Yet the meaning of many terms may not always be clear. Words such as *love, freedom, honesty,* and *decency* can have several meanings.

## Hidden meaning

"You walk fast," the 5-year-old girl said to her father. This was not a simple observation, the father realized. It was a request. He smiled, relaxed his pace, and asked, "Is this better?"

A 4-year-old boy was visiting his grandmother for the weekend. After dinner he said, "We always have ice cream at home for dessert." Understanding his meaning, the grandmother went to the freezer and asked, "Would you like chocolate or vanilla?"

These preschool children have the vocabulary needed to ask directly for what they want. They have already learned, however, that it is polite, and sometimes safer, to state requests indirectly. In fact, Wood (1981) points out

### Are You a Good Communicator?

Answer by circling (0) *rarely,* (1) *sometimes,* or (2) *often.*

| | Rarely | Sometimes | Often | | Rarely | Sometimes | Often |
|---|---|---|---|---|---|---|---|
| 1. In a conversation with someone, how frequently do you interrupt? | 0 | 1 | 2 | 4. When you don't understand something, do you dislike having to ask questions? | 0 | 1 | 2 |
| 2. How often do you joke, saying in a funny way something that is really important to you? | 0 | 1 | 2 | 5. How often do you hint about things you want rather than asking directly? | 0 | 1 | 2 |
| 3. Do you think that if your partner really cared about you she or he would understand your needs without your having to explain everything? | 0 | 1 | 2 | 6. How frequently do you say "yes" when you really want to say "no"? | 0 | 1 | 2 |
| | | | | Total | | | |

### Interpretation

If your score is around three, you are an above average listener and communicator. You understand and get your message across. If you score around six, you are like most people. Sometimes you do not understand what another person wants or you are not able to get your own meaning across. Scores of eight to ten suggest that you frequently do not communicate well. A careful reading of this chapter should help you listen and speak much better, greatly increasing your ability to communicate and to enjoy good relationships (Cahn, 1987; Pearson, 1985).

that by the time they are in school, many say "no" when they mean "yes," particularly in matters of sexual attraction. "Do you like Johnny?" one young girl asks another. "No, I hate him!" is the response. But we, knowing how children can express their feeling indirectly, have reason to suspect that the second girl actually likes Johnny a great deal. Words and phrases cannot always be taken literally, at face value. It is necessary to also consider subtle, hidden meaning.

Adults often use indirect means of communication. At a social gathering, if we want to meet another person we frequently initiate a neutral-sounding conversation. We make a comment about the warmth of the room or how nicely it is furnished. We may discuss recreation, current events, or gossip about the lives of celebrities. Underlying the conversation is the statement, "I'm interested in you." The words and topic talked about are unimportant. It is the fact that we are talking that indicates we are motivated to know one another.

**Joking**   Joking frequently has a hidden meaning. It may be used to convey intimate interest. The words are actually quite direct but because they are humorous, they are supposedly not to be taken literally. Here is a sexual invitation spoken by one worker to another in an office. "Um, you look terrific today. What d'ya say, we run off together to Acapulco this weekend?" The joking invitation has the advantage of sparing the person who makes the proposal from being embarrassed when the invitation is ignored or turned down. She or he was "only joking."

Joking can be tricky. What one person insists is a good-humored invitation another may experience as harassment. We will look at the different forms harassment may take in Chapter 20.

A second form in which joking may communicate more than one meaning is through the telling of an off-color story. This is historically an indirect male way of probing female sexual availability. A few generations ago, men commonly, and erroneously, believed that a woman who laughed at an erotic story was signaling her sexual availability. A "real lady" never laughed at a "dirty" joke. It was more appropriate to blush, leave the room, or even faint (Chapter 1).

If the woman who laughed at an "adult" joke was uncommon at the beginning of this century, the woman who herself told such a story in the company of men was a rarity. Only the most daring woman, so the prejudice held, was bold enough to tell a sexy story. Today, many contemporary women will laugh at or tell a joke with an erotic content and not intend a hidden sexual message. But the bias concerning the propriety and significance of women laughing at or telling a sexy story is still so powerful that even now far fewer women than men tell such jokes (Pearson, 1985; Tavris, Wade, 1984).

Like the child who told her father that he walked fast, adults often use words and phrases that have other than their apparent meaning. We all know that sometimes the question "Would you like to come up to my place for a drink?" can be a sexual invitation. The real message is fairly clear. In contrast, the boss who asks an employee to work late, after the others have left, may think the erotic intent is obvious. But the hidden meaning of these words may be entirely missed. Words, spoken language, are an excellent way to communicate clearly, but they are not perfect. Words may have hidden meanings, possibly leading to misunderstanding and embarrassment.

### Voice

How words are said may influence meaning as much as the words themselves. In the first year of life **voice** is more significant than words as a means of exchanging thoughts and feelings between infant and caretaker. One concept learned quite early is that Mommy and Daddy make sweet low sounds that are associated with cuddling, warmth, and pleasure. In fact, whether we observe people in Kenya, China, or Pocatello, Idaho, moderated, soft, cooing tones are an invariable part of parenting. For infants and also for adults these soft low sounds mean affection and care (Knapp, 1980).

All of us learn early in life that voice is often a more valid carrier of mean-

Talking, communicating, getting to know each other.

ing than words. In an experiment with fifth graders, children were asked to explain what a "TV teacher" was really saying. The "teacher" on a video monitor uttered various messages in which the words, the voice, and the body were communicating different things. In one case, the teacher said, "You did a real good job, children!" but her voice was negative and sarcastic. The children's response to this conflicting message was direct. Many stuck their tongues out at the video monitor. It was plain that these children did not trust the words but believed that the true message was in the voice (Wood, 1981).

When someone greets us with an ordinary brief "hello" it is little more than a courteous recognition. But when "hello" is spoken slowly and with a lilt it may well suggest personal interest. Knapp (1980) has described vocal qualities that show different feelings. By varying qualities such as loudness, pitch, timbre, and rhythm, sounds alone without words can convey anger, love, and most other emotions (Table 10-1). The lesson for us is that we need to be aware of what our voice, as well as what our words, is saying.

*Table 10-1*

**Conveying Emotions Through Voice**

| Vocal Quality | Affection | Anger | Sadness |
|---|---|---|---|
| Loudness | Soft | Loud | Soft |
| Pitch | Low | High | Low |
| Timbre | Resonant | Blaring | Resonant |
| Rate | Slow | Fast | Slow |
| Inflection | Steady, slight | Irregular, up and down | Downward |
| Rhythm | Regular | Irregular | Irregular |
| Enunciation | Slurred | Clipped | Slurred |

# UNSPOKEN COMMUNICATION

Although words and sentences can deliver the most complex human messages, we mention spoken communication only briefly. We do so because in sexual-affectional matters there is often a reluctance to speak plainly. Unspoken signals frequently become very important. If we doubt the potency of unspoken communication, folk wisdom long ago recognized its power by expressions such as "If looks could kill," or "inviting smile." We can also demonstrate to ourselves how well we can read nonverbal cues by turning off the sound on the television. We will then be replicating several experiments in which subjects are shown films of people in normal conversations but without sound. Participants are then asked to judge the emotions portrayed. Basing their decisions only on facial expression and hand and body movements, the judges were highly accurate in labeling the feelings they observed (Hall, 1985).

People differ in their ability to interpret nonverbal cues. A few women and men are extraordinarily perceptive and can pick up even subtle emotions from another person's facial or bodily movement.

### Explicit messages

Unspoken communication may be explicit or implicit. **Explicit** unspoken language is for the most part learned. Different national and cultural groups have their own signs and symbols. The hitchhiker's thumb is unmistakable to people from our own society. Italians say goodbye with their arms extended and their hands palms up, closing, although to us it looks as if the person is signaling come here. Most Europeans, despite spoken language differences, recognize the thumb rubbing over the forefinger as a sign for money.

*explicit*
Fully or clearly expressed; signals that are intended, overt, and generally learned.

The customs of the Polynesian Islands in the South Pacific have changed a great deal. A few decades ago, however, sexual signing was well developed. In some of the islands whether an earring was worn on the left or right signaled availability or not. If a woman was interested in a man she might drop a flower in front of him (Mehrabian, 1981).

In our own society and time there are very few unspoken clear sexual signals. A couple interviewed about alternate life-styles reported a custom found among some partners who exchange spouses for sexual relations (Chapter 12). In their midwest area, interested couples met by answering advertisements. When a couple was invited to the other's home for possible sexual exchange, it was up to the women to signal yes or no. If they quietly removed their shoes, it meant yes. If one of the women kept her shoes on it meant the evening would be a social one. The signal, shoes off or on, saved all the embarrassment of asking in words whether there was to be a sexual exchange that night.

### Implicit messages

The unspoken communications just described are taught and learned. **Implicit** nonverbal messages ("body language") are in part **innate**. It is likely that long before humans evolved a spoken language they conveyed messages by various postures, signs, and displays much as animals do today. Female gorillas, for example, signal by their stance that they are ready to copulate. The gorilla presents her rear to the male, showing she wants to be mounted (Wallace, 1980).

*implicit*
Implied, assumed, signals that are largely not learned.

*innate*
Inherent or inborn.

Human beings also have some signals that seem to some extent to be built-in. In nearly all nations of the world, people use similar facial expressions and body stances to convey happiness, depression, anger, and love. Whether they come from a highly technological society, or one still undeveloped, men and women laugh, smile, frown, and weep. Even children born blind who have never seen the expressions of others react with body and face much as do sighted individuals (Wood, 1981).

Scheflen (1981) describes a combination of body signals that shows sexual interest. He believes they may be partly biological in origin. He writes that the person who is courting, that is, signaling intimate intent, evidences motivation by a state of high muscle tone. Sagging decreases, the torso becomes more erect, eyes seem to be brighter, and preening, such as smoothing one's hair, is likely to occur. Women may sit and expose a thigh, cross and uncross their legs, and cock their head to one side. Men may stroke their face, unbutton or readjust their coats, and look interestedly over the woman's figure. Occasionally, too, either sex may lick their lips, ostensibly moistening a dry mouth, but in reality making a biologically basic sexual gesture.

Monica Moore (1985) made a similar observation. She observed women flirting, apparently trying to interest a man, in places such as singles' bars and a university snack lounge. The signals typically used included smiling at a man, pouting, flipping or brushing back her own hair, making darting but intensive glances, leaning toward the man or brushing against him.

**Smiling**  Smiling is one of the first ways in which infants learn to communicate that all is well. In adults, smiling is ordinarily a harmless way to signal interest in or warmth toward someone. But smiling may also have somewhat different meanings for men and for women. Men may smile because they want to get acquainted and assume that the woman smiling back at them is similarly motivated. The assumption may be correct, but it may also be erroneous.

Frieze et al. (1978) has pointed out that women smile more than men. She believes that much of this may be a learned attempt to seek approval in a male world. Such female smiling, Frieze suggests, could have a negative meaning; it is the kind of fixed smile used by a servant who feels obligated to look good for his or her employer. It is possible, then, that even when a woman seems to

Preening, posing, and other body signals may indicate sexual interest.

return another person's smile it does not necessarily mean she is expressing pleasure or interest.

**Eye contact**   Looking at another person, particularly eye to eye, can have several different meanings. Among many primates as well as humans, staring is a biologically rooted dominance gesture. It is a way of demonstrating prestige and status. The ape who first turns its eyes away backs down and acknowledges that the other is boss. In a human social setting, "catching" someone's eye is ordinarily interpreted as a sign of interest. When someone returns another's gaze, whether in a bar, church, classroom, party, or any other appropriate social context, it indicates that at the least a conversation will soon begin (Moore, 1985; Wilson, 1980).

Knapp (1980) describes eye contact as a frequent learned signal in some homosexual men. In bars, recreational facilities, or other meeting places, homosexual men who want to meet might use an in-group slang expression or a subtle hand or body gesture. Extended eye glances, however, may be the most important signal. In public places, uninterested men will avoid such long lingering looks while those who maintain eye contact may be communicating their interest (Chapter 13).

**Touch**   Touch is almost magical in its ability to convey feelings. Experiments with monkeys and other **primates** have shown that when infants are well cared for but denied their mother's or a mother substitute's touch, they grow up to be highly aggressive and maladjusted. Montagu (1986) suggests that touch may be our earliest infantile communication experience, reassuring us that all is well and secure.

*primates*
The biological order of which humans, apes, and monkeys are members.

Touch can convey reassuring and loving feelings.

Some women believe they are touched too often and too freely by men. They may consider all touch, even if the man believes it is friendly, unwanted and intrusive (Chapter 20).

A demonstration of the potency of touch was reported by April Crusco and Christopher Wetzel (1984). Over 100 customers in two restaurants were lightly touched at the end of the meal when the waitress returned their change. Diners who had been fleetingly touched on the hand or shoulder left bigger tips than customers who had not been touched at all. Touch may motivate generous as well as good feeling among people.

There are different kinds of touches. Some are merely polite, others are friendly. Still others show status, such as when the boss puts his arm on your shoulders. The distinction between sexual touch and affectional touch is often unclear to both women and men. Girls may be a little more attuned to affectional touch, since during their growing years they are far more likely to be warmly cuddled, kissed, and stroked than boys. Consequently, women may feel freer to hug and kiss a woman friend, knowing they are expressing warmth and caring. Many men, on the other hand, who have been caressed and touched less during their childhood years, are not as comfortable in communicating friendship through touch. Their adolescent experience can teach them that touch is largely sexual. There are thus a wide variety of touches, and meanings, not always understood. This may well set the stage for the two sexes to misread each other's touch signals (Thayer, 1988).

**Space**  The more successful or dominant the animal, the larger its territory in which to find food and reproduce. Humans similarly define their space, and it, too, is often correlated with power. The boss has the largest office and can enter the space, that is, office, of any employee. In contrast, the employee may not enter the boss's space without specific permission (Mehrabian, 1981).

The space indicating power and status even surrounds the person's own body. The boss may lean over an employee sitting at a desk, but the reverse is not permissible. Social scientists have defined several zones of space; each non-

The distance maintained among people who are talking often reveals their degree of intimacy.

verbally signals a specific degree of intimacy (Gambrill and Richey, 1985; Wilson, 1981).

In our culture, *social distance* means that two people talk with about 4 to 7 feet of space between them. This distance is usually maintained in formal business situations or at a conservative social gathering. It suggests little warmth or interest. *Personal distance* involves about 1 to 4 feet of space between people and is commonly reserved for friends or spouses in public places. The gap between the two allows for some touching, some whispered confidentialities, but is still not so close as to exclude others.

The ultimate in closeness is *intimate distance*. At this point people are a foot or less away from each other. This distance, in a social setting, often communicates an intense interest in the other person. Consider two people sitting on a couch. The first person has moved closer. If the partner is very interested she or he may have moved closer too. But if the second person backs off a bit, the message is, "I do not want to get that 'cozy' at this point."

**Dress, posture**   Men and women can communicate in dozens of ways without speaking. We will describe briefly two other means that often convey an affectionate or sexual message.

Personal appearance may communicate a sexual message. The biological roots of this type of communication are evident in almost every animal species, but perhaps most dramatically among male peacocks. Their ornate feather displays encourage the females to gather around. Humans do not grow feathers, but we often dress to look erotically inviting. Clothing that reveals a good amount of skin or emphasizes secondary sexual characteristics (Chapters 3 and

In many European nations people talking stand closer to one another than is customary in the United States and Canada. Some American tourists have felt uncomfortable because an Italian or French person seemed to move too close when speaking.

Leaning forward may communicate interest in another person.

## Flirtation

Flirtation involves the communication of friendly, possibly sexual interest using both spoken and unspoken signals. Flirtation may take the form of admiring remarks, probes about after work activities, coy glances, and touches. Males often start the flirtation, although increasingly women are the initiators. Generally the initiator begins with a bit of flattery, a joking invitation, or a touch. The person who is the object of this attention ordinarily responds by what has been called "ritualized flight." The one starts the flirtatious ritual and pursues, the other artfully dodges the advances.

Most flirtation usually signals some degree of sexual interest, but its objective is not always erotic. More than most other sexual signaling, flirtation may be directed to any one or a combination of goals. These flirtation objectives can be described as exploratory, recreational, or manipulative.

### Exploratory

Many relationships that may ultimately prove substantial begin with a seemingly light flirtation. This type of flirtation is used to find out whether the other person is interested without risking serious rejection.

### Recreational

Flirtation that is recreational makes both participants feel desirable and attractive. It is a confirmation, regardless of their age, weight, status, or beauty, that they are sexual beings. This is the kind of flirtation that people working together, old married friends, or sometimes even strangers engage in simply as an entertainment. A 54-year-old office worker said, "It makes the day go a lot faster. It's nicer working with those young kids. Sometimes when I dress extra nicely they'll give me a wink and tell me I look sexy. I know they're kidding me along, but it's fun." Recreational flirtation is a game in which willing participants understand that entertainment, not intimacy, is the goal. It is also possible, however, that what one person believes is recreational flirtation is interpreted by another as a sexual advance.

Erotic pictures, meaning materials intended to be sexually stimulating, are described in Chapter 19.

4) is likely to send a sexual message. The erotica industry clearly understands the importance of clothing. For example, although garter belts and very tight "T" shirts are not commonly worn, pictures of women in this attire are frequent in magazines oriented to male readers. The sexual appeal of men is often conveyed by having them wear casually open oriental robes or softly textured shirts.

Posture, like dress, may also suggest mood and attitude. At a party, a woman standing straight and erect gives a less approachable message than one standing with her hip rolled. The man sitting with his arms crossed in front of his chest may be stopping conversation. Another who leans forward toward

## Manipulative

A son-in-law's flattering comments to his wife's mother may be calculated only to win some financial or personal favor. A daughter may wrap her father around her little finger by being coyly flirtatious. In both cases sexuality is being used, but the goal is clearly not erotic. The two people want something and know they have a better chance of getting it by appealing to the vanity of their relatives.

The manipulative uses of flirtation are endless. A woman may smile and demurely preen herself while a police officer considers giving her a speeding ticket. A salesperson may dress and groom particularly carefully and lightly touch a buyer to get a bigger order. Like recreational flirtation, manipulation runs the risk of being misunderstood as a sexual overture (Gambrill and Richy, 1985).

## Are You a Flirt?

Now that you have read about flirtation, be as honest as you can and answer the following Yes or No:

*Circle*

Y N 1. Do you enjoy making admiring remarks to friends and acquaintances, commenting on how good or attractive they look?

Y N 2. Do you often hint to friends and acquaintances that you particularly like them?

*Circle*

Y N 3. Do you frequently put your arm around a friend's waist or shoulders?

Y N 4. Do you occasionally pat, touch, or caress friends in a sexy or affectionate way?

Y N 5. Do you frequently act "sexy" toward a friend but not really intend an actual sexual overture?

Y N 6. Have you been told by others you are a flirt?

Y N 7. Do you often "kid around" in a sexually provocative way?

Y N 8. Do you tend to flatter people so that they'll be friendlier to you?

Y N 9. Are you able to tease almost anyone into doing a favor for you?

Y N 10. Do you sometimes smile or wink at strangers just to see them become interested in you?

It is often difficult to draw the line between friendliness, warmth, and flirtation. But if you got a score of seven or more Yes, you may well be quite flirtatious. It is also possible, however, that you are often honestly but mistakenly being friendly. A score of four to six suggests that you occasionally may unknowingly be inappropriately flirtatious. Look at how you answered each question and try to understand whether that behavior might be offensive to someone.

another person may be inviting talk. Posture often communicates whether a person wants to talk, is trying to dominate the situation, or wants to be left alone (Hall, 1985).

---

Communication is the process by which people come to know and understand each other. Most human communication uses spoken words. Words cannot always be taken literally because they may have different or hidden meanings. The way in which words are said and the voice quality that accompanies speech also adds meaning to spoken communication.

*In Sum*

In sexual-affectional communication there is often reluctance to speak directly, so that unspoken communication can become especially important. Explicit nonverbal communication is usually learned and shared by a culture. Implicit signals may be partly innate, such as the facial expressions that indicate happiness or anger. Humans use many different unspoken signals to indicate sexual-affectional interest, such as smiling, eye contact, touch, and dress.

## COMMUNICATION FAILURE

In their book, *The Longest War,* Tavris and Wade (1984) point out "The battle of the sexes is not only the longest war, but the oldest mystery." Perhaps part of the war and the mystery can be explained by faulty communication. In one study women and men were asked, "When you interact with a person of the other sex, what kinds of misunderstandings do you have?" Nearly all the answers pointed to poor communication. The research subjects felt that the other sex hid information, did not listen, or misled them. These are three common sources of communication failure that we will examine (Cahn, 1987; Sherman and Haas, 1984).

### Hiding

We are verbal creatures and have a vast array of words that permit us to ask our partners if they want to dance, play tennis, or have sexual intercourse. But when we want to communicate our most intimate needs, we often rely heavily on hints and unspoken cues. We share a cultural heritage that virtually forbids direct talk concerning sex. We invent polite substitutes for invitations to coitus. Friends are asked to come to a late dinner at our apartment or go for a long drive.

A second cause of hiding is that when you seriously verbalize your sexual interest in a person there is no way to cover up your intent. But if you communicate desire indirectly and the request is not reciprocated you can pretend that you did not mean what you signaled in the first place. Rejection can be hidden.

Much of the stress couples experience is due to poor communication.

*Fear of rejection* leads to all sorts of inventive strategies for erotic probing without actually seeming to do so.

Another reason hints and signals are so often used to communicate sexuality is that many people do not know how to talk about sex. Like young adolescents worrying if they should kiss their date, many men and women anxiously wonder if and how they should speak about sex. In a study by Naomi McCormick (1979) on how college students **"come on"** to each other, only one in ten talked about their intent directly. Most tried to get their message across by depending on unreliable techniques like music, candlelight, body language, and hinting by dress. Nearly a decade later, in 1987, Perper and Weis did not find much improvement. Most subjects studied still depended on unspoken communication. Open and honest discussion was employed only by about one in ten (Table 10-2).

How to cope with and handle rejection is discussed in Chapter 11.

*come-on*
Slang for a seductive sexual approach.

*Table 10-2*

**Come-Ons: Communicating Sexual Intent**

| Strategy | Male (%) | Female (%) |
| --- | --- | --- |
| Seduction (music, talk, candlelight) | 39 | 30 |
| Straightforward discussion | 12 | 11 |
| Relationship/feeling talk | 9 | 10 |
| Body language | 6 | 28 |
| Hinting by dress, games | 5 | 12 |

Percentages based on combined data from McCormick (1979) and Perper and Weis (1987). Percentages do not equal 100 since some strategies were omitted.

### Crossed signals

A crossed signal occurs whenever a person intends one message but the receiver understands another. An interviewee gave an example of such a communication error. The woman informant went for the first time to a Quaker religious retreat. Before the first meal a customary Quaker grace took place. This meant that all stood, held hands, and bowed their heads in silence for a minute. The woman stood next to a man and at the end of the grace the man squeezed her hand briefly. Later that evening, the woman confided to a friend that the man sitting next to her seemed to be personally interested. "I think he's got a thing for me. He squeezed my hand during grace." This story caused the friend to burst out laughing. The explanation was that a Quaker grace is frequently ended with the participants squeezing each other's hand. It is a sign that the moments of silence are ended, nothing more.

Crossed signals often occur because men and women have learned to interpret some unspoken behaviors differently. We wrote earlier about women being taught to smile, so that this "forced" smile does not necessarily indicate pleasure or acceptance. Perhaps the area in which there is the greatest potential for crossed signals is touch. A man may think putting his hand around a woman colleague's shoulder a sign of friendship. The woman may feel that women have too long been "public property," with every man entitled to touch them. What one sex sees as an accepting gesture, the other may view as an exploitation (Abbey, Melby, 1986; Pearson, 1985). In many instances today, especially in the workplace, touch is often unwanted, inappropriate, and could be considered harassment (Chapter 20).

### False signals

Some intimate signals are in part deliberately misleading. We sometimes seem to want to convey a sexual message, but also deny it. Perhaps we want to flirt

Clothing can send many different messages. One outfit a person wears can say "I'm a dependable businesslike person." Dressed differently the person can communicate the image of a fun-loving, easygoing, carefree adult.

People respond very differently to touch that is wanted and touch that is not wanted.

or be noticed, but our motivation is largely unconscious. When we are made aware of what we are communicating we become uncomfortable and retreat. A woman reported she had stopped wearing a particular light pink outfit because it seemed to result in flirtatious comments. A man stated he switched aftershave colognes because whenever he wore his favorite some of the women he worked with would tease him by saying he smelled like a **gigolo.**

Teachers are sometimes vulnerable to false communication. Students may be flattering, flirtatious, and manipulative and still want to be seen as honest and academically serious. In her article on sexuality in colleges, Munich (1978) quotes a harassed male professor: "The girls come into my office flashing their thighs, wriggling about in the chair, talking about poetry . . . . Perhaps they're doing what nature tells them to do. Perhaps they don't know what they're doing. But I know—and I notice it."

*gigolo*
A man who provides social and sexual companionship to women for financial rewards (Chapter 19).

## IMPROVING COMMUNICATION

We have described the several means through which people communicate intimate needs. Nonverbal signaling can sometimes be effective, but in most situations such behaviors should be supplemented by words. In her massive survey, Hite (1987) for example acknowledged the centrality of spoken communication for a couple to feel intimate and sexually satisfied. Eight out of ten of Hite's respondents cited as their chief complaint that their partner did not listen. They did not communicate, and as a result a good relationship was difficult. As a basic rule, then, if we want to improve communication, we should use spoken language. However clumsy we may feel, it is through language—words and sentences—that we send our clearest messages.

People who are hearing impaired may become adept at communicating effectively through Sign Language (see Chapter 18).

In this section we have additional suggestions about how individuals and especially couples can communicate more clearly and effectively. Good communication more than any other factor enriches affectional and sexual relations (Cahn, 1987).

### Ground rules

When partners want to improve their relationship through better communication, they need to agree on ground rules. There are at least four cardinal guides. First, while it is recognizably difficult to talk about sex, intimacy, grievances and hidden needs, do try to be open and explicit. Make what you say as clear as possible and give examples as necessary. Instead of saying, "I like you to be freer when we make love," be detailed. Perhaps what you really want to say is, "I like it when you swivel your hips, moan and scratch my back." Use whatever words and examples you feel comfortable with but say what you mean.

A second important ground rule to establish is to be **nonjudgmental.** Encourage your partner to talk freely and fully. Do not judge what is said or how it is said. Do not correct her or his language or speech. There should be no disapproving frown, no comment indicating anything said is "dirty," inappropriate, or offensive.

*nonjudgmental*
Accepting without indicating whether something is good or bad, right or wrong.

A third rule involves the place and setting for communication. There are usually two places in which sex talk occurs. Some takes place while the couple is intimate. In this erotic setting, talk is brief and typically more nonverbal communication takes place. During coitus, the woman may signal to have her breasts caressed. The man may indicate with his body that he wishes to change coital positions. These are valuable and important messages, but they are short and based on momentary wishes.

Complex communication cannot take place in an erotic setting. When one partner has begun sexual relations and is physically and/or emotionally aroused it is not the time or place to say, "I wish you could spend more time making me feel desired, like maybe undressing me like you used to before we were married." Such communication should take place in a conversational setting. The partners might talk over a cup of coffee, while out driving, or walking. The point is that most communication about affectional and sexual needs requires time, careful listening, and questioning.

A couple may want to set out several other ground rules that will govern their sexual communication, but we will mention only one other: Define and focus the area of discussion. We recognize that the relationship of every couple is complex. There is much more to discuss than sex. Probably sooner or later every doubt, jealousy, and conflict should be explored. The point is that if a couple is motivated to improve their sexual/affectional satisfaction they will have to focus their communication. Each time they should select a specific topic and stick to it.

### Warm-up

Nearly everyone finds it difficult to talk about sex. For this reason, to overcome shyness and hesitation, it is frequently worthwhile for couples to begin their communication by warm-up exercises. One simple and safe way to start is to talk about famous actors and actresses, and what does or does not make them "sexy."

A more provocative and sometimes amusing warm-up task is for the couple to think of the slang they know for intercourse, penis, vagina, and other sexual terms. Recognize, however, that naming sexual body parts can cause anxiety, so proceed slowly. You can also explore how you want to talk about sex. Will you use clinical terms or common ones. Be sensitive to each other's needs and work towards a vocabulary with which you both feel comfortable (Carnog, 1986).

Another warm-up is to talk about fantasies (Chapter 8). At first the fantasies may seem relatively restrained. But after a while it is likely both partners will be more and more revealing.

> I finally told my husband that I've imagined making love to two men. But I don't want to be unfaithful. So I had figured out I would get very aroused by another man and then make love to my husband. I wanted to go see a male stripper. One that takes everything off and then you give him dollars and he goes in the audience and sits in your lap and squirms and lets you touch him. Then my husband is waiting outside and after I'm very excited we make love in the car in the parking lot.

> Something real kinky I finally told my friend was that I wanted to lift her dress and spank her gently. She'd be wearing black, silky panties, very tight and see-through.

*(Author's Files)*

One communication specialist advises "talk to yourself." Rehearse what you want to say. It will help you organize and clarify your thoughts.

*Focus*

### No Means No

"No" is a complex and difficult word, especially when it is used in reference to sexual and/or affectional relations. All of us sooner or later receive an invitation for friendship, a date, or even sexual intimacy that we do not want. We may also be at the other end, asking for a date or sexual relations and being told "no." When the latter is the case, it is neither considerate nor usually accurate for a man or a woman to assume the partner's "no" is simply an invitation to be more forceful. When a woman, or a man, says "no" to a request, no matter how you personally interpret the "no," assume that it clearly and simply means "no" and act on that basis.

What should we do when we are given an invitation and we want to say "no?" Granted, it is easier to turn down a request to play tennis than it is for intimate relations, especially if we have given our partner the impression we are quite interested in him or her. But you can and should unambiguously say "no" whenever you are in doubt. To make it easier, keep these rules in mind:

1. It is usually appropriate to indicate appreciation for the opportunity, but say you have to decline. ("Thank you, but I can't now.") You are not ready and will need time to decide.

2. If you want to continue the relationship, emphasize your interest in getting to know the person better and at a later time discussing your feelings about sexual intimacy.

3. Do not let a relationship go on that you are really not interested in perpetuating. This simply puts you in the position of saying "no" over and over. Be honest and say that you feel that you want to explore other alternatives.

Another valuable warm-up task for couples who are very close, is telling your history. Detailing your sexual development may require talking about unhappy, perhaps even abusive experiences. But often as not, telling about what has been painful helps both persons open up.

### Listen and reciprocate

One of the best ways to get another person to talk is to indicate we are listening. This means we maintain eye contact without staring, and study the speaker's expressions. We also need to respond. In addition to nodding, saying "yes," or "uh huh," we may rephrase what the other is saying. "What you're saying, as I understand it, is you really want me to go a lot slower. Not to touch your genitals until you have warmed up. Is that right?" Repeating, or rephrasing in this way, using the speaker's words, is a potent way to increase your own understanding and reassure the speaker you are listening actively.

Communication is one-sided when we talk to a psychotherapist or member of the clergy. We tell them our fears, worries, and transgressions, but they tell us nothing about themselves. We accept their remaining distant, but we would not accept our partner telling us nothing about himself or herself. We expect our partners to **reciprocate;** to reveal to us as we have revealed to them.

Reciprocity does not mean that we barely let our partners finish so that we can excitedly tell all about ourselves. We need to listen, repeating the other's thoughts and demonstrating our empathy. Then after our partners have said

*reciprocate*
To give to others as they have given to us.

Full and honest
communication is essential
to a good relationship.

what they wanted to say, we disclose ourselves. Each partner must feel both are giving and getting almost equally, (Floyd, 1988).

### Teach and question

Every person relies on many different motions, postures, expressions, and sounds to convey sexual meaning. But as we pointed out earlier, unspoken communication—body language—may be difficult to read and easy to misinterpret. For this reason a couple should teach each other what their unspoken cues mean. Here are some examples:

> In the morning when we wake up and I snuggle up to you it doesn't mean I want sex. I just want to feel the warmth of your body and have you hug me, that's all.

> When I seem to be eyeing you a lot during the evening, looking at you and sort of half smiling, it means I'm pretty interested in sex. I'd like you to give me a sign back or say something positive, like you'll take a shower early. If you're not interested then you should say something like you're going to bed extra early because you're tired.

> I find it hard to open my legs until I'm very aroused. If you try to open my legs with your hands or your body it really just turns me off. Frankly I get frightened. I'll open them by myself but it takes a while. It's not deliberate, I'm not holding back.

*(Author's Files)*

Additional tips: Use "I" language. Say how you yourself feel. Always try to temper criticism with praise and understanding.

Questions can distract a speaker and interfere with communication. They should be asked only when the speaker pauses and appears ready to handle a question.

Teaching and questioning are inseparable. Questions should be direct and open-ended. "What can I do to help you feel aroused and open your legs?" This question permits the partner to describe a full range of feelings. Notice how a yes/no question, "Do you like to make love in the morning?" leaves only two alternatives. Another question to avoid is the accusatory one. "Don't you like to make love in the morning?" puts the partner being questioned on the spot. Questions need to be as positive and understanding as possible (Gambrill and Richey, 1985; Hall, 1985; Wilson, 1980).

## Female and Male Speech

Women and men seem to use the same words and speak the same language. There are ways, however, in which the speech of the two sexes may differ. Knowing the distinctive ways in which men and women sometimes talk can help the sexes better understand and communicate with one another.

In response to a statement or question, women are more likely to be reflective and men informative. Women tend to echo the speaker's feelings and men more often try to give help. To the statement, "I'm not happy with my diaphragm," a woman might answer, "Yes, they can be such a nuisance." A man's response is likely to be, "Well, you could switch brands, or try the pill."

Another difference is that even when an area is important to them, women are more likely to

hedge, to qualify a statement, "I don't know, sometimes I wonder if I can get that sexually excited in the morning." A man making the same statement is more likely to say, "I don't get turned on in the mornings."

Women are often more expressive in conversations. They describe their emotions in words. "It's pure joy walking with you in the fresh evening air." Men tend to talk less about their feelings and be more prosaic: "It's not very dark tonight."

Men and women frequently talk about intercourse and name body parts differently. Simkins (1982) asked college students to name the genitals and describe coitus in four different social contexts. Both men and women tended to use formal terms *(penis, sexual intercourse)* in mixed-sex company and with parents. With other males and sometimes with their wives, the men often used slang terms *(cock, lay)*. Women, however, tended to continue using formal terms with members of their own sex and with their spouse or lover. A man may feel the woman is too anatomical if she says "penis," and the woman may object that the word *cock* is vulgar.

Women and men frequently use distinctive words and phrases. The two sexes sometimes approach exchanging information, questioning, and making requests fairly differently. The possibility of misunderstanding is ever present. By being alert, patient, and aware of communication differences, women and men can learn from one another and enjoy more satisfying relationships (Sherman and Haas, 1984; Pearson, 1985).

---

Communication failures occur because we often try to hide or obscure sexual messages. We may also fail to communicate because signals get crossed; the meaning intended by one person is misperceived by the other. Sometimes, too, false signals are sent. Most relationships can be improved by good communication. Communication can be enhanced by active listening, reciprocal self-disclosure, proper questioning, and other techniques. Good communication can measurably increase affectional and sexual satisfaction.

*In Sum*

## Summary

Human beings primarily use speech to learn and get to know and understand one another. Words may seem simple but they may actually have many different meanings depending on their context. Voice, how words are said softly, evenly, or harshly, also conveys different meanings.

In communicating about sexual-affectional matters, many people depend heavily on unspoken communication. Often explicit signals are used, signs and gestures learned and shared by a culture. Much sexual-affectional unspoken communication depends on implicit messages that may be in part innate. Behaviors such as smiling, making eye contact, standing or sitting very close to someone, preening, and gentle touch may all signal erotic interest in another person. We may also indicate our availability nonverbally by our posture, by the way we sit and dress, and through flirtation. In addition to being an exploratory probing of another's interest, flirtation may also be recreational or manipulative.

Communication fails and relationships suffer when meanings are hidden or covered up, signals are crossed or misperceived, or there is a deliberate intent to transmit false information.

Improving communication can enhance the quality of a relationship. In most instances it is probably best to rely mainly on spoken rather than on unspoken communication. Sexual-affectional communication and relationships can also be helped by techniques such as being specific and active listening.

## For Thought and Discussion

1 Words and phrases can have many different meanings depending on how they are spoken. Give several examples using different vocal qualities to express emotions such as love, anger, and boredom.

2 Describe and give examples of how sexual messages may be conveyed while seemingly talking about other topics.

3 What explicit spoken and unspoken sexual signals are commonly used? Are you familiar with others not mentioned in the textbook? In your view would it be better if we had clearer and universally recognized explicit sexual signals?

4 According to the textbook, what implicit behaviors often communicate sexual interest? Describe how the following may indicate sexual interest and also how they may have other meanings: smiling, touch, eye contact, space between people, dress, and posture.

5 What are the sexual and nonsexual uses of flirtation?

6 What are common causes of communication failure? How can sexual-affectional communication be improved?

## References

Abbey, A., Melby, C., and Pearson, J.C. The effects of nonverbal cues on gender differences in perceptions of sexual intent. *Sex Roles*, 1986, *15*, 283-298.

Brehn, S.S. *Intimate relationships.* New York: Random House, 1985.

Cahn, D.D. *Letting go: a practical theory of relationship disengagement and reengagement.* Albany, N.Y.: State University of New York Press, 1987.

Carnog, M. Naming sexual body parts: preliminary patterns and implications. *Journal of Sex Research*, 1986, *22*, 393-398.

Crusco, A.H., and Wetzel, C.G. The Midas touch: the effects of interpersonal touch on restaurant tipping. *Personality and Social Psychology Bulletin*, 1984, *10*(4), 512-517.

Floyd, F.J. Couples' cognitive/affective reactions to communication behaviors. *Journal of Marriage and the Family*, May 1988, *50*, 523-532.

Frieze, I.H., Parsons, J.E., Ruble, D.N., and Zellman, G.L. *Women and sex roles*. New York: Norton, 1978.

Gambrill, E., and Richey, C. *Taking charge of your social life*. Belmont, Calif.: Wadsworth, 1985.

Hall, J.A. *Nonverbal sex differences: Communication, accuracy, and expressive style*. Baltimore, Md.: Johns Hopkins, 1985.

Hite, S. *Women and love: a cultural revolution in progress*. New York: Knopf, 1987.

Knapp, M.L. *Essentials of nonverbal communications*. New York: Holt, Rinehart, & Winston, 1980.

McCormick, N.B. Come-ons and put-offs: unmarried students' strategies for having and avoiding sexual intercourse. *Psychology of Women Quarterly*, 1979, *4*, 194-211.

Mehrabian, A. *Silent messages: implicit communication of emotions and attitudes*. Belmont, Calif.: Wadsworth, 1981.

Montagu, A. *Touching: the human significance of the skin*. New York: Columbia University Press, 1986.

Moore, M.M. Nonverbal courtship patterns in women: context and consequences. *Ethology and Sociobiology*, 1985, *6*(4), 237-247.

Munich, A. Seduction in academe. *Psychology Today*, February 1978, Reprint No. p-452.

Pearson, J.C. *Gender and communication*. Dubuque, Iowa: Wm. C. Brown, 1985.

Perper, T., and Weis, D.L. Proceptive and rejective strategies of U.S. and Canadian women. *The Journal of Sex Research*, November 1987, *23*(4), 455-480.

Scheflen, A.E. *Interactions*. In B.R. Patton & K. Giffin (editors): *Interpersonal communication in action* (3rd ed.). New York: Harper & Row, 1981.

Sherman, M., and Haas, A. Man to man, woman to woman. *Psychology Today*, June 1984, 72-73.

Simkins, R. Male and female sexual vocabulary in different interpersonal contexts. *The Journal of Sex Research*, 1982, *18*, 160-172.

Tavris, C.A., and Wade, C. *The longest war*. New York: Harcourt Brace Jovanovich, 1984.

Thayer, S. Close encounters. *Psychology Today*, March 1988, 31-36.

Wallace, R.A. *How they do it*. New York: Morrow, 1980.

Wilson, J. *Sexpression: Improving your sexual communication*. Englewood Cliffs, N.J.: Prentice-Hall, 1980.

Wood, B.S. *Children and communication: verbal and nonverbal language development* (2nd ed.). Englewood Cliffs, N.J.: Prentice-Hall, 1981.

---

*Suggested Reading*

Brehn, Sharon S. *Intimate relationships*. New York: Random House, 1985.
A practical textbook geared to helping college students understand and make the most of their relationships. Has a very worthwhile section on verbal and nonverbal communication in relationships.

Frey, S. *Nonverbal communication: analyzing patterns of behavior in dyadic interactions*. Lewiston, New York: Hans Huber, 1988.
A careful analysis that is quite informative and rewarding.

Hall, J.A. *Nonverbal sex differences: communication, accuracy and expressive style*. Baltimore, Md.: Johns Hopkins, 1985.
This authoritative book is packed with information, and can help women and men better understand their own and the other sex.

*Chapter 11*

# Love and Attraction

**When you finish this chapter, you should be able to:**

Distinguish among the different kinds of love, such as erotic, friendship, and parental.

Describe the characteristics of love: companionship, caring, intimacy, romance, sex, and commitment.

Explain how love may be biologically rooted and influenced by learning.

Describe how people fall in love and select the person to be loved.

Evaluate love's problems and suggest ways they may be overcome.

The word love has almost magical powers. Think it and you are likely to smile. Say it to someone and both of you will smile. Of all the emotions, it may be the one that is talked about most. Turn on the radio and listen to popular music. The songs are about love. Listen to religious sermons and again the focus is love. Even political leaders talk about love. But although much is said about it, love is not well understood.

Do we love by degrees: "She loves him more," or is it an either/or phenomenon: "She loves me; she loves me not"? Do we learn to love, or is it a built-in biological process? Does love change with age? How is the affection shared by lovers like or unlike that felt by parents and children? Scholars and poets have tried to answer these questions and often raised even more. Realizing that we are probing a delicate area, we will try to shed some light on what is commonly called love. We will start with a definition and describe some of the forms and characteristics of love.

# THE FORMS OF LOVE

Love takes many forms. Parents love their children; people love their country; husbands love their wives. However different, these and many other types of love, all involve similar feelings and attitudes. We can use the same word, love, to describe them. *Love* is an intense, affectionate, loyal emotion. When we go beyond this skimpy definition, we begin to talk about the several varieties of love. If we add physical passion to our definition, then we are really discussing erotic love. If we add phrases like "sharing hopes and fears," but exclude sexuality, then we are discussing friendship. Love takes many different forms and we will review several of these.

## Erotic love

**Erotic love** is physically and emotionally intense. Its cardinal feature is a passionate drive for sexual and emotional intimacy with another. There seems to be a biological "chemistry" that binds the two lovers together and leads them to marry or establish another form of enduring partnership (Fisher, 1982).

Dorothy Tennov (1979) finds the term "romance," often used to describe erotic love feelings, inadequate. She prefers to call these passionate emotions **limerence**, a highly aroused state that most typifies the *early* stages of a relationship. Individuals experiencing limerence have specific sexual and psychological longing for a loved one. They are preoccupied by their love, thinking about the other constantly. The lovers in limerence may also become emotionally uneven. They are happy and buoyant when the loved one reacts favorably, downcast and depressed when the loved person seems disinterested or reject-

*erotic love*
Sexually and emotionally intense love that often leads to a binding partnership.

*limerence*
Tennov's (1979) invented term for sexual, passionate, romantic love. A useful word, but not widely employed.

Erotic love is characterized by powerful needs for sexual and emotional intimacy.

ing. As erotic love ages, its intensity declines. For most couples, however, its continuation at a lower level is sufficient to keep them together for life (Chapter 12).

### Friendship

Love between friends may be deep and intimate but it is not physical. Davis (1985) evaluated the attitudes and experiences of 250 college students and found lovers and close friends very much alike. Both rated trust, mutual assistance, and enjoying each other's company almost identically. In fact, the research participants rated both friendship and love relationships alike on 13 out of 17 qualities. The main areas in which lovers differed from friends were in sexual intimacy, exclusiveness, and fascination. Lovers are more likely to insist on exclusiveness, loving no other person, than are friends. Fascination refers to the preoccupation lovers have with one another. Unlike friends, they seem to almost constantly think about their beloved.

Most friendships are between members of the same sex. This may be partly a result of men and women being more familiar with the experiences their own sex encounters. Perhaps it also simplifies the relationship, because sexual intimacy is usually ruled out. But about half of all women and men have had a best friend of the other sex (Davis, 1985). Often such relations require explaining to others: "We're just friends. There's nothing going on between us." Apparently most such man-woman friendships remain **platonic.** At times, however, such friendships slowly evolve to include sexual relations.

### Other forms of love

Many people speak of loving their god, their nation, or their ethnic group. Profound and caring emotions may center about faith, country, and group identity. This *devotional* love does not involve physical contact, not even a soothing pat on the back. But for many ancient peoples, such as the Athenians 2000 years ago, or some modern societies, the homeland calls forth the highest form of love.

The love between parent and child is the first encounter all of us have with this compelling emotion. For some, no other person—friend or spouse—will ever be loved in as intense and committed a way as their parent or child. Freud (1959) wrote that parental love contains a sexual element. He argued that the fact that children sometimes say they want to marry the parent (Oedipus complex, Chapter 2) clearly reveals the erotic component. Today few support the Freudian view, but physical contact, including closeness, stroking, and touching, is important in building parental love. Infants and children need to be held and touched both to feel love and to learn to love in return (Montagu, 1986).

People spend hours going house to house collecting money for charity. They volunteer to visit patients they do not know in hospitals. Therapists have strong positive feelings for the person they are treating. All of us have the capacity for **altruistic** love, the emotion that makes us feel close to and want to help other people. Some say altruistic love and parental love are similar. Parental love may simply be a special case of altruistic love—a generous giving of oneself.

---

Are people who are "just good friends" and sexually intimate really lovers or still only friends? There is no universal answer because different couples have varying replies to this question.

*platonic love*
Love that does not include sex.

*altruism*
A selfless concern for the welfare of others.

# THE CHARACTERISTICS OF EROTIC LOVE

Love has many meanings and takes different forms. As we noted earlier, there is love between parents and children, love between friends, and there are spiritual affections. In this section we will concentrate on erotic love. We will see that it involves more than sex and affection. Over the years several different scientific and literary descriptions of this kind of physical-emotional love have emerged. We draw from writers who have applied both statistical analysis and insight to the understanding of love. Based on their work, erotic love seems to be associated with six characteristics: companionship, caring, intimacy, romance, sex, and commitment.

## Companionship

Being with another person, sharing life experiences and emotional support, is called *companionship*. Companionship is not a passionate or driving feeling, but a quiet contentment. It is the feeling we often get when we are with a valued friend or sibling. The ancient Greeks referred to this as *philia*. (This is why Philadelphia is known as *The City of Brotherly Love*.)

To find just how important companionship feelings are, Rowe and Vazquez (1987) investigated the "love-state" of 104 individuals. The researchers asked subjects to rank their present marital happiness on a scale of 1 to 7, and also to complete a questionnaire that best described how they felt while they were still dating.

When subjects said "yes" mainly to items such as "had common interests," "were best of friends," "we had a mutual understanding between us," they were revealing that they had emphasized the companionate aspect of love. When items such as "head over heels in love," "possessive," "consumed with thought of partner," were marked "yes," they were interpreted as reflecting love states, such as sex or romance. Rowe and Vazquez found that individuals who described the love they felt for their spouse before marriage in terms of

Lovers who recognize that they have few interests in common often doubt if they are suitable for one another. They may not say it in words but they wonder if they will be good companions.

Men and women can be friends and companions.

### Love, Then and Now

Through the ages philosophers, scholars, and poets have tried to identify and define love. A glance back shows some of the origins of our views of love today.

#### Agape

The Judeo-Christian religious view holds, "God is love." In Buddhism followers are told, "Let a man overcome anger by love." To Plato, about 500 years B.C., this religious love was *agape (ahgap-ay)*. It was an altruistic and spiritual love, considered to be much more valuable than physical love of the flesh.

#### Courtly love

A thousand years after the concept of agape was propagated, the notion of courtly love arose. Courtly love came from the Middle East, carried into Europe during the twelfth century by wandering troubadours and musician-poets. They sang long epic poems about the desires of lovers for their noble ladies. Four stages were described. First the lover was a *fegnedor*, one who falls

helplessly in love with his lady from afar. In the second stage, the lover became a *precador*. He had worked up the courage to tell his desired his hopes and ambitions. If the lady acknowledged her suitor and permitted him to write songs expressing his deepest emotions, he became an *entendedor*. This was often as far as the courtship went. To take the next step required considerable passion as well as courage.

Up until he became an *entendedor*, the third stage, the involvement was considered pure love. Devoid of physical contact, pure love did not compromise the reputation of either a virgin or a woman married to another man. It was in the fourth stage, when the courtier became *drut*, that sexual love took place.

For hundreds of years during the Middle Ages it was widely believed by aristocrat and peasant alike that intercourse could be good only after you reached *drut*, the highest stage of courtly and romantic emotion. Sexual relations without love were believed to be obscene and dishonorable.

companionship were among those more happily married. They not only ranked themselves higher on the seven-point happiness scale, but believed that many of their pleasing courtship activities carried over into their marriage.

Based on her research evaluations of couples, Tennov (1979) draws a similar conclusion. She sees the romantic and sexual correlates of erotic love often fading. Companionship may not be as exciting, but it provides friendship, and caring. Unlike some of the other love correlates, it usually endures and continues to provide satisfaction.

### Caring

**caring**
The desire to do things for and to help others.

Many believe that "really loving someone is wanting what is best for him or her, not what is best for ourselves." **Caring,** or the selfless desire to do things for another person without thought of personal profit, is obviously a critical element in parenting. But according to Rubin and McNeil (1981) caring is also significantly related to the satisfaction spouses or partners feel with one another. The degree to which each partner feels selflessly looked after seems directly related to happiness with the relationship.

In regard to selfless caring the question is often raised: "Doesn't the person

### Rational and romantic love

By the 17th century in Europe the concepts of courtly love had been largely discarded. There was also considerable disagreement about agape. The school of philosophers known as *Rationalists* held intelligence and reason to be all important. Led by renowned thinkers such as John Locke (1632-1704) they believed that people did not just happen to helplessly fall in love as courtly tales implied. Love could be cultivated at will between almost any two people. For example, marriages were usually arranged and young adults often resisted such couplings. Nevertheless, after years together a man and woman frequently loved one another.

A century later, other eminent writers such as Johann Goethe (1749-1832) argued for romantic love. *Romanticists* were influenced by the old notion of courtly love and valued emotions. They also looked to nature to understand the essence of human beings. In the natural world, they argued, growth, health, and beauty occur when every element, all the parts, fit together. With humans too, love, the perfect natural emotion, will be ignited when the proper "chemistry" is present. When each person has just the right elements and parts for the other, then the two will be emotionally and physically drawn to each other. It is important to note that the 18th century Romantic philosophers were in stark contrast with the Victorians, who less than a century later virtually cleansed romance of all sexual elements (Chapter 1).

Courtly love remained an ideal through much of the Middle Ages.

get something out of giving?" In other words, is there such a thing as pure altruistic caring? Sigmund Freud (1959) observed that being kind, doing things for others, even if there is no apparent personal gain, does give the donor conscious and unconscious rewards. Perhaps, for example, in a love relationship the caring may be an investment that presupposes that one will be cared for in return.

Russel Vannoy (1980), University of Buffalo philosopher, suggests it may well be beneficial to limit the amount of unselfishness. If we are cared for no matter what we do, then are we actually loved for ourselves? Vannoy writes that no one wants to be loved out of a pure sense of charity or generosity. Each person wants to feel worthy. So although altruistic caring in a love relationship is an important ingredient, perhaps it may sometimes be best to temper it with a little selfishness.

## Intimacy

*Intimacy* is the desire for close and confidential communication with another person. It involves sharing thoughts, feelings, fears, and hopes with one special person more fully than with anyone else. Many lovers note that their loved one knows them better than anyone. They feel that they can tell their lover everything.

But intimacy has not always been the same for both sexes. A generation ago, the consensus was that it was fine for a woman to reveal her innermost thoughts, but no "real" man needed a confidant. "Women express; men repress." Studies confirmed that women talked openly to both their husbands and female friends, while many men kept their deepest concerns to themselves (Chapter 10).

This decade has seen considerable change. In one survey dating couples were asked how much they told their partners about their work, friends, sexual feelings, and so forth. The extent of intimate revelation seemed substantial. Seven out of ten of the women *and* the men reported that they fully disclosed highly personal feelings, including their sexual attitudes (Rubin, McNeil, 1981).

The couples' love was also measured on a love inventory. The greater the couple's love for one another, the greater the mutual self-disclosure. It seems that men as well as women are becoming increasingly intimate, particularly in loving relationships.

## Romance

To talk of love and omit romance is like describing a sunrise in black and white. It is *romance* with its surging affections, daydreaming, and passions that comes to mind when we think of the early stages of erotic love. When love seems to consist of romance and possibly sex, and lasts only a short time, it is sometimes called, usually with some degree of sarcasm, **infatuation.**

Romance is a critical component of erotic love for most in our society. If we do not feel romantic stirrings we may not believe we are in love. Many women and men agree with the Romanticists of an earlier age. They expect that when they meet the right person, their hearts will race, their breathing deepen, and their remaining years of life be a constant pleasure.

The stereotype has it that women are much more inclined to be romantic. Supposedly they agree with:

Love at first sight.

Love is all you need.

When you're in love you know it.

You can only truly love one person at a time.

Nothing should stand in the way of love.

Contrary to common supposition, women are not more romantic, but are slightly more realistic than men. On questionnaires where both sexes are asked to agree or disagree with statements such as those above, men usually answer in the more romantic direction. Women also seem more cautious in courtships. They appear to hesitate more than men before involving themselves in a relationship (Rubenstein, 1983).

"Love is all you need" and other romantic beliefs may have little validity, but most people still like romance. In her survey, Rubenstein (1983) found that 96% of women and men have some faith in romance. They want the excitement, fascination, and joy of love. Romance may not be the best basis for beginning a marriage or cohabitation, yet it persists as the spice in erotic love that nearly all seem to crave.

---

Some people value intimacy very highly. They say they can only love someone who makes them feel so comfortable and accepted that they can share everything.

*infatuation*
Term commonly used to describe a romantic attraction held to be foolish, childish, and unreasonable. This emotion shares many of the characteristics of erotic love including daydreaming, preoccupation, and physical passion.

*Focus*

### Madonna, Prostitute, Saint, and Sinner

Although most people seem to prefer to have sexual intercourse within the context of a loving partnership, love and sex do not always go together. A person may have satisfying sexual relations with someone who is only a casual acquaintance. There are also some people who prefer not to have sex, or are not able to have sex, with someone whom they love.

In men, the *madonna-prostitute syndrome*, a psychiatric condition, may prevent them from having sexual relations with a woman they love. The background and experiences of such men have taught them that good women, the kind you love and marry, are supposedly disinclined toward physical sex. The woman you love is a madonna, a pure and untainted creature with whom you do not do anything as obscene as sexual intercourse. Such men have sex with prostitutes or women who are alleged to be "loose" or "bad."

The *saint-sinner syndrome* is a similar condition found in women. Such women perceive ordinary men, good people one can love and marry, as "saints." Other men who are addicts, criminals, aggressive, or just "no good" are "sinners." With them these women, often from sheltered and inhibited backgrounds, feel they can do something as "dirty" as having sexual relations.

These conditions may result in a partner not being able to be sexually adequate with a normal, "good" person. A frequent result for women and men with these syndromes is many different and difficult relationships. Such people seem continuously in one or another relationship and often involve themselves with others who mistreat and abuse them.

### Sex

Sex sometimes seems to be at the core of erotic love. New couples typically find their sexual relations a central source of satisfaction. Coitus and other sexual activities occupy a considerable portion of the couple's time and thought. Wolfe's (1981) extensive survey showed that couples who have intercourse most frequently also report the happiest relationships. Partners whose sexual satisfaction is low may still continue to care for one another but often say they experience considerable physical and emotional frustration. They may need professional counseling to help them overcome sexual problems (Chapter 17).

As important as sex is in a loving relationship, there are couples whose physical satisfaction is minimal or absent. Nevertheless they may report they love one another and that their partnership is a good one. Such people can be any age, but more usually they are disabled or elderly (Chapters 12, 18).

At the other extreme Blumstein and Schwartz (1983) found that sex alone, even when it is highly pleasurable, does not seem sufficient to keep an otherwise difficult relationship intact. Sex is pivotal in the lives of all couples, cohabitants, marrieds, and homosexual partners. It is an important component of erotic love. But there are several other correlates that can determine whether a partnership will be a happy one.

Chapter 12 examines the sexual aspects of marriage and similar relationships in more detail.

### Commitment

Any relationship will contain some conflict and some moments when one wonders whether it is worth continuing. Commitment is the aspect of love stated in

## The Characteristics of Erotic Love

What is important in your relationship? Is sex, intimacy, or commitment the quality you value most highly? Review the meaning of each of the erotic love characteristics found on pages 287 through 292, and rate their importance to you on a scale ranging from one to five. Have your partner do the same, independently without knowing your ratings. Then compare results.

| | 1<br>Not<br>Important | 2<br>Slightly<br>Important | 3<br>Important | 4<br>Very<br>Important | 5<br>Extremely<br>Important |
|---|---|---|---|---|---|
| Intimacy | 1 | 2 | 3 | 4 | 5 |
| Romance | 1 | 2 | 3 | 4 | 5 |
| Sex | 1 | 2 | 3 | 4 | 5 |
| Commitment | 1 | 2 | 3 | 4 | 5 |
| Companionship | 1 | 2 | 3 | 4 | 5 |
| Caring | 1 | 2 | 3 | 4 | 5 |

### Interpretation

If you and your partner's ratings are fairly similar you may have the basis for a good relationship. If there is considerable disagreement, that is, three or more points apart on at least four of the six characteristics, you may want to discuss the compatibility of your values and ideas. You may be expecting very different satisfactions from your relationship. Maybe you should reconsider or try to obtain the help of a trusted friend (Rowe and Vasquez, 1987; Tennov, 1979).

---

the marriage vow as "In sickness and in health, till death do us part." *Commitment* means perseverance through times of difficulty and willingness to overcome conflict and nurture a partnership.

It has been suggested that commitment is only the contractual part of a relationship and has nothing directly to do with love. Kelley (1979) sees it as almost the reverse. Commitment is the component that gives erotic love a chance to grow and consolidate. Commitment is pictured as being as much a part of love as water is a necessity for gardening. Withdraw water from a flower and however beautiful the plant or rich the soil, the blossom soon dies.

Sometimes commitment seems to be the only characteristic of love that keeps a relationship going. The partners have made an agreement to stay with each other and they stick to it despite anger, hurt, or boredom. But couples who remain together through periods of stress, through times when they feel little affection or sexual desire, can find that their overall love for each other becomes stronger through the experience (Loudin, 1981).

The person who is least committed, least willing to preserve and nurture a relationship, usually controls it. He or she is the one who most often says "Do it my way or I leave."

### Love's three faces

We have mentioned six elements of erotic love. One of the most interesting and provocative explanations of the dimensions of love is that proposed by

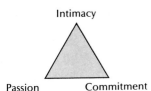
Intimacy

Passion  Commitment

Intimacy

Passion

Commitment

*Figure 11-1*
Sternberg and Barnes, (1988) have suggested a triangular representation of the dimensions of love.

Yale University professor Robert Sternberg (Sternberg and Barnes, 1988). He suggests that love has but three components—intimacy, passion, and commitment. When all three qualities are abundantly present, love is deep, lasting, and substantial. When intimacy alone is present, Sternberg says "that's liking." Two people simply like one another as friends. Passion alone is no more than infatuation. It is the kind of love that makes a young teenager stare longingly at a teacher but never approach her or him in any meaningful way. Empty love is the phrase used when there is just commitment. A couple may have experienced passion and intimacy at one point but both qualities have eroded. All that is left is the decision to stay together.

In this theory, two love elements may combine and yield several different forms of love. Intimacy and passion together give romantic love. This is like a summer affair or a shipboard liaison that will end when the partners return home. Passion plus commitment give superficial love. This is the continually repeated Hollywood theme of boy meets girl, and after a whirlwind week together they walk off into the sunset, supposedly marry, and live happily ever after. We know, of course, that their marriage, lacking intimacy, is not likely to survive the first disagreement.

Love is an affectionate emotion that takes different forms. Parental, devotional, altruistic, and friendship love may be very intense, but they do not involve sexuality. Erotic love includes sexuality and several other components: companionship, caring, commitment, intimacy, and romance. The emphasis couples place on each love quality varies. Some may report that the commitment aspect is most important, while others are likely to emphasize intimacy or companionship. For nearly all, romance seems critical at the beginning of a relationship but it usually recedes as the years go by. Sex is crucial in most erotic love relations, but alone may not be able to determine a couple's happiness.

*In Sum*

## THE ROOTS OF LOVE

Love is an emotion found around the world. This is not to say that every society equally emphasizes every form of love. In the Western nations, erotic love often seems extraordinarily important. In other countries and at other times, friendship or devotional love may have had priority positions. Despite the varying degree to which different love forms are accentuated, love is universal. Are people born loving or do we need to learn this complex affection?

Even though love may be
biologically rooted, a
person may have to have
been loved, in order to
love.

## Biology

There is considerable evidence that in animals and also to an extent in human
beings, aggression is to some degree biologically rooted. If we angrily strike
out when we want something, it may be partly the result of the testosterone
(Chapter 4) circulating in our blood. Love may also have some biochemical
roots. Fisher (1982) sees erotic love, for example, as having adaptive survival
value. It helps assure reproduction. If the man and woman who momentarily
join together for sex stay affiliated for at least a while, it maximizes the possibility that future coitus will eventually result in pregnancy. Even more important, because the human infant needs considerable care, it is advantageous to
have more than one parent available. Love may be an inherent tendency to
bond. It unites father, mother, and child, so that protective care is assured for
several years.

The hormone associated
with aggression is
testosterone (Chapter 4). It
also seems to be related to
sexual desire in both sexes
and might thus have some
bearing on erotic love
(Chapter 17).

Biologists see chemistry triggering love and cite parental affection as an example. They claim that most new mothers, whether human beings, apes, or
white laboratory rats, act maternally because of the hormones produced during the pregnancy and birth process. It is biochemistry that results in the infant
being fed, held, stroked, cleaned, and protected—behaviors people call affection or love (Montagu, 1986).

## Learning to love

For psychologist Harry Harlow, love seems to be learned. In a series of classic experiments with rhesus monkeys, Harlow and his colleagues (1979) raised groups of newborn monkeys in isolation from their mothers and from each other. Essentially, the monkeys grew up all alone.

When the monkeys were mature, they were put together to see if they would interact. If the monkeys had a strong inborn tendency to relate to one another, to "love," then despite their isolation they should form attachments. As a whole, however, the monkeys who were isolated did not join together. They did not touch or groom each other's fur. What is even more dramatic, some monkeys raised in isolation tended to become aggressive and violent. From these studies, Harlow concluded that it is necessary to experience care and love to express love in any of its several forms.

There also appeared to be a developmental love progression. Specifically, the infant had to experience a mother's love before it could express love toward the mother. If these two kinds of love occurred, the monkey youngster could then express love for a playmate, "friendship." The next level of affection the "loved" monkeys developed was heterosexual. Having experienced play together, the monkeys seemed able to form bonds, pair up, and mate.

Findings based on animal research may be applicable to human beings in only a limited way, but there is also some human evidence of the importance of learning to love. Children raised in institutions with few caring human contacts often seem to have their ability to relate to others seriously impaired. Youngsters from homes in which they were harshly rejected or neglected often find it difficult to trust and love when they are adult. There is considerable evidence that to love we must have experienced love ourselves, since earliest childhood (Sternberg, Barnes, 1988).

Does the evidence that love in its various forms seems to be learned rule out a possible biological root? Probably not. As with many human behaviors, there is likely an interaction. Both our genetic heritage and our early experience determine our ability to love.

The ability to love may depend on the caretaker-infant interaction. The caretaker may be the mother, father, sister, or any other person who consistently looks after the child.

## ATTRACTION: FALLING IN LOVE

How does love start, and how often can one fall in love? Most people agree that they have had a "falling in love" experience. It is not known precisely how often the average person falls in love. Surveys of college students show that before they finish their studies most will have fallen in love once or twice. At the college age, men have been found to fall in love more readily than women. This may be contrary to common belief, but it is consistent with our earlier assertion that men may be somewhat more romantic than women (Loudin, 1981; Rubenstein, 1983).

For many people, falling in love is a **euphoric** experience. They are not only happy with the person they have met, but begin to look at the whole world in an uncritically optimistic way. Of course, they may also paint their beloved in glowing colors, exaggerating assets and overlooking weaknesses. Sometimes, too, people who are in a falling in love phase actually experience physiological changes. They may feel flushed, excited, feverish, restless, and have digestive symptoms. But as the song says, "You're not sick, you're just in love."

*euphoric*
Totally pleasing, wonderfully good.

Nearly everyone has experienced "falling in love."

For many people, love takes time to develop. They need to know their partner for months or even years before they feel they are in love.

Exactly what happens when a person falls in love is not entirely clear nor is it the same for everyone. We know that very often the "falling" occurs suddenly, climactically. Some fortunate evening, at a crowded party, you stumble across someone who is thoroughly captivating. You spend hours together and you suspect that you may be in love. At other times, falling in love is a little less sudden and romantic. The acquaintanceship builds up gradually and sex is likely, although not necessarily, to play a prominent role. At the same time, intimacy increases, subtly at first, and then more noticeably. Gradually a transformation takes place. Attraction, sex, caring, and numerous other components come together to form a deep and binding emotion; you are in love.

## Loneliness

Some psychologists explain the erotic falling in love experience not so much as an attraction, but as a flight. Falling in love is running away from aloneness, the feeling of being separated from the human community. Women and men are seen as being driven to find a partner to ease their loneliness. For some, almost any partner is sufficient; the only requirement is that this person be willing to accept them. Freud (1959) speculated that for many adults the partner sought needs to remind the person of a parent—someone who could assure them, like their father or mother once did, of being totally accepted and never alone anymore.

## Is love blind?

One reason why some people fall or stay in love is that they seem to misperceive and idealize each other. Johnson and Leslie (1982) examined this phenomenon and tried to trace its causes. They asked 419 undergraduate and graduate students to list their friends and describe their interaction with them.

Some women and men, old and young, may be motivated to find a partner to ease feelings of aloneness.

The research team then measured each participant's degree of erotic love involvement on a scale that varied from occasional dating through engagement to marriage. As suspected, the more a person was emotionally involved with another, the fewer friends were listed. Students who were engaged or married listed the least remaining friends; some even withdrew from all old friendships.

The importance of this emotional isolation, according to Johnson and Leslie, is that the fewer friends, the less chance for anyone to correct the lover's idealizations. Many students even eliminated friends if they did not agree with them about the beloved's qualities. The end result for many people who are in love or moving toward it, is that they rely only on their own observation. They construct all sorts of positive qualities and overlook negative ones in the woman or man with whom they are falling in love. Erotic love might just sometimes be blind.

### Love stages

Dorothy Tennov (1979) explains falling in love as occurring in several stages. First comes admiration for a person who possesses the qualities for which we look. Then comes sexual attraction. Soon afterwards there is a "spark." The couple are at dinner or a dance. The attractive person makes a gesture, says some words, or gives a look that triggers the feelings of falling in love. Now the person falling in love needs confirmation. Is the other also powerfully physically and emotionally attracted? If the other does not reciprocate, hesitates, or rejects, the disappointing process of falling out of love begins. Sometimes each stage is slow and distinct while at other times all seems to happen rapidly and

*Figure 11-2*
Circular model of erotic
love described by Reiss.

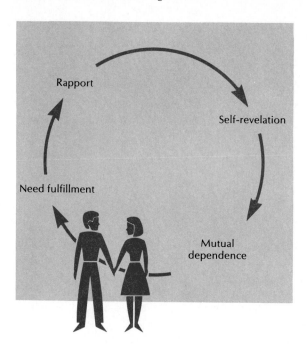

at once. Nevertheless, for Tennov, every woman and man in love has experienced such a progression.

**Love circle**  One of the most detailed analyses of the development of erotic love was described by Ira Reiss (1980). According to Reiss, erotic love progresses through circular stages. First there is rapport. The lovers seem to understand one another, get along well, and like their interaction. Self-revelation follows. The couple tell each other about themselves. The communication becomes deeper as each discloses more (Chapter 10). The joint self-disclosure leads to mutual dependence. The couple wants and needs to be together. They have to talk, touch, experience, and share. The final stage is need fulfillment. The partners want to feel trusted, valued, and loved. Reiss suggests that these four components feed into one another in a circular way. Thus in stage four, need fulfillment feeds into stage one, increasing rapport, which then leads to further self-revelation, and so forth. The "love wheel" may not be the ultimate explanation, but it does seem to illustrate how many people in our society fall in love.

## SELECTING THE LOVER
### The ideal

With whom do we fall in love? Will anyone do? Many people have an ideal in their minds, someone with certain characteristics that would make this person highly desirable. Using undergraduate students as subjects, Kemper and Bologh (1980) obtained a picture of what most young women and men perceive as ideal. Subjects were asked to rate each of 58 qualities on a 5-point scale moving from "He/she must be," to "He/she must not be." The following were some of the characteristics that were considered very important, "must be," for *both* men and women:

Attractive body
Has a mind of his/her own
Sense of humor
Simple, not sophisticated

Men's concepts of an ideal woman included these characteristics:

Smart, brainy
Would make a good parent
Even-tempered, calm
Needs you
Athletic, active
Can suffer in silence

Women idealized men who were:

Ambitious, hardworking
Intellectual, a thinker
Lets you be independent
Sensitive to your emotions
Emotionally strong
Likes art, music, books
Affectionate, warm

Kemper and Bologh suggest that the ideal concept can come about in any one of three ways. (1) We fall in love with someone who meets the preconceived notion of what is ideal. (2) We attribute the ideal characteristics to our loved one, whether or not this person actually has them. (3) After we fall in love, we idealize the characteristics of the loved one and this forms the basis of our ideal. We suspect that for most persons, part of all three processes is involved in the erotic love experience. We find some of the ideals we want, and in one way or another accept or construct a favorable image of the person available to us.

*A few pages back we asked "Is love blind?" People who are in love often isolate themselves from their friends. In this way they make it easier to idealize their love.*

## Looks or personality?

Kemper and Bologh's (1980) subjects emphasized the personality qualities they looked for in their ideal lover. People generally say they want to meet someone with a desirable personality. Dating services spend a good deal of time trying to match women and men based on their traits, habits, and hobbies (Chapter 9). However, the evidence suggests that a great many people do not do as they say.

Susan Green and her associates (1984) studied the selections of clients at a video-dating service. Clients were rated on factors such as age, physical attractiveness, humor, and warmth. The study found that physically attractive men were most likely to be asked for a date. Women who were younger and more attractive were similarly most likely to be asked for a date by the men.

It may not be fair, but physically attractive people, both men and women, seem to have an edge in many aspects of life. For example, research has shown they tend to have more enduring relationships. In addition, good-looking people are rated by others as smarter, healthier, more desirable, and more important. "Attractive people are viewed as being happier, more sensitive, more interesting, warmer, more poised, more sociable, and as having better character than their less attractive counterparts" (Cash and Janda, 1984; Margolin, White, 1987).

Characteristics often mentioned as attractive for both sexes include slimness, clear skin, smiling features, and clean appearance. In men average height or taller and a beard often are considered to add to appeal. In women, a feminine figure and breast size were considered important.

Kleinke and Staneski (1980) hypothesized that breast size seems to suggest personality traits to some people. They asked 282 men and 276 women undergraduates to look at pictures and physical descriptions of women whose bust sizes appeared small, medium, and large.

In four different experiments in which the rating and presentation conditions were varied, a significant proportion of the men and women attributed similar personal characteristics to women with different bust sizes. Those with medium breasts were rated most attractive and liked the best. Women who were larger were viewed as relatively unintelligent; those who were small in bust size were more likely to be described as bright and modest.

Needless to say, breast size, like hair color or height, has nothing to do with personality, competence, intelligence, or worth. But many people try to select partners generally considered more physically attractive. We should caution, too, that beauty preferences change. Standards for attractiveness in the 1980's or 1990's may well seem strange to young adults in the year 2005, looking at pictures of their parents.

### Similarity, need

We tend to rate our own attractiveness as high, medium, or low, and seem to choose potential lovers whose physical appeal we evaluate as similar to ours.

We are likely to fall in love with someone whom we consider attractive and who comes close to our ideal. Studies of friends and other love relationships have shown that the concept of who is ideal and attractive is modified by the degree to which they are similar to ourselves. We tend to be drawn to people whose attractiveness we rate as close to our own. We want to share our opinions on political, economic, and personal issues. We like someone who, coming from a similar social and educational background, has the same attitudes about crime, abortion, and politics. Similar interests in terms of work and play are also vitally important. We may even be drawn to people who resemble us physically. People tend to select those similar in height, body type, and weight. Simply put, "like attracts like." A tendency that may increase the chances for a happy relationship (Kurdek and Schmitt, 1987; Murstein, 1988).

Our parents typically met and married people living only a short distance away. Today at our jobs or in college we are likely to meet people from all parts of the nation and world. This means that relatively few couples will marry and settle in their hometown.

Similarity in area of residence can also be important in helping a love relationship get started. A generation ago more than half of all married couples had lived within walking distance of one another before marriage. Presently, despite a more mobile society, and the majority of young adults attending college away from home, *propinquity,* meaning nearness, still plays a leading role. The fact that college students sit in the same class, or live in the same dormitory, may well stimulate the beginning of a relationship (Murstein, 1988).

The *need-complementarity* view holds that similarity is necessary, but not sufficient to bring people together. To begin erotic love, both must feel they are getting something they want from a relationship. A partnership can only start, it was argued by Winch, (1955), when the would-be partners serve each other's needs. One gives what the other lacks. For example, a quiet person and someone who speaks a great deal might have complementary needs. The quiet

We tend to be most attracted to people whose interests are similar to our own.

one might enjoy the conversational energy of his or her partner, while the talkative one might be happiest in a situation where he or she does not have to compete in order to speak. According to need-complementarity theory, the more the couple depend on each other to give and get what is desired, the more the relationship is likely to begin and endure (Murstein, 1988).

The need-complementarity theory has not found much support as the years have passed. But occasionally evidence that "opposites attract" does emerge. One study evaluated whether Type A personalities (competitive, tense) get along better with Type B people (relaxed easygoing) or with their own kind. Surprisingly, people who had been dating for a year and whose personality differed from their partners felt more comfortable with and committed to their relationship. They were, in fact, more likely to marry. The investigators concluded that, by their definition, people whose personalities complement one another, rather than being identical have better chance of making their relationship work (Strube and Boland, 1987).

## Filtering

Murstein (1988) has supported the filtering view of finding an erotic love partner. *Filtering* means that we imagine sifting prospective lovers through increasingly fine sieves to evaluate their compatibility. Filtering is described as involving three stages: stimulus, value, and role. In the stimulus period, anyone who meets our criteria of attractiveness is acceptable. We get "good vibrations," being drawn to someone whom we consider appealing.

At the value stage, the prospective lover must have similar values, interests, and background. Those who share very little with us, different outlooks, opinions, and activities are likely to be weeded out.

### First Moves and Opening Lines

Every relationship needs a beginning; one person has to indicate interest in another and then hope the other responds. Although they may dislike being the initiators, men ordinarily think they should make the "first move," approaching the woman and starting a conversation. Monica Moore (1985), however, found that women very often are the initiators. Most of the time their flirtation is nonverbal (Chapter 10). They indicate with their bodies that they are approachable. Moore reports that the woman making the first move in a lounge might lean toward a man, sit with her skirt slightly up, stand up and sway or dance alone to music. More directly, she might look at a man and smile at him. In all, Moore calculated that at a singles' bar, women averaged more than 70 flirting, inviting, acts per hour. Sooner or later, most men seem to respond to the cues. They move closer to the woman, smile, and begin to talk to her.

Once the man speaks up, the responsibility to meet shifts to him. Kleinke et al. (1986) have found what is said can make or break a first meeting. College students were asked to evaluate the appeal of "opening lines" that might be used to get to know someone. The 100 most frequent openers were presented to raters who judged them from "terrible" to "excellent." Most women and some men tended to prefer direct and ordinary remarks such as "Hi, I'd like to meet you," or "What do you think of the band?" Cute or flippant comments put many people off. These included: "Is that really your hair?" and "Your place or mine?"

In general, phrases that sound like polite everyday comments are much preferred over remarks that seem false, offensive, or too rehearsed. Honest opening lines may be the best policy.

---

The "role" stage resembles need-complementarity, described earlier. Both ideas suggest that a couple needs to define whether their wants and expectations are in agreement.

If the stimulus and value criteria are met, role is added as an additional dimension for filtering. At this third level, individuals determine whether the role expectations that they each have are compatible. For example, a woman who is career-oriented and wants to be mobile to the exclusion of having children would not be appropriate for a man who is looking forward to having a large family.

The filter theory holds that romantic, sexual attraction is the impetus for starting a relationship. But enduring love supposedly develops and grows only when values and roles are harmonious. It should be pointed out that this is not always the progression. For example, some couples find one another because of similar values. They belong to the same hiking club or church, or work for a planned parenthood group. They know because of their membership that they share many basic attitudes. Such couples may find that it is their psychological compatibilities that first encourage erotic love. In such instances, physical and sexual attraction may come second. In short, selecting or finding one's love may start in any number of ways and take many and varied routes.

---

**In Sum**     Love may have biological roots and also involve learning. Research suggests that people need to experience love from infancy onward for them to be able to love. Most people have "fallen in love" at least once. Erotic love may be partly motivated by loneliness and encourage an idealization of the loved one. Love may proceed in stages, beginning with attraction, advancing to reciprocal disclosure, and culminating in the feelings characterizing emotional-sexual love. Most people select someone to love based on an ideal; often a person who is somewhat similar to themselves. People whose needs are different but congruent are also selected. The selection process filters out those whose qualities are undesirable and those who do not reciprocate our feelings.

## THE PROBLEMS OF EROTIC LOVE

Love may be the most exalted of human emotions, but it is also one of the most difficult. Perhaps it is because our society values erotic love so highly that when it is challenged, painful despair and even violent rage can follow. We will look at three major problems: rejection, jealousy, and losing the feelings of love, and suggest ways to handle them.

### Handling rejection

Everyone who wants a friend, who desires love or a partnership, risks **rejection**. That is, their hope for care and affection could be turned down. To begin with, there is fear of rejection. Such people anticipate being rebuffed and as a result hesitate to ask for a date or to be someone's friend. This fear and some ways in which to cope with it are described in Chapter 9.

*rejection*
Being turned down by another person.

Rejection is actual when a person has asked and is refused. The rebuff is minor when someone refuses to dance. It is major when an offer of marriage or cohabitation is declined. Rejection that follows a simple request may be unpleasant but is usually easily shrugged off. Rejection of a significant emotional or sexual overture can cause considerable despair and anger.

Coping with rejection is difficult and sometimes professional help is required. But there are also ways in which people can assist themselves. The following suggestions should prove useful.

- *Try again*. Focus your motivation and try again. Do not be aggressive or unpleasant, but reasonable further tries are always in order.
- *Positive self-regard*. There is a natural tendency for people who have been rejected to consider themselves inadequate and unlovable. These feelings have to be combated by what therapists call *positive self-regard*. Think of your strong points, your assets, and your abilities. The person who rejected you probably knows little about your capabilities and will lose because she or he has not given you a chance.
- *Talk*. Whenever possible talk about the rejection. Review the material in Chapter 10 on improving communication. Consider with your partner the reasons for the rejection and explore what might be done to rehabilitate the situation.
- *Learn*. Without blaming yourself, analyze the situation. Think about your motives, what you said and how you acted. Was your proposal appropriate? Were you understood? Look at this rejection as an experience from which you can learn.

## Jealousy

Some people consider erotic love finite. Each person has just so much love to give. If some love is given to another, less is left for the primary lover. Someone truly "in love," according to this common view, can only show romantic-erotic interest in one person. Jealousy is partly the product of such an exclusive view of love. If there is just a limited amount of love to go around, it seems reasonable to want all the loved one has to give (Loudin, 1981).

Jealousy has also been explained by using an economic metaphor. Monogamy involves a contractual arrangement that specifies that all the sexual and emotional income, like cash dollars earned, shall be shared only by the partners. All works well until one partner gives some of the desired goods—dollars, sex, or love—to an outsider. This denies the intended partner money (or love) he or she should be getting and also violates the contract. The outcome is the kind of pain and fury we label jealousy.

Another view of jealousy sees this emotion as a sure and deep sign of love. Jill Tweedie (1979) cites the following example: ". . . [a] woman, only recently married, is immensely flattered and continually boasts about her husband's jealousy. 'John's so *jealous,*' she says, blushing prettily. 'Why, last week we went to a party given by a man I've known for donkey's years and he kissed my cheek as we came in. Well, John's sulked for almost a week since.' " Tweedie explains, "She offers this information as if it were the highest of compliments and indeed John's jealousy (and her own reaction) is already hardening into the bond that may keep them together for years." (pp. 156-157). We may see such jealousy as a reflection of the person's insecurity or controlling attitude, but many couples think envy is a necessary and binding aspect of their love.

Is jealousy universal? There are societies where jealousy is minimal. It is reported that among the Eskimo and the Lobi of West Africa there is little jealousy among lovers or couples. Spouses, or other couples in our own society who have an "open" relationship, permitting "affairs" with others, (Chapter 12), contend that they experience little or no jealousy. Most couples, however, report that jealousy is at least an occasional problem.

Jealousy is a painful emotion. Marriage counselors are virtually unanimous in suggesting that a partner avoid deliberately stimulating this potentially destructive feeling.

Distrust, jealousy, and other anxious emotions may accompany feelings of affection and love.

One of the most thorough probes of jealousy was carried out by *Psychology Today* magazine (Salovey and Rodin, 1985). Nearly 25,000 people, mainly in their 30s, were surveyed. They answered questions such as how important they considered sexual/emotional fidelity, how often they secretly go through a spouse's or lover's phone book, belongings, etc. Not surprisingly, the majority of respondents had experienced marked bouts of jealousy. Both sexes, too, shared much the same jealous feelings and behaviors. They might envy their partner's friends, as well as their confidence, appearance, and personality. The researchers also asked their subjects how they coped with jealousy, and found several strategies. Many tried simply to "grin and bear it," living with and adjusting to their jealous feelings. Others tried either to ignore what was happening or to think of positive things instead. Most found these techniques worked poorly. Strategies that may help people cope more adequately follow.

**Handling jealousy**   The time to handle jealousy is when it first stirs the emotions. People who wait, who save up their envy, are liable to attack their partner explosively. It is not likely that much will be solved by such traumatic encounters. Try to handle jealousy as soon as it appears.

1. The first step in handling jealousy is to understand what may be motivating it. Are you distrustful of your lover and afraid of losing him or her? Perhaps you are looking at your partner as a possession and resent almost any time she or he is away from you. Often jealousy can end at this level. An examination of your motives may convince you your fears are unreasonable. You can begin to see your partner as a complex human being who wants and needs a little time alone or with others.
2. Talk about your feelings with your partner. Do not be accusative. Listen actively so that there can be an open and honest exchange. Learn your partner's feelings and perceptions and help her or him understand your emotions.
3. The third step may be negotiation. Couples often have to agree that one will do "A" providing the other does "B." "I will spend less time with Gene, but I'd like you to spend more time with me playing tennis." The partners who fully discuss how they feel and what they expect can usually come to a productive agreement.

### When love fades

Most couples who have felt erotic love early in their relationship find that as time passes the magic seems to fade. Seeing one's love as perfect, as someone who is totally enchanting, does not appear to last more than a few months or several years at most (Tennov, 1979).

What makes love fade? Perhaps it is the constant intrusion of reality that makes us see our partners as just other human beings. They have the same annoying habits, weaknesses, and limitations as any other ordinary person. Familiarity may also take its toll. The person whose newness and potential once fascinated is now just part of our routine.

What happens when erotic love ends can vary. A considerable group of women and men drift apart, separate and divorce. A small number of couples try alternative life-styles, staying together but involving themselves sexually or

The suggestions for effective communication in Chapter 10 can be applied to a wide variety of situations. These techniques can be used by couples to discuss jealousy, sexual needs, parenting, future plans, and almost all other topics.

## Tip

### When Love Fades

Erotic love will fade, although it is more accurate to say it will change. Change, growth, and maturation are the essence of life. It is no more reasonable to expect passionate love to remain the same as it is for the seasons to stop with a perfect day in spring. A first tip then is that when you feel erotic love changing, perhaps diminishing, consider this a normal, expected event. Unfortunately, many couples sensing their relationship altering think they have "fallen out of love." They believe their job is now to separate and look for someone new. They do not realize how much they can do to bring about a more satisfying union.

A second tip is to continue romance. In Chapters 5 and 12 we discuss how women and men can maintain variety in their sexual relationship, preventing it from becoming routine. At this point we suggest an old-fashioned recipe for retaining romance: concern and courtesy. Each partner should try to do the little things the other one wants and enjoys. "Pamper one another now and again" is the way one older couple put it. What considerations, what courtesies will make the other happy?

Finally, we should seek out the strength in our partnership. Perhaps the other correlates of erotic love, which may not have been at their full potential years before, can now be cultivated. Intimacy and caring can increase, with a couple finding in each other a depth of understanding never thought possible. Companionship may ultimately be the strongest of all the qualities of love. A companionate couple, like the best of friends, enjoy being with each other. Their togetherness gives them pleasure they do not ordinarily experience alone (Loudin, 1981).

Caring and understanding partners can encourage their love to evolve and grow.

There are couples who, despite the decades they have been together, still have a physically and emotionally rewarding relationship. Often such people are generally enthusiastic, warm, and understanding in all areas of their life.

emotionally with others (Chapter 12). Some partners continue in what have been described as "boring," "loveless" unions. They stay together out of convenience, a sense of commitment, or concern over the children. Others may continue their partnership because they fear being alone and on their own. The famous English writer and cynic Oscar Wilde (1854-1900) proposed that most marriages are without passion and are held together only by fear or stubbornness.

Yet there are people who, when the initial erotic love fades, seem to create a new emotional bond. In fact it has been argued that married couples are not truly free to engage in an adult, warm, and tender relationship until after they have "fallen out of love." Kelly (1981) notes: "The common first passionate phase of loving, the all consuming infatuation, always ends, and if it has not been replaced by the deeper and more complex process of working at 'being in love,' the loving relationship will also end" (Kelly, 1981, p. 404).

*Summary*

Love is a complex emotion that usually involves affection, warmth, and caring. There are at least five different forms of love: erotic, friendship, devotional, parental, and altruistic. All are similar, but erotic love involves sexual relations. Erotic love has other qualities as well: companionship, caring, intimacy, romance, and commitment. The importance of each component varies in different relationships. Romance is frequently critical at the beginning of a partnership. Sex often continues to occupy a central position.

Love seems to have biological roots and to be significantly influenced by learning. Research has shown that love has to be experienced during childhood if a person is to develop the capacity to give and receive affection.

Falling in love may be motivated by loneliness, physical or emotional attraction, or other needs. It often proceeds through stages involving attraction, mutual disclosure, and culminating in a partnership. Many people seem to have an ideal person whom they want to love although most compromise their image. Physical attractiveness is a major quality in selection. Ultimately the compatibility of needs and other similarities turn out to be highly important. Selection is a filtering process in which the person finally chosen has the qualities desired.

Love is a happy emotion, but there are also problems. Jealousy can be severe and disruptive. Although some people and cultures experience little jealousy, most in our society insist that their lover be emotionally and physically faithful. There are ways jealousy may be understood and minimized. Another difficulty is that erotic and romantic love may fade. Often, however, other love qualities such as companionship can become prominent and enable a relationship to continue.

*For Thought and Discussion*

1 What does the word "love" mean to you? Describe how your feelings of love differ for a friend, lover, and relative. Give examples of the various forms of love, such as spiritual, romantic, sexual.
2 Describe situations in which you knew, almost instantly, that you loved someone. Contrast this with a situation in which you learned, or tried to learn, to love. What biological and psychological processes may have been involved in both instances?
3 Think of couples you know well and try to describe the importance of companionship, caring, intimacy, commitment, romance, and sex in their lives.
4 What is your opinion of Vannoy's belief that love should not be too giving but retain a little selfishness?
5 How do you know you are falling in love? What physical and personality qualities in the other person are most likely to trigger an affectional reaction in you?
6 How do you find love and handle its problems, such as jealousy and the breakup of a relationship? Can a couple really stay in love for 10, 20, or more years? Do you believe that people are capable of changing the love they experience early in their relationship to a growing and mature love years later?

*References*

Blumstein, P.W., and Schwartz, P. *American couples.* New York: William Morrow & Co., Inc., 1983.

Cash, T.F., and Janda, L.H. The eye of the beholder. *Psychology Today,* December 1984, 46-52.

Davis, K.E. Near and dear: friendship and love compared. *Psychology Today,* February 1985, 22 ff.

Fisher, H.E. *The sex contract.* New York: William Morrow & Co., Inc., 1982.

Freud, S. *Collected papers.* New York: Basic Books, 1959.

Green, S.K., Buchanan, D.R., and Heuer, S.K. Winners, losers, and choosers: a field investigation of dating initiation. *Personality & Social Psychology Bulletin,* 1984, *10*(4), 502-511.

Harlow, H.F., and Mears, C. *The human model: primate perspectives.* Washington, D.C.: V.H. Winston & Sons, 1979.

Johnson, M.P., and Leslie, L. Friends and lovers. *Psychology Today,* 1982, *16,* 78-79.

Kelley, R.K. *Courtship, marriage, and the family.* New York: Harcourt Brace Jovanovich, 1979.

Kelly, G.F. Loss of loving: a cognitive therapy approach. *Personnel and Guidance Journal,* 1981, *59,* 401-404.

Kemper, T.D., and Bologh, R.W. The ideal love object: structural and family sources. *Journal of Youth and Adolescence,* 1980, *9,* 33-48.

Kleinke, C.L., Meeker, F.B., and Staneski, R.A. Preference for opening lines: comparing ratings by men and women. *Sex Roles,* 1986, *15,* 585-600.

Kleinke, C.L., and Staneski, R.A. First impressions of female bust size. *Journal of Social Psychology,* 1980, *100,* 123-134.

Kurdek, L.A., and Schmitt, J.P. Partner homogamy in married, heterosexual cohabiting, gay, and lesbian couples. *The Journal of Sex Research,* May 1987, *23*(2), 212-232.

Loudin, J. *The hoax of romance.* Englewood Cliffs, N.J.: Prentice-Hall, 1981.

Margolin, L., and White, L. The continuing role of physical attractiveness in marriage. *Journal of Marriage and the Family,* February 1987, *49*(1), 21-27.

Montagu, A. *Touching: the human significance of the skin.* New York: Columbia University Press, 1986.

Moore, M.M. Nonverbal courtship patterns in women: context and consequences. *Ethology and Sociobiology,* 1985, *6*(4), 237-247.

Murstein, B.I. A taxonomy of love. In R.J. Sternberg and M.L. Barnes (editors), *The psychology of love.* New Haven: Yale University Press, 1988, pp. 13-27.

Reiss, I.L. *Family systems in America* (3rd ed.). New York: Holt, Rinehart & Winston, 1980.

Rowe, K., and Vasquez, C. Marital satisfaction: effects of nuptial love-state, age of marriage, and courtship duration. *Psychological Reports* (In press), 1987.

Rubenstein, C. The modern art of courtly love. *Psychology Today,* July 1983, 40-49.

Rubin, Z., and McNeil, E.B. *The psychology of being human.* New York: Harper & Row, 1981.

Salovey, P., and Rodin, J. The heart of jealousy. *Psychology Today,* September 1985, 22-29.

Sternberg, R.J., and Barnes, M.L. *The psychology of love.* New Haven, Conn.: Yale University Press, 1988.

Strube, M.J., and Boland, S.M. Type A behavior pattern and the self evaluation of abilities. *Journal of Personality and Social Psychology,* May 1987, *52*(5), 956-974.

Tennov, D. *Love and limerence: the experience of being in love.* New York: Stein & Day, 1979.

Tweedie, J. *In the name of love.* New York: Pantheon, 1979.

Vannoy, R. *Sex without love: a philosophical exploration.* Buffalo, N.Y.: Prometheus Books, 1980.

Winch, R.F. The theory of complementary needs in mate selection: final results on the test of the general hypothesis. *American Sociological Review,* 1955, *20,* 552-555.

Wolfe, L. *The Cosmo report.* New York: Arbor House, 1981.

Ehrenreich, B. *The hearts of men: American dreams and the flight from commitment.* Garden City, N.Y.: Anchor/Doubleday, 1984.
  An analysis of couple relationships in which the author believes that men are often forced into stifling the traditional male role of breadwinner.

Gordon, B. *Jennifer fever: older men, younger women.* New York: Harper & Row, 1988.
  The relationships that develop between younger women and middle-aged men are examined in a breezy, sometimes humorous, and occasionally dramatic way.

Liebowitz, M. *The chemistry of love.* Boston: Little, Brown & Co., 1983.
  Many people talk loosely about a "chemistry" attracting people to one another. The author explains how biochemical and neurological events may play a role in attraction, affection, and sexual arousal.

Reik, T. *Of love and lust: on the psychoanalysis of romantic and sexual emotions.* New York: Farrar, Straus & Giroux, Inc., 1984.
  A good example of how a well-known and sometimes controversial psychoanalyst looked at and explained love. Often interesting and sometimes captivating.

*Suggested Readings*

# Chapter 12

# Couples
## Marriage and Alternatives

---

**When you finish this chapter, you should be able to:**

Identify some of the major reasons why people marry.

Describe the frequency of coitus and other sexual behaviors in marriage and cohabitation.

Evaluate the reasons for and the effects of extramarital relations.

Describe how a couple can keep their relationship sexually satisfying.

Identify factors that are and are not important in determining a couple's happiness.

Describe the causes and effects of breakup and divorce, and point out alternatives.

Explain how affectional and sexual relations may change in older couples.

Traditionally, the adult years meant marriage. For most of the last two centuries, 9 out of 10 adults married and established a family. In 1990 the popularity of marriage continues, but the once standard combination of husband as wage-earner, wife as homemaker, and children constitutes less than a fifth of all households in the United States. In contrast, more people than ever before live alone. The American family has changed. In this chapter we will examine contemporary marriage, couples at different life stages, and divorce.

## MARRIAGE

Marriage is a practice that seems as old as the human race itself. The union of man (or men) and woman (or women) in a rite defined by social custom and law and carrying with it specific economic, sexual, and child-care responsibilities is very ancient. The little evidence we have of practices tens of thousands of years ago (Chapter 1) suggests that in different regions marriage came in several forms. A few men, perhaps relatives or from the same clan, could be united with several women, a group marriage. Monogamy (one wife/one husband), polygny (several wives/one husband), and occasionally polyandry (several husbands/one wife), were also possible. There were rules, too, concerning whether a person could marry someone from another tribe and whether relatives could unite. If ancient myths are any guide, then among the early Incas in South America, the Egyptians, and some African and Chinese groups, brother and sister were sometimes permitted or perhaps even obliged to marry.

Two thousand years ago, marriage practices still differed markedly from one culture to another. In India monogamy had become the common practice, but the bride was expected to be one-third the age of the groom. A girl of eight was considered the ideal match (arranged by parents) for a young bachelor of twenty-four. Although there may have been a formal wedding ceremony, the child bride usually did not live with her husband until she reached puberty.

The Romans had three different forms of marriage. *Confarreatio* was a highly ceremonious monogamous wedding and, much like Catholic unions today, very difficult to dissolve. A second form was *coemptio*, a simple inexpensive ritual where the bride's father gave her fully to her new husband who now controlled not only her property but all of her life. He could virtually, at will, keep her or cast her out. The third Roman form was *usus*, a sort of trial marriage. The couple had to remain together at least one year before they qualified for marriage. During their one year together, a relationship we would today call "cohabitation" (Chapter 9), either the woman or man could leave with few if any restrictions or consequences.

· During the same distant era, in the Middle East, the Hebrew peoples had also largely shifted to monogamy. The Old Testament patriarch Abraham and the renowned King Solomon may have had dozens, even hundreds of wives, but the land of Israel into which Jesus was born was monogamous. Marriage took place early, the new husband and wife were usually not yet twenty, and their commandment was "to be fruitful and multiply." Large families were the goal of the early Judaeo-Christian faiths. In this same region, a third major faith, Islam, retained the Biblical emphasis on polygny. Still today, in many Moslem nations, men may have more than one wife.

Marriage today, in the Western nations, reflects our Judaeo-Christian heritage. There are variations among the several denominations but all insist on monogamy, sexual and affectional fidelity, and emphasize the permanence of matrimony. Marriage outside one's faith is often discouraged, and the importance of children is emphasized. Increasingly, however, nearly all Judaeo-Christian groups recognize the new equality between the sexes. Most marriage vows, for example, no longer include "obey" (as in "I promise to love, honor, and obey") in the phrases echoed and affirmed by the bride.

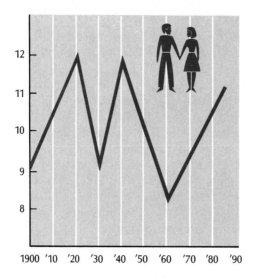

*Figure 12-1*
Since the beginning of this century the marriage rate has continued to rise and fall. Numbers on the left represent marriages per 1000 people in the United States. (Data from *Statistical Abstract of the United States*, 1988.)

We saw in Chapter 9 that more than 2 million couples *cohabit* (live together without being married).

### Why marry?

A generation ago, women often married primarily to gain financial support. Men purportedly sought a sexual partner. Today, while most women still earn less than men, over 40 million women are capable of supporting themselves. In fact, approximately 10% of those who are employed earn more than their husbands. The increasing financial capability of women would seem to lessen the need for traditional marriage.

In addition to greater economic freedom, dramatic changes in mores provide sexual satisfaction for many without marriage. Well over three fourths of young adults have sexual relations before marriage (Chapters 8 and 9).

Despite women's entry into the job world and the availability of nonmarital sexual relations, marriage has not disappeared. In fact, after reaching an all-time low in 1960, the marriage rate has climbed steadily upward. People are now marrying at slightly older ages and quite a few cohabit, but marriage remains a relationship that most people experience (U.S. Bureau of the Census, 1988a).

A great many pressures, incentives, and needs guide people into matrimony. Society and religion both advocate and prompt marriage. Much of this interest in marriage centers about children. Legal and spiritual authorities want continuity. They want their traditions to be carried on. One result is that many unmarried couples who live together contentedly, reconsider and marry when they have children. In one survey, a third of the couples questioned listed the desire to have children as one of the main reasons they married (Safran, 1985).

A second reason for marriage is that despite a more permissive sexual climate, quite a few people still depend on marriage for sexual relations. Sherwin and Corbett (1985) found over a third of the women and a fourth of the men on an Ohio college campus had not had intercourse. Large-scale *Redbook Magazine* and more intensive individual surveys have found similar results. Almost one fourth of all adult women have had only one sexual partner, their spouse, and were just as sexually satisfied as those who had several partners

Marriage remains a relationship that most women and men experience.

(Davidson and Darling, 1988; Rubenstein and Tavris, 1987). The readers of another magazine, *Playboy,* reported that although most single adults have sexual intercourse before marriage, the frequency is low (Cook et al., 1983; Petersen et al., 1983). Often it is hard to find a partner with whom to have relations regularly (Chapter 9). As a result, for many women and men, the opportunity for regular sexual contact provided by marriage still appears to be an important motivator.

There are numerous other reasons for marrying. Some say they marry for companionship or because they are lonely. According to Safran (1985), about 46% of her sample mentioned emotional security as one of the reasons they married. Still others marry for worldly reasons such as money or prestige. Sometimes marriage is motivated by little more than an impulse to imitate friends. Others are doing it, so it seems to make sense to do it too. People influenced by such example may literally marry the first willing person.

Most people marry for a combination of reasons, often including sexual and affectional attraction and a quest for security and companionship.

We must not forget one other very important reason for marriage, however, and that is love. Most people have been in love. They have experienced a compelling mutual attraction. They feel good together; they share sexual pleasure, thoughts, and feelings with one another. The growing closeness of a trusting, affectionate relationship finally leads to marriage (Chapter 11).

How many couples marry for love? Safran's survey of 799 men and women reported in *Parade* magazine gives us a good clue. Most of those evaluated were in their 30s and were college educated. They were a little younger and more affluent than American couples in general, but their responses are fairly typical. Almost two thirds said they married because of strong physical and sexual attraction and ability to share emotions. They wanted to be together. In a word, they were in love. This also leaves one third whose motives may have included some degree of affection, although they were also driven by several of the other needs we have mentioned.

In many countries of the world, marriages are arranged, or at least negotiated, by parents. The belief is that parents better know the personal qualities that make for happy marriages and are also more able to select the appropriate spouse for their child.

## Are You Ready for Marriage?

Circle your answer for each question and then add up your score.

| | Disagree | Agree | Strongly Agree |
|---|---|---|---|
| 1. Most of the time I would rather be alone and not bother with anyone. | 0 | 1 | 2 |
| 2. I really don't understand the other sex. | 0 | 1 | 2 |
| 3. I don't like a lot of touching and hugging. | 0 | 1 | 2 |
| 4. Men are more interested in sex than women and should always take the lead in getting things started. | 0 | 1 | 2 |
| 5. I don't ever want to have children. | 0 | 1 | 2 |
| 6. When I'm married I might have an affair, but I would keep it quiet. | 0 | 1 | 2 |
| 7. If people really love each other they can pretty well guess what the other person wants sexually. | 0 | 1 | 2 |
| 8. After the first year of marriage, sex is not very important. | 0 | 1 | 2 |
| 9. I can't stand being criticized. | 0 | 1 | 2 |
| 10. I don't think I'll ever be as close to my spouse as I am to some of my friends. | 0 | 1 | 2 |
| 11. If a marriage doesn't work, the couple should get divorced. | 0 | 1 | 2 |
| 12. Happy marriages are made in heaven. There's not much you can do if you're stuck with the wrong person. | 0 | 1 | 2 |

Total _____

### Interpretation

Although it is not a scientific instrument, this checklist can help you spot areas that might provoke some difficulty in marriage. It is common to agree or strongly agree with up to four questions. At the same time, any of the four with which you strongly agree could be a source of marital dissatisfaction and should be discussed. A total score of ten or more reveals several attitudes that might interfere with a good marital relationship.

Higher scores, such as sixteen or above, indicate that it is time to think and talk seriously, particularly about the questions answered "strongly agree." Even with high scores, you and your partner may still be able to talk honestly and reconcile many of your attitudes and feelings (Blumstein and Schwartz, 1983; Lauer and Lauer, 1985). (See Chapter 10 on hints on how to communicate effectively.)

## A time to marry

The age at which people marry depends heavily on social standards and expectations. In technologically advanced nations where economic independence is stressed marriage often occurs relatively late. For example, in Ireland, men are expected to be able to support a wife and child financially before entering marriage. Partly as a result, the average age for women to first marry in Ireland is 26; that for men is 31. In other parts of the world where little education is required and income expectations are low, such as in parts of India, women marry in their middle teens, and men are about 20. In order to limit population increase the official government *recommended* age in the Peoples Republic of China is 28 for men and 25 for women. (McWhirter, 1988).

In the United States, the age at first marriage has risen fairly steadily for most of this century. During the 1800s, farming and other rural occupations enabled young men to earn a livelihood early. Further, sexual standards of propriety and morality were strict. There was little premarital sex. The age of marriage, as a result, was low. Both sexes were ordinarily under 20 when they married. By 1950, a half century later, men were 22 and women 20 years old (Kinsey et al., 1948, 1953).

By the late-1980s the median marriage age had climbed to almost 26 for men and 23 for women. About one fifth of women and a third of all men now marry for the first time at about age 30. After 30, the number of first marriages for men and more so for women drops considerably. This has given rise to what some single adults regard as the "now or never—age 30 crisis." Figure 12-2 shows marriage prospects: the odds a person will marry at each age (U.S. Bureau of the Census, 1988a).

## Sex and marriage

Cynics have said that the quickest way to kill sexual desire is to get married. Outside of marriage women and men may go to great lengths, and even take

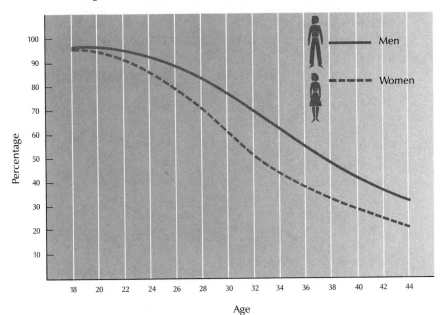

*Figure 12-2*
Marriage prospects: the curve shows the approximate percentage of single people at each age who will marry. About half of all women in their early 30s and men in their late 30s, who are still single, will marry. (Data from Statistical Abstract of the United States, 1988.)

considerable risks, to have intercourse. After marriage, when the spouse is readily available, intercourse may actually be avoided. Just how often do married people have intercourse and how satisfying is it?

Marriage is the one relationship in which intercourse is not only permitted and encouraged but even required. In nearly all countries, as in the United States, lack of coitus following marriage is grounds for annulment. The marriage has not been **consummated,** and as far as the government and the major religions are concerned, the marriage is erased as if it never happened.

*consummated*
Sexual intercourse has taken place.

**Frequency**   As might be expected, young couples, those in their 20s, are the most sexually active. On the average these couples have intercourse three to four times weekly. By the late 30s coitus drops to roughly twice a week and for those approaching 50 to about once weekly. In addition to age, *length of marriage* has a similar effect on coital frequency. For most couples, how often they have intercourse decreases with the length of time they have been together. Early in marriage they may have had sexual relations two to four times a week, but after 10 years it decreases to twice a week and in another ten years to once per week. Of course, these are averages, and many people have intercourse much less or much more than their comparison group. In fact, at every stage there is considerable variation with some people having intercourse more than daily, while others may engage in coitus only once a month or so (Blumstein and Schwartz, 1983; Wolfe, 1981).

One of the most interesting discoveries in the last decade has been that the number of times all couples have intercourse has increased considerably over the last generation. Improved birth control techniques, particularly oral contraceptives, as well as a more sexually enlightened atmosphere have probably encouraged married couples to engage in coitus more freely and frequently.

*Table 12-1*

**Sexual Variety: Percentage of Married Couples Using the Following Techniques**

| Technique | Percentage |
|---|---|
| Fellatio | 60 |
| Cunnilingus | 65 |
| Coitus, woman on top | 50 |
| Coitus, rear vaginal entry | 20 |
| Coitus, sitting or standing | 10 |

Data from Blumstein and Schwartz, 1983, and others.

Different positions for intercourse and other coital variations were discussed in more detail in Chapter 5.

**Variety**   Just as the frequency of coitus has increased, so has variety. More couples now include fellatio and cunnilingus in their activities (Chapter 5). Approximately two thirds of the couples in the Blumstein and Schwartz (1983) studies sometimes used such oral techniques in contrast to only about half as many surveyed a decade earlier. Contemporary couples also tend to vary the positions they employ during sex. Among half of all couples, the woman often lies over the man. Another 10% to 20% sometimes have intercourse standing or sitting or engage in vaginal entry from the rear (see Table 12-1).

The time involved in intercourse seems to have lengthened. A generation ago, *foreplay,* the petting and sexual stimulation before intercourse, typically lasted less than 5 minutes. Judged from the reports of contemporary investigations, kissing and sexual caressing have increased. The breasts, penis, vagina, and other erogenous areas are likely to receive a good deal of attention. Many couples emphasize the excitement, closeness, and pleasure felt during touch. Intercourse itself also seems less hurried so that many couples spend 15 mintues or a half hour or more in sexual pleasuring (Blumstein and Schwartz, 1983; Kinsey et al., 1948, 1953; Petersen et al., 1983; Rubenstein, Tavris, 1987; Sarrel and Sarrel, 1981).

The person initiating intercourse has also shifted. Traditionally sex was both the business and the pleasure of the husband. He indicated his interest and the wife complied. The Victorian tenet that it was indecent for a woman to show pleasure in sex, much less initiate it, held firm until well into this century (Chapter 1). Currently, according to Blumstein and Schwartz (1983), husbands still initiate sex in about half of all couples. But in 14% the wife frequently makes the first sexual overture. Perhaps more revealing, in well over a third of couples either the wife or the husband may start sexual activity (see Table 12-2).

### Marital affairs

**Masturbation**  Strictly speaking, masturbation, since it does not involve a partner, is not quite the same as an extramarital affair. But masturbation is seen by some spouses almost as an infidelity. As a rule adolescents and single adults tend to accept masturbation (as normal behavior) and are likely to acknowledge it (Chapter 8). It seems to be a reasonable practice when no sexual partner is available. But marriage provides a partner. Surely, the erroneous logic goes, there has to be something "wrong." Many wives and husbands have been startled to happen on their spouse and see them masturbating. Often an immediate panicked assumption is that their sexual and/or affectional relationship must be deficient. "What's wrong with me," the puzzled spouse asks "that you do this?"

Some psychologists have added weight to this reasoning by describing masturbation, particularly within marriage, as unhealthy or immature (Freud, 1959). Even some contemporary researchers have contributed to the notion that marital masturbation signals difficulty. Tavris and Sadd (1977) reported that masturbation suggests unsatisfactory marital sexual relations. In their survey they said they found that only 10% of wives who masturbate describe their sex lives as "very good." At the other end, one third of men who report that their sex lives with their wives are poor also report that they masturbate.

Masturbation within marriage or cohabitation is common. Petersen et al. (1983) found that at least two thirds of spouses masturbate occasionally. Furthermore 22% of women and twice as many men in a committed relationship masturbate at least once a week. This is not a recent phenomenon. About 40 years ago the Kinsey studies (1948, 1953) showed that close to half of all spouses, whether or not satisfied with their relationship, sometimes masturbate.

Masturbation may signal a troubled relationship. More often, however, it serves a great many other needs. Sometimes it is a substitute for coitus when the spouse is ill, absent, or otherwise unavailable. At other times men and women report their sexual relations are good but that they want additional sexual excitation. Or masturbation may be considered on its own merits. Husbands and wives may masturbate simply because they enjoy doing so.

Masturbation may also be used as a supplement for a wife who has not had an orgasm through marital coitus. The husband may help her to climax or she may masturbate. At still other times a couple may jointly masturbate as a variation of their sexual play and pleasuring. In all it seems that in most instances masturbation within marriage, like masturbation in general, is a normal and often helpful practice (Cook et al., 1983; Petersen et al., 1983; Rubenstein, Tavris, 1987; Wolfe, 1981).

*Table 12-2*

**Who Usually Initiates Sexual Relations?**

| Spouse | % of time |
| --- | --- |
| Husband | 50 |
| Wife | 14 |
| About equal | 36 |

Data from Blumstein and Schwartz, 1983, and others.

Some of the ways in which women and men masturbate, using their hands, electric vibrators, and other means, are discussed in Chapter 8.

**Extramarital sex**  The extent to which women and men have sexual relations with people other than their spouse or cohabitant is not easy to measure. A generation ago the Kinsey studies (1948, 1953) startled the nation when they showed that by age 40 half the married men and one fourth of the married women had experienced extramarital sex.

More recent investigations have been inconsistent. Surveys by *Cosmopolitan* (Wolfe, 1981) and *Playboy* (Petersen et al., 1983) magazines have shown the incidence of extramarital relationships may be over 60% for women and 75% for men. On the other hand, Blumstein and Schwartz (1983) found in their survey that only a third of the married men and a fourth of the married women had had extramarital relations. The magazine surveys and investigations by Blumstein and Schwartz may be evaluating somewhat different segments of society. The readers of sexually sophisticated magazines such as *Cosmopolitan* and *Playboy* may be more extramaritally active than other groups. The younger Blumstein and Schwartz couples may not yet be married long enough to obtain a full picture of fidelity. It might be best to take a compromise position. It seems most likely that close to two thirds of all men and up to half of all women have at least one extramarital relationship some time during their marriage (Richardson, 1986).

Despite the relative frequency of extramarital relations revealed by these statistics, such activity is strongly disapproved in our society. In many states, adultery is a misdemeanor punishable by up to a year in jail, and it is often considered grounds for divorce.

Not all cultures share the American view of extramarital sexual relations. Among 130 tribal societies close to a majority approved of or tolerated extramarital relations. To be sure most also hedged their approval. It is usually men but not women who are permitted to have an extramarital affair. In most of these societies, the extramarital liaison must be very discreet and conducted so as not to embarrass anyone.

A few American couples try to have an "open" marriage, permitting themselves to have extramarital sexual relations. We will describe these practices later in this chapter.

Some cultures devise means to facilitate extramarital coitus. Among the Eskimos "douse the lights" is played. This is a game in which couples exchange partners when the lights are off. It is reported that there is much talking and joking about who was with whom and what was done when the lights are on again. Among the Turu of Tanzania, it is believed that it is difficult to preserve sexual love with one's spouse. Special meeting places are set aside for women and men to have an *mbuya*, a romantic lover. Thoughtfulness is also expected, and flaunting an affair is in bad taste (Ford and Beach, 1980).

*Why?*  The cliché has it that men and women are interested in extramarital sex only if their marriage is in some way inadequate. Sexual or emotional dissatisfaction may indeed be the motive for an extramarital affair. The husband and wife may be in serious conflict and have a poor sexual relationship. But unhappy marriage may not account for most extramarital involvements. Atwater (1982) interviewed 50 educated women, admittedly a limited sample, and found that the majority were not driven by unhappy marriages. They were women who by and large had a tolerant outlook on extramarital sex and in the main did not regret it afterward.

Extramarital relations may also be the result of illness. Perhaps the husband or the wife is physically or mentally ill and has not been available for a long time. Allied to this are marriages in which a spouse's career forces her or him to work or live some distance away, coming home only on weekends. This unavailability may help steer a lonely spouse into an extramarital relationship.

In recent years, the so-called "mid-life crisis" has received considerable attention. This phrase describes people moving into their 40s and fearful of losing physical appeal and sexual vigor. However, a close look at the statistics describing extramarital affairs does not show any sudden increase during the late 30s or in the 40s. Instead the incidence of extramarital relationships rises steadily, beginning in the first few years of marriage and progressing gradually. A few men and women may be motivated to have an affair to reaffirm their appeal, but the number does not seem large.

Two major reasons for extramarital affairs may be curiosity and a wish for variety. The partnership may be a good one, but an opportunity has arisen to experience sexual relations with another person who is appealing. Reiss, Anderson, and Sponaugle (1980) suggest that a person with a generally liberal attitude is more likely to accept such reasons for extramarital coitus. In this study people who had a permissive attitude toward premarital sex were much more likely to be open to extramarital sexuality.

As more and more married women work outside the home, the opportunity for both sexes to meet, spend considerable time together, and become interested in one another, increases. Places of work have become a major meeting ground. Laurel Richardson (1986), who studied 700 women who had affairs, put it

> . . . she acts as if the time she spends with her . . . lover were strictly business. By not altering the usual routines, she can see him fairly frequently and openly — or at least that is what many of the women in my study believed. One woman routinely stays late at the office with her lover and accompanies him on business trips, just as she had before their affair began; another, a teacher, continues to spend considerable public time preparing classes with her lover, a member of the teaching group. Both believe their romances are totally camouflaged by the cloak of routine work activity . . . (p. 25).

In Lynn Atwater's (1982) view, the extramarital affair progresses through a series of stages. First, most spouses and cohabitants who have affairs have a generally tolerant outlook on this possibility. The second step is detecting opportunities. There is someone or a situation that appears inviting. Third, there are extramarital models, people to imitate, from whom to learn. Perhaps the person knows someone who has had such a relationship. Or a model may be provided by television or a novel. The fourth step is mental rehearsal. "What will I do? What will I say? Where will we go?" After that the last step, actual consummation, takes place.

*Range*   Extramarital relations may range from an impersonal encounter with a prostitute to a deeply loving relationship that continues for years.

> I was in Japan for 8 weeks for my company. I got involved twice with a prostitute. When I told my wife about it she thought I was stupid to risk a venereal disease. But it didn't really cause a lot of upset at home. It was very remote. It didn't affect our marriage.
>
> *(Author's Files)*

Many other affairs are more personal than this. They may involve a person with whom one works, a friend, or an acquaintance. As long as there is no

Sometimes when marital intercourse is limited by illness or distance, a spouse may quietly accept the partner's extramarital relations as long as the affair is discreet and not obvious.

Extramarital relations are often motivated by a combination of an open attitude and an opportunity.

major commitment, the affair is likely to be considered casual by the participants.

> I went skiing without my husband. I went to bed with the ski instructor three times. It was a lark. I never told him about it, but now 4 years later, I think he'd appreciate my honesty. It wasn't a big deal. I've forgotten about it. But I don't think I will tell. It would not break us up. That's for sure. But why upset him now?

*(Author's Files)*

When extramarital partners are emotionally very intimate and in love with one another, ending their affair can sometimes be almost as troubling and painful as divorce.

Perhaps the most serious extramarital relationship is the "meaningful affair." The couple is motivated as much, or more, by emotional longing as by sexual needs. According to Blumstein and Schwartz (1983) half of the affairs of wives, and about a third of those of husbands are meaningful. The two partners care about one another and feel deep affection. This is not just a sexual encounter but a meeting of lovers.

The nature of an affair does not always denote its impact. A marriage may be seriously disrupted by even the briefest and most impersonal outside encounter. But it is most likely that the greater the personal involvement of the participants, the more meaningful the extramarital affair, the greater the threat to the original partnership. Meaningful affairs, more than any other extramarital relation, may end a marriage (Reiss et al., 1980; Atwater, 1982).

*Effects*    Most extramarital affairs are not discovered by the other partner. But they do not usually last long. They stop because one or both participants tire of the relationship. To begin with, the logistics of secret affairs are often difficult. Where to meet? What restaurant or motel is safe to go to? Is the home or apartment of one of the lovers available and can the couple feel secure knowing they will not be discovered?

In addition, lying is necessary to assure the unsuspecting spouse that all is well. Excuses have to be made about why one is coming home late or away at

Extramarital relations often require secret meetings in out-of-the-way places.

odd hours. Eventually the continual deceptions and the difficulties of arranging a secret place to meet can become very burdensome. The extramarital relationship may not seem worth all the effort (Atwater, 1982).

The majority of people disapprove of extramarital sex. According to Reiss et al. (1980), three fourths of couples say, firmly, extramarital sex is wrong. Safran (1985) found an even higher number, 91%, saying marital fidelity is important or very important. Such couples were likely to let their partner know that if they become extramaritally involved they could end the marriage.

Despite threats and pronouncements, every marriage or cohabitation in which an affair is discovered does not end. One partner may feel betrayed, lied to, and cheated. There may be intense anger and resentment. But despite such powerful and painful emotions, extramarital affairs are a relatively infrequent cause of divorce. They directly account for only about 10% to 20% of divorces. An extramarital relationship may cause a couple or one partner grief and rage, perhaps for months or a few years, but the marriage usually endures (Alvarez, 1982).

In many instances an extramarital affair that is discovered may ultimately strengthen a couple. It may prompt them to reexamine their own relationship and their priorities. However difficult the process, married and cohabiting partners can use the stimulus of an affair to help them search for a stronger and happier relationship.

*Consensual affairs, swinging*   Extramarital relations are not disapproved of or conducted in secret by all couples. Some married (or cohabiting) men and women allow one another to have other partners. Such **consensual affairs** are usually the result of an agreement. The rules the couple devise usually prohibit extended or heavy emotional involvement. Sometimes the new lover is also encouraged to be a friend to both members of the couple. In almost all cases, dishonesty and expressions of jealousy are not permitted.

Despite such rules, a degree of conflict is common. A spouse or cohabitant may become uneasy about a partner's new relationship or feel lonely and rejected because nothing promising has developed for him or her. As a result, many couples find consensual affairs difficult to manage and soon try other marital arrangements, including traditional fidelity and swinging (Whitehurst, 1985).

Couples who agree to together meet other couples for the purpose of sexual exchange are **swinging**. Estimates of the number who swing have been as high as one in six (Petersen et al., 1983). This statistic seemed to represent the activities of select young couples, all of whom were readers of *Playboy* magazine. More representative samples have been investigated by Blumstein and Schwartz (1983), Davidson (1988), and Wolfe (1981). Data from these investigators suggests that although many couples may try swinging a few times, only about 1% swing for any substantial period.

Swinging takes several forms. Many couples simply start a sexual relationship with friends or neighbors. Typically a husband (it is usually the male who proposes swinging) introduces the idea that perhaps their good friends Marie and Sam might be interested in an exchange. Such ideas are often floated hesitantly and, at first, frequently rejected by the other spouse. But once the ice has been broken, often over the course of several months, the suggestion reemerges, and finally the spouses agree to sounding out their friends.

During the Victorian era it was often quietly accepted that married men might visit a prostitute or if affluent enough, keep a mistress (Chapter 1).

*consensual affair*
Couple agreeing they may have sexual relations outside their own relationship.

*swinging*
Exchanging partners with other couples for sexual relations.

*party house*
A club, house, or apartment where swingers meet for sexual exhange.

Other swinging couples find partners by advertising in special magazines, or meet new people recommended by other couples who share their life-style. Still another way swinging couples meet is by attending a **party house** or club where swingers gather. The most famous of these, and also the largest, and now closed, was Plato's Retreat in New York City. At clubs, swingers gather for an evening of food, drink, and sex. The more elaborate facilities have saunas, swimming pools, and dance floors. There are also dozens of individual rooms for sexual privacy and large rooms for people who like to take part in group sex (Talese, 1980).

***Reasons for swinging*** Traditional morality recognized that a woman or man might sometimes have an extramarital affair. But this was usually seen as a sign of moral weakness or trouble within the relationship. The notion that a couple might freely consent to having sexual intercourse with people they may just have met at a party or club strikes many almost as bizarre. To substantiate these claims, some early studies of swingers did suggest that they were deviant. Swingers were often described as coming from unhappy family backgrounds, prone to abuse alcohol and drugs, and politically radical. But according to Richard Jenks (1985) what was really happening was that the one disapproved trait, swinging, negatively colored the perception of many investigators.

Jenks carefully evaluated and compared 342 swingers and 134 nonswingers. Most of the swingers were white and had above average levels of education and income, a finding corroborated several times previously. The most important result of this study, however, was the conclusion that swingers "basically differ with respect to their swinging." They are not much different in terms of their drinking habits, politics, and other characteristics from nonswingers from the same socioeconomic background.

Swinging, and we include consensual affairs, seems to have both negative and positive effects on marriage. On the negative side, many couples find that they are more conflicted about or jealous of their partner's activities than anticipated. Other women and men find sexual relations with people who are new acquaintances difficult and unsatisfying and make them apprehensive about AIDS (Chapter 16). They may have spent the evening having intercourse with two or three different people but report that the experience left them feeling empty and worried rather than pleased. In her book, *The Agony of it All*, Joy Davidson (1988) describes people who want multiple partners as sexual thrill-seekers, distorting the natural drive for excitement into a self-defeating melodrama. On the positive side, many men and women state that swinging has opened them up sexually. It has led them to drop inhibitions and added to the excitement, and solidity of the relationship with their own partner. For a few couples, swinging provides an entertaining and full social life (Atwater, 1982; Talese, 1980).

Fear of AIDS does not seem to have had much effect on the number of couples who swing only with close friends. Judging from the advertisements in swingers' magazines, however, it does seem to have very considerably reduced the number of "party houses," and couples who exchange with new acquaintences. Many swingers also now insist on the use of condoms (Chapter 16).

***Threesomes*** Polygamy, multiple marriage, as we pointed out earlier, is not uncommon. Many African nations, most Moslem countries, in fact, well over a half billion people in different nations of the earth permit polygamy. The most common pattern is for the man to have several wives, although in a few instances, several husbands are allowed (Chapter 1). In North America only those of the Mormon faith practiced polygny, a custom now forbidden both by Church law and civil authorities. Yet from time to time, a family or small community that is polygynous is reported in the media. Typically the police "raid" the premises taking the parents and children into custody. More often than not, soon after the furor dies down the news no longer appears in the paper or on television and the people involved quietly resume their life-style.

In a well-documented book, Arno Karlen (1988) reports what might actually be a form of polygamy that is appearing in the United States—threesomes. These are sexual/affectional relations involving three people. For many participants the threesome is little more than a single experience, a "one-night-stand." For others, the combination started with a sexual or friendly relationship that became affectional, and the triple partnership endured. Karlen's 20-year investigation seems to suggest that while little is said about intimate three-way relationships, they may be more common than thought. Several hundred thousand couples have added a third partner at least occasionally, and for a few this arrangement continues (Cook, et al., 1983; Petersen, et al., 1983).

## Marital stages

No two marriages are alike, just as no two personalities are the same. But neither are people or marriages totally different. In both we can identify basic needs, patterns, and developments. In marriage, when we look closely at couples, we can often discern developmental stages. Marriages, like people, grow. And at each stage there are characteristic features and changes.

**Honeymoon**   The first year or two of marriage or cohabitation can be called the honeymoon period. Two people must make obvious and sometimes difficult adjustments when they begin to live together. But the happiest time for most Americans, according to their own descriptions, is when they are first married and do not have any children. For many men and women, part of the happiness in the early period of marriage is related to a feeling of achievement. They have started a home, secured another's affections, and are enjoying a newfound sexual pleasure.

**Career, parenting**   Several years after the wedding, the marital relationship may become secondary. Two new goals emerge that interfere with the couple focusing all their attention on one another. The wife or husband may become more job or career conscious, trying to go as far as she or he can in work or business. One or both may now also shift attention to the children as parenting becomes a major goal. One possible result is that many couples talk increasingly about being tired or preoccupied and sexuality seems to retreat. There is less touch and less caressing, and the frequency of intercourse may decline by nearly half (Blumstein and Schwartz, 1983).

**Stability to growth**   Marriage can reach a third stage. Ten or more years after the wedding, the difficult decisions and adjustments concerning children, household responsibilities, and career aspirations have been more or less resolved. Husband and wife may not share equally in power, work, or money, but the couple is satisfied. Both have come to recognize their own and their partner's contributions as well as limitations.

Campbell (1980) labels this stage *stability* and sees it as a time for contentment and tranquility. It provides a stress-free family setting. Children can grow up in a secure, safe, and healthful milieu. In this stage sexual relations often

### Keeping Sex in Your Relationship

The acclaimed Irish writer George Bernard Shaw (1856-1950) is supposed to have described sexuality in marriage as combining a maximum of opportunity with a minimum of temptation. It is true that most couples begin their marriage by experiencing sex as a frequent and exciting pleasure. But as the years go by, many couples report that sex becomes less frequent and more routine.

The sexual relationship is just one of many factors contributing to the happiness of married and cohabiting couples, but it is an important one. It can be improved and is worthy of some thought and effort.

First, a satisfying sexual relationship should be a priority for both partners. No television program, social obligation, or housekeeping task should stand in the way of good relations. Whether the couple prefers coitus, pleasuring, caressing, or oral-genital relations, the day should be arranged to allow time for unhurried erotic and affectional activity.

A second rule is variety. We all enjoy different foods, entertainment, clothing, and music. Many men and women also want to bring variety into their sexual relations. This may mean reemphasizing arousal, focusing on noncoital sexual enjoyments, or changing the place where the couple habitually have intercourse. Perhaps the living room may be appropriate, or sometimes even the kitchen. New positions for intercourse may also help. Some couples experiment with sitting positions either face to face or with rear vaginal entry (Chapter 5). Some introduce variety by wearing different clothing and undressing partly or not at all. A few couples try sexual toys, such as vibrators, furs, and other props, to add stimulation and pleasure. Still others enjoy erotica in the form of sexually appealing films, books, or similar entertainment (Chapter 19). Affectionate pleasuring or foreplay not routinely leading to coitus is still another variation that some couples enjoy (Chapters 5, 17).

A third suggestion is spontaneity. Sexual urges sometimes occur at odd or seemingly inopportune times—when driving home from a party or movie, or taking a bath or shower. A couple can be tuned into such spontaneity and if at all reasonable go ahead with sexual relations even if the time and place are unusual. One couple reported impulsively stopping at a motel only 4 miles from their home. They found this so rewarding that they have done it several times since. In fact, many couples find that just being away from home, camping or in a hotel room, is a pleasant, exciting sexual stimulus.

Fourth, communicate! Most women and men like to hear their partner say "I love you." Others may want a good deal of explicit sexual talk. Still others want to discuss ideas, hesitations, or concerns about their relations. Communication, as we discussed in Chapter 10, may well be the most critical element of all in assuring a continually satisfying sex life.

A final note: even a conscientious, loving couple who try to enrich their sexuality may sometimes find disappointment. Sexual interactions are complex and sometimes unpredictable. Both partners should good-naturedly expect occasional problems and shortcomings and accept them as inevitable. If there are continuing and serious problems, treatment may help (Chapter 17).

Spontaneity, a sense of fun and play, can help keep sex in a relationship.

continue to recede. Yet a core group of couples remains who despite aging are sexually active and innovative. Brecher's (1984) survey as we will see later in this chapter, suggests that a fourth of middle-aged couples show little if any decrease in interest or activity.

Some couples move past acceptance into a fourth stage, one of mutual growth. This may come when the children are older or in college. It may be a response to the parents experiencing the **empty nest syndrome**; the children are independent and have left the home. At this point, the partners again sense their own and each other's individuality. Each spouse feels free to suggest ideas and innovations in their work, home, and relationship. As one of the respondents put it in a survey of 300 happily married couples, "My spouse has become more interesting" (Lauer and Lauer, 1985).

*empty nest syndrome*
The lonely, sad feelings some parents have after their children are grown and have left home. Conversely, many parents feel this stage provides new opportunities.

---

*In Sum*

Nearly everyone marries; reasons include financial, sexual, affectional, and social motives. The age of first marriage has increased so that the early to mid-20s is now typical, although many wait until they are older.

Sexual intercourse in marriage has increased in frequency since the last generation and is highest among younger couples. As the marriage continues and the couple ages, the amount of coitus usually declines. Masturbation in marriage is common and does not necessarily indicate trouble. Extramarital intercourse is now more frequent and almost half of all women and two thirds of men have had such contact. Extramarital affairs may be motivated by marital dissatisfaction, curiosity, or a need for variety. In most instances extramarital relationships are strongly disapproved although relatively few result in divorce. A few couples consent to openly having individual extramarital relations or jointly exchanging partners. Marriage can be described as progressing through stages from the early honeymoon phase to stability and growth. Couples can work together to keep their relationship sexually and affectionally satisfying.

---

## Marital satisfaction

Nearly every poll and survey has found that married people are usually happier than those who are single, divorced, or widowed. The validity of this common finding has recently been challenged and just getting married is by itself no guarantee of happiness (Glenn and Weaver, 1988). But certainly for many persons and perhaps even for most couples, their marriage is their single greatest satisfaction. In this section we will talk about factors that have been shown to contribute most to an enjoyable, happy marriage.

**Background**   When couples are interviewed, a very revealing finding is that happiness in marriage is not always gauged equally by both people. Partners often see their relationship differently. Not only may they not agree about how satisfied and happy they are, but they even have varying perceptions of such details of their lives as who balances the checkbook and how often coitus takes place. In extreme instances this results in one partner asking for divorce, while the other cannot understand the partner's discontent. A first indicator of mar-

Couples who communicate poorly, who seldom talk and listen to one another, may not know their spouse does not consider the marriage satisfactory.

Few relationships are as thoroughly satisfying as a happy marriage.

ital happiness, then, is the degree to which both spouses agree that their partnership is a good one.

A second important background factor is the couple's parental home. Generally women and men who come from happy homes enter marriage with a positive model and attitude. Safran (1985) believes that happily married parents teach their children the importance of doing things together. They show how to be a couple and enjoy the partnership.

A third factor is similarity. Just as it is in attracting people to one another (Chapter 11), similarity in age, income, education, and social background frequently makes it easier to establish a good relationship. People who are different from one another can get along very well, too, but those who are fairly similar often feel more in touch, more capable of mutual understanding and empathy (Kurdeck and Schmitt, 1987).

**Sex**  Sexual satisfaction seems important, but not critically so to couple happiness. Ninety-two percent of Safran's (1985) respondents indicated that sex is important, while only 32% stated that it is very important. They ranked good communication and doing things as a couple ahead of sex. Both Lauer and Lauer (1985) and Blumstein and Schwartz (1983) got similar results. Sex was a priority for most happy couples, but it was not seen as indispensable in determining overall satisfaction.

Although sex was not solely responsible for a couple's happiness, most satisfied partners also said they made an effort to keep physical relations alive. As an illustration the Lauers (1985) note that for quite a few happy couples, even those together for decades, sexual activity is frequent and varied. Blumstein and Schwartz (1983) add that men who receive or perform oral sex frequently, and women who are more tenderly and considerately aroused, are most likely to be the happiest couples.

## Men Doing Housework

The traditional marriage required the woman to take care of home and children while the husband went out to work. Today when two thirds of wives are employed outside the home the old patterns are changing. Husbands now do housework. In two-career younger and more educated couples, men without children average about 10 hours of housework a week and fathers do about twice as much. Women still contribute more hours but now for the first time many men are cleaning, shopping, cooking, and diapering.

When a man does housework does it contribute to or detract from a couple's satisfaction? Partners who divide chores more or less amicably rate themselves higher on scales of marital happiness.

When both spouses are involved in home, job, and childrearing tasks they have a *role sharing* and usually a more gratifying union.

But this does not seem to be the case when traditional wife-husband roles are totally reversed. Blumstein and Schwartz (1983) found that when the woman was employed and the man remained full-time in the home, most couples (although not all) became "dreadfully unhappy." There was often conflict and confusion about power, prestige, roles, duties, and privileges. Being in charge of the home does not seem to suit all men, just as it does not appeal to all women. A major factor in contentment with the "househusband" role appears to be whether it was chosen or imposed on the individual. Most of the unhappy men taking care of their home had been fired from jobs or were unable to find suitable employment (Benin, Agostinelli, 1988; Smith, Reid, 1986).

Related to sex, physical attractiveness should be mentioned as a potential source of marital happiness or discontent. Spouses who pay little attention to their body, are markedly overweight, or poorly groomed, may not seem to be very appealing persons. A large number of studies have shown that males more than females pay close attention to physical attractiveness in the other person in friendship, dating, and courtship. This interest in attractiveness, a nice face, well proportioned body, and a clean and healthy appearance, continues to play a role in marriage. In one analytical study, the decrease in physical good-looks normally associated with aging apparently affected husbands more than wives. Married women lost some sexual interest and rated their marital satisfaction lower when they saw their husband as becoming unattractive, but men did this to a greater degree. Husband's sexual interest, happiness with the relationship, and perhaps even the inclination toward extramarital relations were affected by how attractive the wife was perceived to be. This study seems to support the folk wisdom that counsels couples who want to stay together to work on staying as physically fit and attractive as possible (Margolin and White, 1987).

**Attitudes** Jeanette and Robert Lauer (1985) trace the happiness of partnerships to several key attitudes. They interviewed 300 couples who said they were happily married and found companionship feelings very strong. Both husbands and wives said their spouse was their best friend. They totally enjoyed each other's company, confidence, and loyalty. Klagsbrun (1985) studied 87 happily married people and found personality traits that parallel the Lauers' reports. She found that happy marriages resulted from characteristics such as mutual respect, trust, and sharing.

All investigators also point to the importance of two other factors in marital satisfaction: communication and commitment. The first lets couples share and understand. The second, commitment, motivates them to work at creating a satisfying partnership. The Lauers (1985) put it this way:

> A . . . key to a lasting marriage was a belief in marriage as a long-term commitment and a sacred institution. Many of our respondents thought that the present generation takes the vow 'till death us do part' too lightly and is unwilling to work through difficult times. Successful couples viewed marriage as a task that sometimes demands that you grit your teeth and plunge ahead in spite of the difficulties. 'I'll tell you why we've stayed together,' said a Texas woman married for 18 years. 'I'm just too damned stubborn to give up.'
>
> (Lauer and Lauer, 1985, p. 24).

Chapter 11 discusses the characteristics of erotic love. Both companionship and commitment are correlates most couples believe are very important.

## BREAKUP AND DIVORCE

More people divorce today than ever before. By 1990, projections suggest, that for every 10 people in an intact marriage, there is one person who is divorced and not remarried. Looking at the statistics another way, about one third of first marriages end in divorce, and an equal proportion of second marriages dissolve. Figure 12-3 graphically shows these patterns of marriage and divorce in the United States. (U.S. Bureau of the Census, 1988a).

### Causes

Conflict in a relationship is inevitable. Despite their best intentions two people soon discover they have some interests, habits, and preferences that do not agree. To better understand some of these conflicts, Straus, Gelles, and Steinmetz (1980) studied 2143 couples around the country.

They found that one third had disagreements about such things as cooking, cleaning, and repairing the house. A fourth of couples stated they always dis-

*Figure 12-3*
Marriage and divorce. (Data from U.S. Bureau of the Census, 1988a).

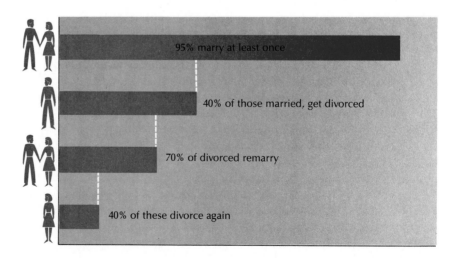

95% marry at least once

40% of those married, get divorced

70% of divorced remarry

40% of these divorce again

agreed about sex, social matters, or money. One fifth were consistently in conflict about children. The woman's job can also be a source of dispute. Among two thirds of younger couples the woman is employed outside the home and for some partners this means marital challenges and responsibilities that are not always handled well. (See Focus: Men Doing Housework.)

Whether or not these conflicts or other ones, or a partner's discovery of an extramarital relationship will result in divorce depends on a host of contributing factors. One reason for the increase in divorce in these last several decades is probably that most states are making divorce easier. A husband or wife no longer has to prove adultery, cruelty, or abandonment. **No fault** statutes are common, permitting the couple to dissolve their marriage without either accusing the other of objectionable conduct.

*no fault divorce*
Divorce legislation that requires only that both partners agree to end their marriage.

Related to this is the fact that divorce has become more socially acceptable. The divorced person is no longer ostracized. There is, too, a whole new network of formerly married people. So many millions of couples have divorced that the formerly married are a substantial group who have created a variety of social and counseling services in every community. People contemplating divorce have a culture to identify with, one that will welcome and help them when they are alone (Chapter 9; Johnson, 1988).

Another important reason for more divorce may be the ability of many wives to support themselves. Many unhappy wives once stayed married because they could not maintain a decent standard of living alone. With greater economic opportunity for women, fewer and fewer feel compelled to stay in an unsatisfactory marriage.

A fourth factor that may account for a high divorce rate is that many couples now expect a good deal more from marriage than people once did. They want a relationship that continues to be emotionally, sexually, and personally fulfilling. The media, numerous authorities and writers on marriage, seem to have helped create a climate that promises marriage to be almost more than it can be. A marriage counselor commented, "Our grandparents were satisfied with companionship, a bit of love and pleasure, and a little responsibility. We expect to find romance, excitement, achievement, and growth".

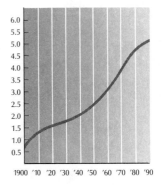

*Figure 12-4*
The divorce rate: Numbers on the left represent the number of divorces per 1000 people in the United States. (Data projected from Statistical Abstracts of the United States, U.S. Bureau of the Census, 1988b.)

### Grief

Albrecht (1980) has written:

> For the person who goes through a divorce, an entire life is often turned topsy-turvy. Intimate bonds with another person are broken; relationships with children are changed; friendship patterns are disrupted; different living arrangements must be established.

The result of marital breakup is typically shock and grief. Depressed, anxious emotions are evoked that are in many ways similar to those that occur when faced with death. Elisabeth Kübler-Ross (1969), a prominent psychiatrist, has described how terminally ill patients react when they learn their illness is fatal. Their emotions run through five stages from denial to acceptance. A similar progression of feelings is often observed when a partnership ends.

At the beginning the partner who learns that the other wants to end the relationship typically denies what was said. The partner is seen as simply making threats or trying to shock. But as the reality of the dissolution becomes ap-

Marital breakup and divorce can trigger intense feelings of anger, grief, and depression.

parent, there is often intense anger. At this point, exceedingly hostile accusations, argumentation, and even fighting may occur. The aggrieved, rejected partner may physically attack the other. Murder followed by suicide is even possible in a few instances.

After anger, or perhaps along with it, there is bargaining. One or both of the couple may attempt to negotiate new rules. The person who wants to leave the relationship may say she or he might stay but only under certain conditions. The person who is being left may offer all sorts of inducements if only the rejecting partner stays. "Just tell me what you want; I swear I'll do it," is a promise often heard during the bargaining stage.

The Kübler-Ross stages—denial, anger, bargaining, depression, and acceptance—may follow one another, or a person may alternate back and forth through these feelings.

In the last stage at the end of a relationship the person moves through depression toward acceptance. Slowly, time and other interests and activities heal the wounds of the breakup. Depression recedes and acceptance becomes the most prominent feeling. But the healing is not steady nor is it dependable. For a while a new life may seem to be beginning, but then suddenly there are surges of loneliness and fear. Often it takes a long time for people to be free of occasional recurrences of anger and depression.

### Children

The current high divorce rate has in effect restructured the family. In this decade, one of every five children lives in what is essentially a single-parent family. Although they may stay briefly with their fathers from time to time, over 90% of these children live with their mothers. One estimate is that by the end of this century half of all children under 18 will spend some time in a female-parent-only family (U.S. Bureau of the Census, 1988a). This situation has led to predictions of significantly increased sexual problems, juvenile delinquency, and emotional and psychological maladjustment.

## Coping With Breakup

The end of a relationship, whether it is a marriage terminated by divorce or a cohabitation ended by rejection, is always a wrenching and painful experience. The following tips suggest both alternatives to break-up and ways to cope with it.

1. Talk first. Try to deal effectively and directly with the conflicts. The old notion had it that it was good for a couple to fight. But anger can beget anger and even lead to violence. The happily married couples in the Lauers' (1985) investigation recognized the damaging effects of intensely expressed anger. The great majority said that they cooled off before discussing a controversial issue. They were aware that freely venting their fury was as likely to damage their relationship as to improve it. Therefore, cool off first, then talk and discuss fully and freely.

2. A second alternative is to obtain the help of a *qualified* counselor, psychologist, or psychiatrist. Notice the emphasis on the word qualified. Some people who have little training or competence represent themselves as counselors. For this reason a couple should insist on verifying the counselor's training and licensing (Chapter 17).

3. A third alternative is to have a trial separation. Sometimes only a few weeks apart can convince a couple that it is far better to work together than to go it totally alone. It is generally better to plan the rules of such a trial quite firmly. Will the individuals see others? What are the responsibilities for the children? There should also be a time limit, perhaps a month or two, after which the partners reunite and discuss their situation again.

4. If the breakup does occur, allow time for grief and healing. When a relationship ends, people are often tempted to become as socially and sexually active as possible immediately. This can be a way to express anger and relieve pain. But it can also cause frustration and despair. A better solution for many men and women is to acknowledge the grief the dissolution has caused and give oneself time for healing. Six months to a year of quietly continuing one's life and solidifying friendships typically helps the rejected partner establish a new equilibrium.

A qualified counselor can help couples in conflict reestablish a satisfying relationship.

How accurate are these forecasts? Noval Glenn (1985) pooled the data from eight national surveys conducted over a period of 10 years. He summarized findings on 703 adults who had been children when their parents divorced. These adults were compared with 1042 persons who had experienced the death of a parent during childhood and with 7954 people who were raised by both natural parents. All subjects were evaluated on tests of psychological well-being, general health, and happiness and satisfaction with various aspects of their lives. Glenn found that many of the adults whose parents had divorced when they were young did a little less well in almost all areas compared to the other two groups. They were not as happy, healthy, achieving, or satisfied as those from two-parent homes or those experiencing death of a parent during childhood.

This does not mean that divorce and single parenting necessarily caused the children's difficulties. It is possible, for example, that the parental conflict that led up to the divorce may have been responsible. It is also important to note that Glenn found a fair proportion of adults from divorced homes who were as competent and happy as anyone else. A single parent can be a loving and capable mother or father and raise healthy children. Grandparents too, are becoming increasingly important, helping to stabilize the one parent home. But some children, particularly younger ones, from divorced homes do present special educational and psychological problems that should be recognized and treated (Johnson, 1988).

### New relationships

Divorce or the breakup of a seemingly durable cohabitation presents numerous problems, not the least of which is eventually establishing a new relationship. We pointed out in Chapter 9 that social and sexual relations following divorce can range from never to "all the time." Jane Woody (1983) sees many of the extreme reactions to partnership dissolution as the result of a damaged self-concept. The woman or man who has been rejected starts to believe that she or he must be incompetent, unlovable, and a failure. Before trying to build another relationship, Woody suggests repairing this negative self-image. Friends, productive work, time to think, perhaps education or counseling can lead to a new feeling of self-worth and purposeful direction.

Eventually nearly all divorced people and separated cohabitants in their 20s to 40s find a new partner. Seven out of 10 of the divorced remarry. And over half report that their second union is better and happier than the first. The frequency of sexual intercourse often also exceeds that with the former partner. The remarried 40-year-old woman or man who was used to intercourse once or twice a week is likely now to average two to three times. Remarried people also seem somewhat more innovative, trying a variety of sexual activities that they did not usually attempt with their former spouse. The new partnership seems to have given these people an opportunity to explore their sexuality with interest and vigor (Alvarez, 1982; U.S. Bureau of the Census, 1988a).

## THE OLDER COUPLE

We are an aging population. In 1900 only 1 person in every 25 was over age 65. Today 10% of the people in the United States, 25 million women and men, are over this age. If old age begins in the 50s, then the number of seniors increases to almost 40 million. Most older women and men are married, although there are also 11 million who are widowed (Chapter 9). Sexual interests and activity remain an important concern for most. Many older people date, are sexually active, and just like young adults, may fall in love, and experience all the joy and uncertainty often called forth by this emotion (Brecher, 1984).

Despite their numbers, and the good health of most older women and men, younger people seem unaware of the sexuality of the aged. Ask most college students if there is much sexual activity among people in their 50s and you will

Divorce was looked at from the perspective of the single adult in Chapter 9. Re-entry fears, concerns about sex, and children were discussed.

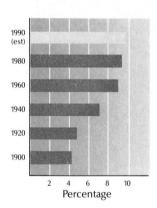

*Figure 12-5*
Percentage of the population over age 65. (Data from U.S. Department of Health and Human Services, U.S. Bureau of the Census, 1988b.)

be told, "No, I really don't think there is much." To determine just how young women and men see the older generation, Pocs et al. (1977) surveyed 239 male and female college students. Their purpose was to find out what the students believed about their parents' sex lives.

The survey uncovered a number of surprising perceptions. Only a fourth of the students thought their parents experienced oral-genital contact. But based on studies by Brecher (1984) and others, the frequency is at least 2 to 3 times as high. Two percent thought their parents had extramarital relations, while the number is actually 20 times higher. Most students estimated that their parents had intercourse about twice a month. A fourth in the study believed that their parents had intercourse only once a year. In contrast, studies show that the frequency in the 40- to 50-year-old group is about twice a week.

College students obviously underestimate the sexuality of their parents. In part this is the result of the discomfort children experience in thinking about their parents' sexual behavior. In a much larger measure, it is the result of the socially encouraged perception that people in their 50s and beyond are no longer sexually alive.

It is rare for television or motion pictures to show older women and men enjoying healthy affectional and sexual pleasure. This persuades many people that love and sex are inappropriate in the elderly.

### Sexuality and aging

Physical changes inevitably accompany aging. Fifty- and sixty-year-old women and men have a few wrinkles, graying hair, perhaps some stiff and painful joints. Sixty-year-olds, even in the best of condition, are generally unable to run as far and as fast as they could when they were 30. Tolerance for stress decreases as do vigor and resistance to illness. At the same time, stereotypical concepts of older people as necessarily ill or feeble are unfair and erroneous. Most older people are in relatively good health.

Many men and women in their fifties and older are just as sexually satisfied, and sometimes even more so, as when they were younger.

Vaginal lubrication is discussed in Chapter 3. Scant moisture may be caused by a variety of factors and can often be compensated for by using saliva or a commercial gel such as K-Y. Estrogen replacement therapy, either pills or vaginal creams, can alleviate some vaginal problems.

There are sexual biological changes that accompany aging. Masters, Johnson, and Kolodny (1986) note that in the 50s, lower levels of hormones in women may be associated with a shortening of the vagina and lesser vaginal expansion and lubrication. The number of vaginal contractions during orgasm also tends to drop to two or three, about half those reported by much younger women.

In nearly all men past their 50s, physiological changes mean that the time to erection becomes longer and frequently the partner needs to directly stimulate the penis to achieve arousal. For about 20% of men in their 60s erection seldom occurs or stops completely. The number of ejaculatory contractions also decreases and the semen is expelled with very little force. The refractory period lengthens so that while a man in his 20s may resume sexual activity a few minutes after ejaculation, most older men need to wait an hour or sometimes much longer.

For both sexes, the frequency of sexual behavior is lower. For many, whether the sexual activity is masturbation or heterosexual or homosexual relations, it may occur only once a week at age 60—less than half as often as at age 30. The sex flush (Chapter 5), the intensification of body coloring that appears in many people during peak excitation, is also seen less often. Ultimately, by the 70s, about a third of all couples have stopped coitus (Brecher, 1984).

Biological sexual function declines for both sexes, but movement in the other direction can also be seen. Masters, Johnson, and Kolodny (1986) note that clitoral response and the character of orgasmic vaginal contractions in many older women is like that found in those who are younger. Older men are often able to maintain an erection and not ejaculate considerably longer than those who are younger—prolonging the pleasure of sexual relations. Most interesting, both Masters and Johnson and Brecher (1984) observe that those who stay most sexually active show fewest physical and behavioral signs of aging. Women who often have sexual relations tend to lubricate about as well as women many decades younger. Men who continue intercourse once or twice weekly tend to erect more rapidly and to have shorter refractory periods.

To obtain a more accurate idea of the sexual capabilities of older people, science writer Edward Brecher (1984), in association with *Consumer Reports,* surveyed 4246 women and men who ranged in age from 50 to well into their 80s. Subjects each took about an hour to fill out a comprehensive questionnaire about their sexual activities, needs, and opinions. Despite some age-related problems, most older men and women were still very interested in sex. A sample of Brecher's findings:

1. Over three fourths of the couples aged 50 to 70 had intercourse at least once a week.
2. Extramarital sexual activity occurred in about a fifth of the couples. One percent of the partners jointly agreed to having separate affairs—"open marriages."
3. Sexual variety was common. Half of the couples had oral-genital relations and half frequently had intercourse in the morning or afternoon. About 1 in 15 had participated in group sexual activities after age 50.
4. Most women and men were usually orgasmic. But most also rated sexual and affectional relations without orgasm or ejaculation as pleasurably contributing to their marital happiness.

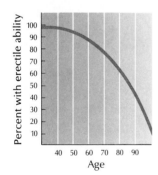

*Figure 12-6*
As men get older the ability to achieve and sustain an erection declines. Nevertheless, two thirds of all men are still erectile until their late 70s. (Based on Brecher, 1984; and others.)

5. Forty percent of the single women reported a relationship with a married man. A third thought it acceptable for an older man or woman to have a much younger lover.

Brecher points out that most older people continue to enjoy sexual relations in every variety well into their 70s and often beyond. It also seems that continued sexual activity not only leads to greater life satisfaction, but may have health benefits as well. Those who are more sexually active are also usually healthier. It may be, however, that health and sex interact. The more either is present, the more the other is encouraged.

Finally, we need to make two important points. Most studies of sex and aging concentrate on coitus. This emphasis appears to argue that sexuality consists of vaginal sexual intercourse and not much else. Actually, sexuality among older couples, as among women and men of all ages, involves a great deal more. Many older people masturbate. Quite a few have orgasmic dreams. Kissing and caressing are present in nearly all and at very advanced ages. Sexuality consists of much more than coitus, and a close look at older women and men suggests that nearly all continue some form of intimate and affectionate relations (Table 12-3).

Chapters 5 and 17 describe a variety of noncoital sexual pleasuring techniques.

A second significant point worth underlining is that sexually active people tend to remain sexually active for very long periods. George and Weiler (1981) looked at the sexual behaviors of married couples in their 50s and then reexamined them when they were well along into their 60s. In nearly all instances the frequency of coitus and the variety of sexual activities engaged in during middle age persisted into the older years. Declines were seen in those very advanced in age. But here, too, those most active earlier tended to show the least decrease in sexual interest and behavior.

**The widowed** No discussion of sexuality in older couples would be complete without recognition of the fact that because men die earlier, the number of widowed women continually climbs as the years advance (Chapters 7 and 9). Among people over 50, there are over 2 million widowed men and more than 8 million women. This means that many older women may have to consider several alternatives if they want a male sexual or companionate partnership.

*Table 12-3*

**Sex at age 60**

| | Percentage participating | |
|---|---|---|
| **Activity** | **Women** | **Men** |
| Masturbation, at least occasionally | 30 | 60 |
| Coitus with spouse, averaging about once every week or two | 80 | 80 |
| Orgasm while sleeping, occasional | 20 | 15 |
| Caressing, kissing, petting | 90+ | 90+ |

Data from Adams, Turner, 1985; Brecher, 1984; and others.

Some writers have suggested that older women who are alone and want sexual relations should consider younger male friends. Many women are not opposed to this, but few are able to establish such relationships. On the other hand the older man with a younger woman is not a rare partnership. This further increases the disparity between the number of single older women and men. There are other possibilities that might be suitable for some who are widowed. These include lesbianism and masturbation. In Brecher's (1984) sample, about 2% of women first had a homosexual relationship after age 50. Catherine Adams and Barbara Turner (1985) report that masturbation occurs among a fourth of older women. But it was apparently not a satisfactory substitute for a human relationship. The authors comment:

> Regarding the suggestion that masturbation might be a solution for the presumably unmet sexual needs of older women (and men), masturbation was not the favorite sexual activity of most of those who reported engaging in it. . . . For a minority of respondents, masturbation is currently a pleasurable and preferred sexual option. However, 85% of the women and 89% of the men preferred an interpersonal rather than a solitary sexual activity. In old age, as earlier, sex is an interpersonal activity (p. 139).

About a fourth of the older women and men who are alone move away from sexuality. They become asexual, saying they have lost interest in physical sex. They may, however, establish good nonsexual friendships with both sexes. Such friendships can provide intimacy, social and intellectual stimulation, and a degree of physical closeness and warmth (Essex, Nam, 1987).

Single people, whether young, old, divorced, or widowed, share many of the same problems and concerns. These are covered in Chapter 9.

## In Sum

Married people are often found to be happier than those who are single. Marital happiness seems to depend on communication, companionship, the model provided by parents, and sexual satisfaction. Partnership conflict has several sources, with housekeeping, sex, and money commonly named. Divorce is now legally easier and more socially acceptable than it once was. In addition many women are financially independent and both spouses are likely to expect a great deal from marriage. All these factors may contribute to current high divorce rates. Divorce is often a traumatic process for the spouses and for the children so that alternatives should be considered. Eventually 7 out of 10 of those who divorce remarry and most report greater marital and sexual satisfaction.

## Summary

Over 9 of every 10 American men and women eventually marry. Their motives are numerous and usually include a combination of incentives, such as love, emotional security, sexual access, and companionship. First marriages in the United States occur around the middle 20s, although many couples choose to wait until they are older. After age 30 the proportion of the eligible population that marries declines continuously.

Marital sexual activity is higher and more varied today than in previous generations. It is highest among younger couples and tends to decline as the years accumulate. Extramarital sex is also more frequent and may involve up to half of all women and two thirds of men. The motives for extramarital relations may include marital dissatisfaction, although many affairs are the result of curiosity and a quest for variety. Couples commonly strongly forbid extramarital involvements, but most marriages do not end because of an affair. About 1% of all partnerships permit extramarital relations through swinging. Masturbation continues into marriage with most women and men involved at least occasionally. Wives and husbands often hide masturbation from one another although it is a common and normal practice.

Marital happiness seems to involve several key attitudes and characteristics. Couples who are good companions, feel committed, and communicate well seem to be happiest. There is also a tendency for sexual satisfaction to be important in marital happiness.

The divorce rate remains high with about a third of marriages ending. Couples often have conflicting positions regarding sex, money, their children, and housekeeping chores. Additional factors may contribute to the divorce rate. These include the growing economic independence of many women, the social acceptability of divorce, and no-fault divorce statutes.

The dissolution of a partnership is often a painful experience leaving one or both partners feeling many emotions similar to those associated with death. Children from divorced homes may have special educational and psychological problems. There are alternatives to a couple's breaking up and these include honest and open discussion and trial separations. Over 70 percent of divorced people remarry and most report happier second marriages and an increase in marital sexual activity.

As men and women grow older, sexual activity slows down, decreases, and may cease altogether. On the other hand, despite social and psychological barriers, and often some health concerns, many couples remain sexually active throughout their lives.

---

1 How similar or different are the reasons you might decide to marry to those described in the text? What are the advantages and disadvantages of remaining single or cohabiting?

2 Based on your own observations, characterize the marital stage of several couples you know. What are some ways to help move marriage out of the career-parent stage into the growth stage?

3 Sexual relations in a long-term relationship can be a source of stress for many couples. How can a couple keep their sexual relations appealing? Distinguish the various forms of extramarital intercourse and give your opinion on them.

4 To what extent is it practical and important for women and men to divide the role of breadwinner, homemaker, and parent? What kind of role and power division would make a satisfactory relationship for you?

5 Which factors related to marital satisfaction are within, and which are outside of, the couple's control?

6 Describe the effects of serious conflict and of divorce on the couple themselves, their children, and society. What are some ways in which conflict can be resolved and divorce prevented?

7 What changes in sexual and affectional relations often take place as a couple age?

*For Thought and Discussion*

*References*

Adams, C.G., and Turner, B.F. Reported changes in sexuality from adulthood to old age. *The Journal of Sex Research*, May 1985, *21*, (2), 126-141.

Albrecht, S.L. Reactions and adjustments to divorce: Differences in the experiences of males and females. *Family Relations*, January 1980, *29*, 59-68.

Alvarez, A. *Life after marriage: an anatomy of divorce.* New York: Simon & Schuster, 1982.

Atwater, L. *The extramarital connection: Sex, intimacy, and identity.* New York: Irvington, 1982.

Benin, M.H., and Agostinelli, J. Husbands' and wives' satisfaction with the division of labor. *Journal of Marriage and the Family*, May 1988, *50*, 349-361.

Blumstein, P., and Schwartz, P. *American Couples.* New York: William Morrow & Co., Inc., 1983.

Brecher, E.M. *Love, sex, and aging.* Boston: Little, Brown, 1984.

Campbell, S.M. *The couple's journey: intimacy as a path to wholeness.* San Luis Obispo, Calif.: Impact Publishers, Inc., 1980.

Cook, K., Kretchmer, A., Nellis, B., Lever, J., and Hertz, R.: The *Playboy* readers' sex survey (Part 3). *Playboy*, May 1983, 126.

Davidson, J. *The agony of it all.* Los Angeles: Jeremy B. Tarcher, Inc., 1988.

Davidson, Sr., J.K., and Darling, C.A. The sexually experienced woman: multiple sex partners and sexual satisfaction. *The Journal of Sex Research*, 1988, *24*, 141-154.

Essex, M.J., and Nam, S. Marital status and loneliness among older women. *Journal of Marriage and the Family*, February 1987, *49*, 93-106.

Ford, C.S., and Beach, F.A. *Patterns of sexual behavior.* Westport, Conn.: Greenwood Press, 1980.

Freud, S. *Collected papers.* New York: Basic Books, 1959.

George, L.K., and Weiler, J.J. Sexuality in middle and later life. *Archives of General Psychiatry*, 1981, *38*, 919-923.

Glenn, N.D. Children of divorce. *Psychology Today*, June 1985, 68 ff.

Glenn, N.D., and Weaver, C.N. The changing relationship of marital status to reported happiness. *Journal of Marriage and the Family*, May 1988, *50*, 317-324.

Jenks, R.J. Swinging: a replication and test of a theory. *The Journal of Sex Research*, May 1985, *21*, 199-210.

Johnson, C.L. Postdivorce reorganization of relationships between divorcing children and their parents. *Journal of Marriage and the Family*, February 1988, *50*, 221-231.

Karlen, A. *Three-somes: studies in sex, power, and intimacy.* New York: Beech Tree Books, William Morrow, 1988.

Kinsey, A.C., Pomeroy, W.B., and Martin, C.E. *Sexual behavior in the human male.* Philadelphia: Saunders, 1948.

Kinsey, A.C., Pomeroy, W.B., and Martin, C.E. *Sexual behavior in the human female.* Philadelphia: Saunders, 1953.

Klagsbrun, F. *Married people: staying together in the age of divorce.* New York: Bantam, 1985.

Kübler-Ross, E. *On death and dying.* New York: Macmillan, 1969.

Kurdek, L.A., and Schmitt, J.P. Partner homogamy in married, heterosexual cohabiting, gay, and lesbian couples. *The Journal of Sex Research*, May 1987, *23* (2), 212-232.

Lauer, J., and Lauer, R. Marriages made to last. *Psychology Today*, June 1985, 22 ff.

Margolin, L., and White, L. The continuing role of physical attractiveness in marriage. *Journal of Marriage and the Family*, February 1987, *49* (1), 21-27

Masters, W.H., Johnson, V.E., and Kolodny, R.C. *Masters and Johnson on Sex and Human Loving.* Boston: Little, Brown, 1986.

McWhirter, N. (editor). *Guinness book of world records.* New York: Sterling Publishing Co., Inc., 1988.

Petersen, J.R., Kretchmer, A., Nellis, B., Lever, J., and Hertz, R. The *Playboy* readers' sex survey (Parts 1 and 2). *Playboy,* January 1983, 108; March 1983, 90.

Pocs, O., Godow, A., Tolone, W., and Walsh, R.H. Is there sex after forty? *Psychology Today*, June 1977, Reprint No. p-407.

Reiss, I.L., Anderson, R.E., and Sponaugle, G.C. A multivariate model of the determinants of extramarital sexual permissiveness. *Journal of Marriage and the Family*, 1980, *42*, 395-411.

Richardson, L. Another world. *Psychology Today*, February 1986, 22-27.

Rubenstein, C., and Tavris, C. Special survey results: 26,000 women reveal the secrets of intimacy. *Redbook*, September 1987, *169*, 147.

Safran, C. Why more people are making better marriages. *Parade Magazine*, April 28, 1985, 16 ff.

Sarrel, P., and Sarrel, L. The *Redbook* report on sexual relationships. *Redbook*, October 1980, 73-80 and February 1981, 140-145.

Sherwin, R., and Corbett, S. Campus sexual norms and dating relationships: a trend analysis. *Journal of Sex Research*, 1985, *21*, (3), 258-274.

Smith, A.D., and Reid, W.J. *Role-sharing marriage*. New York: Columbia University Press, 1986.

Strauss, M.A., Gelles, R.J., and Steinmetz, S.K. *Behind closed doors: Violence in the American family*. Garden City, NY: Doubleday, 1980.

Talese, G. *Thy neighbor's wife*. New York: Doubleday, 1980.

Tavris, C., and Sadd, S. *The Redbook report on female sexuality*. New York: Delacorte Press, 1977.

U.S. Bureau of the Census. *Marital status and living arrangements: Current population reports*. Washington, D.C.: U.S. Government Printing Office, 1988a.

U.S. Bureau of the Census. *Statistical abstract of the United States*. Washington, D.C.: U.S. Government Printing Office, 1988b.

Whitehurst, R.N. There are a number of equally valid forms of marriage, such as multiple marriage, swinging, adultery, and open marriage. In Feldman, H., and Feldman, M. (editors), *Current controversies in marriage and family*, Beverley Hills, California: Sage, 1985.

Wolfe, L. *The Cosmo report*. New York: Arbor House, 1981.

Woody, J.D. Sexuality in divorce and remarriage. *Family Therapy Collections*, 1983, No. 5, 62-81.

*Suggested Readings*

Klagsbrun, F. *Married people: staying together in the age of divorce*. New York: Bantam Books, 1985.

Based on interviews with 87 couples who have been married for at least 15 years, Klagsbrun identifies a number of abilities and characteristics that are frequently found in people with strong marriages.

Krantzler, M. *Creative marriage*. New York: McGraw-Hill, 1981.

In an area flooded with them, this is one of the better advice books. Contains many insights and ideas suggesting how a couple may keep their relationship fresh and vital.

Scarf, M. *Intimate partners*. New York: Ballantine, 1988.

The author presents some creative ideas to improve marriage, and keep it a more exciting and productive relationship.

Smith, A.D., and Reid, W.J. *Role-sharing marriage*. New York: Columbia University Press, 1986.

Presents relationships in which both wife and husband are equally responsible for earning a living, caring for the home, and raising children.

*Chapter 13*

# Homosexual Relationships

**When you finish this chapter, you should be able to:**

Define homosexuality and the mix of homosexual and heterosexual behaviors in many people.

Contrast how psychiatric views concerning homosexuality have changed.

Describe the coming out process and the concerns that may be involved.

Explain how homosexual and heterosexual physical and emotional relationships are similar and different.

Evaluate the different explanations of homosexuality.

Explain how present attitudes toward homosexuality have been shaped by previous beliefs.

People's identities are not well defined by their sexual orientations. If someone were introduced as heterosexual, we would know very little about their personality, aspirations, shortcomings, or strengths. So, too, when we speak of individuals as homosexual, we should understand that this tells us little about them. We would know only that a good deal or perhaps all of their sexual and/or affectional interests are with members of their own sex. In this chapter, we will examine the meaning of homosexuality, its frequency, background, lifestyles, and social context.

*Test Yourself*

---

### What Do You Know About Homosexuality?

Mark the following statements *true* or *false*. Answers are located in the Appendix on p. 580.

| | True | False |
|---|---|---|
| 1. Homosexual behavior is very rare. | — | — |
| 2. Psychiatrists consider people who are homosexual mentally ill. | — | — |
| 3. Homosexuality is the result of children being seduced by adults who are homosexual. | — | — |
| 4. Some homosexual people marry and have children. | — | — |
| 5. In ancient Greece homosexuality was fully accepted and found in the majority of the adults. | — | — |
| 6. Most women and men who are homosexual are unhappy with their orientation. | — | — |

| | True | False |
|---|---|---|
| 7. AIDS is found among homosexual men but rarely among homosexual women. | — | — |
| 8. The term *gay* usually refers to homosexual men and the term *lesbian* refers to homosexual women. | — | — |
| 9. People who are bisexual, having sexual and affectional relations with both men and women, are often in transition, drifting toward one sexual orientation. | — | — |
| 10. Homosexuality like heterosexuality may be in part the result of prebirth hormonal influences. | — | — |

**Interpretation**

Most people are not well informed about homosexuality. If you got nine or ten correct, your score is excellent. A score of seven or eight is also very good. An average score is five or six correct.

If the number of correct answers is below this, you may have received more misinformation than accurate knowledge about homosexuality.

## DEFINING HOMOSEXUALITY

The term *homosexuality* suggests a broad range of attitudes, affections, social expectations, and standards. It is a complex and subtle concept. *Homosexual behavior,* on the other hand, lends itself more readily to definition. It is a specific instance of same-sex contact—two women or two men having sexual relations.

To help us reach a good understanding, we also need to distinguish between sexual behavior and gender identity (Chapter 6). Many people assume that homosexual behavior is the outcome of crossed gender identification. Men who prefer male sexual-affectional partners are thought of as feminine. Women whose relationships are primarily with other women are believed to behave like men. In actuality, homosexual women and men generally identify with their own biological sex. Homosexual people are *not* transsexual, that is, they do not want to be the other sex. Homosexual men think of themselves as men and homosexual women feel and act like women (Bell et al., 1981; Blanchard, 1988).

Another clarification is necessary. A great many people imagine homosexual relations. They may have met a person of their own sex who was attractive to them. They may be motivated to try a homosexual experience but never act on their needs. Schwartz and Masters (1984) found the major portion of the heterosexual men and women that they studied had experienced a homosexual fantasy. Homosexual people, too, sometimes had heterosexual fantasies. Were we to say that heterosexuals with homosexual fantasies were homosexual, we would have to argue the reverse also. Homosexuals with heterosexual fantasies would then be called heterosexual. An occasional fantasy, heterosexual or homosexual, does not define sexual orientation.

### Experimentation and situational behavior

We need to look at two more circumstances before reaching a workable understanding of homosexuality. During the adolescent years, there is a good deal of sexual experimentation. As we saw in Chapter 8, about 20% of teenagers engage in behaviors that can be called homosexual. For the most part these same-sex experiences are limited to one or a few occasions and do not predict adult homosexual behavior (Bell et al., 1981).

There are also situations that may produce homosexual experiences. When men and women are segregated, such as might occur in a school or in prison, there is often a good bit of homosexual activity. Prisons are the most segregated of all institutions and people are forced to live only with their own sex for many years. Half of all prison inmates are homosexually involved. For some prisoners this situation perhaps provides an opportunity to express needs otherwise repressed or hidden. For most others, the homosexual behavior is situational. The men and women are in a circumstance where almost the only way to express themselves sexually and affectionally is through relations with members of their own sex. Once out of prison the large majority of ex-offenders resume heterosexual behaviors (Bell and Weinberg, 1978; Bullough, 1981).

### Incidence

Sexual preferences and behaviors do not necessarily remain the same throughout a lifetime. Adolescent experimentation with homosexuality may be followed by a lifetime of heterosexuality. Even women and men in their 30s or older may ultimately adopt sexual behaviors that were not part of their previous history. Kinsey et al. (1948, 1953) found that 10% of adult males and about half as many females seem to be homosexual for a period of several years and may then shift their preference. Given this degree of fluidity of sexual expression, the number of people who can be thought of as homosexual is at best an educated estimate.

Many researchers define persons whose sexual-affectional interests and behavior are consistently and predominantly directed toward members of their own sex as homosexual. In terms of numbers this means that about 4% of the adult population might be considered homosexual. This number might be a bit low for men and a little high for women but it is a reasonable approximation (Bell et al., 1981; Blumstein and Schwartz, 1983; Bullough, 1981).

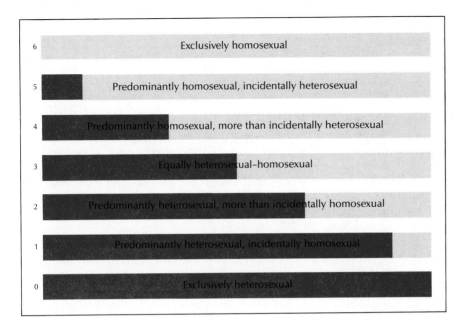

This percentage means that among the 200 million adults in the United States in 1990, approximately 8 million can be thought of as homosexual. This is a substantial minority. The homosexual community in the United States is in fact larger than the population of many countries including Denmark, Honduras, Israel, and Switzerland. This community is big enough to have its own magazines, resorts, city neighborhoods, and political leaders. Homosexual men and women constitute a significant portion of the population and want their interests and concerns considered.

### Bisexuality

The understanding of homosexuality and heterosexuality might be simplified if people were entirely consistent in their behavior. But this is not the case. The pioneering sex researcher Alfred Kinsey and his group (1948, 1953) were for the most part surprised to learn of the mix of sexual interests in many people's backgrounds. In their view, over one fifth of adults who thought of themselves as heterosexual had some homosexual experience. At the same time, almost two thirds of those who consider themselves homosexual have had heterosexual experiences (see Figure 13-1).

To better understand the combination of sexual behaviors the Kinsey group devised a seven-point scale. The first rating, 0, is for a person whose behavior is exclusively heterosexual. The woman or man whose interactions are predominantly heterosexual and infrequently homosexual is given the next rating, 1. The gradations go up to 6—exclusive homosexuality. The middle of the scale, 3, represents people whose history seems a balance of both heterosexual and homosexual activities.

The Kinsey studies and the Hunt update (1974) suggested that 1 in every 20 people might be considered **bisexual**. This interpretation is based on the inclusion of people with just "incidental" (points 1 and 5 of the Kinsey scale) bisex-

In most larger cities there are neighborhoods in which many homosexual people live, but the majority of homosexual women and men do not limit themselves to special residential areas.

*bisexual*
A person who has an almost equal amount of heterosexual and homosexual experience.

### Psychiatry and Homosexuality

For most of the century, psychiatry considered homosexuality a mental disorder. It was included in the official psychiatric *Diagnostic and Statistical Manual of Mental Disorders (DSM)* as a sexual deviation. Beginning in the 1970s homosexual rights groups and mental health workers began contesting this view. They asked that psychiatric practice be changed and that homosexuality be seen simply as an alternative sexual orientation.

Those who wanted homosexuality removed from the list of sexual deviations argued that homosexual women and men could be as well adjusted, socially productive, and responsible as those who are heterosexual. The discussion continued for a decade until the American Psychiatric Association declared that a homosexual orientation is not a mental disorder. This meant that employers, government agencies, and the law could no longer justify measures against homosexual people by saying that homosexuality is a mental illness.

Psychiatry did not entirely remove itself from diagnosing sexual practice. It introduced a new term, *sexual disorder*, for a person distressed by homosexual, heterosexual, or any related form of behavior. Since powerful negative societal attitudes toward homosexuality exist, a homosexual person may be persuaded that her or his sexual-affectional needs are deviant. The result may be considerable internal conflict, anxiety, and stress (Harris, 1988).

The proportion of homosexual women and men who could be considered distressed by their sexuality is not precisely known. The Bell and Weinberg (1978) studies may give some lead. Two groups the authors called *asexual* and *dysfunctional* seemed troubled. The dysfunctional group had problems becoming sexually aroused or satisfied and were unhappy with their orientation. The second group, the asexual, avoided sexual relations and tended to have few friends. Together these two groups accounted for about a fifth of homosexual adults. These authors, however, also found that most of the 1000 homosexual men and women they interviewed maintained satisfactory relationships and were comfortable with their sexuality.

ual behavior. Masters and Johnson (1979) did not subscribe to this position. They agreed that many people may in the course of years have both heterosexual and homosexual experiences. But this is not enough to warrant the term bisexual. Masters and Johnson suggest that most people who appear to be bisexual eventually seem to settle largely into one orientation or another.

This qualification enables Masters and Johnson to distinguish the very few people they believe are consistently bisexual from those they call *transitional.* These are people whose sexual-affectional behavior only appears to be mixed. What is really happening is that it is shifting to just one orientation. Typically these are young adults who over the course of several years, possibly due to circumstances, increasingly drift to homosexuality. They might be thought of as emerging homosexuals. If we limit the definition of bisexual to people who consistently and genuinely respond with equal interest to both sexes, the incidence is probably under 1%.

## LESBIAN AND GAY

What shall we call a person who is sexually attracted to her or his own sex? From the point of view of many thoughtful people, homosexual or heterosexual, it should *not* be necessary to label a person because of sexual preference. When we describe a new acquaintance we do not usually begin with "Gladys is heterosexual." If we have to say something about Gladys at all, it will probably be, "Gladys is a law student; she seems very intelligent." Homosexual people, too, are law students, cab drivers, physicians, dock workers, writers, bank clerks, and law enforcement officers. They are black, white, Catholic, Baptist, and Hispanic, and come from every other ethnic and occupational group. They may also be fathers or mothers, bright or dull, and mentally or physically healthy or ill. In short, homosexual people are a very diverse group and their sexual preference is but one aspect of their identity. Let us recognize, then, that describing someone as homosexual tells us nothing about personality, occupation, age, or any number of other characteristics and behaviors. It just points to a person's sexual behaviors.

The term *homosexual* has been used for most of this century and its meaning is clear. The word itself comes from the Greek *homo*, meaning same. A person who is homosexual is interested in others of the same sex. Over the last decade many homosexual men have preferred the term *gay*. They have argued that the term *homosexual* is both too clinical and too negative. They suggest instead a word they hold to be more positive, one that affirms a life-style — gay.

Homosexual women often elect to use the term *lesbian*. The word comes from *Lesbos*, a Greek island where in ancient times young women were supposedly schooled in feminine and erotic arts. The head of the school, Sappho, according to surviving literature and poetry, encouraged romantic and sexual preferences for women. We will use all three terms. When we say homosexual

A person may find women, men, or both sexually attractive (painting by Paul Gauguin).

it can refer to either or both sexes. We reserve the term gay exclusively for homosexual people who are male. (Many people, however, use gay synonymously with homosexual, to refer to either sex.)

### Behavior

The stereotype has it that homosexual women and men can easily be recognized. The men allegedly act feminine. Their manner and voice supposedly simulate those of women. According to the stereotypes, lesbians dress like men and have bold, assertive postures. There are some homosexual people whose appearance and conduct come close to the stereotype. Gagnon and Simon (1973) point out that effeminate behavior sometimes appears in young homosexual men around the time they are **coming out.** This may sometimes be a way for some gay persons to throw off the traditional appearance and behavior of men and confirm their homosexuality.

Just as there are some homosexual men who act feminine, others appear supermasculine. They may ride motorcycles, wear leather, or earn a black belt in karate. Lesbians, too, may convey an image of extreme femininity or of masculinity. Most homosexual adults, however, eventually develop their own personal style. Like heterosexual people, homosexual people have appearances, traits, and characteristics uniquely suitable to themselves as individuals and do not copy the behavior of others. The result is that most gay and lesbian people do not fit a stereotype.

## COMING OUT

Human beings seem to have a powerful need to define themselves and seek others who share their identity. Many, probably most of us, think of ourselves as "Catholics" or "runners" or "musicians" and try to behave according to these labels. During adolescence a good deal of the search for self-definition focuses on one's sexuality. Evolving a sense of personal and sexual identity, whether it is heterosexual or homosexual, can be a difficult, awkward, and even painful process.

According to Bell et al. (1981), among people who eventually identify themselves as homosexual, fairly clear homosexual feelings occur around age 13 in boys and at about 16 in girls. But it is likely another year or two will pass before there is actual physical sexual contact with a member of the same sex. By late adolescence, however, 80% of individuals who are ultimately gay or lesbian have had homosexual relations.

Becoming aware of one's homosexual orientation might be easier if only same-sex physical and emotional experiences occurred during adolescence. But this is usually not the case. The majority of all gay and lesbian people recount being heterosexually aroused during adolescence. Peplau (1981) found that 80% of her lesbian interviewees had at least one sexual or romantic relationship with a man. Among homosexual men two thirds had sexual intercourse with a woman.

Self-awareness is also complicated by social standards. Young gay or lesbian persons may not want their apparent sexual and affectional preferences to violate social norms. They may repress or rationalize their homosexual desires. As a result they may date the other sex with considerable enthusiasm. Or they

*coming out*
The process of becoming aware of, and disclosing, one's own homosexuality.

may claim that whatever homosexual experiences they have had took place while they were drunk or against their will. But as homosexual needs and experiences recur there is increasing awareness. During middle adolescence a first significant romantic or sexual affair often accelerates self-recognition.

> I was fifteen. I had some sexual experience with a girl. She masturbated me and I played with her. I had also done some childish things with two boys. I thought about being homosexual. I knew more or less what it meant. But it did not become clear to me until I got involved with Billy. He was skinny, pimply, not very attractive. But I developed a fantastic crush. I used to wait across the street from his apartment house in the morning. I just wanted to see him come out . . . eventually we became lovers, that is, as much as 15-year-old boys can really be lovers.
>
> *(Author's Files)*

In about a fifth of homosexual women and half as many men, recognition of homosexual needs does not seem to occur until adulthood. A man or a woman may be married, be a parent, and seem firmly established in a heterosexual orientation. But homosexual preferences eventually surface.

Whether it occurs in adolescence or adulthood, recognizing one's homosexuality may progress fairly evenly. Studies suggest that young men and women who grow up in an accepting and supportive environment define their homosexuality earlier and adjust well sexually and socially. In many other instances, awareness of homosexual needs may provoke conflict and anxiety that can often be helped by competent counseling (Coleman, 1982).

One way in which a few people resist recognizing their own homosexual needs is to seem to be very opposed and hostile toward gay and lesbian people.

## Disclosure

When adolescents or young adults have defined themselves as homosexual, an urge to disclose, to tell others, often follows. But who should be told and when should the information be shared? People who are heterosexual often seem to

Honest and caring parent-child relations make communication possible, even about difficult topics.

announce their identity during midadolescence by letting their increasing interest in the other sex be very evident. Given social pressures and restraints, very
few adolescent homosexual boys and girls can similarly let their preferences be
known. Affirming one's homosexual identity to others, coming out is often a
more subtle process.

Coming out during adolescence typically involves first letting some heterosexual friends know. Other disclosures often wait until early adulthood. Estimates suggest that eventually half of all homosexual men disclose their orientation to neighbors and employers. The proportion of women who disclose appears to be much less. The sexuality of a young or older woman living alone or
with a female friend is often less likely to be questioned.

The most difficult disclosure may be to parents. Eventually most homosexual women and men tell close family members. Some parents accept the disclosure with equanimity and love. They understand their son's or daughter's orientation. At the other extreme are parents whose reaction is depression, fear,
or even fury. They may feel personally violated or believe their child's orientation is a stubborn rebellion against them (Coleman, 1982).

> When my parents found out, my father especially, he was furious. He hit me.
> He said that in his old country, where he was born, a father had the right to kill
> a deviant daughter. They have a strong sense of family loyalty and shame. I had
> no sense of shame. I was disloyal and hateful.
>
> *(Author's Files)*

A new dimension has been added by AIDS, the fatal *acquired immune deficiency syndrome,* discussed later in this section and more fully in Chapter 16.
A few gay people have found their parents giving an extra washing to their
plates, reluctant to use the bathroom after them, or outright terrorized that
they might become infected. For many parents and homosexual persons, AIDS
has opened up old wounds, anxieties, and distress. Ultimately, however, the
large majority of parents regain their equilibrium and once again treat their
homosexual child with concern and affection (Robinson et al., 1987).

## SEXUAL RELATIONS

Homosexual and heterosexual relations are both similar and different. Penile-
vaginal intercourse cannot be included, but kissing and caressing are as universal among homosexual couples as they are among heterosexual couples.
Nearly all homosexual partners, like most heterosexual ones, also touch and
stimulate erogenous and genital areas by hand and mouth (Chapters 3, 4, and
5). Cunnilingus and fellatio appear frequently among homosexual couples,
with eight out of ten often using these techniques to reach orgasm. Anal intercourse is common too, with about half of all male couples often reaching orgasm in this way (Cook et al., 1983).

Lesbians are often thought to strap on rubber or plastic penises or use some
other phallic devices to stimulate each other's vaginas. Actually only about
15% occasionally use such equipment. Many, however, sometimes employ a
vibrator, an electric stimulator, that may be touched to the clitoris. A sexual
technique that is frequent, used by about half of all lesbians, is body to body
rub. The genital area of one partner may be massaged against the other's body,

*Table 13-1*

**Techniques Frequently Used by Homosexual Women and Men**

| | Percentage* | |
|---|---|---|
| | Women | Men |
| Kiss and caress | 100 | 100 |
| Stimulate genitals by hand | 90 | 90 |
| Stimulate breasts by mouth or hand | 90 | 25 |
| Cunnilingus | 80 | — |
| Fellatio | — | 80 |
| Anal intercourse (stimulation) | 5 | 50 |
| Genital/body rub | 50 | 35 |
| Dildo (object into vagina) | 15 | — |

*Figures reported are approximate percentages derived from Blumstein and Schwartz, 1983, and others.

leg, or thigh. A variation of this technique is **tribadism.** The women lie face to face on top of one another. The genitals touch and the partners move to stimulate them (Coleman et al., 1983).

The frequency of sexual relations among homosexual partners is close to that reported for heterosexual pairs. For both groups about 30% to 40% of those who have been together 10 years or less have relations two to three times a week. After 10 years a difference emerges. Nearly half of married heterosexuals still have intercourse two to three times weekly. The proportion of homosexual women and men having sexual relations as often declines to about a fourth. This difference hints that in the later years the sexual element may continue to be more prominent in some heterosexual relations. It may also partly reflect the greater likelihood of homosexual couples having outside partners (see Figure 13-3) (Blumstein and Schwartz, 1983; Coleman et al., 1983).

Homosexual women and men sometimes report more satisfying sexual relations than those described by heterosexual couples. The frequency of orgasm

*tribadism*
Homosexual activity in which partners lie on top of one another, genitals touching and stimulated by rubbing.

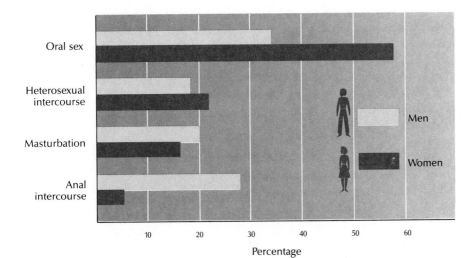

*Figure 13-2*
The percentages indicate the proportion of homosexual women and men who reported the activity as their source of best orgasm. (Modified from Cook et al., 1983.)

for lesbian partners has also been reported to be higher than for heterosexual women. Investigators have sometimes noted, too, a difference between homosexual and heterosexual foreplay. Some homosexual partners seem to arouse one another more slowly and deliberately and to talk more. They especially tend to be quite detailed in giving each other sexual instructions and directions (Coleman et al., 1983; Sakheim et al., 1985).

These observations have not been confirmed by all investigators. Bell and Weinberg (1978) write that about half of all gay and lesbian interviewees report a lack of satisfying orgasm for themselves or their partners was sometimes a problem. Masters and Johnson (1979) also note that whatever the claims, differing degrees of sexual excitation and orgasm as the result of homosexual or heterosexual relations cannot be physiologically distinguished. It may be true, however, that on a personal level, sexual stimulation and orgasm that are the result of more thoughtful and provocative arousal may be more psychologically satisfying, whatever their source (Chapter 5).

### Traditional sexual roles

In most younger homosexual couples, both partners are employed outside the home. This makes it likely that both will share household tasks and responsibilities. Neither will be just the active (traditional husband) or passive (stereotypical wife) partner.

Common belief has it that one person in every homosexual couple is consistently active, meaning plays the male role, and the other is traditionally femininely passive. The active person supposedly plays "husband" while the other enacts the stereotyped role of the conventional "wife." Actually such gender roles are seldom adhered to. Blumstein and Schwartz (1983) asked homosexual women and men who most often initiates sex. For both gay and lesbian couples, the figures divided fairly neatly into thirds. About a third of the interviewees said that they often, but not always, initiated sexual relations. Another third of the interviewees reported that their partners often did. The last third reported that both partners initiated sexual activity equally. These statistics make it appear that in most homosexual relationships neither partner plays what were once rigid and traditional male and female sexual roles.

## COUPLES

The affectional and emotional relationships of homosexual and heterosexual couples are parallel. Some gay and lesbian people remain single for all their lives (Chapter 9). Others find a permanent partner by their late teens or in their 20s. It is more common for lesbians to form emotional bonds that start earlier and last longer. Letitia Peplau (1981) studied a sample of 254 adult homosexual women and men and found 61% of the lesbians and 41% of those who were gay in binding relationships.

*fidelity*
Faithfulness; having sexual relations only with one partner.

Another study contrasted **fidelity** among couples of both orientations. Among heterosexual couples married 10 or more years, roughly a fourth had been involved in an extramarital affair. Among homosexual men who had been in a relationship for more than 10 years, over 90% had been involved in outside sexual relations. For homosexual women the outside affair count was close to 50%. These figures indicate that fidelity may have different levels of significance for homosexual and heterosexual people (Blumstein and Schwartz, 1983).

Another explanation for the higher rate of outside relations for homosexual couples may lie in the different patterns found among lesbian and gay people.

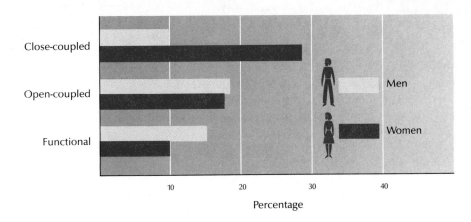

*Figure 13-3*
Relationship patterns
among homosexual women
and men: close-coupled
describes a faithful,
enduring relationship;
open-coupled describes an
enduring and open
relationship; functional
describes those who are
single and well adjusted.
Percentages do not equal
100 since about half the
adults interviewed could
not be simply fitted into
any one classification.
(Data from Bell et al.,
1978, 1981.)

Bell and Weinberg (1978), after study of nearly 1000 homosexual men and women, were persuaded that it is misleading to use only one word, *homosexual,* to describe lesbian and gay life-styles. The authors saw different homosexual relationship patterns.

According to Bell and Weinberg, 30% of lesbians and 10% of homosexual men were described as *close-coupled.* They were generally content with both their sexual orientation and their relationship. They were usually faithful to one another, did not have any significant psychological problems, and in most other ways seemed like heterosexual couples who were in satisfying relationships.

Approximately 20% of lesbian and gay people were *open-coupled.* These homosexual women and men had a steady partner with whom they lived, but they also had friends outside their primary relationship. Many saw no contradiction in having sexual or affectional relations both with their partner and with other lovers. They were much less likely, too, compared to heterosexual couples who tried "open" relationships (Chapter 12), to feel jealous or envious, (Salovey, Rodin, 1985).

About 10% to 15% of homosexuals were called "functional" by Bell and Weinberg. They were essentially single people although they might couple up for brief periods. Both the men and the women in this category appeared to be well adjusted. They were in fact quite similar to heterosexual single adults, sharing most of their life-style patterns and finding the same advantages and disadvantages of living alone (Chapter 9). As among many single people, the men, much more than the women, spent considerable time **"cruising,"** looking for new sexual partners.

### Married homosexuals

People who are homosexual may, nevertheless, marry a person of the other sex. In fact it has been estimated that as many as a third of lesbians and a fifth of homosexual men marry. The difference may be accounted for by the fact that some lesbians seem to become aware of their sexual orientation somewhat later than men. During the prime marital years, the 20s, more homosexual women than men have not firmly fixed their orientation (Bell and Weinberg, 1981).

Over the last decade the proportion of close-coupled relationships for men has considerably increased due to awareness of the threat of AIDS.

*cruising*
Going to bars, baths, or parties to seek new sexual partners. This term may be used to refer to this behavior among heterosexuals and homosexuals.

Homosexual people marry for a number of reasons. First, they may love their heterosexual partner and believe they can be heterosexual or bisexual. They may also want children and a conventional family life or be motivated to disguise their homosexual needs. Whatever the reason for marriage, most married homosexual people continue some homosexual activities. Men, more often than women, may have a secret lover or keep in contact with a small circle of homosexual friends (Coleman, 1982; Masters and Johnson, 1979).

Are homosexual-heterosexual marriages happy? Bell and his coauthors (1978; 1981) note that the frequency of marital sexual relations for homosexual spouses is quite low and dissatisfaction often high. Ten percent of such couples have very little or no marital intercourse. Another indicator that many of these unions do not work out well is that about half end within 3 years. On the other hand for some men and women such marriages seem relatively happy. They have much the same problems and rewards as those experienced by married heterosexual couples. Approximately a third of homosexual-heterosexual partners report their marriage is quite satisfying. It should also be noted that in many—likely in most—the heterosexual partner is unaware of their spouses homosexual-bisexual needs (Blumstein and Schwartz, 1983; Hill, 1987).

A caring relationship.

## Partners

Some homosexual men and, less frequently, homosexual women have a substantial number of sexual partners. Just exactly how many people lesbians and gays have sex with is difficult to determine. Bell and Weinberg (1978) contend that 60% of the homosexual men they interviewed had more than 250 partners. Blumstein and Schwartz (1983) report that only 43% of their respondents had more than 20 partners. Bell and Weinberg investigated the San Francisco area where the proportion of gay people is high. Blumstein and Schwartz tried to get a more nationally representative sample. Recognizing the limitations of both research studies and the precautions now forced by AIDS, a reasonable estimate suggests that most gay and lesbian people may have between 5 and 30 different sexual partners during their adult years, with homosexual women being on the low end of the distribution. It seems too that only a small portion of the gay population continues to have sexual relations with a new partner every several weeks (Richwald, et al., 1988).

The number of different partners for lesbians is not much different from that of heterosexual women (Chapter 9). The statistic for homosexual men needs explanation, however. Peplau (1981) begins her explanation by noting that she found that most homosexual men and women say they want a faithful, enduring relationship. They want to find a partner with whom they can communicate, share interests and objectives, and build a lasting union.

A major reason that many gay couples do not reach these objectives, according to Peplau, is that they, like heterosexuals, have been socialized to the "double standard" (Chapter 8). Heterosexual relationships are a compromise. The socialization of the woman encourages courtship, affection, and trust before beginning sex. The man's training encourages casual sex. Gay behavior is seen as male sexuality unmodified by the female courtship ritual.

A second reason that many gay people may not achieve faithful, enduring relationships is that the majority community exerts strong pressure against homosexual couples. Homosexual partners are discriminated against, and their union is seen as aberrant. Conversely, society does all it can to encourage the stability of heterosexual relations. Everything from the marriage ceremony to tax laws and the presence of children helps a heterosexual union endure.

A third set of factors involves established institutions within the homosexual community itself. Like all singles (Chapter 9), whether homosexual or heterosexual, the unmarried adult's way of meeting and socializing may discourage enduring partnerships. For this reason, some homosexual couples avoid gay bars and the like, feeling the atmosphere may interfere with the quality of their own relationship.

A fourth possible explanation is that homosexual people, as a group, may have more "open" attitudes toward sexuality than heterosexual people. Blumstein and Schwartz (1983) found homosexual men and women more likely to approve of "sex without love" than comparable heterosexuals. About 60% to 80% of homosexuals and 40% to 50% of heterosexuals consented to sexual relationships motivated mainly by physical interest.

Finally we need to be aware that much has been written about, and a good deal of media attention has been paid to, the fact that some homosexual men have had sexual relations with a large number of partners. This interest in variety, whatever its roots, is *not* distinctively a homosexual phenomenon. It is

The Coolidge effect (Chapter 5), an inborn drive for different sexual partners, perhaps found more prominently in males, has been hypothesized to account for the larger number of sexual relations among some gay people.

found among heterosexuals too. Swinging couples, heterosexual men and women who exchange partners, may also have a substantial number of sexual intimates (Chapter 12). A few swingers still go to a "party house," almost every week or two. There, both women and men can have intercourse with several people in one evening. By the end of a year a hundred partners may have been experienced. As Helen Fisher (1982) points out, there may well be a potent biological drive for a diversity of sexual experience. When restraints are minimized or when social conditions encourage sexuality, some heterosexual and some homosexual people may be very active.

## THE HOMOSEXUAL COMMUNITY

Some of the 8 million men and women in the United States whose behavior is substantially homosexual live in specific communities within the United States. Estimates suggest that in the New York City area, there may be one quarter of a million gay and lesbian people. San Francisco may have 150,000 and most major cities in the United States have at least a hundred thousand homosexual inhabitants.

Homosexual neighborhoods are generally male environments. New York City, for example, has its Greenwich Village area, and San Francisco has its Castro and Polk districts. In these gay neighborhoods there are a variety of facilities directed toward serving homosexual needs, styles, and tastes. There may be theaters offering homosexual films, and bookstores, churches, and baths, as well as lawyers, doctors, and stockbrokers.

It is important to understand that many homosexual women and men do not affiliate with the subculture. They do not live in gay neighborhoods, use homosexual slang, attend lesbian or gay groups, or think of themselves as members of a distinct minority. Their partner is of the same sex, but otherwise, they act and feel like any other person with their religious or socioeconomic

Homosexual people constitute a small but significant portion of the population and want their concerns considered.

## The Impact of AIDS

*Acquired immune deficiency syndrome (AIDS) is* a fatal sexually transmitted disease we will describe in detail in Chapter 16. Since AIDS has significantly affected homosexual men, it has had an impact on the gay community and life-styles. Many heterosexual people have reacted with hostility. Attempts have been made to prohibit homosexual employment in schools, hospitals, restaurants, and other areas where there is some degree of personal contact. In Texas, legislation was suggested that would detain or imprison homosexual men "until and unless they can be cleansed of their medical problems" (Brandt, 1985).

Overall, however, punitive reactions toward homosexual people have been limited. The reverse has also occurred. Homosexual and heterosexual people and groups have volunteered and organized to educate the public about AIDS and provide care and support for its victims (Chapter 16).

The disease has brought about changes in life-styles for some gay people. Many bathhouses have closed for lack of attendance or because of local legal action. Most homosexual men also have fewer sexual partners and adopt hygienic precautions when having relations with a new person. In one study, for example, 807 men were interviewed as they left seven bathhouses in the Los Angeles area. Almost all were aware of the dangers of AIDS, and the great majority had modified their sexual activities to minimize the chances of infection. Most had fewer partners, and only 10 percent engaged in receptive and/or insertive anal sexual intercourse without a condom—behavior associated with a greatly increased risk of AIDS transmission (Chapter 16; Richwald et al., 1988). An emphasis on durable couple relationship and fidelity has also appeared among homosexual, as well as bisexual and heterosexual people (Monette, 1988; Richwald et al., 1988; Turner, 1985).

background. When such people are asked "Who are you?" they are most likely to answer "a man," or "an Episcopalian," or "a lawyer," and so on. The fact that they are homosexual is not foremost in the minds of all gay and lesbian people.

### Bars and baths

The homosexual bar is sometimes seen as the hub around which much of the social and sexual life of many lesbian and gay people revolves. Homosexual women and men go to bars to socialize, dance, and feel at home. The male bar often has a more explicitly sexual element. It may be a place in which to meet new partners. If there is a sexual theme in lesbian bars, it is much more subtle. Gay bars also outnumber lesbian bars. In New York City some estimates suggest that there are 100 or more male homosexual bars. Some of these bars attract a younger crowd, some attract older people, some cater to "macho" men dressed in leather and chains, and some cater to people in the entertainment industry, or to other interests. In contrast there are only a dozen or so lesbian bars in New York City, and they tend to be less differentiated along social or age lines.

In a gay bar men can feel free to dance with one another.

It is important to understand that the role of the bar for homosexual people is similar to its function for single heterosexual women and men (Chapter 9). It is a place to relax and meet new people. The baths, however, are a distinctly male homosexual institution. Bathhouses are not just places to go if one wants to sit in a sauna or steam room or get clean. Homosexual bathhouses date back at least 2000 years, to Athens and Rome. Today the baths may include a disco dance floor, but since ancient times a pool, steam room, lounge, bar, and many small rooms furnished with beds or mats have been standard. The purpose of the baths is sexual. The steam baths are places to meet other men and engage in a sexual liaison.

---

### In Sum

Homosexual and heterosexual behaviors are on a continuum. Many people have both sexual experiences in their background. A homosexual person is one who consistently has sexual and affectional relations with people of her or his own sex. Homosexuality is no longer considered a mental illness, although people who are dissatisfied with their orientation may need counseling. Many homosexual women and men prefer the terms lesbian and gay. For some, becoming aware of one's own homosexuality and disclosing it may be stressful. Except for penile-vaginal intercourse, gay, lesbian and heterosexual physical and affectional relations are similar. Many homosexual men and women find partners with whom they may continue for many years or a lifetime. Generally, gay couples, much more than lesbian and heterosexual couples, put a lower priority on fidelity.

# EXPLANATIONS

The search for an explanation of homosexuality should really be an attempt to understand the roots and development of all sexuality. But this has seldom been the case. Heterosexuality as such was until recently relatively poorly investigated. This neglect may reflect the view that heterosexuality is a given, and requires no explanation. In actuality, we need to recognize that homosexual orientations will be explained best when the nature of *all* sexual needs and directions is understood.

Through the centuries, theories to explain homosexuality have been plentiful. In medieval Europe people who were homosexual were believed to be possessed by demons and likely to be banned from the village (Chapter 1). In the nineteenth century, physicians looked for the infection that was supposedly shriveling male testes and producing a different orientation. Current research is more enlightened and points in several directions, but we do not yet have a definitive explanation.

In ancient Athens homosexuals were at one time thought selected by the gods to convey images of beauty and creativity.

## Psychoanalysis

For the past 50 years, the psychoanalytic explanations of homosexuality have dominated the thinking of many researchers and writers. Sigmund Freud (1959) and other psychoanalysts saw homosexuality as the product of a seductive, dominating mother and a weak or passive father (Chapter 2). Irving Bieber (1984) has reported that over the last 20 years he has studied 850 male homosexuals and 50 pairs of parents. "In not a single case was there a good father-son relationship . . . . Mothers tended to . . . openly prefer their son to their spouse."

Freud spoke little of the development of lesbianism (Gay, 1988). Later psychoanalysts, and particularly his daughter Anna Freud, attempted to correct this omission. Lesbianism was seen almost as a mirror image of male homosexuality. It was said to be the outcome of a distant and **ambivalent** mother. In her studies Wolff (1980) reported she often found an indifferent mother in the background. The result may be that because of the lack of love from her mother, the daughter is led to continually seek such love from other women.

*ambivalent*
Characterized by both love and hate—attraction and repulsion.

Are these hypotheses valid? One of the most comprehensive studies was conducted by Bell and his associates (1981). They interviewed 1500 homosexual and heterosexual people and contested most psychoanalytic hypotheses. They report that in many families one parent does tend to be dominant, but this does not usually result in homosexual offspring. Ross and Arrindell (1988) are even more conclusive. Their measures of the parental rearing style of heterosexual and homosexual men led them to say, "We have demonstrated that parental rearing patterns experienced by homosexual men are not necessarily different from those experienced by heterosexual men . . . and that any implied causal links between parental rearing patterns and a subsequent homosexual orientation are not supported by these data."

## Biology

Bell et al. (1981) in their extensive interviews with gay and lesbian people in the San Francisco area were struck by how far back in almost every life they

Some young boys may appear effeminate, whereas some girls are called masculine. There is often a good deal of overlap in the behaviors of young children, and adopting some of the interests of the other sex often says little about future sexual orientation. In other words, effeminate boys and masculine girls will not necessarily be homosexual adults.

could trace homosexuality or heterosexuality. For most people there seems to be evidence which orientation is developing even in early childhood. "Our findings suggest that homosexuality is as deeply ingrained as heterosexuality, so that the differences in behaviors or social experience of pre-homosexual boys and girls and their pre-heterosexual counterparts reflect or express, *rather than cause*, their eventual homosexual preference."

A similar view is held by several other investigators. A survey of over a thousand adults under the auspices of the Kinsey Institute concluded that male homosexuality is first evident in early childhood, signaled by *gender nonconformity*, boys playing with dolls, dressing like girls, and so on. An intense psychiatric study, over almost an entire generation came to the same conclusion. Three fourths of gender nonconforming boys are homosexual or bisexual as adults (Green, 1987) (Chapter 2).

The first place to look for deeply ingrained behavior is biology, specifically at the hormones associated with femininity and masculinity. Do boys and girls, adolescents and adults have different amounts of estrogens and androgens (Chapters 3 and 4) determining their sexual orientation? Some homosexual men have been found with higher estrogen balances. Lesbians may have more testosterone than heterosexual women. But the evidence has not been consistent. There are homosexual men who have higher testosterone levels than heterosexuals and lesbians with more estrogen than heterosexual women (Goodman, 1983).

Giving a heterosexual man estrogens may depress his sex drive but is unlikely to affect his orientation. Testosterone may elevate a woman's libido but not affect her orientation either.

*prenatal*
Before birth

Garfield Tourney (1980) reviewed a large number of research studies and found the results much too contradictory to rule in or rule out a role for hormones in sexual orientation. He also notes that the most telling argument against hormones playing a direct role in determining adult sexual orientation is that neither homosexuality nor heterosexuality has been consistently altered by hormone injections. Neither a homosexual nor a heterosexual adult is likely to be reoriented by hormonal treatment.

Perhaps the biological solution lies in the brain. Investigators have long been aware that the sexual response of animals may be changed by **prenatal** hormonal treatments. Unborn male rats who are temporarily deprived of androgen by experimentation imitate the mating behavior of females. This happens despite the fact that they are born physically male and eventually have the appropriate hormonal makeup. It remains to be proven, but it is suspected, that the balance of estrogens and androgens in the uterine environment during the first several months of pregnancy may influence sexuality long after birth. John Money (1988) contends that this hormonal ratio programs the brain in a homosexual, bisexual, or heterosexual direction. Sexual orientation may be influenced after birth by social conditions or psychological decisions, but the prenatal months play a leading role.

## Learning

According to psychologists, most human behavior is learned. The learning may occur in any of several ways. First behavior that is *reinforced* tends to be learned. This means that whenever we do something that has a favorable outcome, we are likely to do it again. For example, if a child is rewarded by a cookie every time he or she says please, the youngster will learn to say please. Learning may also occur through *imitation*. People tend to dress and behave in

One disputed explanation of homosexuality holds that girls encouraged to act like boys, and vice versa, may adopt the values and orientation of the other sex.

ways that resemble others who serve as models. In this way, girls may choose to wear dresses and a particular style of shoes if they see other females with whom they identify attired in this fashion. There are many other ways in which humans learn, but all methods have one thing in common. Learning is a way of *acquiring behavior* through *experience*. Learned behavior is *not* inborn, inherent, or instinctual. It is obtained through our interaction with others (Chapter 6).

Whitam (1980) examined several hundred subjects across different cultures including the United States, Brazil, and Guatemala. He too, found that adult homosexuality was frequently preceded by gender nonconformity in childhood, particularly in males. Such boys persistently played games like house, "dress up," and preferred the company of women. The learning view explains Whitam's findings in terms of early experience. Boys "playing like girls," it is contended, will adopt the values and behaviors of girls. Similarly a girl growing up almost exclusively in the company of boys whom she admires may copy their male behaviors up to and including sexual orientation.

What used to be called "homosexual seduction" is also explained in learning terms. Bell et al. (1981) found two thirds of the men and women in his sample had a homosexual experience before age 19. Sometimes they were courted or "seduced" by an older person or sometimes by someone their own

Learning advocates suggest that what "turns us on" about another person—a gentle manner, dark eyes, or a beautiful figure—is largely the result of early experience. Biology advocates contend that what we find sexually arousing may be physically programmed in our brain.

age. From the learning perspective, children and adolescents have an incompletely formed sexuality. They are ready to learn any number of patterns. If a pleasing homosexual experience is one of the first physical sexual encounters, that reinforcing relationship may set in motion a preference that could last for a lifetime.

Learning explanations also point to *negative conditioning*. Cook et al. (1983) reported that half or more of lesbian women had unpleasant sexual experiences that in a few instances included abuse or violence by men. A few men have stated that consistent rejection by women, or their intense fear of them, motivated their homosexuality. Interestingly the opposite may also occur. People who begin a homosexual life-style may have unpleasant experiences and start a heterosexual pattern. It is estimated, for example, that a fifth of all women who have lesbian experiences become disillusioned and consciously switch to a heterosexual orientation (Bell and Weinberg, 1978). Thus from the learning viewpoint, dissatisfaction with one sex supposedly could lead a man or woman to experimentation and perhaps to sexual or affectional relations with the other sex.

Another learning view is proposed by Michael Storms (1981). Unlike many other theorists, Storms attempts to describe the development of both heterosexuality and homosexuality by tracing the path children may take to these orientations. Storms sees most children developing sexual interests during later puberty. At this time the peer group is likely to include both girls and boys. This means that sexual and affectional attachments can be encouraged by society toward the other sex.

In contrast, some children develop erotic feelings early, by age 10 or 11, when the play group is most likely to consist only of members of the same sex. In that case these children may learn to feel sexually and affectionally attracted to their own gender.

If these hypotheses are correct, then children growing up in sex-segregated environments like private schools should more often be homosexual. Further, lesbian and gay adults should be able to report sexual and affectional feelings earlier in childhood than heterosexuals. Both observations have received only very limited support (Bell et al., 1978, 1981).

## Conclusion

Sexual orientation, homosexual as well as heterosexual, is not easily explained. We know that much that has been hypothesized needs reevaluation. Most dominant mothers do not have gay children, nor do cold mothers inevitably produce lesbians. Boys who play girls' games and girls who prefer the friendship and activities of boys do not necessarily become homosexual. Sexual experiences with the other sex that are negative, and positive ones with the same sex, seem to play only a very minor role in producing sexual orientation. Hormones do not account for adult homosexuality, but whether prebirth biochemical conditions do is speculative. Perhaps biology, family conditions, and learning interact. Prenatal biochemical programming may lay down heterosexual or homosexual potential. When one or another orientation is firmly rooted, few if any subsequent family, social, or learning experiences will divert it. In other instances when a homosexual or heterosexual biological potential is relatively flexible, childhood and adolescent experiences and decisions may help set one or another sexual pattern. Much still needs to be learned so we can better understand the sexuality of women and men.

## THERAPY

Sexual and affectional needs and behaviors sometimes prove problematic. In Chapter 17 treatment for sexual difficulties largely of concern to heterosexual people is described. In this section therapy that may be appropriate for some homosexual women and men is discussed.

For many years homosexuality was treated as a psychiatric illness. Therapists tried to help gay or lesbian persons reorient themselves. Traditional Freudian psychoanalysts sometimes spent years helping homosexual patients resolve their love-hate feelings toward their parents, a conflict supposedly generating their "inversion"—the psychiatric term for homosexuality (Chapter 2; Gay, 1988). In more recent years, behavioral techniques have been attempted. To teach a homosexual man to become aroused by women and disinterested in men a form of punishment training called *aversive therapy* might be used. Sitting alone in a darkened room while physiological apparatus recorded penile arousal, blood pressure, respiration, and other signs of excitement, increasingly seductive pictures of women were shown. If the patient became aroused, pleasant background music quietly began. When erotic pictures of men were put on the screens, signs of patient arousal were met with a harmless but unpleasant electric shock. This was supposed to teach gay patients to desire women and end the sexual appeal of men (Harris, 1988). One patient commented, "I couldn't imagine how dumb the behavior therapist really is. All those pictures did was teach me to associate sexy men with a bit of pain. It added to my turning on to men. The women did nothing for me."

Attempts have been made to take treatment away from considerations of orientation and concentrate more on behavior. Why not look at homosexual behavior in the same way one regards all sexual activity? Is it functional? Does it enhance a person's life? With this view, Masters and Johnson designed a 2-week therapy program for bisexual and homosexual adults that in basic ways resembles that available to heterosexual people (Chapter 17). Homosexual people learn about both sexes, have fears allayed, and are taught arousal and coital techniques. The focus of the clinic was the same for everyone: the functional well being of the person."

When therapy with gay and lesbian adults did not focus on orientation as such, but on pleasurable functioning with specific partners, male or female, Masters and Johnson stated they had a high success rate. In one series of investigations, 54 homosexual men and 13 homosexual women, who were motivated to include heterosexual activities took part in the standard 2-week program. Several long-term follow-up studies claimed that, for most participants, heterosexual behaviors were still continuing 5 years later (Masters et al., 1988; Schwartz and Masters, 1984).

Therapy for some lesbian and gay people may also be directed at easing self-acceptance and providing means to deal more effectively with social pressure. For others it may lead to greater self-discovery and increased sexual sat-

Masters and Johnson's results have been questioned. They may have been successful with people who were actually bisexual or already considerably inclined toward heterosexuality.

isfaction and make for more productive relationships. For all people in need—heterosexual, bisexual, or homosexual—therapy can provide a means toward a richer and more fulfilling life.

## ATTITUDES

Judging from ancient Egyptian, and some Asian and European illustrations, homosexuality has always been part of human history. It seems, too, that in some of these distant societies homosexual people often had special duties reserved for them. They may have been entertainers, caretakers, doctors, or priests. Sometimes they played unique and valued roles in their community. In many traditional American Indian societies, for example, *berdaches*, men who dressed like women and may have been homosexual, were believed to possess supernatural powers. They often served as guardians of the history and culture of their people. Overall, however, acceptance of homosexuality has not been universal (Williams, 1987).

### Judaism-Christianity

Three thousand years ago the Hebrew people were emerging as a nation. To help differentiate themselves and their faith from others, they carefully regulated a variety of personal acts. Special rules governed prayer, eating, dressing, and sexual conduct. They seemed particularly intent on controlling homosexuality. "If a man also lie with mankind, as he lieth with a woman, both of them have committed an abomination: they shall surely be put to death" (Leviticus 20:13).

The Biblical story of Sodom was held to illustrate the consequences of forbidden practices. The Old Testament relates that Sodom with all its people was totally destroyed by fire and brimstone that rained from the heavens. The usual interpretation of this event is that Sodomites were punished for engaging in animal and homosexual intercourse. The legal term *sodomy,* meaning unlawful sexual relations comes from this source.

Early Christian leaders also outlawed homosexuality. Augustine (354-430) described it as a perverted lust and advocated capital punishment. But despite strong condemnation, homosexuality continued, even among supposedly celibate clergy. Given the frequency of such sexuality, severe punishment seemed unreasonable. As a result, there were often gradations of reprimand. A seventh century Penitential from France is representative of the manuals used by the clergy to guide them (Tannahill, 1981).

| | |
|---|---|
| Simple kissing | Six special fasts |
| Kissing with embrace | Ten special fasts |
| Mutual masturbation | Forty days penance |
| A second offense | One hundred days penance |
| Fellatio | Four years penance |
| Anal intercourse | Seven years penance |

### Greece and Rome

The early Greek and Roman worlds often seemed to be more tolerant of homosexuality. In both societies 2000 or more years ago there were relatively few

The ancient Eastern faiths such as Buddhism and Hinduism said relatively little about homosexuality. Islam, the Moslem faith, strongly forbids homosexuality and gives death as possible punishment.

Homosexual relations have been recognized since earliest times. Detail from a Greek vase circa 500 BC.

rules regulating sexuality. All sexual behaviors were not necessarily approved, but there were no governmental rules against them. Much of Plato's writing, particularly in his *Symposium*, seems to extol homosexual love. Sappho, as we mentioned previously, did the same for lesbian affection.

In Rome, Emperor Egalabalus, in the third century, was reported to prefer to dress in silk, make up his face, and keep a number of homosexual lovers. At this time, too, homosexual weddings were permitted so that late in his life Egalabalus married one of his lovers.

Greek and Roman civilizations are often cited as being understanding of a variety of sexualities. There is no doubt that homosexuality and other lifestyles were a part of the culture of both nations. But according to Robert Flaceliere (1962), sexual tolerance did not endure. In less than a century, diversity and intellectual, artistic, and personal freedom faded. Acceptance of homosexuality and other alternate life-styles "was never very prevalent except in one class and over a quite limited time period."

## Today

Attitudes toward homosexuality today reflect the religious Judeo-Christian tradition and the intellectual heritage of Greece and Rome. As such, most people's feelings seem a mixture of acceptance and suspicion, hesitation and curiosity (Pagels, 1988). Different faiths and clergy, too, interpret biblical writings in varying ways. Some see the Old and New Testaments as accepting homosexuality, whereas others see it as strictly forbidden.

Although many homosexual men have experienced harassment or arrest and gay bars and baths were sometimes raided, homosexual women have usually not been bothered. Some believe this is because the sexuality of women is often "politely" overlooked or is not considered by many authorities important enough to warrant attention.

Warmth and sharing are a part of all intimate relationships.

During this last decade, several dozen groups of homosexual women and men have formed to advance a sense of dignity and pride. They seek also to help one another, and to be affirmative about their orientation. Perhaps the major goal is the enactment of nondiscriminatory legislation concerning employment, housing, education, and other civil rights. Up to this point several dozen cities have adopted laws that broaden their nondiscrimination statutes to include sexual orientation along with race and religion. The Federal Civil Service Commission and many corporations have also established nondiscriminatory hiring and promotion programs. In 1988 the election platform of the Democratic Party urged nationwide legislation to prohibit discrimination based on sexual preference.

"Consenting adult laws" have also been a focus of concern. Many states have statutes that prohibit homosexual (and some forms of heterosexual) contact (Chapter 20). In previous years hundreds of homosexual men were arrested in sweeps of bars and other homosexual gathering places. Statutes forbidding homosexual contact no longer are commonly enforced, but they are seen as a potential threat. At this point about half of the states in the United States have adopted laws that legalize private sexual behavior between consenting adults. At the same time, in 1986 the Supreme Court upheld a Georgia sodomy statute aimed particularly at anal and oral homosexual relations, even when they are private and at home. This decision, however, has had little or no effect on states that have consenting adult laws.

## Homophobia

Many people regard homosexual women and men with suspicion, and quite a few feel personal disgust. They have an irrational fear of those who are lesbian or gay and may harbor violent impulses toward them. They are **homophobic.** People who are highly punitive toward homosexuality, an attitude that may be growing (Kim, 1988), often justify their opinions on the basis of strict religious precepts. Or they may explain their feelings by repeating the erroneous bias that homosexuals seduce or molest children. Another ungrounded fear is that homosexual people cannot be trusted in government or critical corporate jobs or that they wantonly spread AIDS (Chapter 16).

*homophobia*
Fear and hatred of homosexuality

Such convictions often lead to social and job discrimination and may encourage harassment and assault. But homophobia does not always express itself violently or result in obvious discrimination. Often it can be subtle. People may communicate their unease by avoiding working with someone who is homosexual or who just seems to be gay or lesbian. Sometimes, too, a person may tell jokes and stories that are offensive to homosexual people, yet deny they had any such intent. In one investigation, heterosexual subjects were given couple profiles to read. The couple descriptions were essentially identical and were of heterosexual, gay, and lesbian partners. A significant portion of the heterosexual readers stated that the homosexual couples were "less in love" and "less satisfied with their relationship." These heterosexual subjects may have been unwittingly biased in their perception of homosexual individuals, perhaps habitually viewing them with distrust (Testa et al., 1987).

Knud Larse and his coworkers (1983) looked for the correlates of negative feelings toward homosexuality. They administered several attitude scales to 314 subjects. They found that people who had more open attitudes toward heterosexuality were more often positive about homosexuality. People who had liberal attitudes toward premarital or extramarital heterosexual intercourse tended to be more understanding of gay and lesbian sex. Those who were religiously orthodox, and those whose opinions were described as antiminority, however, were nearly all very critical of homosexuality. In the researchers' view, these findings reflect the fact that antihomosexual attitudes are part of a broader syndrome of feelings that are antagonistic toward sexuality and minority groups in general.

---

To understand the roots of homosexuality, an understanding of all sexuality is helpful. Some psychoanalysts hypothesize that parents, particularly mothers, play a critical role in bringing about a heterosexual or homosexual orientation. Learning explanations suggest that those who have positive homosexual relations, models, or experiences may be more likely to be lesbian or gay. Biological theorists say hormone biochemistry, particularly before birth, may set a relatively permanent sexual orientation. Homosexual people who feel stressed may seek treatment and be helped to accept their preference or sometimes be reoriented. Current attitudes toward homosexuality reflect many traditions particularly our Judeo-Christian religious heritage. People who are homophobic are fearful of and antagonistic to homosexuality. During this decade lesbian and gay groups have organized and worked for legislation to assure equal rights and treatment.

*In Sum*

*Summary*

Homosexual and heterosexual behaviors are on a continuum, with many people having some of each in their background. Homosexual people who consistently have sexual and affectional interactions mainly or only with members of their own sex constitute about 4% of the population. People who are bisexual have both heterosexual and homosexual experiences.

Many homosexual men prefer the term *gay*, and many homosexual women prefer the term *lesbian*. Most lesbian and gay people do not have the stereotyped dress and manner reputed to identify them as homosexual. Most appear like other people of their age and background. Recognizing and disclosing one's own homosexuality is called "coming out." This may occur during the adolescent years or not until adulthood. Coming out may sometimes be difficult for the person and for close relatives.

Homosexual and heterosexual physical and emotional relationships are similar. Both couples kiss and caress, although homosexuals rely more on hand and mouth genital stimulation. Half of all gay couples frequently practice anal intercourse. Most lesbian and gay couples have sexual relations about three times weekly. Most homosexual partners initiate sexual relations about equally and share other responsibilities.

Social pressures on homosexual partnerships may contribute to the short-lived nature of some. The gay community and its patterns of socializing may also provide an environment that encourages shorter rather than longer lasting partnerships. However, many homosexual men, and even more women, find long-term partners. These relations may endure for a few years or for a lifetime. Some gay couples attach a lower priority to sexual exclusivity and see no conflict in having sexual and affectional relationships outside their own partnership.

Why people are homosexual or heterosexual is not yet entirely clear. Psychoanalytical explanations have pointed to the role of the family and parents. Mothers who are cold were said to contribute to lesbianism and those who are seductive were said to contribute to male homosexuality. Biological arguments suggest that hormones, particularly before birth, may program the brain so the person is neurologically set to become interested in and aroused by one sex or the other. Learning explanations propose that positive homosexual or negative heterosexual experiences, or both, contribute to homosexuality.

Some homosexual people seek treatment. Masters and Johnson claim success in sex reorientation. They and other therapists, however, also help lesbian and gay people live more satisfying lives within their orientation.

Current attitudes toward homosexuality reflect Judeo-Christian tradition as well as the intellectual influence of Greece and Rome. Some heterosexual people are homophobic; they have a strong dislike and fear of homosexuals. Lesbian and gay groups are working for legislation to prohibit discrimination in employment, housing, and other areas. Many communities have passed such statutes.

*For Thought and Discussion*

1 Describe the attitudes toward homosexuality that you have encountered among your friends and acquaintances. Discuss your own feelings toward homosexuality, and how they have changed as a result of this course.

2 People often have different attitudes toward male and female homosexuality. Describe some of these differences and consider the origins of these feelings.

3 What experiences, biological traits, and other factors have been thought to play a role in determining heterosexual and homosexual behavior?

4 What could heterosexual and homosexual people do to increase understanding and acceptance between the two groups?

5 How are homosexual couples and their sexual and affectional partnerships similar and different from heterosexual ones?

6 How do you think many heterosexual people feel when they see a homosexual couple holding hands or kissing in public? How do you think homosexual adults feel when they see a heterosexual couple kissing in public?

*References*

Bell, A.P., and Weinberg, M.S. *Homosexualities.* New York: Simon & Schuster, Inc., 1978.

Bell, A.P., Weinberg, M.S., and Hammersmith, S.K. *Sexual preference: its development in men and women.* Bloomington, Ind.: Indiana University Press, 1981.

Bieber, I. A discussion of "Homosexuality: the ethical challenge." In Rubenstein, J., and Slife, B.D. *Taking sides,* Guilford, Conn.: The Dushkin Publishing Group, Inc., 1984.

Blanchard, R. Nonhomosexual gender dysphoria. *The Journal of Sex Research,* 1988, *24,* 188-193.

Blumstein, P.W., and Schwartz, P. *American couples.* New York: William Morrow & Co., Inc., 1983.

Brandt, A. *No magic bullet.* New York: Oxford University Press, 1985.

Bullough, V.L. *Homosexuality: A History.* New York: American Library Publishing Co., Inc., 1981.

Coleman, E. Developmental stages of the coming out process. *Journal of Homosexuality,* 1982, *7* (2/3), 31-43.

Coleman, E.M., Hoon, P.W., and Hoon, E.F. Arousability and sexual satisfaction in lesbian and heterosexual women. *Journal of Sex Research,* 1983, *19* (1), 58-73.

Cook, K., Kretchmer, A., Nellis, B., Lever, J., and Hertz, R. The *Playboy* readers' sex survey (Part 3). *Playboy,* May, 1983, 126.

Fisher, H.E. *The sex contract.* New York: William Morrow & Co., Inc., 1982.

Flaceliere, R. *Love in ancient Greece.* New York: Crown Publishers, Inc., 1962. (Translated by J. Cleugh.)

Freud, S. *Collected papers.* New York: Basic Books, Inc., Publishers, 1959.

Gagnon, J.H., and Simon, W. *Sexual conduct.* Chicago: Aldine, 1973.

Gay, P. *Freud.* New York: W.W. Norton & Co., Inc., 1988.

Goodman, R.E. Biology of sexuality: inborn determinants of human sexual response. *British Journal of Psychiatry,* September, 1983, *143,* 216-220.

Green, R. *The "Sissy-Boy Syndrome" and the development of homosexuality.* New Haven, Conn.: Yale University Press, 1987.

Harris, S.E. Aversion therapy for homosexuality (letter to the editor). *Journal of the American Medical Association,* June 10, 1988, *259* (22), 3271.

Hill, I. (editor): *The bisexual spouse: different dimensions in human sexuality.* McLean, Va.: Barlina Books, Inc., 1987.

Hunt, M. *Sexual behavior in the 1970s.* Chicago: Playboy Press, 1974.

Kim, J. Are homosexuals facing an ever more hostile world? *New York Times,* July 3, 1988, E-16.

Kinsey, A.C., Pomeroy, W.B., and Martin, C.E. *Sexual behavior in the human female.* Philadelphia: W.B. Saunders Co., 1953.

Kinsey, A.C., Pomeroy, W.B., and Martin, C.E. *Sexual behavior in the human male.* Philadelphia: W.B. Saunders Co., 1948.

Larse, K.S., Cate, R., and Reed, M. Anti-black attitudes, religious orthodoxy, permissiveness, and sexual information: a study of the attitudes of heterosexuals toward homosexuality. *Journal of Sex Research,* May, 1983, *19* (2), 105-118.

Masters, W.H., and Johnson, V.E. *Homosexuality in perspective.* Boston: Little, Brown, & Co., 1979.

Masters, W.H., Johnson, V.E., and Kolodny, R.C. *Crisis: heterosexual behavior in the age of AIDS.* New York: Grove Press, Inc., 1988

Monette, P. *Borrowed time: an AIDS memoir.* New York: Harcourt Brace Jovanovich, Inc., 1988.

Money, J. The development of sexual orientation. *The Harvard Medical School Mental Health Letter,* February, 1988, *4* (8), 4-6.

Pagels, E. *Adam, Eve, and the serpent.* New York: Random House, Inc., 1988.

Peplau, L.A. What homosexuals want in relationships. *Psychology Today,* March, 1981, 28-38.

Richwald, G.A., Garland, R.K., Gerber, M.M., Morisky, D.E., Kristal, A.R., and Friedland, J.M. Sexual activities in bathhouses in Los Angeles County: implications for AIDS prevention education. *The Journal of Sex Research,* May, 1988, *25* (2), 169-180.

Robinson, B., Skeen, P., and Walters, L. The AIDS epidemic hits home. *Psychology Today,* April, 1987, 48-52.

Ross, M.W., and Arrindell, W.A. Perceived parental rearing patterns of homosexual and heterosexual men. *The Journal of Sex Research,* 1988, *24,* 275-281.

Sakheim, D.K., Barlow, D.H., Beck, J.G., and Abrahamson, D.J. A comparison of male heterosexual and male homosexual patterns of arousal. *Journal of Sex Research,* May, 1985, *21* (2), 183-198.

Salovey, P., and Rodin, J. The heart of jealousy. *Psychology Today,* September, 1985, 22-29.

Schwartz, M.F., and Masters, W.H. The Masters and Johnson treatment program for dissatisfied homosexual men. *American Journal of Psychiatry,* 1984, *141,* 173-181.

Storms, M.D. A theory of erotic orientation development. *Psychological Review,* 1981, *88,* 340-353.

Tannahill, R. *Sex in history.* New York: Stein & Day, Publishers, 1981.

Testa, R.J., Kinder, B.N., and Ironson, G. Heterosexual bias in the perception of loving relationships of males and lesbians. *The Journal of Sex Research,* May, 1987, *23* (2), 163-172.

Tourney, G. Hormones and homosexuality. In Marmor, J. (editor): *Homosexual behavior,* New York: Basic Books, Inc., Publishers, 1980.

Turner, W. AIDS impact wide in San Francisco. *The New York Times,* May 28, 1985, 87.

Whitam, F.L. Childhood predictors of adult homosexuality. *Journal of Sex Education and Therapy,* 1980, *6* (2), 11-17.

Williams, W.L. *The spirit and the flesh: sexual diversity in American Indian culture.* Boston: Beacon Press, 1987.

Wolff, D.G. *The lesbian community.* Berkeley, Calif.: University of California Press, 1980.

*Suggested Reading*

Hill, I. (editor): *The bisexual spouse: different dimensions in human sexuality.* McLean, Va.: Barlina Books, Inc., 1987.

Interesting, enlightening, and insightful case histories and commentaries on heterosexual-bisexual couple relationships.

McWhirter, D.P., and Mattison, A.M. *The male couple.* Englewood Cliffs, N.J.: Prentice-Hall, 1984.

Lacks some degree of objectivity but insightful and interesting to read.

Monette, P. *Borrowed time: an AIDS memoir*. New York: Harcourt Brace Jovanovich, 1988.
   A highly personal story of a man taken ill with AIDS is poignant and sensitively written.

Spong, J.S. *Living in sin*. San Francisco: Harper & Row, Publishers, Inc., 1988.
   An Episcopal Bishop examines religious and social attitudes toward homosexuality and the church's position concerning committed gay and lesbian couples.

Wolf, D.G. *The lesbian community*. Berkely, Calif., University of California Press, 1980.
   A worthwhile and insightful description of the development of a lesbian community and of female homosexuality.

*Part Five*

# REPRODUCTION

*Chapter 14*

# Family Planning and Birth Control

**When you finish this chapter, you should be able to:**

Describe the different forms of contraception and their advantages and disadvantages.

Explain why there are so many unintended pregnancies despite a variety of easily obtainable contraceptive methods.

Evaluate the alternatives available for unplanned pregnancies.

List the types of abortion and suggest when they may be used.

Describe the factors involved in impaired fertility and cite the options available to couples who want children.

Biologically, sexual intercourse has reproduction as its goal. But women and men who have coitus do not always want to become parents. At the opposite pole are those who want to have children but have not been able to conceive. In this chapter we will consider the means available to prevent birth as well as to facilitate it. We will describe contraception, abortion, and fertility.

## FAMILY PLANNING

### Historical perspective

Birth control has a long history. Most of it is a narrative of attempts to limit childbirth in opposition to religious or social demands. Some early civilizations, knowing almost nothing about the process of conception, practiced *infanticide*. Girls were more likely to be killed than boys, as were children of both sexes who seemed underweight or injured. The ancient Hebrews who guessed coitus was responsible for birth often used withdrawal; the man having coitus withdrew just before ejaculation. During this same period, the Egyptians mixed honey, gums, and fabric. This compound was inserted into the vagina in an effort to block the semen from entering the cervix (Tannahill, 1981).

Margaret Sanger.

**Margaret Sanger**   Today many different birth control means are available, but contraception did not come to North America easily. Its introduction and acceptance were in large part the work of Margaret Sanger (1883-1966). She was one of 11 children raised in a restrictive Victorian community, yet by parents who encouraged her individuality and growth. Margaret Sanger's mother died at age 49, prematurely worn out, in her daughter's view, from the endless round of pregnancy and childrearing.

Both her own background and later her nursing experience working among the poor in New York City convinced Sanger that the most vital issue the newly emerging feminist movement should focus on was birth control. The root cause of the subjugation of women, according to Sanger, was that they had virtually no control over their own bodies. Too many were little more than reproductive machines.

In Sanger's time, for most poor and uneducated Americans, the only effective methods of birth control were abstinence and illegal abortion. The former caused enormous frustration and the latter, Margaret Sanger contended, was an unconscionable assault on life.

Sanger's quest for a safe technique led her to the Netherlands where contraceptive advice centers, staffed by midwives and physicians, had developed the diaphragm. It was a simple, inexpensive, and reliable technique that also had the great advantage of making the woman independent. She no longer had to rely on the male's use of a questionable contraceptive or quick withdrawal before orgasm.

When she returned to the United States in 1916, she opened a birth information center in Brooklyn. Within days the police closed it, and Sanger was jailed. At the same time her books and pamphlets were banned from the mails. Information about contraception was considered lewd and obscene.

The 1873 Comstock Law (Chapter 2) forbade the mailing of obscene literature. Birth control information was considered lewd (Chapter 20).

Despite immense legal and social pressure, including several imprisonments, Sanger did not cease campaigning nor fund raising. Eventually her energy brought some physicians, philanthropists, and political leaders to her side. Their help enabled Margaret Sanger to open Planned Parenthood Centers and issue publications that contained birth control information. It was not until the late 1930s that contraceptive literature could be legally mailed. A decade later, contraceptives became increasingly available and medically and ethically accepted (Chapter 1).

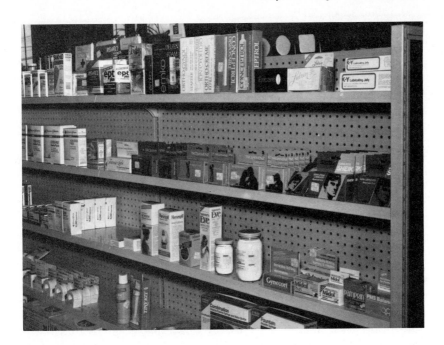

In most drug stores, contraceptives are on open shelves and readily available.

## Contraceptive decision

It appears logical that nearly everyone not wanting to become a mother or father would use some form of contraception. In pharmacies throughout much of North America spermicidal foams, creams, and condoms in all kinds of packaging are on shelves in plain view. It seems easy enough to choose one of those products just as one selects and uses a deodorant. But birth control is not practiced by all men and women. A third of all pregnancies in adult married women are unplanned. Half of all teenagers do not take any contraceptive measures (Chapters 8, 15; Tanfer and Horn, 1985).

**Why contraceptives are not used**   For many younger and single people, contraception is not used because guilt, shame concerning acknowledgment of sexuality, and similar obstructive feelings often stand in the way. Poor planning, cost considerations, and lack of access also play a role in the inconsistent or nonuse of contraception. A few people seem to neglect using contraception because they may actually unconsciously want a child. About a fifth of adolescent and single young adults say they do not want to become pregnant but wouldn't mind if they did. These people have birth control methods available—a diaphragm, condom, or pill—but often fail to use a technique so that pregnancy occurs.

Several religious groups, some strict Protestant and Hasidic Jewish faiths, and most well known of all, the Roman Catholic Church, oppose most contraceptive means. In 1984 Pope John Paul II delivered a special series of discourses strongly reaffirming the church position on birth control. He declared that Roman Catholic couples must reject all artificial means of birth control. They must make a true spiritual evaluation of their sexual relations and express mature "availability to fatherhood and motherhood."

Those who want contraceptive devices sold in all stores and vending machines, say that it would greatly reduce the number of unintended pregnancies. Opponents argue that it would lead to an increase in adolescent coitus.

In Chapter 15 we discuss some of the factors involved in deciding whether or not to have a child.

Religion, however, may not be a great barrier to birth planning. The National Center for Health Statistics found, for example, a majority of Catholic women under age 45 have used birth control methods the church did not approve (Ostling, 1984).

A couple may fail to use contraceptives because they are uninformed. Parents do not commonly teach their children about condoms and diaphragms. Sex education courses in high schools may be nonexistent or avoid mention of birth control methods (Chapter 8). Adolescents and young adults may also be misinformed. This is particularly true of adolescents from unstable homes or with lower educational backgrounds. Such youngsters may assert that they can not get pregnant because they are too young or do not have intercourse often enough. Actually every time a young couple has intercourse without contraception there is a 1 in 20 chance that they will conceive. If they continue intercourse twice a week for several months, the probability for pregnancy is 80% (Forste and Heaton, 1988).

Sex is sometimes unpredictable. The married couple who has sexual relations mainly in bed and at night knows when and where coitus will take place. A single person does not necessarily know in advance that sexual relations will take place. Some adolescents and young adults say they do not want to "broadcast" their interest in sex by carrying a diaphragm or condom. They do not want to "give away" their intentions nor seem accepting of the possibility of sexual relations when they have a date. This attitude is totally contrary to the suggestion by many health and birth planning authorities who urge "ABC." ABC (always bring condoms) is suggested as a wise precaution for *both men* and *women*. Condoms can be easily purchased and inconspicuously pocketed. They are immediately available as a contraceptive if a situation develops that leads to coitus.

The double standard is another obstacle to the consistent use of contraceptives. The traditional view has been that birth control is a woman's responsibility. But when the man in a partnership shows little concern regarding birth control his partner may also do nothing. Each person in the pair holds the other responsible for birth control, a situation likely to result in neither doing anything.

The double standard may be on the way out. Fox (1983) interviewed middle-class adolescents concerning contraceptive practices. Two thirds of the male youths assumed or were ready to assume full contraceptive responsibility. They acknowledged that they, as well as their female partner, had to plan for and use contraception.

**Conditions for contraception**  Don Byrne (1983) and his coworkers examined adolescent and young adult birth control attitudes. They concluded that several conditions need to be met before a person uses contraception. First there has to be a recognition that coitus, even a single liaison, may lead to pregnancy. A second condition that must be met is that it must be acknowledged that intercourse could occur. Many couples, even those who have known each other for a while, do not want to recognize the likelihood of coitus.

> I want it to be spontaneous; just to happen because we both want it. I don't want to prepare for it.

*(Authors' Files).*

The third condition that must exist before contraceptive use is likely is awareness of alternatives. The man and woman who want contraception must know what is available, effective, and suitable. If all three conditions are met—knowledge that coitus could lead to pregnancy, acknowledgment of sexuality, and awareness of contraceptive alternatives—birth control will follow.

## CONTRACEPTION

There are a dozen or so birth control methods in common use. Some are highly effective while the reliability of others is low. All the techniques described, however, are better than doing nothing. Every method mentioned is more effective in preventing conception than luck or hope. Some of the birth control means may not be personally acceptable or may be rejected for moral or religious reasons. But the range of choices is now so extensive that nearly everyone, whatever his or her needs or convictions, can find a suitable method. We will present each form of contraception, show how it is used, and discuss convenience, effectiveness, and safety. Remember, too, that a particular method need not be chosen for life. As circumstances and needs change, a person or couple may find different contraceptive techniques more suitable.

### Abstinence and noncoital sexual relations

It goes without saying that not having sexual intercourse, abstaining from coitus, is guaranteed to prevent conception. It is also approved by every religious faith. At the same time, abstinence is unpopular. Few men and women are able to use this method with any degree of consistency. Abstinence, although a theoretically perfect means of contraception, must in reality be rated quite unreliable.

Noncoital sexual relations are an extended form of foreplay and arousal. In an adolescent context, the term "heavy petting" is often used (Chapters 5 and 8).

Knowledge of how contraceptives work and awareness of alternatives, is most likely to lead to effective birth control.

While abstinence is often frustrating and unreliable, a similar technique that is very effective is frequently ignored. *Noncoital sexual relations* have the advantage of preventing conception and still permitting couples pleasure and affection. Noncoital intercourse includes mutual masturbation, fellatio-cunnilingus, penis inserted into closed thighs, or any of the other nonvaginal and pleasuring techniques mentioned in Chapter 5.

### Fertility awareness

A woman is fertile when she ovulates. There is variation, but often ovulation occurs approximately 14 days before the next menstrual period. Because the egg remains viable for a full day and the sperm may remain alive for 2 or 3 days, there are about 5 days a month when fertilization could occur (Chapter 15). Birth control techniques that rely on **fertility awareness** attempt to pinpoint the fertile period so that coitus during these days can be avoided.

Fertility awareness methods, also called *rhythm methods,* do not require ingesting a hormone or using a diaphragm or condom. They rely only on detecting the body's natural fertility rhythm. For this reason the Catholic church and other groups that reject "artificial methods" approve of fertility awareness. Determining the fertile or "unsafe" days and those that are "safe" may involve any of several procedures.

**Calendar method**   In the calendar method women keep a personal record of their menstrual cycle for at least 9 months. To find their earliest possible day of ovulation they subtract 18 days from the length of their shortest menstrual cycle. The last day of fertility is found by subtracting 11 days from the length of the longest cycle. Let us assume that a woman always has an exact 28-day cycle. Subtract 18, leaves day 10. Subtract 11, leaves day 17. Based on this, fertilization of the egg could occur between days 10 and 17 (the unsafe days). If a woman's menstrual period begins like clockwork every twenty-eight days then she would be "safe" for a total of 20 days, seemingly leaving ample time for coitus. However, few women have precise periods, and ovulation does not always take place exactly in the middle of the menstrual cycle. The result is that while calendar timing is definitely better than doing nothing, the **failure rate** is about 15% to 20% (see Table 14-1).

**Basal body temperature method**   Ovulation brings about a slight but measurable change in the basal body temperature (BBT). Women are instructed to take their temperatures using a special BBT thermometer, every morning on waking, before any activity. One to 3 days before ovulation the base body temperature will drop 0.2° F to 0.4° F and remain slightly lower than normal. Ovulation will be signaled by about a 0.4° F rise in temperature for 3 days. When this entire period has clearly ended, coitus may be resumed.

Unfortunately temperature fluctuations may have causes other than ovulation and sometimes ovulation is not accompanied by a discernible change in body temperature. Nevertheless the BBT method is a slight improvement over the calendar technique (Figure 14-1).

**Cervical mucous method**   Mucous secretions from the cervix change over the course of a typical menstrual cycle. For several days before and after men-

*fertility awareness*
More popularly called the *rhythm method*. It includes any of several timing techniques that identify the period of a woman's fertility, and the avoidance of sexual intercourse during those times.

*failure rate*
The contraceptive failure rate is measured by the number of pregnancies in 100 women using a specific technique for 1 year.

Fertility awareness techniques are being helped by new technology. Electronic and chemical sensors that can reliably detect ovulation are being developed.

*Table 14-1*

**Contraceptive Failure Rates: Pregnancies Per 100 Women in 1 Year**

| Method | Typical users | Careful users | Comment |
|---|---|---|---|
| Tubal ligation | Fails in fewer than 1 woman of every 2500 yearly | | Expensive, usually irreversible but effective, safe, and convenient |
| Vasectomy | Fails in less than 1 man out of 600 yearly | | Expensive, usually irreversible but effective, safe, and convenient |
| Combination pill | 2 | Fails in less than 1 in 200 women yearly | Very reliable, independent of coitus but may have side effects |
| Progesterone (minipill) | 2 | 1 | Fewer side effects but a bit less reliable than above |
| Condom with spermicide | 4 | 1 | Partners can share responsibility |
| IUD | 4 | 2 | Reliable and once in place needs no daily care. Cramping, bleeding, and other possible side effects. |
| Diaphragm with spermicide | 10 | 2 | Reliable and no significant health risks; may interrupt sexual relations for some; objections to taste |
| Cervical cap | 10 | 2 | Reliable, but insertion sometimes difficult |
| Condom | 10 | 2 | Reliable, no health risks but interferes with sexual relations for some |
| Sponge | 12 | 3 | Reliability good and gives 24-hour protection; objections similar to diaphragm |
| Spermicide | 15 | 5 | No health risks, easy to use but reliability lower and objections similar to diaphragm |
| Fertility awareness | 20 | 15 | Acceptable to Catholic and most faiths, natural and little cost; no side effects but not too reliable |
| Calendar | 20 | 10 | |
| BBT | 25 | 10 | |
| Mucous | | | |
| Withdrawal | 30 | 20 | Withdrawal and douching cost little or nothing but are frustrating, inconvenient, and very unreliable |
| Douche | 40 | | |

Data from Hatcher, 1985; Kolata, 1988; Roberts, 1988; Silber, 1987; Wills, 1985.
NOTE: *Typical users* describes people who sometimes forget to use their contraceptives or do so incorrectly. The *careful users* describes people who consistently and correctly use contraceptives.

struation there is little or no mucous secretion. It is considered safe to have coitus during the "dry" phase. Gradually mucal secretions begin, changing in character from thick and white or yellow to watery and clear, like egg white. The days when the mucous resembles egg white are called *peak symptom days.* Women usually ovulate about a full day after the last peak symptom day. This means coitus is unsafe from the first day mucous appears watery and clear until 4 days after the last peak symptom day. At this time, too, the mucous again becomes thicker and white or yellow.

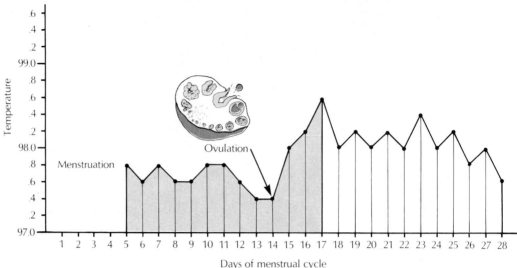

Menstruation

Ovulation

Days of menstrual cycle

*Figure 14-1*
Daily record of basal body temperatures; days 5 through 17 (shaded) are "unsafe."

*ovutimer*
A device used to judge the nature of cervical mucous to determine the probable time of ovulation.

*"the pill"*
Oral contraceptive.

Oral contraceptives are very small tablets that are tasteless and easy to swallow.

It requires practice and expertise for a woman to read her cervical mucous. She must insert her finger into her vagina; after withdrawing the cervical mucous she should touch her wet finger to her thumb and then, pulling the two fingers apart, study the color and quality of the mucous. To assist this procedure an **ovutimer** is available in some pharmacies. Mucous methods like other fertility awareness techniques are modestly effective. If all three fertility techniques are combined, their effectiveness can considerably improve.

### Oral contraception

When oral contraception, **"the pill,"** became available in the early 1960s, it freed coitus from the routine of taking temperatures or interrupting sexual relations by putting on a condom. It permitted women who took the pill regularly to have sexual relations anytime and be virtually assured that pregnancy would not occur.

Today the pill consists of any of several different hormones and dosages. The *combination* tablet is the most common. It contains estrogen and progesterone and is marketed under names such as Ortho-Novum and Modicon. One combination pill is taken every day for 21 days beginning with the fifth day of the menstrual cycle (Chapter 3). The woman then waits for 7 days, or takes a nonhormonal reminder pill for each of those days. Bleeding similar to menstruation occurs during this time. The estrogen-progesterone combination blocks ovulation and impedes the development of the endometrium, the nutrient layer of the uterus, preventing implantation (Chapter 3).

The *biphasic* pill (Ortho-Novum 10/11) also requires taking one tablet every day for 21 days. All 21 pills contain estrogen. The first 10 tablets also contain a small amount of progesterone, and the last 11 contain a larger amount of this hormone. This hormonal combination is held to more closely resemble the body's own menstrual cycle and thus minimize side effects.

The popular *minipill* (Micronor, Ovrette) consists solely of a small amount of progesterone and is taken every day without a break. The pill works by

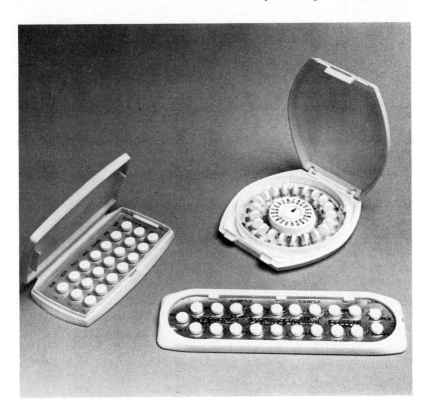

Oral contraceptives.

making the cervical mucous impervious to sperm, and it also alters the endometrium, blocking implantation of any possible fertilized egg (Chapters 3 and 15). The minipill is not quite as effective as the combination product, but because it does not contain estrogen, it causes fewer side effects.

**Advantages and disadvantages**   Oral contraceptive tablets can be taken at any time, as long as they are taken daily, and they do not interfere with sexual relations. They may also reduce cramping formerly associated with menstruation. There is considerable evidence, too, that oral contraception can relieve breast tenderness caused by cysts and perhaps reduce the chances of uterine cancer. Most important, perhaps, oral contraception is very effective. Consistent use rarely fails to prevent pregnancy.

Oral contraception is not inexpensive. The cost of the hormone pills themselves—between $10 and $30 dollars per month—may seem modest. But added to this is the expense of at least one yearly visit to a physician and possibly more. As such, the medication can add up to several hundred dollars per year.

There are also some possible mild side effects. The pills may increase facial skin pigmentation resulting in the so-called mask of pregnancy. They may also cause nausea, weight gain, some edema of arms and legs (swelling caused by retention of water), breast congestion, spotting (irregular vaginal bleeding), and an increase in blood pressure.

The more serious, although uncommon, side effects of oral contraceptives

Forgetting to take a pill for 1 day may not increase the risk of pregnancy. Some physicians recommend that two pills be taken the following day. Forgetting for two or more days, however, may seriously interfere with the pills' effectiveness, and another form of birth control should be used for the rest of that cycle.

Whenever we take a medication or undergo any other form of medical treatment we need to evaluate the risk/benefit ratio. For nearly all contraceptive measures the benefit far outweighs the risk.

include heart attack and blood clots. Most of these difficulties have a greater probability of occurring in women who smoke a pack of cigarettes daily and are over 35 years of age. The Alan Guttmacher Institute points out in its report *Making Choices* (Ory, 1983) that the death rate from pill use in younger women who do not smoke is very low, about 1 in 50,000.

Benson (1989) and Potts and Diggory (1984) suggest that oral contraception is reasonably safe for most women. But those who have any of the following characteristics might best consider an alternative birth control measure:

1. Age 35 or over
2. One pack a day or more cigarette smoker
3. Blood or cardiovascular disorder
4. History of genital or breast cancer
5. Diabetes

### Spermicides

*spermicides*
Contraceptive products that destroy sperm and may also be useful in helping to prevent some types of sexually transmitted diseases.

**Spermicides** are chemicals that kill sperm. They may come in the form of suppositories, aerosol sprays, or in tubes. Whatever type, all have instructions and applicators that allow the woman to insert the chemical into her vagina. Most require vaginal placement a few minutes before coitus and no further in advance than a half hour. The spermicide must then be left in place, not douched out, for 8 hours following coitus.

A few users sometimes find spermicides irritating to genital tissue, causing a burning feeling, a rash, or inflammation. Often this can be alleviated by trying several different products until one is found that does not cause any problems. A few couples also object to the messiness or taste of spermicides. To counter this, neutral and also pleasantly scented and flavored spermicides are available.

Several years ago early reports suggested a potentially serious effect of spermicides. It seemed there were more miscarriages and birth defects among women who used spermicides. It was hypothesized that these chemicals might damage sperm but not kill them. The injured sperm might then fertilize an egg and deliver an impaired chromosomal contribution. Oakley (1982) looked carefully at the evidence and found little support for this hypothesis. It looks as if the possibility of spermicides causing fetal damage is an extremely remote one.

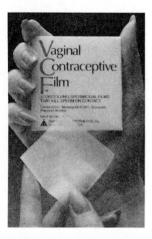

Vaginal contraceptive film is a type of "condom" for women. Film fits over cervical opening, releases spermicide, and gradually dissolves over several hours.

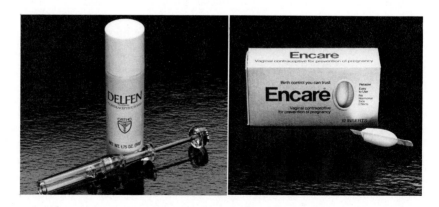

Spermicides.

**Advantages and disadvantages**   The advantages of spermicides are that they are fairly effective and available in pharmacies without a doctor's prescription. They are also inexpensive, about $5 for 5 to 10 doses. The spermicides may also give some limited degree of protection against vaginal infection. The chemicals appear to retard the growth of bacteria responsible for some infections and sexually transmitted diseases (Chapter 16). Applying the spermicide may interrupt foreplay when the woman has not previously inserted the cream. Some partners also complain that the spermicide is messy, does not taste pleasant, or interferes with the natural lubrication of the genital organs.

## Diaphragm

The **diaphragm** is a small circular rubber or plastic dome, about 2 to 4 inches in diameter, that is inserted into the vagina so that it covers the cervix. Since there is variation in the dimensions of women, medical practitioners take internal measurements and prescribe a diaphragm that fits. Some women, although

*diaphragm*
A small dome-shaped object placed in the vagina covering the cervix and serving as a contraceptive.

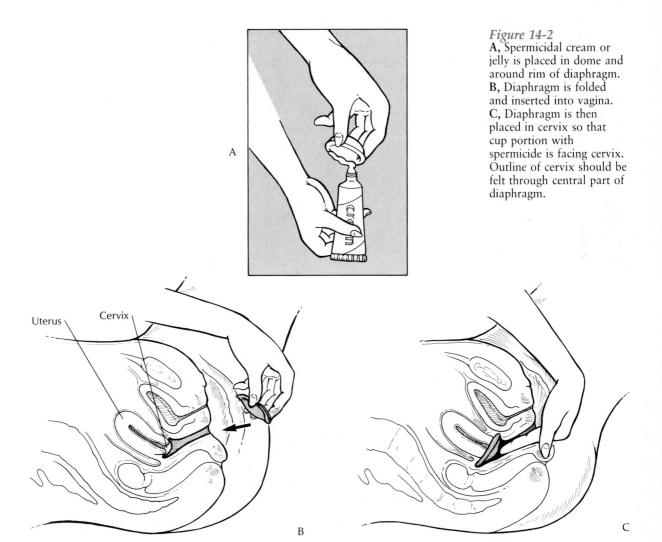

*Figure 14-2*
**A,** Spermicidal cream or jelly is placed in dome and around rim of diaphragm.
**B,** Diaphragm is folded and inserted into vagina.
**C,** Diaphragm is then placed in cervix so that cup portion with spermicide is facing cervix. Outline of cervix should be felt through central part of diaphragm.

normal, have a pelvic structure or uterine position that will not allow the diaphragm to fit securely. They are not able to use this birth control device.

Before the diaphragm is inserted, the rim must be covered with a spermicide. About half a teaspoon of spermicidal cream or jelly is also put in the middle of the side of the diaphragm that will face the cervix. After insertion the woman puts a finger into her vagina and feels that the dome is properly in place (see Figure 14-2).

The diaphragm can be put into the vagina as much as 2 hours before coitus. Either partner can insert and check it, and this step may be a part of foreplay. After coitus the diaphragm should remain in place for 6 hours. If coitus occurs again during these 6 hours, the diaphragm must stay in place and more spermicide must be put in the vagina before resuming intercourse.

**Advantages and disadvantages**   The use of a diaphragm is quite effective and inexpensive. The equipment and one-time visit to a doctor are normally about $75. The additional yearly expense is for spermicide, which may cost another $50 to $100 a year. Perhaps the major advantage of the diaphragm is that it produces no substantial side effects.

Disadvantages of the diaphragm begin with its being large and, some say, slippery with the added spermicide. It may be difficult to insert. Its size is also suspected of pressing against the vaginal wall close to the urethra. This could encourage the growth of bacteria, causing cystitis, a common urinary infection among women (Chapter 18). Some men also say that it is felt by their penis during coitus. Both of these objections can often be relieved by refitting with a smaller diaphragm if this is feasible. In any case, new measurements must be taken following childbirth or other period of significant weight change in the woman.

### Cervical cap

The **cervical cap** is similar to the diaphragm. It is smaller—about 2 inches in diameter—and usually made of hard rubber or plastic. The cap is inserted farther into the vagina than the diaphragm and fits snugly against the cervical tip by suction.

**Advantages and disadvantages**   An advantage of the cap is that it may be left in place for 48 hours. Disadvantages include difficulty of placement and questions concerning its long-term effectiveness. The cervical cap has obtained some popularity in Europe, but its use in the United States was approved by the Food and Drug Administration (FDA) the United States government agency evaluating and regulating health products, only in 1988 (Nightingale, 1988).

### Sponge

The small 2-inch wide polyurethane **sponge** is saturated with a spermicide that is released gradually once it is inserted in the vagina and moistened. The sponge is put in up to 6 hours before coitus, left in place for 6 hours afterward, then removed before 24 hours. While it is in place intercourse can occur as often as a couple wishes without adding a spermicide. Couples need to remember, however, to remove the sponge. Leaving the sponge in place more than a full day could encourage a vaginal infection.

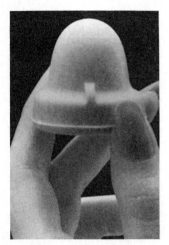

Cervical cap.

*cervical cap*
Firm circular contraceptive device that is placed into the vagina and against the cervical opening.

*sponge*
A contraceptive device containing spermicide, which is inserted into the vagina.

Contraceptive sponge.

**Advantages and disadvantages**  The sponge has several advantages. Carefully and consistently used it fails to prevent pregnancy in only 1 out of 30 women per year. It is not too expensive, costing about $1 to $2 per sponge. It does *not* require a prescription, and one size fits all. The sponge is also compactly packaged, can easily be carried, and is more quickly and easily inserted than a diaphragm. On the negative side, some women note that the sponge may shift positions internally, and its effectiveness may not be as high as early studies suggested.

Combining contraceptive techniques can increase their effectiveness substantially. Unintended pregnancy is very unlikely with a condom-spermicide or condom-spermicide-diaphragm (or sponge) combination.

## Condoms

Condoms are long, balloonlike sheaths. They are probably the most universally familiar birth control method. Over 1 billion are sold in North America every year. Some boys as young as 5 can identify condoms and describe their function. In every nation condoms are extensively used and often the subject of humor. Surprisingly, perhaps, condoms are an effective method of birth control. With reasonable care, it is uncommon for a condom to tear, slip off, or break during intercourse.

Condoms are made of thin rubber, latex, or plastic. Some more expensive ones are made of animal intestines. The latter are supposed to give a more natural skinlike feeling. Most are packaged rolled, some lubricated, and some colored or otherwise embellished. To add to their effectiveness, some are lubricated with spermicide. Condoms are generally 7 inches long and 1½ inches in diameter. The condom is fitted over the man's erect (not flaccid) penis by either partner *before* intromission (see Figure 14-3).

A half minute or less, after the man's ejaculation, and *before* he has *fully lost* his *erection*, the condom, with the penis still inside it, should be removed from the vagina. The rim of the condom is held against the base of the penis as

Always check that the condom is in an intact package and has not dried or deteriorated with age. When rolling it on, gently squeeze the top to make sure no air is caught. It should fit the penis snugly (Figure 14-3).

Condoms.

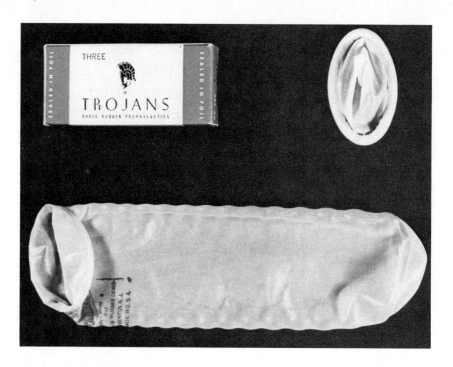

the man withdraws. The point is not to spill any semen collected in the condom into the vagina.

In addition to the standard condom we have described, newer and more innovative models are on the market. Some condoms have rubber "ribbing" supposedly making the penis feel larger or providing extra stimulation to the partner. Another condom covers only the tip or head of the penis, thus allowing greater sensation for the male. The newest product is a female condom. This contraceptive is inserted like a tampon and lines the woman's vagina, extending out over the labia. The effectiveness of these novel condoms is questionable, and they should not be used unless thay have been cleared as reliable by the Food and Drug Administration.

**Advantages and disadvantages** During coitus condoms may get dry; even the lubricated ones may lose their moisture. Usually a bit of surgical jelly, K-Y, or saliva added to the sheath or its equivalent will alleviate dryness. Do not use Vaseline, baby oil, or skin lotions. They can damage the rubber in a few minutes. Putting on condoms is also said to interfere with the flow and intimacy of sexual relations. A few women and men complain that condoms diminish sexual feeling or become a barrier to sensation during intercourse.

On the positive side, condoms have no adverse side effects for either sex. They are inexpensive, and none require a doctor's prescription. They are easily purchased and are often found on public display on pharmacy counters. An important additional advantage is that if they are used in *combination* with a diaphragm (and spermicide) or a sponge, contraceptive effectiveness is excellent. An additional advantage of these sheaths is that they prevent direct contact between the penis and vagina. In this way they can help block the spread of sexually transmitted diseases (Chapter 16).

Condoms can prevent the transmission of several sexually infectious diseases. Many health authorities suggest they be used routinely with every new sexual partner until alternate means of contraception can safely be employed (Chapter 16).

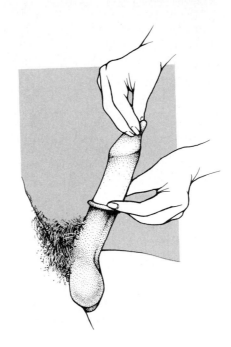

*Figure 14-3*
Condoms may be put on
by oneself or one's partner.

### Intrauterine devices

**Intrauterine devices (IUDs)** are small, about 1-inch in size, variously shaped and made of metal or plastic. They are placed by a health care specialist into the uterus. Most come packaged in an insertion tube for easy entry through the vagina and cervix. The shape selected is generally a matter of trial and error with the client and contraceptive specialist agreeing about comfort and fit. Intrauterine devices seem to work because they are intrusive, causing an inflammatory effect in the uterus. Defensive uterine biochemical changes occur that make the endometrium inhospitable to implantation.

**Advantages and disadvantages**   An advantage of the IUD is that it is totally independent of coitus. It is also an inexpensive way to ensure contraception for many years. The IUD is effective, too, with failure rates of only about 2% to 4%.

Serious drawbacks exist. Some women find insertion of the IUD painful and experience cramping and bleeding for some time following placement. Uterine and pelvic infection is another possibility. The presence of an IUD can also significantly increase the chances of miscarriage and other birth complications.

Because of the problems that may be encountered with intrauterine implants, their popularity has considerably decreased. Few physicians in the United States or Canada now recommend them. In technologically less developed nations however, such as in Africa and Asia, the IUD continues to be fairly common since it can prevent pregnancy for years at little cost.

The one IUD that is still sometimes prescribed in North America for women who do not want more children is the T-shaped insert that slowly releases minute amounts of progesterone or copper, thus supposedly enhancing

The Progestasert IUD (left) and the Copper-T (380A) IUD (right) are recommended by a few physicians in the U.S.

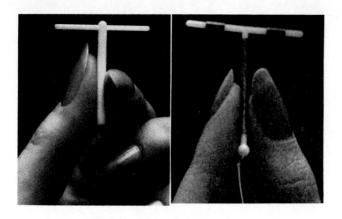

its contraceptive effectiveness. These devices, respectively called Progestasert and Paragard, are claimed to be able to remain in place for up to 4 years (Klitsch, 1988).

**Warning** The *Dalkon Shield,* (Figure 14-4) was used by more than two million women despite increasing reports the device was difficult to place and resulted in numerous complications. Finally, almost a decade after its introduction, it became clear that this IUD directly caused thousands of uterine infections and two dozen deaths. Over 10,000 liability suits have been filed against the manufacturer, (A.H. Robins, Co.), and this IUD has been withdrawn from use.

### Sterilization

Sterilization has become the nation's and the world's most frequent form of contraception. According to the United States Center for Health Statistics (1988), 20 million adults, nearly equally divided between men and women, have been sterilized. It is now widely recognized that sterilization is a highly reliable means of reproduction control.

In men sterilization is accomplished by a **vasectomy,** a 15-minute office procedure. The physician injects an anesthetic into the scrotum and locates the vas deferens. A small incision is then made and a tiny segment of the tubes is cut and removed (see Figure 14-5). This operation permits sperm to continue to be produced, but they can no longer traverse the vas and be ejaculated. Instead they accumulate in the testes and epididymis and are reabsorbed (Chapter 4). Since sperm only account for about 10% of the ejaculate, most men do not notice any difference when semen is expelled during orgasm. CAUTION: Viable sperm may remain in a man's system for some time after a vasectomy. Alternate means of birth control should be used until the ejaculate is tested for the absence of live sperm, usually about 2 months after surgery.

Sterilization in women usually involves **tubal ligation,** tying or severing both fallopian tubes. This procedure may accompany abdominal surgery or a caesarean section. When sterilization alone is the object, it may be performed with the help of a *laparoscope,* an optical tube that permits the physician to see inside the abdominal cavity. The surgeon makes a small incision near the

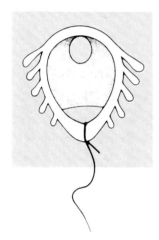

*Figure 14-4*
The Dalkon Shield.

*vasectomy*
Male sterilization performed by cutting the vas deferens.

*tubal ligation*
Female sterilization performed by severing and tying the fallopian tubes.

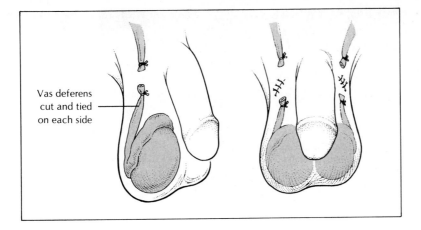

Vas deferens
cut and tied
on each side

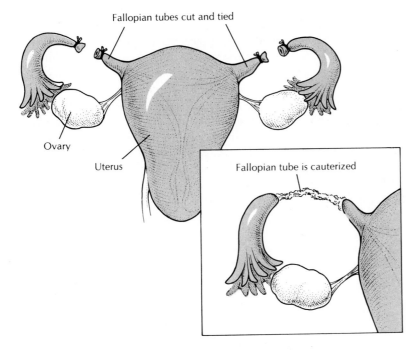

Fallopian tubes cut and tied

Ovary

Uterus

Fallopian tube is cauterized

*Figure 14-5*
A vasectomy requires small incisions in the scrotum. The vas is then located, cut, and cauterized. It is replaced in the scrotum and the incision sewn up. Tubal ligations are frequently performed with a laparoscope. Typically the surgeon makes a small incision near the navel and inserts the lighted hollow laparoscope to locate the fallopian tubes. The tubes can then be cut and cauterized.

navel and inserts the laparoscope to locate the tubes. Next, a cutting or cauterizing instrument may be threaded through the laparoscope to sever the fallopian tubes. There are numerous sterilization techniques, but the objective of all is to definitively cut the fallopian tubes, and prevent the meeting of the sperm from below and the egg from above.

A tubal ligation may be performed on an outpatient basis but very often an overnight hospital stay is required. If local anesthesia has been used, recovery may take place in a day or two. General anesthesia is also often employed and this may necessitate several days' rest. Coitus can usually be resumed in a week. In all, female sterilization is a more complex and physically demanding procedure than vasectomy. The risks are slight but greater than in sterilization for men.

Local anesthesia involves only a small circumscribed area that is anesthetized by injections. General anesthesia involves loss of consciousness. General anesthesia carries a slightly greater risk than local anesthesia.

**Advantages and disadvantages**   The major advantage of sterilization is its excellent reliability. Once someone is sterilized, no further precautions against pregnancy have to be taken. There are no more pills to be swallowed, condoms to be purchased, or temperatures to take. Coitus can take place anytime with no concern about pregnancy.

The high initial cost of sterilization may seem a disadvantage. Vasectomies may cost around $600 and ligations over $2000. These costs may seem less formidable when apportioned over 10 to 20 years. Sterilization is surgery, and this means the possibility of complications. Medical problems are rare but could include infection, excessive scarring, bleeding, or inflammation. Vasectomy almost never results in a fatal outcome, but tubal ligation carries the slight risk of one death per 50,000 procedures (Danforth, 1985).

The major disadvantage of sterilization surgeries is that they are difficult to reverse. One can always stop using oral contraceptives or a diaphragm, and fertility will be restored. Attempts to repair a tubal ligation have met with limited success. At best only one in four fallopian tube ligations is successfully reversed. Among men, new microsurgery techniques have been credited with reestablishing the function of the vas deferens in as many as half of all patients. But there is a second hurdle. The absorption of the unejaculated sperm often produces antibodies to the man's own sperm. Even when the vas is repaired, the antibodies may continue to damage sperm for a year or longer. In essence while some sterilization operations have been reversed, the man or woman who chooses them should think of the procedures as permanent (Benson, 1989; Roberts, 1988; Silber, 1987).

### Ineffective methods

The list of ineffective birth control methods is very long. Masturbating before intercourse to reduce the sperm count is unreliable and difficult for most men. Sperm are temperature sensitive but a very hot bath before coitus is both time consuming and minimally useful. Shaking a bottle of warm Coca Cola and then squirting it into the vagina after sexual relations is useless and a potential source of infection. There is no food or vitamin that will reduce sperm production, inhibit ovulation, or prevent pregnancy.

Two birth control means that are practiced by a few people are *withdrawal* and *douching*. Both are unreliable. A man may not always manage to withdraw just before ejaculation. Semen and sperm may already have been introduced from Cowper's secretions, as we saw in Chapter 4. Douching, that is, flushing the vagina with water and vinegar or a commercial compound, after coitus often fails to kill all the sperm deposited. Douching and withdrawal (*coitus interruptus*) are also frustrating and very easily neglected. As a result almost 4 out of 10 women who rely on these techniques will get pregnant.

Both coitus interruptus and douching may be better than doing nothing, but their effectiveness is too low to be relied on as a frequent method.

### Trends

No contraceptive method is perfect. All involve some slight degree of physical or psychological discomfort and some could produce unwanted side effects. Thus the search for simple, universally acceptable, reliable, and hazard-free contraception continues. Experimental work has been done on a *male pill.* Hormone combinations have not proven very acceptable since they often depress male sexual desire. *Gossypol,* a plant derivative, is promising since it interferes with sperm production. It has had some use in China but has not been accepted for distribution in the United States. Another proposed male contraceptive, *danazol,* is reported to significantly reduce the number and mortality of sperm yet not affect sexual drive or desire. The World Health Organization has been sponsoring clinical trials, but it is unlikely that a decision about whether to introduce the contraceptive for wide-scale use will occur until the early 1990s (Wiest and Webster, 1988).

*Depo-Provera* is the most prominent of several "long-acting" chemical contraceptives. Depo-Provera is a synthetic progestogen that suppresses ovulation. A single injection of the drug prevents pregnancy for 3 months. Thus the hormone seems to combine excellent reliability with convenience and total reversibility. It is used in over 80 countries around the world but has not been approved for the United States by the Food and Drug Administration.

One of the most innovative new techniques makes use of small plastic tubes filled with synthetic progesterone implanted under the skin. The hormone is then slowly released and absorbed by the body. Progesterone thickens cervical mucous, blocking the passage of sperm, and alters the endometrium, inhibiting implantation. The device has been named *Norplant* and has been tested on women in several countries. These preliminary evaluations show that Norplant may remain in place and be effective for 5 years. The indications are also that side effects are minimal.

---

A variety of birth control methods are available, but many people, particularly adolescents, are misinformed about contraception and do not use it consistently. The most reliable means are sterilization and oral contraception. Techniques that are less effective but still very good include the diaphragm, condom, sponge, and spermicides. Fertility awareness is seldom better than fair, but has the advantage of being acceptable to nearly all religious faiths and others who oppose artificial techniques.

*In Sum*

---

## UNPLANNED PREGNANCY: OPTIONS

The discovery of an unplanned pregnancy can be a trying time for men and women, young or old, single or married. After early guilt and fear, emotions often also include affection and pride. Shostak and McLouth (1985) found the great majority of the men, as well as the women, experienced conflict about the pregnancy and were concerned about its outcome. Such mixed emotions can make the decision of what to do difficult and complex.

### Marriage or single parent

When an unmarried couple has an unplanned pregnancy, the traditional first option has been marriage. For many this is not a hardship since eventual matrimony may have been part of their plans anyway. When marriage is forced and the pair are pressured to marry to "legitimize" their offspring, the prospects for a satisfactory relationship are dim (Chapter 12).

A second option is to be a single mother, or sometimes a single father. Sin-

Unplanned pregnancies frequently result in marriages.

gle motherhood is no longer rare. A generation ago only a tiny fraction of 1% of all families were maintained by never-married mothers. Today close to 10% of families are headed by single women who have at least one child. But while social acceptance of single parenthood has increased, the financial and emotional strains can still be considerable. Sometimes parents, friends, or relatives assist the single parent in the decision to go it alone. At other times, help needs to be sought from public agencies. Still, raising a child who has not been planned can be a gratifying experience for the single parent (Chapters 8, 12, and 15; U.S. Center for Health Statistics, 1988).

### Adoption

Most single mothers and fathers come to their status through divorce and find the early years alone quite difficult. After some time, however, most report that they and their children are satisfied and happy (Chapter 12).

Each year there are 200,000 adoptions. About half occur through established government agencies, and the rest are private placements usually arranged by a physician or lawyer. Sometimes a close relative or the parents of the man or woman will ask to raise the child, making the decision to give up the child relatively simple. At other times the knowledge that complete strangers will raise the child provokes painful emotions that make a decision very difficult.

Most involuntary parents, adolescents and older single mothers are increasingly choosing to raise rather than relinquish their children. In one survey of teenagers (Folkenberg, 1985), the majority stated that a mother should be responsible for her baby and not give it to others to raise. There was often pressure by friends and relatives to keep the child. Black and Hispanic adolescents expressed an additional reluctance to give up children for adoption. Since minority children are not as often adopted as those who are white, minority adolescents believed that giving their babies up sentenced them to childhoods of foster or institutional care.

The girls in the study who did give up their babies for adoption tended to be more achievement oriented than those who kept their unplanned infants. They also seemed more self-confident and had realistic plans for education and careers. They were reluctant to have an unplanned pregnancy interfere with their goals and futures (Kaunitz et al., 1988).

## Abortion

Induced abortion is now chosen in nearly a third of all pregnancies. It is often assumed that mothers who choose abortion are frightened, unmarried teenage girls. Actually 70% of all women who elect to abort are over 20 years of age; 25% are married. A majority are white, have been pregnant less than 9 weeks, and do not have any other children. Abortion is an alternative to birth that is elected by women of all ages and marital and family statuses.

The decision to abort is not an easy one for mothers or for fathers. Shusterman (1979) interviewed nearly 400 clients in two Chicago abortion clinics before the operation. Most women reported feeling anger concerning their pregnancy and anxiety as they contemplated their abortion. When relations with the father were good, negative feelings tended to be moderate. But when the relationship with the partner suffered as a result of the pregnancy, fear and foreboding increased.

The reactions of men to abortion were probed by Shostak and McLouth (1985). They interviewed 1000 men in 30 abortion clinics throughout the nation. The majority shared many of the mothers' emotions. They, too, expressed a range of feelings including fear, uncertainty, ambivalence, and distress. Nearly all, too, supported the mother in her decision to abort. At the same time half of the interviewees felt the unintended pregnancy and the abortion had seriously impaired their relationship.

Despite the uncertainties before the abortion, reactions afterward are fairly uniform. The Shusterman and the Shostak and McLouth studies are in agreement with nearly all other research. After the abortion the most common feeling in women, and usually their partners, is relief. There is a marked absence of guilt, sorrow, or resentment regarding the decision. Nearly all say that if they had to choose once more they would again decide to abort. They were satisfied with their choice.

**Vacuum curettage** The *vacuum curettage* method of abortion is usually used when pregnancy is only advanced 1 to 3 months (Table 14-2). The cervix is dilated, often under local anesthesia, to permit access by a thin vacuum hose. Suction of the uterine wall takes less than 10 minutes. Afterward the client rests in a recovery room for an hour or so and may then be driven or drive home. Bleeding is likely to continue for a few days, and there may also be some cramping. It will be several weeks before healing is complete and coitus can be resumed.

Suction abortion methods are relatively painless, and recovery is quick.

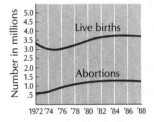

*Figure 14-6*
In recent years there has been approximately one abortion (1,250,000 total) for every three live births in the United States. (Data from U.S. Center for Health Statistics, 1988).

First-trimester abortion procedure.

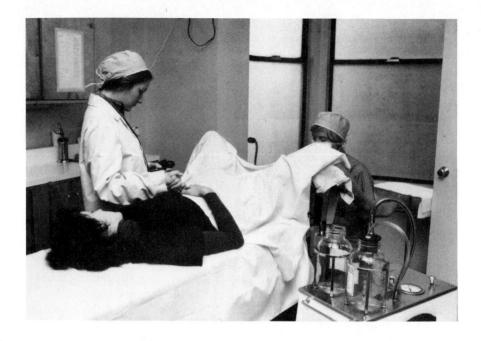

Complications such as hemorrhage, perforation, or incomplete removal of uterine materials are infrequent. Infections do sometimes occur, heralded by fever, pain, and an off-color vaginal discharge. These are successfully treated by antibiotics. Vacuum methods are also reasonably priced, ranging from $300 to $1000.

**Dilation, curettage, and evacuation** From the second to fourth month of pregnancy, *dilation and curettage* (D & C) may be performed. Before vacuum techniques became familiar, this was the most common method of abortion. Dilation is accomplished by inserting rods of successively increasing diameter into the cervix. Curettage means scraping of the uterine lining.

D & C may be performed for reasons *other* than abortion. It is frequently used to help diagnose or relieve a number of gynecological disorders.

D & C procedures require general anesthesia and an overnight hospital stay. Complications are not frequent but slightly more common than in vacuum methods. There is a possibility of infection, incomplete uterine evacuation, and future pregnancy difficulties. Following the D & C most women experience a degree of discomfort for a day or two and some bleeding beyond that. With 2 days of hospitalization, an anesthetist and a surgeon, the cost can easily exceed $2000.

During the second pregnancy trimester *dilation and evacuation* (D & E) may need to be employed. During the fourth and fifth month the fetus is already more than half its potential birth size. This necessitates that the cervix be dilated to allow the passage and entry of a forceps (grasping tool) and a curet (scraping tool). After the fetal mass is broken, it is extracted along with associated uterine tissue. Complications, postoperative care, and costs of a D & E are similar to those for a D & C.

**Amniotic injection** Throughout the second trimester abortion may also be performed by amniotic injection. After a local anesthetic is infused into the ab-

*Table 14-2*

**Induced Abortions**

| Method | Advantages | Disadvantages |
|---|---|---|
| **First Trimester** | | |
| Administration of estrogens, progesterone, diethylstilbestrol | May be administered within a week following coitus; technically not an abortion | Undesirable side effects; cannot be delayed |
| Vacuum curettage | Performed on outpatient basis; may be used up to third month of pregnancy | Can cause bleeding, cramping, infection |
| **Second Trimester** | | |
| Dilation, curettage, and evacuation | May be performed up to fifth month | In-hospital procedure, usually requiring general anesthesia; uterus could be perforated and infection possible |
| Amniotic injection | May be performed from third to sixth month of pregnancy | Possible bleeding, infection, and reaction to injected chemicals |
| **Third Trimester** | | |
| Hysterotomy | May be performed during fifth to eighth month; often important for preserving mother's health. | Fetus may be born alive; entails risks of major surgery |

domen, a hollow needle is placed through the abdomen and into the amniotic sac. Some amniotic fluid is withdrawn and replaced by a saline (salt) solution. This kills the fetus and within a day or two it will be delivered. A similar technique makes use of prostaglandin hormones (Chapters 3 and 4). These may be injected into the amniotic sac and usually cause expulsion of the fetus within 1 day. A possible complication of prostaglandin use, particularly if employed toward the end of the second trimester, is that the fetus may be born alive. This could confront the parents and staff with a difficult ethical and medical decision.

Amniotic injections are done later in pregnancy and as a result carry the risk of more complications. Saline can be toxic to the mother and result in high blood pressure, brain damage, or death. Prostaglandins may cause vomiting, headaches, pain, and respiratory difficulties. Amniotic injection techniques can require several days of hospitalization.

**Hysterotomy**    If abortion is necessary quite late in pregnancy, a hysterotomy is performed. This is similar to a caesarean section (Chapter 15). It requires an abdominal incision through which to open the uterus and remove the fetus.

Hysterotomy must be considered major surgery. A fifth of patients experience some complications. The cost is high, too, since this operation necessitates a week of hospitalization. Hysterotomy is infrequently performed and must be considered an emergency procedure (Danforth, 1985).

**Morning-after techniques**    Sometimes postcoital contraception can be accomplished a few days after unprotected coitus has taken place. These so-called morning-after contraceptive methods may be prescribed for a woman who has been raped, for a contraceptive failure, or when pregnancy cannot be risked because of health. Postcoital methods can be thought of as preventing pregnancy, rather than aborting it. They interfere with the passage of the sperm in the fallopian tubes, or if an egg has been fertilized, they prevent its implantation (Chapter 15).

There are a number of medications that can stop a possible pregnancy. Diethylstilbestrol (DES) may prevent pregnancy up to a week after coitus. It is effective, but there are also potentially hazardous complications that have to be considered. Estrogen may be useful given up to 3 or 4 days after coitus but undesirable bleeding, pain, and other side effects are also possible.

A new chemical called RU-486, an antiprogesterone, blocks the maturing of the uterine lining and causes menstrual bleeding within 48 hours after administration (Chapters 3 and 15). This means that if a fertilized egg is present, it, too, will be expelled. Dr. Etienne-Emil Baulieu, the French physician who pioneered the development of RU-486, points out that the medication may be taken once a month, just before menstruation is normally expected. In this instance a woman having intercourse without contraception need not know if a fertilized egg were expelled. Or, RU-486 might be taken shortly after a period is missed and/or a pregnancy confirmed to induce abortion. RU-486 is being used in France and several other countries, but it may be years before it will be approved for use in the United States. The procedure has become the focus of battle with "pro-choice" and "right-to-life" advocates set for prolonged debate and court hearings.

Research has suggested that RU-486 is quite safe when used regularly. Like other "morning-after" techniques, it has a failure rate of 10 to 20 percent. Side effects in some users include dizziness, painful uterine contractions, and hemorrhaging. Some physicians suggest that postcoital contraception is probably best thought of as an emergency procedure and not included in routine family planning (Danforth, 1985; Shostak and McLouth, 1985).

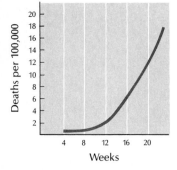

*Figure 14-7*
Abortion safety: The number of maternal deaths per 100,000 abortions is indicated along the left of the graph; the week of pregnancy during which the deaths occur is at the bottom of the graph. Note that 9 out of 10 abortions occur during the first trimester of pregnancy. (Data from U.S. Center for Health Statistics, 1988).

**Safety**    An abortion is a medical-surgical procedure and, like all such interventions, it carries risks. All abortions result in some bleeding and pain and the other possible complications mentioned. In terms of mortal risk to the mother, current statistics show that before the end of the first trimester the death rate for abortion is about 1 in 50,000. When a woman is into the second trimester, the abortion risk increases, with mortality about 1 in 20,000.

To get some perspective on these numbers, the mortality rate for women who deliver their babies should be compared. Healthy young women who carry their children full term to delivery have about 1 chance per 20,000 of dying as a result of childbirth. Most induced abortions then are as safe as or even safer than childbirth (see Figure 14-7).

### Three Views on Abortion

All societies have wrestled with the problem of unintended pregnancies. When no one wanted an infant, people in some nations have practiced infanticide (killing the baby). Abortion has been a solution for people in most cultures since ancient times. Today political, women's, and religious groups that identify themselves as "pro-life" liken abortion to infanticide. Organizations that support abortion advocate "choice." They say a woman has a right to determine what will happen to her body and to her person. Three views follow:

DOCTOR: I speak against abortion because in plain terms it is taking a human life. Within a few minutes after conception a multicelled structure has evolved that is the beginning of a complete human being. Within 3 weeks a very tiny but clearly human person is present in the uterus. When we abort as early as 6 weeks after conception, we kill a recognizable person.

MINISTER: I am for abortion as an option, because it is a woman's inalienable right to decide for herself, seeking any counsel she wishes to determine what will happen to her own body. I think it is clear to all of us that women will get abortions whether they are legal or not. I ask that safe, affordable abortions be available to all women, rich and poor, so they do not have to be butchered.

LAWYER: I don't think we are ever going to settle the abortion issue to everyone's satisfaction. I for one cannot buy either argument: that all abortion is killing nor that a woman must have complete choice over whether or not she carries an infant to term. A pregnant woman is carrying a life and therefore has responsibilities to her infant and to society as well as to herself. In my view, abortion should always be an option early in pregnancy, but should not be one later on. Just when the abortion option should end I would leave to wisdom and science. The choice would be made in terms of the risk of abortion and the degree to which the embryo or fetus has become more of an actual, rather than a potential being.

*(Author's Files)*

**Future of abortion**   Abortion in the United States has become safe, effective, and relatively accepted. Ten percent of American women have had an abortion. There is one abortion for every three live births, for a total of one and a quarter million abortions every year (see Figure 14-6). This is, incidentally, not a world record. Several nations including Japan, Hungary, and the Soviet Union have a higher number of abortions (Yankelovich et al., 1981).

Most women approve of elective abortion. Yankelovich et al. (1981) sampled a cross section of 1015 women from all ethnic and social groups throughout the United States. The researchers found that 67% of all the women agreed that anyone who wants an abortion should be able to obtain it. Only a minority, about 25%, clearly opposed all induced abortion. Yankelovich and his associates also found that while some religious groups strongly oppose abortion, the number of women who were in favor of the procedure was about the same for all major faiths.

In 1973 the United States Supreme Court issued the original ruling (Roe vs. Wade) legalizing induced abortion (Chapter 20). A decade later most major nations of the world had taken similar action. Yet attempts to halt abortion

The earlier an abortion is done, the simpler, safer, and cheaper it is. This is a good reason why a woman and her partner should be aware of her menstrual cycle and know when she has missed a period. An early home pregnancy test (Chapter 15) or other medical consultation may be necessary if an unplanned pregnancy is suspected.

### Surrogate Parenthood

A surrogate is a substitute. A surrogate mother is a woman who agrees to be impregnated, usually through artificial insemination with the sperm of another woman's husband. In a few instances surrogates have been implanted with another couple's fertilized egg. Whatever the procedure, the surrogate agrees to bear another couple's child and give it to them after birth.

Surrogate parenthood is uncommon, and negotiations through a physician or attorney are frequently difficult. Yet there may be a thousand children who have been born by surrogate arrangements. Most surrogates are sincere and healthy women who are attracted for a number of personal as well as financial reasons. They have enjoyed their previous pregnancies and look forward to helping another couple become parents. They may also need the $10,000 to $30,000 fee that is usually offered.

Surrogate parenthood can involve problems. The surrogate mother who has agreed to give up the child may change her mind after its birth. Or the couple waiting for the child may refuse it, especially if there is a birth defect.

There has also been professional opposition to surrogate arrangements. In England, in 1983, an ethics committee of the Royal College of Obstetricians and Gynecologists recommended against the use of surrogate mothers. They reasoned that surrogate women, and waiting parents, cannot predict beforehand what their attitudes toward the child will be.

In 1988, Michigan became the first of several states to outlaw surrogate agreements. In these states, a contract, even if legally prepared, for a woman to bear a child for another person or couple is not enforceable. Criminal sanctions have also been considered for such arrangements. Surrogate parenthood may continue, although very likely on a reduced scale since there seems to be limited public acceptance and support (Chesler, 1988; Dunn et al., 1988; Kane, 1988).

AID and IVF parents typically express delight and satisfaction on becoming mothers and fathers.

### Adoption

Couples and sometimes single people who cannot conceive or risk childbearing may choose to adopt. A few people also elect to adopt since they feel they are helping a needy child or contributing to the solution to poverty and overpopulation (Dunn, et al. 1988).

Adoption is not simple. To begin with, healthy infants available for adoption are in short supply. This is especially true of white babies. Most unmarried or very young mothers, as we saw earlier in this chapter, do not choose to make their child available for adoption. The result is that waiting lists are often 5 or more years long.

Most governmental and religiously based adoption agencies also insist that the couple be legally married and in a standard family relationship. Single people and those who are gay or lesbian have applied to become adoptive parents and have sometimes been successful. Most, however, are likely to be challenged by the agency or refused.

Since formal agencies often move slowly and adoption of a child can take many years, some couples make private arrangements. Frequently an obstetri-

Children do not have to have the same religious or ethnic roots as the adopting parents. Such adoptions can work out just as well as when parent and child are from the same background.

Adopted children, whatever their background, can help make a happy family.

cal health care specialist or an attorney knows a mother who wants to place her infant or young child. Occasionally young women who are unintentionally pregnant may be exploited by a person who persuades them to give up their child. Such private placements are often expensive, costing $5000 to $20,000. They are also fraught with legal hazards because the placement may be considered illegal by the courts. Sometimes parents who have made such private arrangements have had to return the child even several years after adoption (Kaunitz, et al., 1987).

People contemplating adoption are often concerned with whether the child will be physically and psychologically normal. Kathryn Marquis and Richard E. Detweiler (1985) looked at the research and discovered that many studies reported poor psychological fitness in adopted children. When they looked more closely, however, they concluded that this was largely a result of biased sampling. For example, several investigators drew conclusions about the mental health of all adopted children based on the few they had seen for psychotherapy.

In their own study of 167 adopted adolescents, Marquis and Detweiler found that adopted children are generally similar to birth children. In fact "the adopted may be different by being more positive rather than more negative than their nonadopted peers." They seem to have a happier and more optimistic outlook on their lives and on their relationships with their adoptive parents.

Should parents tell children that they are adopted? Most experts say a child should be informed from the beginning. Should a grown adoptee look for his

## Birth Planning

Check each question either *Yes* or *No*.

                                          Yes   No

1. Do I need a contraceptive right away? ____ ____
2. Do I want a contraceptive that can be used completely independent of sexual relations? ____ ____
3. Do I need a contraceptive only once in a great while? ____ ____
4. Do I want something with no harmful side effects? ____ ____
5. Do I want to avoid going to the doctor? ____ ____
6. Do I want something that will help protect against sexually transmitted diseases? ____ ____

                                          Yes   No

7. Do I have to be concerned about affordability? ____ ____
8. Do I need to be virtually certain that pregnancy will not result? ____ ____
9. Do I want to avoid pregnancy now but want to have a child sometime in the future? ____ ____
10. Do I have any medical condition or life-style that may rule out some form of contraception? ____ ____

### Suggestions

If you have checked *Yes* to number:

1. Condoms, sponges, and spermicides may be easily purchased without prescription in any pharmacy.
2. Sterilization, oral contraceptives, cervical caps, and fertility awareness techniques do not require that anything be done just before sexual relations.
3. Diaphragms, condoms, sponges, or spermicides can be used by people who have coitus only once in a while. Fertility awareness techniques may also be appropriate, but require a high degree of skill and motivation.
4. IUDs should be avoided. Sometimes oral contraception also results in some minor discomforts and it may also have harmful side effects. Consider the condom, sponge and diaphragm.
5. The sponge, condom, and spermicides do not require a prescription from a physician.
6. The condom and, to a lesser extent, spermicides and the sponge may help protect against some sexually transmitted diseases.
7. The cost of sterilization is high, but there is no additional expense for a lifetime. Those who have coitus daily or more often may find the diaphragm, oral contraception, or a cervical cap more economical than other methods.
8. Sterilization provides near certainty. Oral contraception or a diaphragm-condom-spermicide combination also gives a high measure of reliable protection. Fertility awareness, withdrawal, and douche methods should be avoided.
9. While it is sometimes possible to reverse sterilization, it requires surgery and is more complex than simply stopping use of any of the other methods.
10. Smokers and people with a history of blood clots should not use oral contraceptives. Some people have an allergic reaction to a specific spermicide and should experiment with another brand. Some women cannot be fitted with a diaphragm or cervical cap because of the position of the uterus. The woman and her health care provider will then need to select another suitable means of contraception.

NOTE: There may be more than one method of birth control suitable for you. Study the methods suggested above and consult Table 14-1 to determine what techniques may be most appropriate.

or her parents? The answer is, again, *yes,* if he or she really wants to. If a young man or woman who has been adopted is curious about his or her birth parents, many agencies are now helpful. At one time all records were sealed, sometimes even destroyed, so that there was no way of tracing one's original mother and father. Today many legal agencies assist adoptees who have reached the age of 21 to find information about their birth parents.

---

*Summary*

Safe and reliable contraception in the United States owes much to Margaret Sanger who introduced the diaphragm early in this century. There are now many worthwhile contraceptive methods available. Abstinence and noncoital sexual relations could be totally reliable, but most couples use these means too inconsistently. Sterilization, oral contraceptives, condoms, sponges, and diaphragms are all quite good. Fertility awareness methods are fair but might be more worthwhile if calendar, temperature, and mucous methods were combined and employed conscientiously. Withdrawal and douching are too unreliable to be recommended but are better than doing nothing.

An unwed couple who is faced with unplanned pregnancy has several options including marriage, being a single parent, abortion, or giving the child for adoption. Few choose adoption but more and more are electing to be single parents. Abortion is chosen by over a million married and single women yearly, and most are pregnant less than 9 weeks. Many couples make the abortion decision hesitantly and with uncertainty, but almost all feel relief and satisfaction afterward.

Most abortions occur during the first trimester, and vacuum curettage is employed. After this trimester, dilation and curettage, evacuation, or amniotic injection methods may be necessary. Toward the end of pregnancy an emergency abortion can be performed with a hysterotomy. Pregnancy may sometimes be avoided by taking particular prescribed medications or hormones within a few days following coitus. Early abortions are very safe, and even by the beginning of the fourth month of pregnancy maternal mortality is 1 in 20,000. Abortion was legalized in the United States in 1973 but still arouses vigorous opposition.

About 15% of all couples are involuntarily childless. In men, impaired fertility is often the result of low sperm count or poor sperm development. Among women, failure to ovulate or tubal blockages are the most frequent causes. In men too, the ducts for sperm may be blocked by scarring, infection, or growth. Medical treatment can alleviate almost half of all involuntary childlessness.

Artificial insemination by donor or husband is a common and usually an effective pregnancy technique. In vitro fertilization has now accounted for thousands of successful pregnancies and is increasing in frequency. Both methods are safe but often provoke legal and moral questions. Surrogate parenthood has become increasingly controversial.

The adoption alternative is often frustrating because it may involve many years of waiting and investigation by social agencies. Minority children and those who are handicapped are more readily available. Adopted children should be informed from the beginning. Despite fears to the contrary, adopted children and their new parents tend to adjust well.

---

*For Thought and*
*Discussion*

1 List the different contraceptive methods in terms of their reliability. Which do you feel are most acceptable and why?

2 What are some of the reasons you have heard for people who are sexually active to not use contraception? How valid are their reasons or arguments? How might one best educate or persuade these people to use contraceptives?

3 There are several alternatives available for an unintended pregnancy. Give your view of each and explain how your attitudes were shaped by your own background and experience.

4 If you were involuntarily childless and wanted to be a parent, what option would you choose? What are some of the advantages and disadvantages of each? Might you employ a surrogate mother? Could you be one?

---

*References*

Andrews, L.B. Yours, mine and theirs. *Psychology Today,* December, 1984, 20-29.

Benson, R.C. *Handbook of obstetrics and gynecology.* Los Altos, Calif.: Lange Medical Books, 1989.

Byrne, D. Sex without contraception. In Byrne, D., and Fisher, W.A. (editors). *Adolescents, sex, and contraception,* Hillsdale, N.J.: Lawrence Erlbaum Associates, Inc., 1983.

Chesler, P. *Sacred bond: legacy of Baby M.* New York: Random House, Inc., 1988.

Danforth, D.N. *Obstetrics and gynecology.* Philadelphia: J.B. Lippincott Co., 1985.

Dunn, P.C., Ryan, I.J., and O'Brien, K. College students' acceptance of adoption and five alternative fertilization techniques. *The Journal of Sex Research,* 1988, 24, 282-287.

Folkenberg, J. Teen pregnancy: who opts for adoption? *Psychology Today,* May, 1985, 16.

Forste, R.T., and Heaton, T.B. Initiation of sexual activity among female adolescents. *Youth & Society,* March, 1988, *19*(3), 250-268

Fox, L.S. Adolescent male reproductive responsibility in a white, middle-class sample. *Social Work in Education,* 1983, 6(1), 32-43.

Gleicher, N., et al. *Fertility: a guide for the couple with infertility problems.* New York: Irvington Publications, 1988.

Glendon, M.A. *Abortion and divorce in Western law.* Cambridge, Mass.: Harvard University Press, 1988.

Hatcher, R.A., et al. *Contraceptive technology 1984-1985.* New York: Irvington Publishers, 1985.

Kane, E. *Birth mother: the story of America's first legal surrogate mother.* San Diego, Calif.: Harcourt Brace Jovanovich, 1988.

Kaunitz, A.M., Grimes, D.A., and Kaunitz, K.K. A physician's guide to adoption. *Journal of the American Medical Association,* December 25, 1987, *258* (24), 3537-3541.

Klitsch, M. The return of the IUD. *Family Planning Perspectives,* January/February, 1988, *20*(1), 19.

Kolata, G. Birth control: new devices on market raise hopes of experts for wider U.S. choices. *New York Times,* June 9, 1988, B17.

Lasker, J.N., and Borg, S. *In search of parenthood.* Boston: Beacon Press, 1987.

Marquis, K.S., and Detweiler, R.E. Does adopted mean different: an attributional analysis. *Journal of Personality and Social Psychology,* April, 1985, 48(4), 1054-66.

Nightingale, S.L. Cervical cap approved. *Journal of the American Medical Association,* July 15, 1988, *260*(3), 315.

Oakley, Jr., G.P. Spermicides and birth defects. *Journal of the American Medical Association,* May 7, 1982, 247(7), 2405.

Ory, H.W. *Making choices.* New York: Alan Guttmacher Institute, 1983.

Ostling, R.N., et al. A bold stand on birth control. *Time Magazine,* December 3, 1984, 66.

Potts, M., and Diggory, P. *The textbook of contraceptive practice.* New York: Cambridge University Press, 1984.

Raymond, C.A. IVF registry notes more centers, more births, slightly improved odds. *Journal of the American Medical Association,* April 1, 1988, *259* (13), 1920-1921.

Roberts, G. (compiler): *A small library in family planning.* New York: Planned Parenthood Federation of America, 1988.

Shostak, A., and McLouth, G. *Men and abortion.* New York: Praeger Publishers, 1985.

Shusterman, L.R. Predicting the psychological consequences of abortion. *Social Science and Medicine,* 1979, *13,* 683-689.

Silber, S.J. *How NOT to get pregnant: your guide to simple, reliable contraception.* New York: Charles Scribner's Sons, 1987.

Simon, J.A., Danforth, D.R., Hutchinson, J.S., and Hodgen, G.D. Characterization of recombinant DNA derived—human luteinizing hormone in vitro and in vivo: efficacy in ovulation induction and corpus luteum support. *Journal of the American Medical Association,* June 10, 1988, *259*(22), 3290-3295.

Snarey, J. Men without children. *Psychology Today,* March, 1988, 61-62.

Tannahill, R. *Sex in history.* New York: Stein & Day, Publishers, 1981.

Tanfer, K., and Horn, M.C. *Family planning: family planning perspectives.* New York: Alan Guttmacher Institute, 1985.

Tilton, N., et al. *Making miracles: in vitro fertilization.* New York: Doubleday & Co., 1985.

U.S. Center for Health Statistics. *Vital statistics of the United States, Annual.* Washington, D.C.: Superintendent of Documents, 1988.

Wiest, W.M., and Webster, P.C. Effects of contraceptive hormone, Danazol, on male sexual functioning. *The Journal of Sex Research,* 1988, *24,* 170-177.

Wills, J. Comparing contraceptives. *FDA Consumer,* May, 1985. Department of Health and Human Services Publication No. (FDA) 85-1123, U.S. Government Printing Office.

Yankelovich, D., Skelly, R., and White, A. Abortion: women speak out. *Life,* November, 1981, 42-52.

---

*Suggested Readings*

Alan Guttmacher Institute. *Making choices: evaluating the health risks and benefits of birth control methods.* New York: Alan Guttmacher Institute, 1984.

A very careful and thorough listing of birth control options and their benefits and risks. Well written and reassuring.

Goldstein, R.D. *Mother-love and abortion: a legal interpretation.* Berkely, Calif.: University of California Press, 1988.

A thoughtful examination of both sides of the right-to-life vs. freedom-of-choice conflict is presented.

Kane, E. *Birth mother: the story of America's first legal surrogate mother.* San Diego, Calif.: Harcourt Brace Jovanovich, 1988.

Describes thae anxieties, joys, and attachment that may accompany pregnancy and childbirth.

Roberts, G. (compiler): *A small library in family planning.* New York: Planned Parenthood Federation of America, 1988.

Suggestions, techniques, and sources of information are provided to assist in thoughtful family planning.

*Chapter 15*

# Pregnancy and Birth
## *Life Changes*

**When you finish this chapter, you should be able to:**

Explain the advantages and disadvantages of having children or being childfree.

Describe fertilization, conception, and the stages of pregnancy.

Explain how mothers and fathers react to and can prepare for pregnancy and childbirth.

Evaluate the medical-surgical and prepared-birth approaches to pregnancy and childbirth.

Describe good prenatal health practices that help to ensure a normal pregnancy and infant.

Describe how pregnancy and birth affect a couple's affectional and sexual relationship.

As little as a generation ago, it was a foregone conclusion that when a couple married they would soon have children. Today more and more women and men cohabit, and quite a few who are married choose not to have children. The result is that the number of births in the United States started a marked decline a generation ago. It has only recently turned up again. But while the birth rate is lower, most married men and women still want to become parents. Over half of all pregnancies among married and cohabiting partners are intended. The parents have planned and are looking forward to the birth of their child. In this chapter we will look at the choices and the physical and psychological processes involved in pregnancy and birth.

# FAMILY PLANNING

Every couple is faced with numerous family planning choices. Once it has been decided to *plan,* an acceptable contraceptive method must be agreed on. An even more fundamental decision is whether or not to have children. This is not easily arrived at, nor is the decision made entirely by the couple themselves. Our society is *pronatal,* meaning *for* birth. Couples are encouraged to have children by their religious faiths, their own parents, and friends and government. Many European nations give birth bonuses; they reward the birth of a child with sums of money. At the beginning of this century President Theodore Roosevelt compared women who avoided pregnancy to men who refused to serve in the armed forces. It was the duty of women to procreate as it was the solemn obligation of men to fight for their nation. The social pressure to have children may be subtle or direct, but it is continuous.

China has a huge population of well over a billion people. Unlike nations that have offered monetary incentives to encourage births, China now discourages them. Couples are offered bonuses and privileges if they have only one child.

## Becoming a parent or remaining childfree

Wanting children may express an innate need. Reproduction is, after all, an apparent biological priority in all species. But men and women may describe their desire for children as based on their love for one another. A woman and man may feel that becoming parents will be a maturing fulfillment. Sharing themselves with their child will intensify their own bond and affirm their love. Mothers and fathers also talk of the joy of participating in their child's delightful discovery of the world about them. It gives adults a chance to feel young and new again. Perhaps the rewards of parenthood do not have to be listed. One father put it, "I've wanted children from the time we were married. I wanted to be a father and now that I am, it just makes more sense to me than anything I've ever done."

Nearly everyone says that they want to have children. Mosher and Bachrach (1982) surveyed 17,000 married women and found that 98% wanted to become mothers. But while people *say* they want to be parents, more and more are electing to remain childfree. These same researchers found that 15% of their respondents continued to put off having children. Thus the proportion who actually want motherhood may be about 80% to 85%.

The minus side of having children begins with restrictions they may impose on one or both parents. A child is a responsibility; with the birth of a child the mother and father have to curtail their recreation and mobility. A couple has almost 50% less time together after the birth of their first child. Some parents also expect too much from parenting. Children often add meaning to a partnership, but becoming parents is expensive, and it is not likely to repair a marriage that is troubled. A child is much more likely to intensify stress and conflict than to alleviate it (Genevie, Margolies, 1987).

In her book, *Childless by Choice,* Marian Faux (1983) argues that while children can make a couple immeasurably proud and happy, they also have the capacity to hurt parents more than anyone else. She cites a newspaper columnist who asked readers to write whether they would have children if they could make the decision all over again: 70% of the 50,000 people who replied voted "no." This may not qualify as a scientific poll but it does give some indication that many more people might choose to be childfree if they had sufficient information and were encouraged to think thoroughly about their decision.

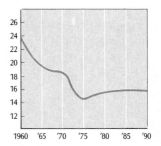

*Figure 15-1*
The number of births per 1000 United States residents. (1990 estimate, data from U.S. Bureau of the Census, 1988.)

The couples that make an informed choice apparently make the best choice. Holahan (1983) surveyed 62 women who were considering having children. These women read about various options and, most importantly, talked to couples who had chosen to be or not to be parents. Holahan found that because they made an informed choice, these women were happier parents as well as marital partners.

### When to have children

When planning a family, a couple needs to decide when to have the first child. A few decades ago, when few women worked outside the home, children started arriving fairly early. The median age for first motherhood in 1950 was 21. Now more than half of all women are employed and many choose to get a solid start in their careers before considering childbirth (see Figure 15-10). Husbands who take an active part in child care may also be motivated to wait. They want to feel financially and occupationally secure before taking on new responsibilities. The end result is that in this decade the number of first births to women in their 30s has increased by 60% (U.S. Bureau of the Census, 1988).

In many respects the best time for motherhood is in the 20s. Mothers who are adolescents experience a disproportionate share of health and emotional problems. Teenaged mothers and fathers are often not very adequate parents (Chapter 8). At the other end of the scale, older parents may find it more difficult to conceive and to have healthy children. Ninety-five percent of couples in their early 20s intending conception will be pregnant within 1 year. When the women are in their late 30s, the percentage drops to 70% (Chapter 14).

A careful study of the effect of age on pregnancy was carried out in Sweden (Forman et al., 1984). Since the standard of living and medical care in the United States is similar to that of Sweden, statistics from that nation provide useful information. Data from nearly a half million births were carefully tabulated and analyzed. This enabled a comparison of younger (age 20 to 24) first mothers, with older (age 35 to 39) first mothers. The analysis clearly showed that older mothers having their first child were likely to encounter more birth

*Figure 15-2*
Two thirds of all births are to mothers under age 30. (Data from U.S. Bureau of the Census, 1988.)

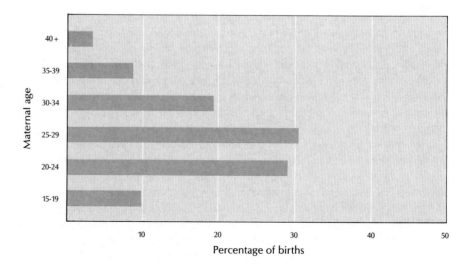

Having a child involves work and responsibilities as well as pleasure and rewards.

hazards. Fetal deaths, low birth weight, and prematurity were about twice as high in older compared to younger mothers.

Young adulthood is an ally of fertility, pregnancy, and birth. But this does not mean that one has to be 25 to become a parent. About 20% of women who become mothers for the first time are between 30 and 35. Somewhat more than 10% of women are in their late 30s and even beyond when they have their first child. There are additional risks at these ages and counseling or special tests are often appropriate. But the overall statistical odds are still in favor of older parents having healthy children (Gillespie, 1987; Rindfuss, et al. 1988).

Couples who plan, who make conscious choices when or whether to have children, are usually more satisfied than those who leave what happens to chance.

## PREGNANCY

We may think of sexual intercourse as an expression of love or a means of satisfying a physical drive. In the simplest physical terms the purpose of coitus is reproduction. During sexual relations when the male ejaculates he releases hundreds of millions of sperm into the vagina. Once in the vagina the sperm can begin their journey through the cervix, into the uterus, and finally to the fallopian tubes where they can fertilize the egg (Chapters 3 and 4).

### Fertilization

In the female reproductive tract most of the hundreds of millions of sperm that have been ejaculated begin moving in numerous directions. Half or more will spill out of the vagina never reaching the cervix. Many others are defective and their motion soon stops. The relative few that survive may reach the fallopian tubes in as little as an hour or more than a full day or two later. Here many more millions will be lost. Some swim into the duct that is eggless. Others stop moving at the bottom half of the fallopian tubes (Chapters 3, 4).

## Do You Want to be a Parent?

Score each question (0) if you disagree, (1) if you agree, and (2) if you agree strongly.

| | Disagree (0) | Agree (1) | Strongly Agree (2) |
|---|---|---|---|
| 1. When I have an opportunity to watch children or play with them, I enjoy it very much. | ___ | ___ | ___ |
| 2. Our relationship as a couple is durable enough to take on the responsibility of having children. | ___ | ___ | ___ |
| 3. I'm ready as an individual to give up whatever time and freedom are necessary in order to be a good parent. | ___ | ___ | ___ |
| 4. I daydream a lot about how wonderful it will be to have a child, but my expectations are completely realistic. | ___ | ___ | ___ |
| 5. My partner and I have planned who will be primary caretaker for the child. | ___ | ___ | ___ |
| 6. My partner and I have planned which child care jobs and activities are assigned to each of us and which we can share. | ___ | ___ | ___ |
| 7. We agree about childcare: sitters, daycare, split shifts, etc. | ___ | ___ | ___ |
| 8. Even if I had to raise a child alone, I know that I would still very much want to be a parent. | ___ | ___ | ___ |
| TOTAL | | | |

### Interpretation

No informal questionnaire can precisely predict whether you should or should not have children. Some people are happier remaining childfree; others enjoy being parents. Your score on this test may help stir your thinking.

A score of twelve to sixteen suggests that you have given being a parent a good deal of thought. You seem prepared for the experience and will most likely enjoy it. A score of seven to eleven suggests that you have planned for children and are probably as ready as most people who are hoping to be parents. As you get closer to the possibility of being a parent your enthusiasm may grow. Scores between four and six suggest several doubts and hesitations about having children. You may be helped to make up your mind whether to have children or be childfree by talking to and observing people with young and older children. A score of under three probably means that you would rather be childfree.

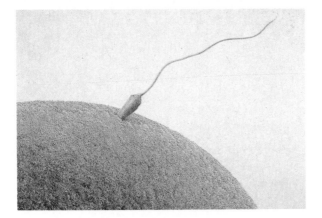

Fertilization: the union of ovum and sperm resulting in a fertilized egg; conception.

Ultimately, dozens of sperm swarm about the egg, where many seem to undergo a biochemical process *(capacitation)* that enables them to penetrate the egg. Sperm and egg now act together to assist fertilization, also referred to as conception. The sperm secretes a substance dissolving the protective jellylike coating of the egg, and the egg, in turn, extends tiny hair-like growths pulling one sperm inside and moving its own nucleus to meet that of the sperm. Once a sperm and egg combine, electrochemical changes on the surface of the egg ordinarily result in a coating that bars the entry of other sperm.

The fertilized egg is called a **zygote.** After about 30 hours, this single-celled, fertilized egg divides into two cells, then four, eight, and so on. This multicelled organism is called a **morula.** During the next 4 days, it will travel down the fallopian tube and enter the uterus.

It now transforms and creates a fluid-filled cavity in its center and is called a **blastocyst.** Inside the uterus the blastocyst undergoes further growth, receiving nourishment from uterine secretions. Just a few days later the blastocyst *implants,* that is, it attaches to the rich, thickened endometrial uterine lining (Chapter 3). The entire process of implantation is usually complete a week (plus or minus a day or two) after fertilization. For some women, implantation results in a little bleeding, possibly leading them to believe they have menstruated, making them unaware for another month that they are pregnant.

Once the blastocyst is anchored, growth and development accelerate. Parts of the blastocyst, now little bigger than a dot on this page, will differentiate into cells that eventually form the nervous system and skin, the digestive, respiratory, circulatory, and reproductive systems, and the muscles. Still other cells contribute toward the development of the **placenta** and the fetal membranes. The placenta is the organ through which the baby will obtain oxygen and nourishment from the mother's bloodstream. The infant will in turn pass its waste products through the placenta to the mother for disposal.

The *fetal membranes* consist of an inner *amnion* and outer *chorion* and compose a thin, transparent sac that encloses the baby. Within the sac several pints of *amniotic fluid* surround the baby, keeping it relatively free from the bounces and shocks of the mother's movements and stabilizing the temperature.

Rereading sections of Chapters 3 and 4 will help in understanding the role of the sperm, egg, uterus, and associated structures in pregnancy.

*zygote*
The cell produced by the union of ovum and sperm.

*morula*
The mass of cells formed as a result of cell division of the fertilized egg.

*blastocyst*
A spherical mass of cells, produced soon after fertilization, with a hollow, fluid-filled inner core.

*placenta*
The tissues surrounding the embryo.

*Figure 15-3*
Fertilization and implantation. At ovulation an egg is released from its ovarian follicle and finds its way into the fallopian tube. Sperm that were deposited in the vagina as little as an hour, or more than a day before, have swum into the fallopian tube. There, one penetrates and fertilizes the egg, now called a zygote. The zygote divides, becoming two cells, then, four, and so on. This multicelled structure is called a morula and remains tiny. It moves slowly through the fallopian tube and then, as a blastocyst, implants in the uterine wall.

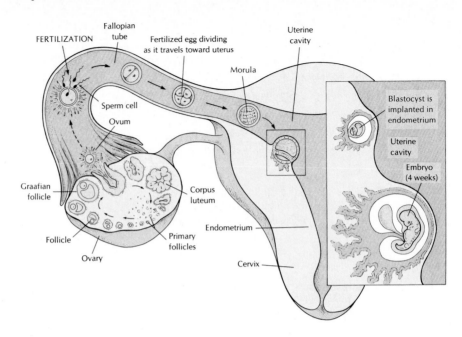

Most birth specialists avoid using medication to treat nausea since drugs may injure the embryo. Sipping ice water, decaffeinated tea, or orange juice before arising and during the morning is often recommended for nausea.

### Signs of pregnancy

The first sign of pregnancy for nearly all women who have fairly regular menses is a missed period. But one missed menses is not sufficient proof of pregnancy. It is not unusual for even the healthiest woman to skip a period because of some temporary illness, stress, or a change in routine. But when a missed period has been preceded by coitus and birth control techniques have not been used, or unreliable methods were employed, the probability of pregnancy increases (Holzman, et al., 1988).

As pregnancy progresses, within a matter of weeks, other signs develop. Some women experience nausea, *morning sickness,* a condition that may be caused by anxiety or triggered by physiological changes affecting the gastrointestinal system. Nausea, incidentally, usually clears up without treatment within 2 months. Other indications of pregnancy include breast enlargement, darkened areolas, frequent urination, and fatigue. Some women report that during the first months of pregnancy they cannot go on without napping during the day. All of these signs certainly seem to point to pregnancy; but like a missed period, they are not absolutely positive.

By the second month of pregnancy, two menstrual periods are missed. In addition to the subjective signs, there will be changes in the placement, shape, and size of the uterus. After another month or so, a special stethoscope will be able to detect the faint but rapid fetal heartbeat. A little after 4 months, the mother's abdomen may still not be very large, particularly if this is her first

*Table 15-1*

**Signs of Pregnancy**

| Sign | Comment |
|------|---------|
| Missed menstrual period | A missed period in a woman under 40 who has been having sexual relations and does not use contraceptives may well indicate pregnancy. |
| Morning sickness | Nausea in the morning, or sometimes during other times of the day, may occur during the first 2 months of pregnancy. By itself this sign means little. |
| Breast tenderness or tingling | Increased estrogen production during the first weeks of pregnancy may produce breast sensitivity. This is a good indicator of pregnancy only when it accompanies the preceding signs. |
| Frequent need to urinate | After a month of pregnancy, urinary symptoms often appear. By themselves, these do not signal pregnancy. If they appear with other signs, they are a positive indicator. |
| Uterine enlargement | After 2 months the uterus can be felt and will be about the size of a chicken egg. At 3 months the uterus will be the size of a grapefruit. Usually this points to pregnancy. |
| Fetal heart tones | Ultrasound equipment can detect delicate fetal heart tones as early as 2 months after conception. This is a clear sign of pregnancy. |
| Quickening | Feeling fetal movement, which usually begin after 4 months, is a certain indicator of pregnancy. |

child. But subtly at first, and then without any doubt, she begins to feel fetal movements, called **"quickening."** (See Table 15-1.)

**Pregnancy testing**    A missed period and uncertain bodily changes may leave considerable doubt about pregnancy. In this instance chemical tests can be useful. Most of the tests depend on detecting the presence of *HCG, human chorionic gonadotropin*. This is a hormone that increases rapidly after the implantation of the fertilized egg and appears in small amounts in the urine. Self-testing pregnancy kits are available *without* prescription in most pharmacies in North America.

The self-test, "at home," pregnancy kits simply require a sample of urine in a test tube. One common technique requires a chemical to be added to the urine and the mixture left to stand for several hours. If there is HCG in the sample, a brownish ring forms. This is a substantial indicator of pregnancy. At-home tests are useful only after a period has been clearly missed. If a more precise and earlier pregnancy test is required, procedures performed in medical laboratories are available.

Remember all tests can give misleading results. Laboratory exams are quite accurate, but at-home kits have a margin of error: 5% of the time they may read positive when you are not pregnant. They may also be falsely negative;

*quickening*
The sensation of movement of the developing fetus perceived by the mother.

about 15% of the time they fail to detect a pregnancy. It is important, therefore, to *repeat* at-home testing after waiting 2 days. If the results still seem doubtful, the more exacting laboratory tests may be required (Danforth, 1985).

## FETAL DEVELOPMENT

Prenatal development is usually described in terms of three periods of time, each 3 months long. During each **trimester,** distinctive maturational changes take place.

*trimester*
One of three 3-month periods from conception to birth.

Three weeks into the first trimester the embryo is still little more than a mass of cells rapidly differentiating into vital body organs. Nevertheless, although only 2 cm (about ½ inch) in length, it looks as if a head, body, and limbs are beginning to be discernible. Just a little later, after 5 weeks, the beginnings of arms, eyes, and ears can be seen in the large embryonic head, and a backbone is evident. The heart, sexual organs, and digestive and nervous systems are also being established. There is, too, a small tail that will disappear within a month.

During the second month following conception, the **umbilical cord** forms and is attached to the embryo at one end and the placenta at the other. Since the mother's and child's blood systems remain separate, this cord will play a major role in transporting nutrients, oxygen, hormones, and some drugs and microorganisms via the placenta to the infant.

*umbilical cord*
The cord connecting the embryo or fetus with the placenta through which nutrients and wastes are exchanged.

*embryo*
The developing organism during the first 8 weeks after fertilization.

At 8 weeks the **embryo** is a little over an inch in length, has a steady heartbeat and detectable brain impulses. The arms have hands with fingers, and the legs are complete with knees, feet, and toes. Teeth, lips, eyelids, and genitals are in place. Internally the kidneys, intestines, and other organs are beginning to function and the lungs take in and expel amniotic fluid. At this point, at the beginning of the third month, the embryo is now called a **fetus.** This miniature human is 10 cm (4 inches) long and weighs about 30 grams (1 ounce).

*fetus*
The developing infant during the second and third trimesters of pregnancy.

### Second and third trimesters

If the fetus enters the second trimester, it has survived the riskiest period of pregnancy. It now has a very good chance of being born full term and healthy.

Prenatal development at 7 weeks and 3 months after conception.

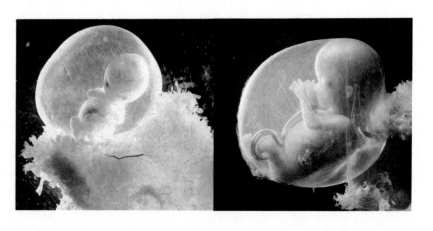

During this trimester the fetus grows in size and the body parts become refined. By the fourth month, the head constitutes about one fourth of the full body length, just as it will at birth. The fetus is about 9 inches long, weighs about 6 ounces, and makes its presence known to the mother through its movements.

During the fifth month the fetus first opens its eyes, and periods of sleeping and waking can be detected. The fetal heartbeat can be heard simply by pressing an ear to the mother's abdomen. Hair now appears on the eyelashes, eyebrows, and head. In fact, the whole body is covered by a downy hair called *lanugo* that usually disappears some time before birth. By the end of this trimester the fetus can make a fist and suck its thumb. It now weighs a little over a pound and is about 14 inches long. If born at this time, the infant has a chance of surviving.

During the third trimester, the fetus seems primarily to be gaining weight. Fat forms beneath the skin, body hair disappears, while head hair often grows. It has fully developed reflexes and can cry, breathe, and swallow. The internal organs are readied to sustain an independent life. Toward the end of this trimester most fetuses have turned to the head-down position preparatory to birth, although about 3% of full-term babies are born in the *breech* or feet-first position. A full-term baby is born about 9 months after pregnancy began. Ninety-nine percent of full-term babies born in the United States survive. There is variation, but on average the newborn weighs about 6 to 8 pounds and is about 18 to 22 inches long. Girls tend to be somewhat lighter and smaller than boys (Danforth, 1985).

A head-first delivery is preferred. Feet-first and other turned deliveries can be challenging but ordinarily do not injure the child or mother.

### The birth day

Babies are "supposed" to be born 266 days after fertilization. Since few parents accurately know when this happened, the day of birth is usually approximated. One technique is to count 280 days from the beginning of the last menstrual period. Another technique used by many is called *Nägele's rule*. Add 7 days to the first day of the last mentrual period. Subtract 3 months and add 1 year. For example, if the last period began December 11, 1989, and 7 days are added, you have December 18. Subtract 3 months and you get September 18. Add 1 year and the baby's estimated time of arrival is September 18, 1990.

Nägele's rule is based on a 28-day menstrual cycle with ovulation occurring on the fourteenth day. If a woman's cycle is shorter or longer, she should add or subtract a few days from the birth day obtained by this formula. Expectant parents should also be aware that only about 10% of infants are born within a day or two of the predicted time. Another 6 out of 10 births occur within 1 or 2 weeks of the expected arrival day.

## MOTHER AND FATHER

As the infant develops, both the mother and father experience changes that may be physical as well as psychological. They, like the fetus, are preparing for birth. When pregnancy is confirmed, the reactions of both the mother and father may range from joy to panic. A couple who have been planning and hoping for a child are delighted. Another couple perhaps young, conflicted, or who did not want to conceive may be depressed and frightened. They may need the

Pregnancy provides new
opportunities for closeness
and warmth.

help of an intelligent friend or counselor (Genevie, Margolies, 1987; Robinson, 1988).

> Sometimes I felt on top of the world. I was going to be a mother and it felt great. At other times I became scared of the enormous responsibility. Many days I was swept between joy and fear.

*(Author's Files)*

Fathers often share their partner's concerns and sometimes their physical symptoms. Among some preliterate societies, such as the Australian aborigines, a practice known as *couvade* was common. This required fathers to take to their beds and enact labor before their wives gave birth. Lipkin and Lamb (1982) found that 23% of the American fathers they surveyed also seemed to share some of their wives' early pregnancy signs. They were tired, urinated frequently, and most common of all, reported morning nausea. The researchers label this tendency for a father to share some of the signs of pregnancy with his wife the *couvade syndrome*.

Today, pregnancy is much more a shared experience than it was a generation ago. Most fathers participate to some extent both in the pre-birth planning and with their partner's diet and exercise. During labor and delivery, as we will note in later pages, they can offer guidance and assistance, and just their touch and presence can be reassuring. Not least of all playing a positive role in the pregnancy and birth can greatly help the bonding between the partners and the child.

I was scared. It meant a lot of new responsibilities, money, and time. There was some jealousy, too. How would I like Marylin spending so much time caring for the baby? I was already a little envious of the attention she got. But taking part in the birth classes and exercises, being there and helping Marylin deliver, made me feel 'This is my baby.' I felt I had just given birth.

*(Authors' Files)*

When fathers take an active part in pregnancy, birth, and the subsequent care, feeding, and sustenance of their child, it may powerfully strengthen the family bond. It can provide healthy models for all the family's children. It should be pointed out, too, that a couple need not be married for both parents to play an important role in child care. Parents may be cohabitants, or even live apart, and still manage a gratifying interaction during pregnancy and after (Entwisle, 1988; Robinson, 1988).

### Later pregnancy

Toward the middle of pregnancy, after about 4 months, the woman may for the first time feel the infant moving about. This is often a time of great excitement with the father and friends being asked to put their hands on the mother's abdomen to feel the baby "kicking."

Near the end of the second trimester, it is likely that the woman will look quite pregnant. Her waist increases in size and maternity clothing may have to be purchased. The skin over her abdomen is stretched, her breasts have enlarged, and the areola has darkened. Facial pigmentation may also increase. A darkened forehead and cheeks, often called the *mask of pregnancy,* is frequently evident. The nipples may ooze an occasional drop of **colostrum,** a watery yellowish fluid that will eventually become milk.

Fathers may have become quite involved in the pregnancy by the second trimester. They can participate in classes preparing parents for the birth and

*colostrum*
A thin, watery, breast fluid that within a few days becomes milk.

Position in which to rest legs and reduce swelling and edema.

after birth period. They may take an active role in helping their partner exercise and maintain a diet.

Toward the end of pregnancy some discomfort may be experienced, especially by new mothers. The fetus may also do a good deal of tossing and kicking, sometimes even interfering with the mother's sleep. The increasing size of the fetus may also displace some internal organs, resulting in digestive discomforts such as heartburn and constipation. There can be considerable water retention, too, causing the legs, hands, and face to appear puffy and enlarged. A large fetus may also throw the mother off balance. Walking and getting in or out of a chair, bed, or car may seem an awkward ordeal.

### Conclusion

We do not want to leave the impression that pregnancy is a time of physical and emotional stress. The Victorians seemed to believe it was (Chapter 1). Women were often isolated and confined to bed during much of their pregnancies. Given the fearful attitudes of a century ago, pregnancy could be a period of anxiety for the mother, while the father ignored much of what was happening. Today a healthy woman in good condition is likely to have some discomfort, but overall she will probably feel well and continue her usual work, most sports, and recreations. She can look forward to bearing a child who will be robust and thriving and to adding a new dimension to her life and that of her partner. Most parents too, look forward to their infant with considerable pride and pleasure (Genevie, Margolies, 1987).

## CHILDBIRTH

Childbirth signals itself several weeks before labor and delivery. In new mothers, two weeks or so before actual labor, the infant *engages,* that is, its head settles down into the pelvis for birth. Among women who have given birth previously, engagement (also called "dropping" or "lightening") is likely to occur during labor itself. Once engaged, the mother feels lighter and balanced again. About 2 weeks before labor, cervical effacement and dilation begin. *Effacement* is the retraction and resultant thinning of the cervix; *dilation* refers to the opening of the mouth of this organ.

Labor during first childbirth is usually slow, often lasting 12 hours to a day or more. Subsequent births may move forward quite rapidly. After the onset of labor, delivery may be as little as 1 or 2 hours away.

A fairly reliable sign that labor may start in a few hours or a day is the appearance of a small bloody vaginal discharge, the "show." This is the result of the release of the mucus plug that had blocked the cervical opening, preventing the entry of microorganisms. About 10% of women also experience a flow of warm amniotic fluid from the uterus before labor. The thin membranous amniotic sac that had protectively surrounded the infant has ruptured, an event commonly spoken of as "breaking of the bag of water." Labor is almost certain to begin within hours. In most instances, however, the "bag breaks" only when labor is already under way.

What prompts labor to begin is not yet clear. Several biochemicals may be involved, but prostaglandin, a complex hormone that is found in both sexes, certainly plays a role (Chapters 3, 4). Even fractional amounts cause powerful muscular and uterine contractions. In addition, prostaglandin concentration has been reported high toward the end of pregnancy. It is also possible that the infant contributes to the onset of labor. Fetal membranes may possess chemical triggers that could induce prostaglandin manufacture in the mother. Once uterine contractions start, labor has begun, although it may seem to stop and start several times. This process is usually divided into three stages.

### First stage

During the start of labor, contractions of the uterus are usually felt about every 15 to 20 minutes. They last slightly less than a minute, and are only mildly uncomfortable. As this stage progresses, the contractions increase to just minutes apart and may be intense and painful.

Internally contractions are effacing and dilating the cervix. When the cervix is completely effaced, its thickness has decreased from 2 cm (3/4 of an inch) to about the thickness of a thin piece of cardboard. Dilation, the opening of the mouth of the cervix, is often announced by the birth attendant. When it reaches 10 cm (4 inches), it is large enough for almost any infant to be born.

The first stage of labor is the longest. Women giving birth for the first time may spend 12 or more hours in labor. A rule of thumb states that the first labor stage will last half as long in second pregnancies. It should not be assumed that women have powerful contractions throughout the 12 or more hours of this stage. During most of this period the contractions are mild and relatively far apart. Most women sit, walk about, read, or talk. It is only the last hour or so that can be uncomfortable.

### Second and third stage

When the cervix is fully dilated, the infant's head, shoulders, and body begin to pass through and down the vagina. During this stage, the woman is encouraged to "bear down" with the abdominal muscles in order to assist the spontaneous contractions. When the infant's head is visible at the vaginal opening,

In Chapter 3 the role of prostaglandins in the menstrual cycle are discussed. During childbirth these hormones stimulate muscle contractions.

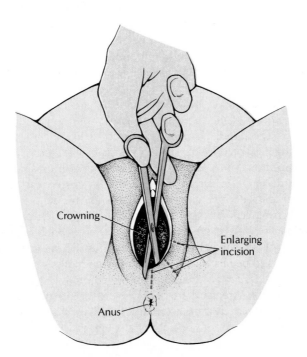

Crowning

Enlarging incision

Anus

*Figure 15-4*
Episiotomies, incisions to enlarge the vaginal opening, frequently are made to provide the baby's head a larger passageway and to prevent tearing. The routine use of this procedure has been criticized; it should be employed only when clearly necessary. The cut may be made in any *one* of the three areas indicated.

Birthing chair.

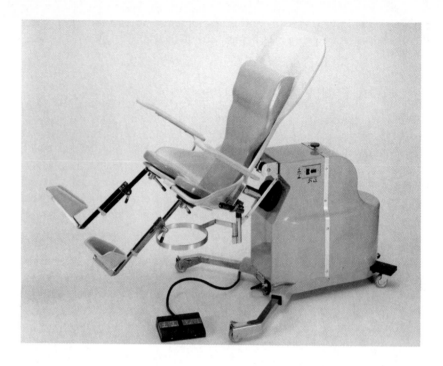

*crowning*
The showing of the infant's head at the vaginal opening during birth.

*episiotomy*
A cut in the skin in back of the vagina, intended to prevent tearing of the vaginal tissue during childbirth.

**crowning** is said to have occurred. The entire second labor stage may take as little as a few minutes or last an hour or two. It is often less stressful for the mother than the last hour of the first stage of labor.

During the second stage, an **episiotomy,** or cut in the skin in back of the vagina, is sometimes performed. The episiotomy provides a larger vaginal opening for birth, and prevents tearing of the vaginal tissue as the infant emerges. The area may be anesthetized and the cut sewn closed immediately following birth. This procedure has been criticized as unnecessary and some health care providers have stopped the practice. Gentle massage of the perineal area sometimes has been found to help relax the vagina, increasing expansion and permitting the infant to pass through without an incision or tear.

The standard birth position for delivery is for the mother to lie supine. During advanced labor, she lies on her back, knees bent, legs wide apart. But other positions may be more effective and comfortable. The mother may lie on her side or be in a crouch position. An obstetrical or *birthing chair* may also be employed. Such chairs were common for centuries and are only now being re-introduced. Birthing chairs allow the mother to sit with her legs apart while she delivers the infant through the cutaway of the chair.

When the baby is completely outside the mother, it takes its first breath of air and begins to cry. Most infants breathe or cry spontaneously. They do not need a slap on their bottom as commonly depicted. In fact, when an infant needs assistance there is suspicion that its development or the obstetrical procedure may not be normal. As the last steps, the infant's mouth and nose are suctioned, the umbilical cord is cut and tied, and the infant is cleaned, examined, and clothed.

*Figure 15-5*
Delivery.

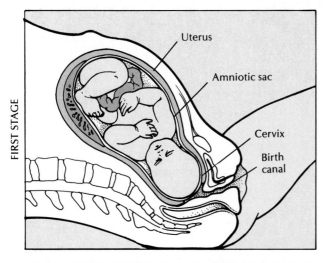

FIRST STAGE

Uterus

Amniotic sac

Cervix

Birth
canal

Uterine contractions
thin the cervix and
enlarge the cervical
opening

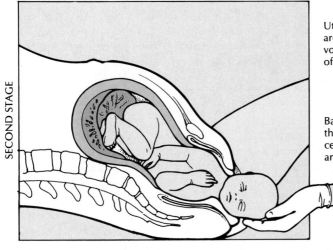

SECOND STAGE

Uterine contractions
are aided by mother's
voluntary contractions
of abdominal muscles

Baby moves
through dilated
cervical opening
and birth canal

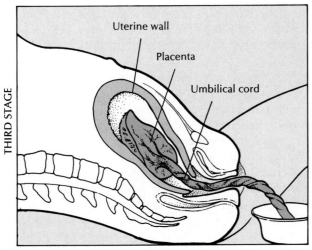

THIRD STAGE

Uterine wall

Placenta

Umbilical cord

Placenta detaches
from uterine wall
and is delivered
through the vagina

*Figure 15-5*
Delivery.

## Apgar Scores

Immediately after birth and again in 5 minutes the newborn infant's physical health may be evaluated. Obstetrical attendants commonly use a system developed by Virginia Apgar.

| | Score | | |
|---|---|---|---|
| | 0 | 1 | 2 |
| A Appearance (color) | Blue, pale | Body natural, extremities blue or pale | Completely pink, brown, or natural |
| P Pulse (heart rate) | Absent | Less than 100 | More than 100 |
| G Grimace (response to foot stimulation) | No response | Grimace | Cry |
| A Activity (muscle tone) | Limp | Some Flexion | Active motion |
| R Respiration | Absent | Slow, irregular | Good, crying |

An Apgar score of ten is perfect but attained by few infants. About 90% of infants score between seven and nine immediately after birth. When the Apgar score is taken again after 5 minutes, 98% score seven or above. An Apgar score of five or below suggests the possibility of a serious defect perhaps requiring treatment (Benson, 1989).

During the third labor stage, the *afterbirth* is expelled. This consists of the placenta, fetal membranes, and the rest of the umbilical cord. This final delivery usually takes 10 to 15 minutes. During this stage, too, the uterus is already beginning to reduce markedly in size.

## METHODS OF DELIVERY

In North America various childbirth points of view and procedures compete with one another. The objective for all is the birth of a healthy child with a minimum of discomfort for the mother. The different approaches and techniques provide couples with alternatives, among which they can choose what seems best for them.

### Medical-surgical

The medical-surgical approach begins long before childbirth. Women are instructed to visit their obstetricians as soon as they believe they may be pregnant. At that point the prospective mother will be advised about prenatal care. Many obstetricians give their patients an assortment of booklets and may suggest classes in which nutrition, exercise, and other good health care practices are encouraged. Toward the end of pregnancy, both parents are likely to be asked to attend classes in which the prospective father and mother are instructed in exercises helpful in relieving maternal discomfort and assisting birth. Most husbands are also encouraged to participate and be in the labor and the delivery rooms with their wives.

In the hospital the woman will likely spend most of her time in the labor room. While she is there, she may be examined both for her pregnancy and also for her general health. Some hospitals will require that her pubic hair be shaved and an enema, to cleanse her gastrointestinal tract, be administered. Sophisticated electronic equipment may also be utilized to monitor the progress of her labor and detect the heart sounds and condition of the fetus.

If labor is prolonged beyond a day or there is evidence of fetal distress, **oxytocin** (trade name: Pitocin) may be injected to induce labor. The possible benefits of this procedure must be weighed against the risks such as hemorrhage or heart irregularities. Few will argue with the administration of the drug when the mother or her infant is in danger. But if the induction seems to mainly suit the work schedule of the obstetrician or staff, the oxytocin may not be warranted.

At the end of the first stage of labor the mother and father or other partner move to the delivery room. At this time the medical team will prepare for the birth. *Forceps* (long tongs) may be readied to help move the baby's head out of the vagina if delivery is slowed or irregular. If the amniotic sac has not broken, it may be carefully incised to accelerate delivery. Anesthesia is likely to be used, usually sparingly, to relieve the mother of pain.

It was once common to employ general anesthesia. Gases might be inhaled by the mother or drugs might be injected so that the delivery proceeded while she was totally unconscious. But rendering the mother unconscious could also affect the infant. Many chemical anesthetics, such as the barbiturates (sleep medication), cross the placental barrier and subdue or damage the infant. As a result most physicians use very light anesthesia or limit themselves to regional sedation. They may for example inject sedatives in the spinal region or around the pelvic area so that pain sensations are diminished. In this way much delivery discomfort can be relieved, but the woman is not heavily anesthetized and her baby is not adversely affected.

**Caesarean section**    The surgical procedure known as **caesarean section** may be the most controversial medical intervention. In this technique the woman is sedated and an incision is made in her lower abdomen so the uterus can be surgically opened. (If possible, a "bikini" incision is made. This low horizontal abdominal cut can be hidden by the shorts of a two-piece swimsuit.) The baby is then lifted out of the uterus and the cut repaired. In 1970 caesarean sections accounted for about 5% of all deliveries in the United States. By 1988 the rate of caesarean section was estimated to be almost 5 times as high (U.S. National Center for Health Statistics, 1988).

Caesarean section may be recommended for many reasons. The major ones are prior caesarean, prolonged or complicated labor. Herpes occasionally is an indication for caesarean (Chapter 16). The mother with an active infection in her vagina may be delivered through an abdominal-uterine incision. In this way the infant does not pass through the vagina and thus avoids contact with the herpetic lesion (Tseng, et al., 1987).

Caesarean sections undoubtedly have saved the lives of some mothers and infants. They have minimized infant difficulties associated with lack of oxygen and prevented physical injury during difficult vaginal deliveries. But maternal death in childbirth occurs 2 times more often in caesarean than in vaginal delivery.

*oxytocin*
A biochemical that encourages uterine contractions and facilitates birth.

*caesarean section*
A surgical procedure in which an incision is made in the mother's lower abdomen so the uterus can be opened and the infant removed.

*Figure 15-6*
The number of caesarean
deliveries per 100 births in
the United States. (Data
from Gleicher 1984; U.S.
National Center for Health
Statistics, 1988.)

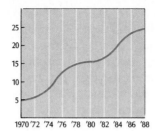

Norbert Gleicher (1984), an obstetrician with Mt. Sinai Medical Center in Chicago, believes the current rate of caesareans is unacceptably high. To stem this increase, Gleicher suggests that physicians should be subject to a careful peer review process. Their decisions and actions should be critically studied and evaluated to limit abuse of the caesarean birth method. Turner et al., (1988), propose physicians be better trained to manage labor both medically and psychologically and resort to surgery only as a last alternative.

### Prepared birth

In non-Western cultures, and in our own history, childbirth was a religious, festive, or ceremonial event. Babies were born at home. Assistance was provided by women, and no one ordinarily believed a doctor, or a man, was necessary to ensure a healthy mother and child. In this century childbirth moved from the home and *midwives*, women trained to help birth, to physicians and hospitals. By the early 1900s childbirth had become a medical event. Mothers and infants were in a hospital, just as if they were ill.

There were numerous health advantages to medicalizing pregnancy and birth. But the hospital environment with its emphasis on drugs, anesthesia, surgery, and confinement may also have produced its own problems ranging from anxiety to unnecessary medical intervention.

The first physician to try to move childbirth away from the medical arena was Dr. Grantley Dick-Read (1932). He coined the term **natural childbirth.** He maintained that if women knew what to expect and were taught to relax and to strengthen their abdominal muscles, birth could occur with minimal medical help. If they chose, they could still go to a hospital. But since they had conditioned themselves for **prepared birth** (the term now preferred to Dick-Read's phrase), their deliveries would be easier.

**Lamaze** Two decades after Dick-Read, a French obstetrician, Fernand Lamaze, extended the "natural" birth method. A month or two before birth, mothers were taught what to expect and specific techniques such as *relaxation, breathing,* and *stroking* of the abdomen. Instruction in exercises included squatting in a "tailor" fashion and pelvic contraction. The expectant mother also had to be accompanied by a coach, her husband or other support person, who remained close at hand during labor and delivery. The coach provides encouragement, as well as helping guide proper breathing, relaxation, and so on.

*natural childbirth*
Method of childbirth preparation undertaken to minimize the need for anesthesia and other medical intervention.

*prepared birth*
The term now preferred to describe natural childbirth and similar methods that stress prenatal exercises and learning for the mother, and couple, to minimize medical birth procedures.

The point of all this activity, Lamaze contended, was that it broke the conditioned link that automatically coupled childbirth effort with pain. Lamaze taught that childbirth was hard, strenuous work, but not necessarily painful.

The Lamaze techniques are currently quite popular. Many births, regardless of the setting in which they take place, employ these or similar methods. During the first stage of labor, shallow breathing and panting are usually suggested. During the second stage the patient is often asked to sit in a tailor position holding her knees from the outside and alternately pushing and panting. At the same time, the support person may lightly massage the woman's back and offer encouragement. Finally, a most important part of the entire procedure is that the coach, commonly the father, participates fully throughout the birth. This not only offers the mother reassurance, support, and intimacy, but gives the father an immediate sense of participating and being needed (Benson, 1989; Lamaze, 1972).

**Leboyer**　Frederick Leboyer, focuses on what he believes are the needs of the newborn. Although the infant may be born in a hospital, every effort is made to make the passage from the womb into the world as gentle as possible. Leboyer says that ordinarily the child is traumatized by being harshly pushed and pulled into the world and greeted with bright lights, noise, cold, and pain.

To bring about a *Birth Without Violence* (1975), Leboyer designs the delivery room to accommodate the child. The room is very warm; lights are dim; voices are soft; and noise is minimal. The baby is gently bathed in warm water and cuddled by the mother almost immediately after birth. Supposedly painful procedures such as severing the umbilical cord, administering antibiotic medication to cleanse the baby's eyes, or giving an injection of a blood coagulant (a frequent medical procedure) are delayed as long as possible.

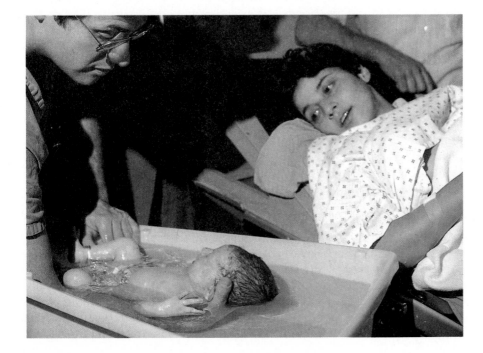

A Leboyer-style bath.

Couple preparing for
childbirth.

Prepared birth methods have moved from being considered eccentric alternatives to acceptance. Many traditionally trained obstetricians who would routinely practice medical-surgical delivery now encourage patients to learn these techniques. Birth can be made "more natural," more comfortable, and feel less medical and foreign. Mothers and their partners prepared through education and exercise can experience birth as a wholesome, joyful event that aids the psychological bonding of parent and child (Wideman and Singer, 1984).

### Location and provider

In addition to a choice of birth procedures, parents now also have options on locations and birth professionals. A woman may give birth in a hospital, or *maternity* or *birth center*—facilities designed just for childbirth. If the mother has had a difficult birth history or expects complications, a hospital may be the best choice. If a birth center is well equipped and professionally staffed, it might be strongly considered. Home birth may be appropriate for healthy women when no complications are expected and expert care will be present. The soundest decisions are made when the expectant mother's health and pregnancy are carefully monitored and she discusses her options and choices with an informed and competent health care provider (Ryan, 1982).

Government regulations and licensing of birthing centers and obstetrical care providers vary from state to state. Before using a facility or person, thoroughly check qualifications, experience, and provisions made for emergencies.

Who shall provide obstetrical care? In the United States, male obstetricians have been the rule. But increasingly obstetricians are women and many non-physicians have entered the field. In some states registered nurses may be trained for childbirth and a few states have revived midwife licensing. Actually the nurse-midwife is not new. It has been a standard profession in Europe for hundreds of years. In the United States it gained popularity during the depression years in the 1930s. Nurse-midwives provided obstetrical and infant care

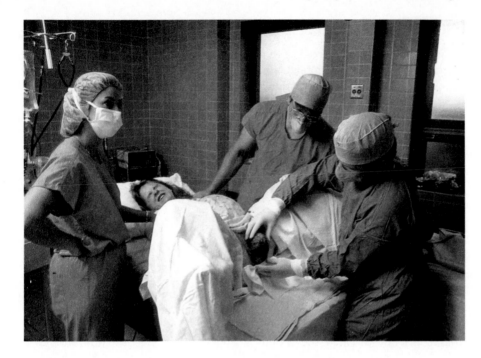

Prepared birth may take place at home, in a birthing center, or a hospital.

to those living in rural and impoverished regions. Whether or not a midwife or a physician is chosen should depend on both the obstetrical health providers' expertise and the mother's or parents' personal needs and viewpoints.

*In Sum*

Most married couples have children. Those who carefully decide whether or not to have children are most satisfied with the presence or lack of offspring. After conception fetal development is divided into trimesters. The first trimester is a period of rapid growth with the development of every organ and system. Maturation continues during the second trimester and there is a chance for a live birth at the end of 6 months. Toward the end of the last trimester, the fetus moves lower in the pelvic cavity and physiological preparation for birth begins.

Pregnancy is signaled by a missed menstrual period and other signs. Home pregnancy test kits can confirm a pregnancy 2 weeks after the first missed period. Prospective parents may react with pleasure or anxiety. As pregnancy proceeds, mothers may experience some discomfort, but both partners usually feel more secure about becoming parents. Childbirth is divided into three stages, with the first being marked by uterine contractions. During the second labor stage, the infant moves through the cervix and vagina and is born. The afterbirth is delivered in the third stage. Most deliveries are in hospitals and are medically oriented. More than one in five births is by caesarean section. Increasingly parents are also choosing prepared birth using Lamaze and other techniques.

## PREGNANCY COMPLICATIONS

In most instances pregnancy proceeds smoothly to the birth of a healthy child. Serious complications are not common, but their warning signs should be known. If a problem occurs, treatment can often save the pregnancy.

### Miscarriage

*miscarriage*
Expulsion of the embryo or fetus during the first months of pregnancy before it is viable.

**Miscarriage,** also called a spontaneous abortion, occurs in about a tenth of all pregnancies. Most expulsions of an embryo or fetus that cannot survive take place within the first 4 months after conception. If the fetus is almost full term and born dead, it is called *stillbirth,* an uncommon occurrence today. Miscarriages may be the relatively normal result of the body rejecting a seriously impaired embryo or fetus or could be a consequence of hormonal or structural deficiencies in the mother.

Estimates suggest that up to a third of all miscarriages are hidden since they occur during the first month of pregnancy. Most of these are perceived by the woman as little more than an unusually heavy or uncomfortable menstrual period that is several weeks late. The blastocyst or embryo that is rejected is so small that the mother does not realize she has miscarried.

Miscarriages herald themselves by bleeding and cramping. Most miscarriages do not threaten the mother's life, but medical attention should be sought. A woman who miscarries still has a very good chance of subsequent pregnancies being completed and then giving birth to a healthy child (Benson, 1989).

### Prematurity

A premature infant is one who is born early in the last trimester and weighs 5 pounds or less. Premature infants require special hospital care and are often

Premature infants are often kept in an incubator until they are sufficiently developed.

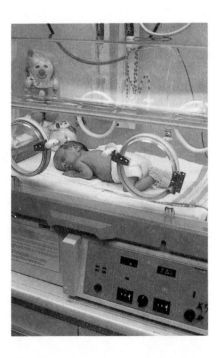

kept in an incubator. With this equipment, temperature and oxygen can be carefully controlled and the baby can be protected as much as possible from infection. Premature babies who are larger, 4 to 5 pounds, have an excellent chance of doing well. Those who are quite small, 2 or 3 pounds, may not survive. In these latter infants, there is also a substantial risk of mental retardation, paralysis, or other handicap.

## Toxemia

About 5% of women develop *toxemia* of pregnancy during the last trimester. The usual symptoms are headache, dizziness, edema (swelling of limbs and face), high blood pressure, convulsions, and coma. The cause is not known, but malnutrition, particularly a diet very low in protein, often plays a role. The usual treatment involves encouraging birth, bed rest, sedatives, and a special diet (Benson, 1989).

Excessive weight gain, as well as improper eating, plays a role in toxemia. This underlines the need for a well-balanced and appropriate diet during pregnancy.

## Ectopic pregnancy

In about 1% of all pregnancies, the fertilized egg plants itself in the fallopian tube, or other organ, and not in the uterus where it is supposed to grow. In such **ectopic pregnancies** (meaning abnormal location), the embryo may develop for a month or two before symptoms indicate that something is wrong. In tubal pregnancies, the most frequent form of ectopic development, the woman may have ceased menstruating, and tests confirm a pregnancy. A tender mass may be felt in the lower abdomen along with severe cramping. When this occurs with heavy or unusual bleeding, ectopic pregnancy is a likely possibility. Since hemorrhage is life threatening, surgery is usually necessary. With surgical intervention, however, most women recover fully and retain their ability to become pregnant and give birth.

*ectopic pregnancy*
Development of the fertilized egg in the fallopian tube or elsewhere outside the uterus.

## Rh incompatibility

The majority of people have a blood factor described as Rh positive. About 10% to 20% of the population is Rh negative. It is possible, therefore, for an Rh-negative mother with an Rh-positive husband to be pregnant with an Rh positive infant. This does not usually present any problem in first pregnancies. But the following could happen: if sufficient blood cells from the Rh-positive infant pass to the Rh-negative mother, her defensive system could be triggered and produce antibodies; in subsequent pregnancies these defensive antibodies could accumulate and large numbers could cross the placental barrier to attack the blood structure of the fetus; the result for the child could be anemia and neurological and liver damage. Today, however, the Rh factor is seldom a problem. First, good prenatal care, including blood tests, will detect this possibility. Second, the immunological system of the mother can be temporarily neutralized by an injection of RhoGAM so that she does not build up antibodies. In a few instances blood may also be transfused to the fetus while it is still in the uterus.

Rh incompatibility could present a problem, even if the first pregnancy does not result in childbirth. A brief period of pregnancy followed by miscarriage or abortion may be sufficient time for the antibodies to develop in the mother.

## False pregnancy

False pregnancy, **pseudocyesis,** is an infrequent medical-psychological condition in which a woman becomes convinced she is pregnant. Usually there is a marked conscious or unconscious wish to have a child, and the body seems to

*pseudocyesis*
False pregnancy. It may be a result of marital conflict or unconscious needs. Often both partners can benefit from counseling.

respond to the motive. Such women stop menstruating, breasts enlarge, morning sickness occurs, and there may even be abdominal swelling. Obstetrical tests that clearly show there is no pregnancy may not be believed. But when, after months, menstruation returns and there are no valid signs of fetal existence, the pseudocyesis ends. It usually leaves a disappointed and depressed person. Psychotherapy is often needed.

## PRENATAL CARE

It is well known that a healthy mother is most likely to give birth to a healthy baby. But many people assume that the mother need not concern herself until she is pregnant. It certainly is important to have exercise and good nutrition and avoid alcohol, drugs, and tobacco when pregnancy is confirmed. It is of even greater advantage for health care to begin for both parents before conception.

It may come as a surprise, too, but the United States, which in many ways provides better medical help than most nations of the world, seems to lag in prenatal care. Part of the reason is the continuing high teenage pregnancy rate (Chapter 8). Many adolescents deny or hide their pregnancy for months, not seeking professional care or advice. Prebirth care is also deficient in many socioeconomically low and inner-city areas where prenatal services are either not available or avoided. The result is that many other Western nations, such as Canada, Sweden, and France, have a significantly better record of healthy births. Currently, the infant mortality rate, the number who die during their first year, is 8 per 1000 among white parents and double that for minority parents. A major educational effort plus adequate funds and facilities must be available to critical segments of the population so that they, too, get good prenatal care and substantially increase the chances for a healthy child and mother (Tanfer and Horn, 1985; U.S. National Center for Health Statistics, 1988).

### Genetic counseling

Who we are and what we will become is in part determined *before* we are born. The genetic makeup of the egg and the sperm that unite determine a vast number of physical and perhaps psychological characteristics of the child. For this reason, it is important for every couple to understand the genetic contribution they may make to their offspring. For most women and men, searching their physical heritage will reveal nothing startling. Perhaps they will discover that they come from a long line of red-haired or short, muscular people. Their offspring then have a good likelihood of having some of these characteristics. A few men and women will find genetic defects that may require careful professional evaluation.

The impairment in the family background may be one in which the genetic contribution is only marginal, as is the case with arteriosclerosis. Or the disorder may have a substantial tendency to be inherited as is the case with **Tay-Sachs disease;** in these instances, a physician or trained genetic counselor usually suggests that the parents undergo physical and chromosomal examination. Such an evaluation will enable the counselor to inform the couple of the pos-

Good prenatal and pregnancy care assures most parents of a healthy child.

*Tay-Sachs disease*
A rare and fatal neuromuscular disorder present at birth.

sible consequences of a pregnancy. It is then up to the prospective parents to decide what risks they are willing to take, whether to consider abortion, or perhaps forgo having their own biological children in favor of adoption.

**Amniocentesis** is a diagnostic method that can identify at least 100 different fetal defects. In this procedure a syringe with a thin, 3½-inch needle is inserted through the abdomen and into the uterus. Preceding this operation, sound waves, ultrasonography, produce a picture of the fetus. This step permits the doctor to determine where to insert the needle so as not to injure the fetus.

Almost an ounce of fluid is withdrawn from the amniotic sac and then sent for laboratory study. In the lab, the fluid itself is tested for the presence of biochemicals that could suggest cystic fibrosis, Rh incompatibility, as well as numerous difficulties affecting the liver, lungs, or the development of the brain and spine. There are also cells shed by the fetus in the amniotic fluid, and these are cultured for 2 to 4 weeks. When matured, the cells can be examined to detect the fetus' sex and conditions such as Down's syndrome and other abnormalities.

Overall, amniocentesis is a highly reliable and relatively safe procedure. A serious complication (premature birth or infection) occurs in less than 1 in 100 cases. In most instances the side effect, such as vaginal bleeding or fluid leakage, is minor. But because there is a very small risk, amniocentesis should not be considered for trivial reasons, such as just to find out the sex of the fetus. Currently physicians follow these guidelines. Amniocentesis is probably indicated under the following conditions to *help* make a *decision whether* or not to *abort:*

1. A previous child with a hereditary or congenital disorder
2. A parent who has an abnormality or who is carrying a defective gene that could affect the child
3. A mother who is over 35 years old

A major disadvantage of amniocentesis is that to be performed effectively the woman must wait until the sixteenth week of her pregnancy. After the procedure the prospective parents may have to wait several more weeks for the laboratory report, so that it is possible for the pregnancy to be advanced 5 months before results are known. By this time the pregnancy is approaching the outer limit for abortion.

**Chorionic villus sampling**    CVS is a new procedure for detecting embryonic abnormalities. As early as 8 weeks into pregnancy a physician can insert a plastic catheter through the vagina and cervix into the uterus, guided by an ultrasound monitor. A tissue sample from the chorionic villi (thread-like protrusions from the fetal membrane) is withdrawn for analysis and the results may be available a week or so later. This means that the parents and physician can know the condition of the child being carried as early as the first trimester.

Chorionic villus sampling usually takes about 15 minutes, does not require anesthesia, and is just mildly uncomfortable. Tens of thousands of procedures have been performed, and it seems as if it is about as reliable and safe as amniocentesis. If further studies confirm CVS validity, it may replace amniocentesis since results are available much earlier, easing the difficulties of making a decision (Goldsmith, 1988).

*amniocentesis*
A diagnostic method that can identify fetal defects by extracting and analyzing the amniotic fluid.

Ultrasound techniques have been criticized for their potentially injurious effect on the fetus. Current studies have shown, however, that ultrasound is safe when properly used by trained personnel.

*Figure 15-7*
Chorionic villus sampling.

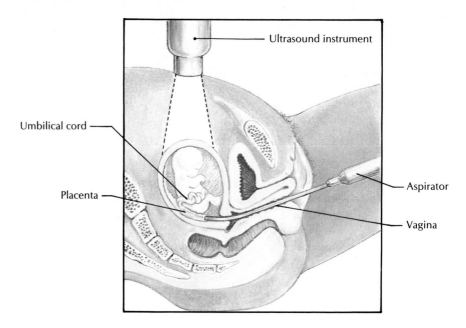

Ultrasound instrument

Umbilical cord

Placenta

Aspirator

Vagina

### Intrauterine environment

We all recognize that the environment a child is born into has a critical effect on its development. A child given good educational, physical, and emotional care is likely to be more accomplished and healthier than one denied these advantages. But environment does not begin at birth. It starts 9 months before, when the sperm and egg unite.

**Nutrition**    Nutrition plays a critical role in the child's intrauterine life. The mother who is malnourished is 5 to 10 times more likely to have a miscarriage and will almost certainly give birth to an underweight infant in precarious health. To avoid these consequences, pregnant women are advised that unbalanced diets and, just as important, overeating should be avoided. Expectant mothers require only about 300 additional calories a day (a small cheese sandwich) and total weight gain should range between 15 and 25 pounds.

Vegetarians need not become meat eaters to have a healthy child. Vegetarians who eat fish or dairy products can get all the protein and associated nutrients from sufficient quantities of these foods. Women who are strict vegetarians can still have a diet ample in protein by including brown rice, whole wheat, tofu (bean curd), soy, and other beans.

**Drugs and medications**    Drugs are potentially perilous during pregnancy. Most chemicals pass the placental barrier so that a short time after the mother has used the drug she has involved the fetus. A generation ago, physicians prescribed thalidomide to pregnant women to reduce nausea and facilitate relaxation. The drug was deemed safe. A year after the drug was widely used it became evident that the medication caused both fetal death and *phocomelia*. The latter is a severe birth defect in which infants are born without limbs, and hands are attached directly to the trunk.

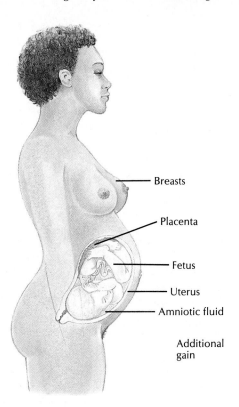

*Figure 15-8*
Normal weight gain in
pregnancy ranges between
15 and 25 pounds.

Breasts

Placenta

Fetus

Uterus

Amniotic fluid

Additional
gain

The thalidomide experience and the known potential of many medications and recreational drugs to be dangerous have made many health care providers extra cautious. Many now urge that no drugs of any kind be taken unless they are necessary and are medically supervised. This rule is especially important during the first trimester of embryonic and fetal life when vital organs are being formed and the possibility for damage is greatest. The possible effects of some common drugs are summarized in Table 15-2.

**Disease**   The placenta is an effective barrier for most microorganisms. Even the bacteria causing severe and life-threatening infections such as pneumonia are blocked by the placenta. But the placenta does not offer perfect protection. Many viruses, which are much smaller than bacteria, cross the placenta and attack the infant. There is suspicion that the virus responsible for mononucleosis (Chapter 16), a common disease among college students, may damage the fetus. Even the viruses responsible for the common cold and influenza have been suspected of sometimes causing embryonic or fetal damage.

Rubella (German measles) is a mild and harmless disease in adults. However, the German measles virus seems to have a particular affinity for the brain and central nervous system of the embryo. In 1964 a rubella epidemic infected nearly a million Americans, some of whom were mothers in their first trimester of pregnancy. The result was that 50,000 seriously mentally retarded children were born in 1965. A few years after this epidemic, a vaccine was developed. Women who are vaccinated are protected against the disease (Shephard and Shephard, 1985).

*Table 15-2*

**Pregnancy, Drugs, and Medication***

| Substances | Possible effect on embryo or fetus |
|---|---|
| **Medications** | |
| Antibiotics—penicillin, streptomycin, tetracycline | Impaired hearing, dental discoloration, spontaneous abortion |
| Aspirin | Bleeding |
| Sleep medications—barbiturates, Dalmane | Bleeding, facial malformation |
| Tranquilizers—Librium, Valium | Blood disorders, skeletal defects |
| Vitamin D | Heart defects, bone malformations |
| **Hormones** | |
| Androgens | Masculinization of female fetus, infertility |
| Diethylstilbestrol (DES) | Vaginal or testicular cancers |
| Estrogens | Feminization of male fetus, infertility |
| Oral contraceptives | Genital-reproductive organ malformation, heart defects |
| **Illicit and recreational drugs** | |
| Alcohol | Low birth weight, facial and limb malformations, cardiovascular and neurological defects, possible *fetal alcohol syndrome* |
| Caffeine | Suspected of possibly causing cardiovascular defects |
| Heroin, cocaine | Convulsions, embryo/fetal addiction and death |
| Tobacco smoking | Underweight, prematurity |

Data from Creasy and Resnick, 1985; Goldberg, Leahy, 1984; and others.
*NOTE: This is only a partial list of drugs and medications that adversely affect the embryo and fetus. Many nonfood substances, particularly if taken *in large amounts,* may injure the developing infant.

**Age** The age of the parents is an important prenatal factor. As we pointed out at the beginning of this chapter, more older women are becoming mothers for the first time. The age of first fatherhood has also advanced. With advancing age, the number of male sperm decreases and the proportion that are malformed rises. But while the age of the mother has been documented as contributing to pregnancy complications and birth defects, the role of the father is not yet clear. One hypothesis suggests a chromosomal deterioration in the ova with advancing age. Women are born with a full complement of eggs, one of which ripens every month, ready for fertilization. Sperm, in contrast, are constantly produced; they do not age for 20, 30, 40 or more years as do eggs (Chapters 3 and 4).

A dramatic example of the effect of maternal age on the embryo or fetus is illustrated by *Down's syndrome*. This is a serious form of mental retardation ordinarily caused by failure of proper chromosomal division during fertilization. The result is an extra chromosome (47, instead of 46) in all body cells. Down's syndrome may vary in severity, but those with marked features are usually short in stature; their heads and faces may seem flattened, and their eyes appear slanted. IQs are typically between 40 and the 60s. This means that although most people with Down's syndrome can speak fairly clearly, their vocabulary and more sophisticated communication skills tend to be somewhat limited. Most do only simple counting, and many are unable to read even simple material.

At age 20 a mother has only one chance in 2000 of giving birth to a child with Down's syndrome. By age 35 the odds have shortened to one in 300. By age 40 the odds are about one in 90, and by age 45 a woman's chances of having a child with Down's syndrome are 1 in 40. We could also, of course, look at these numbers more optimistically. Even a 45-year-old mother has better than a 95% chance of *not* having a child with Down's syndrome. In fact the very large majority of mothers, young and old, have normal pregnancies and healthy children (Gillespie, 1987).

**Work and exercise**   Work and exercise are indispensable parts of good prenatal care. A generation ago pregnant women were advised to stop working and many employers had rules against continued employment. Today it is recognized that in a healthy pregnancy a woman can stay with her job until the last month. The only exceptions are especially strenuous or exceedingly hazardous jobs such as bricklaying or firefighting. In such instances it may be advisable to take maternity leave early.

During pregnancy, women are also counseled to continue their normal exercise. Sports such as tennis, jogging, and swimming can be engaged in safely

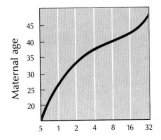

**Figure 15-9**
The number of infants with Down's syndrome per 1000 births is indicated on the bottom of the graph. The incidence of Down's syndrome and many other birth problems rises steadily with age, but most older women have normal births and healthy children. (Data from Shephard and Shephard, 1985; and others.)

Good prenatal care begins early. Modern ultrasound procedures are harmless and can produce a picture showing the development and position of the fetus.

### Having a Healthy Pregnancy and Birth

| | |
|---|---|
| 1. Plan ahead | Before you become pregnant, read, talk to friends, look at the alternatives, and be reasonably sure you want a child. Then seek health professionals who are thoroughly trained, well experienced, and understanding. You want a facility that is competent and a staff with whom you can communicate. |
| 2. Prenatal care | Before you are pregnant, practice good nutrition and develop a well-toned, fit body through sensible (not excessive) exercise. You may jog a mile or walk 2 miles, four or more times a week; or you may choose an equivalent amount of exercise by swimming, dance, tennis, or other sports. When you become pregnant, start regular visits to your health care provider and follow her or his advice. |
| 3. No drugs | Use no drugs unless medically prescribed and clearly necessary. Although an *occasional* modest drink of alcohol, caffeine beverage such as coffee, tea, or cola, or a cigarette may not be harmful, they are addictive. For this reason, the Surgeon General of the United States advised women who are pregnant to stop all smoking and drinking, and particularly emphasized the importance of *abstinence during the first trimester.* |
| 4. Early is easier | If it is possible, if your work responsibilites and life situation can be arranged to permit it, try to become pregnant earlier rather than later. Women in their forties usually have healthy babies, but the odds are more favorable and the pregnancy may be easier when you are in your twenties. |
| 5. Rest | During pregnancy, there are often days or weeks with periods of marked fatigue. Do not be a hero and insist on finishing your work or doing other arduous chores. Frequent naps may be advisable. While most women can continue their work for most of their pregnancy, even those who are very fit and able may need extra periods to relax. |
| 6. No sexual adventures | While you are pregnant, do not begin a new sexual relationship. Although a new partner may not have any sexually infectious disease, he may carry some microorganisms of which he is not aware. Pregnancy is not the time to have a vaginal or uterine infection. If coitus with a new partner does occur, he should at the least use a condom. |

by a healthy mother until the last month or two. Very demanding activities such as scuba diving or long distance running, or potentially dangerous sports like rock climbing, may best be curtailed quite early in pregnancy.

There are also exercises that are recommended during pregnancy. Generally it is advised that expectant mothers at least walk and stretch to remain physically fit. A large number of specific routines are advocated. The Lamaze techniques are quite popular. Lamaze involves squatting, sitting on the floor "tailor" fashion, abdominal and pelvic muscle contractions, and proper breathing.

Most pregnancies are healthy, but complications can occur. These include miscarriage, ectopic pregnancy, and prematurity. Good prenatal care, sometimes including genetic counseling or amniocentesis, maximizes the chance for a healthy infant. To ensure the best intrauterine environment, mothers must be properly nourished and avoid drugs and medications. Normal activity plus some special exercises are usually recommended.

*In Sum*

## AFTER BIRTH

The *postpartum* period, the days and months after birth, is typified by physical and psychological changes. If the birth was uncomplicated, not a caesarean, the mother will be out of bed the first day following birth, and within 3 or 4 days she will very slowly start resuming her routine at home. On the second or third day her breasts will start lactating, the colostrum (described earlier in this chapter) having changed to a sweetish, thin, whitish milk.

Uterine healing and contraction take place relatively rapidly and are marked by a reddish brown discharge called **lochia**. Within a week or two this flow decreases and turns yellowish. Another physical sign often reported is fatigue that lasts for several weeks. Psychologically most mothers can expect a mixture of emotions, including happiness and apprehension. Childbirth is physically and emotionally strenuous, and caring for a newborn, even with the help of a partner or friend, can be demanding.

*lochia*
A red or brownish vaginal discharge following birth.

### Exercise

Postpartum exercises assist the mother to regain abdominal muscle tone, proportions, and a feeling of well-being. Postpartum routines usually involve supine head and leg raises, sit-ups, and cat backs (on elbows and knees curve back up and down). Again, these exercises are best learned under experienced supervision.

Most exercise that is not excessively strenuous can be continued until the last months of pregnancy.

Many women learn the *Kegel exercises* after giving birth. These were originally devised by a gynecologist, Arnold Kegel, to help postpartum women who were experiencing urinary incontinence, a common problem. When they coughed, laughed, or strained, a small splash of urine might be involuntarily released. But it was soon found that the Kegel exercises not only remedied this problem, but the improved vaginal tone also sometimes increased the woman's feelings of sexual pleasure during coitus. As a result Kegel exercises are now also used in the treatment of sex problems (Chapter 17).

The Kegel exercises center about strengthening the pubococcygeal (PC) muscle (Chapter 3). This is done by several days of practice stopping and starting the flow of urine. This routine helps the woman become conscious of her PC muscle so that she can sense its contraction and relaxation. Next she alternates tensing the PC muscle for 3 seconds and then relaxing it for 3 seconds and does this routine a dozen times, three or four times daily. After several weeks the flutter variation is practiced. This involves tightening and releasing the PC muscle in rapid succession. The third exercise, added after 2 months, is to imagine a finger at the vaginal opening and drawing it up into the orifice. The fourth Kegel exercise is a bearing-down activity. Picture pushing an object like a tampon out of the vagina and bear down as you do so.

The Kegel exercises should be done a dozen times four times daily. They can usually be practiced unobtrusively. Kegel exercises may be done, for example, while waiting in line, sitting in a car, brushing teeth, or talking on the phone. Many women find that they accelerate the return of good vaginal muscle tone and continue the exercises for many months or years.

### Breast-feeding

A decision that should be considered before birth is whether to breast- or bottle-feed. Earlier in this century, nearly all mothers breast-fed. By the 1940s and 1950s, however, breast-feeding had fallen out of favor and was looked at with some embarrassment. A number of factors contributed to this shift. Manufacturers of bottles and milk formulas promoted the idea that their products were cleaner and healthier. The breast was glamorized as a sexual organ; it seemed improper to think of its mammalian feeding function. Hospitals and doctors impatiently urged mothers to bottle-feed. It saved them time and seemed so much more orderly.

The tide began to swing back toward breast-feeding in the 1970s as "natural" birth movements gained acceptance and strength. Organizations like La Leche League formed to advocate breast-feeding and educate parents. In 1978, the American Academy of Pediatrics strongly recommended breast-feeding as desirable.

Nursing provides the proper nutrients and helps protect the baby from some diseases by transmitting antibodies. It also stimulates the uterus to contract and return toward its prebirth size and location. In addition breast-feeding offers some degree of protection from pregnancy. *Lactation,* the production of milk, is stimulated by the release of prolactin, a hormone secreted by the pituitary (Chapter 3). High levels of prolactin inhibit ovulation and menses. Many women will not be impregnated while nursing and for some months thereafter. But be cautioned; nursing *cannot* be depended on to confer reliable protection. Other birth planning methods need to be considered (Chapter 14).

An infant can feel equally loved and cared for whether fed by breast or bottle.

On a personal level, many mothers enjoy nursing. It brings them a unique feeling of emotional warmth and closeness with their child. Breast-feeding may also feel sensually pleasing to the mother. It also reduces work; bottles do not have to be prepared. The proper milk need not be purchased and the infant does not have to be watched to see if she or he responds well to cow's milk or is allergic or sensitive to it.

Nursing also has disadvantages. Some women's breasts easily become tender or sore, and infants can suckle quite firmly. The milk flow may also be low or uneven, insufficient for the infant's needs. Another disadvantage for women who want to return to work outside of the home is that nursing may be a barrier. A few employers with day-care facilities on the premises, however, are permitting nursing mothers flexibility in their workday to feed their infants.

A possible disadvantage of breast-feeding is that many drugs enter the mother's milk and may have an adverse effect on the infant. Antibiotic medications and hormones, such as those found in oral contraceptives, can affect the breast-fed infant. Alcohol consumed by the mother appears in her milk quite quickly. A mother who drinks a cocktail 5 to 15 minutes before nursing gives her baby several milliliters of alcohol. An old folk remedy to quiet a crying child was for the mother to drink a glass of wine 10 minutes before nursing. This practice is *not* recommended because even small amounts of alcohol can be toxic and addictive to the infant. The nursing mother is well advised to refrain from all drugs and medications unless health demands make them absolutely necessary.

Some fathers prefer that their wives do not breast-feed. They may want to participate in the feeding of their child, and they may feel excluded during nursing. (Others, however, participate by bringing the infant to the mother.)

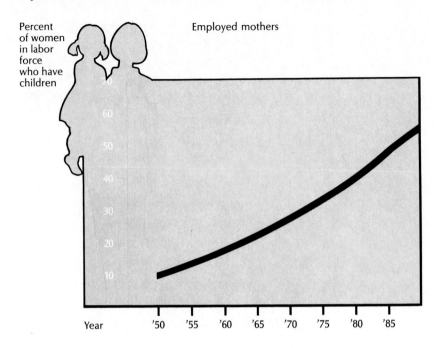

*Figure 15-10*
While many mothers may want to stay home with their infants for some time, having children need not keep mothers from outside employment. During the last fifty years the proportion of working mothers has steadily increased. (Source: U.S. Bureau of the Census, 1988.)

Some men (and women) may also not be happy with the bodily changes related to lactation.

Today over half of all new mothers nurse for at least several months. But the decision to breast-feed cannot be made on a statistical basis. Infants who are not nursed can be just as well nourished and just as affectionately cared for as those who are. Studies suggest little if any difference in the long-range health and emotional well-being of children who have been nursed and those who have been properly bottle-fed. The parents' and infant's needs and goals should be taken into consideration when deciding whether to breast-feed or bottle-feed (Reeder et al., 1983).

### Depression

Pregnancy and birth often induce mixed emotions. The first day or two are characterized by relief and happiness. Congratulations and good wishes are generously bestowed on all. But the mother and father can also be fearful. They now have to consider their new responsibilities and limitations. The birth itself may have seemed anticlimactic, almost disappointing. The baby arrived with less drama than was supposed. It may not even have been very hard work. But once the child is born the prolonged labor begins. Feeding, diapering, carrying, even cuddling the infant may not always be enjoyable. They are work. What is more, new parents can count on having their sleep interrupted. Added to these tensions are marked hormonal alterations in the mother. For example progesterone and estrogen levels drop rapidly after birth, decreasing to less than one tenth the amount found during pregnancy.

*postpartum depression*
Feelings of sadness emotional let-down following the birth of a child.

The combination of physical and psychological changes results in nearly all new mothers feeling at least a little **postpartum depression.** The infant they are taking care of doesn't look round and cherubic as in the advertisements and does not even smile at them. (At about 1 month of age infants begin to smile responsively.) As a result, many new mothers have periods when they feel sad and moody. They may have crying spells, be irritable, and have problems with sleep. For most, these symptoms exist simply on an annoyance level and within several weeks the mother feels herself again. A few new parents have more marked symptoms and would benefit from seeing a qualified counselor or therapist.

A very few individuals become so depressed and disturbed after giving birth that weeks or months later they become violent toward the child, perhaps even killing it. **Infanticide** is very rare, despite the fact that the media have often dramatized it. Mothers who have very hostile feelings or uncontrolled bursts of temper should seek immediate psychiatric help (Goldman, 1988).

*infanticide*
Killing an infant.

Fathers, can also experience emotional let-down. They may feel excluded, envy the closeness of the mother and infant and act helpless and incompetent. No matter how well they prepared to be an equal caretaker, they may feel overwhelmed by the challenge of being a parent. They tend, too, to judge their own competence by the baby's adjustment. Thus a difficult infant may unfairly depress the mother and erroneously make the father doubt his adequacy (Entwisle, Doering, 1988).

Sometimes a mother or father who seems depressed can be helped when a relative or friend aids in caring for the new baby. Sharing responsibility with another person is often good treatment.

### Sexual relations

During pregnancy some couples greatly decrease or even end sexual relations. Attitudes vary widely. Ford and Beach (1980) report Pacific Ocean societies in which sexual intercourse during pregnancy is seen as superfluous and damaging. Among other societies the semen ejaculated during coitus is considered necessary to nourish the fetus. Sexual relations are encouraged and are frequent.

Women who limit sexual relations during pregnancy often cite increasing physical discomfort and fear of injuring the fetus. A few say that they feel awkward and unattractive. Men give similar reasons. At the same time there is also considerable individual variation. A few men and women find their sexual interest heightened by the pregnancy. This increase appears most frequently soon after pregnancy is confirmed. Sometimes, however, there is a temporary surge of libido and responsiveness during the second trimester (LaRossa and LaRossa, 1981).

The interest in the safety of the fetus is realistic. Women who have a history of miscarriage or bleeding may have to significantly curtail sexual activity. Expectant mothers who are in good health and have been reassured by their obstetrical care provider are usually able to have intercourse and orgasm throughout most of pregnancy. There are two cautions. It may be unwise to have coitus with new partners, particularly if they do not use condoms. This could introduce bacteria or other microorganisms into the vagina and result in an infection (Chapter 16).

A second suggestion is to try coital positions that are less strenuous. The vaginal rear entry positions can be much easier and more relaxing for a pregnant woman than face-to-face coitus. Nonvaginal entry techniques may also be used. The penis, vagina, breasts, and other areas can be stimulated by hand or mouth. The two persons may rub genital areas against one another as described in Chapter 5. With these methods sexual pleasure may continue until the last days of pregnancy.

When should coitus end? White and Reamy (1982) reviewed a number of research studies conducted over the last decade and concluded that a general ban on coitus is not warranted. But to err on the side of safety, it should probably stop about 2 weeks before expected delivery.

**Resuming coitus**  For many weeks following birth the new mother's genital area may be quite tender and sensitive. If an episiotomy has been performed, full healing may take 4 weeks. These feelings combined with the diminished level of estrogen that typifies the first postpartum month or two often results in little interest in sexual intercourse. The obstetrical provider is also likely to recommend that the couple wait 6 weeks before resuming coitus. While coitus may be ruled out for a month or more, affection, tenderness, and perhaps sexual relations that do not involve penile-vaginal entry may be especially appropriate.

It has been reported that mothers who nurse, in contrast to those who bottle-feed, resume sexual activities earlier. Nursing can be a physically pleasing experience. But whether it is the physical pleasure of nursing, the hormones stimulated through breast-feeding, or the woman's attitude is not known. Sylvia Close (1985) reports that mothers who bottle-feed tend to wait about 2 months before resuming sexual relations while those who breast-feed wait about 1 month. In both cases partners are advised to resume coitus only when they feel completely comfortable. Men should be instructed, to always use a condom until all vaginal discharge has stopped and internal healing is complete. This precaution is an additional safeguard against vaginal infection for the months following birth. Women who breast-feed should not use oral contraception until after the baby has been weaned, since pills that contain estrogen inhibit milk production.

*A few women and men seem to lose all interest in sex for many months following childbirth. Sometimes treatment as described in Chapter 17 is appropriate and helpful.*

---

## Summary

Society encourages married couples to have children and most do. But increasingly couples are weighing the advantages and disadvantages of being parents and many choose to remain childfree. Many other couples defer starting a family until they are older. Older parents may find it more difficult to have a child and there could be more birth complications. Nevertheless the majority of children born to older parents are normal and healthy. The first sign of pregnancy is usually a missed menstrual period.

Pregnancy begins with fertilization, the union of sperm and egg. About a week later the fertilized egg implants in the uterus. During the following 2 months, the embryo grows rapidly. At 8 weeks arms, hands, feet, genitals, and vital organs have developed. After 4 months fetal movements are felt by the mother. During the next 5 months, body parts and organs are refined and the infant grows and gains weight.

Following the birth parents have many different reactions ranging from delight to panic. Both may attend birth classes, learning how to participate in the birth and be good parents. Most mothers and fathers feel well during pregnancy and continue their usual work and activities.

The fetus engages 2 weeks before labor and cervical effacement and dilation begin. When labor is well under way, the mother feels uterine contractions every 15 to 20 minutes. The pace quickens over several hours and when contractions are 2 minutes apart birth is imminent.

There are several birthing methods. The medical-surgical approach is followed by most obstetricians, and more than 20% of all children are delivered by caesarean section. Prepared-birth alternatives stress the importance of maximal participation by the woman and her partner. Many parents are now also choosing to deliver in a birthing center or at home.

The most frequent pregnancy complication is miscarriage. It terminates about 10% of anticipated births. Good prenatal care may include genetic counseling and amniocentesis. Mothers must be well nourished and guard against excessive weight gain. It is advisable to take medication or drugs only if absolutely necessary.

Following birth about half of all mothers breast-feed. Babies who are bottle-fed can be nourished and cared for just as well as those who are breast-fed. Many mothers and fathers feel somewhat let down after the birth.

During pregnancy the frequency of sexual relations between the couple generally declines. Coitus may continue in a normal pregnancy until a few weeks before labor. It can be important to express sexual and affectional interest by techniques not involving penile-vaginal entry. Full sexual relations can usually be resumed 4 to 6 weeks following the birth of the child.

---

*For Thought and Discussion*

1 What are the advantages and disadvantages of having or not having children?
2 Explain why the first trimester of pregnancy is often called the period most critical to the healthy development of the infant. What physical developments take place during the second and third trimesters?
3 Be an advocate of the medical-surgical approach to childbirth, listing all its advantages and the disadvantages of the prepared birth alternatives. Then switch sides, and do the same for the prepared approaches.
4 Miscarriage, depression, and ectopic pregnancy are all complications of childbirth. What can medical-surgical and natural birth procedures contribute to their treatment?
5 How can a mother ensure the best possible intrauterine environment? What role can genetic counseling, diet, amniocentesis, and chorionic villus sampling play in avoiding complications and defects?

---

*References*

Benson, R.C. *Current obstetric and gynecological diagnosis and treatment.* Los Altos, Calif.: Lange Medical Publishers, 1989.

Close, S. *Sex during pregnancy and after childbirth.* Hollywood, Calif.: Newcastle Publishers, 1985.

Creasy, R.K., Resnick, R. *Maternal-fetal medicine: principles and practices.* Philadelphia, Pa.: W.B. Saunders, 1985.

Danforth, D.N. (editor). *Obstetrics and gynecology.* Philadelphia, Pa.: J.B. Lippincott, 1985.

Dick-Read, G. *Childbirth without fear.* New York: Harper & Row, 1932/1959.

Entwisle, D.R. The emergent father role. *Sex Roles,* 1988, *18* (3/4), 119-142.

Faux, M. *Childless by choice: choosing childlessness in the eighties.* New York: Anchor Press/Doubleday, 1983.

Ford, C.S., and Beach, F.A. *Patterns of sexual behavior.* Westport, Conn.: Greenwood Press, 1980.

Forman, M.R., Meirik, O., and Berendes, H.W. Delayed childbearing in Sweden. *Journal of the American Medical Association,* Dec. 14, 1984, *252* (22), 3135-3139.

Genevie, L., and Margolies, E. *The motherhood report: how women feel about being mothers.* New York: Macmillan, 1987.

Gillespie, C. *Primelife pregnancy: all you need to know about pregnancy after 35.* New York: Harper & Row, 1987.

Gleicher, N. Caesarean section rates in the United States. *Journal of the American Medical Association,* Dec. 21, 1984, *252* (23), 3273-3276.

Goldberg, L.H., and Leahy, J. *The doctor's guide to medication during pregnancy and lactation.* New York: Morrow, 1984.

Goldman, H.H. *Review of general psychiatry.* Norwalk, Connecticut: Appleton & Lange, 1988.

Goldsmith, M.F. Trial appears to confirm safety of chorionic villus sampling procedure. *Journal of the American Medical Association,* June 24, 1988, *259* (24), 3521-3522.

Holahan, C.K. The relationship between information search in the childbearing decision and the satisfaction for parents and nonparents. *Family Relations,* 1983, *32,* 527-535.

Holzman, G.B., Ling, F.W., and Laube, D.W., et al. *Comprehensive Gynecological Review.* St. Louis, Mo.: The C.V. Mosby, Co., 1988.

Lamaze, R. *Painless childbirth: The Lamaze method.* New York: Simon & Schuster, 1972.

LaRossa, R., and LaRossa, M.M. *Transition to parenthood: How infants change families.* Beverley Hills, Calif.: Sage, 1981.

Leboyer, F. *Birth without violence.* New York: Knopf, 1975.

Lipkin, M., Jr., and Lamb, G.S. The couvade syndrome: an epidemiologic study. *Annals of Internal Medicine,* 1982, *96,* 509-511.

Mosher, W.D., and Bachrach, C. Childlessness in the United States. *Journal of Family Issues,* 1982, *3,* 517-548.

Reeder, S.R.; Mastroianni, L.; Martin, L.L.; and Fitzpatrick, E. *Maternity nursing,* ed. 15. Philadelphia: J.B. Lippincott, 1983.

Rindfuss, R.F., Morgan, S.P., and Swicegood, G. *First births in America: changes in the timing of parenthood.* Berkeley, Calif.: University of California Press, 1988.

Robinson, B. *Teenage fathers.* Lexington, Mass.: Lexington Books, 1988.

Ryan, K.J. Hospital or home births. *Harvard Medical School Health Letter,* November 1982, *8,* 3-4.

Shephard, B.D., and Shephard, C.A. *The complete guide to women's health.* New York: New American Library, 1985.

Tanfer, K., and Horn, M.C. *Family planning perspectives.* New York: Alan Guttmacher Institute, 1985.

Tseng, H.C., Villanueva, T.G., and Powell, A. *Sexually transmitted diseases: a handbook of protection, prevention, and treatment.* Saratoga, Calif.: R & E Publishers, 1987.

Turner, M.J. Active management of labor associated with a decrease in the Cesarean section rate in nulliparas. *Obstetrics and Gynecology,* 1988, *71,* 150-154.

U.S. Bureau of the Census. *Statistical abstract of the United States.* Washington, D.C.: U.S. Government Printing Office, 1988.

U.S. National Center for Health Statistics. *Vital Statistics of the United States.* Washington, D.C.: U.S. Government Printing Office, 1988.

White, S., and Reamy, K. Sexuality and pregnancy: a review. *Archives of Sexual Behavior,* 1982, *11* (5).

Wideman, M.V., and Singer, J.E. The role of psychological mechanisms in preparing for childbirth. *American Psychologist,* Dec. 1984, *39* (12), 1357-1371.

Brothers, J. *The successful woman: how you can have a career, a husband, and a family—and not feel guilt about it.* New York: Simon & Schuster, 1988.
> Dr. Joyce Brothers presents a lively, readable discussion of ways of managing marriage, parenthood, and a job.

Close, S. *Sex during pregnancy and after childbirth.* Hollywood, Calif.: Newcastle Publishers, 1985.
> Encouraging and useful information that helps couples keep their sexual relationship joyful during and after childbirth.

Faux, M. *Childless by choice: choosing childlessness in the eighties.* New York: Anchor Press/Doubleday, 1983.
> All couples do not want to have children. This book gives some of the reasons for and advantages of being childless. It also helps couples explore their own motives and capabilities and come to a reasoned decision.

Jones, R.E. *Human reproduction and sexual behavior.* Englewood Cliffs, N.J.: Prentice-Hall, 1984.
> A solid textbook that can provide couples and prospective parents with much of the information they need.

Rindfuss, R.F., Morgan, S.P., and Swicegood, G. *First births in America: changes in the timing of parenthood.* Berkeley, Calif.: University of California Press, 1988.
> Americans are tending to become parents for the firts time at older ages, and many remain childless. The authors analyze the implications of current trends and make some cross-cultural comparisons.

*Suggested Reading*

# *Part Six*

# SEXUAL HEALTH

## Chapter 16

# Sexually Transmitted Diseases
## *Infection and Prevention*

*When you finish this chapter, you should be able to:*

Distinguish between the myths and the realities of sexually transmitted diseases.

List the symptoms and treatments of the major sexually infectious illnesses.

Explain how to communicate with one's partner about sexual health and illness.

Evaluate the relative seriousness of disorders such as herpes, gonorrhea, trichomoniasis, and chlamydia.

Reduce the chances of contracting a sexually transmitted disease.

The sexual organs, the reproductive and related systems are durably healthy. But occasionally, as in other parts of the body, disorder may occur. In most instances the problem is easily diagnosed and can be cured. Still, since many people are anxious about sex, signs of ill health related to sexuality are often hidden or ignored. To encourage understanding and effective action the symptoms and treatment of sexual infections are presented. We will also emphasize good health practices and prevention.

## Test Yourself

### What Do You Know About Sexual Infections?

Check each question either *True* or *False*. Answers are located in the Appendix on p. 581.

| | True | False |
|---|---|---|
| 1. Herpes is a very serious disease that forces most sufferers to lead celibate lives. | ___ | ___ |
| 2. You can get syphilis and most other sexually transmitted diseases from a toilet seat or a hot tub. | ___ | ___ |
| 3. You can get rid of crabs or lice in the genital hair by a good hot shower. | ___ | ___ |
| 4. You cannot get any sexually infectious disease from just kissing. | ___ | ___ |
| 5. Birth control pills protect you from sexually infectious disease. | ___ | ___ |

| | True | False |
|---|---|---|
| 6. Only people who are not clean get gonorrhea and trichomoniasis. | ___ | ___ |
| 7. Using a condom will help prevent catching a sexually transmitted disease. | ___ | ___ |
| 8. Vaginal discharges can be cured at home by douching with water and vinegar. | ___ | ___ |
| 9. Gonorrhea, chlamydia, and other sexually infectious diseases can seriously impair a person's fertility. | ___ | ___ |
| 10. AIDS is only transmitted by anal intercourse. | ___ | ___ |

### Interpretation

A score of nine or ten is excellent. You are well informed about sexual health. Seven or eight correct is also good and above average. Most people who have not had a course in human sexuality get a score of around five or six. If you score four or less, it is probably because you have not had a chance to learn much about sexual health from very reliable sources.

## SEXUALLY TRANSMITTED DISEASES: FACT AND FALLACY

Not long after Christopher Columbus returned to Europe following his discovery of America 500 years ago, a deadly plague emerged. A new epidemic disease, **syphilis,** was claiming tens of thousands of lives every year. Europeans were frightened and desperate. It was recognized that the disease was related to sexual intercourse, but there was no treatment and no cure. Soon the anxiety turned to blame and accusations were hurled against prostitutes, Columbus's crew, and other sailors and foreigners for causing the hopeless affliction.

Syphilis and another **venereal disease (VD),** gonorrhea, remained as mysterious and sinful infections for hundreds of years. Today, both are readily diagnosed, treated, and cured. We also no longer use the term venereal disease, since it is misleading. First of all, in the minds of many people the term suggests that disease is caused by the very act of intercourse itself. It implies that just having sexual relations outside of marriage will somehow, in retribution, produce infection. The fact is that you only get a venereal disease from a per-

*syphilis*
A sexually transmitted disease that if left untreated may eventually result in heart or brain damage.

*venereal disease (VD)*
A disease that is transmitted through sexual relations. (The term is now outdated.)

son who has one. A venereal illness may be transmitted only if the person with whom you have intercourse is in an infectious state.

A second fallacy is that the term *VD* usually refers only to gonorrhea or syphilis. But there are at least a dozen other infections that can be passed on by sexual activity. We are ready, then, for a new and more inclusive term. We want a phrase that clearly points to the fact that some diseases are passed, *transmitted,* by sexual relations.

The term used by health professionals today is **sexually transmitted disease** (**STD**). STDs are illnesses resulting from some form of sexual contact. In a sense, the common cold could be an STD, since if you kiss a person with this ailment you are likely to wind up with a cold yourself. But colds can also be passed by being in a room with a sick person and inhaling the millions of viruses exhaled or sneezed by him or her. Consequently, the disorders that are labeled *STDs* are those that are *primarily* transmitted by sexual relations.

Anyone and everyone, excluding those who are celibate, can get an STD. Even a "nice" person and one who is totally faithful to her or his sexual partner can get an infection. It may be contracted from the partner, who may have gotten it from someone with whom he or she had sexual relations. People who are spotlessly clean may also contract or transmit an STD. STDs are also not the result of sitting on a dirty toilet seat. Sexual infections are the result of person-to-person transmissions.

## Statistics

It is difficult to obtain precise figures about STDs. Some STDs, such as AIDS and syphilis, must be reported by law. Physicians must report every case to the Centers for Disease Control in Atlanta, Georgia. But while STDs are supposed to be reported, it does not mean that they are. Public clinics keep fairly accurate counts, but many private physicians do not. Often patients ask a physician whom they have known for years to keep their STD quiet to protect them. One

*gonorrhea*
A common infectious disease, sexually transmitted, and often causing urinary symptoms.

*sexually transmitted disease (STD)*
The preferred term for a disease that is primarily passed person-to-person through sexual relations.

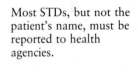

Most STDs, but not the patient's name, must be reported to health agencies.

*Figure 16-1*
Because it is difficult to obtain an accurate count of the number of people with sexually transmitted disease, there is some variation in the frequencies reported by different writers and agencies. Thus these estimates are based on several sources. The arrow at the end of the herpes bar indicates ten million "old" cases of herpes (i.e., people who continue to have recurrent lesions). (Data from Bingham, 1984; Centers for Disease Control, 1990; and others.)

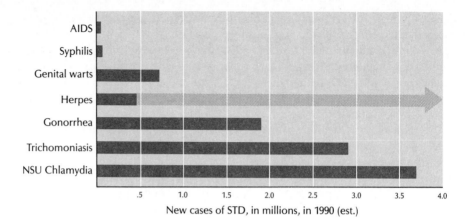

New cases of STD, in millions, in 1990 (est.)

physician related that whenever he finds an STD in one of his private patients he writes *prostatitis, vaginitis,* or *dermatitis* (rash) on the record with a secret code mark known only to himself. In this way he hides the real disorder from his staff, the insurance company, the patient's employer, and ultimately, the Centers for Disease Control.

The discrepancies in record keeping and reporting of STDs mean that all numbers for STDs are, at best, estimates, educated guesses. In this text we consider the numbers collected by public health clinics, but realize these figures represent only a small portion of those actually ill. We also include studies of sample populations and counts made by cooperating physicians in private practice.

## BACTERIAL SEXUALLY TRANSMITTED DISEASES

Bacteria (singular: *bacterium*) are microorganisms that are round, rodlike, or spiral in shape. Almost all are readily seen under a microscope and easily grown in laboratory cultures. The great majority of bacteria are also harmless, living harmoniously in their human hosts. A few, however, can attack human cells and tissue and cause illness. In this section we will describe sexually transmitted diseases caused by bacteria and similar microorganisms.

### Syphilis

Until a few generations ago, syphilis was *the* most feared sexually transmitted disease. As Brandt (1985) points out, it was seen as a dreaded, shameful, and life-threatening affliction, surely created as a terrible punishment for those wicked enough to commit a sexual misdeed. For centuries, everyone blamed everyone else for introducing the malady. The English called it the *French disease;* the French whispered it was the *Italian pox,* and many historians insisted that the Indians in the New World gave it to Christopher Columbus. His crew, it is alleged, then spread it all over Europe. In truth, as best as can be determined, syphilis has been with human beings since before recorded history and was not the exclusive problem of any one nation or people.

In the United States today, syphilis is one of the least common STDs. There are about 100,000 cases annually, which is a significant number, but it is

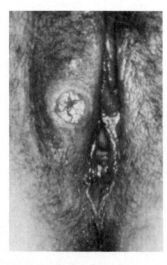

Syphilitic lesion in a female.

dwarfed by the several million cases of other STDs. Several centuries ago, syphilis was much more common. During the sixteenth century, an apparently unusually dangerous form of the bacteria gripped Europe. Millions seem to have been afflicted. The symptoms—rashes, pustules, and fevers—were severe, and death was not an infrequent outcome (Brandt, 1985).

Syphilis is caused by a bacterium called the *Treponema pallidum,* a microorganism that looks like a spiral, and, because of its shape, is called a *spirochete.* Given its character and appearance, the spirochete can corkscrew itself into the skin where sexual contact is prolonged. A break in the normal skin or an opening, such as is usually needed in gonorrhea, is not always necessary for *T. pallidum.*

Once contracted, the disease progresses slowly, taking anywhere from a couple of weeks to several months before it makes itself known. The first sign of what is called *primary syphilis,* meaning the earliest stage of the disease, is an infectious lesion on the skin called a **chancre.** This "sore" is usually painless and may appear on the genitals or on the lips, wherever the spirochete first entered. As a result syphilis may be transmitted by kissing, coitus, and oral-genital relations.

*chancre*
An infectious lesion, often on the lips, or genitalia, or in the mouth; it may be the first sign of primary syphilis.

The chancre heals within a month or two but the infection has not ended. *T. pallidum* has been spread by the bloodstream throughout the body. During this *second stage,* symptoms could include rash, fever, large genital warts, and joint pains. Even without treatment, these second-stage symptoms also improve and within several months a person may be free of obvious syphilitic signs.

The majority of untreated patients do *not* advance into *third-stage* syphilis. They become symptom free and are no longer contagious. But in perhaps a third of all patients, the bacteria slowly, over the course of 10 to 30 *years,* invade several body organs. The heart muscle and the central nervous system seem to be particularly favored targets for *T. pallidum.* In the former instance, the patient may eventually die because of an injured heart, and in the latter instance, the patient may develop nerve and brain damage resulting in **general paresis.**

*general paresis*
A mental condition resulting from brain damage that sometimes develops a decade or much longer after initial syphilitic infection.

Third-stage syphilis and its serious organic damage are very rare today. Diagnostic blood tests for syphilis are a frequent part of ordinary medical examinations and are required in many states before marriage. The result is that the disease is usually caught early, long before serious physical damage has occurred. But at whatever stage syphilis is detected, it can be successfully treated with penicillin and other antibiotic medication.

## Gonorrhea

Gonorrhea, with nearly 2 million cases annually, ranks as one of the most often encountered sexual infections. It is caused by a bacterium, *Neisseria gonorrhoeae,* a germ that thrives in wet, mucous-lined body areas such as the vagina, rectum, and genitourinary tract. In order for the microorganism to be transmitted, contact has to be close and prolonged, since the gonococci need warmth and moisture to survive. This makes sexual relations, in any of its several forms, an ideal mode for transmission.

The signs of gonorrhea in *men* are usually obvious within 2 or 3 days following exposure. There are a burning sensation during urination and a cloudy

*Table 16-1*

**Sexual Activity After Symptoms**

| | Men | Women |
|---|---|---|
| Genital discharge | 16% | 46% |
| Painful urination | 17% | 32% |
| Average number of partners in past month | 2 | 1 |

Data from Kramer, Aral, and Curran, 1980.

or puslike discharge from the penis. In a few instances gonorrhea is fairly silent. There are minimal symptoms and they are easy to overlook. When this is the case, men may not be aware that they have gonorrhea until complications occur.

In most *women* the early symptoms of gonorrhea—urinary burning and discharge—are either absent or slight enough not to be noticed. But even if a woman does not have obvious symptoms, she may still be contagious for several weeks. In fact, since the majority of women are asymptomatic, many first become aware that they have gonorrhea when they have infected their male partner (Woo, 1987).

The lack of direct and early symptoms of gonorrhea in most women and in a few men may make them carriers, unknowingly transmitting the disease. It is also true that even when men and women know something is amiss and are actually aware of symptoms, a great many nevertheless continue sexual activity. Table 16-1 shows that between 16% and 46% of patients at an STD clinic continued intercourse after noticing venereal symptoms that resulted from different genital infections. They had intercourse at a time when they knew they might be ill and also when they were highly infectious (Kramer, Aral, and Curran, 1980).

It is not unusual for people to seemingly ignore signs of genitourinary infection. Such evasion is as often motivated by anxiety and guilt about sexuality as it is by lack of information. For this reason education concerning STDs is more effective when its goal is enlightenment rather than fear.

Gonorrhea is not always limited to the genitourinary system. It may be rectal. This is more often found in homosexual males, but the condition may also occur in heterosexual couples as a result of anal coitus. In some women rectal gonorrhea results simply from the spread of the disease from the vaginal to the anal area. Gonococcal sore throat is possible too, following prolonged oral contact with infected genitalia, but this is less common.

Infection of the eyes is also possible if a person touches the puslike discharge from the genitals and then rubs his or her eyes with the same fingers. While this condition is rare in adults, eye infections of newborn infants were once frequent. The mother who had gonorrhea, whether she had obvious symptoms or not, might infect the child as it passed through the cervix and vagina and was born. For this reason, most states still require that all newborns at birth have medication put in their eyes to prevent gonorrhea.

**Complications and treatment**   Men who are not treated or who receive inadequate therapy risk having the bacterial infection move through the urethra to the prostate, epididymis, and seminal vesicles. Serious pain and fever are likely to follow, and tubal scarring may impede fertility (Chapters 4 and 14).

In about one fourth of *untreated* women, over the course of months, the gonococci may migrate to the uterus, ovaries, fallopian tubes, and other reproductive structures. Any combination of organs may become infected, and when several are involved, the term *pelvic inflammatory disease* (PID) is often used. This complication can cause sterility, as when a fallopian tube becomes inflamed and scarred or the hormonal function of the ovaries becomes damaged.

In both women and men, untreated gonorrhea, in a few cases, results in a spread of the infection through the bloodstream to several parts of the body. One consequence of this is skin eruptions. Such lesions begin as small, red, raised areas and eventually become large and filled with pus. The microorganism may also invade the joints, making them swollen and painful, a gonococcal arthritis.

Gonorrhea can be effectively treated and *cured* whether it is detected in the first week or fifth week or even later. The treatment of choice is penicillin. When the microorganism is resistant to penicillin, and this sometimes happens, an alternative such as tetracycline may be recommended. Whatever the medication used, symptoms will markedly decrease within a day. But it is important to abstain from sexual relations until laboratory tests, after treatment, confirm a cure (Sargent, 1987).

> PID may be caused by a number of different microorganisms that invade the pelvis. The condition is also not always the result of an STD. PID may have nonsexual origins.

> There are strains of gonorrhea that are very resistive to treatment and require a great deal of medical ingenuity to cure.

### Chlamydia, nonspecific urethritis

**Chlamydia,** sometimes called *nonspecific urethritis,* is an STD that resembles gonorrhea. The strange negative name, nonspecific urethritis, comes from the fact that until recently some genitourinary symptoms, almost like those of gonorrhea, could not be explained. The person seemed ill, but no gonorrheal bacteria could be cultured. Then, only a few years ago, careful laboratory studies showed that what were thought of as vague symptoms were actually due to the presence of a sexually transmissible bacteria called *Chlamydia trachomatis.*

Once identified, accurate diagnoses could be made of what had seemed to be a puzzling sexual disease. It also became apparent that chlamydia is an extremely frequent infection. The Centers for Disease Control estimate that over 3 million adults, including possibly 10% of all college students, currently have the infection (Wallis, et al., 1985) (see Figure 16-1).

The early symptoms of chlamydia resemble those of a mild case of gonorrhea. Men tend to have a little urethral discharge and some burning on urination. Women may have similar symptoms but more often are unaware of the infection. A few women and men just notice a vague discomfort or a tingling-like feeling with urination. Occasionally the only sign may be that the urethral meatus (opening) seems a bit reddish and swollen.

The consequences of not treating chlamydia in men are similar to those for gonorrhea. There may be prostatic and testicular inflammation, and fertility could be impaired as a result. In women, chlamydia may infect the uterus and fallopian tubes and, as in gonorrhea, eventuate in pelvic inflammatory disease. In addition chronic chlamydial infections can interfere with pregnancy. They may scar the fallopian tubes, cause cervical blockage, and increase the possibility of miscarriage and ectopic pregnancy (Chapters 14; 15).

## Lice and Mites

*Pediculosis pubis* is an impressive medical term for what are commonly knowns as *crabs,* but more accurately called *lice.* Pubic lice can be sexually transmitted. While a couple lies together, a louse living in the pubic hair of one partner may crawl over to the hair of the other. But lice, particularly head lice, can also be contracted by using infested combs, towels, or sheets, and through similar nonsexual means.

Pubic lice are not really a disease. They do not cause fever, infection, or any serious complications. But they do itch. Once or twice a day they pierce the skin and feed on a tiny bit of blood. Their bite and the chemicals they leave behind are irritating and create a desire to scratch.

Crabs are visible even without magnification. They are about the size of a period on this page. If they are picked off the pubic hair and put on a fingertip, their little legs can be seen waving about. Ordinary washing, shampoo, and extra cleanliness are useless against lice. They hook strongly on to the pubic hair and skin and glue their eggs firmly.

The *scabies mite* is a tiny bug only one tenth the size of a period on this page. The mite digs itself underneath the skin, making a burrow that is sometimes visible as a tiny, half millimeter long, grayish streak. Scratching the itch can transfer the scabies mite or its eggs under the fingernails from one body site to another, thus spreading the affliction. Scabies, like pediculosis, are *not* necessarily sexually transmitted. Children may pick up the organisms through rough and tumble play or by adults sharing infested clothing or the like.

Scabies and pediculosis can be cured by a prescription shampoo, gamma benzene hexachloride (Kwell). This kills *both* organisms, the louse and mite, and their eggs. In addition, an over-the-counter pediculicide, A-200 Pyrinate, destroys crabs, but may be useless against scabies. Also, since the lice and mites may infest bedsheets, underwear, and so on, it is advisable to give these objects a thorough hot laundering. A note of caution: Kwell and other pediculicides contain powerful chemicals that can provoke a rash or other allergic reaction. They should not be used routinely and directions must be followed precisely.

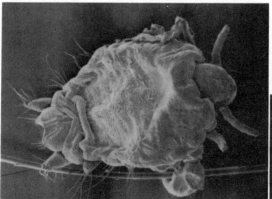

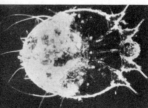

The pubic louse and the scabies mite. The actual size of the pubic louse is about equal to a dot on this page, and the scabies mite is a tenth as large.

Chlamydia is a difficult and widespread disease because its symptoms are often subtle. It also tends to mimic gonorrhea. The latter situation can trigger treatment for gonorrhea, which is penicillin, an antibiotic ineffective against chlamydia. On the other hand, when the symptoms remain subtle, no treatment may be instituted. People who suspect they have this bacterial infection or men and women who have had many different sexual partners should request examination for chlamydia. New laboratory tests are quick, simple, and reasonable in cost. If the results are positive, treatment with tetracycline, or another antibiotic, is usually successful (Nettleman and Jones, 1988).

### Trichomoniasis

**Trichomoniasis** is a sexually transmitted disease that typically causes few if any symptoms in males while most women notice an unusual vaginal discharge. The ailment is caused by a tailed *protozoan,* which can often be seen under a microscope with relatively low magnification. Trichomoniasis usually shows itself a few days to a few weeks after coitus with a contagious partner. In most women, the major symptom is a yellow-greenish frothy discharge that is fairly odorous.

Trichomoniasis (pronounced with the accent on "trick") is a frequent STD with close to 3 million cases annually. Estimates suggest that another 6 million may harbor the protozoa in their vaginas but do not get obvious symptoms. In addition, most men have symptoms that are so slight, perhaps a little urethral itching, that they may carry the microorganism for years without being aware of it. In this way, men can unknowingly be reservoirs for the disease, infecting their partners. It should also be apparent that since the condition may be relatively quiet in both men and women for a very long period of time, it can be a mistake to "blame" a new sexual partner for transmitting the malady.

The trichomonads seldom cause pelvic inflammatory disease or seriously infect other organs. The protozoa may, however, cause sufficient infection and swelling in the lower reproductive tract in some women as to make sexual intercourse uncomfortable or even painful. Thus it is always wise to obtain a medical examination if intercourse is difficult rather than to automatically assume the cause is psychological (Chapter 17).

Women often attempt to treat trichomoniasis with vinegar or other douches. These home remedies may be soothing, but they are not curative. The only effective treatment at present is a medication called metronidazol (Flagyl) or a similar drug. Flagyl may be given in tablet form in one large single dose, or several pills may be taken daily for a week. There has been some question about the safety of metronidazole since large doses can cause malignant tumors in laboratory rats. There is no evidence, however, that prescribed use by humans triggers cancerous tissue changes (Woo, 1987).

Men who have trichomoniasis are almost always symptom free. Nevertheless, as in most sexually transmitted diseases, the partner must be treated simultaneously. Otherwise the infection can "ping pong" back and forth between the treated and untreated one of the pair. One other caution: metronidazole and alcohol are chemical antagonists. When the two are consumed together, severe gastrointestinal cramps and even convulsions may occur. For this reason alcoholic beverages are strictly forbidden during treatment with metronidazole.

*trichomoniasis*
Trichomonads are technically not bacteria but simple-celled microorganisms called *protozoa.* They are discussed under the heading of Bacterial Sexually Transmitted Diseases because the symptoms they cause and the treatment directed against them are similar to those for bacteria.

*Figure 16-2*
The microorganism causing trichomoniasis. It is a single-celled organism that has flagella (strands) whose whiplike motions propel it.

## Candidiasis

There are a great many bacteria or similar microorganisms that may cause vaginal discomfort and discharge. Further, not all discharges are infectious or pathological. Many simply reflect the normal and healthy activity of the vagina and reproductive organs (Chapter 3). A common, sometimes annoying, and persistent vaginal discharge is caused by a yeast cell.

*candidiasis*
A vaginal discharge caused by an overgrowth of yeast cells normally residing in the vagina.

*Candida albicans* is a fungus that lives harmoniously in the vagina, but then something may occur that tips the ecological balance. The triggering mechanism may be oral contraceptives or a medication such as penicillin prescribed for a sore throat. These substances can disturb the vaginal environment and prompt an overgrowth of yeast cells. The result is that within a few days the woman will notice signs of **candidiasis** (also called *moniliasis*). Itching and soreness, often most noticeable during intercourse, are the main symptoms. Discharge is whitish with curdlike flecks, and it may be scant or plentiful.

Candidiasis is sometimes sexually acquired in women, and it can be transmitted to men. In males symptoms include penile irritation and burning and a reddish rash on the glans (Chapter 4).

Women often find douching soothing and men may be prescribed saline baths. Cure, however, is dependent on antifungal medications, such as nystatin (Mycostatin). These may be prescribed as ointments, suppositories, or tablets.

---

***In Sum***

STDs are common and are contracted through sexual intimacy with an infected person. Gonorrhea, trichomoniasis, and chlamydia are the most frequent bacterial illnesses. All can be successfully treated with antibiotic medication. If untreated, numerous complications can occur including sterility.

---

## VIRAL SEXUAL INFECTIONS

Viruses are extremely small particles of matter. They are visible only under the most advanced electron microscope. They do not possess a cellular structure and are often thought of as bits of protein molecules. When a virus invades the human body, it frequently takes over command of the cell in which it resides and dislodging or destroying it is difficult. In fact, there are no medications that easily destroy viruses. As a result any of the numerous diseases that they cause, including the common cold, influenza, measles, and genital herpes, are essentially incurable. Patients have to recover on their own.

### Genital herpes

*herpes genitalis*
A common STD that may be very annoying and is characterized by blister-type sores on the genitals.

Genital **herpes** is one of the more feared sexual infections. Many people become almost irrational when the infection is diagnosed. In 1985, a 3-year-old child in Maryland, who sometimes had herpes lesions, was withheld from school. The parents of the other children would not allow their youngsters to attend school unless this child was expelled. The *New York Times,* a responsible media voice, editorialized, "With a virus so common, and symptoms so minor, it makes little sense to try to avoid it by staying away from work or school" (1985).

Herpes is the name of a family of viruses. The specific virus that causes genital lesions is the *herpes simplex virus,* usually abbreviated HSV. This very

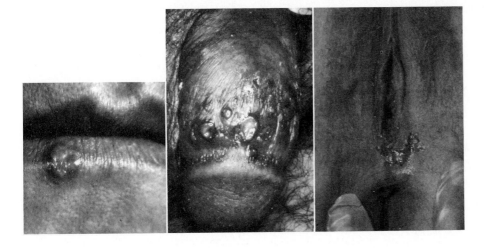

Herpes lesions on the mouth, penis, and vagina.

same virus also causes lesions on the lips and in the mouth. When HSV lesions appear in the mouth area, they are commonly called cold sores or fever blisters. These identical lesions on the penis or vagina are usually called herpes genitalis. Whether it appears on the lips, cheeks, penis, labia minora, or vaginal wall, it is still an HSV lesion.

Until the 1960s, the HSV was responsible mainly for ordinary cold sores around the mouth. There were also genital herpes lesions, but the number of people affected were very few. Then a decade or so ago, the HSV virus seems to have become more active and more contagious. Very likely a viral mutation occurred and a new strain evolved. We are unable, however, to see any microscopic difference between an HSV visualized today and one photographed 30 years ago. In any case, the virus began to appear increasingly in the genital area. Very careful analysis also identified two HSV types. HSV I often produced lesions above the waist. HSV II usually caused sores below the waist. This distinction has become blurred. Research shows that HSV I and HSV II may appear in any location on the body (Balfour and Heussner, 1984).

The herpes simplex virus is one of the most common causes of infection. Eight out of ten people have had an HSV cold sore in the mouth or surrounding area. Ten million people in the United States are estimated to have had at least one episode of an herpetic lesion on the genitals. Another 400,000 new cases are probable every year (Centers for Disease Control, 1990).

When the herpes lesion appears on the lips it may be unsightly and unpleasant. When it appears in the genital area it is likely to create fear. The combination of sexual guilt and media hype has managed to produce anxious emotions, all out of proportion to the significance of the illness. From a medical perspective, herpes is a minor illness and rarely has serious consequences (Kilby, 1986).

The herpes eruption typically begins with an itchy, tingly, painful feeling. At the same time, the patient may feel achy, fatigued, and feverish. Lymph glands in the groin or neck, or both, may also be enlarged and tender. The lesion itself may consist of one or two pea-sized blisters or a host of pinhead-sized eruptions. If the blisters are in the mouth or throat, there may be pain on talking and swallowing. If the blisters are in or near the urethra or the vaginal folds (Chapters 3 and 4), there may be a stinging, burning feeling on urination.

Herpes is not unique among viruses in the way in which it recurs. Many viral illnesses such as the common cold and influenza repeat periodically.

*Figure 16-3*
Herpes: yearly new cases.
(Data from Centers for
Disease Control, 1990.)

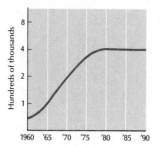

A genital herpes lesion
could have a nonsexual
origin. If you have a cold
sore on the lip and rub it
and then touch your
genitals, you might
autoinoculate.

During the eruption and blister stage, hundreds of millions of viruses are in and around the lesion; this is the most contagious period. If the blisters are left alone, within 2 to 4 days they break down and form a hard crust or scab. Contagion is now considerably reduced and some individuals begin sexual intercourse again using a condom. After a week or so the crust falls off revealing healed skin underneath. It is safe to resume sexual relations. The entire herpes episode may take as little as 1 week or as much as 3 weeks.

Throughout the attack the lesion is best left alone, not covered by any sort of bandage. No cream or ointment should be applied unless prescribed. It is important, too, particularly during the blister stage, not to touch, rub, or scratch the area. If viruses get on the fingers, and the fingers touch another part of the body, the HSV may be transferred to a new site. This is called *autoinoculation* (self-infection). It is important to point out that the cornea of the eye is particularly vulnerable to herpetic infection so that care should be taken never to autoinoculate this site.

After the lesion is healed the virus has retreated deep into the nerve endings and migrated to the base of the spinal cord. There it remains dormant for months or years. As a result, about a third of all people who have a herpes lesion will only have a recurrence every few years. Another third may have repeat episodes every few months.

There has been concern about cervical cancer and birth damage. To be sure there is a slight correlation between cervical cancer in women and the presence of HSV. But the correlation is modest, and its meaning is not entirely clear. Since correlation is *not* cause (Chapter 2), it could be that both herpes and cervical cancer are linked through a third set of circumstances about which we now know very little. Nevertheless, it is good preventive care for a woman who has herpes, or a woman whose partner has herpes, to have a yearly Pap test (Chapter 3). Cancer of the penis is very rare, and found just as infrequently in men with or without HSV infections.

The HSV virus and many other viruses, including those that cause mononucleosis and influenza, may damage newborn children. Infants have few immunological defenses against viruses. These microorganisms may attack the child's central nervous system, destroy neurological and brain tissue, and damage other vital organs. A mother who is in labor and has an active herpetic lesion may transmit the virus to her baby as it passes through the birth canal. For this reason a woman with an HSV history should alert her obstetrician. Signs of a herpetic lesion in the vaginal area of a woman giving birth mandate a caesarian delivery, which avoids passing on the infection to the infant (Chapter 15).

This description should not induce future mothers to believe that because they have had herpes lesions their childbirth will be dangerous and difficult. Even women who have herpes lesions that recur do not usually have an active infection during childbirth. Thus despite the large number of women of child-bearing age who have herpes genitalis, an infant whose health is impaired because of HSV is rare. Balfour and Heussner (1984) estimate that about 1 in 10,000 infants is adversely affected by genital herpes in the mother. This number looks even smaller when compared to the number of infants impaired by those mothers who smoke or drink (Chapter 15).

For most people as the HSV lesion recurs over the years it becomes less bothersome, heals more rapidly, and breaks out less frequently. In short, there is no reason to regard oral or genital herpes with dread. HSV lesions very seldom cause genital cancer or birth defects. For the large majority of people, the HSV infections are a nuisance, sometimes uncomfortable, frequently unsightly, but all in all rarely dangerous (Haynes, 1987).

> Herpes lesions tend to recur when the site is irritated, the person's resistance is low, or when she or he is under considerable stress.

**Treatment** The recurrence of herpes, even if the usual site tingles expectantly, is unpredictable. Some people have one attack a year, and a few others have almost one a month. Even without treatment, recurrences gradually diminish and become less bothersome. This situation is tailor-made for the promotion of all sorts of cures. Everything has been advocated from vitamin C to meditation to lysine (a milk product protein and a health food favorite). There is no evidence that any of these nostrums are effective.

There are a few antiviral drugs such as acyclovir, which in ointment form reduce the severity of herpetic attacks. In pill form acyclovir (Zovirax) can be taken daily by people who often have very uncomfortable herpes episodes. It seems to substantially reduce the frequency and severity of attacks. Herpes infection can be moderated but no cure is yet available (Mertz, et al., 1988).

Herpetics Engaged in Living Productively (HELP) is an organization that has chapters in many major American cities. It tries to assist people who have social and sexual problems related to herpes. Arrangements differ, but most chapters have weekly meetings to talk over their concerns and offer solutions and encouragement.

Herpes treatment and support groups have been credited with relieving the depression and loneliness of many of their members. They encourage people to live productively despite their illness. They also serve as a meeting place for women and men. New friendships can be started and both parties spared the ordeal of educating the other about herpes (Gillespie, 1982).

Support groups have also been criticized. The advice given concerning herpes may be quite inexpert and erroneous. The major criticism of the herpes groups, however, is that they perpetuate the myth that there is something horrendous about genital herpes. Just the fact that there is a support group seems to validate the perception that herpes sufferers need to be isolated and treated with care. If herpes is to be seen realistically, as a relatively minor disease, meetings should be replaced with efforts to educate the public (Brandt, 1985).

> Sometimes a herpes lesion is triggered by too much friction during coitus. The use of a lubricating gel (such as K-Y jelly) may help reduce irritation.

### Genital warts

*condylomata*
Genital warts caused by the papilloma virus.

Genital warts, also called **condylomata**, are usually painless growths that occur on or near the genitals and/or the anus. They are caused by a sexually transmitted microorganism called the human papilloma virus (HPV). For many years these warts were relatively uncommon and considered more of a nuisance than a serious health problem. Currently, however, the Centers for Disease Control (1990) estimates that there are over a half million new cases a year. It is also suspected that in a small number of instances, and depending upon the type of HPV, they may contribute to cervical and genital cancer. For this reason, if for no other, the presence of genital warts merits a medical examination and accurate diagnosis.

The warts themselves may be flattish, more or less the size of a pea, and often appear in clusters. Their surface has been described as cauliflower-like, and they may range in color from pinkish to deep brown. The infection may be transmitted by coitus, or oral or anal intercourse. Since they may be contagious as long as they are present, sexual relations should be avoided.

Treatment is directed at removing the warts and is usually successful, although repeated attempts may have to be made. Removal may be through freezing, electrocautery (burning), or laser surgery. In most instances these are office procedures and only moderately uncomfortable (Kilby, 1986).

### Mononucleosis

*mononucleosis*
A disease caused by a virus found primarily in the saliva. Symptoms usually include fatigue, slight fever, general achiness, and sore throat.

**Mononucleosis** stands on the border between a sexually and nonsexually transmitted disease. The virus causing mononucleosis appears primarily in the saliva; extensive and intimate kissing is a mode of transmission. Contagion may also occur through the use of an infected person's toothbrush, fork, spoon, and so on. Since the latter modes of transmission are less likely, mononucleosis has been called the "kissing illness." Mononucleosis is caused by the

Mononucleosis may be transmitted by kissing.

*Epstein-Barr virus,* a member of the now familiar herpes virus family. Like other herpes viruses, the Epstein-Barr virus is troublesome but usually not serious.

Mononucleosis usually announces itself by a sore throat, mild fever, achy, tired feelings, and lymph gland tenderness in the neck and under the arms. There is no specific medication, but rest and aspirin or similar drugs to help the patient feel better are usually recommended. Most patients recover in several weeks.

## Hepatitis

There are several types of **hepatitis,** a liver disease. The hepatitis A virus (HVA) attacks the liver and is ultimately transported to the colon. Here it inhabits the feces and eventually appears in the anus. This means you can contract this form of hepatitis by eating food prepared by a contagious person who has not washed his or her hands after going to the bathroom. Eating raw or uncooked shellfish such as oysters and clams that come from sewage-contaminated waters is another way of getting hepatitis.

A *small* number of cases of HVA are sexually transmitted because the virus in an infected person may live in the anus or in the moist, warm area adjacent to it. As a result, oral-anal or genital-anal relations followed by oral-genital activities may spread the infection. Because of the nature of this transmission hepatitis type A is found more often in homosexual men.

The hepatitis B virus (HVB), like HVA, also appears in the anus. But this virus is found, too, in saliva, blood, semen, vaginal fluids, and sweat. This means that HVB may be spread in several different ways. As in HVA, sexual relations involving the anus provide a good means of transmission. Because the virus appears in the blood, blood product users such as hemophiliacs and transfusion recipients may become ill if they receive infected blood. Intravenous drug users who share a needle or syringe with an infected person may also become ill.

Finally, since HVB appears in a number of body fluids, men and women may contract the disease if infected body fluid is deposited in the mouth, anus, vagina, or any body opening. This means coitus and oral-genital relations, as well as kissing, sharing a spoon, fork, or glass, and many other nonsexual contacts, could spread the disease. HVB is thus a disease that may well be transmitted nonsexually as well as sexually.

The symptoms of hepatitis and the course of the illness are relatively mild for HVA and more pronounced for HVB. Nausea, fatigue, achiness, fever, and an enlarged tender liver are common. After a week or more jaundice, a yellowish skin color, may occur. Most patients need to remain home and rest, and some may be confined to bed. As with other viral illnesses, there is no specific medication, but good nutrition, no alcohol, and no smoking are emphasized. The illness usually lasts 1 to 4 months and all but 1% to 2% recover.

The incidence of hepatitis has increased steadily; there are now several hundred thousand cases each year. There is good news too, however. Since 1985, a vaccine has been available that protects against hepatitis. Blood product users and medical personnel who work with hepatitis were among the first to be effectively immunized. It is recommended that homosexual men and heterosexual men and women who have many partners, and are therefore at greatest risk, also receive vaccination (Bingham, 1984).

*hepatitis*
An infectious inflammation of the liver that may sometimes be transmitted through sexual intercourse.

*acquired immune deficiency syndrome (AIDS)*
An STD that is fatal.

## Acquired immune deficiency syndrome

**Acquired immune deficiency syndrome (AIDS)** is a disease without precedent in modern times. By the early 1990s a total of more than a quarter million people will have AIDS in the United States, and half this number will have died. Tens of thousands of other patients and fatalities are reported in 40 nations around the world. There is currently no cure for AIDS, and death seems inevitable.

A major difficulty in understanding AIDS is that the time between infection and clear symptoms is very long. A computer analysis by Salsberg, et al., (1988) suggests that 20% of patients will have obvious AIDS symptoms within 2 years of infection. Another 15% will have medical symptoms within 5 years, and more than half of all those infected with the AIDS virus will be sick within 10 years. Once serious AIDS symptoms develop, these authors calculate, the average remaining lifetime is about 20 months. It should also be noted that there is evidence that a small proportion of those infected with the virus causing AIDS may take longer than 10 years before becoming ill or just possibly never succumb at all (Langone, 1988).

It is not yet clear when the patient who is infected with the virus causing AIDS is most contagious. At present it seems that infectivity is at a maximum in the year or so before clear AIDS symptoms appear. But according to

Safer sex practices help prevent all STDs.

William Haseltime of Boston's Dana-Farber Cancer Institute, contagion studies show prolonged infectivity. "Once infected, a person is infectious. It's not safe to assume otherwise" (Clark et al., 1985).

**Transmission**   AIDS is caused by the *human immunodeficiency virus* (HIV). The AIDS virus attacks lymphocytes—white blood cells that play a major role in defending the body against disease. This means that ultimately the body is left without any effective immune system. It is helpless against illness. Any "opportunistic" infection that comes along may overwhelm the person. The two most common forms of AIDS-produced infections are a cancer called *Kaposi's sarcoma* and a pneumonia called *Pneumocystis carinii,* both ordinarily rare diseases.

The early signs of AIDS include fever, weight loss, swollen lymph glands, skin growths, and rashes. These symptoms are quite general and may point to any number of illnesses. They do not necessarily indicate AIDS. In 1988, estimates suggested that 300,000 Americans showed some mild preliminary symptoms of AIDS. Whether these preliminary symptoms, called *AIDS-related complex (ARC),* will eventuate in full-blown AIDS for all patients, or spare a small proportion is not yet certain (Langone, 1988).

ARC symptoms include swollen glands, fatigue, night sweats, and diarrhea.

AIDS is transmitted in almost the same way as hepatitis. The AIDS virus has been found in blood, semen, mother's milk, and vaginal, anal, and other body fluids. As a result, taking these fluids directly into the body might result in transmission of the virus. HIV is not found in the exhaled air of patients. This means that infection via a sneeze, cough, or the like is not a means of contagion.Unlike hepatitis AIDS is *not* transmitted by shared dishes or eating utensils, etc.

Unlike hepatitis AIDS is *not* transmitted by shared dishes or eating utensils etc.

Prior to 1985, people who used blood products—hemophiliacs and kidney dialysis and surgical patients—were at risk for contracting AIDS. A tiny fraction of the blood donated contained the AIDS virus and resulted in the transmission of the disease to blood product users. Since 1985, however, this source of contagion has virtually ended. In 1985 a test to detect the presence of HIV antibodies in donated blood became widely available. Today all blood is screened and infected products are removed (Centers for Disease Control, 1990).

Intravenous drug users also are at risk for contracting AIDS, if they share needles and syringes or go to "shooting galleries" for their drugs. Here they purchase the drug they want and rent or borrow a needle that has been used and possibly contaminated by an AIDS-infected addict.

The people most at risk for possible infection by AIDS are sexually active homosexual and bisexual men. There are two reasons for this. First, of all sexually active groups, (young singles, college students) AIDS happened to initially strike gay men in the late 1970s; because gay men tend to have sexual relations mainly with other homosexual men, the disease remained confined to this community for several years, from about 1978 to 1983.

The second reason is that AIDS, like hepatitis, is seemingly well transmitted by anal intercourse, a frequent practice among homosexual men (Chapter 13). This has been well documented by considerable research. For example Zachariae, Ebbesen, and Stenbjerg (1985) studied 14 AIDS-infected hemophiliac men and their families. None of the 29 parents, children, or wives of the infected men, despite close household and spousal contact showed evidence of AIDS.

The only person who did contract the virus was a girlfriend of one of the infected men who regularly was the recipient of anal intercourse.

All of this, so far, fits in with the fact that the majority of AIDS patients have been homosexual men. But being the recipient in anal intercourse is not the only means of transmission. By 1990, several thousand people with AIDS were exclusively heterosexual and most did not practice anal sexual relations. In several studies of heterosexual patients with AIDS, Redfield and his colleagues (1985) hypothesized that HIV can be transmitted by heterosexual contact. They found that in the majority of heterosexual cases the virus was apparently transmitted by vaginal intercourse or fellatio, or both.

In 1988, Masters, Johnson, and Kolodny (1988) in a very controversial book, reported their study of 800 heterosexual adults. These adults were neither bisexual nor users of intravenous drugs. The authors reported that in 400 individuals who had long-term monogamous relationships, only one had AIDS. In contrast, among those who had 10 different heterosexual partners, 8% were infected. Masters, Johnson, and Kolodny concluded that AIDS had entered the heterosexual population in a major way, and that in the coming years the infection would snowball.

It should be pointed out that the Masters and Johnson statistics are contested. Studies by the Centers for Disease Control suggest that the incidence of AIDS among single heterosexual people who have several different partners per year is about 1%. While this may seem reassuring, it should be noted that this means, of the total sexually active singles' population, at least about a half million people are infected. Given the lengthy incubation period for AIDS, few show symptoms yet.

Further evidence of the heterosexual transmission of AIDS comes from Africa. In central Africa most of those with AIDS are heterosexual. In Zaire and Rwanda the incidence of AIDS is higher than in New York City and San Francisco. But unlike these cities in which the greatest number of patients are homosexual men, in these African nations the greatest number of patients are heterosexual men and women (Langone, 1988).

**Risk behaviors**   There is a tendency, often reinforced by the way in which media report on AIDS, to assume that only homosexual men and intravenous drug users will become ill. It is true that people in these groups have been most affected. But it is *not group identity*, it is *behavior* that leads to AIDS. Anyone—heterosexual, homosexual, old, young, woman, man—who practices risk behaviors may get AIDS. The following are *risk behaviors* that may communicate AIDS:

- Anal intercourse without a condom
- Sharing intravenous needles
- Vaginal intercourse without a condom
- Oral-genital sexual relations
- Sharing objects (like a vibrator) inserted into the anus or vagina
- Intercourse, without a condom, with multiple partners, with someone who has multiple partners, or a history of risk behaviors

There are also *safer sex behaviors*. The AIDS virus needs to be conveyed directly *into* the body so that erotic touching, stroking, and light kissing are ordinarily not likely to communicate the HIV. Sexual relations can also be made much safer by the use of a condom. The word "no" may also prove very useful in declining sexual contact, particularly with a person who is relatively unknown (Fineberg, 1987). Other preventive measures will be described at the end of this chapter.

**Treatment and counseling**   AIDS has been declared the "number-one health priority," by the head of the Department of Health and Human Services. Currently, AIDS is treated at two levels. First, opportunistic infections, diseases that take hold because the body's immune system has been impaired, must be remedied. For example, pneumocystis pneumonia, which so frequently occurs in HIV infected patients, is handled with potent antibiotics. The cancerous lesions of Kaposi's sarcoma respond to chemotherapy. Unfortunately, however,

Over a thousand children have AIDS. It was most likely transmitted during pregnancy by a mother who was ill or incubating AIDS. Contagion is also possible through mother's milk while nursing.

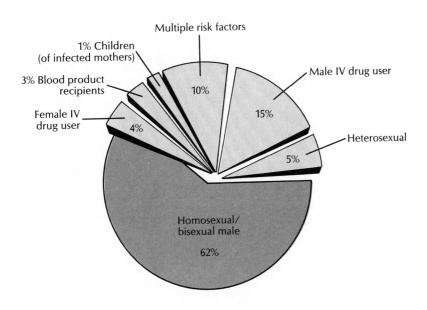

*Figure 16-4*
AIDS patients in the United States. (Source: Centers for Disease Control, 1990 estimates.)

## The Ethics of AIDS

Since AIDS is both an infectious and a terminal disease, it poses numerous ethical questions not evoked by less serious sexually transmitted illnesses. As is usually the case with complex dilemmas, it is easier to state the questions than to arrive at satisfactory answers.

### Are AIDS Tests Accurate?

When AIDS testing is called for, the technique usually used is the *enzyme immunoassay* (ELISA). Overall it fails to detect HIV infection (false negative) or calls a well person ill (false positive) in less than 3% of cases. When the ELISA is positive, the results are usually double checked with the *Western blot* test. Confirmation on this second test makes it close to certain that AIDS has been correctly diagnosed. False negatives, though rare, may occur on both tests. Both detect the presence of AIDS antibodies rather than the HIV. As a result, a person infected with HIV for only a few months, who has not yet developed antibodies, may slip by, falsely registering as uninfected.

### Routine Screening

The combination of AIDS diagnostic tests is quite accurate. Should they be required for people getting married? In this way the spouse and future children could be protected. Is it reasonable for future employers, insurance companies, and schools to test applicants for AIDS? This could assure that the applicant is in good health and will bring financial and productive benefits. Those who oppose such testing argue that HIV diagnoses are a dangerous intrusion into the right of privacy. Further, employment, school, and insurance opportunities should exist for everyone without discrimination.

### Confidentiality

By law and tradition, physicians are supposed to keep a patient's record confidential. But what should a physician do if the patient's lover or spouse calls and asks for the AIDS test results? Should the patient's identity be given to state or federal government agencies concerned with health matters? If the patient is positive, should the doctor inform medical colleagues so that if they ever treat the patient they can take proper precautions? Many physicians have argued that the rule of confidentiality is not total, that when persons' lives are at stake they may reveal critical information. The other side asserts that if the rule of confidentiality has a tiny hole in it, it—like a balloon with a pinprick—is useless.

### The Courts

All the questions asked, and many more, have been raised in many different courts. Few arguments have been definitively settled. Some courts have ruled that an HIV infected person who has intercourse with an uninformed partner is committing a criminal act. Other courts have held that reluctant surgeons and dentists must perform necessary medical procedures even if their patient is HIV infected. Several state governments and private employers have won the right to test all prospective employees for HIV and *share* this information with related agencies. The American Civil Liberties Union, meanwhile has won court decisions denying mandatory testing. The legal and ethical challenges posed by AIDS are far reaching and can touch the lives of all of us. It may well be another decade before consistent, reasonable, and effective guidelines emerge (Barry, 1987; Dickens, 1988.)

even when the first attack of illness is relieved, further episodes follow that eventually result in death.

The second level is to attempt to treat the AIDS infection itself. Compounds such as gamma-interferon have been tried in an attempt to bolster the patient's failing immune system.. Antiviral agents have also been used. Drugs like ribavirin and dideoxycytidine have had inconsistent results. The most promising drug is azidothymidine (AZT). It seems to help prolong the life of AIDS patients and be especially useful to ARC patients in slowing the pace of their disease. AZT has serious side-effects such as weight loss and anemia, thus limiting the frequency and dosage that may be employed with patients. While none of these antiviral drugs are very effective, the outlook is encouraging. By the end of the 1980s there were at least 30 different drugs to treat AIDS in various stages of clinical testing and development (Langone, 1988).

The best hope may lie in the development of a vaccine to immunize against AIDS. The difficulty in developing an HIV vaccine is that this virus tends to assume several different forms so that an effective vaccine developed today might be ineffective tomorrow. Nevertheless, there is preliminary evidence of certain "regional" constancies in the HIV molecule that might be responsive to a vaccine.

In 1988, the first AIDS vaccine was approved for clinical trials. It utilizes

A health crisis center provides counseling about AIDS.

AIDS patients who receive counseling, assistance, and support appear to deal more effectively with their illness. Often a sympathetic and caring friend or relative is as helpful as a trained counselor.

the HIV envelope precursor protein and is produced by MicroGeneSys in Connecticut. Over a thousand adults volunteered and several hundred have participated in the various phases of the study. The first years of testing evaluated the vaccine's safety, and it will probably be the early 1990s before it is known whether the vaccine is effective (Raymond, 1988).

There is no definitive medical treatment for AIDS but psychological help has been found as necessary as physical treatment. AIDS patients may react to the illness with many different emotions. Some deny the seriousness of their situation; others become suicidally depressed. More common feelings include guilt, anxiety, and anger. Most of all, AIDS patients usually want to talk, to develop a rapport, and to have their needs and doubts considered.

A special problem is presented by the patient with AIDS-related complex (ARC). For the patient with AIDS-related complex there is a high possibility of full-blown AIDS as well as perhaps a small possibility of improvement. Morin et al. (1984, p. 1290) quotes a patient who has the early signs of ARC. He lives in an uncertain world, not knowing what to do or which way to turn.

> I don't know how to live my life anymore in the most basic ways. If I'm going to get AIDS and die within a couple of years, then I'd rather not continue with school. I'd want to use the time left differently . . . . I don't even know if it's all right to kiss my lover anymore . . . . Maybe the worst part of this is just not knowing . . . . Waiting for the other shoe to drop is just hell.

**Social impact**  AIDS is not transmitted by a handshake or a sneeze. Yet, according to a *Newsweek* poll, one fourth of parents who learned an AIDS-infected child was attending school with their child would keep their own child home or ask to have the other child expelled. Another fourth would instruct their own child to carefully avoid contact with the AIDS victim (Clark, 1985).

Sometimes concern takes extreme forms. A few police and fire personnel have refused to touch or transport AIDS patients. Prison guards have picketed, demanding that AIDS patients be removed from their prison. At the other end, there have also been people who have been extraordinarily helpful and sympathetic. In San Francisco General Hospital, 13 nurses volunteered and expressed a particular interest in working with AIDS patients (Morin et al., 1984).

In the gay community many baths and other places for sexual liaisons have shut down, (Chapter 13). A few heterosexuals who have many sex partners, such as swingers (Chapter 12), also seem to be limiting their activities. In New York, Los Angeles, and other large cities, several swinging clubs have closed for lack of attendance. In a study of college students and another of homosexual men attending bath houses, half or more interviewed said that their sexual behavior had considerably changed because of their concern with AIDS. Both groups had fewer partners and/or typically used sexual techniques considered safer, less likely to spread any possible HIV infection. But still there are people, homosexual and heterosexual, who deny the reality of AIDS or take a fatalistic stance. They continue their sexual life-styles and say they are not worried (Carroll, 1988; Richwald, et al., 1988).

Considerable concern has also been evident that AIDS may set back efforts at sexual equality and increase homophobia (Chapter 13). Some clergy have spoken of AIDS as a punishment. Others have suggested that it comes as a

At the present moment, AIDS is the subject of active research efforts in the United States, France, England, Sweden, and a dozen other nations. It is projected that by 1990, well over 10,000 scientists may be working on the treatment and prevention of AIDS.

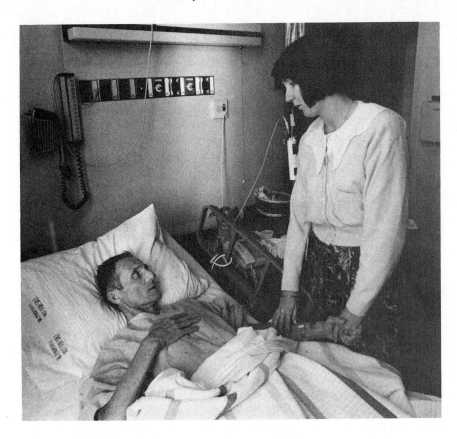

A counselor confronts a fatally ill AIDS patient.

Educational efforts have resulted in a significant shift toward safer sexual practices, particularly in the homosexual community. As a result, the incidence of AIDS among homosexual men is slowing. Cases of AIDS among intravenous drug users, however, seem to be increasing.

guide to encourage homosexuals toward heterosexuality and punish all who are "promiscuous." At the same time, it appears as if most people have responded with sympathy and understanding. Religious and social groups are increasingly offering supportive care and informational and referral services. In a nationwide Gallup poll, sampling the opinion of 759 adults, the majority believed that the fact that AIDS affected so many homosexual men has led to greater acceptance of this orientation (Clark et al., 1985).

---

The viral illnesses are difficult to treat and most medication is ineffective. Genital herpes is a very frequent STD. It can be annoying but seldom causes serious consequences. Hepatitis may be sexually contagious and can be a debilitating infection lasting several months. AIDS is a fatal viral illness and there is currently no effective treatment.

*In Sum*

---

## PREVENTING SEXUAL INFECTION

The presence of AIDS has caused some people to forget to be cautious about the other much more common STDs. "I don't engage in anal intercourse, so I'm all right," one student said. The belief was that by eliminating one central risk behavior the student was safe from gonorrhea, herpes, and the other sexually transmitted illnesses. This is, in fact, not a rare attitude. The result is the frequency of STD has not declined a great deal. People tend to take one or a few precautions for AIDS and forget that the other STDs still remain and are far more common. If we use good general preventive measures all the time, then we would be less likely to contact AIDS or any of the other STDs (Cates, 1988; Tseng et al., 1987).

A physician specializing in sexually transmitted diseases has commented, "If everyone had sexual relations with just one partner for the next 5 years, I'd quickly be out of business." The point the doctor was making is that sexual infections are contagious illnesses. You cannot get gonorrhea or herpes unless you have intimate contact with a person who has this infection. It follows that the more different partners, the greater the chances of having relations with one who has a sexual infection. This suggests the first rule of prevention: limit sexual relations to one person or as few as possible.

A related rule follows from the first: try to avoid sexual relations with a person who has a very large number of partners or engages in risk behaviors. You may have only one partner, but if she or he has sexual relations with many other people the chances for the transmission of a sexually infectious disease considerably increase.

If you or your partner has an STD, scolding or finding someone to blame is useless. Instead, talk honestly about your relationship. Consider ways to prevent futher infection and get medical treatment.

Another important preventive measure requires learning and looking: know the symptoms of the major STDs. When you are aware of the signs of trichomoniasis, gonorrhea, hepatitis, and so on, you are ready to look. Does your partner seem fatigued, or look ill and feverish? Is there a lesion or signs of a discharge? Looking during foreplay cannot and should not be a military medical inspection nor can it guarantee to detect all STD symptoms. But do try, before beginning sexual relations, to look casually at your partner and the genital organs. If you have some doubt, mention it, and wait to have sexual relations another time when the condition has been resolved.

Sexual diseases are transmitted through contact with mucous membranes primarily in the vagina and anus. Or the microorganism may be plentiful in semen and vaginal fluids. This means that contact with these tissues and fluids should be avoided. A condom (Chapter 14) is likely to prevent the transmission of bacterial infections. It may also block viral diseases (herpes, hepatitis, AIDS). But its effectiveness in this latter respect is not perfect. Further, latex or plastic condoms are probably more reliable in blocking viruses than those made of animal intestine like *Naturalamb* and *Fourex*. The latter are good as contraceptives but not as good in preventing STD. In any case, if a condom were always used with a new partner, the incidence of STDs would very substantially decline.

The spermicide *nonoxynol* found on some condoms also helps disable infectious viruses.

Women may get a measure of preventive protection from a diaphragm or sponge together with a spermicide. The spermicide may help inactivate some viruses and bacteria and the barrier may protect the cervix from receiving semen that contains microorganisms. If, during coitus, the woman uses a barrier and spermicide and the man uses a condom, protection from possible STDs will be considerable. Many couples continue this practice until the safety of coitus is established and other contraceptive arrangements have been made.

There are postcoital preventives. Washing reasonably soon after sexual relations may be helpful, but it is far from a certain means. Urinating may aid

Honesty in discussing a sexually transmitted disease can lead to greater intimacy and trust.

too. It could clear the urinary tract of bacteria that may have been introduced during coitus. If a condom fails during coitus, immediately inserting spermicide into the vagina, as high as is safely possible may be helpful.

A special precaution has arisen because of the increasing incidence of AIDS. Some people not trusting the preventive effectiveness of condoms, follow a very stringent rule with new partners. They do not enter any body cavity, do not kiss, and do not exchange bodily fluids. They may, however, massage, caress or masturbate or climax by sliding their genitals along the partner's leg or other skin surface (Chapter 5).

**Questions and answers about AIDS**   AIDS education is now mandated in many state school systems. The following are probing questions asked an AIDS expert by senior high school students.

*Q.* Is it safe to kiss?
*Dr.* Usually yes. The AIDS virus, or viral particles, is not usually found in saliva. But if an AIDS-infected patient has a tiny bleeding lesion in her or his mouth, it is possible that kissing will exchange blood. Blood is the richest source of HIV. In this latter case, though the likelihood remains low, AIDS could be spread by prolonged deep kissing.
*Q.* Is cunnilingus going to give you AIDS?
*Dr.* The HIV is found in low concentration in vaginal fluids. The person performing cunnilingus probably has a small chance of contracting AIDS. The woman receiving cunnilingus has very little chance of contracting AIDS—unless the person performing has bleeding lesions in her or his mouth.

*Q.* How about fellatio?

*Dr.* The person receiving fellatio is unlikely to contract AIDS unless the person performing has bleeding mouth lesions. The person performing fellatio is likely to get semen into his or her mouth, or swallow it. Semen contains the virus and thus there is a chance of contracting AIDS.

*Q.* Who is most at risk in anal intercourse?

*Dr.* The person receiving anal intercourse, particularly if the performer ejaculates deep in the anus, is at very great risk for AIDS. The person performing anal intercourse is also at risk, though less so than the receiver.

*Q.* Are you at risk in anal or vaginal intercourse if your penis does not have a tiny cut or sore?

*Dr.* Yes you are at risk. Apparently there does not have to be a tear or cut in the skin. In the case of the penis the HIV may enter through the urethra, or possibly even through unbroken skin.

*Q.* Do condoms really work?

*Dr.* Yes, but they make sex *safer,* not guaranteed safe. To make latex condoms even safer try wearing two, and make sure they have *nonoxynol* or another antiviral (spermicidal) lubricant.

*Q.* We'd like to get married but want to know that we don't have AIDS. What do we do?

*Dr.* Make an appointment with our county clinic. We'll test you and whatever the results, also give you personal counseling. Incidentally, it's free and the results are confidential.

These rules may have provoked some anxiety. It should be remembered, however, that most sexual relations do not result in an infection. Further, over 90% of all STDs are treatable and, if detected early, relatively mild. Being alert and educated to the signs of STDs can ensure a healthier and more pleasurable life (Balfour and Heussner, 1984; Langone, 1988; Hearst, Hulley, 1988).

---

## Summary

Sexually transmitted diseases are often regarded with dread, although most are relatively mild and treatable. They are also common, with over 10 million cases of sexual infections in the United States every year.

Syphilis is an infrequent illness today. It usually begins with a genital lesion. If left untreated, in the course of a decade or two it can result in heart or brain damage or both. Gonorrhea and chlamydia are very frequent infections. The symptoms of these diseases, urinary pain and discharge, are usually evident in men, but in women the signs may be more subtle or even absent. Because of this, both infections may progress to a potentially serious pelvic inflammatory infection in women.

Trichomoniasis and moniliasis often cause a vaginal discharge. The former is always a result of sexual transmission, while the latter rarely is. Both can be effectively treated. Since men may be asymptomatic carriers, they should be treated also.

Sexual infections caused by viruses range from mild to fatal. None are easily treated since effective medication to destroy viruses has not been developed. Genital herpes is a viral disorder that causes lesions on the penis or vagina. These cold sores may recur and can be uncomfortable and frustrating. But genital herpes is a relatively minor illness and rarely produces complications.

Mononucleosis is transmitted by kissing, and hepatitis may be contracted through sexual relations. The former can result in several weeks of fever, malaise, and fatigue. The latter will produce similar symptoms that can last for several months. Mononucleosis is found most often among college students, and hepatitis is seen with some frequency among homosexual men.

AIDS is a new STD most easily spread by anal intercourse, sharing intravenous needles and other risk behaviors. There is no effective treatment today, and death seems the usual outcome.

AIDS has brought about changes in sexual life-styles and encouraged some individuals to speak out particularly against homosexuality. Most people, however, seem sympathetic to the impact of AIDS and have supported treatment and counseling efforts.

There is a likelihood that STDs can be avoided by following cautions. These include limiting the number of sexual partners, using a condom and diaphragm or sponge, or engaging only in skin-to-skin sexual relations.

---

1  Explain the different meanings and attitudes suggested by the terms venereal disease and sexually transmitted disease.

2  What are some false beliefs about STDs that are mentioned in the textbook or that you have heard or held in the past?

3  Why has so much misunderstanding and anxiety been built up around herpes? Contrast attitudes toward herpes with those toward another viral illness, hepatitis. Which is more serious?

4  In men and women what are the principal symptoms of and treatments for gonorrhea, nonspecific urethritis, trichomoniasis, syphilis, hepatitis, and AIDS?

5  In which ways can you personally help prevent STDs? Suggest some ways in which you can make a public health contribution to help limit the spread of STDs?

*For Thought and Discussion*

---

Balfour, H.H., Jr., and Heussner, R.C. *Herpes diseases and your health*. Minneapolis, Minn.: University of Minnesota Press, 1984.

Barry, M.J. AIDS tests: when and for whom? *Harvard Medical School Health Letter,* September 1987, 5-9.

Bingham, J.S. *Sexually transmitted diseases*. Philadelphia: Williams & Wilkins, 1984.

Brandt, A. *No magic bullet*. New York: Oxford University Press, 1985.

Carroll, L. Concern with AIDS and the sexual behavior of college students. *Journal of Marriage and the Family.* May 1988, *50,* 405-411.

Cates, Jr., W. The "other STDs": do they really matter? *Journal of the American Medical Association,* June 24, 1988, *259* (24), 3606-3608.

Centers for Disease Control. *STD statistics, 1988*. Atlanta, Georgia: U.S. Dept. of Health and Human Services/Public Health Services, 1990.

Clark, M., Gosnell, M., Witherspoon, D., Hager, M., and Coppola, V. AIDS. *Newsweek,* August 12, 1985.

Dickens, B.M. Legal limits of AIDS confidentiality. *Journal of the American Medical Association,* June 17, 1988, *259* (23), 3449-3451.

Fineberg, R. Newly defined infectious disease problems. In Branch, W.T. (editor), *Office practice of medicine,* Philadelphia: W.B. Saunders Co., 1987.

Gillespie, O. *Herpes: What to do when you have it*. New York: Grosset & Dunlap, 1982.

Haynes, H.A. Genital lesions. In Branch, W.T., (editor), *Office practice of medicine,* Philadelphia: W.B. Saunders Co., 1987.

Hearst, N., and Hulley, S.B. Preventing the heterosexual spread of AIDS: are we giving

*References*

our patients our best advice? *Journal of the American Medical Association,* April 22/ 29, 1988, *259* (16), 2428-2432.

Kilby, D. *Manual of safe sex.* Burlington, Ontario: B.C. Decker, Inc., 1986 (Distributed by The C.V. Mosby Co., St. Louis, Mo.).

Kramer, M.A., Aral, S.O., and Curran, J.W. Self-reported behavior pattern of patients attending a sexually transmitted disease clinic. *American Journal of Public Health,* 1980, *70,* 997-1000.

Langone, J. *AIDS: the facts.* Boston: Little, Brown, & Co., 1988.

Masters, W.H., Johnson, V.E., and Kolodny, R.C. *Crisis: heterosexual behavior in the age of AIDS.* New York: Grove Press, 1988.

Mertz, G.J., Jones, C.C., Mills, J., Fife, K.H., Lemon, S.M., Stapleton, J.T., Hill, E., Davis, L.G., and the Acylclovir Study Group. Long-term acyclovir suppression of frequently recurring genital herpes simplex virus infection. *Journal of the American Medical Association,* July 8, 1988, *260* (2), 201-206.

Morin, S.F., Charles, K.A., and Malyon, A.K. The psychological impact of AIDS on gay men. *American Psychologist,* November 1984, *39* (11), 1288-1293.

Nettleman, M.D., and Jones, R.B. Cost-effectiveness of screening women at moderate risk for genital infections caused by *Chlamydia trachomatis. Journal of the American Medical Association,* July 8, 1988, *260* (2), 207-213.

*New York Times.* False fears of contagion. *New York Times,* November 15, 1985, 18.

Raymond, C.A. New population, new HIV vaccine in clinical trials. *Journal of the American Medical Association,* March 4, 1988, *259* (9), 1290-1291.

Redfield, R.R., et al. Frequent transmission of HTLV-III among spouses of patients with AIDS-/Related Complex and AIDS. *Journal of the American Medical Association,* March 15, 1985, *253* (11), 1571-1575.

Richwald, G.A., Kyle, G.R., Gerber, M.M., Morisky, D.E., Kristal, A.R., and Friedland, J.M. Sexual activities in bathhouses in Los Angeles County: implications for AIDS prevention education. *The Journal of Sex Research,* May 1988, *25* (2), 169-180.

Salsberg, A.M., Runser, R.H., Dolins, S.L., and Salsberg, D.H. Male-to-female transmission of HIV. *Journal of the American Medical Association,* December 18, 1987, *258* (23), 3386.

Sargent, R.K. Penile discharge and urethritis. In Branch, W.T. (editor), *Office practice of medicine,* Philadelphia: W.B. Saunders Co., 1987.

Tseng, C.H., Villanueva, T.G., and Powell, A. *Sexually transmitted diseases: a handbook of protection, prevention, and treatment.* Saratoga, Calif.: R & E Publishers, 1987.

Wallis, C., Boyce, J.N., and White, H. Chlamydia: the silent epidemic. *Time,* January 4, 1985, 67.

Woo, B. Vaginitis and cervicitis. In Branch, W.T., (editor), *Office practice of medicine.* Philadelphia: W.B. Saunders Co., 1987.

Zachariae, E., Ebbesen, P., and Stenbjerg, S. Anal intercourse as a possible factor in heterosexual transmission of HTLV-III to spouses of hemophiliacs. *Journal of the American Medical Association,* March 28, 1985, *312* (13), 857.

Brandt, A. *No magic bullet*. New York: Oxford University Press, 1985.
An engrossing book that traces the history of American attitudes toward sexuality and sexually transmitted diseases over the last 100 years. Shows how negative and punitive beliefs have hindered educational and medical efforts.

Cooke, C.W., Dworkin, S. *Ms. guide to women's health*. New York: Berkley, 1981.
A reasonably complete and often useful guide to most health issues of concern to women.

Kilby, D. *Manual of safe sex*. Burlington, Ontario: B.C. Decker, Inc., 1986 (Distributed by The C.V. Mosby Co., St. Louis, Mo.).
This highly readable and realistic book provides valuable, detailed information on birth control and sexually transmitted diseases.

Langston, D. *Living with herpes*. Garden City, N.Y.: Doubleday, 1983.
A good discussion of the herpes virus and the diseases it causes. Puts genital herpes in perspective and is realistic, practical, and reassuring.

Monette, P. *Borrowed time: an AIDS memoir*. New York: Harcourt Brace Jovanovich, 1988.
This highly personal story of a man ill with AIDS is poignant and sensitively written.

*Suggested Readings*

## Chapter 17

# Sexual Problems and Solutions

**When you finish this chapter, you should be able to:**

Describe the sexual problems that often concern men and women.

Discuss medical, relationship, background, and other factors as causes of sexual problems.

Describe the treatment methods used by Masters and Johnson and other therapists.

Explain ways couples can help themselves resolve a sexual difficulty they are experiencing.

List what to look for to select a qualified sex therapist.

Sexual problems are conditions in which a person finds it difficult to become sexually stimulated or satisfied. Difficulties may be related to desire, arousal, and/or orgasm. Both women and men may be affected and the problem may occur only occasionally or it may be continual. Sexual problems are common and can be psychological and/or physical in origin. In many instances professional therapy is necessary. In other situations women and men can help themselves to a more satisfying sex life.

## PREVALENCE AND ORIGINS

Sooner or later most women and men will experience some sexual problem. When adults are interviewed, the majority recall periods in their lives when they were troubled by low sex desire or orgasm difficulties. Concerns about arousal seem to increase with age. Middle-aged and older people say erection and vaginal excitation are likely to take longer or to be less certain (Chapter 12).

Couples as young as their 20s also have sexual difficulties. Frank, Anderson, and Rubinstein (1978) surveyed 100 educated, younger couples who said they were happily married. Nevertheless, they found that half of the men said they sometimes had problems with erection or ejaculation and orgasm. Among the women at least three fourths occasionally had difficulty with arousal or orgasm. About two thirds of both sexes said they sometimes felt tense during sex or went along with their partner even if they themselves had little desire (see Table 17-1). People do not often talk about their sexual problems with one another, but if they did they would quickly discover that sexual questions and concerns are troubling to many women and men, both those who are older or as young as college students (Spencer, Zeiss, 1987).

### Medical

In this age when most people are aware of the psychological roots of many seemingly physical problems, it is too often assumed that all sexual difficulties are emotional. Psychological and social factors do play large parts in determining sexual well-being, but physical causes should not be overlooked. In a study at Beth Israel Hospital in Boston, for example, 105 men complaining of erection problems were carefully examined. One third were found to have unsuspected hormonal disorders, usually too little testosterone (Chapter 4) (Harvard, 1980).

Similar reports come from Baylor College of Medicine in Texas. Sleep research has shown that nearly all males have four or five erections and females have similar episodes of vaginal arousal during a normal night's sleep (Chapters 3 and 4). Arousal does not happen, however, when there is an underlying physical problem. In one investigation a plastic sleeve was fitted around the penis to measure sexual arousal during sleep. It was found that two thirds of men complaining of erection problems were also not aroused during sleep. The conclusion was that most probably had medical deficits accounting for the arousal dysfunction (Karacan, 1981).

The list of possible physical causes is very long. There are at least two potential areas of difficulty. First, drugs and medication must be considered. Continued and immoderate use of alcohol probably heads the list of physical causes of erection problems. "Street" drugs such as heroin and cocaine can also markedly depress sexual function. Prescribed medications such as tranquilizers and sedatives are very likely, too, to interfere with arousal and orgasm (Ende, 1984).

Second, ill health can lead to sexual problems. Hormonal imbalances, diabetes, neurological disorders, or injuries can block sexual interest or response. Sexually transmitted illnesses (Chapter 16) may cause lingering infections that make coitus uncomfortable. Conditions such as chlamydia and trichomoniasis

The potential for drugs to interfere with sexual response is often overlooked. Prescription medication given for conditions such as insomnia, high blood pressure, and allergies may impair sexuality.

may cause pain in the penis or the vagina. Growths in the vagina or scrotum may be harmless but cause discomfort in the genital area. All of these can quickly lead to a loss of sexual desire or ability.

The evidence that a good portion of sexual problems are medical in origin is persuasive. A conservative estimate is that, overall, a third of all cases of diminished desire, and arousal and orgasmic difficulties are medically caused (Harvard, 1980; Kaplan, 1983).

### Relationships

Some sexual activity, notably masturbation, involves only one person. No one else needs to be pleased nor is the cooperation of a partner important to the person's satisfaction. But when sex involves two people, the quality of the overall relationship can affect the sexual experience. As a result many sexual difficulties reflect conflicts within a partnership. Alone a man or woman may have no difficulty with arousal or orgasm, but together with a particular partner, they may not function well.

See Chapter 10 for a review of couple communication problems and suggestions for increasing information and understanding.

The relationship factor that may contribute the most to sexual interactions is *communication*. Sexual questions and affectional concerns between two people are numerous. How often does each person want coitus to occur? How do they want to be approached, touched, and stimulated? What does each find especially pleasurable or uncomfortable or even annoying? The answers to these questions cannot be guessed, nor will they be conveyed by evasive shrugs of the shoulder. Hite's (1987) survey of over 4,000 women was certainly scientifically flawed (Chapter 2), but it did illustrate how, in the large majority of couples, communication is often meager or inadequate.

Another relationship impediment to good sexual function revolves around *uneducated sexual attitudes*. A couple may be on good terms, but because they really know so little about sexuality they fail in their attempts to establish a healthy sexual adjustment. Wolfe (1981) found that up to a third of men and women are uninformed of the necessity and length of foreplay; they attempt coitus far too soon. A few couples believe that it is important that orgasm be simultaneous, and distort the easy flow of sexuality to reach an almost unattainable goal. Many men believe women must have a coital orgasm. They think something is wrong with their partner or themselves if they do not have orgasm during intercourse. Still others have stereotypical notions of what each gender is properly to do or not to do. The attitude that women only do this while men do that is not likely to lead to harmonious sexual enjoyment (Chapter 6; Hawton, 1985).

Closely related to uneducated attitudes are unrealistic *performance expectations*. Myth has it that men are potent, and ever ready sexually. The first time a man fails to erect because he is tired or disinterested, or for whatever reason, may result in fear if not panic. The next time the man may approach sexual intercourse as if it were a challenge. He will be on stage and his act must impress his partner. Unfortunately, this self-conscious attitude induces *performance anxiety,* fear that he will not erect again—that once more he will fail to carry out his role. The likely result is a diminished erection. Thus the vicious cycle begins: fear of failure, diminished erection, increasing fear of failure, increasing erectile impairment, and so forth.

The performance attitude means watching oneself or one's partner instead of unself-consciously participating in sexual relations.

Women, too, may make unrealistic performance demands on themselves.

Even happy couples can sometimes have sexual problems.

They may try to be irresistibly sexy, or they may feel they must demonstrate an orgasm, lest their partners reject them or feel rejected. Just as with men, a vicious cycle may arise: fear of being nonorgasmic, anxiety that blocks orgasm, increasing fear of orgasm failure, and so on. As Masters, Johnson and Kolodny, (1986), suggest, the more idealized, the loftier the sexual expectations, the greater the chance of disappointment.

> Mimi came to the college counseling center very distressed that her marriage, planned for June, would never take place. Her boyfriend Rudolph had increasingly avoided sexual relations with her. The last several times his erection had been incomplete, and he had wanted to stop intercourse. Mimi believed that Rudolph no longer found her attractive. "I don't know how to make myself sexy for him," she complained.
>
> *(Authors' Files)*

A fourth relationship factor that subverts sexual function is *power struggle*. Couples who are contesting control of the relationship, who are angry and manipulative, are not likely to find their sexual relations satisfying. The partner who feels she or he never gets her or his way about money may unconsciously exercise control in sexual relations. Here she or he can be demanding and distant, making the partner feel unwanted and unappealing. The Blumstein and Schwartz (1983) studies of couples point out that the rapport, warmth, and cooperation that exist before intercourse begins can determine how pleasurable later sexual relations will be.

We do not want to leave the impression, however, that couples who do not get along will have poor sexual relations and those who do get along will be sexually satisfied. Lorne Hartman (1980) used carefully constructed rating scales to evaluate the personal and the sexual relationships of 20 couples. Like Frank (1978), whom we mentioned earlier, Hartman found that sexual function and satisfactory relationships were somewhat independent of one another. There were couples who were not getting along well but were sexually satisfied. More interesting, there were couples who had a good partnership but whose sexual harmony was quite low. A happy partnership does not automatically mean good sexual function. Even happy people and loving partners may have sexual difficulties and problems.

## Stress

Physical and psychological pain, emotional and environmental demands, in a word *stress,* can have a significant impact on sexual capability. The spouse who comes home tired from work and declines the partner's invitation to sex may not just be making an excuse. Stress and frustration on the job are real and can result in debilitating fatigue and disinterest in sex. The sources of stress are varied and plentiful (Maier and Laudenslager, 1985). They include the following:

> Fatigue itself, just being plain tired from long hours of work or other effort, without stress, can decrease sexual interest and capability.

Death of a close family member
Difficulty in school
Unemployment
Difficult work or supervisor
Business or financial problems
Unsatisfactory living conditions
Birth of a new child or childrearing problems
Victim of crime or attack

The body's reaction to stress is both physical and psychological. Psychological reactions to stress are depression and feelings of helplessness and despair. Often anger and violent impulses are not far behind. Physical reactions to stress may be fatigue and a general feeling of not being well. Sometimes, too, stress-related illnesses such as a peptic ulcer, high blood pressure, or colitis may occur. Often as not, sexual interest and responsiveness are rapidly affected by stress. Schumacher and Lloyd (1981, p. 49) hypothesize that

> In the hierarchy of systems of the body, sexual function has a low status since it does not appear essential for the individual's life or health. Therefore when the body is under threat from physical and/or psychological stress, sexual functions may be sacrificed to foster the systems that are more important for survival or health.

## Background

The experiences we bring into a sexual relationship, our own personal history, as well as our present partnership, affect sexual feelings and function. The single most important factor, according to Kaplan (1983), is *anxiety.* The person who is fearful about sexuality is likely to impair her or his desire, arousal, and/or orgasm.

> Chapter 4 describes the way in which erection can be blocked by neural impulses that are triggered by anxiety.

Anxiety may be obvious or hidden. Sometimes a past traumatic experience—rape, incest, or some other sexual exploitation—has left a fearful psychological imprint. Anxiety could also be the result of mixed feelings concerning heterosexuality or homosexuality. A person may be uneasy with her or his

## Can You Handle Stress?

Stress is an important cause of sexual problems that is often overlooked, but not everyone is equally disturbed by specific stressors. Some people respond to difficulties in school or on the job with relative calm and equanimity. Others be- come preoccupied with their troubles and lose interest in sex and the normal pleasures of living. To see how well you handle stress answer the following questions *Yes* or *No*.

|  | Yes | No |
|---|---|---|
| 1. I have strong religious or ethical beliefs that are a comfort to me. | — | — |
| 2. I always take time out, every day, to relax and enjoy myself. | — | — |
| 3. I have a good sympathetic friend to whom I can talk about anything. | — | — |
| 4. I get a good night's sleep, about 8 hours, every night. | — | — |
| 5. I drink (or smoke) very little or not at all and do not habitually use any drugs. | — | — |
| 6. I take care of my health and weight and eat regular meals. | — | — |

|  | Yes | No |
|---|---|---|
| 7. I exercise or participate in active sports at least a few times every week. | — | — |
| 8. I have a friend (or spouse) whom I love and who loves me. | — | — |
| 9. I have my days pretty well organized and I work fairly efficiently. | — | — |
| 10. I manage my money well so that I never feel I'm deeply in debt or broke. | — | — |

### Interpretation

This test provides an informal guide to how well you are prepared to handle stress. If you have eight to ten *Yes* responses, your life seems to be quite well ordered and healthy. You should be able to handle ordinary stresses better than most people. A score of five to seven is an average response. Stress may discourage you, but you have the resources to muster your abilities and recover. Scores under five suggest you are vulnerable to stress and that it may impair aspects of your psychological and sexual function. A look at the questions to which you have answered *No* may suggest corrective measures. (Data from Maier and Laudenslager, 1985.)

orientation. At still other times, anxiety may result from fears concerning contracting a sexually transmitted disease. The causes of anxiety are legion, but whatever the roots, anxiety is almost certain to interfere with satisfying sexual function.

A background factor related to anxiety is a *sex-negative* attitude. Children may be told that touching their genitals is sinful or dirty. Sex-negative emotions can be conveyed subtly too, by parents who imply that it is wrong to feel the sensual pleasure of an embrace. Children as young as 1 or 2 years old who are scolded for running naked from bath to bedroom may begin to question the wholesomeness and worth of their bodies. Children who learn that sex is degrading become fearful, shy, unloving adults (Gilmartin, 1987). Freud

The changing gender roles and expectations of women and men may sometimes result in sexual problems.

(1959) said that we are all forced to carry a suitcase: it is filled with useless habits, misperceptions, and disabling fears. Only through insight and diligent effort can we begin to empty the suitcase and rid ourselves of the burdens our own history has forced us to assume.

An important background factor that should not be overlooked is *changing gender roles*. A generation ago, the double standard dictated that women were expected to be sexually attractive but passive. Men were expected to be the aggressors. Single women and men followed a fairly precise dating ritual. Whether older or younger, men, not women, telephoned and made dates. The woman's job was to act as gatekeeper. She determined the type and amount of sexual activity that would be allowed (Chapters 8 and 9).

The women's movement in the last two decades has meant both greater equality for the two sexes and recognition of female sexuality. Women no longer necessarily confine themselves to traditional gender roles, and they may want more in their sexual lives. These new developments can threaten both sexes. Some men see their masculinity challenged. Others perceive the new woman as less sexually available but more demanding of satisfaction. Women may believe that they are expected to be more knowledgeable and also more readily orgasmic. Hite (1987) suggests that these perceptions and attitudes often lead to distrust, and self-doubt. When gender roles are in transition, the uncertainties in both sexes may sometimes lead to difficulties in sexual interactions and relations.

## SEXUAL PROBLEMS

Sexual problems may be the result of medical, relationship, personal, and health concerns and affect desire as well as satisfaction. A decade ago a man who had little sexual interest or experienced erectile difficulties was usually de-

scribed as impotent. A woman similarly uninterested or one who did not usually have an orgasm was called frigid. Despite the fact that both sexes could be
potent and orgasmic when masturbating, they were labeled incompetent. Both
terms, *impotent* and *frigid,* implied a pathology that permeated each person's
entire personality and being. The frigid woman and the impotent man con-
jured up pictures of chilly, inadequate people.

When the inappropriateness of both words was recognized, psychiatry introduced the term **dysfunction.** Women whose orgasmic response was uncertain were described as orgasmically dysfunctional. Men might be said to have
an arousal or erectile dysfunction. The term dysfunction is an improvement
over frigidity and impotence, and the word is often useful, but it is primarily a
medical term that suggests an organ is unhealthy.

For these reasons, we and many therapists prefer to see concerns about orgasm, arousal, and desire described as *problems*. They are, questions and dilemmas that reflect personal needs and attitudes. Their solution often lies not
just in mending a person's organs but in teaching reasonable ways to understand oneself and one's partner and to interact (Floyd, 1988).

*dysfunction*
Failure of an organ, sys-
tem, or part to work
correctly.

### Problems in sexual desire

The drive, some say the appetite, for sex varies considerably. Most younger
people want sexual relations three or four times a week, yet a few prefer sex
weekly, and still others every day. We also need to recognize that sexual desire
may be quite low during periods of stress or pregnancy and much higher during vacations. All these changes in libido (sexual desire) make the definition of
what constitutes a problem in desire somewhat difficult (Chapters 5, 12).

Consider a couple in which the wife wants intercourse three times a week
and the husband only once. She says that he has a low sex desire problem.
When this couple divorces, the woman finds a partner who wants intercourse
daily. This man says that *her* libido is too low. Let us recognize that what constitutes low (or high) sex drive is often in the prejudiced eyes of the partner.
There are normal variations in desire and most couples are not exactly
matched in libido. Differences in sexual desire are frequent, but most otherwise
compatible couples manage to accommodate such variations and still maintain
a good relationship (Chapter 12).

Another consideration is that low desire may not be a unitary problem. It
could be a symptom composed of a number of difficulties. According to Lo-
Piccolo (1988), what appears as low sexual desire may be hormonal, due to
depression, relationship conflict, stress, or any combination of these. Still other
underlying concerns might include sexual inhibition, the inability to recognize
and/or deal with one's own sexual arousal or subtle but disabling negative sexual signals from one's partner (Rosen, Leiblum, 1987).

What then is low sexual desire? Exact numbers cannot be pinpointed. A
person who wants sexual relations once or twice a month may function just as
well and be as healthy as one who desires relations daily. But sexual desire is a
problem when the level of interest is persistently low or absent. In this case, the
person wants sexual relations so rarely that it causes the partner considerable
strain and dissatisfaction. Using this definition, then, about one third of
women and one sixth of men can be said to have had some extended period in
their life marked by low sexual desire (see Table 17-1).

What appears to be low
desire may sometimes be
boredom; a person no
longer finds the same
partner interesting. In
Chapter 12 we describe
ways to overcome
boredom and monotony in
"Keeping sex in marriage."

**Nymphomania and satyriasis**  Just as some people have a problem with low sexual desire, a few others supposedly have too high a level of sexual need. The man whose on-the-job performance suffers because he locks himself into the bathroom four or five times a day to masturbate may have a high-libido dilemma. A woman who daily risks assault by scouting bars for a succession of new lovers might have a similar sex desire difficulty. People whose sex drive is so high that it seriously interferes with their work, relationships, health, and safety may have sex desire problems.

The old terms used to describe high sex need were *nymphomania* for women and *satyriasis* for men. Both words fell into disuse partly because they have a judgmental quality. The terms imply that it is wrong to have more interest in sex than is traditionally prescribed for men and women. More important, sexologists began to doubt whether high sex drive is really a diagnosable condition. Perhaps people whose interest in sex is very high are just more active and healthier than most.

Patrick Carnes, a sex therapist, estimates that 1% of the population is sexually excessive. These people want sexual activity several times a day and often with a variety of partners. In his book *The Sexual Addiction* (1983), Carnes shows the similarity between drug and sexual addiction. In both instances, the addictive goal dominates the person's thinking and much of her or his day. A daily routine is developed to get the drug or have the sexual encounters. The addict seeks out contacts, cruises likely bars and streets, and feels a compelling need to "score." The addictive behavior continues even in the face of threat, punishment, and intense feelings of remorse or guilt.

Another writer (Trachtenberg, 1988) sees some aberrant sexual behavior as compulsive. He labels six different possible sexual scenarios followed by people psychologically forced to reenact their sexual script. The *hitters* are experts at one-night stands and the *drifters* similarly wander from one sexual encounter to another. The *romantics* are intensely seductive, while *nesters* yearn for domesticity which they flee should they ever attain it. The *tomcats* are married yet constantly on the prowl, while the *jugglers* try to manage any number of simultaneous relationships. This overlapping classificatory scheme has limited scientific support, but it does illustrate a range of sexually addictive behaviors.

Not all therapists see all high sexual desire as necessarily pathological. So long as a person's libidinal interest and activity are satisfying and do not have negative consequences, it may not be a problem. Deciding where a healthy and robust interest in sex ends and addiction begins is not a simple task.

### Problems in arousal

Arousal problems manifest themselves in men quite dramatically. Despite foreplay and sexual interest, the penis does not erect or seem firm enough for coitus to take place. At other times the penis becomes erect but does not stay hard long enough to begin intromission.

In women the arousal difficulty is less obvious. The vagina does not expand and lubricate in preparation for coitus. Unlike the man with an erectile problem, the woman who is not lubricated may still have coitus if she wishes. She may use a lubricant to enable the penis to be admitted easily and intercourse to take place.

For both women and men, arousal problems are common, although they

Surgical gels such as K-Y are good lubricants. Saliva is also a good lubricant. *Vaseline,* baby oil, *Nivea,* and petroleum products are not recommended; they can damage a condom or a diaphragm.

Arousal problems are common and often temporary.

may be temporary or only occur once in a while. Such momentary difficulties are not likely to necessitate treatment, but if arousal is persistently problematic—occurring in a fourth or more of all sexual interactions—professional help should be considered (Table 17-1).

## Orgasm and ejaculation problems

Whether or not a man or a woman really has an orgasm problem can depend on one's definition. As we saw in Chapter 5, about two thirds of all women usually or frequently experience orgasm as a result of coitus. Does this mean that the other third of women, most of whom have orgasms through oral or manual touch, have orgasm difficulty? Few sexologists today would make such an assertion. The more common view is that a woman is orgasmic if she climaxes a good part of the time whether through coitus, masturbation, cunnilingus, or whatever other means is preferred.

The women who may have the clearest problem are the 10% who supposedly seldom or never have an orgasm. They have been dubbed *anorgasmic* (meaning "without orgasm"). A more accurate description might be *preorgasmic;* the technique or situation, or both, that will lead to climax has not yet been discovered (Chapter 5). Among men, orgasm appears unattainable in only about 2%. These men rarely or never climax (Rosen & Leiblum, 1987) (see Table 17-1).

Jerome Wakefield (1988) argues that too many women are erroneously labeled anorgasmic. First, many may be thought of as nonorgasmic when in fact their sexual problems lie elsewhere, such as in low desire or difficulty becom-

*Table 17-1*

**Percentage of Men and Women Reporting a Sexual Problem at Some Time in Their Lives**

| Problem | Percentage of women | Percentage of men |
|---|---|---|
| Low sexual desire | 30 | 15 |
| Difficulty attaining or maintaining arousal | 40 | 30 |
| Reach orgasm too quickly | 10 | 15 |
| Frequently unable to have orgasm | 15 | 2 |
| Genital pain | 15 | 5 |

Estimates are based on data from Ende, Glasgow, 1984; Frank, Anderson, and Rubinstein (1978); Spencer, Zeiss, 1987)

ing aroused. A second group have not masturbated and thus discovered their orgasm. They may feel awkward or uninformed about masturbation, or religious or moral beliefs may prohibit them. Wakefield sees undesirable consequences from the overdiagnosis of anorgasmia. It tends to label and exaggerate a difference between the sexes. It focuses undue attention on only part of women's sexual and affectional function. From Wakefield's perspective, given the proper circumstances, very few women are anorgasmic.

Orgasm problems in both sexes often center around time. A woman or man may require a good bit of sexual stimulation, perhaps an hour or more before climax. The woman may then be diagnosed as having *delayed orgasm* and the man as exhibiting *delayed* (or *retarded*) *ejaculation*.

When **rapid ejaculation** occurs, the man or his partner may feel it is a problem. One in six men believe they have at some time climaxed too rapidly (Table 17-1). What is too fast? The definition used to be that the man who has an orgasm just before coitus or within a minute or so of being admitted to the vagina is ejaculating prematurely. Those who were more concerned with the satisfaction of the man's partner extended the definition. A man was said to be climaxing too rapidly if he customarily ejaculated before his partner had an orgasm. This could mean that ejaculation was "premature" even after 20 minutes of coitus if the partner had not climaxed.

Realistically, it is unreasonable to expect a person to delay his or her orgasm for as long as it takes for the partner to climax. As we pointed out previously, the goal of simultaneous orgasm is a troublesome delusion. With this in mind, orgasm may, however, be too rapid if it occurs within minutes after the beginning of coitus so frequently that it is a frustration for one or both partners.

*rapid ejaculation*
Premature ejaculation; orgasm and seminal emission occur so rapidly it frustrates one or both partners.

Jimmy, age 20, had met "the woman of my life." He was convinced the two were just right for each other and would some day marry. On four occasions they had attempted coitus, but Jimmy ejaculated before intromission. He then felt embarassed and would not continue even after the encouragment of his girl friend. A careful history revealed that throughout high school, Jimmy's sexual experiences consisted largely of "heavy petting"; the couple touching, caressing, and rubbing one another's sexual organs, while fully clothed, until orgasm. Jimmy was helped to understand how these early learning experiences led to his current situation and the couple was counseled on techniques to help alleviate their sexual problem.

*(Authors' Files)*

### Genital pain

Discomfort during intercourse may occur once in a while to most men and women. The solution is usually simple. Relax, talk, and perhaps rest a bit before trying again. When pain is persistent and serious, it is called **dyspareunia.** The term is usually applied to women but may be used to include men. In women the pain may be experienced inside the vagina, the cervix, the clitoris, or the outer lips. In men the scrotum, the penis, or the urethra may hurt. The ache can be sharp or dull or have a burning feeling.

The vagina opens to facilitate coitus (Chapter 3). It may also close quite tightly. In **vaginismus,** the muscles associated with the vagina go into spasm. They contract and close the organ so effectively that even inserting a small lubricated finger may be difficult or uncomfortable. Typically the vaginal spasm occurs as foreplay intensifies, but it may happen at any time. The vaginal spasm may be a reflexlike response to dyspareunia. The organ is guarding itself from coitus and pain. The origin of vaginismus may also be psychological: a reaction to fear or disgust concerning sexual relations.

*dyspareunia*
Painful sexual intercourse.

*vaginismus*
Spasm of the muscles causing closing of the vaginal opening.

Even if vaginismus occurs during coitus, the penis will not be caught. It will just be pushed out. Vaginal penis-capture is necessary for reproduction in dogs and other mammals but very unlikely in humans.

---

*In Sum*

Sexual problems, such as difficulties in arousal or orgasm, may be the result of drug use, illness, or stress. The causes of sexual difficulties may also lie in a couple's relationship, background factors, misinformation, or anxiety. People who seldom or never have any sexual appetite have a desire problem. Men who frequently do not have an erection and women who do not respond vaginally have arousal difficulties. Orgasm and ejaculation problems occur when the climax is excessively rapid, delayed, or infrequent. Genital pain is uncommon but may impair sexual function for women and men.

---

## TREATMENT APPROACHES

Most adults with sexual problems do not seek help. When they do ask, often with some embarrassment, they are likely to consult their gynecologists, family physicians, or psychologists. Unfortunately, however, few health professionals have specific training in sex therapy. The help and advice obtained may not be very useful. If nothing else seems to be available, there are always the "back of the magazine" advertisements. There, creams and pills are promised that allege that they will make a man stay erect (Chapter 19). Women are offered drugs that will "inflame" their desires. Looking at this situation one can become discouraged. But there are excellent sex therapists and worthwhile treatment programs. In this section we will describe therapy approaches that are reliable and effective.

## Masters and Johnson

William Masters and Virginia Johnson, the sex research team whose pioneering work has contributed substantially to sexology (Chapters 2 and 5) are major figures in therapy (Masters, Johnson, and Kolodny, 1986). Two decades ago they introduced treatment techniques that were new, original, and daring. They announced results that encouraged initially hundreds and ultimately tens of thousands of couples to apply for admittance to their program in St. Louis.

Masters and Johnson's treatment directly addresses the sex problems themselves. If a man has erectile concerns, he and his partner learn to sexually touch and stimulate to help overcome this difficulty. In contrast, before Masters and Johnson, the treatment of sexual complaints was most often indirect. Psychiatry and psychology had taught that orgasm and erection problems were only symptoms. They were considered the surface manifestations of deeper, unconscious conflicts and motives. It was no use to try to eliminate a symptom since the underlying disorder would then just produce another complaint. The only way to resolve sexual problems, according to psychotherapists, was to get to the core of the psychic pain. This process could involve years of weekly psychotherapy meetings.

Masters and Johnson agree that sexual problems can be symptomatic of anxiety and maladjustment traceable to childhood. They argue, however, that women and men can be helped here and now by using specific treatment techniques. What is required is not 3 years of psychoanalysis, but 2 weeks of co-operative activity by the couple involved.

**Opening session**   Masters and Johnson began the treatment of sexual problems by requiring that both partners meet with both of them or with other female and male co-therapists. During these initial sessions, clients talked about their childhood and adolescent years. Particular attention was paid to how their sexual information and attitudes were shaped. These opening sessions also involved physical examination by a separate medical staff. If the sexual

Sex therapists teach, guide, and discuss treatment with their clients. They do not watch or have sexual relations with them.

couple may masturbate together and/or stimulate each other in order to learn from one another.

**Penis squeeze technique**    Squeezing the penis to avoid climax can be traced back to ancient Greece. The second century physician Galen mentioned it as a way of preventing conception. Masters and Johnson use it to teach ejaculatory control (Figure 17-2).

The **penile squeeze** necessitates that the man or his partner manually stimulate the penis until it is fairly close to ejaculation. If the man is with a woman, he tells her orgasm is very close. At this point the woman takes the man's penis, places her thumb just below the coronal cleft on the bottom, and puts her other fingers opposite. She then squeezes gently but firmly for about 4 seconds. This usually stops the ejaculatory-orgasmic impulse. After a rest of a minute or so, arousal and stimulation may begin again followed by the penile squeeze to stop ejaculation. This exercise can be safely practiced three or four times per session. It usually results in the man learning to delay his ejaculation.

*penile squeeze*
A method of delaying male orgasm by applying pressure to the underportion of the penis just below the coronal cleft.

### Helen Kaplan

Helen Kaplan (1983) suggests that a sex problem often can be helped simply by giving accurate information and clearing away false ideas. For example, a couple may need to learn that most women do *not* usually "ejaculate" fluid with orgasm (Zaviacic, et al., 1988). At other times psychotherapy, rather than physical sex treatment, may be needed. It might seem, for example, that the reason a woman is not having orgasms is because of a lack of genital stimulation. Actually the free talk and analytic probing that go on in psychotherapy might reveal that the woman had abusive sexual experiences when she was 11 years old that eventually culminated in her adult orgasmic difficulty.

Kaplan also believes that frictions and conflicts in a couple's relationship may be central to their sexual problem. What may seem to be low desire could actually be an expression of hostility between the two partners. The sexual problem will not be resolved, no matter how clever the technique, until both people in the relationship are willing to come to grips with their feelings.

Kaplan has questioned, too, the need for both a man and a woman therapist. Many clients say they feel more comfortable having both. They appreciate the rapport possible with a member of their own sex and also value the understanding that comes from the other. But Kaplan has observed that most clients seem to adjust easily to either a man or a woman. Marks (1981), who surveyed the research literature, supports Kaplan's view. He finds little evidence that having a woman and man as joint therapists is either necessary or especially beneficial. There may be, in fact, an important advantage of having just one therapist. Only one therapist can mean the client's cost is cut nearly in half.

Kaplan has also questioned whether it is always necessary for a couple to come to treatment. Granted that most sexual problems are in a couple context; it is only when they are together that one of the partners has difficulty with arousal or orgasm. But there are also sexual problems that are not couple-dependent. A person may have low sexual desire, and although single, be disturbed by a lack of libido. Another unmarried person may have arousal difficulties and because of them not have a steady partner to bring to sex therapy.

Many sex therapists no longer treat only heterosexual couples. They also treat homosexual partners and single people.

## Goal-Free Pleasuring

A variant of Masters and Johnson's sensate focus that Helen Kaplan and other sex therapists believe is helpful for most problems of arousal or orgasm is *goal-free pleasuring*. Sexual relations ordinarily go from arousal to coitus to orgasm (Chapter 5). This progression "requires" that each partner be prepared and ready at critical points along the way. After arousal the man must be erect; after some time in coitus the woman is expected to climax.

A goal-free approach emphasizes the pleasure, affection, and closeness derived from each sexual interaction itself. A goal-oriented experience proceeds from kiss to hug to intromission to orgasm. A goal-free experience may follow a different sequence: kiss, hug, kiss, caress, oral-genital, kiss, manual-genital, caress, and so on. Orgasm may occur, but it is neither a goal nor essential.

Some couples and social scientists have criticized goal-free pleasuring. They claim that the technique may be frustrating. There has been little research in the area. One of the few studies was conducted by Caroline Waterman and Emil Chiauzzi (1982). They questioned 42 couples with arousal or orgasm problems, who had goal-free and more traditional sexual treatment. Many found goal-free pleasuring to be difficult and discomfiting. It did not fit in with the rhythm of their sexual relations. They seemed to want techniques more pointed toward the arousal, intercourse, orgasm sequence. A few other couples, however, responded favorably. These women and men said that they enjoyed some aspects of sexuality more when their interactions were not just directed toward orgasm. They liked the continuing caressing, stimulation, and variety that typified pleasuring.

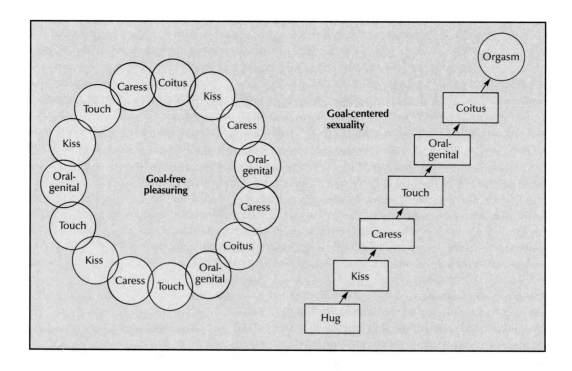

Kaplan modifies her sex treatment techniques to enable her to work with individuals without partners. She believes that women and men on their own can be helped as much as those who come as couples.

## Behavior therapy

Behavior therapists are little interested in discussing their clients' childhood or how well they get along with their partner. From the **behaviorist** perspective, a sexual problem, whatever its psychological roots, is the result of faulty learning. This means, too, that erectile, orgasmic, and other sexual difficulties are behaviors that can be changed by new learning.

Behavior therapists use many different learning techniques. One that might be employed to help a woman who wants to have coital orgasms involves **shaping.** The behavior that is desired is gradually shaped a tiny bit at a time. In this instance the woman may be instructed to masturbate almost to orgasm and then have coitus during the final moments. Gradually the period of masturbation is shortened and coitus is prolonged. Eventually she should be able to have orgasm through coitus alone.

Another technique frequently used by behavior therapists is **systematic desensitization.** This teaches the client to associate pleasant and relaxing responses with behaviors that once evoked anxiety. In this way, it is hoped, the feared behaviors will slowly lose their negative quality. (See Focus: Try systematic desensitization.)

The desensitization method works well on a therapist's couch. It does not always, however, transfer easily to real life. But having made progress in the safe confines of the therapist's office, clients are often encouraged to face their real life fear situations (Marks, 1981).

**PLISSIT**   A useful behavior approach to the treatment of sexual problems, developed by Jack Anon (1976), is described by the acronym PLISSIT. Anon points out that not all women and men who seek help with sexual difficulties need similar treatment. Whereas one couple may need extensive assistance developing appropriate techniques and attitudes, another may require only "permission." PLISSIT describes four levels of treatment: *Permission, Limited Information, Specific Suggestions,* and *Intensive Therapy.*

Anon points out that in many cases permission—the therapist reassuring the couple—and perhaps some limited information (meaning education) is sufficient. Other people need further help such as specific suggestions concerning coital positions, pleasuring, touch, or sensate focus. Relatively few people need to go on to intensive therapy. Those who do will get help dealing with their relationships, personal conflicts, and many other psychological problems. PLISSIT has the advantage of meeting each couple at a basic level and advancing therapeutically with them as far as they need to go.

## Medical treatment

A little over a third of all sexual problems have a physical cause and may require drugs or surgery. The latter is usually needed when structural abnormalities of the penis and vagina cause sexual difficulties. Medication is necessary for infections (Chapter 16). Hormones may also be useful when an endocrine

*behaviorism*
The psychological approach that deals only with observable behavior. Behaviorists contend that learning—more than unconscious needs, motives, or conflicts—brings about behavior.

*shaping*
Gradually modifying a behavior bit by bit.

*systematic desensitization*
The association of pleasant and relaxing responses with behaviors that once caused fear or anxiety.

*PLISSIT*
A four-level behavioral approach to sex therapy in which couples receive *Permission, Limited Information, Specific Suggestions,* or *Intensive Therapy* as needed.

## Try Systematic Desensitization

Many fears can be alleviated through systematic desensitization. First a fear hierarchy has to be constructed. List, one by one, in increasing order, the situations you fear. Next learn to relax. Lie down, close your eyes, loosen your muscles, breathe slowly, and feel calm and good. In order to desensitize, you need to be relaxed and simultaneously imagine the first fearful situation; this is step one. You may have to practice staying calm while visualizing a fearful situation for a day or two. But once you can do this, feeling totally at ease while thinking about the fearful experience, you are ready to move ahead. Again lie down, relax, and think about step two of the fear hierarchy. In this way you eventually work your way to the most feared event and still stay relaxed. Systematic desensitization is best done with the help of a therapist, but some benefit can be obtained on your own.

The following fear hierarchy was constructed by a young man who had sexual anxiety. He became extremely fearful, often to the point of dizziness and nausea, when he was in an intimate situation with a woman. It took him 4 weeks to work through the entire fear hierarchy. At the end, however, he was able to date and enjoy the company of women with much less anxiety.

### Fear Hierarchy

1. I'm sitting in the dining hall, and I'm having a cup of coffee with a woman who I know likes me.
2. I walk a woman to her class.
3. I take a walk with a woman and she holds my arm.
4. I'm at a party and a woman is sitting close to me, talking, and touching me.
5. I'm doing a slow dance with a woman, and we're holding each other tightly.
6. I'm sitting with a woman in a corner of the room at a party, and we're necking a little.
7. We're necking quite a bit. It's too much to do in public.
8. We go to my apartment and we're alone and lying on the bed kissing.
9. She's taking off my shirt, kissing my bare chest. I have my fingers in her hair.
10. We're taking each other's clothes off. We're going to have intercourse.
11. We have intercourse.

deficiency or imbalance is the cause of a sexual difficulty (Chapters 3 and 4). At other times drugs may be used to help erection and arousal. Recently, for example *clomipramine* has been found helpful in the treatment of rapid ejaculation (Assalian, 1988).

A new direction in medical treatment emphasizes **prostheses.** Women who have lost breast tissue may have prosthetic implants that give the breasts a normal appearance (Chapters 3, 18). Men who have arousal problems may have prostheses that can bring about an erection.

One frequent implant technique surgically places slim, hollow cylinders in the penis. A small fluid-filled reservoir is put in the abdomen and a pump is put in the scrotum. When erection is wanted, the man pumps the fluid into the cylinders. When he releases a reservoir valve, the fluid leaves the cylinders and his penis becomes flaccid again. For some this way may sound like too much mechanical technology. Kessler (1980), however, questioned users and found that nearly all were very satisfied with the device and reasonably enjoyed coitus.

*prosthesis*
A device that supplements or replaces a part of the body.

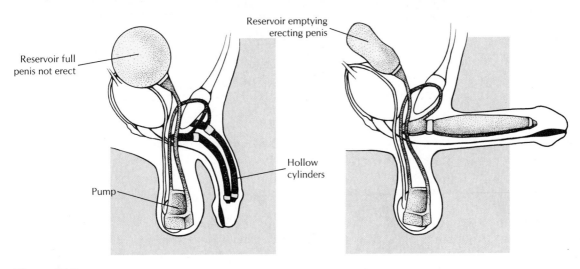

*Figure 17-3*
An inflatable penile
prosthesis.

**Fitness and exercise**  The role and importance of fitness and exercise as treatment for sexual problems are often overlooked. Consider a 36-year-old man who is considerably overweight, smokes a pack of cigarettes a day, and drinks too much alcohol. He has a sedentary job, gets no exercise, and is easily out of breath and fatigued. He believes he has a sexual problem since his erections are not as firm as they once were and he takes much longer to ejaculate.

Many people who assume they have a sexual problem may only need counseling concerning good health habits and exercise. Frauman (1982) found a direct relationship between physical well-being and the desire for, and level of, sexual activity. The people in poor shape had the least sexual activity and were also the least satisfied. Those who were in good general health, reasonably active and fit, also did very well sexually. They had the most rewarding sex lives.

A minimum exercise program to ensure at least a modest level of physical fitness was described by the *Harvard Medical School Health Letter* (1985). They suggest a half hour of sustained activity three to four times a week. Providing the person has been medically cleared, this means running, bicycling, swimming, tennis, or other sustained, vigorous sport. The benefits are numerous. They include strengthening the heart, muscles, bones, and circulation, and fortifying every bodily system and organ. Well-exercised people, the Harvard report points out, combat stress, depression, and anxiety. They function more effectively and satisfactorily in all aspects of their lives, including sexual aspects.

### Finding a sex therapist

Most states in the United States have few or no laws regulating who may be called a sex therapist or counselor. The result is that in many areas poorly qualified, or even completely untrained, people hold themselves out to be therapists. This means that clients need to exercise great care before beginning treatment with anyone. Often another professional, a family doctor, lawyer or therapist can suggest several qualified people.

Professionals in a variety of fields may have received sufficient training to be sex therapists. These include the following:

Psychiatrists—persons with an MD degree with special therapy training

Psychologists—persons with a Ph.D. degree who specialize in counseling and psychotherapy

Social workers—persons who have received a master's degree in social work (MSW) and have special training in therapy

Registered nurses—persons who are licensed RNs and have specialized in counseling

Marriage or family counselors—persons who may have a master's or doctorate degree

Most qualified sex therapists are professionals in one of the above or similar specialties. They have advanced training in sex therapy and can document this. Many sex therapists are members of the American Association of Sex Educators and Therapists (AASECT). A note to AASECT at Suite 220, DuPont Circle, NW, Washington, DC 20036 will give the addresses of some therapists in your area. Other qualified therapists may not belong to AASECT but are members of their own professional societies (Chapter 2).

No legitimate professional will be offended if you ask for her or his training and professional background. Most insurance carriers require certain licensing and credentials before they reimburse for sex therapy. A therapist who is not eligible to receive payment for services from insurance companies may not be qualified.

Pay attention to the first treatment session. Does the therapist act in a responsible, forthright, professional way? Does he or she make extravagant promises? Are personal, sexually suggestive remarks made? A competent sex therapist is realistic, does not try to be ingratiating, and discusses fees, outcomes, and procedures in a clear and objective manner.

Finally, it must be emphasized, sex therapists should never have sexual contact with clients. Such contact between therapists and clients has been shown to have negative effects, is unethical, and is usually illegal. If the therapist suggests sexual intimacy, the client should clearly refuse, end therapy, find another therapist, and report the incident to the state licensing board.

> Sex therapists usually charge between $60 and $100 per hour. Medical insurance often pays for most of this.

## In Sum

Contemporary sex therapy has been substantially influenced by the pioneering work of Masters and Johnson. Their techniques and innovations are now used by many sex therapists. These procedures include an interview during which couples talk about their backgrounds and are taught specific methods such as giving and receiving, sensate focus, and penile squeeze.

Other sex therapies such as that of Kaplan may focus more on a couple's experiences and relationship and try to resolve difficulties in these areas. Behavioral therapy teaches new sexual responses, and medical treatment may involve drugs, surgery, and prostheses. Before selecting a sex therapist, his or her qualifications and competence should be evaluated.

Legal authorities questioned whether hiring a person for sexual relations, even if under the heading of therapy, was not actually prostitution. Therapists criticized surrogates because the sexual intimacy was said to risk having the client becoming emotionally attached and ultimately having to be rejected. Newspapers, magazines, and radio and television shows seized on surrogate therapy as a rich source for sensationalistic stories. As a result, Masters and Johnson and most other sex therapists have curtailed or eliminated surrogates. Albert et al. (1980) for example, has replaced partners with fantasy. His exercises require clients to fantasize as realistically as possible. They live their sexual problems and solutions in their imaginations and slowly transfer this learning to reality.

Despite the efforts to minimize the use of sex surrogates, sometimes their contribution appears indispensable. Dean Dauw (1988) reports an integrated psychotherapy/sex therapy plan called surrogate-assisted sex therapy (SST). The 24 surrogates investigated had at least a Master's degree and had received over 100 hours of additional intensive therapy training. All were female and treated an average of 20 cases, which included arousal and ejaculation problems and low sex desire. The surrogate services were part of a complete team treatment program, and the SST was closely supervised. Outcome studies of the 489 clients involved showed that nine out of ten were successfully treated. Dauw believe this success rate is substantially higher than is ordinarily expected from sex therapy programs not employing SST.

## Success

Masters and Johnson not only announced an innovative approach to sex therapy but stated that it was highly successful. Among men and women seen for various sexual problems, over 80% were reported to be successfully treated (Masters, Johnson, and Kolodny, 1986). However, doubt has been cast on these results. Desire, arousal, and orgasmic problems may have appeared to have improved, but did the results last? Reevaluation of the Masters and Johnson data and follow-up examinations suggested that success was sometimes a little scarcer than it appeared. Schumacher and Lloyd (1981), for example, looked at 83 men who had apparently been successfully treated for erectile problems: 6 months after therapy only half had retained their improvements.

Sex problems can be resistant to treatment and the success rates are not as high as early optimistic reports indicate. It is probable that three fourths of patients who stay with treatment are greatly improved or cured. People who work diligently with a competent therapist may not have a guarantee that they will be helped but their outlook for improvement is reassuringly high (Hawton, 1985; Kaplan, 1983).

## How to help yourself

Sexual problems are common and often do not require professional help. But genital pain, the complete inability to become aroused, or other evidence of possible physical disturbance should prompt a visit to a physician. If self-help seems not to work, then it is also time to seek professional care.

This text, like others, is filled with statistics: 10% of couples have sexual intercourse standing up. A third of women and men say oral-genital relations

Self-help can aid a couple
in overcoming their
problems.

Sometimes knowing what
other people do can be
helpful. Such information
can be obtained from good
text and sexual advice
books (Chapters 5, 12).

*Communication* may be
the most important
technique in helping
yourself. Be honest, open,
talk, and listen as
suggested in Chapter 10.

gives them their best orgasm (Chapter 5). But *do not compare* yourself or your partner to others. Be yourself. You or your partner may want something few others do, or you may dislike what nearly everyone wants. It is important for you and your partner to be yourselves and to talk about your likes and dislikes.

*Be informed.* This involves three steps. First *read* so that you will understand your own and your partner's sexual anatomy and function. Second, look at your genitalia in a mirror (Chapters 3 and 4). Study what your own organs look like. Touch them to see how they feel and respond. Third, when you are thoroughly familiar with your own genitalia it is time to bring in your partner. Show what you have learned. Guide your partner's hand to touch, feel, and understand your structure as well as he or she knows his or her own.

Know your partner. Do a little amateur psychoanalysis. Tell how you learned about sex and ask your partner to tell you her or his experiences. What happened in your growing-up years that gave you the preferences, attitudes, and problems you have today? Share your backgrounds, histories, thinking, and feelings.

Like professional sex therapists, set aside a quiet time to help each other. You may also borrow techniques from sex therapy, such as hand-over, sensate focus, massage, goal-free pleasuring, and so on. In addition, couples can devise their own methods. One couple found that a man who frequently had erectile difficulty at night almost never did in the morning. By shifting sexual relations to morning, this problem was resolved. A woman whose orgasms were infrequent found that when her partner used a vibrator as part of foreplay, orgasm almost always followed later during coitus. A couple cooperating with one another can devise techniques sometimes more creative than those suggested by a sex therapist.

Finally, both partners should resolve to *give a little*. One partner may ask something the other feels is silly, unimportant, or embarrassing. Your partner may ask for a toe to head massage with perfumed oil and you may feel this is messy and unhygienic. But as long as it is important for your partner, it should be something you give. Many women and men request certain kinds of touch, caress, positions, arousal techniques, dress, or undress when they have sexual relations. As long as it harms no one, however eccentric it may sound, give a little. Without each partner going out of the way to do something the other wants, self-help will not get very far.

---

*Summary*

Sexual difficulties, once labeled impotence and frigidity, are more accurately described as problems concerning desire, arousal, and orgasm. Problems concerning desire are characterized by little or no interest in sexual relations. In a few instances there is excessive sexual need, sex becoming almost addictive. Arousal problems manifest themselves in men by frequent erectile failure and in women by lack of vaginal excitation. Orgasm problems in women are usually the result of a climax that is too delayed or infrequent. Men more often complain of orgasm occurring too rapidly. Genital pain during coitus and spasmodic vaginal closing are infrequent problems, but they are distressing.

Masters and Johnson proposed a direct approach to the treatment of sexual problems. They suggested a man and woman therapy team work together with clients who come as couples. Treatment begins with an interview and medical examination. Later patients are taught techniques such as sensate focus, masturbation, and the penis squeeze. Therapists do not watch their patient in intimate relations and do not have sexual contact with them.

Other therapists use many of the techniques introduced by Masters and Johnson. They may also, like Helen Kaplan, require weekly meetings for many months to work out background or relationship factors that are causing sexual difficulties.

Behavior therapists teach clients to unlearn faulty sexual habits, replacing them with ones that are desired. Physicians use medication and surgery to alleviate sexual difficulties. Prosthetic devices have also been introduced.

Some people who claim to be sex therapists have little or no training. Chances for obtaining a qualified sex therapist are best if one insists on a professional with an advanced college degree and a state license.

Medical and physical problems that affect sexual function should be considered first. Relationship difficulties and inadequate sexual information also need attention. Following this, low sexual desire and arousal and orgasm problems often benefit from an emphasis on noncoital, nondemanding sexual pleasuring. Exercise and maintaining good physical health can also make positive contributions to sexual well-being.

Studies show that the large majority of patients in competent programs are helped. A woman and a man can also do much on their own to alleviate their sexual difficulties.

*For Thought and Discussion*

1 If there are large differences in the desire for sexual activity between two partners, does the one with less desire have a sex problem? How low should the libido be before a therapist might say there is a problem? Should a person with little or no sexual desire (or someone with a very high level of desire) be considered to have a problem if she or he feels content and comfortable with her or his sexuality?

2 Several psychological causes for sexual difficulties are mentioned in the chapter. Can you think of additional ones? How might sex therapy be used to treat a person whose dilemma is the result of underlying conflict with the partner and another one whose complaint is the result of anxiety and inhibition?

3 What are the advantages and disadvantages of treatment using a sex surrogate?

4 Discuss how sexual problems in desire, arousal, and orgasm may be similar and how they are different.

5 How could children be raised, or our environment and society changed, to minimize sexual problems?

*References*

Albert, H.D., Olds, D.D., Davis, D.M., and Hoffman, J.S. Sexual therapy for patients without partners. *American Journal of Psychotherapy,* 1980, *34* (2), 228-239.

Anon, J.S. *The behavioral treatment of sexual problems: brief therapy.* New York: Harper & Row Publishers, Inc., 1976.

Assalian, P. Clomipramine in the treatment of premature ejaculation. *The Journal of Sex Research,* 1988, *24,* 213-215.

Blumstein, P., and Schwartz, P. *American couples: money, work, and sex.* New York: Wm. Morrow & Co., Inc., 1983.

Carnes, P. *The sexual addiction.* Minneapolis, Minn.: Compcare Publishers, 1983.

Dauw, D.C. Evaluating the effectiveness of the SECS' surrogate-assisted sex therapy model. *The Journal of Sex Research,* 1988, *24,* 269-275.

Ende, J., Rockwell, S., and Glasgow, M. The sexual history in general medical practice. *Archives of Internal Medicine,* 1984, *144,* 558-561.

Floyd, F.J. Couples' cognitive/affective reactions to communication behaviors. *Journal of Marriage and the Family,* May 1988, *50,* 523-532.

Frank, E., Anderson, C., and Rubinstein, D. Frequency of sexual dysfunction in "normal" couples. *The New England Journal of Medicine,* 1978, *299,* 111-115.

Frauman, D.C. The relationship between physical exercise, sexual activity, and the desire for sexual activity. *Journal of Sex Research,* 1982, *18,* 14-46.

Freud, S. *Collected papers.* New York: Basic Books, 1959.

Gilmartin, B.G. *Shyness and love: causes, consequences, and treatment.* Lanham, Maryland: University Press of America, Inc., 1987.

Hartman, L.M. The interface between sexual dysfunction and marital conflict. *American Journal of Psychiatry,* 1980, *137* (5), 576-579.

Harvard Medical School, Department of Continuing Education. Impotence—all in the mind? *Harvard Medical School Health Letter,* July 1980, *5* (9), 5-6.

Harvard Medical School, Department of Continuing Education. The medical forum: exercise and well being. *Harvard Medical School Health Letter,* April 1985, *10* (6), 3-5.

Hawton, K. *Sex therapy: a practical guide.* New York: Oxford University Press, 1985.

Hite, S. *Women and love: a cultural revolution in progress.* New York: Alfred A. Knopf, Inc., 1987.

Kaplan, H.S. *The evaluation of sexual disorders: psychological and medical aspects.* New York: Brunner/Mazel, 1983.

Karacan, I. Sleep and sex. *Science Digest,* July 1981, 68.

Kessler, R. Surgical experience with the inflatable penile prosthesis. *The Journal of Urology,* 1980, *124,* 611-612.

LoPiccolo, L. Low sexual desire. In Lieblum, S.R., and Pervin, L.A. (editors), *Principles and practices of sex therapy,* New York: Guilford Press, 1980.

Maier, S.F., and Laudenslager, M. Stress and health: exploring the links. *Psychology Today,* August 1985, 44-49.

Marks, I. Review of behavioral psychotherapy (II): sexual disorders. *American Journal of Psychiatry,* 1981, *138,* 750-756.

Masters, W., Johnson, V.E., and Kolodny, R.C. *Masters and Johnson on sex and human loving.* Boston: Little, Brown & Co., Inc., 1986.

Montagu, A. *Touching: the human significance of the skin.* New York: Columbia University Press, 1986.

Nutter, D.E., and Condron, M.K. Sexual fantasy and activity patterns of females with inhibited sexual desire versus normal controls. *Journal of Sex and Marital Therapy,* 1983 (Winter), *9* (4), 276-282.

Rosen, R.C., and Leiblum, S.R. Current approaches to the evaluation of sexual desire disorders. *The Journal of Sex Research,* May 1987, *23* (2), 141-162.

Schumacher, S., and Lloyd, C.W. Physiological and psychological factors in impotence. *The Journal of Sex Research,* 1981, *17,* 40-53.

Spencer, S.L., and Zeiss, A.M. Sex roles and sexual dysfunction in college students. *The Journal of Sex Research,* August 1987, *23* (3), 338-347.

Trachtenberg, P. *The Casanova complex.* New York: Poseidon Press (Simon and Schuster), 1988.

Wakefield, J. Female primary orgasmic dysfunction: Masters and Johnson versus DSM-III-R on diagnosis and incidence. *The Journal of Sex Research,* 1988, *24,* 363-377.

Waterman, C.K., and Chiauzzi, E.J. The role of orgasm in male and female sexual enjoyment. *The Journal of Sex Research,* May 1982, *18* (2), 146-159.

Wolfe, L. *The Cosmo report.* New York: Arbor House, 1981.

Zaviacic, M., Zaviacicova, A., Holoman, I.K., and Molcan, J. Female urethral expulsions evoked by local digital stimulation of the G-spot: differences in the response patterns. *The Journal of Sex Research,* 1988, *24,* 311-318.

*Suggested Reading*

Barbach, L. *Women discover orgasm: a therapist's guide to a new treatment approach.* New York: Macmillan, 1980.
Good description of specific techniques to help women become orgasmic. A sympathetic and affirmative book.

Brooks, M.B., and Brooks, S.W. *Lifelong sexual vigor: how to avoid and overcome impotence.* New York: Doubleday, 1981.
A short book filled with reassuring and practical suggestions.

Fisher, R., and Brown, S. *Getting together.* Boston: Houghton Mifflin, 1988.
How, step-by-step, a couple can build a relationship that permits each to get what they want and need.

Hay, L.L. *You can heal your life.* New York: Hay House, 1988.
A counselor's prescription for regaining one's affectional, sexual, and psychological self-esteem and confidence.

*Chapter 18*

# Health
## *Ability and Disability*

**When you finish this chapter, you should be able to:**

Describe how social and psychological attitudes towards health and disability may affect sexual activity.

Evaluate the effects of neurologic, cardiovascular, and other health problems on sexual and affectional relations.

Explain how lack of information, and medication may interfere with sexual fulfillment in ill and disabled people.

Identify techniques that may enable disabled people to experience pleasurable affectional and sexual relations.

Health and sexual/affectional function are closely related. The person who is ill or severely disabled may find sexual relations difficult or show little interest. In addition there may be social and psychological barriers to sexual fulfillment. Often, too, health practitioners pay little attention to the sexual needs of their patients. Yet health problems need not necessarily end sexual and affectional pleasure. Often education and appopriate encouragement can help even people with serious physical or developmental limitations enjoy a satisfying and responsible sexuality.

## ATTITUDES: ABILITY AND DISABILITY

In Chapter 17 we saw how psychological inhibitions and obstacles may hamper the sexuality of otherwise healthy women and men. In Chapter 12 it became apparent that older couples who maintain interest in sexual activity also encounter personal and societal barriers. Friends, relatives, the media, and even professionals may poke fun at a seventy-year-old who expresses interest in affection and sexuality.

The area in which misconception is often greatest may well be health. Often, men and women who have health problems or are disabled find little sympathy or support for their sexual needs. Peers as well as health care workers are likely to avoid mention of their erotic potential and may even consider their expression of sexual motives as shameful.

Whether the person has a spinal cord injury, a sensory loss, heart problems, or is developmentally disabled, the message conveyed frequently seems to be that sex is not appropriate. Often the result is *sex-negative* attitudes that can frustrate emotional and physical sexual needs and capabilities. People who have health problems and disabilities need first, therefore, to gain confidence that they can experience and enjoy sexuality.

### Cardiovascular problems

**Cardiovascular** problems, diseases of the heart and blood vessels and high blood pressure, afflict many millions of women and men. Each year, hundreds of thousands of cardiovascular patients, most in their 50s and 60s, emerge from coronary care hospital units. Inevitably they are afraid of resuming sexual relations in case the exertion should cause crushing chest pain, otherwise stress their heart, and bring on a life-threatening attack.

*cardiovascular*
The heart and associated blood vessels.

Cardiovascular problems are common in older people but need not mean the end of sexual interest or activity.

For a long time, data by Masters and Johnson (Masters et al., 1986) dominated the thinking of educators and physicians. These sex researchers showed that during intercourse and particularly orgasm, heart rate speeds up by 50% to 100%, blood pressure increases markedly, and breathing doubles or triples. All of this sounded hazardous to cardiovascular patients.

Another warning appeared to come from a persuasive study carried out in Japan a generation ago (Brenton, 1968). It reported a relatively high heart attack rate during intercourse. Closer inspection of this data, however, showed that 8 of every 10 coronary seizures had occurred when the man was with a new partner. A heart attack during sexual relations with a spouse or familiar partner was actually not very common. This information prompted one cynical, poetic cardiologist to suggest:

> If you're concerned with your cardiac rate,
> Then go to bed only with your usual mate

*(Author's Files)*

The advice may not be necessary. Reanalysis of the original Japanese study suggests heart attacks in the presence of a new partner may have been caused more by the heavy eating and drinking that preceded the intercourse than by the coitus itself (Brenton, 1968).

Most cardiologists now see sexual relations as simply one form of exercise. After the coronary recuperation period, coitus can be reintroduced into a patient's life slowly, just as is walking, stair climbing, tennis, and other forms of activity. In addition, because exercise is believed to be a valuable treatment tool (along with dieting, stopping smoking, and so forth) nearly all recovering heart patients are told to gradually resume sexual activities. Neither heart disease nor most other illnesses need ordinarily result in an end to sexual relations (Butler, Lewis, 1986).

The medications used to treat common health problems are often unsuspected, but they, more than the illness treated, might interfere with sexual function.

### Cancer

Cancer may involve any organ of the body and is a serious disease although half of all patients are cured. The disease may strike at any age, but it clearly

*Figure 18-1*
Reconstructed breast following mastectomy.

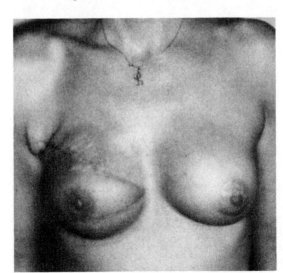

*Focus*

### Controlling Cystitis

*Cystitis,* which is an infection of the urethra and bladder, is a frequent condition among women of all ages and occasionally found in men. It is *not* a sexually transmitted disease, but it can be related to sexual activity. Often, too, its symptoms—urinary frequency, burning, and a dull pain in the lower abdomen—are falsely diagnosed as an STD (Chapter 16). It is important, therefore, for patients to insist on accurate laboratory tests in order to diagnose genitourinary symptoms rather than rely on their own or a physician's guess.

Cystitis is far more common in women because the female urethra is much shorter than that of the male. Consequently bacteria do not have far to travel to get into the normally germ-free bladder. The infection is sometimes triggered by intercourse, particularly after periods of relative abstinence. The term "honeymoon cystitis" has been used because the malady is often found among new brides or a woman of any age in a new sexual relationship. The use of a diaphragm or tampon has also been implicated in cystitis. In some women these objects may push against the urethra, encouraging bacterial growth.

Cystitis can be persistent and annoying and inhibit sexual relations. Sometimes, too, it is difficult to explain since it may occur in women who are not sexually active and no source of infection seems apparent. The following suggestions may help control cystitis.

1. If a diaphragm, tampon, or other vaginal insert could be responsible, consider trying appropriate substitutes.
2. Stay well hydrated. This means drink an extra four to six glasses of water daily. Some women believe cranberry juice is helpful in maintaining a healthy vaginal environment. There is no evidence for this claim, but the extra liquid is worthwhile.
3. Consider you and your partner showering before intercourse. Wearing a condom might also be helpful.
4. Urinate before and after intercourse. This may help remove potentially troublesome urethral bacteria.

When cystitis continues, some physicians suggest taking tetracycline or another antibiotic before coitus. Others have cured cystitis by large doses of antibiotic for about a week and then low level maintenance doses for several months. Cystitis does tend to recur but with intelligent effort it can be cured (Jawetz, 1988).

increases in frequency as people get older. Some of the cancers that have an impact on sexual function are discussed below.

Breast cancer no longer automatically means losing the entire breast, a surgical procedure called *mastectomy.* This is particularly the case when the tumor has been spotted early by self-examination (Chapter 3). Current medical research shows that a *lumpectomy,* taking just the tumor, coupled with radiation or chemotherapy, or both, is an effective treatment for most early cancers. This procedure leaves most of the breast intact. In other cases, when the whole breast is taken, reconstruction is often possible. Abdominal folds or similar tissue can be used to surgically build a new breast (Figure 18-1).

Most women find breast reconstruction or a prosthesis (artificial breast) quite satisfactory.

When breast removal is required, the mastectomy patient is often gripped by anxiety about her desirability as a woman, in addition to the fear about surviving the cancer itself. Single women may be particularly despondent or angry, feeling that their surgery will isolate them socially and sexually. Most find, however, that contrary to their fears, nearly all of their friends, partners, or lovers remain genuinely happy to still share their lives (Merz, 1988).

Prostate cancer is found mainly in men over 55 years of age. Since, in the early stages, it can only be detected by rectal examination (Chapter 4), it is important that men over 50 have a regular check-up. The cancerous gland may be removed by different surgical or radiation techniques depending on its size and the patient's condition. When the cut is behind the testicles, nerves may be severed that are involved in erection. For this reason a small portion of men become physically incapable of an erection following *prostatectomy.*

A common condition following prostate removal is *retrograde ejaculation.* The man retains his erectile capability and has intercourse but notices that there is no ejaculate. The prostate removal has resulted in the semen being expelled into the bladder rather than through the penile urethra (Chapter 4). This causes no difference in pleasurable orgasmic feeling, and the change in direction is harmless. The seminal fluid is later eliminated with the urine. It is important that men understand this, since these physical changes could falsely convince a misinformed man that he can no longer function sexually (George and Weiler, 1981).

Cancer of the cervix or uterus is usually detected by a Pap Test (Chapter 3) and almost always requires an *hysterectomy,* surgical removal of the uterus. Not all hysterectomies, however, are performed to cure cancer. Well over a

*Table 18-1*

**Medication May Affect Sexual Function**

| Medication | Comment |
|---|---|
| Antiallergy (antihistamines) | May cause drowsiness, fatigue, and lower sexual motivation |
| Antibiotics (penicillin, tetracycline) | Used to combat infections and related illnesses; usually have no effect on sexual interest or ability |
| Antidepressants (Elavil, Marplan, Tofranil) | Used to relieve depression; often cause ejaculation problems in men and impaired orgasm in women |
| Antihypertension (Aldomet, Lozol) | Used to relieve high blood pressure and treat heart problems; can diminish sexual interest and arousal |
| Antiulcer (Tagamet, Zantac) | Occasionally trigger some superficial feminine body changes in men and cause problems in sexual arousal |
| Hormones (estrogens, androgens) | Restoring proper biochemical balance may alleviate sexual problems; when hormones characteristic of the other sex are administered, sexual function may be impaired |
| Sedatives and tranquilizers (Seconal, Valium) | Used to help patients relax, sleep, or reduce pain; can interfere with sexual arousal and orgasm |

Data from *Physicians' Desk Reference,* 1989

half-million are carried out every year for noncancerous conditions such as large and troublesome *fibroid tumors* or severe and chronic bleeding. Most hysterectomies include removal of both ovaries, and this means a cessation of the normal monthly hormonal cycle (Chapter 3). Thus when a forty year old woman is operated on, she may enter menopause suddenly and earlier than her age indicates. Many health care experts today advise that if the ovaries are not diseased, both, or at least one, should be retained so that the woman's ovarian cycle continues. It is possible, too, that keeping the ovaries intact helps preserve sexual interest and function. Some women with a hysterectomy including ovarian removal have noted a decrease in sexual interest, although others report no change (Tuomala, 1988).

## Neurological and endocrine disorders

*Multiple sclerosis* (MS) is a chronic neurological disease that begins during early to middle adulthood. Symptoms include blurred vision, numbness or loss of control of limbs, and sometimes inability to become sexually aroused physically and experience orgasm. There is no effective treatment, but typically the symptoms of MS wax and wane. They disappear for weeks or months and then return sometimes in a more marked fashion.

*Parkinson's disease* (PD) is also a long-term illness that worsens as the years go by. In the early stage the symptoms of tremor of arms and/or legs, slowness and stiffness of movement are mild. Later, after several years, the patient may require help in all the activities of daily living. Unlike MS, this neurological illness does not usually directly effect the sexual organs, but the patient's increasing disability may eventually halt sexual activity. In many instances of advanced PD, medication may help ease symptoms.

*Diabetes* is the result of impaired function of the pancreas and includes several million people from childhood to old age. It can usually be controlled by maintaining a careful diet and taking insulin. A fair proportion of diabetics, particularly middle-aged or older adults, suffer circulatory and nerve damage as a complication of the disease which causes loss of the ability to become erect or aroused. Because the disease is so common, it is one of the more frequent medical causes of sexual disability (Schover and Jensen, 1988).

*Alzheimer's Disease* affects about one in every twenty people over the age of sixty. It is a progressive illness with symptoms such as serious memory loss, inability to concentrate, poor hygiene and lack of self-care. Eventually patients may become so disabled that they can not carry out the ordinary activities of daily living or recognize their friends and relatives. In the early years, mild Alzheimer's may not affect sexual function. Later on, as the patient increasingly deteriorates, sexual needs along with psychological and social skills become incapacitated.

---

Social and psychological concerns and fear of failure often play a larger role in bringing about a decline in sexual and affectional relations than physical difficulties themselves. Cardiovascular and neurologic disease, cancer, surgery, and medication can diminish sexual activity. Yet most men and women can continue sexual and affectional relations although accommodations for their health problems may have to be made.

*In Sum*

---

# PHYSICAL AND DEVELOPMENTAL DISABILITY

Disabled people, even if they are young adults, are often looked upon as asexual human beings. Typically, little consideration is given to, or provision made for, their sexual and affectional needs and concerns. Like all human beings however, those with physical or developmental disabilities want to experience intimacy and love, although their handicap may require special techniques.

Men and women who have a handicap are often very much alive sexually, and their number is considerable. According to the U.S. Department of Health and Human Services (1988) 3 million people have brain or spine injuries or suffer from a sensory loss. Add to this total 7 million developmentally disabled and it becomes clear that close to 1 out of every 25 women and men in the United States has a major disability. This is a substantial group whose sexual needs and concerns have to be recognized.

## Developmental disabilities

People who have difficulty learning, who are very slow to master ordinary skills such as speech and self-care, are diagnosed as developmentally disabled or retarded. The large majority of the intellectually impaired have IQs in the 50s and 60s and are called *mildly retarded* or *educable*. Most people in this category are physically normal, but their literacy and social skills are limited. At best they may be able to read, write, and calculate at about a sixth grade level and hold unskilled jobs. Many marry and live relatively independently. Others may receive welfare support, live in sheltered situations, or remain in institutions.

Only a small proportion of the intellectually deficient have IQs in the 20s to 40s. They are considered *moderately* to *severely retarded*. Nearly all are illiterate and many have difficulty in communicating orally. They are also likely to be physically disabled. Their stature is often disproportionate, and their appearance suggests retardation. Down's syndrome is one common form of moderate to severe retardation (Chapter 15).

The moderate to severely developmentally disabled rarely live independently or marry. They are also unlikely to have children. This is the result of a number of factors. They are supervised; their lives are very regulated, they seldom have intercourse, and their fertility is low.

Pregnancy is infrequent among the moderate and severly retarded. It is not unusual among mildly retarded individuals. There is a tendency, too, toward high frequency of unwanted teenage pregnancy. This is not the result of unusual sexual activity or capacity. It is clearly one consequence of ignorance. Most developmentally disabled people have not received any formal sex education. They are ill informed about reproduction and contraception (Baroff, 1986).

Today it is recognized that retarded people, particularly those only mildly impaired, need more than stern prohibitions. Repression of sexual and affectional needs is as likely to distort a retarded person's adjustment as that of a person with average intelligence. As a result, there are now professionals, frequently nurses, social workers, or educators, who specialize in sex education and personal counseling for the developmentally disabled. Groups such as

A generation ago retarded people could be involuntarily sterilized. Many states have repealed the sterilization statutes. Even in states where the forced sterilization of retarded people is still permitted, the operation is now rare.

Developmentally disabled
people too have sexual and
affectional needs.

SIECUS (Sex Information Education Council of the United States, 80 Fifth
Ave., New York, NY 10011) have prepared special curricula, films, illustrations, and additional group and individual instructional material.

Sex education for the retarded often stresses two areas. First, all mildly retarded and many moderately retarded people are able to learn cause and effect.
That is, they can be taught that unprotected sexual intercourse may result in
pregnancy. They can learn that regularly using a condom or daily taking a pill
will prevent pregnancy. Teaching this recognition and motivating developmentally disabled people to habitually use contraception requires very special educational skills and a great deal of patience, but it can be done.

A second area of sex education for those who are developmentally disabled
is teaching appropriate behavior. A few people, particularly those lower in intellectual function, may seem unduly assertive or even aggressive in their sexual or affectional interest. A very few may make masturbatory gestures in public situations. Still others may be untutored about their bodies and be especially vulnerable to sexual abuse by others. With special training and a great
deal of persistence, behaviors that are socially acceptable can be learned
(Hanke, 1987).

Developmentally disabled
people often find a
condom or oral
contraceptive more
acceptable and less difficult
to learn to use than a
diaphragm or spermicides.

### Spinal cord and brain injuries

The spinal cord may be injured as a result of disease, accident, or other
trauma. The result is often *paraplegia,* paralysis of both legs, or *quadriplegia,*
paralysis of both arms and both legs. In many instances spinal cord–injured
men and women lose control of some internal organs so that bowel and bladder function is impaired.

Men who have an upper spinal cord injury will likely retain the ability to
erect and probably ejaculate. But they are unlikely to do so when the injury is

lower. Sexually pleasurable and orgasmic sensations are also impaired in men with most kinds of serious spinal injury. Most injured women continue to menstruate and can also become pregnant. They sometimes retain some genital feelings, although orgasm is often unlikely.

Brain injury may also impair motor and sensory function. *Cerebrovascular accidents,* commonly called strokes, are a frequent source of brain tissue damage in older people. When brain injury occurs before or at birth the condition may be diagnosed as *cerebral palsy.* Both are distinctive diagnoses and have some significantly different symptoms. In both conditions, however, speech, movement, coordination and the use of arms and hands may be quite limited. Some patients may also be confined to a wheelchair.

Despite the severity of the physical impairments, the majority of women and men with cerebral palsy and most who have survived a stroke, are intellectually normal and may have a full range of sexual feelings and responses. Sexual desire, arousal, and orgasm may be virtually intact.

It should also be added that while some brain or spinal injured people find coitus difficult, unsatisfying, or impossible, sex and affection consist of more than genital intercourse. Many couples find lying together, intimate talking, and sharing fantasies can be arousing and psychologically satisfying (Malloy and Herold, 1988).

**Sexual techniques**  Disabled people, like all others, need to know the basic physiological facts and be helped to develop responsible sexual attitudes. People who are spine or brain injured or confined to wheelchairs particularly need to learn special ways to satisfy their sexual needs.

For many of the physically disabled, particularly those whose ability to become physically aroused or orgasmic has been impaired, touch, massage, cuddling, and kissing can be emphasized. Parts of the body that are moveable, (the legs, hands, mouth and tongue, arms, or trunk) can be rubbed or caressed. Often one partner can use a vibrator, if necessary held in the mouth, to stimulate any erogenous or responsive area of the body. Parts of the body not ordinarily thought of as sexual (such as the underarms) may become responsive in those otherwise physically disabled.

The penis may be erected by the use of a prosthesis as described in Chapter 17, or a penis not capable of erecting may be tucked inside a well-lubricated and open vagina. A woman who opens her legs widely can place even a flaccid penis in her vagina and with some practice hold it in by hand while she moves gently. It must be recognized, too, that a penis is not necessary to stimulate the vagina or clitoris, since any body part, beginning with the toes, may be used.

Proper positioning for sexual activity should also be taught. One rule is to place the bed against the wall so that the physically impaired person can move as much as she or he is able yet not fear falling to the floor. Pillows can also be used generously to support legs that are held apart or a person lying supine or trying to lie on one side. The partners should also, as much as they are able, "map" each other's bodies. By touch and other exploration they can learn what spots are sensitive, or pleasurable, or do not have much sensation at all. Sexuality can play a significant role in all lives, and with some ingenuity the physically disabled can gain intimate pleasure and satisfaction.

Penile implants that produce an erection when a pump is activated are popular with a small number of physically impaired men. Sexual partners often report such erections are satisfying, and a few men say they, too, experience a pleasant sensation (Chapter 17).

## Do You Know How to Keep Sexually Fit?

Write down at least four rules that you believe will keep you healthy and sexually fit. Then study the suggestions below. How close were your suggestions to those made? Perhaps you were able to think of rules that add to the tips suggested.

1. _____

2. _____

3. _____

4. _____

There is no secret food, vitamin, or hormone that will keep a man or woman sexually healthy. This is not to say that people have not continued to look for a magical solution. In the Orient, shark livers are said to have restorative powers. In North America, vitamin E has been popular. As we point out in the discussion of aphrodisiacs in Chapter 19, all of these have some placebo value but no valid effect on sexuality.

### Suggestions

1. Stay sexually active. Every investigator who has studied human sexuality has found that those most active in their youth stay most active as they get older.

2. Sex is work; it can be fatiguing. To continue to function sexually requires that one be in sound physical condition. This means that people should walk, jog, swim, bike, dance, or engage in some other carefully planned and medically approved exercise three or four times a week.

3. Watch your diet. Eat nutritional meals and use alcohol and other drugs vary sparingly. Alcohol, cigarettes, and tranquilizing medications such as diazepam (Valium) often depress sexual capacity.

4. Keep a balanced view of sex. Remember that sometimes it may be wonderful and at other times disappointing. Do not focus exclusively on erection or orgasm. Remember pleasuring (Chapter 17). Be affectionate, understanding, and cooperative, and don't hurry.

5. Stay informed. Remember that many health problems need not end sexuality. Make use of books that give sound advice for those with various disabilities.

## Visual and hearing impairment

People with visual and/or hearing impairments have the same sexual needs and affectional feelings as everyone else. Neither visual nor hearing deficits produce any limitations on the physical or emotional aspects of sexuality. Both conditions, however, may have produced a psychological isolation, a distancing that makes sexual/affectional contact difficult to initiate. For example, hearing impaired individuals, since they can not hear themselves speak, often produce words that are improperly modulated, pitched, and enunciated (Merson, 1987).

> "I am very embarrassed to ask a hearing girl for a date, since I sound so funny to them and then have so much trouble understanding their answer."
>
> *(Author's Files)*

A similar concern was voiced by a young woman who needed to wear dual hearing aids.

### Equality for the Physically Disabled

Disabled women and men, those who are wheelchair bound or whose mobility and function are otherwise curtailed, constitute a small but increasingly active minority. In recent years disabled people have asked for fair job opportunities and that stores, transportation, and homes be designed so that they have equal access. They want education, also, both to learn their own capabilities and to make others aware of them. Whatever their limitations, most desire the pleasure and affection that are part of sexuality and intimacy.

The disabled have three main problems in the area of sexuality. The first is being perceived by the able-bodied as sexually interesting, a person who is a potential partner. Many physically able people react to disabled men and women with fear, self-consciousness, or even revulsion. An accountant, a man in a wheelchair because of cerebral palsy, recalled shaking hands with all but one colleague he met at a business convention. Seeing this man draw back with some apparent distaste, the accountant blurted out, "You can shake my hand, this is not catching." Whether we admit it or not, many of us need to learn to be more accepting of all people, however different they may seem.

An allied problem that many disabled people have is seeing themselves as sexual. The person who has been able-bodied and then has a motorcycle accident damaging the spinal cord may believe that sexuality, just like the use of the legs, has been lost. Those who have been disabled since birth may have assimilated the general view that sex is not for someone with physical difficulties. Or they may have been told by parents that they had better put thoughts of intimate relationships out of their minds. People who are handicapped need to learn a more positive attitude toward their own sexuality.

A third problem physically disabled people have is understanding and learning appropriate sexual techniques. Nearly all disabled people have a good deal of contact with physicians. But although most doctors may expertly guide the medical treatment of their patients, they know or do little to help sexuality. Medical schools and sex education and rehabilitation programs have until very recently paid little attention to the sexuality of those who are blind or deaf or who have other physical problems. Only now are sexual pleasuring techniques being taught by newly trained counselors.

"I know I'm supposed to be good-looking and I guess I am. But when I put those things in my ears I feel less desirable; I feel old and handicapped and no man is going to be interested in me."

*(Author's Files)*

People who are hearing impaired sometimes need relatively little special educational care. Their visual skills may have adequately helped them attain a measure of satisfying sexuality. On the other hand, some may feel that their hearing losses have complicated their adjustment and denied them opportunities for learning and experience. Young adolescents who are hearing impaired may have missed their share of "street learning." They may not have learned from hearing children about at least the rudiments of reproduction. Those who are hearing disabled, like those who are visually impaired, may need qualified, empathic teaching to help them toward healthy sexual function and adjustment.

A physical disability need not be a handicap to expressing affection.

People with visual deficits may feel awkward, ignorant, and disadvantaged. Not being able to see the many different faces and forms of other women and men can lead to persistent feelings of aloneness. One important task for teachers or parents who want to help the visually impaired is to describe in considerable detail the enormous human physical variety. Presenting plastic models may also be helpful. At times, as a group exercise, visually disabled people may be encouraged to gently touch and explore one another's faces and bodies.

People blind since infancy are deprived of the opportunity to see the different shapes of women and men.

There is a role, too, that friends can play. A visually impaired person may have become interested in someone, liking how she or he sounds and what is said and yet be unable to imagine what the person looks like. Friends can then tell the impaired individual whether the person is tall or short, thin or chubby, and answer all the questions that the seeing world takes in at a glance. The partners, lovers, or spouses of those who are visually impaired may also need to assume a more leading or direct role in sexual interactions. Often among unimpaired people, one partner arouses the other by smiles, looks, body postures, dress, or other visual sexual signals (Chapter 10). The caring partner of a person with visual deficits learns to be a little more direct and rely on more overt cues, like touching, that their partner can perceive (Strong, 1988).

Women and men who have little or no hearing or sight often socialize with people who are similarly disabled. Within these communities of deaf or blind people, romantic love, jealousies, flirtation, and sexuality blossom and grow just as they do among the hearing and sighted population. A sense of handicap may not be felt by such groups until it is imposed from the outside.

---

Many developmentally disabled people can marry and be self-supporting. With special educational effort, most retarded men and women can understand relationships, contraception, and other aspects of sexuality.

*In Sum*

Physically disabled people, particularly those who are spinal cord or brain injured, often suffer impairment in arousal or orgasm or both. The rehabilitation of physically limited, blind, or deaf people can help them recognize their sexual potential and teach means for experiencing affection and pleasure.

## Summary

Cardiovascular and neurological diseases can restrict sexual function. Often, however, patients' anxieties and social misconceptions are as much an obstacle as the physical disability itself. In fact sexual relations can sometimes be recommended as sound and health restorative exercise. Cancer can result in fear of rejection and medication may block sexual arousal or capability. In most instances adjustments in objectives and techniques and the careful use of prescribed drugs can help women and men have fulfilling sexual and affectional experiences despite significant health concerns.

People who are mildly developmentally disabled are a little more likely to have unwanted pregnancies. Childbirth and sexual activity in the more seriously retarded are very low. Most developmentally disabled people can be taught about reproduction, contraception, and relationships. With proper education, many can live responsible lives.

Physically disabled women and men often see themselves, and are preceived by others, as nonsexual. People who have sustained lower spinal cord injuries are likely to have little or no ability to experience physical arousal and orgasm. Those who are brain injured may still be sexually functional and this is typically the case with cerebral palsy and multiple sclerosis. Nearly all sensorially and physically disabled people can learn attitudes and techniques that can help provide them with pleasurable intimate experiences.

## For Thought and Discussion

1 What are some of the concerns that people may have who have high blood pressure or who have had a heart attack when having sexual relations with a familiar or a new partner?
2 How may cancer of the prostate, uterus, or breast interfere with sexuality? What techniques may be appropriate for women and men who want to continue to function sexually and have had such surgery.
3 Before reading the text, what were your beliefs about the sexuality of physically or developmentally disabled persons? What were the origins of your right or wrong ideas?
4 What social, psychological, and medical changes are necessary to help assure people with health problems that they are entitled to maintain sexual and affectional interests and activities?

## References

Baroff, G.S. *Mental retardation: nature, cause, and management.* Washington, D.C.: Hemisphere Publishing, 1986.

Brenton, M. *Sex and your heart.* New York: Coward McCann, 1968.

Butler, R.N., and Lewis, M.I. *Love and sex after 40.* New York: Harper & Row, 1986.

George, L.K., and Weiler, J.J. Sexuality in middle and later life. *Archives of General Psychiatry,* 1981, 38, 919-923.

Hanke, G.C. Sexuality of clients with mental retardation/developmental disability. *ASHA,* December 1987, 31-37.

Jawetz, E. Infections of the urinary tract. In Krupp, M.A., Schroeder, S.A., and Tierney, Jr., L.M. (editors). *Current medical diagnosis and treatment,* Norwalk, Conn.: Appleton & Lange, 1988.

Malloy, G.L., and Herold, E.C. Factors related to sexual counseling of physically disabled adults. *The Journal of Sex Research,* 1988, 24, 220-227.

Masters, W., Johnson, V.E., and Kolodny, R.C. *Masters and Johnson on sex and human loving* Boston: Little, Brown & Co., Inc. 1986.

Merson, R.M. Sexuality in communicative disorders. *ASHA,* December 1987, 27-28.

Merz, B. Clinical alert gives breast cancer data, revises recommendations. *Journal of the American Medical Association,* July 8, 1988, 260 (2), 153-154.

*Physicians' Desk Reference.* Oradell, N.J.: Medical Economics Co., 1989.

Schover, L.R., and Jensen, S.B. *Sexuality and chronic illness.* New York: Guilford Press, 1988.

Strong, M. *Mainstay.* Boston, Little, Brown & Co., 1988.

Tuomala, R. Hysterctomy. *Harvard Medical School Health Letter,* May 1988, 13 (7), 5-8.

U.S. Department of Health and Human Services, National Center for Health Statistics. *Statistical Abstract of the United States.* Washington, D.C.: U.S. Government Printing Office, 1988.

*Suggested Readings*

Beattie, M. *Codependent no more.* New York: Harper & Row, 1988.
Examines how to solve your own problems while helping other people with their afflictions.

Rabin, B. *The sensuous wheeler: Sexual adjustment for the spinal cord injured.* San Francisco, Calif.: Multi Media Resource Center, 1980.
An easy-to-read book, written with grace and humor and packed with information. Useful for spinal cord injured people, their partners, counselors, and educators.

Siegel, B.S. *Love, medicine & miracles.* New York: Harper & Row, 1988.
Siegel, a surgeon, writes about his experiences with patients for whom love and meditation have contributed toward recovery.

Strong, M. *Mainstay.* Boston: Little, Brown & Co., Inc., 1988.
A moving depiction of life with a chronically ill spouse, and a helpful guide to healthy women and men who are in this situation.

*Part Seven*

# SEX AND SOCIETY

*Chapter 19*

# Sex as Business

**When you finish this chapter, you should be able to:**

Describe ways in which sex has been exploited and commercialized by the media and business.

Identify the different kinds of female and male prostitution and evaluate the degree of exploitation in each.

Describe opposing views of victim and victimless crime.

Explain the difference between pornography and erotica and the possible effects of each.

We may think of sex as a sharing of pleasure between friends, or a reaffirmation of the emotional bond between two people. But sex is also seen as a commodity, merchandise to be used, sold, and bought. The most direct sale of sex occurs in prostitution. The buyer pays a seller for intimate sexual services. Sex can also be purchased symbolically. Books, pictures, and films abound that show and describe every possible type of sexual interaction. Sex sells, and for many it is richly exploitable.

## SEX AS BUSINESS

Sex sells. It is a well-known commercial axiom that whether one wants to merchandise jeans, magazines, motion pictures, or sports cars, "make them sexy." An advertisement with an attractive human model, with a bit of erotic suggestion in appearance, can sell wrenches, watermelons, or wheelbarrows. The sex industry, which ranges from "soft-core" magazines like *Playboy,* to more revealing "R" rated movies, to "hard-core" video tapes that display in graphic detail every possible kind of human sexual activity, is a multibillion dollar enterprise. Commercial sex is an integral part of the financial and employment structure of our society. Much of it is in violation of local or state statutes and strongly opposed by a broad spectrum of religious, political, and social authorities (Chapter 20). Some aspects of it, the marketing of some sexually explicit magazines and films, and some prostitution networks, may be under the control of organized criminal groups. For the most part, however, the sex industry seems to consist of thousands of small business entrepreneurs selling sex as profitably as they can (Kendrick, 1987; Weatherford, 1986).

### Pornography

The word *pornography* comes from the Greek and literally means *writing about prostitutes.* Today, pornography has come to mean an explicit depiction of sex or sexuality. A word frequently used in conjunction with pornography is the legal term **obscene.** Its original meaning was "offensive to chastity and decency." Laws intended to restrict pornography are almost always justified on the basis that the explicit description of people engaged in sexual relations is obscene, meaning *offensive.*

During colonial times in the Americas, there were few laws concerning obscenity in art, literature, and drama. The picture changed dramatically in the late 1800s. Then a self-appointed guardian of morality, Anthony Comstock, led a nationwide campaign to censor and restrict sexual material. The antiobscenity crusade became so vehement that birth control pamphlets issued by Margaret Sanger were labeled obscene and their distribution was prohibited (Chapter 14). Even dramas by Shakespeare and classical paintings by Rubens and Renoir were restricted.

As the twentieth century began, there were a multitude of laws against what was held to be pornography. But there was also a thriving underground commerce in sexual materials. There were no "adult" bookstores such as exist today. But a knowledgeable buyer knew where to find pictures of nudes and, later, 8 mm films of couples in sexual intercourse.

By the 1950s, the early stirrings of the sexual revolution (Chapter 1) resulted in more and more books and pictures once deemed obscene being sold and circulated openly. *Playboy* magazine and a host of competitors were showing women nude. *Lady Chatterley's Lover,* a mildly erotic and time-honored novel by D.H. Lawrence, was being sold in established and legitimate bookstores.

During this period, the issue of the police seizure of *Lady Chatterley* and the prosecution of a bookstore owner eventually found its way to the United States Supreme Court. In a landmark 1957 decision, the court ruled that *Lady Chatterley* may be pornographic, but it is not obscene. The court held that a

*obscenity*
Depictions, writings, or speech that is legally considered offensive.

In past centuries, obscenity laws were primarily directed against materials that questioned or offended Christian religious beliefs. Books or pictures depicting sexual relations were very uncommon.

Pornographic movies on 42nd Street in New York City.

work is not obscene if it has *literary, social,* or *scientific merit.* It can also not be banned as offensive if it is tolerable in terms of local *community standards.*

This ruling meant that none of the great classics or any substantive work would be considered obscene as long as it had artistic or comparable merit. Further, what was found obscene by community standards in Tulsa, Oklahoma, might be acceptable in Los Angeles, Detroit, or Miami.

Today, adult bookstores selling magazines, video tapes, and pictures depicting every sort of heterosexual and homosexual act are common in every major city in the United States. In a few areas, pornographic bookstores have been closed using fire, health, safety, and similar laws, but pornography is still widely available. In New York City, for example, in a 10-block area around West 42nd Street, there are over 100 adult stores featuring pornographic materials from all over the world and catering to every sexual taste.

### Obscene or antisocial

For most of this century opposition to pornography has been based on the perception that the depiction of sexual relations is obscene. During the last decades, the argument against pornography has shifted. It is now held that pornography frequently portrays women and men as little more than sexual objects. Further, the sadistic and manipulative behavior sometimes depicted in pornography encourages violent sexual attitudes. In short, the argument for curtailing pornography now is that it is socially damaging. It harms the health and well-being of children, women, and men.

Is pornography indeed harmful? This is not an easy question to answer. It is clear that some pornography seems to be violent. Charles Winick (1985) analyzed the contents of all 430 magazines found in a New York City adult bookstore. He found 6% of the magazines pictured coercive and sadistic acts. A person, usually a woman, might be tied to a bed and appear to be slapped, pinched, or forced to have sexual intercourse. On the other hand, the large majority of pictures and stories involved people in a variety of voluntary adult sexual activities (Table 19-1).

One of the early answers to the question linking pornography to antisocial acts was provided by the Commission on Obscenity and Pornography (1970) appointed by President Richard Nixon. The commission reviewed dozens of studies, sponsored several of its own, and submitted eight volumes of scientific data. One study compared imprisoned sex offenders with other prisoners and a control group of nonoffenders. Contrary to expectations, the imprisoned sex offenders did not have a history of viewing pornography that was different from that of prisoners convicted of nonsex crimes or nonimprisoned adults.

Another study reported by the commission compared sex crimes in Denmark before and after pornography was legalized there in 1967. Did the number of sex crimes go up when sexual material became widely available? The answer was no. In fact, sex crimes declined in the years after pornography was legalized. Perhaps pornography provided a harmless outlet for antisocial sexual impulses. Looking at all the evidence, the Presidential Commission concluded that there was little if any linkage between pornography and sex crimes or sexual delinquency.

The commission found, also, that the typical consumers of pornography were neither derelicts nor socially undesirable. Customers in adult bookstores were usually middle class, middle aged, nearly always male, and frequently professionals or businessmen, and married.

Despite the seeming conclusiveness of the commission's findings, President Nixon rejected the report. Social scientists as well as spokespeople from religious and feminist groups also questioned the validity of the findings. For example, how could one rely on the honesty of convicted sex offenders? They might say they rarely look at pornography simply because they think saying otherwise might prolong their incarceration.

Still another commission appointed by the President of the United States in 1986 and headed by the Attorney General (1986), Edwin Meese, reviewed extensive research and listened to numerous experts and social and religious lead-

One social scientist, commenting on pornography, asked, "Why is an adolescent allowed to see a motion picture in which people are gruesomely dismembered by a chain saw and not permitted to see another one in which a couple have affectionate sexual intercourse?"

*Table 19-1*

**Pictorial Content of 430 Sexually Explicit Magazines (Winick, 1985)**

| Content | Percentage of pictures |
| --- | --- |
| Photographs of women's breasts, genitalia | 32 |
| Male-female coitus (simulated) | 15 |
| Male-female coitus, oral and other | 15 |
| Male-female coitus (actual) | 8 |
| Bondage (simulated, coerced sadistic acts) | 6 |
| Females with boots, shaved genital hair, wrestling | 3 |
| Oral-genital relations | 3 |
| Group sex, swinging couples | 3 |
| Lesbian sexual relations | 3 |
| Interracial sexual relations | 3 |
| Gay sexual relations | 1 |
| Anal intercourse | 1 |

ers. In its report there was some agreement that investigation showed that violent, aggressive pornography might lead to such attitudes and actions in frequent consumers. There was substantial disagreement, however, about the majority of pornography that is explicit but consensual, the kind viewed by adults when they rent an "X" rated video cassette. Many Meese commission members felt such erotica led to "promiscuity" and weakened family and society. Other commission experts found this erotica harmless and possibly even contributed to more positive and healthful sexuality. Just as the research has not agreed on the effects of sexually explicit material, there have been differing feminist points of view. Catherine MacKinnon (1987), a feminist leader, holds that pornography is no more protected by the First Ammendment (free speech) than is sexual harassment. Pornography, she states, is a form of action requiring the submission of women. It perpetuates the power imbalance of male domination/female submission.

Other feminist leaders have taken a different stand. Betty Friedan (1985) has suggested that most pornography may not be esthetically or emotionally acceptable, but it is usually little more than harmless erotic entertainment. The efforts of the women's movement, she believes, are better directed at more critical issues such as protecting abortion choice and assuring economic opportunity and equality.

Despite disagreement among feminists, a number of groups have come together and campaigned to have legislatures restrict pornographic materials. One organization, Women Against Pornography (WAP), has formulated the following guiding principles (Drucker, 1988):

1. We do not oppose displays of nudity or erotica.
2. We do not advocate censorship.
3. We are protesting the physical and psychological violence in pornography and the degradation of women.
4. We are seeking to make pornography unprofitable.
5. We understand the dangers of government regulation of speech.

## Erotica

The opponents of pornography can be divided into two groups. Many religious and civic groups see all explicit sexual depictions as unethical, immoral, and corrupting. Like the 1986 Attorney General's Commission Report, the so-called Meese Report, they want all pornography restricted or outlawed (Shenon, 1986). The second alliance of opponents—some feminists, educators and social scientists—talk about two kinds of sexual materials. They reserve the term *pornography* for stories and pictures involving children or adults being humiliated or exploited. Such materials, in their view, cause abusive inclinations and hostile feelings concerning sexuality.

This second group carefully differentiates this undesirable pornography from what they term *erotica*. Pornography involves power and injury. Erotic depictions, in contrast, are warm and sensual. They show adults freely engaging in mutually satisfying sexual activities. Erotica, it is argued, teaches empathy and responsiveness. It induces sexual arousal as well as affection. It follows from this perspective that pornography should be restricted, but erotica permitted.

Many would consider the material on the right pornographic, whereas the photograph on the far left is defined as erotic.

## Customers

When sexually explicit material was available only in out-of-the-way adult bookstores and what usually looked like dilapidated "adult" movie houses, the customers were almost exclusively men. Today the picture has changed enormously. The fact that sexually explicit television tapes are readily available in most video stores has encouraged many women to be renters. It is estimated that 10% of all video tapes are pornographic/erotic recordings and that several million are rented every week. This new availability has also meant the closing of most adult motion picture theatres and a sharp decline in the more explicit, "hard-core," magazines.

The question of the degree to which women enjoy and are aroused by sexual material has also become clearer. The typical erotic film played on a VCR (video cassette recorder), is watched by an adult couple. Women may not find every tape arousing or acceptable but seem to prefer those in which the sex occurs in the context of a meaningful story or evolves out of a relationship (Chapter 7). Thus the customers of erotica today are very likely to be ordinary men and women, ranging in age from young adults to those who are advanced in years. There are still many adults who, because of esthetic, political, religious, or other beliefs, will not rent a cassette with erotic content. But it is likely that close to half of the North American adult population has seen such video tapes and a small portion rent them almost weekly (Kendrick, 1987; Lawrence and Herold, 1988; Weatherford, 1986).

**Arousal**   The goal of erotica is arousal—becoming sexually excited (Chapter 5). One common use is for masturbation. The erotica evokes a sexual re-

Sexual problems and treatment are discussed in Chapter 17.

sponse, often with the aid of fantasy and imagination. Couples may also find erotic video tapes a "turn on." The scenes depicted may act as a disinhibitor or suggest activities they might try and enjoy. On occasion a sex therapist may recommend a special erotic film. Such specially prepared tapes could help an individual or a couple to overcome inhibitory barriers, and to learn more about their own and the other sex's erotic capability. The VCR can act as on-the-spot uncritical teacher (Chapter 17).

## Conclusion

Whether or not pornography and erotica, or in fact, any depiction of women and men in sexual intercourse, lead to distorted sexual attitudes, subjugate women, or trigger violence is not simply answered. Since reports from the two Presidential Commisions in 1970 and 1986 have not been considered conclusive, investigations continue. One research team tried to correlate the incidence of rape with the circulation rates of sexually explicit adult magazines. They found little meaningful relationship (Scott and Schwalm, 1988). Other researchers showed college males sexually stimulating photos of women, some of whom were in distress, ostensibly suffering pain. Some of the men said that they found the distressed model, a woman in bondage (Chapter 20), more sexually arousing but many did not (Heilbrun, Jr. and Seif, 1988). Still other investigators are doubtful if there is a sex-to-violence linkage but believe there may be a violence-to-violence linkage. Donnerstein and Linz (1986) reviewed the voluminous literature on pornography and violence and found that, first of all, very little sexually explicit material that is readily available is actually violent (Table 19-1). More important, the reviewers are convinced that it is violence and not sex that promotes and triggers violent behavior. Violence need not be linked with sexual entertainment to promote aggression. Violence in any context in the media tends to incite violent behavior. (See the media section in the following pages.)

Some couples say watching adult videos has taught them gratifying new erotic techniques.

The issue of pornography-erotica will not be easily settled. There is some agreement, a limited consensus, that includes feminists, social scientists, religious groups, and to an extent, free speech advocates. Pornography that enlists children to pose in sexual situations, so called *kiddie-porn,* should be prohibited. These efforts are by and large successful since several prosecutions throughout the nation have made pornography displaying children virtually unavailable. There is a good deal of agreement, too, that sexual material that clearly degrades women or men can probably contribute to disturbed sexual attitudes and perpetuate myths harmful to the full and equal function of both sexes.

After these agreements have been stated, dissension begins. One research effort after another, although it seems momentarily persuasive, ultimately fails. In many instances the sample population is much too small or the questions are emotionally loaded to favor a particular outcome. Often as not the people who participate in research are motivated not to be truthful. When sex offenders and prisoners are questioned, their answers may well be chosen to demonstrate how contrite they are, or to show that they are not responsible for their behavior (Marshall, 1988).

Many investigators also unknowingly have a bias. They come from psychoanalytic, feminist, anti-feminist, religious, free-speech, or other backgrounds and want their research to confirm their points of view. The result of this diversity, Mould (1988) argues, is a plethora of assumptions leading to an accumulation of inconsistent findings. It follows that until we have excellent, unbiased, scientifically impeccable research, confirmed many times over, all present conclusions about the effects of erotica/pornography should be regarded as tentative.

## Erotic toys

In addition to sexually explicit stories and films, many "adult" stores sell a variety of erotic toys. The merchandise can include whips, leather and seductive clothing, sensual oils and powders, and sexual games. One board game is similar to Monopoly except that the players buy a kiss, a massage, oral-genital, or coital relations.

Sexual apparatus—toys to enhance sexual pleasure—have been sold for centuries. During the Ming Dynasty, 500 years ago, wealthy Chinese males slipped jade rings on their erect penises to increase the duration of the erection. Small pea-sized jade *Ben-Wa* balls were found to be pleasurable by some women when inserted into the vagina. Supposedly the movements of walking or dancing tumble the balls, stimulating the woman's genitals.

Some sexual toys are intended to enhance or substitute for sexual intercourse. There are condoms that are ribbed, usually with foam rubber, to make the penis seem larger. There are penis-like strap-on devices, usually called *dildoes,* that a woman can wear enabling her to perform vaginal or anal inter-

This 300 year old Chinese illustration shows an erotic swing, a rare sexual toy, but one that appears in most societies.

course. Life-size inflatable rubber dolls with "realistic" open mouths, vaginas, and/or anuses are available for those who want an instantly available partner who requires no foreplay or communication. Similar mannequins with a penis ("pick the size you want") that vibrates and is constantly erect, are more difficult to find but also available. The number and variety of sexual toys is considerable, and every year seems to bring about new inventions (Weatherford, 1986).

The most widely used contemporary erotic toy is the electric or battery-driven *vibrator*. Petersen et al. (1983) and Wolfe (1981) report that about a third of younger women and about 10% of men frequently use this device in sexual relations or for masturbation. Vibrators may be shaped like a penis, be disc- or cup-shaped, or boxlike with straps for the hand, which is then caused to vibrate.

**Caution**  Most sexual toys, silky underclothes, and vibrators are harmless. Some therapists are concerned, however, that the frequent use of vibrators may bring about dependence. Ben-wa balls and similar vaginal inserts can be very hazardous. They can cause vaginal and uterine infections and in rare instances even require surgery for their removal. All erotic toys, props, and apparatus should be used carefully and with the full knowledge and consent of partners.

## CLOTHING AND THE MEDIA
### Clothing

The emphasis that clothing has given sexuality has varied from one era to the next. Each fashion shift has greatly enriched the manufacturers who caught the

*Figure 19-1*
Codpieces.

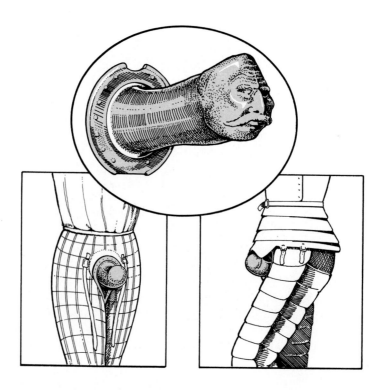

trend in time. Better yet, if by clever advertising the producers initiated the style, then they could start profiting right from the beginning. It is no wonder, then, that we are constantly besieged by erotic, seductive advertising for the latest clothing and underclothing that is daring, revealing, titillating, and stimulating. Men are by no means exempt from the marketers of erotically tinged clothes and accessories. Now they too like women for centuries, are, in the words of Coward's (1985) book, "sought, bought, and packaged."

Actually, erotically suggestive men's clothing is not recent. A few centuries ago English and French gentlemen dressed in silks and ruffles with a flourish we might today look at as feminine. The *codpiece* worn by tight-breeched Europeans from the fourteenth to sixteenth century not only protected the penis, but most important, exaggerated its full dimensions. Today's body hugging men's jeans with their phallic bulge have ample historical precedent.

Women, perhaps more than men, have been persuaded to buy, discard, and buy again. Valerie Steele (1985), in her book on fashion and eroticism, shows that however frequent changes in bustline and hemlines, lingerie and stockings, manufacturers have preserved the rule to conceal yet enticingly reveal. Even the corset, that tightly laced seemingly unglamourous nineteenth century tortuous female undergarment, served a sexual purpose. It greatly narrowed the waist and thereby accentuated the hips and bust. It announced, in Steele's view, both an ample sexuality and maternal potential.

## The media

If all pornography and erotica disappeared tomorrow at noon, if every adult book, magazine, photo, and video tape instantly evaporated, we would still be living in a sex-saturated society. Motion pictures, rock music, advertisements, and particularly television, are filled with sex. Just what is there to be learned from televsion, by far the predominant medium? The average viewer spends between 3 and 5 hours daily with the set on, hearing and seeing, and having his and her thinking and behavior shaped both consciously and unconsciously.

We already know a great deal about the impact television has on the human tendency toward aggression and violent behavior. According to the National Commission on the Causes and Prevention of Violence, the constant gunfire, car chases, and assaults are *directly* responsible for a large portion of the violence we actually experience in our society. Many viewers who have a vulnerability toward criminal behavior are easily triggered into committing a violent act because they have seen it modeled for them on TV. But others, too—those who might never use a gun or knife—are prompted to action by the constant violence of television that trivializes death and makes injury seem acceptable (Strouse and Fabes, 1985).

Television is a powerful teacher. A 30-second commercial suggesting an underarm deodorant or toilet paper will literally result in millions of sales. Just what is this extraordinarily influential medium teaching about sex? In an effort to sell everything from breakfast cereal to eye make-up, commercials, the "soap operas," dramas, and comedies are loaded with sex. According to a study by Louis Harris & Associates, 65,000 sexual references are broadcast every year for an average of 27 per hour. This includes 9 lingering, intimate kisses, 6 sexually toned hugs, and a dozen hints at, or thinly disguised instances of sexual intercourse. Much of this behavior, too, is impulsive, manipulative, or hostile.

Most social scientists agree that television can trigger violence. Why is this rarely, if ever, reported on television?

Three thousand years ago the Egyptian Queen, Nefertite seems to have shaped her eyebrows and wore rouge and lipstick just as is common today.

Despite the frequency of sexual material, responsible conduct is seldom depicted on television. For example, there was only one reference to birth control in 50 hours of broadcasting, and awareness of sexually transmitted disease appeared only once in 10 hours. One media observer stated that the reason the "sex outweighs the sanity by 85 to 1, is that sex sells. There's no money in talking about safer sexual practices" (Blau, 1988).

---

### In Sum

Human sexual needs are exploited to sell all sorts of merchandise and services. Sexually explicit films and stories are popular and have been seen by nearly all adults. Some writers distinguish pornography from erotica, the latter being nonexploitive. Whether pornography leads to antisocial behavior, or if it is the violent content itself—and not the sex—that triggers aggression, are questions not yet conclusively answered by research.

---

**aphrodisiac**
Foods, drugs, or scents that are alleged to increase sexual interest or vigor.

### Aphrodisiacs

All societies have eagerly sought and bought nearly an infinity of devices, powders, liquids, drugs, and chemicals that ostensibly stimulate or increase sexual capability. Goat's testicles boiled in milk were prized in ancient India. Today, powdered rhinoceros horn is still sold in the Orient, and at considerable cost, since it allegedly assures potency. (One side-effect of this intense consumer demand is that the animal may soon become extinct in Africa.)

The most widely used **aphrodisiac** is alcohol. It both increases and decreases sexuality. A small amount of alcohol, such as in one mixed drink, a
medium sized glass of wine or a beer, has a disinhibiting effect. A little light
drinking may create a feeling of warmth, relaxation, and desire. Go a little further and the sedative and physiological depressant effects of alcohol become
obvious. After three drinks desire may still be elevated. But physical ability has
also been markedly curtailed. As a result, the man or woman who has drunk a
good deal may find arousal and orgasm elusive. In fact, many men have their
first erectile difficulty when they attempt coitus after a substantial amount of
alcohol.

Since the 1960s, marijuana use, although illegal, has become widespread in
the United States. Like alcohol, this drug has gained a reputation as an aphrodisiac. Weller and Halikas (1984) interviewed marijuana smokers and found
that two thirds thought the drug increased their sexual pleasure. Half reported
that marijuana enhanced their desire. About a fifth felt that the drug was so
important to their sexual relations that they smoked regularly in preparation
for intercourse.

Marijuana is a mild hallucinogen. It modestly distorts feelings and perceptions, and it is often considered a *mood enhancer*. This means that if you feel
sexy, relaxed, and affectionate, a little smoking is likely to make you feel a bit
more so. When you are physically involved, this same tendency to exaggerate
sensation can make an orgasm seem to last minutes, not just seconds.

Marijuana distorts all feelings, not just good ones. If you approach a sexual
relationship with some fear, smoking is likely to intensify and increase anxiety.
If there is suspicion, doubt, and mistrust, marijuana is likely to distort these
feelings into paranoia. Marijuana is also undependable. Nearly all smokers report that there are occasions when they have used the drug and the effects
were opposite those expected. They hoped that smoking would increase their
desire, arousal, and orgasm. Instead marijuana "flattened" the feelings and
made the smoker feel distant and uninterested.

A legendary aphrodisiac is prepared from a bright green bug called a *Spanish fly*. The beetle is dried and a powder called *cantharidin* is derived from it.
When consumed, cantharidin increases the output of urine and irritates the
bladder and urethra. This urethral tingling is supposed to excite people who
have little sexual desire. But it is questionable whether the burning, itchy discomfort caused by cantharidin is likely to be interpreted by anyone as passion.

Numerous other drugs have also been reported to have aphrodisiac proper-
ties. Amphetamines and cocaine (particularly "crack") are both stimulants and
supposedly energize and prolong sexual relations. Besides being illegal, these
substances can also diminish excitation and orgasm. At the other extreme, barbiturates and methaqualone (Quaalude) are both sedatives. They are said to
relax and disinhibit some users. Many consumers, however, report that these
substances impair arousal and response.

Amyl nitrate is a liquid often kept in a small capsule worn, mainly by men,
on a decorative chain around the neck. The capsule is "popped" and inhaled
along with orgasm. This supposedly magnifies the intensity of climax. Amyl
nitrate is a potent vasodilator. It rapidly expands the blood vessels, drops
blood pressure, produces a flushed hot feeling, and may interfere with the
heart's rhythm and activity. For many people, amyl nitrate is a serious health
hazard (Ray, Ksir, 1987).

The sexual potential of
alcohol is continuously
stressed. One advertise-
ment, showing a cozy cou-
ple in front of a fireplace
reads, "You know the mo-
ment is right when you
share a bottle of Chateau."

Men and women have
been looking for a genuine
aphrodisiac with much the
same intensity and lack of
success with which they
have looked for the
"fountain of youth." Both
goals and frustrations are
thousands of years old.

### Dare to Go Bare*

Nudism and nudist camps, long the subject of ribald jokes and social discrimination, have for many become profitable enterprises. Only a generation ago, nudists were likely to spend their clothes-free weekends at a facility that offered tents, modest trailers, or primitive cabins. Facilities were usually limited to a small pool, volley ball net, and a tennis court. Camps were remote and hard to find; most towns made it difficult for such facilities to operate. Today elaborate complexes in Florida, California, and several other states offer condominium living, saunas, and all the facilities of luxurious resorts.

Nudism began as a "back to nature" movement in western Europe nearly a centry ago. The belief was that clothing hid and corrupted people while nudity compelled honesty, equality, and physical and psychological health. Despite popular myths to the contrary, nudism was and remains a *nonsexual* recreation. In fact, some facilities are so strict that a husband and wife, playfully jumping in the pool holding hands, will be informed that such visible "sexual contact" is not approved.

Many nudists spend their summer vacations and most warm weekends at a facility. There they do essentially what anyone else who is camping or visiting a resort would do. They play games, sun themselves, swim, read, play cards, and chat. The only difference is that they are totally nude. It often comes as a shock to a first-time visitor to find not only are all the guests nude, but also the waiter, life-guard, office clerk, and secretary are not clothed. Furthermore, every variety of human is usually present. Nudists may be children or aged, tall, short, thin, obese, beautiful, or plain. Many times, too, entire families are present.

The American Sunbathing Association, the official nudist membership group, estimates there are nudist facilities in most states, 100,000 "camp" nudists, and several times that number who, on their own, swim nude on deserted beaches, or relax nude in their own backyards.

Nudists do discourage public sex, but they are by no means asexual beings. They may have nude beauty contests for both sexes. In a camp, it is readily apparent that good-looking men and women receive more than their share of appreciative glances. Marylin Story (1987) compared 100 nudists to non-nudists who were otherwise similar. She was interested in exploring just how sexually different and/or permissive contemporary nudists are. She found that nudists had fewer sexual problems and most had richer fantasies about sexual behaviors in which they would like to engage. But the majority seemed no more sexually permissive than non-nudists. Nudists, by and large, seemed like everyone else, except perhaps for fewer problems and a little more creative sexual imagination.

*Bumper sticker some nudists put on their cars.

A persistently popular aphrodisiac, *Yohimbe,* derived from the bark of a tropical tree, supposedly enhances sexual arousal and particularly helps men maintain an erection. The evidence has been inconsistent, yet the drug is still marketed. One advertisement in the *Journal of the American Medical Association* claimed that scientific research had shown that 46% of men with erection problems improved their sexual function. The manufacturer warned, however, that *Yohimex* (1988), the trade name, should not be used by older patients or women, and that side effects such as dizziness, headache, and elevated blood pressure could occur.

**Do they work?**   The Food and Drug Administration (FDA) in Washington, D.C., is responsible for evaluating and monitoring the effects of drugs and similar substances. In a comprehensive review of illegal and nonprescription aphrodisiacs, the FDA declared that *none* had been shown to be *effective* and many were *unsafe*.

The FDA cited the sample of a product called "Big Ox." It is a combination of stimulants and vitamins. Despite graphic and lavish advertising depicting its purported potent effects, the FDA found that the product did not work.

Safety is also a major consideration. Spanish fly, for example, is quite toxic. Its use can lead to genitourinary infection and urethral scarring. Its continued consumption can be poisonous. Eating overly large quantities of vitamins is also NOT recommended. Hypervitaminosis can result. This is a condition marked by nausea, weight loss, and bone, liver, and organ damage. Aphrodisiacs not only do not work, but many carry health risks (Molotsky, 1985).

**Placebo effect**   Hormones administered to people whose systems are deficient may reinvigorate sexual appetite and capability. Various medical interventions to alleviate infections and other physical problems may rehabilitate sexual response. With these exceptions, no drug, food, vitamin, or any similar substance has been shown to effectively alleviate sexual problems or create desire. But having said this, we need to qualify it. Powdered rhinoceros horn, vitamin E, and anything else for that matter can work, if it is believed that it works. Placebos (Chapter 1), help as long as people believe. Men and women who are certain that a little vitamin E or goat glands will enhance their abilities are likely to benefit from such substances. *Placebo effect* describes the ability of useless, harmless substances to sometimes be somewhat effective if there is strong belief in their potential.

Sex sells. Most advertisements try to use sexually appealing men and women to merchandise the product. This may sometimes be interpreted as exploitation.

# PROSTITUTION

A *prostitute* is a person who is paid for sexual services. Typically each sexual service has a price tag. Seventy-five dollars may be enough for conventional sexual intercourse. If oral-genital relations are desired $50 more may be required. For $200 the prostitute may spend a full hour with the customer. If instead a "quickie" is desired (a rapid 10-minute sexual experience) perhaps only $50 will suffice. The point is that prostitutes work for specific fees. They think of themselves as *working girls (or boys)* who offer a service for which they rightfully deserve to be paid.

Prostitution is a very ancient trade. In Athens 2000 years ago, prostitutes were *hetaerae* (Greek for *companions*) and had a valued social function. They were women of intelligence and education and expected to carry out their profession with warmth, imagination, and skill. When they retired they were almost certain to be in great demand as wives. A few hundred years later, as Christianity was adopted by Rome, the lot of prostitutes declined. They were seen as outcasts, forced to wear identifying wigs and tunics so that they could easily be spotted and avoided. By the Middle Ages in Europe, prostitutes were gathered together and often moved out of sight into **brothels** at the far end of town.

In the United States *red light districts,* collections of brothels, (each with a red light over the door) had existed in every major city and many minor ones since the American Revolution. Beginning in the 19th century, however, they were outlawed by state after state supposedly to stop the spread of sexual infections and to protect women. Presently only Nevada has reversed its laws and permits prostitution. Many other nations, including England, Holland, and Japan, once outlawed prostitution but now have more permissive legislation. It can be said, too, that whether outlawed or not prostitution appears in all nations and is usually tolerated as long as it is not too obvious (Carmen, Moody, 1985).

## Life-styles

It is guessed that perhaps 100,000 women and perhaps 5000 men earn all or a good part of their livelihood from prostitution each year. This count does not include another 100,000 or so topless dancers, strippers, nude models, and other sex entertainers, most of whom are not prostitutes (DeWulf, 1983; Carmen, Moody, 1985).

Prostitutes tend to develop distinctive occupational life-styles. Those who are more intelligent, resourceful, and attractive are likely to be **call girls.** They will be independent and have a "book." This is a list of customer names and phone numbers to be called from time to time to suggest another visit. Incidentally, when a call girl leaves the business, her book may be sold to another prostitute for several tens of thousands of dollars.

Call girls earn from one hundred to several hundred dollars for a visit of an hour or two. As a result they have a good income and are considered to be at the top of the economic and status hierarchy of prostitution.

A woman who is a *house prostitute* works with several others and receives customers in a brothel. A variation of the brothel is the *escort service,* where women are sent out on calls. Typically there is a *madam,* or occasionally a male, who runs the house and oversees assignments. Frequently too, the house is thinly disguised as a model or massage studio.

*brothel*
A house or apartment maintained by prostitutes where they receive customers for sexual activity; bordello.

*call girl*
A prostitute who is generally well paid and usually receives customers in her own apartment.

At the bottom of the social and occupational ladder of prostitution are **streetwalkers.** They literally walk the streets. They usually have a favored area and may even stake out a block or two that is specifically their territory. In New York City streetwalkers can be found along most of midtown Eighth Avenue. In Washington, D.C., 14th Street, only a few blocks from the nation's Capitol, is a popular streetwalker area. Streetwalkers usually dress in a conspicuous manner and approach their customers asking, "Do you want to go out?" If the "John" (prostitutes' term for a customer) indicates interest he will next be asked, "How much do you want to spend?" The John who has only $25 is likely to have to settle for a quick "hand job." Those who want more will have to pay more.

Streetwalkers are likely to be adolescents or in their early 20s. They are often lacking in social or vocational skills and are controlled or victimized by a **pimp,** a man who lives with, cares for, and controls prostitutes. Potterat and his associates (1985) closely studied 14 streetwalkers and found a number of identifying characteristics. Their mean age was 23; they had not completed school. They first had intercourse at age 13; most were dependent on drugs or alcohol, had a history of abuse by spouse or boyfriend, and came from an unstable home. Compared also with other prostitutes, they are more likely to have an STD (Chapter 16).

*streetwalker*
A prostitute who picks up customers by soliciting on the street.

*pimp*
A man who shares prostitutes' earnings and usually provides them with protection and care. (Not to be confused with a *procurer,* who finds customers.)

Streetwalkers are the most visible of all prostitutes. They are outnumbered, however, by prositutes that are house or call girls.

Sex entertainers "strip" or dance almost nude to entertain their audience.

Prostitutes themselves are not usually involved in violent criminal activity, but streetwalkers are likely to attract muggers who victimize them and their customers.

## Sex entertainers

*Strippers* are men or women who, accompanied by music, enticingly take off their clothes for an audience. *Topless dancers* are women who dance bare-breasted in bars and other entertainment facilities. There are also hostesses or *B-girls* in bars and cocktail lounges who may sit next to a man and encourage him to buy drinks. All of these people are using their sexuality to amuse and arouse, and they are being paid. But are they prostitutes?

Sometimes the line between an entertainer and a prostitute becomes very unclear. It has become customary for women and men strippers to take off their clothes and then, wearing only a tiny patch over their genitals, mingle with their audience. They sit on customers' laps and for a tip of a dollar or two kiss their customers or allow them to briefly caress parts of their bodies. Bar hostesses may also allow customers to lightly touch and fondle them. To all intents and purposes these entertainers, like prostitutes, are selling sex. But there is a technical distinction. As long as the stripper and other entertainers do not have coitus or oral-genital relations or masturbate their customers, they are not considered prostitutes. They are sex entertainers.

## Entering the life

Prostitutes talk about "the life," meaning their working career. A question, "How did you enter the life?" is most likely to be answered with a shrug and comment such as, "It just happened." What this answer reflects is that more often than not becoming a prostitute is the result of a drift into the life rather than a clear-cut job decision.

Some prostitutes come from the entertainment industry. They may have started as topless dancers or tried to work as actresses, actors, or rock singers. In these situations, which may encourage casual sexual contacts, they may have happened into a paid sexual arrangement.

An important means for entering the life is to have a friend who is already a prostitute. The woman who visits her friend may be asked to accept a "date." "He's very nice and you'll like him. You'll get a hundred dollars and you can keep it all." A less benign way some women enter is by being victimized by a pimp or his associates. Adolescents who are runaways are particularly vulnerable to being befriended by a woman or man who seems to like them and promises to help them. Next they may get involved in the pimp's life-style, drug dependency, petty thievery, and eventually prostitution.

A feminist view of why women enter prostitution generally emphasizes the economic motive. In our culture, it is argued, women and men have been conditioned to view sex as a commodity. It is something a woman dispenses to repay a man's dating expenses. Even spouses may unconsciously view the wife's sexual services as an exchange for her husband's paycheck. In this atmosphere it is not difficult for a woman who has few educational and vocational resources, whose employment is further limited by discrimination, to think that all she has to offer to earn a living is her body (MacKinnon, 1987).

Another opinion holds that all prostitutes are mentally deranged, sexually insatiable, or glumly, like automatons going through their routine. There is little evidence for these perceptions. Prostitutes are neither unrestrained, lascivious women, nor mechanical human beings who always get rid of their customers as quickly as possible. It is true that among some streetwalkers and "house girls" the philosophy that is sometimes enunciated is called the "five gits": "Get paid, get them up, get them in, get them off, get them out." Nevertheless, prostitutes are women who have sexual and affectional feelings, and who have preferences and likes and dislikes just as any other person.

Savitz and Rosen (1988) interviewed 40 streetwalkers, women who very likely have the most difficult and hazardous life of all prostitutes. They found that over half frequently reached orgasm with their customers and nearly all were or- gasmic with their own lover. The women also made distinctions in their sexual conduct. Only about half had oral sexual relations with their customers, but nearly all did with their lover. Most did not consent to receiving anal intercourse with their customers but did with their boyfriend. When asked about their own sexual self-image, most said they were heterosexual, and about a third reported varying degrees of lesbian interest. From the investigators' point of view, prosti- tutes and prostitution should be looked at as a complex of economic, personal, and social determinants that are not easily stereotyped.

There is also some question about psychological illness. Drug abuse, alco- holism, and emotional disturbances are found in many prostitutes and may be particularly frequent among streetwalkers. But studies that compare the many different social levels of prostitutes with controls have shown that similar psy- chological dilemmas can exist in women and men who do not sell sexual ser- vices. At the present time it seems as if psychological problems among prosti- tutes play only a partial role in steering women into this vocation (Potterat et al., 1985).

Perhaps the explanation of why people enter prostitution involves elements of all of these hypotheses. Most prostitutes begin sexual relations early, and frequently they have been abused. Many feel trapped by a lack of schooling and poor economic skills, assets and opportunities. Most seem to have a low image of their character and worth. But these experiences and feelings are not sufficient to propel a person into prostitution. They only make her or him sus- ceptible. What is needed is exposure. Another person has to introduce or co- erce them into the prostitute life-style. As Potterat and his associates (1985) point out, this explanation for entering prostitution involves two distinct con- cepts. Susceptibility comes first, and exposure second. When both are present, the woman (or man) is likely to move into prostitution.

## Customers

The entertainment media and the newspapers so often feature stories about prostitution that one might think it a common experience. However, not only are there relatively few prostitutes, but the number of male customers is also low. Visiting a house of prositition was once fairly common. Two or three generatons ago, probably a fourth of men may have had this experience. To- day it is likely that fewer than 5% of men have ever visited a prostitute and fewer than 1 in 100 males do so with any regularity (DeWulf, 1983).

Most men employ a prostitute for the sake of sexual variety. They want a new partner or to have a sexual experience such as fellatio not offered by their spouse or friend. A few others patronize prostitutes because they are lonely or have no other sexual outlet. These may be men who are physically unattractive or handicapped. Women have continually rejected them and they have to buy sexual release and a small amount of seeming affection.

Robinson and Krussman (1983) looked at the men who patronize prostitutes. They studied 530 customers and found the most requested acts were first coitus and second fellatio. Most men were married and ranged in age from 20 to the 40s, with the average age in the early 30s. People from every educational and vocational level were represented, including laborers, clerks, salesmen, government officials, and every variety of professional. Another finding contradicted earlier studies. It was formerly believed that customers were emotionally maladjusted. The men were thought to be incapable of forming affectional bonds or their psychosexual development was said to be immature. Robinson and Krussman reported no evidence that the men who patronized prostitutes were psychologically any different from men who did not. Sexual relations with prostitutes attract relatively few men, but they seem to come from all social levels and appear relatively normal.

### Male prostitutes

Men who serve as prostitutes to women are rare. There is virtually no equivalent of the streetwalker or house prostitute among men who cater to women. There are occasionally men available through escort services. More typically, however, the few men whose clients are women sometimes appear in jobs such as ski, tennis, or dance instructors. They are in positions where they are likely to meet women and are already being paid for a relatively personal service. Even then, if a relationship becomes sexual, pay is as likely to be a gift as an outright amount of money.

> There are virtually no lesbian prostitutes. Women who sell sexual services to women have been the subject of myths and stories but are rare.

Another form of male prostitution that is also infrequent is for an older woman to "keep" a nice-looking younger man. The man is sometimes disguised as a business assistant, or decorating consultant, and does not live with her. Or the man may live with the woman and be called a friend, or ". . .a college student who helps around the house, and I give him room and board." If the man is known for his tendency to be the temporary companion of older women he will probably be called a *gigolo*. A gigolo typically stays with a woman for a few months or a year or so. Then the relationship fades and he searches for another older woman who will support him and give him money or gifts.

The most common form of male prostitution is homosexual. It is far less frequent than female prostitution, but several thousand adolescents and young men sell their services to homosexual or bisexual males. Like the heterosexual gigolo, many male prostitutes are *kept boys*. They are supported by older homosexual men and are paid with gifts or money. There are also a few *call boys,* young men who like call girls are relatively resourceful, educated, and financially independent.

> *hustler*
> A male prostitute who caters to men. This term may also be used to describe aggressive salespeople.

The most visible form of male prostitution involves **hustlers,** males who may be as young as 12 or 13. Like streetwalkers, hustlers may cruise certain city blocks, or congregate in bars, baths, parks, or public toilets. Some also purport to be masseurs, advertising their massage and related services in sexually oriented newspapers.

Interestingly, unlike the customer of a woman prostitute, the Johns who use male prostitutes often want the prostitute to have an orgasm. They may spend a good deal of time performing fellatio on the male prostitute or demand that he have anal intercourse with them until climax. Many customers of males also insist that the prostitute retain a very youthful boyish appearance. Because of this emphasis on youth, the working life of male prostitutes usually ends by the time they are in their late 20s (DeWulf, 1983).

### Victim or victimless crime

There are occasionally well-publicized efforts on the part of a city government to crack down on vice. At such times hundreds of streetwalkers, other prostitutes, and sometimes customers are arrested. Soon, however, the legal tide runs its course and everyone is back in business. Police, government, and even enlightened social efforts to eliminate prostitution have not been very effective. Recognizing the futility of arrest, most larger cities such as New York, San Francisco, Houston, Montreal, and Chicago ordinarily ignore the activities of prostitutes as long as they are not too conspicuous or a guise for robbery and other crime.

The continuation of prostitution despite occasional police raids and other harassment has led many to point out that legal restraints are futile. It is argued that prostitution is a victimless crime and not a major source for the spread of sexual infections. Both the prostitute and customer are willingly engaging in a buy and sell arrangement. A customer is simply buying a personal service in much the same way that a patron buys a restaurant meal. Why, then, should prostitution be considered a crime if there is no victim?

The counter to this contention is that while the customer may not be a victim, the prostitute is. Some see all prostitutes as women who are being taken advantage of by a society that provides them with few other economic options. Potterat et al. (1985) suggest that prostitution is an end-product of a male-dominated social order that induces vulnerable women to turn to prostitution simply to survive.

A third group agrees that some prostitutes are victims; they are exploited. But others, it is held, are not exploited. Streetwalkers are most likely to be disadvantaged, but call girls may be exercising relatively free choice. Social scientists Gail Pheterson and Judith Walkowitz (1985) distinguish between prostitutes who work under coercive conditions and those who choose their lifestyle. Saying that all prostitutes are abused encourages attitudes and laws "that punish, stigmatize, and deny human rights. . . ." In these researchers' view, the exploitation of some of the women who are prostitutes is not likely to be ended by restrictive laws. A controversial view holds that a just solution would be to extend to prostitutes the status of a legitimate vocation and provide them with safe and sensible working conditions, Social Security, health insurance, and the other benefits of meaningful employment.

Prostitutes now commonly insist that men wear a condom. This may explain why their incidence of sexually transmitted disease and AIDS is relatively low. Fear of AIDS also does not seem to have substantially reduced either the number of prostitutes or their customers.

*Summary*

Sexuality is exploited, bought and sold as a commodity, in numerous ways. Pornography is the explicit depiction of sexual relations in books, pictures, films, or the like. Despite contentions that pornography encourages exploitive and violent attitudes, research findings have been inconclusive. Pornography has been distinguished from erotica; the latter is often seen as a more positive description of sexuality.

Aphrodisiacs are widely promoted as sexual stimulants. It is likely, however, that most, probably all, have only a placebo effect.

Prostitutes are women or men who are paid for their sexual services. Call girls are at the top of the status ladder and streetwalkers are at the bottom. There are also sex entertainers, strippers, and B-girls who provide limited sexual services for money.

Prostitutes enter "the life" by drifting into it, or by being recruited or victimized. Men who act as prostitutes for women are rare. Most male prostitutes cater to other men.

---

*For Thought and Discussion*

1 Is there a difference between pornography and erotica? What makes a story or picture pornographic rather than erotic?
2 What arguments can be made for and against legalizing prostitution? If prostitution were an accepted vocation, with regulated working conditions, minimum wages, and retirement and health plans, how might this change the lives of women who are "in the life?"
3 What kind of childhood or adolescent experiences might help account for people who habitually buy pornography?
4 What suggestions do you have to help prevent commercial sexual exploitation?
5 How would you both protect personal privacy and freedom yet regulate pictures and other sexual enterprises that might be harmful?

---

*References*

Attorney General's Commission on Pornography. *Final Report of the Attorney General's Commission on Pornography.* Washington D.C., Department of Justice, 1986.

Blau, E. Study finds barrage of sex on TV. *New York Times,* January 27, 1988, p. C-26.

Carmen, A., and Moody, H. *Working women: the subterranean world of street prostitutes.* New York: A Cornelia & Michael Bessie Book/Harper & Row, 1985.

Commission on Obscenity and Pornography. *The report of the commission on obscenity and pornography.* Washington, D.C.: U.S. Government Printing Office, 1970.

Coward, R. *Female desires: how they are sought, bought, and packaged.* New York: Grove Press, 1985.

Dewulf, L. *Faces of Venus: prostitution through the ages.* New York: Focus, 1983.

Donnerstein, E.I., and Linz, D.G. The question of pornography. *Psychology Today,* December 1986, 56-57.

Drucker, S.J. The anti-pornography crusade coalition: feminists, the new Christian right, and the Meese Commission. *The Speech Communication Annual,* January 1988, 2, 21-40.

Friedan, B. How to get the women's movement moving again. *The New York Times Magazine,* November 3, 1985, 36.

Heilbrun, Jr., A.B., and Seif, D.T. Erotic value of female distress in sexually explicit photographs. *The Journal of Sex Research,* 1988, 24, 47-57.

Kendrick, W. *The secret museum: pornography in modern culture.* New York: Viking, 1987.

Lawrence, K., and Herold, E.S. Women's attitudes toward and experience with sexually explicit materials. *The Journal of Sex Research,* 1988, 24, 161-169.

MacKinnon, C.A. *Feminism unmodified: discourses on life and law.* Cambridge, Mass.: Harvard University Press, 1987.

Marshall, W.L. The use of sexually explicit stimuli by rapists, child molesters, and nonoffenders. *The Journal of Sex Research,* May 1988, 25, 267-288.

Molotsky, I. U.S. moves to ban sexual nonstrums. *New York Times,* January 16, 1985, p. C11.

Mould, D.E. A critical analysis of recent research on violent erotica. *The Journal of Sex Research,* 1988, 24, 326-340.

Petersen, J.R., Kretchmer, A., Nellis, B., Lever, J., and Hertz, R. The *Playboy* readers' sex survey (Parts 1 and 2). *Playboy,* Jan. 1983, 108; March 1983, 90.

Pheterson, G., and Walkowitz, J. Not all prostitution is forced trafficking. *New York Times,* July 2, 1985, A-18.

Potterat, J.J., Phillips, L., Rothenberg, R.B., and Darrow, W.W. On becoming a prostitute. *Journal of Sex Research,* August 1985, 21(3), 329-335.

Ray, D., and Ksir, C. *Drugs, society, and human behavior.* St. Louis, Mo.: 1988, Times Mirror/Mosby.

Robinson, S.E., and Krussman, H.W. Sex for money: profile of a John. *Journal of Sex Education Therapy,* Spring/Summer 1983, 9(1), 27-31.

Savitz, L., and Rosen, L. The sexuality of prostitutes: sexual enjoyment reported by "streetwalkers." *The Journal of Sex Research,* 1988, 24, 200-208.

Scott, J.E., and Schwain, L.A. Rape rates and the circulation rates of adult magazines. *The Journal of Sex Research,* 1988, 24, 241-250.

Shenon, P.A. A second opinion on pornography's impact. *New York Times,* May 18, 1986, E-8.

Steele, V. *Fashion and eroticism: ideals of feminine beauty from the Victorian to the Jazz age.* Fair Lawn, New Jersey: Oxford University Press, 1985.

Story, M.D. A comparison of social nudists and non-nudists on experiences with various sexual outlets. *The Journal of Sex Research,* May 1987, 23(2), 197-211.

Strouse, J., and Fabes, R.A. Formal versus informal sources of sex education: competing forces in the sexual socialization of adolescents. *Adolescence,* Summer 1985, XX (78), 161-166.

Weatherford, J. *Porn Row.* New York: Arbor House, 1986.

Weller, R.A., and Halikas, J.A. Marijuana use and sexual behavior. *The Journal of Sex Research,* May 1984, 20(2), 186-193.

Winick, C. A content analysis of sexually explicit magazines sold in an adult bookstore. *The Journal of Sex Research,* May 1985, 21(2), 208-210.

Wolfe, L. *The Cosmo report.* New York: Arbor House, 1981.

*Yohimex.* Psychogenic impotence. *Journal of the American Medical Association,* May 20, 1988, 259(19), 2813.

---

Carmen, A., and Moody, H. *Working women: the subterranean world of street prostitutes.* New York: A Cornelia & Michael Bessie Book/Harper & Row, 1985.
    A vivid description of the lives of prostitutes, often reported in an idealized romantic fashion.

Carpenter, T. *Missing beauty.* New York: W.W. Norton & Co., 1988.
    The true story of a Tufts University professor and his love, a high-priced prostitute. A contemporary tragedy.

Faust, B. *Women, sex, and pornography.* New York: Macmillan, 1980.
    A detailed and persuasive book that argues that pornography damages women and men in many ways, including their sexual/affectional relationships.

Smith, B. *Twentieth century masters of erotic art.* New York: Crown, 1980.
    A rich collection of sexually explicit and uninhibited art. Illustrations provide a good example of the difficulty sometimes encountered in determining what is affirmative erotica and what is potentially damaging pornography.

*Suggested Readings*

*Chapter 20*

# Sex and the Law

**When you finish this chapter, you should be able to:**

Explain how sex is one of the most closely regulated of all human behaviors.

Define the paraphilias and identify possible causes.

Explain child abuse and pedophilia and describe the possible causes.

Identify the causes of rape and sexual assault, and describe the effects on victims.

Discuss ways in which children and adults can help prevent being victims of sexual abuse and assault.

In Chapter 19, "Sex as Business," we saw the consumer and the seller of commercial sex may sometimes be victims, being emotionally, socially, or behaviorally scarred. In this section we will address sexual well-being more directly. We will look at the laws regulating sexual conduct and at the people who violate them, forcing sexual behaviors on others. Often the soundness and adjustment of these individuals are disturbed, and they may damage the physical and psychological health of their victims.

## SEX AND THE LAW

Sex is one of the most closely regulated of all human behaviors. Even the most permissive societies make it clear what is and is not sexually acceptable. In the Western world, the American continents and Europe, most laws regulating sexuality can be traced back to the Judaeo-Christian tradition. The Old and New Testaments, and their interpretations, form the basis of our legal statutes (Chapter 1). One central guiding principle has been to prohibit force; no person may compel another psychologically, physically, or through intimidation, to engage in a sexual act. *Rape,* forced sexual relations, is universally illegal. A second common principle is the prohibition of intimate contact between close family members, *incest.* Parents and children, brothers and sisters, may not have sexual relations.

Beyond the prohibitions of rape and incest, laws vary considerably in different regions of the United States. In nearly all, intercourse with an under-aged child, variously defined as 18 or under, is a felony. Many states have laws prohibiting intercourse between nonmarried adults, **fornication,** and extramarital sexual relations, *adultery.* Laws prohibiting *sodomy,* anal or oral-genital relations, are statutes usually directed at homosexual men, but in some jurisdictions even a married couple may be charged. Punishments differ, too. In some states—for example, Arizona, Florida, and Kansas—the sentence for sodomy may be a few months of imprisonment. In several other areas such as Georgia, Maryland, Michigan, and Washington D.C., the incarceration could be for 10 years or more.

*fornication*
The legal term for intercourse between unmarried adults.

Most sex laws, excluding rape, violence, and incest, are infrequently enforced. Occasionally a cohabiting couple or a homosexual partnership is arrested, and even though charges are likely to be dismissed, they have endured the humiliation and harassment that occur from being in the newspapers. Because of the infrequent and injudicious enforcement of sodomy, adultery, and fornication statutes, half of the states have adopted *consenting adult* laws (Chapter 13). These laws **decriminalize** private, voluntary, nonbusiness, sexual conduct between adults. Such laws are in force in California, Connecticut, Illinois, Indiana, New York, Ohio, Pennsylvania, Texas, and 20 other states.

*decriminalize*
To repeal laws that once considered a behavior criminal.

Like many adult taboo behaviors, prostitution and pornography continue to flourish despite legal prohibitions (Chapter 19). Prostitutes are caught in a web of conflicting, often ineffective, state and municipal statutes and differing enforcement philosophies. For many years New York City, for example, which has the largest population of male and female prostitutes in the United States, did little or nothing. Then, a few years ago, in a "clean up the city" campaign, special courts were empowered to rapidly process prostitutes who were arrested. The arrested women, and the occasional man (and sometimes a customer) would be hustled off to court in a van. There they were fingerprinted and photographed and spent most of their time waiting for a judge. After pleading guilty, they paid a fine of $200 and then went right back on the street again. The money paid was simply a "business expense."

With few exceptions, new laws or old, prostitution has continued, and the same can be said for pornography. As soon as some cities passed legislation curtailing adult movie theaters, and the federal government limited sexually explicit materials sent through the mails, the video cassette recorder (VCR) ap-

Street walkers are the most likely of all prostitutes to get arrested.

peared. With the VCR came a flood of sexually explicit films in thousands of rental outlets throughout the United States (Chapter 19).

In the People's Republic of China, the adult video tape brought about extraordinary treatment. According to an Associated Press news release of August 23, 1987, a man who had bought and shown nine sex films to 80 others was sentenced to death in a Shanghai court. Four others associated with him were given life-prison terms. In contrast, efforts to curtail the production, sale, or rental of adult video tapes in the United States have had little if any impact on the millions of customers (*Kingston Freeman,* 1988).

### Sexual victimization

Legal and social attempts to punish or regulate pornography, nonmarital intercourse, homosexuality, and other traditionally disapproved behaviors have been inconsistent and usually met with little success. From a psychiatric standpoint *none of these consenting behaviors is a mental health problem. But psychiatry and the law agree that sexual conduct that victimizes is an aberration* requiring treatment or punishment.

When people's sexual needs involve nonconsenting participants, they are injuring others. They are forcing unwilling partners to satisfy their own psychological and sexual needs. In this section we will consider several different types of illegal victimization. We will describe the behaviors themselves and also pay attention to the effect forced sex has on its victims. Finally we will evaluate the effectiveness of attempts at rehabilitation and treatment.

*paraphilia*
A sexual disorder in which the person is aroused by objects and/or a victim's forced shock, humiliation or sexual compliance.

## PARAPHILIAS

**Paraphilia** is a psychiatric term that comes from the Greek and literally means *a love that is side-tracked*. Paraphilias are troubled sexual behaviors that in the large majority of instances involve coercion. Another person is forced to invol-

## Three Views on Sex and the Law

1. I'm a libertarian; I believe in complete freedom. Sex no longer means risking pregnancy and can be enjoyed for itself alone. All persons, all ages, genders and orientations should be freed from the constraints of law. The only rule should be that sex is consenting; that it is not forced. Then we can be free to enjoy sex with anyone, as part of love, part of friendship, or just because we want to have fun with someone who appeals to us.

2. I guess you would call me a traditionalist. We need laws regulating sexual behavior. Such laws are in fact grounded in Scripture, in the Old and New Testaments. What it really comes down to is that decent sexual behavior between husband and wife is the only kind of sexual expression that should be permitted. The laws against other sexual behaviors should be strongly enforced and punishment should be vigorous.

3. Perhaps the word for me is rationalist, meaning reason. My reasoning tells me there should be laws to protect those who can not protect themselves. I believe, therefore, that most forms of sexual relations between adults, and only between adults, who freely consent to such relations should not be prohibited by law. I also want to see sex take place in the context of a healthy and serious relationship. Sex should not just be a casual pleasure you enjoy with someone you pick up.

untarily participate in some sexual activity. Paraphilial behavior is so common that almost everyone has been a victim—even if only the recipient of an obscene telephone call.

**Exhibitionism and voyeurism**   Many women and men enjoy showing themselves physically by wearing brief or revealing clothing. There are also strippers who take off their clothing for an audience. Neither of these groups are **exhibitionists.** The person who is sexily dressed may like feeling sensuous and the attention it brings. The stripper is a paid entertainer, and while perhaps enjoying the job, is simply performing (Chapter 19). A true exhibitionist behaves quite differently. To begin with, virtually all exhibitionists are men. Second, they typically confront their victim, a girl or adult woman, suddenly and with a degree of hostility. They directly display their penis and it is often erect. Many also masturbate in front of their victim.

> *exhibitionism*
> A paraphilia found in men in which they expose their genitals in public.

Exhibitionism may take milder forms. Some men, or adolescent boys, just approach their victim and make sexual or obscene remarks. A few expose their genitals briefly and then flee by foot or car. Most also do not touch or hold their victim, but about 20% have on occasion become assaultive and attacked the woman.

Exhibitionism is very common. Probably one out of every three or four women has been victimized. *Telephone scatologia,* meaning sexual or obscene remarks on the phone, is a form of exhibitionism. This is so frequent that virtually all women and quite a few men have received such calls (American Psychiatric Association, 1987).

All of us have taken a second look at the minimally dressed bodies on a

Voyeurism.

*voyeurism*
A paraphilia in which a person secretly peeks at women or at couples engaged in sexual activity.

beach. Such looking is not sufficient for a **voyeur**, frequently called a *Peeping Tom.* The voyeur takes the common human tendency to look to the point where it is intrusive. Voyeurs, nearly all of whom are men, secretly peek into windows and through keyholes and any other aperture, hoping to catch a woman undressing, in the bathroom, or with a sexual partner. During the peeping, they may masturbate. Some also tap on the window after they have stopped looking. The victim then knows she has been watched and her fear and humiliation increase the voyeur's excitement. Assault sometimes follows peeping so that the victim who discovers a voyeur should take immediate protective action.

*fetishism*
Disorder in which a person is sexually aroused by objects or body parts.

**Fetishism**   Like *most paraphilias,* **fetishism** is a *normal interest taken to an extreme.* Fetishism involves becoming sexually aroused by an object or a part of the human body. Most of us are mildly stimulated by certain types of clothing. We may also be erotically excited by certain parts of the body, such as hair, buttocks, breasts, penis, or lips. But while such arousal ordinarily accompanies sexual relations, it is the sole objective for a fetishist.

Fetishism is found almost exclusively in men and it is not a very common disorder. Any number of objects may be the focus of the fetish. Some may seem logical to us because they have a sexual connotation. A fetishist who craves brassieres, panties, or hair may appear to be reasonably focused on sex-related materials. But the fetishistic object may also include nail clippings, dirty sneakers, rubber raincoats, used handkerchiefs, navels, and mother's milk.

Fetishists may stroke, caress, chew, or otherwise manipulate the object or body part and then masturbate. Because most fetishistic objects such as underwear are readily available in stores, fetishism may seem like a victimless para-philia. But a new pair of panties is seldom satisfying. Fetishists typically want used and dirty panties, sneakers, and handkerchiefs. They get these by stealing. Most are content to pilfer from baskets of dirty laundry waiting their turn in the laundromat. Others break into homes and burglarize. Fetishists who fixate on hair may snip a few strands from a woman's head in a crowd and run away.

In a few instances fetishism involves setting fires—a form of *pyromania*. Igniting a fire may involve only the fetishistic object: burning hair, panties, or high-heeled shoes. The fire setting may be intended to be specific, but the fire may spread to a woman's clothes closet and eventually involve an entire build-ing. As such, fetishistic behavior may be extremely dangerous (Wilson and Gosselin, 1981).

**Sadism and masochism**  The French Marquis de Sade (1740-1814) and the Austrian writer Leopold von Sacher-Masoch (1836-1895) have given their names to two infrequent psychosexual disorders. De Sade severely abused and tortured his victims and was eventually arrested and committed for life to an asylum. In his novels, Sacher-Masoch lavishly described the exquisite sexual pleasure to be derived from pain.

**Masochists** may be of either sex. They associate sexual pleasure with feeling pain. They may ask or provoke their partner into beatings or other abuse to become sexually excited. They may also involve themselves in life-threatening situations to feel arousal. For example, they might push their car to top speed on a dark, rainy night, going over 100 miles per hour so that the danger and fear will bring about sexual climax. Many masochists are self-mutilating. They inflict scarring injuries on themselves, particularly on their genitals, breasts, and related areas.

Sexual **sadists** are usually men who enjoy inflicting pain. They are likely to beat, cut, burn, or shoot their victim, causing injury and sometimes death. Some sadists are also rapists. They may, however, also rely on persuading their victim to participate with some degree of coerced consent in their activities (Gendel, Bonner, 1988; Wilson and Gosselin, 1981).

**Pedophilia**  In Greek, **pedophilia** means child love. It is the psychiatric term for what is commonly called *child molestation* or *abuse*. Statutes vary from state to state, but sexual contact is generally considered pedophilial when the child is in early adolescence or younger and the molester is adult.

Adults having sexual contact with children, whether supposedly consensual or not, is strongly disapproved, but nevertheless frequent (Chapter 8). In the United States, about 30% of women and 10% of men recall having had some kind of sexual contact with an adult before puberty. In most instances the con-tact occurred only once or twice and was limited to the offender exhibiting himself, kissing and fondling the child, or touching sexual body parts. In a few instances however, the abuse included sexual intercourse (Kohn, 1987).

Most adult contact with children is not with strangers and not the result of force. Most children's sexual contacts are with relatives or friends. In one study 40% of the molesters of girls were their fathers and 15% their adoptive fathers. For boys the adults with whom they had contact were commonly older

*masochism*
Sexual excitement produced by experiencing pain or humiliation.

*sadism*
Sexual pleasure received through the infliction of pain on another person.

*pedophilia*
Adult sexual activity with young children.

Educational materials that deal with the prevention of child abuse are widely available.

male relatives, including siblings, uncles, and fathers. Molestation by female relatives and friends is infrequent but does occur (Crewsdon, 1988).

A small proportion of sexual offenses against children are committed by people who are strangers, individuals who habitually molest children. Such men, and rarely women, may be thought of as true pedophiles. Most are heterosexual, but a few, perhaps 5%, are homosexual men who molest boys. Most pedophiles also limit themselves to exhibitionism or voyeurism and intimately touching children. A few are violent, kidnapping the child and forcing sexual acts including oral-genital contact and coitus. A very few are sadistic and homicidal.

The child's reaction to the pedophilial event depends on a number of circumstances. Some youngsters molested by relatives do not realize that anything distressful and illegal has happened. At the other extreme, those violently attacked, particularly by strangers, can be extremely frightened and emotionally scarred.

**Dealing with abuse**   The way parents handle abuse can be crucial. In situations involving relatives or acquaintances and limited abuse, parents need to recognize the situation yet not exaggerate it. This means that they have to let the child and if possible the molesting adult know that the behavior is totally inappropriate and unwanted. The child must also be reassured that he or she is not responsible for the act and, however distressful the experience, healing will follow.

When the sexual assault has been extensive or perpetrated by a stranger, and particularly if it involved violence, a child may be severely traumatized. Such victimization creates a breach in the child's adaptive milieu. Something totally unexpected and deeply painful has shattered the protective shield created by parents. The child may withdraw; have eating, sleeping, and school problems; be depressed; afraid of strangers; and have any number of other physical and psychological symptoms. Many also suffer long-range effects. Their social, psychological, and sexual adjustment could be impaired well into adulthood. The child who has been deeply hurt will need the concerted help of her or his family and a professional therapist (Van Scoyk, Gray, and Jones, 1988).

A final note: we have become increasingly aware of child sexual abuse and of the importance of detection and treatment. At the same time, we have to be careful not to look with suspicion at every adult who touches or hugs a child. Nor do we want to prompt children to be paranoid about their affectionate relatives. What we need to do is to alert children in a realistic, reassuring, and reasonable way. The suggestions given by the National Committee for the Prevention of Child Abuse in their *Spider-Man* comic book may be helpful (p. 554).

**Other paraphilias**   There are over a dozen less frequent psychosexual disorders. We will limit our description to three that are sometimes encountered. *Frotteurism* is rubbing against an unsuspecting person's body for sexual purposes. The victim and frotteur are dressed and the rubbing usually occurs in very crowded places such as a bus or a milling mass of people in a theater or stadium. Frotteurs are almost always men and they try to brush their body, limbs, or hands against a woman's buttocks, lower abdomen, or breasts. In a crowd this behavior is often overlooked as accidental.

If a person is extremely preoccupied with sex, it may be a psychosexual disorder called *erotomania*. Unlike the person who is sexually addicted, as described in Chapter 17, the erotomaniac does not engage in actual sexual activities. She or he is hypersexual on an imaginative and verbal level. This disturbance may take any of several forms. In one, the person persistently makes sexual comments or constantly talks and jokes about sex.

In another variety of erotomania the person fantasizes about sex with a prominent individual such as a local doctor, member of the clergy, or teacher. This type of erotomania is found much more often in women and is psychiatrically termed *de Clerambault syndrome*. As time goes by, the imaginative person drops hints to others and confides that he or she having a love affair. The delusion is typically embellished by realistic-sounding details. ("We ate and danced at Jacques until midnight and then went to the Holiday Inn in Middletown.") (Munro, 1982).

The least common psychosexual disturbance of the three is *zoophilia*, sexual relations with animals. When people lived on farms and in rural areas as most did a century ago, this behavior was much more frequent. Most people who have had sexual relations with animals are men and they have usually attempted coitus. However, women have been reported to have caressed and stimulated animals in an attempt to insert the penis of a dog or a horse into their vagina (Gendel, Bonner, 1988).

Women who fantasize about secret sexual liaisons with prominent people may convince themselves that the experience was real. One result is that they may accuse the man and cause an innocent person considerable distress.

## Paraphilia or Fun and Games?

Exhibitionism, sadism, and other paraphilial behaviors involve victims, people who are injured physically and/or emotionally. Some fetishism or voyeurism may seem relatively harmless, but more often it is only part of a constellation of disordered sexual needs. In one study of fetishists, 12% had also molested boys, 7% were voyeurs, 20% were exhibitionists, and 19% had committed rape. The average person with paraphilial behavior also seems to be very active. Among a sample of 159 men apprehended for sex offenses, the mean number of different paraphilial and sexually assaultive acts was 520 (Rosenfeld, 1985).

Paraphilial behavior victimizes both children and adults. True sadism or fetishism should not be confused with the "pretend" games played by some couples. When a couple voluntarily ties each other up, it is not paraphilia. The sadomasochistic and fetishistic games people play are as different from a paraphilia as children playing cowboys and Indians is from the Western frontier of 150 years ago. From a mental health perspective, however different, odd, or unusual a sexual behavior, even if it appears to be paraphilial, it is not pathological so long as it injures no one and involves only consenting adults.

### Explanations

People with paraphilias often seem to come from sexually inhibited, anxious, or punitive backgrounds. Most are married but are repressed and consider sex to be dirty and degrading. Typically they are men and have difficulty establishing adequate sexual relations with their wife or other women. Most often, too, they appear angry and confused. As a result men who have been especially socialized to be aggressive may use their sexuality to strike at women. Paraphilial behavior may be motivated more by hostility than by sexuality.

Another theory sees faulty learning playing a prominent role in paraphilias. Most people learn that sexual relations involve physical and emotional interactions with a whole human being. In paraphilia the sexual response is attached to a small part of sexuality. Perhaps this restricted attachment is the result of early conditioning. An exhibitionist remembered that his first masturbation, at age 11, involved the additional satisfaction of knowing that his baby-sitter was

## Sadomasochism, Bondage, and Dominance

According to Wolfe (1981), 2% of her respondents had played *sadomasochistic* (S & M) type games. The Petersen et al. (1983) survey showed 8% of women and men had experienced whipping, tying up, nipple pinching or piercing, and similar painful stimulation.

Spanking is another game that resembles sadism and masochism. The person may be spanked by hand or paddle or caned. Often the person to be spanked is accused of some infraction, scolded, partly undressed, and put across the spanker's knee.

When the pain element is absent, and the partners are dressed in hoods, black stockings, corsets, leather, and fur, the game involves fetishistic elements and is called *bondage and dominance* (B & D). Such scenes may also include master and slave scripts. The slave may be led about on a leash and made to exhibit himself or herself and sexually service the master in numerous subservient ways.

## Urolagnia

The sexual and excretory organs overlap both anatomically and physiologically. This juxtaposition seems to have eroticized eliminatory functions for a few people. Some men are aroused by receiving enemas, *klismaphilia*. A tiny number enjoy feces as part of sexual arousal and intercourse, *coprolagnia*. According to Petersen et al. (1983), 4% of women and men have experienced "golden showers," the clinical term for which is *urolagnia*. As part of sexual relations, they have asked to urinate, be urinated on, or in a few instances swallow their partner's urine.

## Caution!

Sexual games that involve physical restraint, spanking, and domination obviously need to be played with care to avoid injury. Partners who participate must trust one another completely so that they can totally rely on the other to stop a game whenever they are uncomfortable. Games involving excretory functions also carry a health risk. It is particularly important that urinary and fecal material not be introduced into the vagina. The bacteria and other microorganisms that dwell safely in these excretions can cause troublesome infections when brought into other parts of the body (Chapter 16).

secretly watching him. A voyeur recalled the excitement he felt when at 9 years of age he accidentally saw a neighboring couple in their bedroom having intercourse.

Shawn Johnston (1987) reports that her review of the research suggests sex offenders, particularly child molesters, may actually feel and think differently about sex. They tend to be bothered by sexual obsessions and feel unable to control their urges. Many also seem quite self-centered and emotionally immature. While a normal adult who is attracted to someone may think "you turn me on," the sex offender feels a loss of control and responds with "here I go again." The pedophile's sexual confusion, immaturity, disordered thinking, and sexual preoccupation "make him turn to children for sexual gratification."

The biological explanation holds that some men have a stronger and more pervasive sexual drive. As a result they are supposedly ever ready to find new avenues for expressing their erotic needs. The biological hypothesis also sug-

Frotteurs frequent crowded places where rubbing against someone can seem accidental.

gests that this high libido may be caused by an overabundance of male hormones or a greater sensitivity to testosterone (Chapters 4 and 7). We will see later, however, when we discuss rape, that the evidence for this hypothesis is inconclusive at best.

**Don't be a victim**   The paraphilial behaviors that are most likely to be encountered are exhibitionism and voyeurism. Exhibitionists usually accost their victim on the street, or in hallways and parks. Do not converse with or offer advice to the man exhibiting himself. If screaming seems an appropriate way to assure safety, then do so vigorously. If possible leave the scene and head for a safe spot. Try to telephone the police and insist on an officer or car patrolling the location.

Exhibitionistic obscene phone callers are best deterred when they are not rewarded. This means that as soon as you are aware it is an obscene call, calmly hang up. Do not scream at the caller, offer mental health advice, or engage in any further conversation. Then do not answer the telephone if it rings again for another hour or so.

Don't pick up the telephone and blow a shrill whistle into the receiver. You may hurt a friend's hearing, or the obscene caller may later do the same to you.

If a woman spots a voyeur peeking at her, she should call the police. If she feels her home or apartment is not safe, she should go to a neighbor. Again, do not talk to or interact with the voyeur in any way. Voyeurs tend to have favorite routes and routines. Ask the police to patrol and check your area for some time. (Also see the section later in this chapter, "Avoiding Rape.")

### Incest

*Incest* is sexual relations between close family members. This usually means coitus or other intimate sexual activities between parents (or grandparents) and children, or between siblings. Today incest is forbidden in every major nation and society, although the punishment varies from little more than social disapproval to jail sentences.

Incest was not always forbidden. In the distant past, when humans roved in bands of 40 or 50 people, contact with other groups was short and infrequent. Tannahill (1981) believes, "In human society before intertribal contacts began to develop, inbreeding was almost inevitable." More recently, 3000 years ago, some cultures seemed to permit limited incest. The ancient Egyptians encouraged their nobility to intermarry. Brother-sister marriage was held to be a particularly reliable way to assure the continuation of religious and aristocratic characteristics.

Many explanations have been proposed for the incest taboo. Perhaps marrying outside the family unit helps enlarge a clan's influence and survival. Or there may have been some recognition that outbreeding may bring damaging genetic traits to a biological dead-end. Perhaps there is even a learned sexual aversion that close family members have toward one another. Typically girls and boys who have grown up together in the same family or institution, even when they are unrelated, usually (but not always) have little or no sexual interest in one another.

Whatever the origins and usefulness of the incest prohibition, it is not totally effective. The number of people in the United States who have had an incestuous experience has been estimated to be as low as 1% and as high as 20%. Both extremes are probably inaccurate. Wolfe (1981) asked the many thousand *Cosmopolitan* magazine readers who responded to her survey about their experience. Ten percent of the women questioned said they had at least one incestuous encounter. Half of these reported that they had relations with their brother. One third named their father and a fifth said they had been intimate with an uncle.

Other forms of incest are rare. Mother-son incest and homosexual relations between parent and child or among siblings are seen in fewer than 1% of families (Stark, 1984).

Even incest that is not harmful is likely to cause embarrassment and guilt and could hamper future relationships. It is wise for both partners to seek some counseling help.

**Characteristics and consequences**    Sister-brother incest is the most common. In many instances neither the girl nor the boy is seriously maladjusted or has major sexual problems. Finkelhor (1980) questioned 80 college students who had an incestuous experience. Almost half of them said they had an unfavorable reaction to the sister-brother coitus. Thus while some sibling incestuous relations are relatively benign, others may be traumatic.

Incestuous fathers are often diagnosed as psychologically normal although many seem to feel sexually or affectionally frustrated. They may be quite dependent, wanting a great deal of support and emotional and physical care. Still other incestuous fathers are distant and may not even feel that their daughter is their child. She is seen as a woman, a person the father can control and from whom he can demand sexual as well as other gratifications. The most extreme instances are fathers who have significant emotional problems or are violent and generally abusive. Sometimes alcohol or other drug dependence is an accompanying complication. Such fathers may physically compel, that is rape, their daughters.

Father-daughter incest may occasionally have few negative consequences. The daughter and father may feel guilt and embarrassment, but ultimately go on to have satisfying sexual and affectional relations with other people. More commonly, however, father-daughter incest can lead to sexually and affectionally troubled behavior in the victim. Disturbed, distressed, angry, and deeply confused feelings can disrupt healthy relationships and effective life adjustment for many years. Often victims require extensive professional help (Stark, 1984).

## RAPE

*Rape,* meaning sexual relations forced with actual or threatened violence, is a frequent crime. Over 90,000 attacks are reported every year. In addition, according to a United States Justice Department study in which 2 million people were interviewed, only about half of all victims report the crime to the police. Further, the number of rapes continues to increase nearly every year. These statistics mean that 1 of every 50 women born in this decade in the United States will face a violent sexual assault sometime in her life (U.S. Federal Bureau of Investigation, 1988).

The figures for rape are extraordinarily high, but they are only one aspect of what is an enormous criminal problem in the United States. Every year there are 20,000 homicides and 1,500,000 armed robberies and assaults. The total number of serious crimes exceeds 15 million yearly, or one felony for every 16 people. None of several dozen other industrially advanced nations of the world has a crime rate that is comparable. For example, homicides are 500% greater in the United States than in Canada. The United States exceeds the rate in Sweden by 1,000% and of Holland by 2,000%. If these numbers tell us nothing more, they show that the incidence of rape is not likely to be reduced until there is also an intelligent and effective attack on crime in general (U.S. Bureau of the Census, 1988).

One of the major correlates of crime was identified by a President's commission studying the media. The commission concluded that the continual emphasis on violence in films and television was a leading cause of the enormous criminal problem in the United States (Chapter 19).

### Men who rape

Men who commit forcible rape may come from any social class and be any age. The majority, however, are between 15 and 30 years old and come from a background characterized by low income, marginal employment, and inadequate education. Often their home life is typified by neglect alternating with harsh punishment and deprivation. They are likely to have been raised by a relative or a single or foster parent. This same picture that we have painted of the rapist is also true for perpetrators of other serious crimes. Both kinds of offenders come from a subculture marked by despair, force, and violence. They have grown up learning that physical aggression is acceptable and necessary. What particularly marks the man likely to rape, however, is what Briere and Malamuth (1983) call an "aggression toward women" syndrome. Rapists see women as adversaries to be attacked and subdued.

Rapists are not the sexual supermen often portrayed in fiction. Half are married or have an available partner. Yet in most instances their sexual relations with their wives or friends are not satisfactory. With their victims, too, rapists frequently cannot function sexually. Erectile and orgasmic problems are common (Chapter 17).

About one fourth of rapists attack an acquaintance. They assault a person who works for the same firm, or who is a neighbor, a friend, or a date. The large majority of rapists, however, attack a stranger, often a person picked at random. Seven out of ten rapists also victimize a person of the same ethnic background. Black rapists generally attack black women and those who are white have white victims.

One of the best descriptions of men who rape is emerging from the work of Robert Prentky and Ann Burgess. They have been studying 800 convicted rapists and contend that they see four distinct types (Goleman, 1985).

Half of all rapists they call "exploiters." These men decide on rape on the spur of the moment. They may, by chance, find their victim alone, or be in a situation with an acquaintance and want immediate sexual gratification. Such rapists are often not blatantly violent and might be open to reason.

A fourth of all rapists are what Prentky and Burgess call "compensatory." These men feel sexually inadequate and have sexual problems. They believe that ordinarily women would reject their sexual overtures so that force is necessary.

A fifth of rapists are labeled "enraged." They hate their victims; they want to humiliate and dominate women and are little if at all sexually motivated. Their rape is an act of aggression, violence, and anger. Even more dangerous are the 5% that the researchers call "sadistic." These men often make unusual and painful sexual demands and may seem to be acting out a bizarre fantasy. They may fatally injure their victims.

Work such as that of Prentky and Burgess has made it apparent that there is no single cause of rape. Ultimately the solution will have to address a variety of motives and behaviors. Judi Lawson and W.A. Hillix (1985, p. 53) suggest

*Table 20-1*

**Characteristics of Rape and Rapists**

| Location | Percentage |
|---|---|
| Street, park, outside | 35 |
| Rapist's or victim's home | 45 |
| **Rapist** | |
| White | 50 |
| Previous sex offense record | 50 |
| Under 26 years old | 65 |
| Stranger | 75 |
| Acquaintance | 20 |
| More than one rapist | 40 |
| **Rapist behavior** | |
| Weapon used or threatened | 40 |
| Forced vaginal intercourse | 75 |
| Forced fellatio | 25 |
| Forced cunnilingus | 5 |
| Forced anal intercourse | 5 |
| Assault duration 1 hour or less | 70 |
| Severe beating | 20 |

Data based on Holmstrom and Burgess, 1980; Wolfe and Baker, 1980; U.S. Federal Bureau of Investigation, 1988.

that rape is like cancer: "It may involve not a single disease but a collection of pathological behaviors with motivations that span a range from sex to violence."

### Persuasion, coercion, and date rape

Rape is a criminal act and the most extreme form of forced sexual activity. But for every violent rape there are at least 10 times as many incidents of coerced sex. It is not unusual for couples to view their sexual/affectional relationship somewhat differently. Sometimes one feels more in an erotic mood than does the other. When such disagreements occur, partners often talk about their differing needs, and one may try a little friendly persuasion. When does friendly persuasion turn into coercion? When does coercion become rape? These questions are not easy to answer.

Nearly all women and men can recall times they agreed to sexual relations with their friend, lover, or spouse essentially to please the other. Few consider this more than submitting to friendly persuasion. But about half of all college women (and many men too) report instances when they have been unduly persuaded. Sometimes this coercion included some physical intimidation, pushing, or roughness (Gilbert and Cunningham, 1987).

Contrary to popular belief, according to Muehlenhard and Linton (1987), coercive sexual aggression does not usually occur on the first date with a relative stranger. *Date rape,* that is unduly coerced sex, is more likely to occur between partners who know each other fairly well. Many have been acquainted for a year.

The extensive surveys by Petersen and his colleagues (1983) revealed that 10% of the men surveyed and 7% of the women admitted that they had forced sex on a partner. They had significantly pressured an uninterested or unwilling partner to have sexual relations. Many aggressors, particularly males, thought that their partners enjoyed or expected to be coercively pressured. They rationalized date rape as part of the "game" of temptation and teasing that the sexes supposedly play with one another (Byers, 1988; Larsen and Long, 1988).

These self-justifications point to an additional factor in most coerced sex, the *mythology of rape.* The false mythic ideas include that women have to be forcefully swept off their feet, that it is impossible to rape an uncooperative woman, and that it is not really rape unless it is an armed attack by a stranger. Beliefs such as these may help create an atmosphere and attitudes that abet aggression and coercion.

Forced sexual relations are partly the outcome of a society that alienates the sexes. Judi Lawson and W.A. Hillix (1985) believe poor communication plays a central role. Lawson and Hillix compiled 50 different male behaviors designed to **seduce** or coerce a woman into having intercourse. They also gathered 50 female behaviors intended to avoid sexual relations. Experimental subjects, men and women, were then asked to read the male come-ons and rate them on a scale from 1, nonaggressively seductive, to 10, overtly coercive. The women's responses were rated on a similar scale on how strongly and clearly they conveyed a definite "no" or a "yes" to requested sexual relations.

There was a great deal of agreement between the raters of both sexes. In several important instances, however, women rated male come-ons (put his hand on her thigh; said that he "wanted" her) as more coercive than did men.

College and other young women are especially likely to be victims of *date rape.* Some students have begun to wear buttons saying NO MEANS NO to call attention to this problem.

There is no substitute for honest communication. Every couple should discuss what they view as friendly persuasion and coercion.

*seduce*
Entice; lead subtly (into sexual intimacy).

The line between friendly
sexual persuasion and
coercion is sometimes
difficult to define.

Women saw it as force; men believed it to be seduction. Similarly men might see a behavior such as extensive open mouth kissing as being quietly seductive, while a woman might consider it fairly coercive.

The two sexes also had a little difficulty agreeing on what meant "no." When the woman said the man was to stop his sexual advance or she would call the police, both sexes agreed that this was a strong no. But when the woman said she was not in the mood right now, men more often tended to see this as a "yes." For many it was believed to be a request to improve technique and put the woman "in the mood." Many responses, for both sexes, fell into the ambiguous ground between seduction and coercion. No doubt the meaning of these kinds of intermediate behavior depends on the couple's feelings about one another and the circumstances of the encounter (Lawson and Hillix, 1985, p. 52).

Muehlenhard and Linton (1987) also believe that faulty communication is the central problem in coerced sex. Their questioning of 600 college men and women found substantial agreement in both sexes that coercion and aggression usually occurred when one partner felt "led on," and the other did not make it clear "how far" she or he was willing to go. Charlene Muehlenhard and Melaney Linton believe, however, that "no" may not be clear enough. They contend it is better for the unwilling partner to be specific. Rather than just saying "no," she should emphatically declare, for example, "I don't want to do anything more than kiss." The incidence of coercive sex might well decline if communication, sharing, and understanding between the sexes could be increased (Chapter 10).

## Marital rape

Husbands may rape their wives and unmarried men may rape the women with whom they cohabit. Such rapes are not rare. Estimates suggest that 10% of all

## When Men Are Raped

The exposure of the myths surrounding rape has taught us a great deal about the aggressive characteristics of the rapist and the predicament of the women victims. It has also made it clear that men, too, may be rape victims. The assault may vary—from unwanted persuasion from an acquaintance to outright violent assault.

When men are questioned about date rape it has been reported that nine out of ten have felt pressured into unwanted sexual activity by friends. This includes unwanted kissing, petting, genital fondling, and caressing. A survey of 507 young men concluded that 62% had actually experienced unwanted sexual intercourse. Suprisingly, too, men were sometimes pressured by physical force as well as by psychological and social persuasions (Muehlenhard and Cook, 1988).

Outright violent sexual assaults on men are occasionally carried out by a woman or a group of women. But it is far more likely that the perpetrators are other males. It is estimated that 10,000 or so men, *not* in prisons, are victims every year. If all prisoners who were raped are counted, then men as rape victims would number in excess of 100,000.

Groth and Burgess (1980) describe at least two types of male assault. In the first, the assailant traps the victim. He may do this by getting him drunk or drugged and then taking sexual advantage. In the second type of sexual assault the assailant threatens or uses physical force or a weapon. A man may be hitchhiking, for example, and be picked up by two men. They may then pull off the road, beat and threaten the victim with a knife, and force sexual relations.

Men may be sexually assaulted in a college dormitory, on the street, or at home. The most frequent compelled sexual activity is to be the recipient of anal intercourse. The forced performance of fellatio is next most common.

Male victims are much more likely to be gang raped, severely beaten and brutalized, and held captive much longer than women. When they report the incident, most typically also hide the sexual aspect. They claim they were involved in a fight or robbed and simply physically attacked (Struckman-Johnson, 1988).

Women may also be raped by other women. Such attacks are uncommon and usually occur in prisons.

women have been sexually attacked by their partners. Finkelhor and Yllo (1983) divide such spousal rape into several categories. Two distinct types are assaultive and sexually demanding rape.

The sexually demanding rape forces the woman to participate in activities to which she objects. She may be compelled to have anal intercourse, have objects inserted into her vagina, or participate in other nonconsenting acts. The assaultive rape is more common. It often grows out of a relationship already characterized by poor communication and verbal and sometimes physical violence. This atmosphere of anger can lead to coerced sexual relations often accompanied by slapping and beating.

Until a few years ago, in most states a wife could not legally charge her husband with rape. To be sure, she could achieve almost the same results by pressing charges of assault or even attempted murder. Then little over a decade ago, Greta Rideout became the first woman whose charges of spouse rape reached the court. She alleged her husband John had forcibly and against her will compelled her to have sexual relations. Eventually the couple reconciled and John was found innocent. But this landmark case encouraged states to re-examine and revise their rape statutes. A charge of marital rape can now be brought in about half of all states (Finkelhor and Yllo, 1983).

## Statutory rape

Most states forbid intercourse, even if it is fully voluntary and consenting, with an underaged male or female. The age of consent differs from state to state but may be as old as 18 or as young as 14. *Statutory rape* laws are enforced only occasionally and then almost always against men. It may happen, for example, that an 18-year-old boy has intercourse with his 16-year-old girlfriend and they are discovered by her parents. The parents can ask for charges to be brought and the boy may be sentenced to prison.

Statutory rape laws are seen as protecting the young and uninformed, particularly against adults. They are intended to help dissuade older women and men from seducing innocent children. Critics of such statutes point out that most teen-age sexual intercourse involves only adolescents, with partners of almost equivalent age. Furthermore, while adolescent intercourse may not be desirable, statutory rape penalties have not seemed to effectively restrain, shelter, or protect youngsters (Chapter 8). They have instead punished some honest adolescent relationships (Holmes, 1983).

## Victims

Any woman (or man) can be a rape victim. Victims may be aged or be very young children. They may be provocatively dressed or dirty and disheveled. Whether or not a person is considered attractive is also irrelevant. The point is that anyone may be attacked. Statistically, however, most are women under age 30 and also single. This may partly be a reflection of the fact that women in this category are more likely to walk, travel, and live alone and therefore may be more vulnerable.

Following attack, the rape victim is almost certain to have some physical and psychological injury. For most, physical wounds are not severe and will heal within a few weeks. Psychological pain may endure and be substantial for many months and sometimes years. Steven Berglas (1985, p. 44) observes, "Even the most physically and mentally strong are likely to experience shock, anxiety, depression, shame and a host of psychosomatic symptoms after being victimized."

The psychological reactions following rape are called *rape trauma syndrome*. The syndrome (collection of symptoms) may be characterized by fear, paranoia, depression, nightmares, fatigue, crying spells, and eating, digestive, and sleeping problems. Sexual interest and function are also likely to be impaired. The woman may want her partner to be warm and tender, hold her, and be affectionate, but not desire actual sexual relations for some time. It will require a great deal of sensitivity and understanding between the woman and her partner, and sometimes professional counseling, to reestablish a healthy and enjoyable sexuality.

Another problem found in rape victims is self-blame. They often go over every single aspect of the attack again and again trying to understand what they could have done differently. "If only" they had done or said, or not done or said, this or that, it would not have happened. Although most victims are

Do not treat a victim's pain or emotional scars lightly. Reassure the person that with support and professional help she or he can look forward to recovery and resuming her or his life.

### Avoiding Rape

It is a sad commentary on society that women (and men) have to curtail their freedom and mobility to decrease the chances of assault. But as was pointed out at the beginning of this section, rape is only a part of a massive problem of crime and violence in the United States. *All women, men, and children need to be concerned with their own security.* Major changes in our social structure are necessary to relieve these concerns. An effective police and criminal justice system is a priority. Equally important is the need for a thorough understanding and systematic remediation of the causes of crime.

1. A first rule in avoiding rape is to act with confidence. An assertive walk and a tough disciplined manner, particularly when approached by strangers, suggest you are not easily intimidated.

2. Avoid night hours and poorly lit or empty streets or public places. If you are followed, go into the nearest busy store or other safe place and telephone for help. Jog and run only in relatively busy places.

3. Recognize that most rapes occur indoors and avoid lonely elevators, buildings, workplaces, and the like. At home, admit no one without positive assurance of their reliability. For example, if a repairman asks to be let in, telephone his firm and confirm before admitting him.

4. If you have late night duties, arrange for a secure and trusted escort and leave your car in a well-lit area.

5. Do not be taken in by strangers who politely request your help in finding an address, making a telephone call, or the like. For example, if a strange car seems to be stopping near you while you jog or walk, walk away immediately. Run if necessary. An important general rule in avoiding assault is: *Do not be embarrassed* to run, act rudely, or seem too suspicious. It is *better to overreact* than to be careless.

6. Do not take a new acquaintance to your home. Do not go to his home or drive with him. Avoid all lonely or intimate situations with strangers and do not give any false cues that might signal sexual interest.

7. Do not hitchhike, and do not accept rides, even if there is a woman or a child in the car.

---

actually entirely blameless, such self-accusation is common and can be helped by caring reassurance (Rynd, 1988).

The victim of date rape is especially likely to blame herself. She was not a person attacked at random on a street but actually accepted a date with the person who victimized her. She can easily believe she is responsible for creating the situation that allowed the sexual coercion to occur. Often an additional feeling is one of failure. All of the victim's friends seem to have dates and manage them successfully. But she has failed, permitting a social occasion to turn into a painful incident. Victims of coerced sex especially need to be helped to understand and work through their feelings of responsibility and failure.

**Blaming the victim**  Whether the crime is robbery, rape, or assault, many people blame the victim. To reassure ourselves, we look for "mistakes" the victim allegedly made that supposedly provoked the crime. Lawson and Hillix (1985) hypothesized that all crime victims tend to be blamed, but those who are sexually assaulted are particularly singled out. To test this, they asked 219

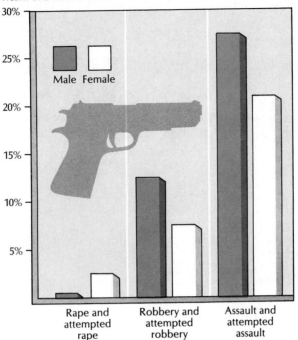

Lifetime chance of being a
victim of a violent crime

*Figure 20-1*
Lifetime chance of being a
victim of a violent crime.
(Data based on U.S.
Federal Bureau of
Investigation, 1986, 1988.)

adults to read several different rape and robbery scenarios. In the robbery stories the victim's behavior varied from timid to assertive and in buying something she displayed either a few dollars or as much as a $100 bill. The rape stories described women who were modestly to very provocatively dressed and shy or aggressive. The experimental subjects read the different stories and then using an 8-point scale assigned the extent to which the assailant and the victim were responsible for the crime.

The researchers expected that responsibility for both crimes, rape and robbery, would be most likely assigned to victims the more they flaunted their sexuality or money. It was supposed, too, that men would identify much more with the sexual assailant and blame the female. Actually, victims who flaunted their wealth or sexuality were assigned only a small inconsequential part of the blame for the crimes. Even more surprising, men as well as women identified very closely with the rape victim and blamed her little if at all for the sexual assault. The authors of the research conclude that current social pressure to recognize the rights of women has been effective. The tendency to blame the victim, particularly in sex crimes, still exists, but there is also an increased awareness that it is the criminal and not the victim who is ultimately responsible for crime.

Do not second-guess a victim's judgment. She, or he, did the best possible under emergency circumstances and now needs our fullest support.

**Resisting attack**   Women who are sexually attacked often attempt to resist. A few plead; some argue with their attacker; and a very few may try karate or the like. Unfortunately, such formalized martial training is seldom effective. The women are usually being confronted by young men, most of whom are

Counseling and medical assistance are now provided to rape victims in most communities.

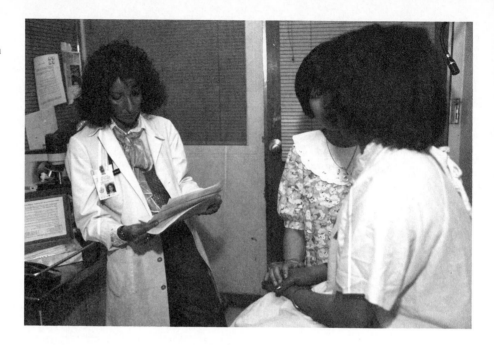

"street fighters" and do not fight by any rules. Prentky and Burgess, who categorized different types of rapists, also suggest a number of tactics that may help (Goleman, 1985).

- When there is more than one assailant, or the person has a weapon and flight or fight is impossible, talk reassuringly. Try to calm the situation and give it a semblance of normalcy. Tell your name; ask his. Tell him you understand his situation and ask him if he can sympathize with yours. Some women have found flattery can sometimes get a conversation going. "You are a good-looking man; why do you do this?" Perhaps the conversation can be led around to a bargain with the assailant. He might be persuaded to put the weapon away and decrease violence in exchange for cooperation.
- Try not to provoke the rapist's anger by what you say. Prentky and Burgess doubt the value of the victim claiming she has a venereal disease or is pregnant. This may simply enrage the rapist. Further, threats of later retaliation are useless and may simply motivate homicidal violence.
- If the rapist is unarmed and alone and you are relatively strong, resistance may work. Fight, kick, gouge, scratch, and scream wildly and without restraint. But do this only when there is hope of help or escape. In other situations, resistance may evoke lethal violence.

If a rape has occurred it should be reported. Most police now have an officer, frequently a woman, trained to sympathetically elicit important information from the victim. The officer can also help guide the victim through the routine of medical examination, making a formal police statement, and receiving psychological counseling. The victim can greatly help the police by trying to recall details of the attacker's appearance, his car, manner of approach, and speech. The woman should also not wash, douche, or change clothes. Her appearance and even material collected from under her fingernails may be useful in arresting and convicting the rapist.

### Assuring justice

For most people, reports of sexual abuse and assault evoke a fearful, agonized response. We are likely to be particularly repelled by the sexual victimization of children. Taking advantage of the physical and psychological vulnerability of children strikes us as especially abhorrent.

Over the past few years, many states have made it easier to prosecute sex offenders. In most areas, rape victims in courts need no longer endure torturous examinations of their entire life history, nor do they need to present numerous witnesses. Court proceedings have also been made less painful for children. They may be permitted to tell their story privately and have their narration video-taped for presentation in court. Much still must be done to ensure that child and adult victims are heard, their charges fairly considered, and that the court process itself does not add to their trauma.

We need to exercise great care, too, that our horrified emotional responses to rape and child abuse do not result in persecution of the innocent. To begin with, an accusation is not proof, although the media sometimes treat it as such. We supposedly no longer live in the "witch-hunting" era (Chapter 1) when an accusation alone was enough to severely punish the person at whom a finger was pointed. Anyone can be erroneously or maliciously accused, and the predicament may be most serious when it involves a child.

In 1983, Lawrence Spiegel, a psychologist in the midst of a bitter divorce, was charged by his ex-wife, with sexual abuse of their 2½-year-old child. What followed was an excruciating legal ordeal that could have cost the father custody of his daughter, Jessica, as well as a long prison sentence. Ultimately Spiegel was vindicated, but only after a harrowing 2-year legal trauma that cost him his home, friends, and attorney's fees of $70,000 (Spiegel, 1987).

Imprisonment and rehabilitation can be an effective treatment for some sex offenders.

A few years earlier, charges of child sexual abuse were leveled at 24 parents, ordinary citizens without any history or evidence of sexual disorder, in the rural Minnesota town of Jordan. Despite the fact that the accusatory stories were inconsistent and some were clearly fantasies, prosecutorial efforts went ahead. Ultimately only one person out of the 24 was convicted. The rest are suing the county for false prosecution.

*In considering possible child sex abuse, great care must be taken both to ensure that the accused is not falsely or maliciously charged and that the children involved are not further hurt by the judicial process.*

Children are not inherently deceptive. They can be counted on, usually, to recall an event or tell about a happening to the best of their intellectual ability. But they can also be influenced by a parent, a lawyer, psychologist, or other adult who suggests a particular story or fantasy.

Carol Grant, a legal coordinator for Victims of Child Sex Abuse, is troubled by the extent to which children's recollections and narrations can be distorted. They can adopt experiences others have had or just fantasized about as their own. Grant points out that children believe in Santa Claus and the Easter Bunny. "Children under five have trouble separating truth from fantasy . . . you find parents program them." The enormous number of reports of sexual victimization urges even greater care be taken to protect the innocent, prosecute the guilty, and care for and rehabilitate the victim (Diesenhouse, 1988; Havgaard, 1988).

---

*In Sum*

Many sexual behaviors are forbidden by society and/or considered psychiatric conditions. Paraphilias are sexual disturbances that victimize others. Most paraphilias are found in men who have a sexually repressed and disturbed background. Although some behaviors, such as exhibitionism and fetishism, may not seem violent, some paraphilial men are also physically assaultive. Pedophiles are usually men and are sexually interested in children. Often it is a close relative who sexually molests a child. When sexual contact is extensive or violent it may be physically and psychologically very damaging. Incest, too, can either have relatively minor effects or be severely traumatizing.

Rape usually results in the victim becoming anxious, depressed, and sexually unresponsive for many months. Most rapists come from a disadvantaged and violent family and environmental background. They are also frequently sexually inadequate and driven by anger. Rape victims are often blamed, but this tendency seems to be decreasing. Some safety precautions in one's home and routine can help avoid rape. If attacked, resistance, cooperation, or talking may be helpful depending on the rapist's motivation and the circumstances.

---

## TREATING OFFENDERS

**Prison**   Throughout the world, in all societies, people who exhibit themselves, assault children, or rape have been considered sex offenders and punished. Historically the punishment for sex offenses has often been death. In more recent times, those who are more violent, such as rapists, are likely to go to prison. Less violent-seeming victimization, such as voyeurism, is likely to lead to a suspended sentence along with compulsory treatment.

How effective is imprisonment in stopping sex offenses? The statistics are equivocal. Men who are middle class and middle aged and apprehended for voyeurism, exhibitionism, or frottage are very likely never to repeat. For such people being caught is typically enough to end the behavior. On the other hand, the more violent offenses are often not stopped by imprisonment. It is not unusual for a person who has sexually assaulted children and adults to have a record of dozens of offenses interspersed with four or five imprisonments. Thus while arrest and the threat of punishment often stops people who have committed lesser offenses, there are many persistent, assaultive offenders who do not seem to be deterred by incarceration (Holmes, 1983).

**Medical treatment**   Medical treatment for sex offenders began at the end of the last century. In many nations, *castration* (removing the testicles) was common. Estimates suggest that since 1900 more than 100,000 such operations have been performed in Europe and the United States (Heim, 1981). Not only is this procedure punitive, but it reduces the level of male hormones (Chapter 4).

Castration was based on the assumption that sex offenders were too sexually driven; they allegedly had too much testosterone and other androgenic hormones. Castration is now uncommon but attempts to reduce androgens continue. More recently *Depo-Provera*, a progesterone (Chapter 3) that helps suppress androgen, has been administered to rapists and others with violent sexual disorders.

Does reducing androgens work? Perhaps to a limited extent. Heim (1981) followed released ex-offenders in West Germany who had been castrated while in prison. Many said they experienced a reduction in sex drive and activity, but a third of the men said they continued sexual relations much as always. Further, these men's subsequent sex offense rearrest record was only slightly different from similar ex-offenders who had not been castrated.

In the long run, androgen reduction therapy by chemicals or by castration does not seem to offer much promise. To begin with, it is very doubtful that sex offenders have higher hormonal levels than most other men. Even more revealing, many sex offenders have problems becoming erect or being orgasmic (Chapter 17). Thus, they may not be "oversexed" but perhaps even "undersexed" (Freeman-Longo, Wall, 1986).

**Psychotherapy**   Counseling and psychotherapy with sex offenders acknowledges that the person with disordered needs is a victim almost as much as the woman or man forced to participate in the behavior. The man who is an exhibitionist and the woman who is a pedophile are psychologically and sexually disturbed and need help. Therapists influenced by Sigmund Freud assume that patients are disordered because their sexual development was blocked at an infantile level (Chapter 8). They try to help them reach an adult level of function (Gay, 1988).

Other therapists see sex offenders as the product of a society and a home in which human and sexual values are distorted, inhibited, and confused. The aim is to help sex offenders rid themselves of sick and erroneous beliefs and work toward healthy relationships.

The effectiveness of psychotherapy seems to depend on whether the client is motivated and stays in treatment, as well as the therapist's competence. Peter Kilmann and his colleagues (1982) reviewed a broad and comprehensive col-

Scene from an erotic film like those that some behavior therapists may have sex offenders watch to encourage positive and healthy sexual fantasy and interests.

lection of studies of the treatment of paraphilias. Without treatment, 8 out of 10 apprehended continued to commit sex offenses. With therapy, most offenders were helped regardless of the treatment assumption or approach. But often long-standing conditions required long-term therapy.

**Behavior therapy**    Behavior therapy techniques make use of conditioning and learning (Chapter 17). In one relearning treatment program, sex offenders who had assaulted children had sensors attached to their genitals and electrodes attached to their bodies. They were then shown films of children playing. If the penile sensors indicated arousal and erection, they were given a mild shock. On the other hand, when they were shown adult sexual scenes, if arousal occurred, there was no shock (Freeman-Longo, Wall, 1986).

There are many different behavioral treatment techniques. Abel, Becker, and Mittleman (Rosenfeld, 1985) studied the effectiveness of three combinations of methods on 192 child molesters. The three included sex education, training in social skills, and encouraging desirable sexual fantasies. The researchers found that while all the techniques were helpful, fantasy was most effective. Patients were taught to think of unpleasant events whenever they were aroused by a paraphilial situation. In contrast, when fantasies involved consenting adult coitus, they were encouraged. In a 1-year follow-up study, 8 out of 10 offenders had stopped their sexual victimization. Given these reports, it appears that behavioral as well as psychotherapeutic approaches can be effective in rehabilitating many sexually disordered people.

## SEXUAL HARASSMENT

Unwanted attention of a sexual nature that clearly creates embarrassment or distress has been called **sexual harassment.** This can take several different forms. In social situations one person may make intrusive sexual comments or annoyingly touch or pat another. In a college setting, faculty, dormitory supervisors, and most often, fellow students may make coercive sexual suggestions or advances. During the college years, about a fifth of all women, and a tenth of men, recall some actions that were harassing. At the same time, many students consider the harassments too minor to mention. Some wonder, too, if they were actually harassed or simply misinterpreted an attempt to be friendly. Often discussing these feelings and pointing to specific incidents with the harassing person or the supervisor is very effective (Somers, 1982).

Perhaps the most pervasive of all harassments are those that occur between employer and employee. A boss or a manager can sometimes be very sexually aggressive. The supervisor may let the employee know that promotion, raises, or even the job itself depends on sexual cooperation. According to a study by a federal civil service agency, the United States Office of Merit Systems (1981; 1988), over 50% of women had experienced at least some harassment as had about 20% of men. Based on the responses of 8,523 employees, harassment took the form of unwanted telephone calls, letters, touching, suggestive looks,

*sexual harassment*
Unwanted attention of sexual nature that creates embarrassment or stress.

A college faculty member who married one of his students was asked how he courted her without it seeming like harassment. He said, "I told her in a friendly way that I would like to get to know her and when the school year was over, I would ask her out for a cup of coffee. She did not have to say yes or no till then."

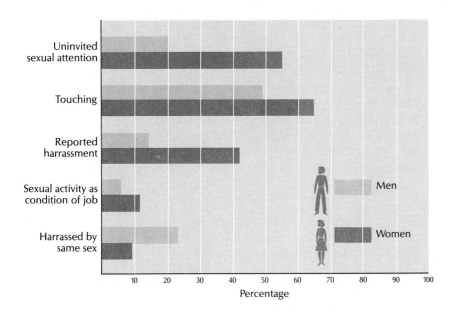

*Figure 20-2*
On-the-job sexual harassment. (Data based on U.S. Merit Systems Board, 1981, 1988.)

sexual jokes, and attempts to make dates. The most frequent unwanted behaviors were sexual remarks, questions, and teasing. The women who reported harassment tended more often to be single, between 20 and 40, and work in nontraditional jobs in a predominantly male environment. The men who complained of harassment were similar in age and marital status and most often worked in a clerical or trainee position in a largely female environment.

Men and women who feel themselves harassed on the job may file a grievance with their company. If this is not sufficient, a complaint to the state Fair Employment Commission, or an equivalent group, should assure a fair hearing. Harassment, whether in school, on the job, or among acquaintances, can be stopped and a sense of equity and respect restored for women and for men.

---

*Summary*

Sexual conduct is closely regulated by society, with nearly all cultures forbidding force and incest. In many states cohabitation, extramarital sexual relations, homosexuality, and many other sexual behaviors are considered illegal. Prostitution and pornography are also prohibited or attempts made at regulation in most of the United States. There are, however, considerable inconsistencies from one area or city to another, and over half of all states have adopted consenting adult laws, decriminalizing most adult voluntary sexual behavior.

Paraphilias are sexual disturbances that victimize others. Most paraphilial behaviors are found in men. Exhibitionists usually expose their genitals and voyeurs secretly watch women. Fetishists become sexually excited by objects associated with women. Sexual sadists are often assaultive and masochists may enjoy experiencing pain and risking their lives. Pedophilia is sexual interest in children. Coerced child sexual activity may be highly traumatic.

Incest is sexual relations between close family members. Most incest occurs between adolescent brothers and sisters. Sometimes it also occurs between fathers and daughters; other forms are infrequent.

Rape is a common crime. Following attack, nearly all victims suffer from fear, depression, and impaired sexual relations. Most victims, however, recover within several months to a year. Men who rape typically come from a background characterized by poverty and violence. Most do not know their victims, although rape between acquaintances and spouses also occurs. Men may also be raped, usually in prison by other men.

Rehabilitation through imprisonment seems ineffective for most rapists and violent offenders. The most effective treatments involve psychotherapy, counseling, and behavior modification techniques.

Sexual touch and comments that are unwanted, are called harassment. Harassment may occur in work or educational settings and can often be corrected by talking with the person or reporting the events to a supervisor.

---

*For Thought and Discussion*

1 Why do men, more often than women, commit sexually motivated crimes? Can a woman be a rapist, fetishist, or exhibitionist?
2 What kind of childhood or adolescent experiences help explain pedophilia, fetishism, exhibitionism, and rape?
3 What suggestions do you have to help prevent sexual victimization and rape?
4 What changes would you make in our police, court, and prison systems, and in our society generally to reduce the enormous incidence of rape and all violent crimes? What evidence do you have that your solutions might be effective?

5 In your own experience, how common is sexual harassment and what forms does it take? How should a person respond to sexual harassment?
6 What roles should society, religion, and psychiatry play in regulating, allowing, or prohibiting sexual behavior?

*References*

American Psychiatric Association. *Diagnostic and statistical manual of mental disorders (DSM-III-R)*, 3rd edition (revised). American Psychiatric Association, 1987.

Berglas, S. Why did this happen to me? *Psychology Today,* February 1985, 44-49.

Briere, J., and Malamuth, N.M. Self-reported likelihood of sexually aggressive behavior: attitudinal versus sexual explanations. *Journal of Research in Personality,* September 1983, *17*(3), 315-323.

Byers, E.S. Effects of sexual arousal on men's and women's behavior in sexual disagreement situations. *The Journal of Sex Research,* May 1988, *25*(2), 235-254.

Crewsdon, J. *By silence betrayed: sexual abuse of children in America.* Boston: Little, Brown & Co., Inc., 1988.

Diesenhouse, S. Child abuse victims face system made for adults. *The New York Times,* March 6, 1988, E26.

Finkelhor, D. Sex among siblings: a survey on prevalence, variety and effects. *Archives of Sexual Behavior,* 1980, *9,* 171-197.

Finkelhor, D., and Yllo, K. Rape in marriage: a sociological view. In Gelles, R.J., Hotaling, G.T., and Straus, M.A. (editors), *The dark side of families: current family violence research.* Beverly Hills, Calif.: Sage, 1983, pp. 119-130.

Freeman-Longo, R.E., and Wall, R.V. Changing a lifetime of sexual crime. *Psychology Today,* March 1988, 58-64.

Gay, P. *Freud.* New York: Norton, 1988.

Gendel, E.S., and Bonner, E.J. Gender identity disorders and paraphilias. In Goldman, H.H. (editor), *Review of General Psychiatry,* Norwalk, Connecticut: Appleton & Lange, 1988.

Gilbert, B., and Cunningham, J. Women's postrape sexual functioning: review and implications for counseling. *Journal of Counseling and Development,* October 1986, *65* (2), 69-71.

Goleman, D. Study lists ways to deter rapists (by Prentky, R., and Burgess, A.). *New York Times,* May 5, 1985, p. 35.

Groth, A.N., and Burgess, A. Male rape: offenders and victims. *American Journal of Psychiatry,* 1980, *137,* 806-810.

Havgaard, J.J. *The sexual abuse of children: a comprehensive guide to current knowledge and intervention strategies.* San Francisco: Jossey Bass, 1988.

Heim, N. Sexual behavior of castrated sex offenders. *Archives of Sexual Behavior,* 1981, *10,* 11-19.

Holmes, R.M. *Sex offenders and the criminal justice system.* Springfield, Ill.: Charles C Thomas, 1983.

Holmstrom, L.L., and Burgess, A.W. Sexual behavior during reported rapes. *Archives of Sexual Behavior,* 1980, *9,* 427-439.

Kilmann, P.R., et al. The treatment of sexual paraphilias: a review of the outcome research. *The Journal of Sex Research,* August 1982, *18*(3), 193-252.

Johnston, S.A. The mind of a molester. *Psychology Today,* February 1987, 60-63.

*Kingston Freeman.* Pornographer facing death. *Kingston Freeman,* August 23, 1987, 1.

Kohn, A. Shattered innocence. *Psychology Today,* February 1987, 54-58.

Larsen, K.S., and Long, E. Attitudes toward rape. *The Journal of Sex Research,* 1988, *24,* 299-304.

Lawson, J., and Hillix, W.A. Coercion and seduction in robbery and rape. *Psychology Today,* February 1985, 50-56.

Muehlenhard, C.L., and Cook, S.W. Men's self-reports of unwanted sexual activity. *The Journal of Sex Research,* 1988, *24,* 58-72.

Muehlenhard, C.L., and Linton, M.A. Date rape and sexual aggression in dating situations: incidence and risk patterns. *Journal of Counseling Psychology*, 1987, *34* (2), 186-196.

Munro, A. Paranoia revisited. *British Journal of Psychiatry*, 1982, *141*, 344-349.

Petersen, J.R., Kretchmer, A., Nellis, B., Lever, J., and Hertz, R. The *Playboy* readers' sex survey, (Parts 1 and 2). *Playboy*, January 1983, 108; March 1983, 90.

Rosenfeld, A.H. Discovering and dealing with deviant sex. (Abel, G., Becker, J., and Mittleman, M.) *Psychology Today*, April 1985, 8-10.

Rynd, N. Incidence of psychosomatic symptoms in rape victims. *The Journal of Sex Research*, 1988, *24*, 155-161.

Somers, A. Sexual harassment in academe: legal issues and definitions. *Journal of Social Issues*, 1982, *38*(4), 23-32.

Spiegel, L. *A question of innocence*. New York: Unicorn Publishers, 1987.

Stark, E. The unspeakable family secret. *Psychology Today*, May 1984, 41.

Struckman-Johnson, C. Forced sex on dates: it happens to men, too. *The Journal of Sex Research*, 1988, *24*, 234-241.

Tannahill, R. *Sex in history*. New York: Stein & Day, 1981.

United States Merit Systems Protection Board. Wide harassment of women working for U.S. is reported. *The New York Times*, July 1, 1988, B6.

United States Office of Merit Systems Review and Studies. *Sexual harassment in the federal work place: is it a problem?* Washington, D.C.: U.S. Merit Systems Protection Board, U.S. Government Printing Office, 1981.

U.S. Bureau of the Census. *Statistical abstract of the United States*. Washington, D.C.: U.S. Government Printing Office, 1988.

U.S. Federal Bureau of Investigation. *Uniform crime reports for the United States*. Washington, D.C.: U.S. Government Printing Office, 1988.

Van Scoyk, S., Gray, J., and Jones, D.P.H. A theoretical framework for evaluation and treatment of the victims of child sexual assault by a nonfamily member. *Family Process*, March 1988, *27*, 105-113.

Wilson, G., and Gosselin, C. *Sexual variations: fetishism, sadomasochism, and transvestism*. New York: Simon & Shuster, 1981.

Wolfe, J., and Baker, V. Characteristics of imprisoned rapists and circumstances of the rape. In C.G. Warner (Ed.), *Rape and sexual assault*, Germantown, Md.: Aspen Systems Co., 1980.

Wolfe, L. *The Cosmo report*. New York: Arbor House, 1981.

---

**Suggested Readings**

Cohen, M. *The sisterhood*. New York: Simon & Schuster, 1988.
Feminism, the women's movement, has made an indelible impression on society and the law. This is the story of four women who helped bring about these changes.

Grossman, R., and Sutherland, J. (Eds.). *Surviving sexual assault*. New York: Congdon and Weed, Inc., 1983.
A helpful and reassuring book detailing the options, rights, and rehabilitation available for victims.

Plummer, C.A. *Preventing sexual abuse: activities and strategies for those working with children and adolescents*. New York: Learning Publications Inc., 1984.
Alerts professionals and other adults to strategies to detect and prevent child abuse.

Westheimer, R., and Lieberman, L. *Sex and morality: who is teaching our sex standards?* Boston, Mass.: Harcourt Brace Jovanovich, 1988.
An interesting look at legal and ethical standards for sexual conduct.

# Appendix

Answers to the Test Yourself on p. 5, Sexual knowledge. Complete explanations are found in the chapters mentioned at the end of each answer.

1. False. Most adolescents, boys and girls, masturbate (Chapter 8).
2. False. Masturbation is common among married adults and usually is not a sign of any problem (Chapter 8).
3. True. Cunnilingus and fellatio are common (Chapter 5).
4. False. Homosexuality is now considered an alternative sexual behavior (Chapter 13).
5. True. Almost a third of adolescent males have had a homosexual experience (Chapter 8 and 13).
6. False. Many virginal women have little or no hymen (Chapters 3 and 5).
7. False. Most women are not irritable and depressed during menstruation (Chapter 3).
8. False. Sexual desire cannot be created by aphrodisiacs such as Spanish fly (Chapter 5).
9. False. Boys and girls are more similar than different in arithmetic and other skills (Chapter 7).
10. False. Withdrawal is a very unreliable birth control technique (Chapter 14).
11. False. Not having an orgasm may be the result of many different factors (Chapter 5).
12. False. A few women seem to produce some moisture along with orgasm. There is debate about whether this is actually an ejaculation analogous to the emission of semen (Chapter 5).
13. False. We do not yet clearly know the effects of living together on marital happiness (Chapter 12).
14. False. Many wives and husbands do not have extramarital intercourse (Chapter 12).
15. False. During a healthy pregnancy intercourse is usually possible until the eighth month (Chapter 15).
16. False. Herpes can be a persistant and discomforting infection, but it is not likely to cause cancer and rarely causes birth defects (Chapter 16).
17. False. Condoms are effective as a birth control measure (Chapter 14).
18. False. Most women who have an abortion feel relieved (Chapter 14).
19. False. About half of all impotence is the result of a physical disease (Chapter 17).
20. False. Exhibitionists do not usually attack their victims (Chapter 20).

## Answers to the Ask Yourself on p. 49, How can sex be scientifically investigated?

1. No scientist can proclaim that sexual intercourse outside of marriage is wrong or right. Those are opinions based on a person's religious, social, or personal background. But a scientists can investigate related questions such as:
   - How does sexual intercourse before marriage affect the satisfaction couples later express (on a questionnaire) with their own marriage?
   - Does having sexual relations with a person other than one's spouse lead to greater or lesser marital satisfaction?
2. *Immature* and *habitually* are not very precise words. One could, however, investigate questions such as:
   - How frequently do people at different ages masturbate? Are people who masturbate more than four times a week more or less psychologically healthy (as measured by tests) than those who masturbate less frequently?
3. In some of the Islamic nations of the world, such as Saudi Arabia and Morocco, men often have more than one wife at a time. This practice was also common in Biblical times. In addition, a few nations, such as historical Tibet, permitted a woman to have two or more husbands. A scientist might be able to investigate whether men and women in multiple marriages rate themselves as more or less happy, on a test of marital satisfaction, than those with just one spouse. But even if this research revealed meaningful differences, there is really no objective way to answer this question. The choice of one or many spouses is not a decision a society makes based on scientific evidence. It is a value judgment that reflects a people's culture, religion, and history.
4. The word *bad* is ambiguous and value laden. It would be better to substitute a phrase such as *mutually unsatisfactory*. A scientist could question several hundred couples about their degree of sexual satisfaction. Several years later the scientist could question every couple again to see if those whose scores were low on sexual satisfaction divorced more often than those whose scores were average or high.
5. The question might better be asked using a survey to explore the following:
   - How many people living in the area are for or against nudity?
   - How many people are opposed to nudity if the area involved is completely shielded from public view?
6. What is too much? A scientist might rephrase this question so that it could be scientifically answered and ask:
   - What is the effect on physical health or on psychological adjustment of having sexual intercourse daily?
   - Are people who have intercourse daily more or less physically healthy than those who have intercourse three times a week or less?

Remember, most questions about human sexuality can be answered scientifically, but it is important that the questions be phrased so that research is possible. Then by using the techniques discussed in this chapter—surveys, observation, and careful statistical analysis—valid information can emerge.

## Answers to the Test Yourself on p. 58, What do you know about women?

1. labia minora and majora
2. clitoris; stimulation
3. Grafenburg
4. menstruation
5. middle
6. removing only the tumor

7. hymen; absent
8. antiprostaglandin

## Answers to the Test Yourself on p. 92, What do you know about men?

1. spongy tissue; blood
2. 200 and 400 million
3. estrogen; androgen
4. prostate
5. menstrual
6. male sex hormone
7. no longer (or not)
8. not

## Answers to the Test Yourself on p. 114, What do you know about sexual intercourse?

1. There is no prescribed time for how long foreplay should last. Most couples seem to enjoy 10 minutes or more of arousal before intercourse. Many women and some men, however, say they would like more foreplay. If you filled in 10 to 15 minutes, count yourself correct.
2. False. A few couples enjoy mutual climax. But trying to have a simultaneous orgasm could be distracting. It is not a goal that needs to be part of intercourse for all couples.
3. False. A woman who does not climax may have been inadequately stimulated or caressed by her partner; however, each person is usually most aware of what is necessary to bring about her or his own orgasm. There is also considerable variability among people and from situation to situation. Outside stress and lack of information may interfere with climax. Further, orgasm may not always be the goal of intercourse. Sexual relations without orgasm can be satisfying for some couples if other objectives such as emotional closeness are met.
4. Oral sexual relations are uncommon in some countries. They are not usually found, for example, in most African nations. In the United States, Canada, and Europe, oral relations are practiced by most young adults.
5. False. Sexual relations serve many purposes ranging from expressing love to physical pleasure. Sexual and affectional pleasure may be obtained without an erection, as well as with one.
6. A person is said to be multiorgasmic when she or he has several *orgasms within a short period of time.* Theoretically, most women and men are capable of having more than one orgasm within an hour or so of sexual relations. Actually, only a small proportion of both sexes have several orgasms regularly.
7. False. For many women orgasms may or may not result as a consequence of coitus. In most instances such variation is normal and should not be considered a sign of sexual problems. Many women enjoy coitus when it is accompanied by clitoral stimulation by hand.
8. The position in which the man is on top and the woman is supine is very frequent and found among all humans throughout the world. Almost every couple uses it at least once in a while. But it is not the only position. Many couples also include woman-on-top, and rear-vaginal-entry intercourse positions.
9. False. Foreplay is often like masturbation, because the genitals may be stimulated by the partner. Masturbation alone, or with a partner, may also help men and women become aware of their sexual needs and responses and lead to more satisfying coitus. Masturbation is normal behavior both for children and adults.
10. A healthy person may be able to have several orgasms daily. Most people find, however, that fatigue, as well as other interests, limits the frequency of their

intercourse. If you picked any number between 2 and 8, count yourself as correct.

### Analysis of the Ask Yourself on p. 153, What is my gender biography?

Sometimes it takes longer, but most boys and girls are aware of their sex by age 2 or 3. Many cannot recall a single event that focused their gender awareness or identity. Others remember their mother telling them when they were 3, "You're a girl, and not supposed to wrestle with the boys." Another child may recall being excluded. One man remembered that at about age 4 a group of girls said he could not play house, because "house is only for girls."

Many boys are teased that they look and act like girls, and many girls are teased that they look and act like boys. Most children are uncomfortable with such teasing, and some become very aggressive or anxious about it. A very few may tend to withdraw from play situations, whereas others may try harder to look and act like other members of their sex.

Many children recall a model—an older friend, a sibling, or an adult—who appeared the epitome of femininity or masculinity. One girl remembered that when she was 6 her family doctor so impressed her with understanding, warmth, and a businesslike but feminine manner that she tried to copy her doctor's behavior for years afterward.

Children sometimes deliberately dress in the clothing of the other sex. Normally they do this to masquerade, entertain, play house, or satisfy some persistent curiosity. In most instances feelings range from defiance to neutral or amused. When dressing like the other sex provides deep, hidden, and significant pleasure, it may sometimes suggest an alternative adult sexual interest.

Thinking about what it might be like to be the other sex is a common and normal experience. Most people who think about it do so only occasionally and are neither particularly frightened nor elated by such feelings. In a very few instances there is an actual wish to be the other sex. The person is dissatisfied with her or his physical body and wants it to be altered. These desires are not common. A very few people who persistently want to alter their biological sex eventually do so with psychological and medical help.

### Answers to the Test Yourself on p. 341, What do you know about homosexuality?

1. False. Homosexual behavior is fairly common. About 4% of adults are homosexual, and over 20% of adolescents have had some temporary homosexual experience in their growing-up years.
2. False. Psychiatry no longer considers homosexuality a mental illness.
3. False. Homosexuality seldom seems to be the outcome of adult seduction.
4. True. About 20% to 30% of homosexual women and men marry a person of the other sex, and two thirds of these have children.
5. False. There were brief periods in ancient Greece when homosexuality was relatively accepted, but even then this sexual orientation was not widely practiced.
6. False. Most homosexual people, like those who are heterosexual, are satisfied with and adjusted to their orientation.
7. True. AIDS is an extremely serious disease that has infected homosexual men. It is extremely rare among homosexual women.
8. True. Many, but not all, homosexual people prefer these terms.
9. True. Most bisexual people seem to drift more and more into just one orientation.
10. True. It is hypothesized that the balance of male/female hormones present in the prebirth months may have a strong influence on future sexual orientation.

**Answers to the Test Yourself on p. 452, What do you know about sexual infections?**

1. False. Herpes is an annoying, sometimes persistent infection, but it is a relatively minor disease. Only infrequently does it have serious consequences.
2. False. It is very unusual to acquire syphilis or any other sexually infectious disease from a wet toilet seat or by bathing in a hot tub.
3. False. Ordinary soap and water are insufficient to destroy crabs. A special medicated shampoo is needed.
4. False. If there is an active lesion in the mouth, then herpes, gonorrhea, and other infections can be transmitted mouth-to-mouth and mouth-to-genitals.
5. False. Birth control pills, by making the vagina less acidic and more hospitable to microorganisms, sometimes increase the possibility of catching a sexually transmitted disease.
6. False. Gonorrhea and trichomoniasis may be found in all sexually active people. Personal cleanliness has little to do with becoming infected or transmitting these diseases.
7. True. Condoms are helpful in preventing the transmission of many sexual infections, but they are not a certain means to prevent all infections.
8. False. Douches may help relieve the discomfort of vaginal infections, but they are rarely sufficient to cure the underlying disease.
9. True. These and other sexual infections may scar the fallopian tubes and testicular ducts, impeding the passage of egg and sperm.
10. False. AIDS may be transmitted by blood transfusion or injection, vaginal intercourse, and possibly other forms of sexual relations.

# Glossary

Numbers in (#) refer to the page on which the term is first used.

**A**

**abortion, induced**   medical and/or deliberate termination of pregnancy (p. 393).

**abortion, spontaneous**   a miscarriage; "loss" of the fetus during pregnancy (p. 430).

**abstinence**   self-restraint in satisfying an appetite; refraining from sexual intercourse (p. 377).

**acyclovir**   a medication used to control herpes (p. 463).

**adolescence**   the period in human life between puberty and adulthood; usually the teen years from about 13 to 18 or 19 (p. 205).

**adultery**   sexual intercourse by a married person with someone other than his or her own spouse (p. 8)

**afterbirth**   the placenta, fetal membranes, and portions of the umbilical cord that are expelled after the infant is delivered (p. 424).

**afterplay**   the affectionate or erotic behavior that follows sexual intercourse (p. 141).

**agape**   an altrustic, spiritual, or religious love (p. 288).

**ageism**   the prejudice that people of another age (usually the elderly) are less compentent and vital.

**AIDS (acquired immune deficiency syndrome)**   a usually fatal disease transmitted through sexual relations, drug needle sharing, and other highly intimate contact (p. 355).

**AIDS related complex (ARC)**   symptoms such as fever, fatigue, weight loss, swollen lymph glands, skin growths, and rashes, which usually seem to lead to AIDS (p. 467).

**altruism**   a selfless regard for the welfare of others (p. 286).

**ambivalent**   characterized by both love and hate, attraction and repulsion (p. 357).

**amniocentesis**   a diagnostic procedure that can identify fetal defects by extracting and analyzing the amniotic fluid of the pregnant woman (p. 433).

**anal intercourse**   insertion of the penis into the rectum (p. 127).

**anal stage**   according to Freud, the second psychosexual stage during which attention and gratification are focused on excretory function (p. 33).

**androgenital syndrome**   a chromosomal female whose adrenal glands overproduced masculinizing hormone (p. 150).

**androgens**   a general term for male sex hormones secreted by the testes (p. 72).

**androgyny**   exhibiting the personality traits that convention usually associates with both men and women (p. 187).

**anorgasmia**   absence of, or inability to experience, sexual orgasm (p. 481).

**anus**   the rectal opening for defecation (p. 87).

**Apgar score**   rating of a newborn's physical condition (p. 424).

**aphrodisiac**   foods, drugs, or scents that are alleged to increase sexual interest or vigor (p. 536).

**areola**   the area around the breast's nipple that is usually pinkish or brownish in color (p. 83).

**artificial insemination by donor (AID)**   the insertion of freshly collected semen into the vagina of a woman who wishes to become pregnant (p.401).

**asexual**   avoiding sexual interaction; nonsexual (p. 344).

**assertiveness training**   courses aimed at helping people overcome shyness and lack of directness (p. 256).

**autoinoculation**   spreading infection from one part of the body to another (p. 462).

**autosome**   a chromosome that does not determine sex but carries other genetic instructions (p. 152).

B

**Bartholin gland**   gland located in the vagina, which secretes a small amount of lubricant during sexual excitation (p. 60).

**basal body temperature method**   a method of birth planning requiring taking one's temperature to detect ovulation (p. 378).

**behaviorism**   psychological approach that deals only with observable behavior (p. 497).

**Ben-Wa balls**   balls inserted into the vagina, which supposedly stimulate the woman while she is walking (p. 533).

**bidet**   a toiletlike fixture used primarily in Europe for washing the genitals (p. 128).

**birth control**   limiting the number of one's children through the prevention of conception; family planning (p. 374).

**birthing chair**   a special chair that permits the mother to sit during the delivery of the infant (p. 422).

**bisexual**   an individual who is sexually attracted to and active with both women and men (p. 343).

**blastocyst**   a hollow spherical mass of cells produced soon after conception by the cleavage of the fertilized egg (p. 413).

**body language**   the message communicated by a person's expression, gesture, posture, dress, and so on (p. 274).

**bombykol**   a pheromone secreted by female moths during their period of sexual receptivity (p. 73).

**bondage and dominance (B & D)**   sexual activities involving restraining a partner and engaging in make-believe sadomasochistic behaviors (p. 557).

**breech birth**   an infant born in a feet first position (p. 417).

**brothel**   a house for prostitutes to receive customers for sexual activity; bordello. (p. 540).

**bulbocavernosus muscle**   muscular tissue around the urethra, which helps control urinary flow (p. 93).

C

**caesarean section**   a surgical childbirth procedure in which an incision is made in the mother's lower abdomen so that the uterus can be opened and the infant removed (p. 425).

**calender method**   birth control based on avoiding sexual intercourse during the days that ovulation is most likely to take place, that is, 14 days before menstruation (p. 378).

**call girl**   a prostitute who is usually well paid and receives customers in her own apartment (p. 540).

**candidiasis**   a vaginal discharge caused by an overgrowth of yeast cells normally present in the vagina (p. 460).

**cantharidin** Spanish fly; a urinary irritant that is alleged to be erotically stimulating (p. 537).

**cardiovascular** pertaining to the heart and associated blood vessels (p. 511).

**caring** the desire and act of doing things for and helping others (p. 288).

**castration** emasculation; removal of the penis and/or testes (p. 33).

**celibacy** abstaining from sexual relations (p. 8).

**cervical cap** a firm circular contraceptive device that is placed into the vagina and against the cervical opening (p. 384).

**cervical mucus method** birth control based on avoiding sexual intercourse during the time when the cervical mucus permits conception (p. 378).

**cervix** the lower and narrow end of the uterus (p. 67).

**chancre** an infectious lesion, often on the lips or genitalia, or in the mouth, which may be the first sign of primary syphilis (p. 455).

**channeling** patterning an individual's environment to produce a certain effect, for example, providing a "male" or "female" type environment (p. 157).

**chlamydia** a fairly common STD, caused by bacterial infection and usually characterized by a slight discharge and burning on urination (p. 457).

**chorionic villus sampling** a method of detecting embryonic abnormality during the first trimester (p. 433).

**chromosome** a threadlike body that carries the genes; found in the nucleus of cells (p. 97).

**cilia** very small or microsopic hairlike structures (p. 68)

**circumcision** the surgical removal of the foreskin of the penis; performed as a religious ritual in several cultures (p. 95).

**climax** sexual climax means the same as orgasm (p. 207).

**clitoridectomy** surgical removal of the clitoris (p. 62).

**clitoris** a small sensitive organ located in front of the vaginal opening, it is a center of sexual pleasure (p. 60).

**close-coupled** a monogamous partnership (p. 351).

**Code of Hammurabi** Babylonian legal code legislating civil and criminal matters 2000 years ago (p. 7).

**coefficient of correlation** a mathematical indication of the degree to which two or more variables are related; a correlation of ± 1.0 means a perfect unvarying relationship; a correlation of 0 means no relationship (p. 48).

**cognition** the act or process of perceiving, knowing, thinking (p. 159).

**cohabitation** living with another person in a sexually intimate relationship without marriage (p. 38).

**coitus** the act of sexual intercourse (p. 6).

**coitus interruptus** an unreliable method of birth control in which the man withdraws his penis from the vagina just before ejaculation; withdrawal (p. 390).

**colostrum** a water, yellowish fluid that is produced before the production of milk (p. 419).

**come-on** slang for a seductive, sexual approach (p. 275).

**coming out** process of becoming aware of and disclosing one's own homosexuality (p. 346).

**commitment** preseverance even through difficulties; pledge (p. 291).

**condom** a contraceptive sheath pulled over the erect penis, which is also effective in preventing the spread of most STDs (p. 385).

**consensual affair** an extramarital relationship that is mutually agreed on and accepted by a married couple (p. 321).

**consenting adult laws** laws that do not prohibit any voluntary sexual behavior between adults (p. 364).

**consummated** a union completed by sexual intercourse (p. 316).

**context**   the physical, psychological, and social environment (p. 203).

**continuum**   a scale used to indicate or measure the degree to which a trait is present (p. 146).

**contraceptive**   a device used to prevent conception, such as a condom, diaphragm, or pill (p. 374).

**contraceptive sponge**   a device that is permeated with a spermicide and placed in the vagina to be used as a contraceptive (p. 374).

**control group**   subjects who are not exposed to any intervention, thus forming a basis for comparison in an experiment (p. 46).

**Coolidge effect**   the ability of a "'new" sexual partner to rearouse (p. 130).

**coprolagnia**   sexual interest in feces (p. 557).

**copulin**   a scented vaginal fluid secreted during periods of sexual excitation and hypothesized to be a pheromone (p. 74).

**corona**   the rim of the head of the penis (p. 95).

**corpus cavernosus**   cylindrical structure in the penis and the clitoris that fills with blood during sexual arousal, causing erection (p. 62).

**corpus luteum**   structure that forms on the ovary, producing progesterone (p. 67).

**corpus spongiosum**   also called the corpus urethra; a cylinder of spongy tissue at the base of the urethra (p. 93).

**courtly love**   the stages of love depicted by twelfth century musician-poets in the Middle East and Europe (p. 288).

**couvade**   males experiencing symptoms of pregnancy and birth (p. 418).

**Cowper's glands**   located below the prostrate, they emit small amounts of clear fluid (often containing some sperm) into the urethra. The fluid tends to neutralize the urethra and serves as a lubricant during coitus (p. 97).

**crabs**   common term for pediculosis pubis; tiny, barely visible lice that may infest pubic hair (p. 458).

**crowning**   the showing of the infant's head at the vaginal opening during childbirth (p. 422).

**cruising**   term used in the gay community that refers to a person going to a bar or to baths to pick up a sexual partner; may also be used to refer to similar behavior among heterosexuals or lesbians (p. 351).

**cunnilingus**   oral stimulation of the vaginal lips and clitoris (p. 118).

**cystitis**   a common infection of the bladder in women causing uncomfortable urinary symptoms (p. 513).

### D

**date rape**   forcible, unwanted, sexual assult by a friend, acquaintance, or "date" (p. 562).

**de Clerambault syndrome**   the fantasy that one is having a love affair with someone and telling others as if it were reality (p. 555).

**decriminalize**   to remove criminal penalities for activities once considered illegal (p. 549)

**deep kissing**   open mouth kissing, which may also involve the tongue (p. 115).

**Depo-Provera**   a synthetic hormone used as a contraceptive (p. 571).

**diaphragm**   a small dome-shaped object placed in the vagina, covering the cervix and serving as a contraceptive (p. 383).

**diethylstilbestrol (DES)**   a synthetic estrogen that may prevent pregnancy. Commonly referred to as the "morning after" pill. Was once used by pregnant women to prevent miscarriages, but it has potentially damaging effects on the children (p. 73).

**dilation and curettage (D and C)**   a procedure used for diagnosis, control of menstrual bleeding, or induced abortion, in which the cervix is dilated and the tissue scraped from the uterine wall (p. 394).

**dilation and evacuation (D and E)**   mainly an abortion procedure used in the second trimester (p. 394).

**dildo**   an artificial penis (p. 348).

**DNA**   deoxyribonucleic acid; the chemical found within the genes, which is responsible for transmitting hereditary characteristics from one generation to the next (p. 148).

**dominance and submission**   sadomasochistic play that some couples engage in for sexual stimulation (p. 557).

**dominant gene**   a gene whose characteristic will be apparent in the next generation (p. 149).

**double standard**   the conventional attitude that permits men more sexual freedom than women (p. 30).

**douche**   to cleanse the vagina with a liquid, usually water and vinegar or a commercial compound (p. 390).

**dysfunction**   impaired function; problems with sexual arousal, desire, or orgasm (p. 344).

**dysmenorrhea**   painful menstruation, often with a physical cause; may be aided by antiprostaglandin medication (p. 77).

**dyspareunia**   painful sexual intercourse (p. 491).

**dysphoria**   unhappiness (p. 168).

## E

**ectopic pregnancy**   the development of a fertilized egg in the fallopian tube or elsewhere outside the uterus (p. 69).

**effacement**   flattening and thinning of the cervix during childbirth (p. 420).

**egalitarian**   equal, fair, and equitable (p. 248).

**ego**   according to psychoanalytical theory, the aspect of personality concerned with understanding reality and acting accordingly (p. 33).

**ejaculation**   the emission of semen associated with male orgasm (p. 97).

**ejaculatory duct**   an area near the urethra that helps propel the sperm through and out of the passageway (p. 97).

**ejaculatory inevitability**   the point at which the male orgasm is certain and cannot be stopped (p. 104).

**embryo**   the developing infant during the first 2 months following conception (p. 77).

**emission**   the first stage of the ejaculatory process; the semen in the glands and ducts is emptied into the urethra (p. 104).

**empty nest syndrome**   the lonely, sad feeling parents may have after their children are grown and have left home (p. 325).

**endometrium**   the inside layer of the uterus composed of mucouslike tissue (p. 66).

**epididymis**   a very thin, 20-foot-long, coiled tube that lies over the testes (p. 97).

**episiotomy**   a cut in the skin in back of the vagina supposed to prevent tearing of the vaginal tissue during childbirth (p. 422).

**erection**   the stiffening of the penis; tumescence (p. 93).

**erogenous areas**   parts of the body that are particularly erotically sensitive to stroking and touch (p. 108).

**Eros**   sexual desire, the Greek god of love (p. 10).

**erotic**   arousing sexual desire (p. 6).

**erotic love**   physically and emotionally intense love that often leads to a binding partnership (p. 285).

**erotica**   pictures, literature, or art dealing with sexual themes and intended to arouse. Erotica often is differentiated from pornography: erotica is held to involve adults in acceptable and consenting sexual portrayals; poronography is defined as violent and exploitive (p. 178).

**erotomania**   extreme preoccupation with sex (p. 555).

**escort service**   arrangements in which male or female companions are provided for a fee; sexual intimacy is included in many cases (p. 540).

**estrogen**   female sex hormones (p. 67).

**ethnocentrism**   believing ones own sexual and social standards are correct and others wrong (p. 25).

**euphoric**   totally pleasing; wonderfully good (p. 295).

**exaltolide**   a scented secretion in male urine and sweat, hypothesized to be a human pheromone (p. 108).

**exhibitionism**   a paraphilia found in men in which they expose their genitals publicly and inappropriately (p. 551).

**experimental group**   subjects who receive treatment in accordance with the purpose of an experiment (p. 46).

**explicit messages**   communication signals that are intended, overt, and generally learned (p. 267).

**expulsion**   the second stage in the ejaculatory process; the seminal fluid in the urethra is expelled from the body (p. 104).

## F

**failure rate**   the contraceptive failure rate is measured by the number of pregnancies in 100 women using a specific contraceptive technique for one year (p. 378).

**fallopian tubes**   two ducts that provide passage from the ovaries to the uterus (p. 68).

**family planning**   limiting the size of the family through spacing and prevention of pregnancies; birth control (p. 374).

**fellatio**   stimulation of the penis by tongue and mouth (p. 118).

**feminizing**   producing the physical, behavioral, and attitudinal characteristics of women (p. 107).

**fertility**   the ability to produce offspring (p. 398).

**fertility awareness**   rhythm method; any of several timing techniques that identify the period of a woman's fertility and prompt avoidance of sexual intercourse during those times (p. 378).

**fertilization**   the combining of the ovum and sperm to form a zygote (p. 68).

**fetal alcohol syndrome**   infants of an alcohol-abusing mother may have symptoms such as stunted growth and intellectual retardation (p. 436).

**fetishism**   the sexual disorder in which a person is sexually aroused by objects (p. 552).

**fetus**   the developing infant during the second and the third trimesters of pregnancy (p. 416).

**fidelity**   faithfulness; having sexual relations only with one's partner (p. 350).

**filtering**   the filtering theory of dating and courtship suggests that people "sift" out incompatible partners (p. 301).

**fimbriae**   fringelike projections coming from the fallopian tubes, which embrace the ovary (p. 68).

**first-stage labor**   the beginning of childbirth in which contractions begin and the cervix dilates (p. 421).

**flagellant**   a person who whips himself or herself as punishment; this behavior may lead to erotic arousal (p. 12).

**Flagyl**   an antibiotic used to treat trichomoniasis (p. 459).

**follicle stimulating hormone (FSH)**   a hormone secreted by the pituitary gland, which stimulates the production of sperm in males and follicle and ovum development in females (p. 71).

**follicular phase**   menstrual phase during which ovarian follicles develop (p. 76).

**forceps**   a tonglike tool that may be used to help in delivery of the infant (p. 425).

**foreplay**   kissing, touching, and other precoital behavior that stimulates the genital organs so that intercourse can take place (p. 115).

**foreskin**   the skin forming a hoodlike fold over the tip of the flaccid penis (p. 95).

**fornication**   sexual intercourse between two people who are not married to each other (p. 549).

**fraternal twins**   two individuals born of the same pregnancy because two eggs were released and fertilized by two different sperm (p. 68).

**free choice**   decision making by the individual(s) involved (p. 210).

**free love**   usually used to mean sexual relations without commitment (p. 236).

**frenulum**   a delicate strip of skin on the underside of the glans of the penis (p. 95).

**frigid**   old term describing a woman disinterested in sex or one who does not reach orgasm easily (p. 487).

**frotteurism**   sexual pleasure from rubbing against other people in a crowded place; frottage (p. 555).

## G

**gay**   used primarily in reference to male homosexuals but sometimes used for female homosexuals (p. 178).

**gender**   pertaining to masculine or feminine or to the biological and learned characteristics that distinguish the sexes (p. 145).

**gender identity**   how one psychologically perceives oneself as either female or male (p. 157).

**gender reassignment surgery**   surgical procedures that change a person's apparent sex (p. 168).

**gender role**   the attitudes and behaviors that most people in a culture consider appropriate for a female or male; also called sex roles, (p. 157).

**gender stereotypes**   commonly held beliefs about the characteristics supposedly appropriate only for women and others only for men (p. 183).

**gene**   the unit of heredity transmitted in the chromosomes (p. 148).

**general paresis**   a mental condition caused by brain damage, developing a decade or much longer after initial syphilitic infection (p. 455).

**genetic counseling**   guidance in the prediction and planning for offspring, which is based on inherited characteristics (p. 432).

**genital stage**   according to Freud, the period during which libidinal energy is maturely focused on coitus (p. 34).

**genitals**   the external sexual reproductive organs (p. 201).

**genotype**   the genetic makeup of an individual (p. 149).

**gestation**   the period from conception to birth during which a developing fetus is in the uterus (p. 417).

**gigolo**   a man who provides social and sexual companionship to women for financial rewards (p. 277).

**glans**   the head of the penis (p. 95).

**goal-free pleasuring**   shared sexual pleasure that does not have orgasm as a goal; useful in treatment of sexual problems (p. 496).

**going steady**   a relationship in which a couple who are dating agree to date only each other (p. 211).

**gonadotropin**   a hormone that regulates a sex gland (p. 71).

**gonads**   sex glands; in males the testes and in females the ovaries (p. 67).

**gonorrhea**   a common infectious disease, sexually transmitted and often causing urinary symptoms (p. 452).

**gossypol**   a plant derivative that may be effective as a male oral contraceptive; still experimental (p. 390).

**graafian follicle**   a vesicle containing a mature ovum and other cells (p. 67).

**Grafenberg area (G-spot)**  an area located within the anterior wall of the vagina, which is highly sensitive to erotic stimulation (p. 64).

**guilt**  the anxious feeling that one has done something ethically or morally wrong (p. 106).

## H

**hand-over technique**  the receiver of sensate focus puts his or her hand over the giver's to guide touch and pressure (p. 494).

**hedonism**  the belief that personal pleasure is the major purpose of one's life (p. 23).

**hepatitis**  an infectious inflammation of the liver, which may sometimes be transmitted through sexual intercourse (p. 465).

**hermaphroditism**  a rare condition in which an individual partly has the genital organs of both sexes (p. 146).

**herpes genitalis**  a common STD, which is marked by blisterlike eruptions in the vaginal area or on the penis (p. 460).

**herpes simplex virus (HSV)**  the virus that causes cold sores or similar lesions on the genitals, lips, or other parts of the body (p. 460).

**heterosexual**  sexual behavior and interest in people of the other sex; a person primarily sexually interested in and active with those of the other sex (p. 87).

**HIV**  the human T-cell lymphotropic virus responsible for AIDS (p. 467).

**Homo sapiens sapiens**  the current human species; from the Latin meaning wise, wise man (p. 4).

**homophobia**  fear and hatred of homosexuality (p. 365).

**homosexual**  sexual contact with individuals of the same sex or a person whose primary sexual interest and activity are with someone of the same sex (p. 240).

**homosexual behavior**  a sexual interaction with someone of the same sex (p. 341).

**hormones**  chemicals that regulate body growth and function; produced by ductless glands and released directly into the bloodstream (p. 67).

**hot flashes**  occasional warm sensations about the head and neck, which are common in menopausal women (p. 81).

**human chorionic gonadotropin**  a hormone found in urine of pregnant women (p. 415).

**hustler**  a prostitute; often used to describe males who serve homosexual men (p. 544).

**hymen**  a mucoid membrane that may partly block the entrance to the vagina (p. 61).

**hypothalamus**  a ductless gland located in the brain (p. 71).

**hypothesis**  a scientific guess based on limited information (p. 156).

**hysterectomy**  removal of the female uterus and, often, associated reproductive organs (p. 514).

**hysterotomy**  an infrequent procedure for late abortion by abdominal incision and surgical removal of the fetus (p. 395).

## I

**id**  according to psychoanalytical theory, primitive sexual and aggressive drives; the "life instinct" (p. 33).

**implantation**  the attachment of the blastocyst to the lining of the uterus (p. 66).

**implicit messages**  communication signals that are largely innate or not learned (p. 267).

**impotence**  old term for the inability to achieve or sustain an erection (p. 487).

**in vitro fertilization (IVF)**  the procedure of fertilizing an egg with donor sperm outside the mother and in a laboratory dish (p. 401).

**incest**  sexual intercourse with a member of one's immediate family (p. 204).

**infanticide**  killing an infant (p. 374).

**infatuation** foolish, irrational, and short-lived romantic love (p. 290).

**infertility** the inability to produce offspring (p. 398).

**innate** inherent or inborn (p. 267).

**insemination** medically placing sperm into a female's reproductive organs (p. 400).

**intercrural** between the thighs (p. 128).

**intergluteal** between the buttocks (p. 128).

**intermammary** between the breasts (p. 128).

**intrauterine device (IUD)** a small coil or shield that is placed in the uterus to prevent conception (p. 387).

**intromission** placing the penis in the vagina (p. 121).

## K

***Kamasutra*** an ancient Hindu book that lists and describes numerous ways of performing loving and sexual acts (p. 10).

**karma** the Hindu and Buddhist belief that and individual's destiny in this life is predetermined (p. 9).

**Kegel exercises** contractions of the pubococcygeal muscles designed to strengthen them (p. 440).

**klismaphilia** sexual excitement achieved through enemas (p. 557).

**Kwell** a prescription shampoo used to treat crabs and scabies (p. 458).

## L

**labeling** assigning a name to a person that relates to her or his identity (p. 160).

**labia majora** the major or outer lips of the vulva (p. 60).

**labia minora** the minor or inner lips of the vulva located inside the labia majora (p. 60).

**lactate** to produce milk (p. 72).

**Lamaze method** a method of preparing parents for childbirth to minimize the need for anesthesia and other medical intervention (p. 426).

**lanugo** downy hair that covers the developing fetus (p. 417).

**laparoscope** an optical tube that permits viewing the inside of the abdominal cavity (p. 388).

**laparotomy** an incision into the abdominal cavity, sometimes used for tubal ligation to effect female sterilization (p. 388).

**latency period** according to Freud, the period from about 6 to 12 years of age when all sexual feelings are dormant (p. 33).

**learned** behavior, skills, or attitudes that are acquired through experiences and are not inborn (p. 154).

**Leboyer method** a method of childbirth in which the newborn is placed immediately with the mother and lights are dim to reduce the shock of transition from the womb to the outside world (p. 427).

**lesbian** a homosexual woman (p. 11).

**libido** sexual interest and desire (p. 176).

**limerence** sexual, passionate, romantic love (p. 285).

**lochia** the reddish-brown discharge following birth (p. 439).

**love** a tender, affectionate attachment; a warm, caring emotion (p. 284).

**lumpectomy** removal of only the malignant lump from the breast (p. 513).

**luteal phase** menstrual phase when the endometrium is ready for the implantation of a fertilized egg (p. 77).

**luteinizing hormone** a hormone secreted by the pituitary, causing ovulation in females (p. 71).

**lysin** a chemical antibody located in the head of the sperm, which helps dissolve the membrane of the female egg and allows the sperm to enter (p. 97).

# M

**Madonna-prostitute syndrome**   a condition in which men are not interested in sex with "good" women and have coitus only with those who are "bad" (p. 291).

**male climacteric**   a sudden decline in sexual interest and energy experienced by a few older men (p. 109).

**mammary glands**   glands located in the breasts, which can be hormonally stimulated to produce milk (p. 83).

**mammography**   x-ray study of the female breast (p. 85).

**masculinizing**   producing the physical and behavioral characteristics of men (p. 106).

**mask of pregnancy**   the darkened facial pigmentation, especially on the forehead and cheeks, which is often associated with pregnancy (p. 419).

**masochism**   sexual excitement produced by experiencing pain and humiliation (p. 553).

**mastectomy**   total surgical removal of the breast, usually as a result of advanced cancer (p. 513).

**masturbation**   self-stimulation of the genitals to the point of orgasm (p. 19).

**mbuya**   Turu of Tanzania term for nonmarital romantic lover (p. 318).

**mean**   the numerical average; the sum of scores divided by the total number of scores (p. 48).

**meatus**   an opening or a channel (p. 93).

**median**   when all scores are ranked from lowest to highest, the median is the middle score (p. 48).

**menopause**   the termination of menstruation as a result of age or surgery (p. 65).

**Menrium**   a commercial estrogenic substance used to regulate the menstrual cycle or relieve menopausal symptoms (p. 73).

**menses**   see menstruation.

**menstrual aspiration**   extraction of the embryo during the first month of assumed pregnancy, using a vaginal suction technique (p. 393).

**menstrual synchrony**   the tendency of women who live together to sometimes follow a similar menstrual cycle (p. 74).

**menstruation**   the monthly vaginal discharge of blood and the lining of the uterus (p. 75).

**minipill**   oral contraceptive containing low dose of progesterone (p. 380).

**miscarriage**   expulsion of the embryo or fetus during the first months of pregnancy before it is viable (p. 430).

**missionary position**   fact-to-face sexual intercourse with the man lying on top (p. 122).

**Mittleschmerz**   midtime pain (German); used in reference to the cramping some women feel during ovulation, which is midtime between menstrual periods (p. 68).

**mode**   the most common or frequently occurring score in a distribution (p. 48).

**modeling**   the acquisition of behaviors through observation and imitation of people (p. 157).

**moniliasis**   see candidiasis.

**monogamy**   the practice of being married to one preson at a time and restricting sexual activity to that person alone (p. 4).

**mononucleosis**   a disease caused by a virus found primarily in the saliva; usually characterized by fatigue, slight fever, and general achiness and sore throat (p. 464).

**mons pubis**   the area in women below the abdomen, which is composed of soft tissue and covered with hair (p. 60).

**mons veneris**   see mons pubis.

**morula**   the mass of cells formed as a result of cell division of the fertilized egg (p. 413).

**Motrin**   a drug used to relieve menstrual discomfort (p. 77).

**mucoid plug**   mucus located in the cervical opening, which may protect the uterus from bacteria and other foreign matter (p. 67).

**mucus method**   see cervical mucus method.

**multiorgasmic**   experiencing more than one orgasm within a single period of sexual relations (p. 132).

**myometrium**   the middle layer of the uterus (p. 66).

**myotonia**   muscular tension and contractions that occur during the sexual response cycle (p. 137).

## N

**natural childbirth**   a method of preparing parents for childbirth to minimize the need for anesthesia and other medical intervention (p. 426).

**natural world**   according to philosopher Rousseau an environment uncontaminated by law and custom in which each person's true and positive essence will emerge (p. 16).

**necking**   kissing and hugging without other erotic touch (p. 212).

*Neisseria gonorrhoeae*   the bacterium that causes gonorrhea (p. 455).

**nipple**   the tip of the breast (p. 83).

**nocturnal emission**   ejaculation occurring during sleep, often accompanied by erotic dreams; "wet dreams" (p. 104).

**nonjudgmental**   acceptance without indicating whether something is good or bad, right or wrong (p. 277).

**nonspecific urethritis (NSU) or nongonococcal urethritis (NGU)**   an STD that may resemble gonorrhea symptomatically but is caused by other bacteria (p. 457).

**Norplant**   a contraceptive technique involving the implantation of hormones under the skin of the upper arm (p. 391).

**nuclear family**   a family consisting only of mother, father, and children (p. 4).

**nurturance**   supportive, care-giving behavior (p. 147).

**nymphomania**   an old term for excessive sexual activity in women (p. 488).

## O

**obscenity**   depictions, writings, or speech that is considered offensive (p. 527).

**Oedipus complex**   the hidden sexual desire of a son for his mother (p. 33).

**open couple**   a partnership that permits intimate relationships outside the pair (p. 351).

**open marriage**   a marriage in which partners consent to intimate relationships with other people (p. 318).

**oral stage**   according to Freud, the first psychosexual stage during which pleasure is derived from activities centered about the mouth (p. 33).

**oral-genital contact or relations**   stimulation of the genitals by mouth and tongue (p. 118); see cunnilingus and fellatio.

**orgasm**   the pleasurable physical and emotional sensations occurring at the climax or peak of sexual relations (p. 64).

**orgasmofib**   pretense of sexual climax when none has occurred (p. 135).

**os**   opening; as in the cervical os (p. 67).

**ovarian follicle**   tissue capsule that houses the ovum (p. 67).

**ovaries**   organs located on each side of the uterus and responsible for the production of sex hormones and reproductive cells or ova (p. 67).

**ovulation**   the release of a mature egg, which is ready for fertilization, into the ovary (p. 62).

**ovulation phase**   menstrual time when the graafian follicle leaves the ovary (p. 77).

**ovum**   egg; female reproductive cell (ova is plural) (p. 67).

**ovutimer**   a device used to judge the nature of cervical mucus to determine probable time of ovulation (p. 380).

**oxytocin**   a chemical used to induce labor (p. 425).

## P

**Pap smear**   a method of testing for cervical cancer (p. 70).

**paraphilia**   a condition in which individuals obtain erotic gratification in ways only partially related to sexual activities and that may harm other people (p. 550).

**participant observer**   a method of studying behavior by actually becoming part of the group to be studied and engaging in that group's activities (p. 45).

**party house**   a club, house, or apartment where swingers meet for sexual exchange (p. 322).

**pediculosis pubis**   see crabs (p. 458).

**pedophilia**   adult sexual activity with young children (p. 553).

**penile squeeze**   a method of delaying male orgasm by applying pressure to the underportion of the penis just below the coronal cleft (p. 494).

**penis**   a male reproductive organ; also urinary outlet (p. 92).

**penis envy**   according to Freud, the jealousy girls feel when they discover boys have a penis but girls do not (p. 33).

**perimetrium**   the outer layer of the uterus (p. 66).

**perineum**   the small sensitive area between the anus and sexual organs (p. 86).

**permissive**   placing few restraints on behavior (p. 204).

**perversities**   deviant or illegal sexual behaviors (p. 225).

**petting**   kissing and erotically stimulating another person without having sexual intercourse (p. 212).

**phallic stage**   according to Freud, the third psychosexual stage during which the child begins to center sexually on the genitals (p. 33).

**phallus**   penis (p. 92).

**phenotype**   the behavioral manifestation or outward expression of a genetic potential (p. 149).

**pheromones**   chemicals produced by the body, which influence and attract others (p. 73).

**philia**   the ancient Greek term for companionate or brotherly love (p. 287).

**pill ("the pill")**   oral contraception (p. 380).

**pimp**   a man who shares prostitutes' earnings and usually provides them with protection and care (p. 541).

**pituitary**   a pea-sized gland located at the base of the brain, which secretes several hormones important to growth and sexual function (p. 71).

**placebo**   a substance having no pharmacological effect but that works because it is believed to work (p. 46).

**placenta**   structure enabling fetus to obtain nutrients and expel wastes (p. 413).

**platonic love**   love that does not include sex (p. 286).

**pleasuring**   erotic stimulation and sexual intimacy that are not necessarily tied to orgasm (p. 493).

**PLISSIT**   a four-level behavioral approach to sex therapy in which couples receive *Permission, Limited Information, Specific Suggestions,* or *Intensive Therapy* as needed (p. 497).

**polyandry**   one woman having several husbands (p. 7).

**polygamy**   a marital arrangement in which one person has more than one partner or spouse (p. 4).

**polygyny**   one man having several wives (p. 7).

**Ponstel**   a medication to relieve menstrual pain (p. 77).

**pornography**   art, literature, film, or the like, which is intended to be sexually arousing; pornography is sometimes differentiated from erotica in that the former is considered exploitive and demeaning, whereas the latter is aesthetically genuine (p. 22).

**postpartum**   the time period following birth (p. 442).

**Premarin**   a commercially sold estrogenic substance used to help regulate the menstrual cycle or relieve menopausal symptoms (p. 73).

**prematurity** the birth, during the last trimester, of a live infant with a weight of 5 pounds or less (p. 430).

**premenstrual syndrome (PMS)** tension, breast tenderness, backache, and other symptoms sometimes associated with the few days preceding menstrual flow (p. 80).

**premenstruation** phase IV of the menstrual cycle, just before menstrual flow (p. 79).

**prenatal** before birth (p. 358).

**preorgasmic** not yet having experienced orgasm (p. 133).

**prepared childbirth** childbirth techniques that prepare the parents through exercises and education (p. 426).

**prepuce** the foreskin of the penis or clitoris (p. 95).

**Priapus** an ancient Roman fertility god (p. 92).

**primary sexual characteristics** the sexual/reproductive organs that define people as women or men (p. 146).

**primate** the biological order to which humans, apes, and monkeys belong (p. 269).

**probability** term used statistically to indicate the likelihood that a certain outcome was not due to chance (p. 51).

**progesterone** female hormones secreted by the ovaries (p. 67).

**progesterone-induced hermaphrodism** a person with some apparent male and female genitalia; caused by hormones taken by the mother (p. 150).

**prolactin** a hormone secreted by the pituitary gland, which is involved in lactation (p. 72).

**proportional selection** carefully selecting subjects, or people, by matching percentage of individuals in specific categories such as age groups, religious affiliations, educational levels, etc. so that the sample resembles the whole (p. 43).

**prostaglandins** hormones that stimulate contractions of the uterus during childbirth (p. 77).

**prostate gland** a gland located below the bladder in men, which secretes an alkaline fluid comprising a major portion of the semen (p. 97).

**prostatis** infection of the male prostate gland, causing uncomfortable urinary symptoms (p. 454).

**prosthesis** a device that supplements or replaces a part of the body (p. 498).

**prostitute** a person who provides sexual intercourse for money (p. 11).

**pseudocyesis** false pregnancy (p. 431).

**psychoanalysis** technique proposed by Freud for exploring and treating psychological disorders (p. 34).

**psychosexual stages** the periods defined by Freud during which libidinal pleasure is focused orally, anally, phallically, or genitally (p. 33).

**puberty** the period of accelerated growth and development culminating in a sexually mature person; the time in which reproductive organs mature (p. 203).

## Q

**quickening** the sensation of movement of the developing fetus by the mother (p. 415).

## R

**random sample** a small group selected by chance procedures from a larger population (p. 43).

**range** the distance between the lowest and highest scores in any distribution (p. 48).

**rape** forcing sexual intercourse against a person's will (p. 560).

**rape trauma syndrome** severe physical and emotional difficulties, usually experienced after rape (p. 565).

**rapid ejaculation** orgasm and seminal emission occurring so rapidly it frustrates one or both partners (p. 490).

**Rationalism** the school of philosophy that believes that reason alone is responsible for our knowledge and feelings (p. 289).

**recessive gene**   a gene, the characteristic of which is manifest only when both parents contribute it to the zygote (p. 149).

**reciprocate**   to pay back; to give to others as they have given to us (p. 279).

**rectum**   the digestive tube leading to the anus (p. 87).

**red light district**   in past times, a section of town containing brothels, traditionally identified by the red light shining in the windows (p. 540).

**reentry fear**   anxiety concerning returning to a situation in which a person once functioned (p. 241).

**refractory period**   the period following orgasm during which further sexual arousal and orgasm cannot occur (p. 131).

**reinforcement**   a rewardlike event that strengthens a preceding behavior or results in its learning (p. 159).

**rejection**   being turned down by another person (p. 303).

**REM**   rapid eye movements; characteristic of relatively light sleep (p. 105).

**representative sample**   a small group selected from a larger population, which is believed to be very much like the entire group (p. 42).

**repression**   the rejection from conscious awareness of thoughts or impulses that are painful, disagreeable, or unhealthy (p. 32).

**rhythm method**   see fertility awareness (p. 378).

**Romanticism**   an emphasis on the nonphysical, spiritual, and ideal aspects of love and sexuality (p. 16).

## S

**sacral**   pertaining to the sacrum, the rear portion of the pelvis (p. 100).

**sadism**   sexual pleasure received through the infliction of pain on another (p. 553).

**sadomasochism (S & M)**   sexual excitement through the infliction and reception of pain (p. 557).

**saint-sinner syndrome**   the condition in which women are not sexually interested in "good" men but are attracted to those who are "bad" (p. 291).

**sampling**   a method for studying a large population by systematically selecting a small segment for research (p. 36).

**satyriasis**   an old term for excessive sexual activity in men (p. 488).

**scabies**   a microscopic mite that may infest the body and burrow under the skin (p. 458).

**scatologia**   concern with excretory function and obscenity; telephone scatologia refers to obscene phone calls (p. 551).

**scrotum**   the sac or pouch behind the penis, which contains the testicles (p. 96).

**secondary sexual characteristics**   physical traits that distinguish women and men but are not essential to reproduction (p. 146).

**seduce**   entice, lead subtly (often to sexual relations) (p. 562).

**semen**   the thick whitish fluid ejaculated from the penis, which carries sperm in a nutrient solution (p. 93).

**seminal vesicles**   saclike structures in the abdomen, which secrete a fluid that activates the sperm (p. 97).

**seminiferous tubules**   the treadlike substances in the testicles, which produce sperm (p. 97).

**sensate focus**   a massage and touch technique useful in treatment of sexual problems (p. 493).

**sensuous**   pleasing to the senses; often used to mean sexually pleasing (p. 110).

**sex**   biological femaleness or maleness (p. 145).

**sex chromosomes**   chromosomes that influence the determination of biological sex (p. 152).

**sex flush**   patches of darker coloring on the skin associated with sexual arousal (p. 140).

**sex-linked trait** a hereditary quality that is transmitted in the sex chromosome (p. 152).

**sex reassignment** surgical change of a person from one sex to the other (p. 168).

**sex roles** see gender roles

**sex stereotype** behavior assumed to be typical of men or women (p. 162).

**sex surrogate** a trained person who is paid to interact sexually with a patient in the treatment of sexual problems (p. 504).

**sexologist** a person who scientifically studies sexual attitudes and behaviors (p. 41).

**sexology** the scientific study of sexual attitudes and behavior (p. 41).

**sexual arousal** heightened state of sexual excitement and interest (p. 63).

**sexual dysfunction** medical term for sexual problems involving difficulty with arousal, intercourse, or orgasm (p. 487).

**sexual harassment** any unwanted attention of a sexual nature that creates embarrassment or stress (p. 573).

**sexual preference** the selection, or choice, or same or other sex individuals as sexual partners (p. 342).

**sexual response cycle** the various phases of sexual relations, including arousal, orgasm, and resolution (p. 135).

**sexually transmitted disease (STD)** an infectious disease such as gonorrhea or trichomoniasis that is spread primarily through intimate sexual contact (p. 252).

**shaping** gradually modifying a behavior one step at a time (p. 497).

**"shot-gun" wedding** a slang term for a marriage forced by pregnancy (p. 315).

**shyness** a persistent feeling of fear and tension in social situations (p. 255).

**sixty-nine** a slang term for simultaneous cunnilingus and fellation (p. 118).

**smegma** glandular secretion that lubricates the foreskin and glans of the penis (p. 95).

**sociobiology** the study of the effects of biology and physical factors on human behavior (p. 154).

**sodomy** a broad legal term for a variety of sexual acts, including oral/genital contact and anal intercourse, which are often considered unlawful (p. 127).

**Spanish fly** see cantharidin.

**speculum** instrument used to hold vaginal walls open during gynecological examination (p. 70).

**sperm** see spermatozoa (p. 93).

**spermatozoa** the microscopic cells in the semen, which are the male reproductive cells (p. 97).

**spermatic cord** the tube that contains the vas deferens, nerves, and blood vessels and travels from the scrotum to the abdominal cavity (p. 97).

**spermicide** a contraceptive product that destroys sperm and also may be useful in helping to prevent some types of STD (p. 382).

**spirochete** a spiral-shaped bacterium—the shape of the syphilis microorganism (p. 455).

**sponge** a contraceptive device containing spermicide, which is inserted into the vagina (p. 384).

**spouse** a husband or wife (p. 318).

**statutory rape** a legal term for sexual intercourse with a minor (p. 215).

**stereotype** biased ideas about the characteristics of particular people or groups (p. 166).

**sterilization** a procedure by which a person is rendered infertile or unable to reproduce (p. 388).

**stillbirth** the delivery of a full-term infant who is born dead (p. 430).

**streetwalker** a prostitute who picks up customers by soliciting on the street (p. 541).

**superego** according to psychoanalytical theory, the part of personality embodying ethical and moral principles learned early in life, which dictate right and wrong; the conscience (p. 33).

**surrogate father**   a man who donates his sperm to the woman of a couple wishing a child (p. 401).

**surrogate mother**   a woman who agrees to be impregnated with a man's sperm and to bear a child for him and his partner (p. 401).

**swinger**   a heterosexual couple who exchange partners with other couples for sexual relations (p. 321).

**syphilis**   an STD that if not treated may eventually result in serious heart or neurological damage (p. 452).

**systematic desensitization**   the association of pleasant and relaxing responses with behaviors that once caused fear or anxiety; a behaviorist tool, usually beginning with relatively simple situations and progressing a step at a time to those that are most anxiety producing (p. 497).

## T

**taboo**   totally forbidden (p. 240)

**Tay-Sachs disease**   a rare and fatal neuromuscular disorder present at birth (p. 432).

**telephone scatologia**   making obscene or sexual comments on the telephone (p. 551).

**tertiary sexual characteristics**   nonphysical, primarily learned traits that are associated with masculinity and femininity (p. 147).

**testes**   the male glands located in the scrotum—pouch behind the penis—which produce sperm (p. 96).

**testicles**   the testes and epididymis (p. 96).

**testicular feminization**   a chromosomal male with inadequate quantities of androgen available or functional (p. 150).

**testosterone**   a male sex hormone secreted by the testes (p. 106).

**thought sharing**   telling another person one's idea, feeling, or observation (p. 256).

**toxemia of pregnancy**   an infrequent complication of pregnancy characterized by high blood pressure, swelling, and possible convulsions (p. 431).

**toxic shock syndrome**   a rare condition in which a vaginal insert produces an overgrowth of life-threatening bacteria (p. 77).

**transsexual**   a person who would prefer to be a member of the other sex but who maintains heterosexual interests (p. 166).

**transudate**   a clear fluid emitted through the vaginal wall during sexual excitation (p. 137).

**transvestism**   cross-dressing; dressing as a person of the other sex (p. 165).

*Treponema pallidum*   the bacterium causing syphilis (p. 455).

**tribadism**   homosexual activity in which partners lie on top of one another, genitals touching and stimulated by rubbing (p. 349).

**trichomoniasis**   a common STD, a major symptom of which is an odorous vaginal discharge (p. 459).

**trimester**   one of the three 3-month periods from conception to birth (p. 416).

**tubal ligation**   severing and tying the fallopian tubes to sterilize a female (p. 388).

**tumescence**   period of building up of sexual energy during arousal; penile erection (p. 100).

## U

**ultrasonography**   a method of using sound waves to produce a picture of the position of the fetus (p. 433).

**umbilical cord**   the cord connecting the embryo or fetus with the placenta of the mother, through which nutrients and wastes are exchanged (p. 416).

**urethra**   the tube through which urine is carried from the bladder to outside the body (p. 60).

**urolagnia**   sexual interest in urine (p. 557).

**uterus** a highly fibrous, elastic structure that contains the developing fetus before birth (p. 61).

## V

**vacuum curettage** a method of abortion during which the uterus is suctioned and scraped (p. 393).

**vagina** the passage in females leading from the uterus to the external vulva; the organ accommodating the penis during coitus (p. 60).

**vaginismus** spasm of the muscles of the outer portion of the vagina, causing closing of the opening (p. 491).

**vas deferens** a tube in the scrotum that transports sperm to the urethra (p. 97).

**vasectomy** male sterilization performed by the cutting of the vas deferens (p. 388).

**vasocongestion** erection or swelling of genital organs of a result of increased blood flow during sexual arousal (p. 137).

**venereal disease (VD)** the old term for sexually transmitted disease (STD) (p. 452).

**vibrator** an electrical device that may be used for massage and sexual stimulation (p. 534).

**Victorianism** attitude of strict morality dating from the nineteenth century reign of British Queen Victoria, in which secrecy, shame, and guilt were associated with sex (p. 18).

**virgin** an individual who has never experienced sexual intercourse (p. 62).

**vocalize** make sound with the voice (p. 189).

**vocational stereotypes** expectations that certain jobs can be done only by certain people; for example, some jobs are for men, others for women (p. 191).

**voyeurism** a paraphilia in which a person secretly peeks at women or at couples engaged in sexual activity (p. 552).

**vulva** the external portion of the female genitalia (p. 58).

## W

**withdrawal** see coitus interruptus (p. 390).

**workaholic** a work "addict"; someone overly dedicated to her or his occupation (p. 231).

## Z

**zoophilia** sexual relations with animals (p. 555).

**zygote** the cell produced by the union of the ovum and sperm (p. 413).

# Subject Index

# Author Index

**PART I OPENER:** *Idyll II* by Lennart Anderson, Courtesy Davis and Langdale Company, New York.

## CHAPTER 1

P. 6, *Venus of Willendorf,* Vienna Museum of Natural History; p. 8, Parke-Davis, Division of Warner-Lambert Co., Morris Plains, N.J.; p. 9 Ira Kirschenbaum/Stock, Boston; p. 11 Alinari/Art Resource: Bernini, *Apollo and Daphne,* Galleria Borghese, Rome; p. 12 Bettmann Archive, New York; p. 14 Bettmann Archive; p. 17 H. Armstrong Roberts; p. 20 The Bettmann Archive; p. 24 Photographic Resources.

## CHAPTER 2

P. 30, 31 Culver Pictures; p. 32 Archive/Photo Researchers, Inc.; p. 35 photograph by Dellenback, reproduced by permission of the Kinsey Institute for Research in Sex, Gender, and Reproduction, Inc.; p. 39 UPI/Bettmann Newsphotos; p. 43 Mark Dobson, St. Louis; p. 48 courtesy of Hewlett Packard/Palo Alto, California.

**PART II OPENER:** Victoria and Albert Museum *Jealousy and Flirtation* by Haynes King

## CHAPTER 3

Pp. 59, 61, 65 David Mascaro; p. 66 From Seidel, H.M., et al.: *Mosby's Guide to physical examination,* St. Louis, 1987, The C.V. Mosby Co.; p. 68 Joan M. Beck; p. 70 (top), (c) Hazel Henkin/Stock, Boston; and (bottom) Lincoln Russell (c) Stock, Boston; pp. 76, 85 Modified from Payne/Hahn, *Understanding your health,* 2nd ed., St. Louis: Times Mirror/Mosby College Publishing, 1989; p. 79 National Library of Medicine, Bethesda, MD; p. 80 Bob Daemmrich/Stock, Boston; p. 86 Douglas Child and Creative Support Systems of California, Santa Barbara, California; p. 87 H. Blume/H. Armstrong Roberts.

## CHAPTER 4

P. 93 (right) From Seidel, H.M., et al.: *Mosby's Guide to physical examination,* St. Louis, 1987, The C.V. Mosby Co.; p. 95 (c) Joel Gordon Photography; p. 98 William Ober; p. 102 Stock, Boston; p. 105 J. Myers/H. Armstrong Roberts.

## CHAPTER 5

P. 116 B. Gunther/Photo Researchers; p. 117 Lynn Hoffman, Photo Researchers; p. 128 Courtesy Kohler, Co., Kohler, Wisconsin; p. 136 (top) Willie L. Hill, Jr./Stock, Boston; p. 136 (bottom) Suggested by Kaplan, H. *Disorders of sexual desire.* New York: Brunner/Mazel, Inc., 1979; p. 137 Adapted from Masters, W.H., Johnson, V.E., and Kolodny, R.C. *Masters and Johnson on sex and human loving.* Boston: Little, Brown & Co., 1986; pp. 138, 139 from Payne/Hahn, *Understanding your health,* 2nd ed., St. Louis: Times Mirror/Mosby College Publishing, 1989.

## CHAPTER 6

Pp. 147, 153, 158, 163 H. Armstrong Roberts; p. 149 from Thibodeau: *Anatomy and physiology,* 1st ed., St. Louis: Times Mirror/Mosby College Publishing, 1987; p. 151 *Clinics in Plastic Surgery.* Philadelphia: W.B. Saunders Co. April 1980, 7 (2), 192; p. 154 Vidic, B. and Suarez, F.R. *Photographic atlas of the human body,* St. Louis: The C.V. Mosby Co., 1984; p. 160 Data from Doyle, J.A. *Sex and gender: the human experience.* Dubuque, Iowa: Wm. C. Brown Group, 1985, and from Maccoby, E.E. *Social development, psychological growth and the parent-child relationship.*

New York; Harcourt Brace Jovanovich, Inc., 1980; p. 161 Bob Daemmrich/Stock, Boston; pp. 164, 165 Photo Researchers; p. 168 *(left)* from Grabb, W.C., and Smith, J.W. (editors) *Plastic Surgery, ed. 3.* Boston: Little, Brown & Co., 1979; and *(right)* from Noe, J.M. Birdsell, D., and Laub, D.R. The surgical construction of male genitalia for the female-to-male transsexual. *Plastic reconstructive surgery,* 53, 511-516; p. 170 FourByFive, Inc.

### CHAPTER 7

P. 176 H. Armstrong Roberts; p. 185 Dave Logan/H. Armstrong Roberts; p. 186 Bob Daemmrich/Stock Boston; p. 189 Photo Researchers; p. 190 *(left)* H. Armstrong Roberts; and *(right)* Kindra Clineff, The Picture Cube.

**PART III OPENER:** Giraudon/Art Resource, CRL 6287, Chagall, *The Model,* Basel, Coll. Mme. Chagall.

### CHAPTER 8

Pp. 200, 218 H. Armstrong Roberts; p. 203 Photo Researchers; pp 205, 223 Stock, Boston; p. 210 Data based on Friday, N. *My secret garden.* New York: Simon & Schuster, Inc., 1984; and Hunt, M. *Sexual behavior in the 1970s.* Chicago: Playboy Press, 1974; p. 211 Lenore Weber, Taurus Photos; p. 213 Data from Coles, R., and Stokes, G. *Sex and the American teenager.* New York: Harper & Row, 1985; and Petersen, J.R., Kretchmer, A., Nellis, B., Lever, J., and Hertz, R. The *Playboy* readers' sex survey (Parts 1 and 2). *Playboy,* January 1983, p. 108; March, p. 90; p. 220 Data from Zelnick, M., et al. *Sex and pregnancy in adolescence.* Beverly Hills, Calif.: Sage Publications Inc., 1981; p. 222 Data from Davis, S.M., and Harris, M.B. Sexual knowledge, sexual interest, and sources of sexual information of rural and urban adolescents from three cultures. *Adolescence,* 1982, 17, 471-492; and Gordon, S. What kids need to know. *Psychology Today,* October 1986, 22-26.

### CHAPTER 9

P. 232 Data from U.S. Bureau of the Census. *Current population reports.* Washington, D.C.: U.S. Government Printing Office, 1984, 1988; p. 233 Arvind Garg/Photo Researchers; p. 234 Ricmor Mason/Photo Researchers; p. 235 Data from DeLmater, J.D., and MacCorquodale, P. *Premarital sexuality: attitudes, relationships, behavior.* Madison: University of Wisconsin Press, 1979; Peplau, L.A. and Cochran, S.D. *Sex differences in values concerning love relationships.* Paper presented at the annual meeting of the American Psychological Association, Montreal, September 1980; and Christopher F., and Cate, R. Factors involved in premarital decision-making. *Journal of Sex Research,* 1984, 20, 363-376; pp. 238, 252 Stock, Boston; p. 243 Photo Researchers; p. 245 H. Armstrong Roberts; p. 255 Video Chemistry, New York.

### CHAPTER 10

Pp. 266, 275 (top) H. Armstrong Roberts; p. 268 R. Krubner/H. Armstrong Roberts; p. 269 Frank Siteman/Stock, Boston; p. 270 Susan Leavines/Photo Researchers; p. 271 Jim Weiner/Photo Researchers; p. 275 (bottom) Based on data from McCormick, N.B. Come-ons and put-offs: unmarried student's strategies for having and avoiding sexual intercourse. *Psychology of Women Quarterly,* 1979, 4, 194-211; and Perper, T., and Weis, D.L. Proceptive and rejective strategies of U.S. and Canadian women. *The Journal of Sex Research,* November 1987, 23(4), 455-480; p. 280 Teri Leigh Stratford/Photo Researchers; p. 281 Stock Boston.

### CHAPTER 11

P. 285 FourByFive, Inc.; p. 286 (c) Suzanne Arms/Jeroboam, Inc.; p. 287 Jeffrey W. Myers/Stock, Boston; p. 289 (c) Mary Evans Picture Library/Photo Researchers, Inc.; p. 293 After Sternberg, R.J., and Barnes, M.L. *The psychology of love.* New Haven, Connecticut: Yale University Press, 1988; p. 294 Erika Stone,/Photo Researchers; p. 296 Harriet Gans/(c) The Image Works; p. 297 Roswell Angier/(c) Archive Pictures, Inc.; p. 298 Based on Reiss, L.L. *Family systems in America*, ed. 3 New York: Holt, Rinehart & Winston, 1980; p. 301 Elizabeth Crews/Stock, Boston; p. 306 (c) Frank Siteman/Jeroboam, Inc.

## CHAPTER 12

Pp. 312, 315, 329, Data from U.S. Bureau of the Census. *Statistical abstracts of the United States*. Washington, D.C.: U.S. Government Printing Office, 1988; p. 313 Robert A. Isaacs/Photo Researchers; p. 316 Data from Blumstein, P., and Schwartz, P. *American couples*. New York: William Morrow & Co., Inc., 1983; Cook, K., et al. The *Playboy* readers' sex survey (Part 3), *Playboy*, May 1983, 126; Hunt, M. *Sexual behavior in the 1970s*. Chicago: Playboy Press, 1974; Kinsey, A.C., et al. *Sexual behavior in the human male*. Philadelphia: W.B. Saunders Co., 1948; Kinsey, A.C., et al. *Sexual behavior in the human female*. Philadelphia: W.B. Saunders Co., 1953; and Petersen, J.R., et al. The *Playboy* readers' sex survey (Parts 1 and 2), *Playboy*, January 1983, 108, March 1983, 90; p. 317 Data from Blumstein P., and Schwartz, P. *American couples*. New York: William Morrow & Co., Inc., 1983; p. 320 Ellis Herwig/Stock, Boston; pp. 324, 333 H. Armstrong Roberts; p. 326 photography by Miro Vintoniv c./Stock, Boston; p. 328 Data from U.S. Bureau of the Census. *Marital status and living arrangements: current population reports*. Washington, D.C.: U.S. Government Printing Office, 1988; p. 330 (c) FourByFive, Inc.; p. 332 data from U.S. Department of Health and Human Services, National Center for Health Statistics. *Statistical Abstract of the United States*. Washington, D.C.: U.S. Government Printing Office, 1988; p. 334 Based on Brecher, E.M. *Love, sex and aging*. Boston: Little, Brown & Co., Inc., 1984; Hobson, K.G. The effects of aging on sexuality. *Health & Social Work*, 1984 (Winter), 9 (1), 25-35; Hunt, M. *Sexual behavior in the 1970s*. Chicago: Playboy Press, 1974; and Starr, B.O., and Weiner, M.B. *The Starr-Weiner report on sex and sexuality in the mature years*. New York: Stein & Day Publishers, 1981; p. 335 Data from Adams, C.G., and Turner, B.F. Reported changes in sexuality from adulthood to old age. *The Journal of Sex Research*, May 1985, 21, (2), 126-141; Brecher, E.M. *Love, sex and aging*. Boston: Little Brown & Co., Inc., 1984; and Starr B.O., and Weiner, M.B. *The Starr-Weiner report on sex and sexuality in the mature years*. New York: Stein & Day Publishers, 1981.

## CHAPTER 13

P. 343 Based on Kinsey, A.C., et al. *Sexual behavior in the human male*. Philadelphia: W.B. Saunders Co., 1948; and Kinsey, A.C. et al. *Sexual behavior in the human female*. Philadelphia: W.B. Saunders Co., 1953; p. 345 Gaugin, *Eh quoi, es-tu jalouse?* Moscow, Pushkin Museum; p. 347 photography by Miro Vintoniv (c) Stock, Boston; p. 349 (top) Data based on Blumstein, P., and Schwartz, P. *American couples*. New York: William Morrow & Co., Inc., 1983; Gagnon, J.H., and Simon, W. *Sexual conduct*. Chicago: Aldine Publishing Co., 1973; Hunt, M. *Sexual behavior in the 1970s*. Chicago: Playboy Press, 1974 and Peplau, L.A. What homosexuals want in relationships. *Psychology Today*, March 1981, 28-38; and (bottom) Modified from Cook, K., et al. The *Playboy* readers' sex survey (Part 3). *Playboy*, May 1983, 126; p. 351 Data from Bell, A.P., and Weinberg, M.S. *Homosexualities*. New York: Simon & Schuster, Inc., 1978; and Bell, A.P., et al. *Sexual preference: its development in men and women*. Bloomington: Indiana University Press, 1981; p. 352 Richard C. Wandel/Bettmann Archive; p. 354 UPI/Bettmann Newsphotos; p. 356 Jerry Berndt/Stock, Boston; p. 359 Blair Seitz/Photo Researchers; p. 363 Art Resource; p. 364 Max Winter/Picture Group.

**PART V OPENER:** *A Bridal Pair*, The Cleveland Museum of Art, Delia E. Holden and C.E. Holden Funds, 32. 179.

## CHAPTER 14

P. 374 F.P.G.; p. 377 H. Armstrong Roberts; p. 379 Data from Hatcher, R.A., et al. *Contraceptive technology* 1984-1985. New York: Irvington Publishers, 1985; Kolata, G. Birth Control: new devices on market raise hopes of experts for wider U.S choices. *New York Times*, June 9, 1988, B17; Roberts, G. (compiler): *A small library in family planning*. New York: Planned Parenthood Federation of America, 1988; and Silber, S.J. *How NOT to get pregnant: your guide to simple, reliable contraception*. New York: Charles Scribner's Sons, 1987; pp. 381, 382, 384, 385, 388 (right) (c) Joel Gordon Photography; p. 383 Adapted from David Mascaro; p. 386 Betsy Cole/Stock, Boston; p. 388 (left): courtesy Alza Corp., Palo Alto, California; p. 389 from Payne/Hahn *Understanding your health*, 2nd ed., Times Mirror/Mosby College Publishing, 1989; p. 392 Flowers by Dierberg's Florist, Creve Coeur, Missouri; pp. 393, 396, Data from U.S. Center for Health Statistics. *Vital statistics of the United States, Annual*. Washington, D.C.: Superintendent of Documents, 1988; p. 394 Erika Stone/Photo Researchers; p. 399 Modified from Silber, S.J. *How to get pregnant*. New York: Charles Scribner's Sons, 1980; p. 400 FourByFive, Inc.; p. 403 J. Whitner, H. Armstrong Roberts.

## CHAPTER 15

Pp. 409, 410 Data from U.S. Bureau of the Census, *Statistical abstract of the United States*. Washington, D.C.: U.S. Government Printing Office, 1988; p. 411 Kara George/H. Armstrong Roberts; p. 413 Francis Leroy, Biocosmos/Science Photo Library/Photo Researchers; p. 414 from Payne/Hahn *Understanding your health*. St. Louis: Times Mirror/Mosby College Publishing Company, 1989; p. 416 Lennart Nilsson, Sweden; p. 413 J. Nettis/H. Armstrong Roberts; p. 422 Photo courtesy of Century Manufacturing Company/Aurora, Nebraska; p. 426 Data from Gleicher, N. Ceasarean Section rates in the United States. *Journal of the American Medical Association*, Dec. 21, 1984, 252 (23), 3273-3276, 1984; and U.S National Center for Health Statistics. Vital Statistics of the United States. Washington, D.C.: U.S. Government Printing Office, 1988; p. 427 Diane Lowe/Stock, Boston; p. 428 Tim Davis/Photo Researchers; p. 429 Photo Researchers; p. 430 Stan Levy/Photo Researchers; p. 436 Data from Creasy, R.K., and Resnick, R. *Maternal-fetal medicine: principles and practices*. Philadelphia: W.B. Saunders Co., 1985; Goldberg, L.H., and Leahy, J. *The doctor's guide to medication during pregnancy and lactation*. New York: William Morrow & Co., Inc., 1984; and Wilson, J.R., and Carrington, E.R. *Obstetrics and gynecology*. St. Louis: The C.V. Mosby Co., 1983; p. 437 (top) data from Shephard, B.D., and Shephard, C.A. *The complete guide to women's health*. New York: New American Library, Inc., 1985; and others; p. 437 (bottom) H. Armstrong Roberts; p. 439 (Mike Malyszko/Stock, Boston; p. 441 *(left)* Erika Stone/Photo Researchers and *(right)* David Weintraub/Photo Researchers; p. 442 U.S. Bureau of the Census. *Statistical abstract of the United States*. Washington, D.C.: U.S. Government Printing Office, 988.

**PART IV OPENER:** Pierre Bonnard, *Y' homme et la femme*, Musee d 'Orsay.

## CHAPTER 16

P. 453 Robert DeGast/Rapho, Photo Researchers; p. 454 (top) Data from Bingham, J.S. *Sexually transmitted diseases*. Philadelphia: Williams & Wilkins, 1984; Centers for Disease Control. STD *statistics*, 1988. Atlanta, Georgia: U.S. Dept. of Health and Human Services/Public Health Services, 1990; Wallis, C., et al. Chlamydia: the silent epidemic. *Time*, January 4, 1985, 67; and Willcox, R.R., and Willcox, J.R. *Venerological medicine*. London: Grant McIntyre, Ltd., 1982; p. 454 (bottom), p. 458 *(left)*, 461 Centers for Disease Control; p. 456 Data from Kramer, M.A., et al. Self-reported behavior pattern of patients attending a sexually transmitted disease clinic, *American Journal of Public Health*, 1980, 70, 997-1000; p. 458 (right) Reed &

Carnrick Pharmaceuticals; pp. 462, 469 Centers for Disease Control. STD *statistics*, 1988. Atlanta, Georgia: U.S. Dept. of Health and Human Services/Public Health Services, 1990; p. 464 Alan Carey/The Image Works; p. 466 Rick Browne/The Picture Group, Inc.; p. 468 Steven Benbow/Stock, Boston; p. 471 (c) Betty Lane/Photo Researchers; p. 473 John Griffin/The Image Works; p. 475 (c) Erika Stone/Peter Arnold, Inc.

## CHAPTER 17

P. 486 Teri Leigh Stratford/Photo Researchers; p. 489 Chester Higgins, Jr./Photo Researchers; p. 490 Ende, J., Rockwell, S., and Glasgow, M. The sexual history in general medical practice. *Archives of Internal Medicine,* 1984, 144, 558-561; Frank E., Anderson, C., and Rubenstein, D. Frequency of sexual dysfunction in "normal" couples. *The New England Journal of Medicine,* 1978, 299, 111-115; and Spencer, S.L. and Zeiss, A.M. Sex roles and sexual dysfunction in college students. *The Journal of Sex Research,* August 1987, 23 (3), 338-347.

## CHAPTER 18

P. 511 J. Myers/H. Armstrong Roberts; p. 512 Bostwick: *Aesthetic & Reconstructive Breast Surgery.* St. Louis: The C.V. Mosby Company, 1983; p. 514 *Physicians Desk Reference,* Oradell, N.J.: Medical Economics Co., 1989; p. 517 (c) Abraham Menasche/Photo Researchers.

**PART VII OPENER:** Marc Chagall: *A ma femme,* Musee National d'Art Moderne, Centre National d'Art et de Culture Georges Pompidou.

## CHAPTER 19

P. 528 Hazel Hankin/Stock, Boston; p. 529 Modified from Winick, C. A content analysis of sexually explicit magazines sold in an adult bookstore. *The Journal of Sex Research,* May 1985, 21(2), 208-210; p. 531 *(left)* Peter Simon/Stock, Boston; and *(right)* (c) Ira Berger/Woodfin Camp & Associates; p. 536 Bettmann Archive; p. 539 F.B. Guenzweig/Photo Researchers; p. 541 Abraham Menashe/Photo Researchers; p. 542 Stuart Rosner/Stock, Boston.

## CHAPTER 20

P. 550 Michael Hanulak/Photo Researchers; p. 554 Spider-Man/Power Pack c. 1984 Marvel Comics Group. All rights reserved. The National Committee for Prevention of Child Abuse publishes and distributes educational materials that deal with a variety of topics, including parenting, child abuse, and child abuse prevention. Written in a conventional style, the publications are excellent for professionals, lay persons, students, and children. Selected publications are available in Spanish. The NCPCA catalog is available free upon request from NCPCA, Publishing Dept., 332 S. Michigan Avenue, Suite 950, Chicago, Illinois 60604-4357, (312)663-3520; p. 556 (c) Sepp Seitz/Woodfin Camp & Associates; p. 558 Hazel Hankin/Stock, Boston; p. 561 Data based on Holmstrom, L.L., and Burgess, A.W. Sexual behavior during reported rapes, *Archives of Sexual Behavior,* 1980, 9, 427-439; Wolfe, J., and Baker, V. Characteristics of imprisoned rapists and circumstances of the rape. In Warner, C.G. (editor). *Rape and sexual assault,* Germantown, Md.: Aspen Systems Corp., 1980; and U.S. Federal Bureau of Investigation. *Uniform crime reports for the United States.* Washington, D.C.: U.S. Government Printing Office, 1988; p. 563 Jeffrey Myers/Stock Boston; p. 567 U.S. Federal Bureau of Investigation. *Uniform crime reports of the United States.* Washington D.C.: U.S. Government Printing Office, 1988; p. 568 (c) Carrie Boretz/Archive Pictures, Inc.; p. 569 Jack Spratt/The Image Works; p. 573 data based on Office of Merit Systems Review and Studies. *Sexual harassment in the federal work place: Is it a problem?* Washington, D.C.: U.S. Merit Systems Protection Board, U.S. Government Printing Office, 1981, 1988.